PRAISE FOR *PATH LIT BY LIGHTNING*

*A *New York Times* Notable Book*

"Throughout a book marked by deep research and expert context-setting, [Maraniss] sifts through the myths about Thorpe and Native Americans, depicting his subject as a proud, complicated man who sought to shape his own destiny, yet was bedeviled by larger forces of racism and hypocrisy. . . . *Path Lit by Lightning* tells his story with skill and integrity."

—Aram Goudsouzian, *The Washington Post*

"Reveals the complexity behind Jim Thorpe. . . . A masterful, in-depth portrait of a monumental figure."

—Louis Moore, *The Boston Globe*

"In the new biography *Path Lit by Lightning,* David Maraniss details the enormous odds that a Native American hero had to overcome. . . . He insists that taken as a whole, Jim Thorpe's story is not one of prejudice, nor the hypocrisy of others. . . . [And] emphasizes that whatever life took from him, Thorpe persisted and trained and worked and learned and succeeded."

—Keith Olbermann, *The New York Times Book Review*

"Goes beyond the myth and into the guts of Thorpe's life, using extensive research, historical nuance, and bittersweet honesty to tell the story of a gifted and complicated man. . . . Maraniss's biography does justice to the struggles and triumphs of a truly great man."

—Mary Ann Gwinn, *Los Angeles Times*

"*Path Lit by Lightning* showcases Mr. Maraniss's abilities as an indefatigable researcher and a deft prose stylist. . . . [Reveals] Thorpe as a man in full, whose life was characterized by both soaring triumph and grievous loss."

—Andrew R. Graybill, *The Wall Street Journal*

"Maraniss not only succeeds in revealing the man behind the fable, but also exposes the shameful treatment that Native Americans endured. . . . [Maraniss] demonstrates both Thorpe's persistence and courage, and the discriminatory policies that tried to keep him down."

—Olive Fellows, *The Christian Science Monitor*

"David Maraniss brilliantly rescues Jim Thorpe from myth and prejudice, restoring something more consequential than the Olympic medals stolen from him by small men—his humanity. This is another masterpiece from the master of biography."

—Jane Leavy, author of *The Big Fella* and *Sandy Koufax*

"*Path Lit by Lightning* is a flat-out masterpiece. The story of Jim Thorpe, one of America's greatest and most misunderstood heroes, is told in riveting detail by David Maraniss, one of our greatest biographers. The result is a portrait as powerful, dazzling, and nuanced as Thorpe himself."

—Jonathan Eig, author of *Luckiest Man, Opening Day*, and *Ali: A Life*

"*Path Lit by Lightning* is a captivating book by a master storyteller. David Maraniss provides new insights into Jim Thorpe, a man who was not only 'the world's greatest athlete,' but a cultural icon complicated by the dynamics of race and celebrity."

—Patty Loew (Bad River Ojibwe), professor, Medill School of Journalism, Northwestern University, and inaugural director, Center for Native American and Indigenous Research

"In different hands I might be dubious, but David Maraniss revives the titanic Jim Thorpe for a new generation with a surgeon's care, the diligence of a great researcher, and the poignance and humanity that is the signature of his writing. *Path Lit by Lightning* is a masterful look at this country's first super-athlete, unflinching from what conquest did to his people, from the rousing and bittersweet journey of fame and identity, and from an American century often far less heroic than the book's protagonist. It's simply brilliant."

—Howard Bryant, author of *The Last Hero: A Life of Henry Aaron*

"I love this book, not only for its evocative account of the unmatched athletic triumphs of the great Jim Thorpe, but even more for the way it powerfully illuminates the larger American Indian experience through the story of his life's struggles and perseverance against all odds."

—Suzan Shown Harjo (Cheyenne and Mvskokvlke), writer, curator, Native rights advocate, and recipient of the 2014 Presidential Medal of Freedom

"Before Shohei Ohtani, before Michael Jordan and Bo Jackson, Jim Thorpe was the world's best athlete, and David Maraniss tells Thorpe's extraordinary, tragic story with all of the power and detail that it deserves."

—Buster Olney, senior writer and analyst, ESPN

ALSO BY DAVID MARANISS

A Good American Family: The Red Scare and My Father

Once in a Great City: A Detroit Story

Barack Obama: The Story

Into the Story: A Writer's Journey through Life, Politics, Sports and Loss

Rome 1960: The Summer Olympics That Stirred the World

Clemente: The Passion and Grace of Baseball's Last Hero

They Marched into Sunlight: War and Peace, Vietnam and America, October 1967

When Pride Still Mattered: A Life of Vince Lombardi

The Clinton Enigma: A Four-and-a-Half-Minute Speech Reveals This President's Entire Life

First in His Class: A Biography of Bill Clinton

The Prince of Tennessee: Al Gore Meets His Fate (with Ellen Nakashima)

"Tell Newt to Shut Up!" (with Michael Weisskopf)

PATH LIT BY LIGHTNING

THE LIFE OF JIM THORPE

DAVID MARANISS

Simon & Schuster Paperbacks

NEW YORK • LONDON • TORONTO
SYDNEY • NEW DELHI

Simon & Schuster Paperbacks
An Imprint of Simon & Schuster, Inc.
1230 Avenue of the Americas
New York, NY 10020

First Simon & Schuster paperback edition June 2023

SIMON & SCHUSTER PAPERBACKS and colophon are registered trademarks of Simon & Schuster, Inc.

For information about special discounts for bulk purchases, please contact Simon & Schuster Special Sales at 1-866-506-1949 or business@simonandschuster.com.

The Simon & Schuster Speakers Bureau can bring authors to your live event. For more information or to book an event, contact the Simon & Schuster Speakers Bureau at 1-866-248-3049 or visit our website at www.simonspeakers.com.

Interior design by Paul Dippolito

Manufactured in the United States of America

2 4 6 8 10 9 7 5 3

Library of Congress Cataloging-in-Publication Data is available.

ISBN 978-1-4767-4841-2
ISBN 978-1-4767-4842-9 (pbk)
ISBN 978-1-4767-4843-6 (ebook)

In memory of Alice Mayhew, the editor whose inimitable voice I still hear in my head, with the wisdom and vigor that kept me going through twelve and a half books . . . and also to the wondrous voices that herald a better future—grandchildren Heidi, Ava, Eliza, and Charlie.

Contents

PATH LIT BY LIGHTNING

Preface

THE LATE REUBEN SNAKE, ONETIME CHAIRMAN OF THE American Indian Movement and member of the Winnebago nation, said that to be an Indian meant "having every third person you meet tell you about his great-grandmother who was a real Cherokee princess" and "nine out of ten people tell you how great Jim Thorpe was." Thorpe, in that sense, was one of the few Native Americans of the twentieth century whom people could cite and praise even if they knew little else about the indigenous experience. From the moment I started telling acquaintances that I was writing a book about Thorpe, the reply was often some variation of "Oh, I read a book about him in fourth grade." Many of those people were in fourth grade long before there was much effort to diversify school libraries. Thorpe was an archetype, a gifted athlete, and a stereotype, the romanticized noble Indian. He was a foundation story of American sports.

As with most public figures of that sort, the man became shrouded in myth. As a biographer, I am interested in both—the making of the man and the creation of the myth. Born in 1887, in the Indian Territory of what later became Oklahoma, Thorpe was the quintessential underdog who rose from nowhere to become the greatest athlete in the world, the Natural who could do anything on the fields of play. He was an Olympic champion decathlete in track and field, a football All-American, a star pro and first president of what became the National Football League, and a major league baseball player, a seemingly indestructible force who ran like a wild horse thundering downhill yet was also a graceful ballroom dancer and gifted swimmer and ice skater.

When people display such rare physical gifts, there is a tendency to lift them into the realm of the superhuman, as if human magnificence is insufficient. That was certainly true with Thorpe. The hyperbolic stories told by writers and sports fans over the decades could fill many notebooks. As is also often the case, there were times when Thorpe became the storyteller of his own legend. Jim loved to recall the tale of how at Carlisle he brilliantly ran a punt back for a touchdown against Army, and when the score was nullified by a penalty, he simply repeated his touchdown gallop on the next play. He was indeed the dominant player in that game, but the back-to-back touchdown runs never happened. Nor is there any truth to his boast that during a baseball game in Texarkana he hit three home runs into three separate states, Arkansas, Texas, and Oklahoma. He did hit three home runs, but the three-state hat trick was a geographic impossibility. Mythmaking in the American tradition of George Washington, Paul Bunyan, Davy Crockett, and Babe Ruth.

But there was another myth at the center of the Thorpe story, a deeper and more pernicious myth that had to do with the history and treatment of the American Indian: the myth that the Great White Father knows best. Thorpe's life spanned a sixty-five-year period when the dominant society believed the best way to deal with Indians was to rid them of their Indianness and make them as white as possible. It was that mentality that shaped Thorpe's life. Much of the territory of his Sac and Fox and Potawatomi people was lost when the federal government moved to strip them of communal property, opening up vast swaths of territory to the land rushes that white Oklahoma settlers and their descendants celebrated as Boomer Sooner frontier derring-do. As a teenager, he was sent away to the Carlisle Indian Industrial School in Pennsylvania, the federal government's flagship Indian boarding school, where the focus was more on forced acculturation than on education and the methods were crude, cruel, and dehumanizing. Football, as a college sport then largely the province of Ivy League good old boys, was considered a central component of the assimilation process.

A biographer's responsibility is to acknowledge the complexity of human existence, its many contradictions, crosscurrents, and nuances. For all of Carlisle's failings and questionable intentions, some of its students considered their boarding school years among the best of their lives. Jim sometimes claimed that himself. It is fair to say that few would know or care about him had he not gone there and shown his unmatched athletic skills to the nation and the world. Whether he would have had a happier life without the surrounding hoopla of fame is another matter. He was not a loner and had a touch of mischief to him, but he was innately modest and comfortable away from the limelight. He was most relaxed while stalking the woods or sitting on a riverbank or ocean pier, hunting or fishing. In the years after his playing skills faded, his life was troubled by alcohol, broken marriages, deferred dreams, lost opportunities, and financial distress resulting from a generosity that lapsed into wastefulness. He was the American nomad, migrating from job to job, state to state, in search of a peace he never found before he died of a heart attack in a trailer park in southern California in 1953 at age sixty-five.

At times Jim was his own worst enemy, yet throughout his life he had to deal with powerful white men who tried to control his fate. Some presented themselves as his savior, others as his moral superior. The most notable example of the savior type was Pop Warner, Jim's coach at Carlisle. In *Jim Thorpe—All-American*, the 1951 movie version of his life, Thorpe (played by movie star Burt Lancaster) is the main character but Warner, who consulted on the script, is portrayed as the hero and wise man who discovered the raw athlete, molded him into a superstar, and then tried time and again in later years to save Jim from his worst impulses. The true story is less flattering. Warner was a hypocrite if not a coward. At the time of Jim's greatest peril, when his Olympic medals were being taken from him because he had played bush league baseball, Pop lied and feigned innocence to save his own reputation while portraying Jim as the ignorant native. There is strong evidence that James E. Sullivan, then the big man of American amateur athletics and the person most responsible for the decision to deny Thorpe his medals and records, was also duplicitous during that ordeal even as he claimed to be upholding the righteous cause of pure amateurism.

And then there was Avery Brundage, once a decathlete himself, a teammate and rival of Jim's at the 1912 Stockholm Olympics. Brundage performed miserably there and dropped out of the competition when the going got tough, an early refutation of his later bromide that in the Olympic ideal participation was what mattered, not performance. He went on to a high-flying career as the holier-than-thou arbiter of all things amateur in the world of sports, and for decades as he rose through the ranks from president of the U.S. Olympic Committee to head of the International Olympic Committee, he consistently refused to reconsider the injustice done to Thorpe, often complaining that he, not Jim, was the victim of unfair treatment. In the long list of Brundage misdeeds, others were more inexcusable, especially his cozying up to the Nazi organizers of the 1936 games in Berlin, but his condescending and dismissive attitude toward Thorpe stood as Exhibit A in the hypocrisy of moral superiority.

Thorpe's unparalleled athletic accomplishments did not make his life triumphant. His days were marked by loss. The loss of tribal lands. The loss of his twin brother in childhood. The loss of his namesake son at age three. The loss of his Olympic medals and records. His loss of money and security and equilibrium. There is a temptation, then, to view his story as tragedy, but I emerged from my study of his life with a different interpretation. It is also a story of perseverance against the odds. For all his troubles, whether caused by outside forces or of his own doing, Jim Thorpe did not succumb. He did not vanish into whiteness. The man survived, complications and all, and so did the myth.

1

"The Stuff His People Are Made Of"

PEOPLE WERE EAGER TO SEE "THE BIG INDIAN" AS SOON AS he returned to America. He was a celebrity now, a global sensation after winning two gold medals at the 1912 Olympic Games in Stockholm, where the dapper king of Sweden was said to have called him the greatest athlete in the world. The first public stop on home soil was in Boston, where a local newspaper heralded his exalted status by suggesting he pose as the Indian on the flip side of the buffalo nickel. Boston's mayor, an avid sports fan nicknamed Honey Fitz, challenged him to a race in the hundred-yard dash at the Elks Club picnic on August 11. John Francis Fitzgerald, almost fifty, and five years away from becoming the grandfather of a future president, jocularly boasted that he might not need a head start to keep up with James Francis Thorpe.

Speechwriters for William Howard Taft, the current president, a sporty walrus who weighed 350 pounds, were already drafting a letter of praise on behalf of the nation, asserting the fond hope that Jim Thorpe's Olympic victories in the pentathlon and decathlon would "serve as an incentive to all to improve those qualities which characterize the best type of American citizen." The White House seemed clueless about the fact that the United States government did not yet consider Thorpe any type of citizen, best or otherwise. From Boston it was on to Carlisle, New York City, and Philadelphia, where exuberant crowds jostled for the best view of the new American colossus.

An American Indian mythologized into spectacle. It was a familiar scene that had played out in strikingly parallel fashion almost eighty years earlier, in 1833, when Black Hawk was paraded through cities on the East Coast. At the height of their fame, Black Hawk and Jim Thorpe, warrior and athlete, were the best-known Indians in America, and they would remain among the most renowned of all time. But the connection was deeper and more spiritual. Black Hawk and Thorpe, both members of the Sac and Fox nation, also came from the same clan, the Thunder Clan; they were connected in lineage through Thorpe's paternal grandmother, *No-ten-o-quah*, who might have been Black Hawk's grand-niece, although the documentation is imprecise. As a boy growing up in the Indian Territory that later became part of Oklahoma, Thorpe was told by his mother that he was the reincarnation of Black Hawk. Both Thorpe and Black Hawk were curiosities to the dominant Anglo-Saxon society, alternately noble and tragic—and often inscrutable, as seen through the distorted cultural lens of whiteness.

Black Hawk, carrying with him a mystical medicine bag made from the skin of the raptor from which he took his name, made his eastern tour as a manacled prisoner of war, an exotic Indian leader who had rebelled against the ever-expanding reach of white settlers into ancestral tribal lands in the Middle West. He lived during a time when an American president, Andrew Jackson, gained notoriety as an Indian killer, and killing Indians was part of the nation's providential plan.

Thorpe, carrying with him the medals and trophies from which he took his fame, made his tour as a prisoner of his own athletic success, an Indian who in his youth had been shipped off to a school in Pennsylvania run by the federal government, the Carlisle Indian Industrial School, where the official policy was to exterminate Indians not in body but in language, dress, behavior, tradition, and soul. Cut their hair and outfit them in uniforms resembling those worn by the enemies of their forefathers, the U.S. Cavalry. *Kill the Indian, save the man.*

WHILE IN BOSTON, Thorpe received a telegram from Pop Warner, his track trainer in Stockholm and the football and track coach at Carlisle. Glenn Scobey Warner was an imposing figure in the athletic world of the early twentieth century, as well known in that subculture as his most prominent player for turning little Carlisle into an athletic marvel that competed on the fields of play with the elite colleges of the East, from Penn to Harvard to Syracuse to Yale to Army. Warner had sailed home from Stockholm with most of the U.S. Olympic delegation directly after the games, disembarking from the SS *Vaderland* in New York on July 30, while Thorpe stayed behind with a few teammates for an extra round of exhibition track meets on the Continent, ending in Paris. Somehow, uncharacteristically, Pop had lost track of his prize pupil and searched frantically for him in New York, thinking wrongly that he must be there, until finally learning from the newspapers that Thorpe was in Boston hanging out with Honey Fitz.

Get to New York soonest, came the message. A welcome home celebration was being planned back in Carlisle that had been delayed once already awaiting the hero's return. When Thorpe reached New York by train he was met by Pop and Lewis Tewanima, a rail-thin Hopi distance runner with uncommon stamina who, as Thorpe's Carlisle teammate, had also excelled in Stockholm, winning a silver medal in the 10,000-meter run. Of more interest to Thorpe was something else Warner brought with him—a passel of letters sent to Jim at the Carlisle address from his sweetheart, Iva Margaret Miller, who had graduated from the Indian school that spring. Since then she had worked at a mission school in Oklahoma before heading out to southern California to live with her siblings. Iva's older brother Earl was especially wary of Thorpe's romance with their intelligent and cultured sister—and had gone so far as to return many of his letters before Iva could see them. Now, with Jim's global fame, the protective family chaperones seemed to be relenting.

The festivities in Carlisle started at two on the soft summer afternoon of August 16 with a parade from the station across from the James Wilson Hotel at the corner of Hanover and High Streets to the Indian school half a mile away. This was the biggest thing that had ever happened in Carlisle, and the "gorgeously decorated" town shut down to celebrate. A carriage carrying Thorpe, Tewanima, and Warner rolled just behind the parade marshals, followed by a marching formation of ninety-one Indian students militarily attired in their cadet uniforms, then an assortment of town bigwigs and council officials and more students accompanied by Moses Friedman, the Indian school's superintendent. The sidewalks were lined ten deep along pockets of the route out to Biddle Field, the new athletic grounds, where the Eighth Regiment band performed as seven thousand students and locals filled the bleachers and grandstands for speeches.

Superintendent Friedman spoke first. He called the day a national occasion of which the entire country should be proud. These were "real Americans," he said of Thorpe and Tewanima, whose forebears were "on the reception committee which welcomed to this soil and this glorious New World the famed first settlers who arrived on the *Mayflower.*" No sooner had Friedman recited the founding fable of racial conciliation than he shattered it, perhaps unwittingly, with an undeniable truth about forced acculturation. His subject was the little runner, Tewanima.

"One of these young men came to this town and to the Indian school five years ago virtually as a prisoner of war," the superintendent said. "His people, the Hopi tribe of Arizona, had been giving the government much trouble and were opposed to progress and education. It was finally decided to send twelve of the men and most influential of the tribe to Carlisle to be educated in order to win them over to American ideals." Tewanima was one of the twelve Hopi prisoners the U.S. government had sent to Carlisle. "They came with long hair and some of them with earrings. They were pagans and opposed to education and American civilization." As he looked toward his Hopi student, Friedman busted with pride about all that Carlisle and that half decade had accomplished. "Louis Tewanima here is one of the most popular students at the school and has an enviable record. You know of his athletic prowess—I wanted you to know of his advancement in civilization and as a man."

Friedman then turned to Thorpe. "There is another here today who is now known over all the world. The world's greatest athlete is also an Indian. We welcome you, Jim Thorpe, to this town and back to your school. You have covered yourself with glory. By your achievement you have immeasurably helped your race. By your victory, you have inspired your people to live a cleaner, healthier, and more vigorous life."

As further testament to Thorpe's achievement, letters were shared from the highest officials in Washington, D.C. There was the one from President Taft, an almost identical letter from Walter L. Fisher, secretary of the Interior, and finally one from Robert G. Valentine, commissioner of Indian Affairs. It was a deputy in Valentine's office who had instigated the letter-writing by noting in a memo: "It seems to me that when an American Indian wins honors of this kind against all the world he has done something to show the stuff his people are made of, at least physically, and that some personal recognition from you might not be amiss."

Warner spoke next. Friedman had introduced him by praising the coach for turning out "clean and strong athletic teams." At the time, Pop was regarded as the father of Carlisle's success, overseer of the Olympians, and responsible for victories on the football field year after year, all of which brought outsize recognition to the school. In a few years, like Friedman, he would depart Carlisle shadowed by scandal. Now, by some accounts, he received the loudest ovation at Biddle Field. He talked about how celebrations for the U.S. Olympic team would be held in many cities, but "none will have a greater right to celebrate than Carlisle." He said that he and Thorpe had "fought it out" over who would speak first until Thorpe relented. Unlikely, given Thorpe's reserved public nature, and that when Thorpe's turn came he limited his speech to twelve words: "All I can say is that you showed me a good time."

That night, after an exhibition baseball game between Carlisle and Chambersburg, another band concert, and an informal banquet in town attended by the chief ethnologist from the government in Washington, the Olympians were escorted back to school by a raucous battalion of students festively dressed in nightshirts and white caps. A team of boys pulled a carriage carrying Thorpe and Tewanima down the streets, hollering as they danced in the glow of bloodred and golden lights, the school colors. The school newspaper described the scene as "somewhat beautiful, and slightly weird, but surely noisy."

Eight days later, on August 24, Thorpe was in New York for an Olympic victory parade, the largest in the city since Admiral Dewey's return from battle in 1899 after the Spanish-American War. "NEW YORK FETES OLYMPIC HEROES," blared the banner headline in the *New York Herald.* "THORPE LIONIZED, Honors Startle Indian; Red Man, All-Around Champ, Chews Gum and Blushes as He Rides Alone."

Sixty Olympic athletes were there, assigned two to a car and aligned in alphabetical order. With one exception. At the last planning meeting held at the Pulitzer Building, P. J. Conway of the Irish American Athletic Club suggested that Thorpe should be placed alone in the first car "where he may be recognized and enthusiastically greeted as he deserves." As it turned out, he was in the second car. The first carried the trophies he brought back from Stockholm. Olympians and dignitaries (including a delegation of Swedes), marching military units, athletic clubs, public and Catholic school athletic teams—all streaming along as the parade moved from Forty-First Street down Fifth Avenue to Waverly Place, across to Broadway, and on to City Hall. Confetti tossed from office windows flecked the air. In the crowd were twelve thousand schoolchildren who came with organized cheers, boys on one side of the street, girls on the other. As Thorpe's car passed, they chanted in phonetic rhythm: "Ray-ray-ray! U-S-A! A-M-E-R-I-C-A! JIM THORPE!"

Press scribes covering the event kept their focus on Thorpe and wrote variations of a theme offered by the *Herald*, seemingly reading his mind: "Jim Thorpe, the Carlisle Indian and champion all-around athlete of the world, sat alone in an automobile in embarrassed silence. He was perhaps the chief attraction in the line, but he pulled his panama hat over his eyes, chewed gum, pinched his knees, and seldom lifted his gaze."

The only time they saw Thorpe animated, newspapermen noted, was when his car stopped in front of the reviewing stand and he bounded out to vigorously shake the hand of James E. Sullivan, who as commissioner of the American Olympic Committee and secretary of the Amateur Athletic Union held singular sway over track and field in the United States. Sullivan was effusive in his praise of "the wonderful Carlisle Indian" whose achievements in the all-around events "stand out at the head of the list" of

American successes in Stockholm. He knew all about Thorpe and Carlisle long before the Olympics. Sullivan was close to Pop Warner and for years had served on the advisory board of the Carlisle Athletic Association. Four and a half months after the glorious New York parade, in the first month of 1913, the relationships between athlete, coach, and sporting potentate would entangle in a less agreeable way.

From New York it was on to Philadelphia. When Thorpe and Tewanima arrived at the Continental Hotel, they were surrounded by reporters, who again took note of their seemingly laconic natures. They were "loathe to tell of their triumphs" and could not be provoked to say much more than that they enjoyed the trip abroad. Another parade the next day, this time followed by a ball game at Shibe Park between the world champion Philadelphia A's and the Detroit Tigers. The stars of both teams, Eddie Collins for the A's and Ty Cobb for the Tigers, were guests of honor at a banquet that night, but popular as major league baseball was, the biggest luminary in Philadelphia was Jim Thorpe, and what drew the most fawning attention were two objects Thorpe brought with him. On display at the Wanamaker department store were two trophies he was given in Stockholm: a silver Viking ship in honor of his decathlon victory, endowed by the tsar of Russia, and for the pentathlon a bronze bust, gift of the king of Sweden. These were Thorpe's prized and hard-earned possessions, at least for now.

EIGHTY YEARS EARLIER, in late October 1832, the artist George Catlin arrived at Jefferson Barracks on the edge of St. Louis to paint portraits of several prisoners of war who were being held there.

They were Indians from the Sac and Fox nation who had been captured at the conclusion of the Black Hawk War, a series of skirmishes in Illinois and territory that would become Wisconsin. For a few months that spring and summer, a contingent of Illinois militia and federal troops had tracked down and killed or captured a rebellious faction of mostly Sac and Fox Indians, led by the warrior Black Hawk, who had tried to return to their homeland after the government pushed them onto reservations on the other side of the Mississippi. It was a violent power struggle perceived differently from opposite perspectives. To white settlers and government officials, it was a bloody incursion on frontier settlements by untamed savages. To Black Hawk and about a thousand followers—including not only warriors but women and children—it was a righteous reclamation of their cultural and property rights after a series of one-sided treaties with the government. Most of the power was with the whites. In the end, most of the casualties were Indians.

The decisive Battle of Bad Axe was more accurately a massacre. It took place on the first two days of August when Black Hawk's haggard band, tired of running and down to fewer than 400 starving and exhausted Indians, tried to recross the Mississippi near the Bad Axe River, about twenty-five miles south of La Crosse, to escape an approaching army. During the first attempted crossing by raft and canoe on August 1, the Sac and Fox were stopped midstream by the military steamboat *Warrior.* Black Hawk tried to surrender, but soldiers aboard suspected a ruse and began firing. At least 25 Indians were killed, and the rest pushed back to the eastern shore. Black Hawk decided the crossing was futile and tried to persuade his band to retreat with him to the north and east. Most refused, and he left with only a score of followers. An attempted crossing by those who remained ended in slaughter the next day, with more than 150 Sac and Fox killed, many of them women and children. U.S. soldiers wantonly scalped the heads of dead warriors amid the carnage—and called them savages. Black Hawk eventually surrendered a few weeks later.

An oddity of the Black Hawk War was that it involved three future presidents—two of the United States and one of the Confederate States of America. Abraham Lincoln, then living in New Salem and about to run for a seat in the Illinois House of Representatives, enlisted in the Illinois Militia in late April and served into July, rising to the rank of captain. He marched and camped but never engaged the enemy, though later would recount how he came upon the scalped remains of several militia comrades. Zachary Taylor was a U.S. Army colonel who had been stationed at several forts in Wisconsin and led the regulars in a decisive battle of the war. When Black Hawk was captured, he was first held in custody at the fort in Prairie du Chien that Taylor had commanded. It was there that one of Taylor's men, a young West Point graduate named Jefferson Davis, was assigned to escort Black Hawk down the Mississippi River to Jefferson Barracks in St. Louis.

Catlin had seen Black Hawk once before, as an unshackled participant at a treaty gathering in 1830. Now he was in chains, a captive subject. Even if he had wanted to, the Indian could not avoid the artist's gaze. But Catlin, who devoted his career to painting Indians, considered him a sympathetic figure. He would not show the chains. When Black Hawk posed at Jefferson Barracks, Catlin recalled, "he was dressed in a plain suit of buckskin, with strings of wampum in his ears and on his neck and held in his hand a medicine bag . . . the tail of which made him a fan which he was constantly using." He sought to idealize Black Hawk, not demonize him, portraying him as the classic noble warrior. And so was Black Hawk reimagined, an early representation of what would happen to leading American Indians many times through the decades of the nineteenth century in paintings and traveling shows and books, from Geronimo to Sitting Bull to Iron Tail to Crazy Horse and on to Jim Thorpe, some defanged, all romanticized, exaggerated yet diminished at the same time.

In whatever way it was perceived, the story of the Black Hawk War of 1832 propelled Black Hawk into American myth and legend, much as the Olympics of 1912 did with Thorpe, his tribal descendant.

Black Hawk's trip east in early 1833 came in two parts, with separate missions. The first was to transport him to Fort Monroe in Hampton, Virginia, where he and the ten other captives, including his charismatic son, *Nasheweskaska*, were to be indefinitely imprisoned. Curious crowds gathered at populated spots along that leg of the trip up the Ohio River to Louisville and Cincinnati, over to Wheeling, West Virginia, and along the Cumberland Road to Frederick, Maryland, then down into Washington. It was in the nation's capital that the Indian captives met the Indian Killer himself, President Jackson, in a brief visit to the White House. Black Hawk referred to him as the Great Father, at least in the translated version of a memoir he later dictated to Antoine LeClaire, a government interpreter. A correspondent for the *Boston Globe* reported that they were received "with great urbanity" and that Jackson told them their futures "would be determined by their behavior"—meaning they must not try to escape.

In his memoir, Black Hawk was more succinct. After describing the president looking "as if he had seen as many winters as I have" (both were sixty-five, though dates with the Sac and Fox were iffy), Black Hawk confessed that he "had very little talk with [Jackson], as he seemed to be busy and did not seem to be much disposed to talk." Not surprising given Jackson's history. He had not only fought and slaughtered the Creek Indians as a major general during his military career, but as president in 1830 he signed the Indian Removal Act that forced all tribes to leave the eastern half of the continent for unsettled lands west of the Mississippi. The Black Hawk War was a failed refutation of that very act.

The indefinite stay at Fort Monroe turned out to be only a matter of weeks. Then came the second mission. The idea was to take Black Hawk and his men on a guided tour of major eastern cities, show them America's full military and economic might, and "impress upon them the nature of our institutions" in an effort to persuade them that further attempts at war would be foolhardy. That was the plan, but not exactly what happened. If Black Hawk was impressed by what he saw, the citizens he encountered were more impressed by him. He became a spectacle. A popular frenzy of curiosity and wonder took hold. It was called Blackhawkiana.

At Norfolk, Virginia, before Black Hawk's delegation boarded the steamboat *Delaware*, a crowd gathered under his hotel window and chanted his name, demanding a viewing of the magnificent Indian, just as his descendant Jim Thorpe would become a curiosity to the public eighty years later. Black Hawk obliged and bowed on the balcony, and the cheers grew louder. As the steamboat plied the Chesapeake Bay to Baltimore, by one account Black Hawk suffered a bout of seasickness. By another, when he heard reports that some passengers thought their money was missing, he insisted that he and his fellow Indians all be searched. "The white men might steal but he would let all know the Sacs were honest," one reporter wrote. As the *Delaware* eased into Baltimore Harbor, raucous chants of

"Black Hawk! Black Hawk! Black Hawk!" rose from the excitable throng gathered at the dock.

Under the watchful eye of Major John Garland, the Indians stayed in Baltimore for several days. They slept at Fort McHenry and ventured into the city to see the sights, including a circus and the theater. The circus amused them; the theater bored them. The title and topic of the theater performance revealed the contradictory strains of race in America and the different ways Indians and blacks were perceived. It was *Jim Crow*, a racist, blackface minstrel show conceived and performed by Thomas Dartmouth Rice, a white New Yorker who traveled from city to city entertaining audiences with his degrading depiction of enslaved people, culminating with the song "Jump Jim Crow." Rice was considered a father of American minstrel, and Jim Crow later became the notorious shorthand name for segregation of the races in the southern states. Native Americans suffered from genocide, neglect, and discrimination of other sorts, but were treated separately from African Americans. Black Hawk's eastern venture was covered extensively and positively in scores of southern newspapers, something unimaginable for a black prisoner of war. During the depths of Jim Crow segregation, his tribal descendant Jim Thorpe traveled freely through Florida, Georgia, Alabama, and Mississippi, often as the guest of honor at gatherings of athletic boosters and men's clubs.

The curious crowds grew only larger and more adoring as Black Hawk and his crew moved through Philadelphia and New York. After watching them at a series of teas, banquets, and tours of military installations and financial enterprises, a correspondent for Philadelphia's *National Gazette* reported that "Black Hawk and his companions bear inspection and suffocation most admirably." He watched in bewilderment as refined, urbane citizens became entranced by the warriors and "ladies emulously grasp tawny hands that have been imbrued with human blood." In New York the wharves again throbbed with spectators as the boat carrying Black Hawk approached. Once he was on land, a reporter recalled, the crowd was so intense that "it was with great difficulty he effected a passage along the streets." Look up, Black Hawk was told, a man was rising to the sky in a hot-air balloon. He had never seen anything like that before. "We watched with anxiety to see if it could be true," Black Hawk recounted in his memoir. "And to our utter astonishment saw him ascend in the air until the eye could no longer perceive him."

The same might be said of Black Hawk. In white America he had ascended to a place where the eye could no longer perceive him. By the time he died five years later, a bereft and bedraggled old man among his Sac and Fox people in Iowa (including the twelve-year-old girl *No-ten-o-quah* who would become Jim Thorpe's grandmother), all that was left was myth and legend, along with the Catlin painting—and a life-sized plaster cast of his head and face that had been inspired by his eastern trip. This was an era when plaster casts had a peculiar use, as a means of studying the habits and characteristics of the human from which they were made. In November 1838, only a month after Black Hawk's death, the *American Phrenological Journal* published an eleven-page article using phrenology to examine thirty-four of Black Hawk's personality traits. Phrenology was a trendy pseudoscience employed by European and American practitioners to establish through an analysis of the shape of the skull and face differences between Caucasians and others, often with the intent of establishing lines of racial superiority and inferiority. It became popular as a means of rationalizing the colonization of Africa and the enslavement of African Americans, and for making Native Americans appear more warlike than the whites seeking to annihilate them in the cause of westward expansion.

The phrenologists admired Black Hawk in condescending fashion. He was their quintessential noble savage. They examined him by studying what they called the various "organs" of his head, face, and skull, which were not organs in any biological sense but merely bumps and shapes. "His head is large, giving much more than an ordinary amount of intellect and feeling, and indicative also of weight of character and extent of influence," the journal asserted. But what was called his "index of causality" was judged moderate at best, "thus too feeble to originate very comprehensive plans and successfully adapt means to ends." This deficiency, they concluded, was common to Indians, and "one of the principal causes" why they could not defeat whites in battle.

Studying the "organs" on the side of his head and around his ears, the pseudoscientific phrenologists noted a bulging appearance that they said revealed the "organs of Combativeness, Destructiveness, Secretiveness, and Cautiousness." In a savage state, they claimed, these produce "cruelty, cunning, and revenge" and make the Indian "a bold and desperate warrior." The phrenologists expressed amazement at what they thought was the accuracy of their own work. It was not until the twentieth century that phrenology was fully debunked, although even then it could be seen as a cousin of eugenics, the attempt to "improve" the genetics of the human population by excluding supposedly inferior races.

LATE IN 1912, Jim Thorpe was put to his own pseudoscientific examination. It came a few months after his return from Stockholm and at the end of that Carlisle football season, where for the second year in a row he was named by Walter Camp as a first-team All-American. This study was demeaning in its own way, though conducted for more benign reasons than the phrenological analysis of Black Hawk—not to prove the Sac and Fox Indian's inferiority, but to account for his athletic superiority. The method now was anthropometry, from the Greek for "human measure," which is precisely what it entailed.

If Thorpe in his early twenties was in fact the world's greatest athlete, what specifications of his physique made him so? How could he perform so many athletic feats so spectacularly? He ran with the fluid speed and force of a racehorse. He jumped as if his feet had springs. He performed the five track-and-field events of the pentathlon and the ten of the decathlon better than anyone alive, to say nothing of what he could do with a ball—carrying it, punting it, kicking it, passing it, hitting it, catching it.

Dr. Ferdinand Shoemaker, a medical inspector for the U.S. Indian Service who had once been the physician at Carlisle, and Professor Forrest E. Craver, physical training director at nearby Dickinson College who also happened to be a close friend of and football scout for Pop Warner, wanted to answer that question. To do so, they spent a full day at Carlisle measuring Thorpe's stripped body in forty-six ways and compared the results to those of the average college student. Anthropometry was so popular in the early years of the twentieth century that physical education departments at high schools and colleges around the country were constantly taking the measure of their students. The noted anthropologist Franz Boas had already spent fifteen years compiling anthropometric data on more than fifteen thousand American Indians. Shoemaker and Craver considered their task with Thorpe so momentous they brought in a notary public and swore under oath that the measurements were "true and accurate."

Weight 181 pounds. Height 71.2 inches. Chest normal 39.7. Chest inflated 41.3. Waist 32.5. Hips 38.2. Biceps right arm 13.2. Biceps left arm 13.1. And on it went, from top of fibula to knee; from left shoulder to elbow; arm reach; right foot, left foot; right leg, left leg; head circumference; neck; nipples; pubis. When it was over, in the presence of the notary, they declared Thorpe "the perfect physical man . . . compared to the average male student superior in all respects." Thorpe was no bodybuilder or circus strongman, they found. He had no "knotted or corded muscles out of proportion to his body to break the symmetry that is the most characteristic feature of his physical makeup." They took note that his right foot, which he used on the football field as the nation's premier drop-kicker and punter, was larger than the left, but that his lower left leg, which he pushed off with in high-jumping and hurdling, was slightly larger than his right.

All science at that point, but then came a subjective assessment, the pseudoscience relying on stereotypes of Indians and people of mixed heritage, like Thorpe, who had some white ancestors on both sides of his family. "Today the master athlete of the world as a type, stands halfway between the sinuous aborigine who has been found at some time or other in nearly every country in the world, and the modern product of civilization with specialized muscular development," the examiners explained. "To outward appearances, the resemblance to the aborigine is certainly more marked. Thorpe's body is gracefully molded and as is characteristic of the American Indian is free of the growths of hair that are the usual accompaniment of tremendous strength."

Long after Thorpe was dead, the artist Charles Banks Wilson was commissioned by the Oklahoma legislature to paint a full-length portrait of him. Wilson was the George Catlin of a later time, so fascinated by American Indians that he once spent a year collecting portraits of every tribe in Oklahoma. For the Thorpe portrait, completed in 1967, he could not look at the subject himself, except in two-dimensional photographs. The Carlisle Indian Industrial School by then had been closed for a half century, so he recruited several Indian athletes from the Haskell Institute in Lawrence, Kansas, to pose for him. Soon he discovered that his best models were nonathletes. He found "Thorpe's forearm on a man whose work was lifting bricks, and a Thorpe-like deltoid on a young farm worker." By then he knew the precise dimensions of Thorpe's body.

At the kitchen table of John Steckbeck, an administrator at Lehigh University who had been amassing Thorpe documents and memorabilia for decades, Wilson had come across the anthropometry report conducted by Shoemaker and Craver in 1912. He took the forty-six measurements of that long-ago examination and reduced them to fractions so he could construct a fifteen-inch clay model. From the clay model he practiced with two small paintings before starting on the eight-foot canvas for the final work. It shows the great Indian athlete standing in the infield of a stadium on a summer day. It is 1912 in Stockholm. Thorpe's body is smooth and symmetrical, an image of athletic grace and perfection. He is outfitted in gray shorts and a white sleeveless T-shirt with the U.S. Olympic team emblem on the front. He cups a discus in his right hand, preparing for one of the ten events of the decathlon, looking out at the world unvanquished, the American colossus, black hair windswept over his forehead, the trace of a smile creasing his broad face.

The painting hangs in the rotunda of the state capitol in Oklahoma City, fifty-three miles from the log farmhouse where Jim Thorpe was born.

2

Path Lit by Lightning

HIRAM THORP HAD FIVE WIVES AND AS MANY CHILDREN AS the maximum number of leaflets found on a single stem of the mature pecan trees that shaded the banks of the North Canadian River. That would be eighteen children. His third wife, Charlotte, had eleven of them, all born in the Indian Territory of central Oklahoma, although only five made it to adulthood. She bore two sets of twins. Margaret and Mary died before they reached age four. Soon after came a pair of boys. They were born on May 22, 1887, in a log house on the Sac and Fox reservation near the tiny town of Bellemont, about sixteen miles northeast of Shawnee. One boy was named Charles for Charlotte's older brother and the other James for Hiram's younger brother. Charlie and Jim. Charlotte, a devout Catholic, saw them baptized at the Sacred Heart Mission Church. They were also blessed with Indian names. Jim was called *Wa-tho-Huk*. Among the variations of how that name can be translated into English, the most poetic is Path Lit by Lightning.

The name was intended not as prediction of future athletic greatness but as a description of the scene outside during the hours after his birth. There were few natural lights along the path of Jim Thorpe's life. His wayward father, who according to census data could neither read nor write but had his surname spelled without an *e* at the end, came and went during Jim's youth, once marrying another woman and siring another child before returning to Charlotte. Jim's beloved twin brother died of typhoid fever when they were nine, followed by the deaths of a younger sister and brother. His mother died after childbirth when Jim had just reached his teens, and Hiram succumbed to a fatal poison, likely from a snakebite, when his son was sixteen. Long before Jim became an orphan, he followed his own path between divided worlds, Indian and white.

He was part of both, yet also apart. Losing a twin at an early age was like losing half of himself, but the fault lines of his split identity were apparent from birth. He had ancestors of Sac and Fox, Potawatomi, Kickapoo, Menominee, French, and English descent. The Potawatomi, Kickapoo, Menominee, and French were on his mother's side; the Sac and Fox on his father's side, through his paternal grandmother, *No-ten-o-quah*, whose name translated to Wind in the Rain. She was the wife of Hiram Thorp the elder, a blacksmith of English lineage who lived among that tribe. By tribal custom Jim was considered Sac and Fox even though there was more Indian heritage, especially Potawatomi, on his mother's side. Blood quantum, a means of defining what comprises the whole of a person by calculating through percentages the ancestral bloodlines, was a concept imposed on American Indians by white society. By that definition, Jim Thorpe would tell people he was five-eighths Indian.

In resolving his self-identity, Thorpe had to adjust to forces outside his native surroundings. The unequal and violent relationship between whites and American Indians was changing dramatically in the very year he was born. That was when forced assimilation became government policy through the General Allotment Act of 1887, more commonly known as the Dawes Act, named for its chief sponsor, Senator Henry Dawes of Massachusetts, chairman of the Senate Committee on Indian Affairs. The specifics of the Dawes Act dealt mostly with land, amounting to one last territorial conquest after centuries of Indian lands being taken by the firepower of the U.S. Army, the unceasing migration of white settlers, and the manipulation of federal treaties.

Here was the government's deal: every adult Indian living on a reservation in the West would be granted 160 acres of land (in the woodland Great Lakes region it was half that amount), with lesser parcels eventually granted to those who were single, orphaned, or under eighteen. With some exceptions, these allotments would be held in trust by the United States for a quarter century, during which time the Indians could earn their way to citizenship by demonstrating their competence, defined in this case as the ability to survive culturally and financially in a white-dominated society. In exchange, all remaining land—meaning most of it—would be appropriated at bargain rates by the government and opened to white settlement. The Indians would not get that land-sale money all at once, as in many real estate deals, but in small yearly severalty payments.

The Sac and Fox were among many Indian nations wary of the deal. One month after Jim was born, an Indian council of delegates from eighteen tribes gathered at Eufaula in Indian Territory to discuss the Dawes Act. While the prevailing tenor of the gathering was that it was time for Indians to "adopt the ways of civilization," the delegates also drafted a memorial letter to President Grover Cleveland opposing the allotment provision. It was, they argued, a detriment to their interests that would soon engulf them in cultural and political catastrophe. "The Indian needs a political identity, an allegiance, elsewhere called patriotism, in order to make true progress in the affairs of life," an essay describing the letter asserted. "The law . . . leaves the balance [after allotment] to others, who will be composed of a class having no sympathy for Indians, who will rush into the new country in their mad race for gain, and crowd out every hope and chance of Indian civilization."

Prescient words, ignored. The Sac and Fox reservation at the time of Thorpe's birth consisted of almost half a million acres between the North Canadian and Cimarron Rivers. Within five years, more than three-quarters of that land was gone to white settlers as part of what was called the Oklahoma Land Rush. The same happened throughout Indian Territory and with other tribes in the plains states. But it was not just people greedy for land who pushed the Dawes Act. Dawes was among those who presented themselves as progressive reformers who believed the only way Native Americans could survive after centuries of decimation was for them to disappear into white civilization. Eliminating their communal reservation lifestyle and turning them instead into private landowners was part of that process, along with the educational acculturation of their children.

A volatile family, growing, dying, leaving; a vulnerable culture the government sought to dissolve; a pressure to conform to the dominant society—this was the world of young Jim Thorpe. His life was shaped by the way he responded to those circumstances, alternately adapting and rejecting.

JIM AND CHARLIE were born into the colors of the Thunder Clan: purple, rose, coal gray, dark blue, and turquoise. The U.S. government, reflecting the mores of white society, divided Indian tribes into two categories then: wild or civilized. The Sac and Fox were placed in the wild category. A government agent reported at the time of the Dawes Act that nearly half of the 2,002 members of the Sac and Fox tribe in Indian Territory were "blanket Indians" who followed old traditions and lived in bark houses. Some others went back and forth between Indian and white dress and housing, and the smallest group, perhaps 15 percent, had adapted to white norms of dress and lodging. Included in that last number were Hiram and Charlotte, who were considered better off than most. Their family by then lived in a log farmhouse, one large room plus a sleeping loft, built amid the cottonwoods and blackjack oaks on a red-clay bluff above the North Canadian, a branch of the Canadian River (named for the French traders from Canada who once camped there). Lush bottomlands provided pastures where Hiram could breed and train horses. The family also raised cattle, chickens, and hogs; collected pecan nuts and wild blackberries that thrived along the riverbank; grew corn, beans, and melons; and hunted for meals of rabbit, wild turkey, prairie chickens, deer, and red squirrel. Fried squirrel with cream gravy became Jim's favorite meal.

Although Charlotte imbued Jim with intimations of Black Hawk's greatness, in appearance it was Charlie who more resembled the Sac and Fox warrior, with his angular face, copper skin, and eagle nose. Jim looked more like his father, ruggedly charismatic with lighter skin, smoothly sloped shoulders, hooded eyes, and a broad forehead. In a word portrait decades later, Jim said his face revealed his heritage, with its "expression of a red man." Family members considered Charlie the more thoughtful and inward of the twins, while Jim was spontaneous and physical, again more like his father. Among the many characteristics of Hiram Thorp, good and bad, he was strong and agile. Jim called him "an athletic marvel" and recalled how on summer nights after dinner he watched his father and other men compete in wrestling, jumping, running, and horseback riding. Hiram, he said, was "the undisputed champion in all these sports." On a hunting trip they took once, by Jim's account, his father shot two deer, skinned them, draped the deadweight carcasses over his shoulders, and hauled them twenty miles back to the log cabin by the river. Maybe an exaggeration, maybe not. Jim would grow up to meet or play against all the greatest athletes of his day, but he said he never met a man with more energy than his father.

Hiram was a big man with an outsize reputation in Indian Territory, a ruffian in a rough land. This is what patrons saw when he entered the Black Dog Saloon, one of his favorite hangouts in nearby Keokuk Falls: the cowboy Indian, a hulking 230 pounds of frontier arrogance in a business suit, with a crowned black hat and straight black hair shading a roustabout mug accented by a handlebar mustache. A silk scarf was knotted around his neck, a long hand-rolled cigar smoldered in one hand, holster and Colt Peacemaker were strapped to his waist, and dusty boots jagged his suit pants. People were never quite sure with Hiram. He loved practical jokes and spent days planning them, but that gun and those big hands and his fondness for whiskey could as easily lead to mayhem. He traveled with a mongrel dog that loved to fight as much as he did. Mayhem was part of daily life around Keokuk Falls.

On the border of Indian Territory, which by federal mandate was supposed to be dry, the town was wet and violent, in contrast to the Sac and Fox leader for whom it was named. Chief Keokuk was a man of accommodation who had adhered to the white man's treaties and tried to dissuade Black Hawk from his fated mission across the Mississippi. The Black Dog, a hangout for outlaws, gamblers, and prostitutes, was one of the Seven Deadly Saloons of Keokuk Falls. According to legend, when the stagecoach stopped in town the driver would crow in the manner of a traveling show barker: "Stay for a half hour and see a man killed!" Hiram saw plenty.

Along with ranching, farming, and horse trading, Hiram was an inveterate bootlegger, crisscrossing Indian lands with gallon jugs of illicit whiskey he hawked from the back of his wagon, usually one step ahead of the law.

Other bootleggers tried at least rudimentary means of deception, posing as egg or dry goods salesmen. Hiram was blatant. At least once Lee Patrick from the Sac and Fox Agency reported him to the U.S. attorney in Guthrie, noting that Hiram introduced "onto this reservation one gallon of whiskey and gave same to Naw-mil-wah, Henry Miller, Parkinson, Sam Brown, Sac and Fox Indians." The next day, he was at it again, selling whiskey to the same characters. "I have the jug in my possession," Patrick reported. "This liquor was introduced during the Sac and Fox payment and created much disturbance. He is very defiant in the matter and I respectfully request that you have him immediately apprehended and prosecute him to the full extent of the law." The respectful request was never fulfilled.

The history of alcohol and Native Americans was a case of the white man giveth and the white man taketh away—or tryeth to. From the time it was introduced to Indians by Europeans soon after they reached what was to them a new world, liquor was a lucrative means of profit for merchants and traders, and a destabilizing force furthering the cause of manifest destiny, a means of perpetuating the drunken Indian myth of people who were childlike and inferior. Get them drunk, then forbid them from drinking anymore for their own good, in the name of civilization. Aside from its condescension, that myth also dealt in the stereotype that all Native Americans were alike rather than a complex assortment of peoples with a variety of physical traits and cultural traditions. The Indians-and-alcohol stereotype persisted deep into the twentieth century before it became accepted science that systemic social conditions were the primary cause of high rates of alcoholism among Native Americans, and that genetically they were not more susceptible than other groups. The roustabout crowd at the Black Dog and the other Seven Deadly Saloons of Keokuk Falls offered ample evidence that white men were equally prone to uncontrolled drinking.

Hiram had a thirst for liquor. And for women. One of his great-grandsons later recounted how the word around Indian Territory was that the man in the black hat and silk scarf "liked to keep teams of two horses and two women at all times." Charlotte came closest to being the exception to that rule. She was strong-willed and big-boned, weighing two hundred pounds herself, only thirty pounds less than her imposing husband. Her face was a pleasant oval, her eyes brown and soft. Intellectually, Hiram was no match for her. Unlike him, she could read and write, according to the 1900 census, skills she learned at St. Mary's Mission in Kansas as a girl. She also had a knack for languages, speaking fluent English, French, Potawatomi, and Sauk, allowing her to negotiate different cultures.

Charlotte came from Kansas as a teenager with her parents and the Citizen Band Potawatomi, who had been practicing Catholics for generations and citizens of the United States since 1861. A quarter century before the 1887 Allotment Act, most members of the tribe, then based in northeast Kansas, had signed a treaty that accomplished much the same thing as the Dawes legislation—to their detriment. They gave up their reservation in exchange for smaller individual landholdings, and in their case immediate citizenship. But white settlers and the railroads pressed in on them, eager to take the land, and the federal government failed to keep its promises of assistance during the transition. By late 1873 so many tribal members had had their acreage seized due to unpaid federal taxes that the Citizen Band decided to move to land in Indian Territory adjacent to their longtime allies, the Sac and Fox.

Another migration in a century of migrations, most forced by treaty and gunpoint. Before the Europeans arrived, the Potawatomi had thrived for centuries in the woodlands around the Great Lakes. White encroachment kept pushing them farther west and south. Charlotte's ancestors migrated from the Green Bay area down to Skunk Grove near Milwaukee before being forced across the Mississippi to Council Bluffs, Iowa, where famine and debts led them to pick up again and traipse south to Kansas. All along the route they were followed by a French trading family founded by Jacques Vieux, whose sons and grandsons married Potawatomi women, one of whom was Jim Thorpe's maternal grandmother. In Kansas, the band that came down from Iowa was joined by a large band from the same tribe that had been rounded up by federal troops in 1838 at an encampment near Twin Lakes, Indiana, and led on a forced march through Indiana, Illinois, and Missouri into Kansas. That march, known as the Trail of Death, started in the heat of early September and ended in the snows of November, with a unit of federal troops pushing 756 Indians and their horses and wagons onward. Often thirsty and near starvation, plagued by fever and pneumonia and tuberculosis, walking as many as twenty-six miles a day, the band lost at least 41 people, including many infants and young children, before they reached Kansas.

Then the final migration from Kansas to Indian Territory—the end of the road. Charlotte Vieux was sixteen when her people reached their new home amid their woodland allies, the Sac and Fox, Kickapoo, and Shawnee. Hiram Thorp and his family were already there.

The trail of forced migrations for the Sac and Fox had followed a similar route from Wisconsin and Illinois to Iowa and Kansas, where they were ravaged by a smallpox epidemic in 1851 that killed more than three hundred people and forced the tribe's blacksmith, Hiram Thorp the elder, to devote his time to constructing burial frames and boxes. Finally, in 1869, diminished in numbers and prospects, they made their final move south to unoccupied land in Indian Territory. The trek was made during a mild winter, men and women on horseback, many grandparents and children walking amid a scampering pack of camp dogs, the infirm riding on wagons that carried personal possessions and farm implements. The legend of that journey was passed down through generations, and some accounts were told to field workers collecting oral histories six decades later. Mandy Starr recalled her parents telling her how "the caravan was headed by government troops and the wagons strung out for four or five miles behind. They grouped themselves into units, twenty wagons to a unit." It was spring when they arrived in Oklahoma. Once there, Starr said, "they camped wherever they wished near river or spring, often eight or fifteen miles apart. In those days everyone knew the Indian name of all his neighbors and even mere acquaintances and where they lived."

Hiram Thorp the blacksmith and his wife, *No-ten-o-quah*, found a spot near the North Canadian. He was in his late fifties, she was in her early forties, and their son Hiram the younger was eighteen.

The descendants of Jim Thorpe were never sure how his parents, Hiram and Charlotte, met. It was likely at a dance or powwow of the friendly neighboring tribes. What is documented is that Hiram the younger by then was already living with two wives, bigamy being acceptable by tribal custom. Not long after he reached Indian Territory, he married Mary James, also Sac and Fox. They had four children, two surviving past childhood. While still married to Mary, Hiram took a second wife, a Creek woman named Sarah LaBlanche, who gave birth to another child. According to a probate report written decades later when the Sac and Fox Agency settled Hiram's estate, "the testimony shows that he lived with Mary . . . and Sarah at the same time." They also left at the same time, in 1880. The reason: Hiram wanted to marry Charlotte Vieux, who said that as a Catholic she considered bigamy out of the question. She would marry him only as his sole wife, or at least the only wife living with him. "I was with Hiram the night he brought Charlotte back to live with him," Alexander Connelly, Hiram's friend, testified at the probate hearing. "And then the other two women he was living with picked up and left him. I drove them to Okmulgee myself."

Jim and Charlie were born to Charlotte on a spring day seven years later when lightning flashed along the river.

"BOOMER SOONER" IS the famed fight song at the University of Oklahoma. The song evokes the history of settlers rushing into Indian Territory to claim land that had been taken from tribes after a series of congressional actions provided the ways and means. First came the Dawes Act of 1887, which forced Indians to cede their reservations in favor of smaller private holdings, then the Indian Appropriations Act of 1889, which officially opened vast swaths of former reservation land to white settlement. People who had been pressing the government for years to open this land were called Boomers. Impatient white settlers who entered prematurely and staked out plots before the government gave its official blessing were called Sooners. "Boomer Sooner"—the celebration of land thieves and their abettors.

Jim Thorpe was four when the Sac and Fox saw much of their reservation go to white settlers. The Oklahoma Land Run of 1891 started at noon on Tuesday, September 22. Hundreds of men and their families had camped along the boundaries of Sac and Fox country for several days waiting for the signal; then a mad scramble began. Paul Gokey was with his parents at a Sac and Fox Drum Dance lodge east of Aydelotte that day, within a few miles of the Thorp farmhouse. "Towards noon we saw a whole lot of people coming from the south but we didn't know what they were there for," Gokey recalled in an oral interview. "We knew the government had given . . . surveyors the right to enter the territory, but this couldn't be they, because there were women and children besides men. They kept coming all day, and they seemed to be very excited. There was a lot of shooting and fighting going on, and I saw several men killed. They burnt the prairies and there sure was a lot of smoke. I found out afterwards that the land had opened to the whites and they were burning the prairie to find the eighty-acre markers. The Indian land was already marked, and they had to find land that didn't belong to the Indians. After all the excitement was over, we continued our dance."

Jim remembered his father and several friends "quietly watching four or five white men peering through their surveying instruments" to map out land for white settlers. Words were exchanged, a challenge made, and by Jim's account Hiram "met the man's challenge with a blow to the chin which sent him against his surveying instrument, toppling it to the ground he had just charted." That is not to say that all white participants in the Oklahoma land runs were violent misfits. Many were families who after struggling with hard times in other states were enticed by the possibility of a fresh start and became unwitting pawns in the larger cause of Indian displacement. Men like DeWitt Dever, who had seen his hardware business go bust in Kansas and was in Missouri with his young and growing family when he read about a land rush in the local paper; Dever traveled to Oklahoma, walked sixty miles over two days to the border of open land, and borrowed a racehorse to reach the property where he staked his claim. He learned about Boomers and Sooners, encountered cheaters with guns who tried to force their way onto property, and was frustrated by U.S. marshals at the land office who, he said, were nothing more than "a bunch of grafters clothed with authority."

Charlotte Thorp was in the eighth month of pregnancy when settlers rushed the land near the homestead, including Czech immigrants who founded a town they called Prague. She gave birth to a son named Jesse three weeks later, but the boy died before turning one, and Hiram left soon after for a new wife, his fourth. Charlotte filed for divorce, but there is no documentation that it was granted. The marriage of Hiram and Fannie McClellan was by tribal custom, not government law. Fannie gave birth to a son, William Lasley Thorp, in 1893, who eventually became so close to his half-brother Jim that he came to be called Little Jimmy. Then Hiram divorced Fannie, again by tribal custom, and returned to Charlotte.

All this coming and going happened during the years Jim and his twin, Charlie, were between four and seven years old. The family rupture never became part of Jim's depiction of childhood, which sounded less traumatic and more idyllic. He told of boys roaming free in the forest, swimming in the "lazy flowing North Canadian," fishing for catfish on the sandy banks of the river, playing Fox and Geese and Follow the Leader, the loser forced to crawl through a tunnel of legs and a human windmill of hard-slapping hands. "Many a time in these games I had to swim rivers, climb barns and jump off roofs, wade streams and ride horses," he once recalled to a magazine writer for an as-told-to account. "Our favorite stunt, however, was to climb to the top of a tall tree that would bend and sway under our weight, swing there, and then leap to the ground."

With the modern world closing in, the Sac and Fox also clung to traditional games and totems. The boys played a dart game called *Mi-qua-pee* in which they tossed two-foot darts at a nearby mound and competed to see how far the darts could bounce. Their elders gathered for long sessions of *Ko-the-ka-no-ke*, a dice game that could involve as many as twenty-four people. The players sat in a circle around a thick pallet of blankets and a wide bowl made from a turtle shell from which the dice were shaken onto the blankets. The two most important dice had animal heads carved into them. Turtle and horse heads were worth ten points. Scores were kept with rows of buckeyes. There was much betting, often fifty-cent games, and with so many people playing, the winner of even one pot felt rich. "It is inherent for Indians to love games," Jim once told a sportswriter.

He remembered feasts lasting ten days, often held after a death in a family or an adoption, and occasional visits to other tribes. Ben Smith recalled trips to Ponca and Osage country. "They would make friends and there would be a powwow for four days," he told an oral historian. "The last day was give-away day. A horse would be given to one you wished to be a friend to. This meant you were the same as a brother to them. Even though you were of different tribes. The next year they in turn gave you something."

Even during the years when Hiram Thorp was with another wife and family, he was not absent from the boys' lives, by Jim's account: "From the time I was six my father would take me with him on hunting trips. It was on one of those trips for wild game that I first learned to shoot and ride horseback. Often we would be gone for weeks. We would pack our kill—mostly deer and bear—on the backs of the horses and then walk home, sometimes twenty or thirty miles a day." When they returned from a hunt, Hiram would dry and hang the meat in a smoke cellar for the winter's supply. Jim loved to hunt so much that even at the height of his athletic fame, after he was acclaimed for his skills in football, baseball, and track and field, he would say that hunting was his favorite sport. "I learned how to wait beside a runway and stalk a deer. I learned how to trap for bear and rabbits, coon and possum. . . . I used to go out by myself with an old dog and hunt coon when I was only eight or ten years old. I would often make camp and stay overnight."

When young Jim misbehaved, his father beat him with his heavy fists or lashed him with a stick or leather strap. There were other methods of punishment meted out by elders of the tribe. Stella Reuben recalled being deprived of food if she did something wrong, or if it was winter her parents might force her to bathe in the icy waters of the North Canadian. "In the midwinter they often had to cut a hole in the ice," Reuben said in an oral history. "They knew the swimming hole and always cut where the water wasn't more than waist high. As the country was settled by whites, we cut it out, never knew when someone was coming upon us when we were taking a bath."

At age seven, Jim and Charlie were sent to the Sac and Fox boarding school near Stroud, a government institution founded by the Society of Friends that covered eight grades. The three-story brick-and-wood red schoolhouse had a gabled roof and wide porches fronting the first and second floors, with a smaller building in back. The girls wore cotton dresses and sweaters and the boys were outfitted in vested suits and black hats. Up at quarter to six, marching to and fro in formation. They performed manual labor during the mornings, often on the school farm, and classroom work in the afternoons. There were eighty students and four teachers along with a superintendent. The students were forbidden from speaking Sauk, even among themselves. English only. A few students arrived knowing only their Indian names and were renamed by the school; one was dubbed after the outlaw Jesse James. One of the teachers was Harriet Patrick, the daughter of Lee Patrick, the government agent for the Sac and Fox who had tracked and reported Hiram Thorp's whiskey bootlegging enterprise. Harriet found Jim "an incorrigible youngster" who was "fidgety, undisciplined, and uninterested in anything but outdoor life," so unlike his twin. Charlie, she said, was "a sweet, gentle boy."

Stella Reuben, who was also a student there, said many of the children "hated the school" because the routine was so different from the "free life on the reservation." Some attended willingly, or at least at the direction of their parents; others were rounded up by government agents and brought to school by the wagonload against their will. In either case, Indian parents had little choice. The year before Jim and Charlie began their educations, Congress authorized the Indian bureau to "withhold rations, clothing, and other annuities from Indian parents or guardians who refuse or neglect to send their children" of proper age to school. Many of those who attended against their will were from so-called blanket Indian families—Sac and Fox who tried to hold on to their traditional lifestyles and avoid the white man's culture. "The blanket Indians often came to the school asking to visit their children," Reuben recalled. "Few of them could speak English, so one of the girls in the school usually acted as interpreter. Quite frequently the parents of children in school camped for months at a time along the creek at the agency so as to be nearer their children."

During Jim and Charlie's third year, typhoid fever raged through the school, brought on by contaminated food or water. The disease struck the superintendent and many students, including Charlie but not Jim. Teachers became nurses, spending their nights making the rounds of ailing children. Harriet Patrick saw Charlie's typhoid bring on pneumonia. "I took care of him at night with the others," she said. "Mr. and Mrs. Thorpe came one night to relieve me and I tried to get some rest." This was through the night of March 9 and into the morning of March 10, 1897. "At 5 a.m. came word that Charlie was worse. I went to him and took him in my arms, put his little feet in mustard water, and sent for doctor. But the poor fellow just lay back and died."

Jim had lost his constant companion and some part of himself. "No two brothers were ever closer," Michael Koehler, one of Jim's grandsons, later wrote. That summer at home, Jim walked alone with his coon dog through their wooded playland, sometimes sleeping in the forest. Sent back to school the next fall, he kept running away, often getting caught and taken back in the government wagon. Jim would later tell the story of how he once made it all twenty-three miles to the farmhouse on the North Canadian, and when his father met him at the door and immediately marched him back to school, he fled again, this time taking a shortcut to beat Hiram home. Myth or hyperbole, the story accurately reflected Jim's determination to escape. Realizing this, Hiram finally told Jim: "I'm going to send you so far away you'll never find your way back."

ON THE FIRST weekend of September 1898, Jim arrived in Lawrence to attend Haskell Institute. He and his brother George, who was sixteen, the oldest of Hiram and Charlotte's children, made the three-hundred-mile journey from Indian Territory up into Kansas by wagon and railroad, making a switch in Kansas City. The Lawrence depot was bustling from before dawn to midnight that weekend. A morning train carried the chancellor of the University of Kansas. A night coach brought the captain of the KU football team. Students by the trainload disembarked and were surrounded by solicitors, some offering to haul luggage to the Jayhawk campus, others trying to persuade them to board at one of the many rooming houses in town. Jim and his brother did not need a rooming house. Haskell, across town from the big state university, was an Indian boarding school, one of the two largest in the country, housing more than seven hundred students.

In the middle of one of Jim's first nights at Haskell, around 3:30 a.m., the students were awakened by an ear-shattering noise. It turned out to be the accidental blowing of the steam whistle at the town's barbed wire plant when a boiler pipe cracked, but it was good training for the regimentation of his new life. Military-style uniforms, reveille at dawn, taps at night, drills and farmwork in the morning, classes in the afternoon. Everything with one purpose in mind—to refashion young Indians in the image of white people. As at all federal Indian schools of that era, the students were not to use their native tongues but speak, write, and think in English. When the school opened in 1884, the superintendent in his inaugural address had spoken of his aspirations for Haskell and its students. "Here we hope them to share with us the blessings of enlightened people," declared James Marvin. "In vision near we see the Indian tribes turning their spears to pruning hooks, the tepee replaced by the cottage, fields of grain and the fragrance of orchards all over that vast land once assigned as the red man's burial ground."

Some students did not want to be saved in that fashion. The newspapers in Kansas at the time Jim enrolled, fourteen years after Haskell's opening, were full of stories about escapes from the school, the prose dripping with a journalistic mix of sympathy and condescension. "NO LIKE SCHOOL," ran a headline in the *Topeka State Journal.* "Tired of living under the roofs of the white man's school, uncomfortable in tight fitting clothes of the American citizen, and with a longing to once again don the soft moccasins, leggings, and red blankets of the tribe, two Indian boys stole away from the Haskell Indian school at Lawrence early Sunday morning before sunrise and started on their journey home to the hunting grounds and tepees of their tribe, the Arapahos in the Indian Territory." The boys were caught in north Topeka and taken to the station house by truant officers who were awarded five dollars for every runaway. "Police court judge Atchison asked 'Why did you run away from school?' " the article went on. "'Don't like it,' was the answer. The prisoners were led back to the cell, stretched themselves on the floor and with only evil thoughts for the white race they are waiting to be taken back to school which to them is bondage."

Readers in the cities and towns of Kansas rarely went a day without seeing something about Haskell. The construction of a new chapel on campus that could hold more than five hundred students at a time was front-page news in many towns, as was the acquisition of one hundred Old Testaments and two hundred New Testaments from the American Bible Society. In contrast, there was the article about the U.S. marshals' efforts to track down and arrest bootleggers who were selling liquor to Haskell students. A writer for the *Kansas City Journal* described the music program with equal parts wit and racist stereotyping: "There is a band of twenty-four men composed entirely of students. They play a fair grade of music in a more or less ensnaring manner. The percentage of trombone players is abnormally large and is to be accounted for by the profound reverence which the Indian manifests for anything capable of producing torture."

Elementary grades at Haskell did not correspond precisely to public elementary schools, but records show that Jim in a sense started over again at a rudimentary level—Grade 1B. Along with working at the school farm and learning mechanical tasks, he was taught to add, read, spell, and write with a steady, looping cursive hand. But in terms of training for his future, the most important interest he developed at Haskell was a love of a game—football.

The season when Haskell started to emphasize football coincided with Jim's first year. The new superintendent, H. B. Peairs, gave football his "hearty support," reasoning that it would promote Haskell to a wider audience while further immersing the boys in a game of growing appeal in white society. Whether football was in fact a civilizing influence and means of enlightenment was another matter to be debated for generations to come. In his effort to bring big-time football to Haskell, Peairs enticed a young but well-known local figure to take over as coach, the first Haskell coach to be paid a salary. It was Will T. Walker, familiarly known as Sal, a former star center at the University of Kansas. Walker started training his new charges in the heat of early fall, laying out a practice field behind the disciplinarian's house. He said he liked what he saw, promising to field the best Indian team west of the Mississippi.

Jim was only eleven when he started at Haskell and thirteen when he left, too young to play on the team, but he became entranced by the game and the Indian players and was a regular on the sidelines watching practice. "It was at Haskell I saw my first football game and developed a love for it, a love I have had through the years," he recounted decades later. "Too young to take part in the football games at the school, I organized a team among classmates my own age. We fashioned a football from wool yarn and occasionally were successful in including one of the older boys to referee our game. We played after school hours on the outskirts of campus. An Indian by the name of Chauncey Archiquette on the regular Haskell squad was my football idol and in our scrub games with the homemade football I always tried to emulate him."

Chauncey Archiquette was an Oneida from the Fox River Valley near Green Bay, the same pocket of northeast Wisconsin that produced the Potawatomi ancestors of Jim's mother, Charlotte. Archiquette was the captain and star of the 1900 Haskell team that won nine games, including a shutout of the University of Missouri. As it turned out, he had already played several years of football at the Carlisle Indian School, and in fact had graduated from Carlisle before enrolling at Haskell and playing several more seasons—possible in that era before governing bodies were established to set eligibility rules. By one account, it was Archiquette, after taking a liking to the young boy, who gave Jim the makeshift football he used in intramural games. With that ball in his hands, even then, Jim was the fastest boy on the field. He had been around horses all his young life and tried to run like one—"head up and feet coming down with a thundering certainty." Before Haskell, he had never thought about his future, but there the intimations of something better in his life began. He thought that someday he might want to be a football coach.

• • •

THE LACUNA IN Jim Thorpe's life came at the end of his Haskell experience and during the year after. The one known constant in that period is that he was increasingly alone in the world.

It started when a classmate revealed that a secret was being kept from Jim, that while in the office of a Haskell administrator the classmate had seen a letter sent to the school stating that Hiram Thorp had been shot during a hunting accident and was dying of a chest wound. Jim would later say that the letter was written by his father, but the 1900 census recorded Hiram as unable to read or write. Was the letter written by Charlotte? Perhaps, although the Sac and Fox Agency annuity rolls of 1899 list her as "Separated from Husband" and Hiram as "Separated from Wife"—indicating he had split again. In any event, Jim's response to the letter was to leave Haskell. He said he "jumped a freight train" in Lawrence, only to discover that it was northbound instead of southbound, so he got off and started to walk. "It took me two weeks," Thorpe recalled. When he arrived at the log farmhouse above the North Canadian, his father was recovered, but as ornery as ever. "One day soon after, my dad gave me a licking that I probably deserved but didn't like so ran away to the Texas Panhandle." The story Jim would tell was that he stayed for a year in Texas, fixing fences and working as a ranch hand.

His account is the only record of that year; there are no documents, no recollections by witnesses. But there was one defining event that happened while Jim was in Texas. Charlotte and Hiram reunited long enough for Charlotte to give birth to another baby on January 5, 1902, the last of her eleven. No sooner had they named him Henry than he died on January 8. Charlotte died from complications of childbirth weeks later. She was only thirty-eight—a large presence gone. Her death reverberated through the broken family and ended up taking Jim, the son she saw as the reincarnation of Black Hawk, along his lightning path.

3

"This Is the Indian's Home"

THE CARLISLE INDIAN INDUSTRIAL SCHOOL HAD BEEN OPerating for twenty-five years by the time Jim Thorpe arrived in early 1904. It was the flagship school of the federal Indian bureau, the first and largest of its kind, a non-reservation school for all tribes. The twenty-seven-acre campus covered a hill in the fertile countryside on the edge of the city of Carlisle, a short hop southwest on the Pennsylvania Railroad from Harrisburg, the state capital. The grounds and many of the buildings had once constituted the Carlisle Barracks, a military installation that traced back to before the Revolutionary War. Most of the forty-nine buildings—dormitories, classrooms, gymnasium, dining hall, and workshops—were painted steel gray. Exceptions were the laundry, the doctor's cottage, and the superintendent's house, formerly the commandant's quarters, which was gleaming white with a roof redone in red and gold, the school colors. The oldest standing structure on the grounds, known as the Hessian Powder Magazine, with its arched roof and limestone walls lined with brick six feet thick, was built in 1777 by Hessian prisoners after George Washington's victory at the Battle of Trenton and used to store gunpowder and cannon shot.

The Hessian captives also built the Guard House next door, a small prison with six cells, two with barred windows and four completely dark. A century and a quarter later the Guard House was still in use as a punishing jail for runaways and misbehaving Indian students. At least once during his time at Carlisle, Jim was among the Guard House's unwilling overnight guests. That was for the older boys, referred to as the Large Boys. There was a less intimidating lockup room in the Small Boys quarters. On the

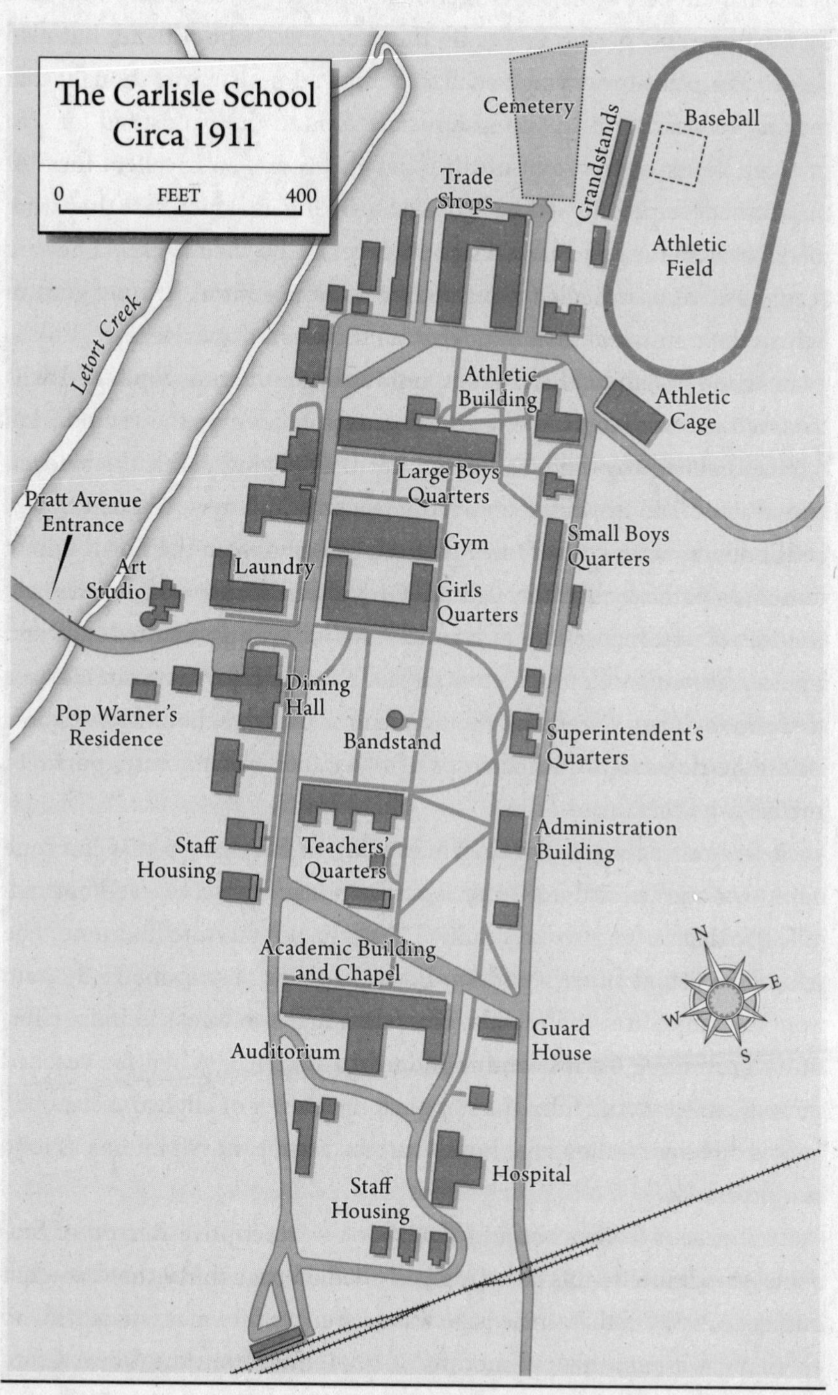
The Carlisle School
Circa 1911
0
FEET
400
Letort Creek
Cemetery
Baseball
Grandstands
Trade Shops
Athletic Field
Athletic Building
Athletic Cage
Large Boys Quarters
Pratt Avenue Entrance
Small Boys Quarters
Gym
Art Studio
Laundry
Girls Quarters
Dining Hall
Pop Warner's Residence
Bandstand
Superintendent's Quarters
Administration Building
Staff Housing
Teachers' Quarters
Academic Building and Chapel
N
E
W
S
Guard House
Auditorium
Hospital
Staff Housing

grassy parade below the superintendent's quarters a bandstand was used for orations and performances by the renowned school band, but also served as a place for paying penance. School administrators thought that making wayward Indian youngsters pace around the bandstand for two or three hours within sight of their classmates was an excellent form of punishment, especially if they had been drinking, in which case they were made to circle the bandstand with a DRUNK sign on their backs. "They are very sensitive to ridicule," explained one administrator. "It only goes to help in the training of their minds . . . a little reproof goes deep."

In good weather, the campus unfolded gentle and copious, lawns trimmed and verdant, wisteria vines draping violet over the veranda, tall oaks and elms providing leafy shade for the walking paths, the beloved Old Walnut Tree towering above the teachers' quarters, fragrant flower beds popping with color. Down past the workshops on the north side of campus, a path wended through the Grove, five thickly wooded acres of willow, walnut, locust, hickory, and sycamore leading to a millrace and an old gray stone mill near Letort Creek. Nearby was the swimming hole at Conodoguinet Creek and the abundance of two school farms where limestone-rich soil produced crops of wheat, barley, oats, corn, potatoes, and garden vegetables.

It was on the warm but drizzly evening of February 6 that Jim rode into town on the local from Harrisburg, the last leg of a twelve-hundred-mile trip that began two days earlier in Stroud, not far from his home. The school's assistant superintendent, Edgar A. Allen, also came in by train from the same direction that day after spending two weeks in Indian Territory promoting Carlisle and rounding up students. When Jim reached campus, an easy walk from the station at the corner of High and Hanover, he was directed to the Large Boys quarters, a three-story building as long as a city block.

In Carlisle's leather-bound ledger book—Descriptive Record of Students As Admitted—his name was recorded on page thirty-three, student number 3205. On that single page was a listing of fifty male students who entered Carlisle in the first months of 1904, boys from the Sioux, Chippewa, Seneca, Onondaga, St. Regis, Sac and Fox, Assiniboine, Delaware,

Shoshone, Arapaho, Cherokee, Ute, Inuit, and Oneida nations. The oldest was David Little Old Man, a twenty-two-year-old, six-foot Cheyenne who suffered from acute bronchitis. The youngest was Jeremiah Horner, a ten-year-old Onondaga who stood three foot three and weighed just over sixty pounds. One Sioux boy, Moses Norbert, ran away before he could be examined. Nearly half, like David Little Old Man, had health problems listed in the remarks. Weak heart. Weak lungs and heart. Half-blind eye. Chronic heart disease. Asthmatic lung disease. Under the listing for mother and father, half were recorded as having only one living parent and one in four was an orphan.

The entry for James Thorpe noted that he was Sac and Fox, son of Hiram, father alive, mother dead. His age was listed as seventeen, which he would not turn until May. The remarks section was blank. Most striking were the measurements of his height and weight: five feet and five-and-a-half inches and 115 pounds. He was soon outfitted in the Carlisle uniform: cavalry cap, light blue slacks with dark stripe down the leg, dark blue jacket, and buffed black shoes that faced regular inspection. From the options for manual training, Jim passed on the blacksmith trade of his grandfather and chose tailoring and painting.

The 860 Indian students at school that year came from eighty-eight tribes, but only 14 were Sac and Fox—10 boys and 4 girls. Jim found a boy from his tribe who gave him the first glimpse of what was expected of him. Reveille at six. Breakfast at seven in the dining hall. Four hours of classwork in the morning. Four hours of farm or industrial shop in the afternoon. A routine he had become familiar with, and had chafed at, during his days at Haskell.

THE EVENTS THAT took Jim to Carlisle—where off and on he would spend the next nine years—started with his return from Texas and the death of his mother, who was buried at the Sacred Heart Cemetery on the Potawatomi reservation near her parents. For a time after Charlotte's death, Jim and his older brother, George, who was nineteen, took responsibility for their younger siblings, Mary, Adeline, and Edward. Jim helped on the farm and enrolled at the local public school in Garden Grove, a one-room and one-teacher school about three miles from home. "It was all book work there," Jim recalled, "and I missed the football games for which I had developed some enthusiasm at Haskell." He also missed watching his mother sew the family clothes and grind corn flour on ancient rocks, and he longed for the slow nights of games and storytelling on the front porch of the farmhouse when she was alive. "Mother's death laid a quiet hand upon the little community in which we mingled." But Hiram did not wait long before marrying again, taking a white woman named Julia Hardin as his fifth wife, and by all accounts she and Jim did not get along.

Two weeks before Christmas 1903, the Sac and Fox agent in Stroud received a letter signed "Hairm Thrope" (Hiram with the letters jumbled and misspelled Thorp gaining an *e*). It was probably written by Hardin, since Hiram Thorp was illiterate. The letter was filled with mistakes of spelling and fact, even making Jim two years younger than he was, but the point was obvious.

> *Dear Sir—*
>
> *I have a boy I wish you would make rangements to Send of to School Some Ware Carlyle or Hampton I don't Care ware. He went to Haskill but I Think it better one of the former plases so he Cannot run away—he is 14 years old and I Cannot do any thing with him So plese at your Earliest Convence atend to this for he is getting worse every day—and I want him to go and make something of him Self for he cannot do it hear.*

A decade later, after Jim Thorpe gained world renown, another version of how Carlisle found Jim emerged. The two stories were not mutually exclusive, and in fact made sense when combined. A federal official named Alex Crain, who worked as the Indian agent in Wewoka in Seminole country but owned a farm near Keokuk Falls, claimed that he "talked the lad's father into sending him to the big Indian school." Carlisle was always scouting Indian Territory for new students. That was the point of the recent visit by the assistant superintendent. And there were occasional letters from the Carlisle administration like the one the Sac and Fox agent in Stroud had received in 1899: "Have you not a small number of exceptionally good boys and girls to send to Carlisle this year?" That inquiry included a not subtle hint that they were especially interested in strong boys who could play sports. Jim was small, but he had already expressed his love of football. It was not just watching his first pigskin idol, Chauncey Archiquette, that stirred him. As a student at Haskell in early January 1900, he had been among the boys who attended a breakfast in the dining hall and gaped in awe at the sight of the powerful Carlisle team when it stopped in Lawrence on a continental train ride east after a game against the University of California.

Haskell was regional; Carlisle was national, the mother ship of Indian schools, and part of the college football elite. It seems probable that Hiram and his new wife, whatever their motivation, got the idea from an agent like Crain, and that the boy was ready to go.

ON THE DAY before Jim arrived at Carlisle, *Red Man*, a school newspaper published every Friday by student apprentices in the printshop, posted a poem titled "This Is the Indian's Home" by A. O. Wright, an educator in the Indian bureau's administration.

Soon the last wild Indian pagan
Will forsake the tribal rule
All the reservations opened
All the children in some school;
White and Indians then united
Make one nation, great and free
One alone will be their country
One their speech and flag shall be.

Here, in mawkish rhyme, was the perfect encapsulation of Carlisle's philosophy, connecting Anglo education and the elimination of reservations as essential to saving Indians by making their homelands and customs dissolve into white society. The Dawes Act took away the communal reservation land; Carlisle and its sister schools would do the rest. It was no coincidence that Senator Henry Dawes and Col. Richard Henry Pratt, the founder and longtime superintendent at Carlisle, were friends and coconspirators in what they considered a progressive and noble effort. Dawes had been a frequent visitor to Carlisle in the years he chaired the Senate Committee on Indian Affairs and at Pratt's request often spoke at commencement exercises. When Dawes needed help persuading various tribes to go along with his reservation-busting act, Pratt, the ramrod-straight cavalryman, became one of his key emissaries traveling out to South Dakota to persuade the Sioux to cede more of their communal land in the name of progress.

At Carlisle, the Dawes Act was celebrated as an annual holiday. Dawes Day, it was called, a day for student assemblies, speeches, and debates over the act's merits and drawbacks. Jim Thorpe had been at school only two days when he experienced his first Dawes Day. As the *Red Man* newspaper noted that weekend: "The 8th of February is recognized as Dawes Day in the Indian service. It was the eighth of February that the eminent senator's bill for the Indians to receive lands in severalty was approved by the president."

Ten days later, on February 18, Jim and his classmates were again called to the assembly in the gymnasium for the school's twenty-fifth anniversary exercise. Scores of parents, dignitaries, and civilian guests were also present. Carlisle was neither a high school nor a college. It was an industrial school that also offered academic courses, but most of all it was a school of assimilation. Most students were in their teens, but their ages ranged from seven to the mid-twenties. The plan was for those in the upper school to stay at Carlisle five years or until they graduated, but that plan was decidedly flexible. Some students needed more time, some less, to reach a stage where the administrators could release them with a reasonable expectation that they would melt into the white world and not revert to the life of a blanket Indian on the reservation. That was the theme of Superintendent Pratt's commencement speech, which he couched in the language of the nation's ideals.

"United States, united people. How can we be made and keep our people united if we educate and train them to differences?" Pratt asked. "Here today we are considering our brother in red. He is not in the family, not part of the united people. He is a prisoner in our hands so we control him absolutely, therefore, his useless dependent condition and segregated situation stamps our brother-of-man-Christianity a myth and our equality and freedom Declaration of Independence a lie. The Indian peoples themselves want to be in our United States family and are willing to develop and exert their powers and are capable of accomplishing it."

Jim and his classmates sat cross-legged on the gym floor, with parents and guests in chairs on the sides. The two main guest speakers at the commencement reflected the crosscurrents of the school and the times, revealing the competing strands of racial violence and reconciliation that coiled and frayed through American history. The first speaker was O. O. Howard, a retired Union general who led troops at Antietam and Gettysburg and served as the right flank on General William Sherman's March to the Sea. Howard was known as "the Christian general," a soldier of piety who commanded respect despite occasional battlefield errors that earned him a second sarcastic nickname—Oh-oh Howard. He was a supporter of black freedom, and after the Civil War was appointed commissioner of the Freedmen's Bureau, playing a vital role during Reconstruction in helping former slaves gain jobs, land, and the right to vote. His combination of evangelism and sympathy for African Americans led him to push for the establishment of a seminary to train black preachers, which resulted in what eventually became Howard University, the historically black college in Washington, D.C., named in his honor.

But what brought O. O. Howard to Carlisle that February day in 1904 was his role as an Indian fighter with the U.S. Army in the West, ending with the campaign against the Nez Perce tribe led by Chief Joseph in 1877. The man who fought to free enslaved blacks and worked to make space for them in the American family was the same man who led an army tracking down and killing Indians. Land was at the center of the Nez Perce War, as with all wars against the Indians, as Chief Joseph's band tried to resist when Howard's army pushed them out of their ancestral home in the Wallowa Valley of northeastern Oregon and chased them into Canada before they surrendered and were taken to a smaller reservation in Idaho Territory. Now here stood Howard at age seventy-four, white-haired and only somewhat repentant, addressing an auditorium of American Indians, including twenty-one sons and daughters of the Nez Perce tribe. He told Thorpe and his classmates that he was "just doing my duty" fighting Indians. "There come times when a fight is a good thing and when it is over let's lay down all our feelings and look up to God and see if we cannot get a better basis on which to live and work together."

When Howard sat down, Pratt introduced the next guest. "I present to you Chief Joseph of the Nez Perces in Washington," the superintendent said. Men from a different time, different century. The two old antagonists brought together at Carlisle. "General Howard and Joseph fought each other in '77, two years before Carlisle began," Pratt continued. "Their line of battle was fourteen hundred miles long. We think Gettysburg a big battlefield and we are proud of it. Joseph would not go on his reservation and had his way for a time. . . . I have always regarded Chief Joseph as one of our great Indians. He kept ahead of General Howard for fourteen hundred miles."

The essential contradiction of how white America viewed Indians was evident in that brief introduction, a peculiar combination of a relentless effort to destroy a people followed by mythmaking reverence of those same people. The Indian was made noble in retrospect, after he was no longer a threat. Chief Joseph had a different perspective. As two students later remembered the scene, when the old chief entered the crowded gymnasium, he walked slowly among the students and gently patted them one by one on the head, blessing them with a whisper. "You are the original red, white, and blue."

Time and circumstance having worn down his resistance, he gracefully handled the face-to-face meeting with his old adversary. "I meet here my friend General Howard. I used to be so anxious to meet him. I wanted to kill him in war," Joseph said. He was talking history to these students, who were toddlers or not yet born when the last of the government wars against their people were waged. "I am glad to meet him and glad to meet everybody here and to be friends with General Howard. We are both old men. Still we live and I am glad. We both fought in many wars and we are both alive. Ever since the war I have made up my mind to be friendly to whites and to everybody. I wish you, my friends, would believe me as I believe myself in my heart in what I say when my friend General Howard and I fought together I had no idea that we would ever all sit down to a meal together as today, but we have and I am glad."

Then Chief Joseph turned to the subject of Indian education. His message could not have been more harmonious to Pratt's ears. "I understand of course that the learning of books is a fine thing, and I have some children here from my tribe that are . . . struggling to learn the white man's ways and his books. I wish my children would learn more and more every day so they can mingle with the white people and do business with them as well as anybody else. I shall try to get Indians to send their children to school. That is all I can say tonight."

It was one of Chief Joseph's last public speeches. He died that September at age sixty-four on the Colville reservation in northern Washington state. The 1904 commencement was also the last hurrah at Carlisle for Richard Henry Pratt. Three months later, he was forced into retirement by officials at the Bureau of Indian Affairs in Washington. Jim Thorpe's rise at the school took place under Pratt's successors, but even as Carlisle entered an era of athletic renewal and ethical decline, the founder's influence would be felt at Carlisle to its final days.

PRATT WAS A long-limbed crane of a man, so lanky at six foot four they had to install larger bathtubs in the superintendent's house. His students called him Father. One commencement speaker praised him as the "Moses of the red man." He was known as a leader "with rough edges"—blunt, harsh, stubborn, arbitrary, and undiplomatic in responding to his enemies, of whom there were many, including not only Indian bureau officials but also religious missionaries and academic ethnologists who dared to challenge his opinions about what was best for Indians. He was also an Old Testament–style idealist and thinker who considered himself a champion of black Americans and Native Americans and fought against racial bigotry. Like John Newton, the former slave trader who saw the light and became the abolitionist Anglican minister who penned "Amazing Grace," Pratt came to regret the Indian killer mentality instilled by the U.S. Army in the West and devoted his life to trying to save Indians through his own definition of amazing grace. He thought he was doing good. In the words of Suzan Shown Harjo, a lifelong Indian rights advocate and cultural archivist, Pratt considered himself "a civilizationist alternative to the exterminationists"—the military leaders who had waged war against Indians in the post–Civil War West, men like George Armstrong Custer and Philip H. Sheridan.

If Sheridan became known for once saying "The only good Indian is a dead Indian," or more likely a less evocative variation of that phrase, Pratt became known for turning that thought around. "A great general has said that the only good Indian is a dead one," Pratt countered. "In a sense, I agree with the sentiment, but only in this: that all the Indian there is in the race should be dead. Kill the Indian in him and save the man." He also used a religious analogy to describe this philosophy: "I believe in immersing the Indians in our civilization and when we get them under, holding them there until they are thoroughly soaked."

Pratt's transformation began in Indian Territory after the Civil War when he served as a lieutenant in the Tenth Cavalry Regiment, a unit comprising black men recently freed from enslavement, known as Buffalo Soldiers, and Indian scouts, mostly Cherokee and Choctaw. It was because of that experience, Pratt said, that he came to appreciate both groups for their intelligence and fearlessness and lamented their subordinate status in American life. His admiration for Indians intensified under unlikely circumstances in 1875 when he was assigned to be the military warden at Fort Marion in northeast Florida of a band of seventy Kiowa, Cheyenne, Arapaho, Caddo, and Comanche warriors who had resisted the U.S. Army along the Red River in the Texas Panhandle. Pratt thought it wiser to try to acculturate them rather than punish them. He freed them from chains, let them monitor themselves, encouraged their skills as artists and craftsmen, and taught them English. The Indian prisoners of Fort Marion became a tourist attraction. White visitors flocked to admire their artwork and capture them on stereopticon cameras. Pratt became a local celebrity.

The Indians themselves were torn between two worlds, a variation of what Jim Thorpe faced a generation later. A Kiowa warrior, Wolf Robe, captured their ambivalence in a self-portrait he drew that showed a buffalo, tepee, and forest to one side of his face and a cow, building, and farm to the other side. But watching his Indian prisoners adapt to Western ways led Pratt to a civilizationist revelation, the concept of a non-reservation Indian school, and he persuaded the War Department to let him start one on the site of the old and mostly abandoned Carlisle Barracks.

ARRIVED SAFELY AT MIDNIGHT PARTY IN GOOD CONDITION, Pratt notified the Indian bureau in Washington by Western Union telegram on October 6, 1879. He had just reached Carlisle with his first recruits, eighty-two Sioux boys and girls from the Rosebud and Pine Ridge reservations in the Dakota Territory, many of them children and grandchildren of prominent chiefs, including American Horse, White Thunder, Two Strike, Red Cloud, Standing Bear, and Spotted Tail. Pratt had hoped his inaugural class would be from tribes in Indian Territory, with which he was more familiar, not Sioux, but the government considered the Sioux troublesome dissidents and thought Pratt might be useful in the effort to temper their hostility.

It was not an easy sell. When he met with Spotted Tail and a council of elders at Rosebud, Pratt discovered that they had already decided among themselves to reject the request. "The white people are all thieves and liars," Spotted Tail told Pratt through an interpreter. "We refuse to send our children because we do not want them to learn such things. The government deceived us on the Black Hills treaty. The government knew that gold was there and it took the land from us without giving us its value, and so the white people get rich and the Indians are cheated and become poor. The government let us keep this plains country and it agreed that the lines should be away out and we should have a large district. Your men are out there now running the lines and they run the lines a long ways inside of where we agreed they should be. Some of our people who lived outside of these lines have been compelled to move inside. The government has always cheated us and we do not want our children to learn to do that way."

The mention of gold had a disturbing meaning to Pratt that Spotted Tail could not know. Pratt's father, who had once been a contractor on the construction of the Erie Canal, had gone to California and got lucky panning for gold on the Feather River during the 1849 gold rush but was robbed and murdered on his way home. Richard was left fatherless at age ten because of gold. Now, in his negotiations with the Sioux, he countered Spotted Tail's irrefutable argument by accepting it and praising him. "Spotted Tail, you are a very distinguished man. Your name has gone all over the United States. It has even gone across the ocean to other countries," Pratt said. "You are the head of these people because you have a strong mind, but Spotted Tail, you cannot read or write. You sign papers and you do not know what you sign." The reason the Sioux felt manipulated and deceived about the gold and the reservation boundaries was that the tribe's leaders could not read the treaties, Pratt said. If the chiefs had been literate, he argued, they would have been able to understand the traps in the treaties and would still have the Black Hills. Spotted Tail relented, as did Red Cloud.

From Spotted Tail's Rosebud band came sixty-six students, with sixteen more from Red Cloud's band at Pine Ridge. Their departure for the east was haunting. Large crowds of parents and relatives camped on the banks of the Missouri River for two days in anticipation of the leave-taking. Wails of sorrow and prayerful chants echoed across the water when the steamer pushed off for Yankton and disappeared around the bend. At Yankton, Pratt had arranged for two special train cars for the trip through Chicago to Carlisle. Three years after the Battle of the Little Bighorn and the Lakota Sioux, Northern Cheyenne, and Arapaho's annihilation of Custer's cavalry, the journey became a tourist attraction—much like Black Hawk's trip east in 1833, except these Indians were not in chains. Thousands of curious Chicagoans turned out to see the Sioux youths when the train reached the station there, and hundreds more were waiting at midnight when they reached the Gettysburg Junction station at Carlisle. Pratt thought he could avoid the crowds by slipping his charges into town at a secondary trunk depot in the middle of the night, but it made no difference once word spread that "the Indians are coming." The "noble savages" again provided a spectacle for white society, and as sympathetic as he was to the Indians' plight and as much as he disparaged their mistreatment, Pratt became an impresario of that spectacle.

In an interview with an eastern newspaper, he described these Indian youths as an exotic species that needed to be tamed: "The first eighty-two came from tepees, there was not an exception. In 1879 the buffalo was still plentiful. The Sioux lived mostly in Buffalo tepees. They were dirty. They were the regular blanket Indians. Some of the young men had buffalo robes. Most of them had deerskin leggings worked with beads. Their hair was braided with beaver skin or red flannel and they wore earrings. They were absolutely wild Indians."

Among the boys he took east on the train was Chief Standing Bear's eleven-year-old son, Luther Standing Bear. "When I went east to Carlisle school, I thought I was going there to die," Luther wrote decades later. "I could think of white people wanting little Lakota people there for no other reason than to kill them, but I thought here is my chance to prove that I can die bravely. So I went east to show my father and my people that I was brave and willing to die for them."

The conditions the young Sioux encountered upon arrival at Carlisle only reinforced their fears. They knew no English. As interpreters, Pratt had brought up several Indians who had been his prisoners at Fort Marion. The interpreters pointed to a two-story building and told them to go there to sleep. The boys were exhausted, looking forward to sleeping on "nice little beds like those the white people had." But the first room they entered was empty, no beds, no bedding, nothing but a coal-oil lamp. The next room was the same. "We had to make the best of the situation so took off our leggins and rolled them up for pillows," Luther Standing Bear wrote. The only coverings were the blankets they had brought with them. They were accustomed to sleeping on the ground, but the floor was rock hard and colder than anything they had experienced. Pratt discovered that the Indian bureau in Washington had neglected to supply his school while he was gone. Not only were there no beds, but there were also no civilian clothes or uniforms, and barely any food. The first meal the students ate consisted of bread and water. When the first crate arrived, it turned out to be an organ for the chapel. A month passed before the first clothing reached the school, and Pratt described it as "the shoddiest of the shoddy."

One day after classwork had started, some men entered the building carrying large chairs; the boys asked their interpreter what they had come for and he said the men had come to cut the Indians' long hair. The boys were called out of the classroom one at a time and came back looking sheepish, hair shorn. Luther Standing Bear said he began to cry when his turn came. "None of us slept well that night, we felt so queer," he recalled. "I wanted to feel my head all the time." The ostensible reason for the haircutting was to make it easier to control head lice. Luther Standing Bear thought there was a more sinister reason having to do with the philosophy of culturally killing them to save them. "The fact is we were to be transformed, and short hair being the mark of gentility with the white man, he put his mark upon us."

A smaller group of students arrived later that month from Indian Territory and the Southwest—Apache, Kiowa, Cheyenne, and Pawnee—to fill out the class. The total that first year was 147. One tenet of Pratt's philosophy was that the more he could blend the many tribes to create a pan-Indian sensibility among his students, the more effective his assimilation process would be. From the arrival of those new tribes onward Pratt separated members of the same tribe as much as possible, eventually reaching a point where the barracks rooms, which could hold three or four students each, would have no more than one from any tribe.

When the one-year anniversary came, Pratt held "a little impromptu gathering" of students, teachers, and outside supporters, including sympathetic women from the Young Ladies' Seminary in St. Augustine, Florida, who had helped him with the Indian prisoners at Fort Marion. He asked for a show of hands from his charges: How many wanted the school to continue? "Every hand went up in favor of continuing, and some boys even stood up and held up both hands," Pratt recounted. "Speeches were in order. Everybody was happy and many reminiscences were brought out and [there was] much incentive to continued effort."

The Indian perspective on Carlisle was far more complicated than that, as it would be from that first year to the last. One might ask what choice the young students had that day when they were instructed to vote with their hands in front of their superintendent and teachers. They were certainly less likely to vote honestly with their hands than with their feet, by trying to run away, which by one calculation more than fourteen hundred boy students did during the school's lifetime, about twenty a year at first but increasing exponentially later. It was enough of a problem for Pratt that he set up a sophisticated alert network within a fifty-mile radius of campus for citizens to contact the school as soon as they spotted a possible Indian truant.

Two of the original group were not alive to participate in that one-year anniversary vote. Amos LaFramboise, age thirteen, had died the day before Thanksgiving, seven weeks after he arrived on that train from Yankton. Cause, unlisted. Pratt sought to bury him in the nearby Ashland cemetery, but it was for white people only. Two months later, a Cheyenne boy who took the name Abe Lincoln at Carlisle died of spinal meningitis. Carlisle in its first three years became a death chamber, especially for young students from the Rosebud reservation. Eighteen of the first 101 youths Rosebud sent east died at the school or were sent home to die, a horrific rate of nearly one in five. "A strange fatality seems to hang over our Rosebud pupils," Pratt wrote in a letter to the Indian bureau, but he took no blame for this tragedy, attributing the death rate to chronic poor health conditions among the Sioux. One of those who died was Chief Spotted Tail's own daughter, Gertrude Spotted Tail, who succumbed to pneumonia while in Philadelphia. She had been at Carlisle less than a year, dead at only fourteen. Pratt asked the Indian bureau to cover his expenses for sending a doctor to attend to Gertrude before her death. The bill was for $65.94.

Before Carlisle closed in 1918, 186 students from fifty different Indian nations died there and were buried in a haunting campus cemetery behind the athletic field grandstands, row after row of rectangular headstones, the remains interred in the east-west position, the families unable to reclaim them and not invited to attend services that were not by tribal custom on sacred ground but with Christian prayers in soil far from home.

Barbara Landis, the Carlisle archivist at the Cumberland County Historical Society a century later, thought the number of Indian students who died during their schooling at Carlisle was many times greater than those 186 headstones in the graveyard; hundreds more were sent back to their reservations to die once the administration realized they were gravely ill, not out of cultural sensitivity but so the death statistics would seem less glaring.

Yet there were many students over the years who came to think of Carlisle as their home, used their schooling as the foundation for successful careers, and developed a strong loyalty to the institution despite the early trauma. Luther Standing Bear himself would become a distinguished writer and Indian spokesman later in life, and while not airbrushing the struggles he went through at Carlisle nonetheless expressed a fondness for the school and even served as a recruiter for Pratt. In a screenplay that N. Scott Momaday, a Pulitzer Prize–winning novelist from the Kiowa nation, wrote about Carlisle, he used Luther Standing Bear to express the depth of those conflicted feelings. "For some the Carlisle experience was bad—it was the theft of an Indian childhood, the annihilation of language, culture, tradition, the sacred. But for others—and for me—it was good," Momaday wrote in the dialogue for Luther Standing Bear. "It gave us purpose and resolve at a time when purpose and resolve were dead in our camps. It gave us the chance to test our bravery and our will to survive and to excel."

From the uncertainty of the first days in 1879, Carlisle grew year by year. Pratt discovered that his students excelled at languages and most of them quickly learned to speak English. Within three years the school had evolved from a War Department project to an Indian bureau school chartered and funded by Congress. The first class of students and several that followed left after three years as part of the bargain Pratt had made to get them to come in the first place, and it took him a decade before he could keep some students long enough to produce his first small graduating class.

The bare-bones academic requirements at the school did not stop

Pratt from assuming the manners of a college president, inviting important politicians from Washington and rich benefactors from Philadelphia, New York, and Boston to visit the school and marvel at the transformation of his Indians into productive young people who could survive in white society. He was a believer in using the media to spread his vision, inviting big-city journalists to the school and bringing in a local photographer to take before-and-after pictures of his little Indians, here wearing moccasins and long hair, there neatly shaved and uniformed, the photos developed in a way that made their skin look whiter. Ladies' clubs and Quaker and Methodist religious societies provided money and moral support to Carlisle to demonstrate their tolerance and humanitarianism. Local ministers took turns leading chapel services at the school. By 1893 Pratt had started to emphasize athletics, including football. At one point he dropped the sport because he thought it was too violent, but then a few years later brought it back, in part at the request of his students and in part because he saw its promotional value, especially after he recruited Pop Warner, a young football whiz from Cornell, to coach the team in 1899.

It was all part of an effort to set his students on a path away from reservations. That some would go back was his greatest fear. "I would have more respect for you, every one of you, if after you went through Carlisle I saw you on the streets blacking boots than I would if you went back," he told the students at one assembly. "There must be a break." What prompted Pratt's lecture were the unwelcome reports, even fifteen years after he opened Carlisle, that many of his students had returned to reservation life. "Pretty soon I shall begin to think that my life work has been without effect and without result," he told one class in a characteristically melodramatic flourish. Pratt, the reformer who had convinced himself that he was helping save a race, felt pressure from all sides by then. His support from Congress and the Bureau of Indian Affairs had been based more on practicality than idealism, and politicians were seeing less value in having a non-reservation school in the east. The western Indians had been defeated and tamed, the prevailing pseudoscience was categorizing them as irredeemably inferior, and Carlisle was more expensive than modest reservation schools. Former students reverting to reservation life, current students running away or dying—none of that, Pratt feared, helped his cause.

THE EARLY MONTHS of 1904 were a time of leave-taking at Carlisle. On January 4, a month before Jim Thorpe arrived, Cooki Glook died of rheumatic heart disease at age sixteen. Cooki was among a group of Inuits who had been recruited to Carlisle from Port Clarence, Alaska, and the first of five of them who would die at school that year. The *Red Man* described her as "a sweet, lovable child endearing herself to the hearts of all who knew her." For several weeks before she died, she was bedridden in pain, leaving her room only on Christmas Day when her classmates presented her with gifts around a miniature tree. The next student buried in the cemetery behind the athletic field was Wade Ayres, a Catawba from Rock Hill, South Carolina, who at age thirteen stood four foot eight and weighed seventy pounds. It was said that Wade took "cold in the arm after vaccination" and died from fever.

Pop Warner took leave of Carlisle in February before getting a chance to meet Thorpe, the athlete who later, after more goings and comings by both, would lift their names together into football immortality. In five years at Carlisle during his first stint there, Warner had led the football team to a point where it was nationally recognized and earning honors from Walter Camp, the arbiter of college rankings and All-American teams. In his last two seasons—1902 and 1903—he had finished 8-3 and then 10-2-1 and his Indians had defeated many of the best squads in the East, including Penn, Cornell, Harvard, and Georgetown. But his brusque manner created tensions with some of his best players, who challenged his authority, and a job offer came along that he could not refuse. Warner decided to return to Ithaca to coach his alma mater. "Our loss is Cornell's gain," the *Red Man* said. One of his former players, Edward Rogers, a Carlisle success story who was studying law at the University of Minnesota, was lured back to replace Warner.

Richard Henry Pratt, after a quarter century as the founder and champion of Carlisle, was also on his way out. His long-running ideological argument with Washington had reached a bitter climax when Indian Commissioner Francis E. Leupp forced him to retire. Leupp was a former newspaperman who had crusaded against non-reservation Indian schools and whom Pratt despised. Leupp's motto for dealing with native peoples was "improvement, not transformation," but Pratt countered that "all basic improvement is inevitably transformation" and asserted that Leupp's support of "perpetual tribalism" was nothing more than a power play to keep the Indians down so that his bureau could have a reason for existing.

In defense of his school and his philosophy, Pratt was never timid about expressing his feelings. In a speech that year at a conference of Baptist ministers in New York he said that "nothing better could happen to the Indians than the complete destruction of the [Indian] bureau"—not the sort of statement that would ingratiate him with his Washington bosses. Always strong-willed and certain of his righteousness, he had finally alienated everyone who held power over him: the Indian commissioner, members of Congress, the secretary of the Interior, all the way up to President Theodore Roosevelt. Although Teddy had at least once been Pratt's guest at Carlisle when he was U.S. Civil Service commissioner, the two men were constantly at odds, which in this case meant "the man in the arena" was frequently disparaged by the pious superintendent, who once had called Teddy nothing more than "a conspicuous and inveterate office seeker." His firing was inevitable, and it came late that spring, making front-page news in the *New York Times.* As part of his departure, Pratt was made a brigadier general.

In a retirement speech to his students, Pratt tried to hide his despair, saying "there is always some good in every action" and that he thought it would all come right in the end. "As it is now it lies in your power to hold the school in its present standard and I hope the good that is expected of you will not become otherwise. I would say more if I could but I will leave you with what I have said so far and though I may not be with you much longer my heart will remain with you each and every student of this school."

Warner left (temporarily) for Cornell; Cooki Glook and Wade Ayres departed permanently for the school cemetery; Pratt was ushered begrudgingly into a twenty-year retirement during which he never stopped promoting his civilizationist cause. Shortly before he departed, there was another mass leaving, but it was an annual event that was one of Pratt's founding ideas. The Outing.

On the first two days of April, 112 boys, large and small, left the Carlisle campus to live and work in farm homes in Pennsylvania and nearby regions of New Jersey, Delaware, and Maryland. The following two days, 68 large and small girls left for similar destinations. "They are going out in search of manly qualities and womanly accomplishments, and the real genuine stick that Colonel Pratt would have us find and hold onto," proclaimed a notice in the *Red Man*. "Every one of them had stick in the eye as he passed out of the gates." These Outings, which had been going on since Carlisle's inception, were as central to Pratt's assimilation philosophy as any of the pedagogy inside the school walls.

The Outing system had been run since its creation in 1880 by Anne S. Ely, the school's institutional memory, and a Pratt loyalist who came to Carlisle soon after its founding and departed soon after Pratt's firing. Ely maintained Outing records in well-ordered files in her office, but also held much of the information in her head. It was said that "she could tell you at a moment's notice the whereabouts of any boy or girl, their standing, experience, conduct, and character." She worked with a boys field agent and a girls field agent whose job it was to find families willing to partner with Carlisle and then match them with suitable students. The idea, according to a school brochure, was to imbed the students in the homes of "the best white families in the east" where they could "imbibe the best of civilization and earn wages." The boys would do farmwork and the girls would help with housekeeping; all would become part of the family that took them in, treated not as servants or farmhands but as equals to the sons and daughters. During the school year, if they were still on Outing, they would be enrolled at the same public school as their family's school-age children.

Along with furthering the assimilation effort, the Outing system was part of Carlisle's financial strategy, equal parts ingenious and manipulative. Sending students out for long periods of time meant that Carlisle did not have to account for their room and board or education, even though they were kept on attendance rolls that determined federal funding. The families paid the Outing students between $5 and $15 a month, but that money did not go directly to them; it was sent to the superintendent and placed in a bank for future use. The students had to follow strict rules: no going to the big city of Philadelphia except for special occasions, no use of tobacco or liquor, no gambling or card playing, no absences without permission. They had to promise to obey their employers, attend church and bathe regularly, write monthly letters back to school, and stay the duration unless their patrons sent them home for misbehavior. While the Outing concept was presented as a boon to the Indian students, in essence it was an exploitative system intended to create a pool of second-class workers for the benefit of whites. School officials could never articulate that reality, but they dealt with the consequences. F. W. Canfield, the boys field agent, was constantly on the alert for difficulties from one direction or the other. He had to be part salesman, part conciliator, his work "in many instances requiring a great deal of diplomacy" as the reality of the program did not always match the promise.

Jim Thorpe met that harsh reality all too soon. He had been at Carlisle two months when word reached him from home that his father had died from snakebite poisoning. Jim's relationship with Hiram had been uneven at best. They hunted and fished together, and fought often, and were separated for long stretches, either Hiram leaving the family or Jim off at boarding school. Carlisle was reluctant to let its students return home, especially in a situation like this where Jim had only recently enrolled. He was forced to stay in Pennsylvania and mourn far from the North Canadian River, an orphan before he turned seventeen. Just as Superintendent Pratt was leaving, Jim left as well, sent on his first Outing. "I was anxious to go for the experience," he said. But not long after he reached the farm of Arthur E. Buchholz in Pennsylvania Dutch Country, his eagerness turned to despair.

Buchholz, a regular patron in the Outing system, was a summertime farmer. Most of the year he worked in Philadelphia as chief inspector of tenement houses for the Department of Public Health and Charities. He was a rigid man who spoke of the need for boys to be around "manly boys and men" and disparaged the "petticoat" style of Carlisle's Quaker matrons, who he believed were guilty of "loving people too much." With Thorpe, it seemed, he presented the worst of all worlds. Instead of outdoor work on the farm, Jim was assigned to be the family's houseboy. He played with the two children when he could, but was treated like a servant, there to wash dishes after meals and cook at times. Buchholz kept him inside and made him eat separately, in the kitchen, rather than in the dining room with the family. He was paid $5 a month for this unpleasant experience. He was at Carlisle but not at Carlisle, supposedly learning how to live in a white world. Seeking independence, instead he felt trapped and smothered and asked to be transferred. He was still looking for his home.

4

High Jump

BEFORE RETURNING TO CARLISLE FOR A LONGER STAY AT the Indian school, Thorpe had worked at the homes of three farm families, only one of which he found agreeable—the truck farm of Harley Bozarth near White Horse, New Jersey, two miles outside Trenton. The Bozarths made regular use of Carlisle's Outing students and were among the most accommodating of the families that benefited from the system. They paid Jim \$8 to \$10 a month to cut asparagus, invited him to eat with them in the dining room, and gave him full run of the house and property, treating him more like a relative than a servant. The two girls and boy in the family, Laura, Hazel, and Harley Jr., became his weekend companions "hurdling fences and jumping ravines" in the verdant countryside. During the school year, he attended the Maple Shade School a mile down the road, one of forty-one grammar students in the upper grades at the new two-room schoolhouse with its sturdy brick exterior topped by a clanging bell that called the students in for study.

But when Jim was transferred to a less friendly household in Yardley, Pennsylvania, a situation that reminded him of his lowly status at the Buchholz farm, where he was restricted in his movements and made to feel like an alien presence, he soured on the Outing life and ran away. Jim arrived back at Carlisle on March 9, 1907, where he went from feeling trapped away from school to being confined at school. "I am sorry to say that James Thorpe is in the guardhouse for running away from his country home," reported one of his Sac and Fox classmates, Sadie Ingalls, in a letter home.

When class assignments for the year were handed out that month, Jim was placed in Room 9, which meant he had not been promoted for the semesters he was on Outing. In Carlisle's unorthodox grade hierarchy, Room 9 was not the equivalent of ninth grade but more like seventh grade, and had no correlation to age, since Jim was nineteen, almost twenty, and there were many younger students in that class. The placement, based on an assessment of his academic skills by principal-teacher John Whitwell and the education staff, surprised and disappointed Jim. It meant he could not graduate in five years as he had hoped, a realization, he said later, that "rankled in my heart for many years." In retrospect, even though he had never shown much interest in classwork, he would explain or rationalize his subsequent obsession with athletics as a way for him to make the administration "sorry for having treated me that way."

His jump to athletic heights sprang from that sense of being underestimated—and with an origin story that took place on a spring afternoon as he passed the high-jump pit on his way to play baseball with his pickup team, the Big Chiefs, on the lower field. The story was recounted in scores of newspaper articles in later years, a recycling loop of information that began with interviews with Jim or his coach, Pop Warner, who had returned to Carlisle that year after a three-year hiatus coaching at Cornell. The tale was refashioned in various ways by imaginative scribes and the two main characters themselves in their as-told-to biographies, "Red Son of Carlisle" and *Pop Warner: Football's Greatest Teacher.* Like most stories that become etched into legend, the essence remained the same in endless retellings but differed in details.

It went like this: On his way to the intramural ball game, dressed in overalls, a twilled-cotton work shirt, and borrowed gym shoes, Jim stopped to watch the track team's high jumpers. Most stories say the bar was set at five feet nine inches. When the team's jumpers one after another failed to clear that height, Thorpe asked if he could try. By some accounts this elicited derisive laughter from the varsity men. *This guy in his overalls?* Probably an embellishment to dramatize the story, but what was not exaggerated was the ease with which Thorpe rose over the bar and descended into the pit. With little effort he had jumped higher than anyone in Carlisle history.

Word of Thorpe's feat quickly found its way to Coach Warner. In "Red Son of Carlisle," Thorpe said Warner heard about it from a fellow student named Harold Archenbald. Close, but there was no student by that spelling. He meant Harry Archambault, a Sioux from the Standing Rock reservation who had been at Carlisle since 1902 and knew Jim from the time the skinny Sac and Fox kid had first entered the Large Boys quarters three years earlier. Archambault was a pole vaulter on the track squad and took photographs for the school paper. Other accounts said Warner was tipped off by one of the school's athletic stars, Albert Exendine, who like Jim was an Oklahoman, though from the Delaware nation. In either case, Warner was always scouring the grounds for athletes and reacted quickly, summoning Thorpe to his office the next day without offering a reason. Jim had never played for Warner, never been to his office, never talked to him before. He feared that he was about to be reprimanded by the coach who, in his second coming, wielded as much power as anyone there, even the superintendent.

In Warner's version of their meeting, Thorpe came in and said, "You wanted to see me, Coach? Have I done something wrong?"

"Son," replied Pop, "you've only broken the school record in the high jump, that's all."

"Pop, I didn't think that [was] very high," Thorpe responded. "I think I can do better in a track suit."

In Thorpe's version, he came into Warner's office and stood there quietly as Pop looked him over. "Are these the clothes you had on yesterday when you made the high jump?" Warner asked.

Thorpe nodded. "I want you to go to the club house, take those overalls off, and put on a track suit," Warner then said. "You're now on the track team."

Warner saw enough promise in Jim to put him under the mentorship of Exendine, who had graduated but returned to town to prepare for Dickinson Law School and was conveniently available to renew his athletic career under Warner. Although Carlisle was no more than a high school in academics, in sports it had been competing at the college level since the 1890s. The track team that spring had dual meets with Penn State, the Naval Academy, Syracuse, and Bucknell, the first and last at home, the middle two away. In preparation for the season, Warner had installed a new cinder track around the athletic field and recruited a squad from the Small Boys quarters to smooth it.

The spring was unusually wet and chilly, limiting practices, but Exendine worked with Thorpe on his high-jump and shot-put techniques. His disciple showed the first hint of all-around promise days before the start of official contests with his performance at the school's annual Field Day competition on the Saturday afternoon of April 19. With students filling the grandstands in clusters, cheering raucously and waving banners for their class's athletes despite the blustery weather, Thorpe's Room 9 finished second in points, most of them earned by him. He won the 120-yard high hurdles, finished second in the 220-yard hurdles, won the high jump, and finished second in the shot put. That showing brought new status to Jim among his classmates, but it was a ceremonial exhibition match that was missing some of Carlisle's varsity track stars.

The day before the first official meet a week later, Jim and his classmates were called to the auditorium for a school-wide assembly. President Roosevelt had established Arbor Day by issuing a "Proclamation to the School Children of the United States about the importance of trees." After speeches by students and teachers and a reading of the president's declaration, the assembly joined in singing "America." By the time they reached the second verse—*My native country thee / Land of the noble free / Thy name I love / I love thy rocks and rills . . .*—eyes turned to a little band of students from the Hopi nation who had arrived at Carlisle only three months earlier, essentially as kidnapped prisoners, noble but not free in their native country, brought to the school against their will in a government effort to control and assimilate the recalcitrant Hopi people. The Hopi boys knew no English until they were taken to Carlisle. Now here they stood, extolling America "in perfect English and good melody." Pop Warner was there, unaware that one of the frailest among the Hopi boys was a remarkable long-distance runner who years later would join Jim Thorpe in leading Carlisle to world fame.

The ceremony ended on the school grounds with each class choosing a spot to plant a tree, seventeen in all. The Hopi planted an elm and named it Hopi, short for *Hopituh Shi-nu-mu*, roughly translated as Peaceful Little Ones. The junior class named an oak after Pop Warner. Jim's class, "gaily adorned with streamers tan and blue," walked together to a spot near the hospital chosen by the school nurseryman and tenderly placed a horse chestnut into the rich soil.

Jim had success that track season, but not dominance. He failed to place in the meets against Navy and Syracuse, finished second in the high jump against Penn State, and placed second in the 120-yard hurdles and high jump against Bucknell. "The No. 9 pupils are proud of their two members James Thorpe and George H. Thomas who did such fine work in the dual meet with Bucknell last Saturday," an item in the *Arrow* noted. It was in the high jump against Bucknell that Jim broke the school record, matching the first jump he had made so nonchalantly in overalls on his way to a pickup baseball game. All that was enough to earn him his first varsity letter, a big yellow C to be sewn onto his red letterman sweater.

Before Carlisle's academic department shut down for the school year in June, three boys in grades ahead of Jim—Michael Balenti, a Cheyenne; William Garlow, an Onondaga; and William Newashe, a Sac and Fox who had known Jim since their childhoods in Indian Territory—left to play semipro baseball for Hagerstown in the Sunset League. Reports about other players at Hagerstown indicated some were paid as much as $75 a month. The three were well-known athletes on campus, and their exploits in summer ball were reported several times in the school paper, including a first-person account from Newashe. This was Newashe's first experience with summer ball, and it surprised him that they played almost every day, he wrote. There were teams in Martinsburg and Berkeley Springs, West Virginia; Frederick and Sparrows Point, Maryland; Hanover and Carlisle, Pennsylvania; and Winchester, Virginia. "The crowds in Virginia and West Virginia were not as good as the crowds in Maryland and Pennsylvania," Newashe observed. "And there is usually some betting done in the game nearly every day." After a weekend game against Carlisle, Balenti slipped away to visit his pals at the school and told stories about his life in semipro ball. The school paper also noted that another student, Jesse Youngdeer, was playing semipro baseball that summer somewhere "in the west."

Their experience was regarded as normal for students who had the talent, and in almost every respect it was. Students and staff at Carlisle knew Newashe, Garlow, Balenti, and Youngdeer, read about their exploits, and welcomed them back later, when they would continue playing baseball or football at school. School records indicate that the experience was considered an Outing, just like going to a sponsor's farm. On the Outing line in Garlow's student file, one of the notations reads: "Hagerstown Baseball Team." As athletic director and head coach of most sports, Pop Warner kept tabs on his athletes every summer and could learn from public reports and his network of scouts who was playing and where. He did not instruct his boys not to play. The fact that Jim's friends and teammates were doing it, that it seemed utterly ordinary, and that Warner likely knew every detail—all of this would become crucial context for the controversial events a few years later involving Jim and semipro baseball that haunted him the rest of his life.

While most of his classmates left for summer Outings, returned home for vacations, or took summer jobs, Jim remained at Carlisle. He and some friends slipped away from campus briefly to hunt and fish at Tagg Run, the school's forested summer camp south of Carlisle on the northern edge of the Blue Ridge range. When he returned, a wisecracker in the *Arrow* wrote that "Thorpe must have been visiting Alaska where the Eskimos live"—implying that he was fond of an unnamed Inuit girl. At school that July and August he worked as foreman of a crew of students slapping fresh coats of paint on old campus buildings, and in the evenings he loped down to the athletic field to play pickup football and baseball. He anticipated the fall football season, and early reports speculated that he would soon be a star in both track and football, but baseball was also piquing his interest. He loved taking the mound for the Big Chiefs in the intramural league. The easygoing mix of work and unstructured play seemed to have a positive effect on his disposition. His friend Harry Archambault, the pole-vaulting Sioux photographer, bought a new camera that July and practiced by taking shots of his friends. When Jim posed for Harry, it was said that "he had on the smile that won't come off."

IN THE YEARS after Richard Henry Pratt was ousted from the institution, the Carlisle Indian Industrial School underwent a gradual change in emphasis. Pratt's successor, Major William A. Mercer, also came out of the U.S. Army, a cavalryman whose last posting had been as an Indian agent at the Uintah and Ouray Agency in Utah, after similar assignments in Wisconsin, Minnesota, and Nebraska. He had been dealing with Indians, first killing them, then overseeing them, since the final Sioux campaign that ended with the massacre at Wounded Knee in South Dakota on December 29, 1890, when at least 250 Lakota people, including many women and children, were slaughtered by the Seventh Cavalry, in which Mercer was a lieutenant. Unlike Pratt, Mercer never underwent a road-to-Damascus conversion about Indians or came to think of himself as their savior. He did not lobby for the job, but was chosen at least in part because he was on friendly terms with Teddy Roosevelt. It was thought he would be less ornery than Pratt and more willing to do the bidding of the Indian bureau.

Mercer was not interested in turning students into brown-skinned white people, had no training in academics, and wanted to focus on the third word in the school's name: *Industrial.* He did not share Pratt's conviction that an Indian could be as intelligent as any white person, or as successful if given the chance. His policies, reflecting those of Commissioner Leupp, came from the notion of white superiority and a belief that the students could grasp only so much; better to "let Indians be Indians" and focus on developing their practical skills. The Mercer administration was a mix of good and horrid intentions, just as Pratt's was, though from a different perspective, but it did offer some benefits to the students that Pratt did not. Under Mercer's tenure less attention was paid to strict notions of Christian obeisance, there were more social gatherings and dances, traditional Indian arts and crafts were encouraged, and competitive sports, especially football, were emphasized more than ever.

The arts program was run by Angel De Cora, a talented Winnebago artist who was given her own studio, the Leupp Art Studio, located near the main gate and across the lane from Pop Warner's house. It was named in honor of the Indian commissioner, who had recruited her. De Cora was well established by then as an artist fluent in two worlds, Indian and white. She had run studios in New York and Boston and had been trained first at the Hampton Institute in Virginia, when it was a school for both African Americans and Native Americans, and then at two prominent white colleges, Drexel and Smith. She refused to be easily categorized and saw herself as a link between cultures, rejecting neither while firmly opposing Pratt's assimilationist philosophy as it applied to art. She saw it as her mission at Carlisle to revive the inherent creative instincts in her students, which she said "had not perished but only lain dormant" in the Indian schools. "The method of educating the Indian in the past was to attempt to transform him into a brown Caucasian within the span of five years," she said. "The educators made every effort to convince the Indian that any custom or habit that was not familiar to the white man showed savagery and degradation."

That changed under De Cora. Rather than instruct her students in the European model, she took them outside to see beauty in their natural surroundings and had them study photographs of their reservation homelands, reconnecting them to their roots as a means of artistic inspiration. To promote their work, she eventually established another school publication, the *Indian Craftsman*, that featured student illustrations and border designs along with poems and stories that were "not only about Indians but by Indians."

Not long into her stay at Carlisle, she secretly married a younger man who would play football with Jim Thorpe while serving as her assistant at the art studio. William H. Dietz was his name, but he called himself Lone Star Dietz, and his life, as would become clear later, was a brilliantly concocted and deceptive work of art all to itself. De Cora was thirty-five when she eloped with Lone Star, eleven years her junior. They lived near the old stone Guard House in a small cottage where Lone Star kept a pack of wolfhounds that he exercised by riding his bicycle up and down the school lanes with the dogs trotting behind him. The marriage would not last long. De Cora's reputation also seemed short-lived; after dying during the great flu epidemic in 1919, she trailed into obscurity for much of the twentieth century, her art dismissed as insufficiently authentic, not Indian enough. But that was an overreaction and eventually her life and work regained stature to the point where the Winnebago nation in Nebraska, her homeland, named the Angel De Cora Museum after her.

If the government in Washington thought Indian schools were a drain on the federal budget, Superintendent Mercer saw it as his responsibility to run Carlisle as a capitalist operation. One aspect of Pratt's old regime that fit into that plan was the Outing system, which provided a cheap labor pool to the region while also saving the school money. Mercer also saw the industrial shops as assets and took it upon himself to hawk the school's products. An advertisement placed in the *Arrow* and Indian bureau newsletters around the country showed drawings of carriages that came out of the wagonmaking shop—a top buggy, a two-seated surrey, and a two-seated mail wagon—with a caption underneath stating "for descriptive circulars and prices address Major W. A. Mercer, U.S. Indian School, Carlisle."

The school's most profitable enterprise was its football team. Many of the newer buildings on campus were built by students and funded by proceeds from football games. All money from ticket sales and guaranteed percentages for away games went through the Carlisle Athletic Association, formed by Pop Warner and run by him again upon his return, enhancing his already formidable status on campus. While the grandstands at Carlisle's home field, even when full, could hold only modest crowds of a few thousand, the team of Indians was a popular attraction on the road against Ivy League schools and top universities in the Midwest, where crowds of twenty to thirty thousand were common and Carlisle benefited from a guaranteed percentage of the gate. As much as Mercer was Commissioner Leupp's man, he was also Coach Warner's. Winning wasn't the only thing to him, but winning while making money from football was, and after Warner returned from Cornell, Mercer did nothing to discourage the coach from recruiting the best players even if they did not fit the normal criteria for Carlisle.

That freedom was the main reason Warner had fled his alma mater to return to the Indian school. He thought the administration at Cornell cared little about football and less about winning. Some of the friction was personal, a lingering grudge between the school president and Warner over his expulsion of the team's most popular player, Lawrence Rice, who Warner thought was undermining his leadership but others considered a model student and sportsman. There was a far larger issue as well—the growing violence of the game. At another Ivy League school, Dr. Charles Eliot, the president at Harvard, equated football with murder and wanted to ban it altogether. Cornell was not that extreme, but less enthralled with the sport and more concerned than Warner about its harmful effects on young men.

Before 1906, there were rules in football, but few to tame its ferocity. The game seemed a case of unnecessary roughness. Teams would line up head-to-head with no neutral zone and bang away at each other, hold, scrap, lock arms for brutal arrow-like flying wedges, slug, bite, pile on, and attack with deadly force. Helmets, more like thin leather straps or bonnets, had been around since the 1890s, but they were not yet mandatory, and few players wore them. From 1901 to 1905 there were 71 recorded deaths in football. In 1905 a Union College back, Harold Moore, died of a cerebral hemorrhage after being kicked in the head while trying to tackle a New York University runner. He was one of 18 players who died that year. An unofficial casualty count of the 1905 season read like a military after-action report: deaths, 18; partially paralyzed, 1; eyes gouged out, 1; intestines ruptured, 2; backs broken, 1; skulls fractured, 1; arms broken, 4; legs broken, 7; hands broken, 3; shoulders dislocated, 7; noses broken, 4; ribs broken, 11; collarbones broken, 7; jaws broken, 1; fingers broken, 4; shoulders broken, 2; hips dislocated, 4; thighbones broken, 1; brain concussion, 2. And these numbers were likely an underestimate.

And Christian reformers encouraged Native American boys to play football, the game of Harvard and the Ivy League boys, because the indigenous game of lacrosse was too savage.

Teddy Roosevelt, whose son had been injured playing football at Harvard, summoned several prominent Ivy League athletic directors to the

White House and told them the only way to save the game, which he loved as much as they did, was to reform it. Walter Camp of Yale, considered the father of American football, was reluctant to change, but several new rules were instituted for the next season, including one that Warner took advantage of as much as or more than any coach in the nation. It was the forward pass, legalized as a means of spreading the field and making each play seem less like a rugby scrum. The pass had been legal for a year by the time Warner returned to Carlisle, and he saw it as the perfect tactic for a team of swift, savvy, fluid, and undersized players.

Warner encountered the Indians "with all the prejudices of an average white man." Some of these dissolved there during his two stints, some remained. He was protective of his players, but also tended to think of them as a stereotyped group rather than as individuals. He thought they played better as underdogs and let up when they were ahead. They had uncommon powers of observation, he said, attributing that trait to centuries of their forefathers living and surviving outdoors. If he had Pratt's zeal, it was toward transforming his charges not into white people, but into invincible players. He was Pop, but no father, not only because he and his wife, Tibb, had no children. His moniker preceded his arrival at Carlisle, given to him when he played football at Cornell and was older than his teammates, hence Pop. His childhood nickname in the farming village of Springville in western New York was less flattering: Butter, the boys called him, not because of his smoothness but for the flab around his belly. The midriff blubber dissolved during his playing days, then returned when he started coaching. He was a stout, gruff, profane man, a chain-smoker of Turkish Trophies cigarettes who spent his life tinkering, equally obsessed with devising new equipment, making a buck, and scratching out innovative football plays and formations on the back of a napkin or by moving salt and pepper shakers around the table.

Warner was an artist, a deft watercolor painter, but also had the brain of a mechanical engineer. He could take apart an auto piece by piece and put it back together. One of his favorite hangouts on the Carlisle campus was inside the industrial shop, where he was his own one-man athletic-wear creator, pounding away with a hammer to fashion longer and wider cleats for surer traction on muddy fields and concocting lighter and less bulky shoulder pads and thigh pads from varnished fiber lined with felt. To protect players with bum knees, he developed a device that became known as the Warner brace. Many of his inventions were bought and popularized by the A. G. Spalding sporting goods company for use by other teams around the country. It was no coincidence that an advertisement for Spalding appeared in every Friday's edition of the *Arrow.*

The engineer and artist in Pop also worked to invent or refine formations and techniques that became standard in the game. His most lasting creation was the single-wing offense—first known simply as the Carlisle Formation or by Warner himself as Formation A—that involved a direct snap to a back, usually the tailback, and the stationing of another back just behind and to the outside of an end, positioning that enhanced both end runs and the passing game. The double-wing formation, screen pass, three-point stance, flying chop block, spiral punt—all those also came out of Pop's laboratory, as did a phantasm of trick plays, including a hidden ball trick once used against Harvard for which he had a running back secretly stuff the ball into a pouch sewn into his uniform.

IN THAT FALL of 1907, Jim's first on the varsity, he and his teammates were granted special privileges and set apart from other Large Boys as they moved into a commodious football dormitory refashioned from the old hospital; it featured two new pool tables and a reading room with racks of newspapers from Philadelphia, Harrisburg, and New York so the players could take in fresh accounts of their sporting exploits. They also had their own dining room stocked regularly with beef, milk, potatoes, and flapjacks—fare the rest of the school was served infrequently. Their special path at school became literal when student masons paved a walkway from their new quarters overlooking the quadrangle down to the playing fields. The fact that football players received elite treatment fostered some resentment among other students, just as it did at many colleges around the nation. Winning and bringing public notice to Carlisle helped ease the discontent, as did Warner's constant presence at school events and his eagerness to entertain groups of schoolgirls by inviting them along in the back of his automobile, one of the few cars on campus.

The first football practice was held on September 2, with twenty-five boys reporting for varsity and an equal number on the "hotshots" scrub team. That was more than enough players in that era, when the eleven starters played both offense and defense, often for an entire game. As Thorpe later told the story, an assistant coach encouraged him to try out, but neither Warner nor the team's trainer, Wallace Denny, wanted him to play: Warner because he was fearful his future track star would get hurt on the gridiron, Denny because he thought Thorpe was too young and too small. That sounds apocryphal; Thorpe had turned twenty that May, hardly too young by any measure, and the student newspaper had been speculating all summer about his promising football future. Estimates of his weight at the time varied, but it was likely in the range of at least 160 pounds, and it is safe to say he was far taller and heavier than the runt who'd first appeared at Carlisle three years earlier, if not as perfectly proportioned as he eventually became. Furthermore, the team's star quarterback, Frank Mt. Pleasant, who was also a track star with hopes of competing in the 1908 Olympics, was shorter and slighter than Jim, but Warner and his assistants had no similar concerns about him.

Jim described his first football outfit as embarrassingly baggy. "When I walked out and joined the scrubs I was given the merry laugh by everybody for my misfit appearance," he recalled. Perhaps, although that seems reminiscent of the supposed snickers greeting his first high jump in overalls. The anecdote more certainly reflected his state of mind. He had something to prove. How he did that, how he made Pop Warner take notice yet again, is another origin story, and like his first high jump, this one was told and retold in various ways with exaggerated dialogue. One of Warner's drills involved giving the ball to a running back and instructing him to run the length of the field trying to dodge tacklers who were lined up at five-yard intervals. When Thorpe "dodged and swiveled" his way from one end to the other without being brought to the ground, a disbelieving Warner told him to try it again—which Jim did, again without being tackled, at which point Warner muttered to his assistants, "He's certainly one wild Indian."

In football, as in track, Exendine was Thorpe's mentor. Ex, as he was known, was a bright student and tenacious athlete, a six-foot two-hundred-pounder who had the respect of Warner and his teammates. He told Jim the key to football success was to remember to be mean, whether running or tackling. Jim was a good student, Exendine recalled. "He was quick at doing things the way you showed him." How much instruction Thorpe needed is an open question. He certainly had enough instruction on how to be mean from Hiram, his ruffian old man, and even during his days at Haskell playing with a makeshift cloth football he had told himself to run with the thundering certainty of a horse. He had already demonstrated enough toughness to be promoted from the scrubs to the second team as left halfback behind Albert Payne, who according to Carlisle documents was twenty-six and had been recruited from the Umatilla reservation in Oregon that fall to play football.

Thorpe's first football season was similar to his experience in track. There were several games in which, as a second-stringer most of the season, he never saw the field, but he gradually earned more playing time and notice. His time on the bench owed not to deficiencies in his game but to the excellence of that team, which Warner later declared his best, if not most famous. The 1907 squad was so stocked with talent it barely needed Thorpe. Considered the most innovative coach in the nation, Warner had players who could master whatever schemes he conceived. For the forward pass, the new way of advancing the ball, he usually turned to Mt. Pleasant. Along with being a nifty runner, Mt. Pleasant could throw a tight spiral for long distances at a time when many teams, in those rare instances when they tried to throw the ball (then a rugby-descended, bloated oblong sphere), were heaving it dead in the air like a shot put or end over end. The squad also had Exendine at end; Pete Hauser, an all-around star at fullback who sprinted around the ends, could throw a spiral nearly as well as Mt. Pleasant, and had a booming leg for punts; and a deep lineup including captain Antonio Lubo, Fritz Hendricks, William Gardner, Wauseka, Little Boy, Theodore Owl, Afraid-of-a-Bear, Albert Payne, and Michael Balenti, a multitalented back who also showed he could throw a tight spiral when he rejoined the football squad after his summer of semipro baseball in Hagerstown. Thorpe was an afterthought.

The Lebanon Valley opener was played in the rain. No contest: 40 to zip, Indians. Jim watched from the bench. Next Villanova visited Carlisle, a better gate attraction. Blanche Warner, the coach's cousin and a strong supporter of "Pop's Indians," ventured down from upper New York State to watch. Major Mercer led a pregame parade of his Indian cadets and tripped on his saber. On the hill opposite the grandstands, Villanova fans parked their Ford Runabouts and Franklin Model D Landaulettes and watched from the sideboards, joining more out-of-town spectators lured from Shippensburg, Hagerstown, and Harrisburg by Warner's paid publicist, Hugh Miller, who also was a stringer for the Associated Press and a New York paper. Another shutout, 10–0. No sign of Thorpe. A midweek game next against Susquehanna would not really count, too lopsided. Indians won 91 to zilch. Then up to Williamsport, a spectacular drive through the fall foliage on a sweet Saturday morning for a game against Penn State. Another Carlisle win, 18–5. Still only bench time for the second-string left halfback. On to Buffalo's Olympic Park for the Syracuse game, where clever little Mt. Pleasant pulled off a long pass to Hauser on a fake punt—Warner was the master of trick plays—and another win, 14–6. Thorpe got in but did nothing to make the papers.

Now came Bucknell, and here was Thorpe at last, running like a downhill horse. In the first half he made a long run but tripped and fumbled on his way to the end zone, and the ball was picked up by his Cherokee teammate Theodore Owl, who ran it in for a score. In the second half Jim did most of the ball carrying and showed Pop how smoothly he could follow his blockers. Another Carlisle shutout win, 15–0. Five games, five wins. The game stories about Carlisle included violent stereotypes, racist descriptions ingrained in American sports culture. The *Philadelphia Ledger* account of the rivalry game against Penn wrote of "a determined horde of Redskins." The *Philadelphia Press* reported that Carlisle's Indians "played with racial savagery and ferocity."

For Carlisle students, October 25, 1907, was a starred date on the calendar, marking for many a road trip to Philadelphia. The band, outfitted in bright red uniforms, marched into town from the hillside campus that morning to catch the train to Philly, joined by a boisterous throng of boys and girls who had been practicing cheers along with a new pep song written by Fannie Charley, a girl from the Peoria nation in Oklahoma. The school's adopted stray mutt, Long Branch, followed the girls to the station but had to be left behind. Once at Penn, they toured the Free Museum of Science and Art, its bottom floor lined with Indian artifacts that anthropologists and archaeologists had appropriated from many of their tribes. When they reached Franklin Field, they were joined in the crowd of twenty thousand by classmates who came in from their Outing homes for the game, filling a section of the stands in a scene the *Inquirer* used for a page-one photograph captioned "Indian Maidens Viewing the Game."

Carlisle defeated Penn handily, 26–6, but the score was secondary to the scene and its meaning. The game illuminated the crosscurrents of Carlisle and college football. It was at once a glorious autumn Saturday spectacle, an occasion of great school spirit for Carlisle, and a moneymaking sideshow for Penn. In a column that was racially degrading yet honest about the role of money in the sport, the *Philadelphia Inquirer* dismissed Penn's defeat as inconsequential. When a prominent eastern university lost to the Indian school, it did not really count, the paper argued, except in the financial ledger. Schools like Penn, Princeton, Yale, and Harvard needed the gate attraction of Carlisle to maintain their big-time football programs. "The game with the Indians is one of the spectacular features of the year and is added to the schedule largely because as a financial proposition it is a winner," the paper asserted. "The Indians are a strong drawing card wherever they go. They are not held down by any eligibility code or amateur rules. They are just Indians, and the best team possible is gotten together respective from where the material comes. Thus to be beaten by the red men is not counted as a blemish upon a college team's escutcheon."

Thorpe's memories of the Penn game showed him to be an unreliable narrator of his own career. "During the first five minutes of play, Payne hurt his knee and had to leave the game," Thorpe recalled. "I was sent in for my first chance. From that game on I remained at the left halfback position during the years I was at Carlisle." Too excited on his first play, he said, he ran headlong into the defensive wall, was thrown for a loss, and looked at the sidelines, afraid that Pop would yank him from the game. But he quickly redeemed himself by racing around the end for a seventy-five-yard touchdown.

Good story, but most of it inaccurate. It was not his first chance—that came against Syracuse and more against Bucknell. Payne was not hurt in the first five minutes but played the entire first half and beginning of the second. Thorpe did not enter the game until Carlisle was winning by three touchdowns, and he did not score, let alone on a seventy-five-yard run. The one thrilling run of the game was a length-of-the-field kickoff return by Fritz Hendricks. The play where Jim was thrown for a loss came later, as the game was ending. Overall, his performance was good if not great, breaking one twenty-yard run and returning a punt to midfield, so there was no discernible need for this exaggeration, though misremembering events is not uncommon among athletes—or soldiers or business tycoons, for that matter—when describing their days of glory, especially when recalling them in as-told-to conversations. For the following weekend's game against Princeton at the Polo Grounds in New York, Thorpe was the starting left halfback, but he and Payne took turns at that position the rest of the season.

The Princeton game was another financial boost for both schools, drawing a crowd of thirty thousand, not just partisans but thousands of New Yorkers curious to see the Indians, who had been an exotic draw in the city since Carlisle first played there in 1895. The teams played in a steady downpour that turned the field into a mud-slop mess. Thorpe kicked some booming punts, but the sloshy track eliminated Carlisle's speed advantage and the slippery ball made it difficult for Pop to pull off trick plays. In what would be Carlisle's only loss that year, they were defeated by Princeton 16–0. That game could have inspired Warner to head to the shops to design bad-weather cleats, but the coach had another explanation for the poor showing, also connected to foul weather. He said the Indians rarely performed well in bad weather because it took the joy out of the game, and they played more for fun than out of any Ivy League notion of school spirit. Princeton's fans reveled in the rain from beginning to end, singing and cheering "heartily as though the sun shone brilliantly upon them." When Carlisle jogged onto the field, the hold-that-Tiger section in the bleachers broke into a song drafted for the occasion. Here again, in a lighthearted ditty, were the contradictions of the Anglo view of native peoples, sympathy and condescension intertwined.

Mr. Indian, he is American
Mr. Indian, he is all right
For he used to be
In North America
When Society
Was out of sight.
As a potentate
Of Yankee real estate
He is just as great
As any man.
He may have beaten dear old Penn
But he can't do a thing to the Princeton men.
Poor Mr. Indian.

JIM WAS PROMOTED that October in the classroom. He and five other students were moved up from Room 9 to Room 10. As a member of the football team, he was away from schoolwork much of the time until after Thanksgiving. Carlisle closed out the season with three time-consuming but profitable road games, first zigging up to Harvard in Boston and then taking the train zag west to face two powerful midwestern universities, Minnesota and Chicago. Jim had been on trains before, but traveling with the football boys on an extended journey was a more raucous experience of card playing, jamming on instruments, and singing into the night. "We had a private car for our trips and stayed in the best hotels," he recalled. "But most of the boys complained about having to sleep in the soft beds.

They preferred hard ones, being used to the uncompromising military beds of the school. Some of the team overcame this soft-bed condition by wrapping themselves in blankets and sleeping on the floors of the hotels or in the aisles on the train." Once, as Thorpe remembered it, a maid opened the door to the room in the morning, saw that the bed had not been slept in, and entered assuming no one was there, then shrieked in fright when a player stuck his head out from under the bed. The maid "fled the room and didn't stop until she fainted in the office of the hotel manager."

Thorpe believed the team played better after a night of singing, so perhaps the music overflowed before those final three games. All were victories over favored opposition for the Indians, who finished the season with a 10-1 record, outscoring their opponents 267–62. Thorpe and Payne shared backfield duties. The game against Minnesota, in which Mt. Pleasant threw a touchdown pass to tackle Antonio Lubo on a fake field goal, was witnessed by hundreds of Indians who came from the reservations in Minnesota and the Dakotas. Mt. Pleasant hurt his thumb later in that game and did not play on Marshall Field in Chicago against the Maroons. That game, won by Carlisle 18–4, was an all-star coaching matchup between two giants of college football, Warner and the Maroons' Amos Alonzo Stagg, both early advocates of the passing game and fiendish football magicians. Instead of the hidden ball trick wielded against Harvard, this time Warner sprang the hidden player trick, having Exendine trot from his end position to the sidelines and behind the opposition bench, then slip back into play thirty yards downfield to haul in a high-arching fling from Hauser. No rule against that—yet.

The next morning, the *Chicago Tribune* overflowed with stories about football, good and bad. One page was devoted to the mounting casualties during this second season of what was called "debrutalized" football, meaning the era that had started with rule changes imposed after the 1905 season intended to make the game less violent. Not much progress on that count, according to the newspaper's investigation, which documented eleven deaths and ninety-eight serious injuries on the nation's college, high school, and sandlot gridirons that year. Under the headline "The Dead and How They Were Killed," *Tribune* readers learned about, among others, Leonard Clarkson of Norwich University, who died from a fractured skull in a game against Dartmouth; and Richard Evans, the left halfback on Wooster University's squad, who was kicked in the abdomen and died of internal injuries after a scrimmage against Ohio rival Western Reserve; and Leo Strohmeyer, a talented young athlete in Iowa City, who was carted off the field on a stretcher during a high school game, neck broken, never to regain consciousness.

Further inside the Sunday paper, several pages were devoted to the Carlisle versus Chicago contest, including a cartoon of an Indian chief in moccasins, leggings, and full headdress, tomahawk in hand, posed as a fearsome statue on a Carlisle pedestal with the caption: "THE SECOND MASSACRE OF FORT DEARBORN." The actual Battle of Fort Dearborn had occurred along the Chicago River in August 1812, when a rebellious band from the Potawatomi nation attacked and killed a smaller traveling party of soldiers and white settlers near the U.S. Army fort. The cartoon was nonchalantly racist, and to use that event as a metaphor for a football game ninety-five years later was questionable. In any case, in terms of events related to Carlisle football, another article appeared in the *Tribune* that day that was more explosive than the report on casualties or the game stories detailing what happened when the Indians beat the Maroons.

5

Athletic Duties above Everything

RICHARD HENRY PRATT WAS MORE THAN THREE YEARS removed from Carlisle by the end of the 1907 football season, but he had not gone quietly into retirement, and his acolytes were still vigorously defending his quarter century of assimilation work against efforts to reverse it by the Bureau of Indian Affairs in Washington and the school's replacement regime led by Major Mercer. The fiercest counterattack from the Pratt side was directed at the football team precisely when Pop Warner's squad was at its zenith—the morning after the season-ending road win over the University of Chicago on Thanksgiving. It came in the form of a guest article written by Carlos Montezuma in the November 24 Sunday *Chicago Tribune.* The paper carried the piece with a one-column headline on the bottom of page twenty-four, but the volatility of the subject matter and the prominence of the author assured that it would not go unnoticed.

Montezuma's column crackled with accusations, portraying the Carlisle team as a professional squad stocked with non-students recruited and foisted upon the college football scene by a superintendent and head coach who—in the interest of winning and gaining fame—failed "to comprehend the underlying purpose of the school." It was a mix of hard truths and exaggerations, and parts of the argument had been made earlier in condescending fashion by various sportswriters, including the *Philadelphia Inquirer* columnist who had dismissed Penn's loss to the Indians as no "blemish upon a college team's escutcheon" because Carlisle did not follow the amateur code on eligibility rules. But Montezuma was a path-breaking doctor in Chicago, not a sportswriter, and one of the most noted Native Americans in the country. His decision to mount a public case against Carlisle forced the Indian bureau and the school to scramble up a defense and at the same time revealed the conflicting intellectual arguments then being waged about "the Indian problem" not just among white policymakers but within the Native American community itself. Montezuma and his complex life story were in the middle of it all.

Wassaja was Montezuma's birth name, translated as "beckoning" or "signaling" in the native tongue of the Yavapai-Apache nation, whose tribal homeland was near Four Peaks in the Mazatzal Mountains of Arizona, sacred land rising from the blistering bed of the Sonoran Desert. At the time of his birth in 1866, in the aftermath of the Civil War, the U.S. Army and white settlers were turning their attention to westward expansion and the Indian resisters in their way. The Yavapai were penned in by military forts, new white settlements, and traditional Indian foes, including the Pima. With an unending series of chases, skirmishes, raids, and massacres, *Wassaja*'s early life, as Yavapai historian Maurice Crandall wrote, was shaped by "extreme violence and terror," culminating when he was captured at age five by Pima warriors and sold to a white man for thirty silver dollars.

His guardian was an Italian-born photographer named Carlo Gentile, who was in Arizona Territory doing ethnographic work. Gentile created a strange new life for his young companion, renaming him Carlos Montezuma and taking the boy around the country as he tried to scratch out a living as a photographer, until the responsibility became too much and he sent Carlos to Urbana, Illinois, to live during his high school years with a pious Baptist minister. A brilliant rise began there, as Monte, as his classmates called him, became the first Native American to attend the University of Illinois, and then Northwestern, and finally earn a doctorate from the Chicago Medical College. On the surface, he seemed to be the avatar of assimilation, the symbol of everything Richard Henry Pratt hoped Indians would become. As Pratt the Indian baptizer would say, Montezuma had been immersed in civilization and held under until he was thoroughly soaked, emerging as a devout Christian who championed education and denounced the Bureau of Indian Affairs, the reservation system, and old tribal customs.

Montezuma's situation was more complex than that, as historian Crandall astutely pointed out; the letters he wrote back to Arizona starting in early adulthood showed him seeking information about his identity, his family, and the Yavapai people, on a quest not just for intellectual understanding but for an emotional homecoming that would be realized in his final days decades later. But that inner search occurred even as he argued for acculturation and developed a close relationship with Pratt, who eventually persuaded him in the mid-1890s to move to Carlisle and become the school physician. He arrived at Carlisle with the conviction that it was time "to fulfill the higher mission than mere physician, that is to prove to the white people there is the same stuff in the Indians as there is in the white people, it only requires the same environments." Treating football injuries became part of Montezuma's portfolio. Like Pratt, he appreciated the role that football played in bringing national recognition to Carlisle and believed that the sportsmanlike conduct of Indian boys would impress white society. He traveled with the team to eastern schools and, even after leaving the school and returning to private practice in Chicago, made the 1900 train trip west for the game against California that included two stops on the way home: first in Phoenix, where Montezuma tried to make his first personal contacts with his Yavapai people, then at Haskell, where young Jim Thorpe gawked at the team at breakfast.

In the yearslong power struggle between Pratt and his detractors in Washington, Montezuma consistently took Pratt's side, even criticizing the establishment of the Leupp Art Studio at Carlisle and the hiring of Winnebago artist Angel De Cora to oversee it. There was "no such thing as Indian art," Montezuma argued, adding that the "attempt to perpetuate this nonexistent thing has a tendency to undermine the foundational purpose of the school." He defined that purpose as "preparing the Indian youths, boys and girls, for absorption into the civilization of the country." In moving away from that philosophy since Pratt's departure, Montezuma said, Carlisle was embracing "hydra-headed faddism." His heated attack on the art studio was overblown, his dismissive attitude toward Indian art condescending, but his diatribe in this instance reflected the intensity of the larger debate, which grew ever stronger as Pratt and then his loyalists at Carlisle were pushed aside one by one. Which leads to the football team and his broadside against Superintendent Mercer and Coach Warner.

One of Montezuma's oldest allies at Carlisle was William Grant Thompson, who had been a school disciplinarian, superintendent of the industrial shops, and athletic manager until he was supplanted when Pop Warner returned in 1907. Thompson was by no means hostile to football. He had traveled with the team for many years and often served as toastmaster at the postseason football banquets. It was his ouster and a mix of personal pique and disillusionment over Warner's recruitment methods that led Thompson eventually to mount a campaign against the football team. Montezuma was enlisted as his most fearsome public weapon. "As you know I have been a strong advocate of clean sport, and as the present Supt. and also the coach care only to win and at any price, I failed to dovetail in their schemes as well as I could have," Thompson wrote Montezuma earlier that year. "The school had degenerated into a school of professional athletes, where everything—the welfare of the individual as well as that of the community—must step aside to gratify the desire of Major Mercer and Pop Warner . . . to win, and create a large account to use as they wish, without supervision from Washington."

Montezuma took up the cause with fervor and used the Chicago newspaper to spread the word to a national audience. He charged that "not more than one-third of the members" of the football team "were in actual attendance at the school as students," a situation he called unacceptable. Some of his facts could be challenged, but the argument he made would echo down through the decades thereafter. The point of football and all sports, he said, was to develop physical and mental proficiency as "a stimulant to their ambitions as students," not in the cause of winning for winning's sake. "There is no reason why the Carlisle students should be proud of the success which in 1907 attended the football efforts of a lot of hired outsiders," he wrote. "There is no reason why the Carlisle Indian

Industrial School should parade under false colors. As conducted this year the school might just as well have farmed out its football work to anybody who would take the job. . . . The Carlisle football team of 1907 might as well be called the 'All Around Redmen of the West,' or any other name that fancy might suggest, and it would mean as much and be as significant in one case as in the other."

The real target of Montezuma's column became clear in his conclusion—the men who had uprooted his mentor, Richard Henry Pratt. Warner and the football team merely represented a larger moral failing at the school, he said. "The mistake in this football matter is due to the present management having lost, or more correctly speaking, never having had, its bearings on the matter of properly conducting the Carlisle school. A failure on the part of those in charge to comprehend the underlying purpose of the school in itself opens the way to failure in any and all directions in the matter of school work, and this football departure is not much out of the order of things in the school as now conducted."

Montezuma's complaint was soon amplified by twenty-two charges presented to the press, including: That the administration would not allow an audit of the Carlisle Athletic Association to determine how its funds were used. That players were paid for their services and given bonuses for good play. That the disciplinarian was ordered not to punish important athletes. That many of the stars, including Exendine and Mt. Pleasant, had already graduated and attended neighboring Dickinson College in preparation for law school. That some of the players had been on the team as long as eight years. That the student calling himself Wauseka was in fact Emil Hauser, who had played three years at Haskell, where he was not a student but an employee who had been discharged for misconduct. That Samuel McClain was playing under the name Afraid-of-a-Bear and had attended Haskell for four years before being induced by money to play at Carlisle. That Little Boy was in fact named Porter and had been at Haskell before that institution discovered that earlier he had been expelled from an Indian school in Nebraska.

While Warner and Mercer scurried to prepare responses, the first return volley came on November 28 from Gus Beaulieu, editor of *Tomahawk*, the official publication of the Chippewa nation's White Earth reservation in Minnesota. Beaulieu, whose tribe had sent many of its boys and girls to Carlisle over the years, took offense at the accusations against one of his people, Little Boy, whose full English name was Scott J. Porter. "It was charged by Montezuma that Little Boy was expelled from Haskell, but this is not true in any particular," Beaulieu wrote. "The player in question is one of the steadiest young men ever sent forth from the reservation and he has never even been open to criticism for his conduct at school." The public records on this back-and-forth reveal a mixed result. Little Boy was by all accounts an upstanding young man who did not drink and later went on to become a police officer. But one Carlisle document—"Descriptive and Historical Record of Student"—has a handwritten note on the back. For a period of time, the note says of Little Boy: "Did not attend school but taking part in athletics."

Later in his response, Beaulieu broke open the argument within the indigenous community over assimilation. Could Montezuma even call himself an Indian? "We are at a loss when we come to analyze the criticism, coming as it does from an Indian, or one who claims to be such," he wrote, adding: "Dr. Montezuma evidently has none of the feelings of kinship with the Indian, and perhaps this is not to be wondered at since he has not been much in contact with his red brethren since his childhood, and because the greater part of his life has been passed within the circles of refined civilization."

The internal dispute about who was sufficiently Indian was of no concern to Pop Warner. His mission was to save his program. He issued a response to Montezuma in a statement published by the *New York Times* one week later.

No one at the school was paying any attention to "these absurd stories," he wrote, "and the public generally are wise enough to understand that these knocks against the Carlisle team came from soreheads and losers." Nonetheless, he felt compelled to "nail some of the lies that have been flying around." Warner asserted that no one on the team had played at Carlisle for a total of eight years, eluding the reality that in the past some had played that long. He did acknowledge that some of his 1907 boys had played for five years but argued that was acceptable because the normal term of enrollment was five years. Then he said from now on they would be limited to four years of eligibility. He denied that anyone attached to the school had traveled the country "recruiting athletic material," a careful answer that evaded the truth that Carlisle officials for years had recruited students and were especially interested in boys with athletic talent. He acknowledged that Exendine and Mt. Pleasant had played for Carlisle while studying at Dickinson College, but only because they were excellent students and Carlisle did not have a law school.

Superintendent Mercer, in response to an inquiry from the Indian bureau, called the controversy a put-up job by Thompson and other disgruntled former Carlisle employees, including Frank Hudson, a former football star and later bookkeeper at Carlisle who had been fired after it was charged that he had embezzled money from the school. Mercer claimed that Thompson and the others had tried to get their charges published through anonymous letters to newspapers but, failing that, "the only way they got them before the public was through Dr. Montezuma, who had them published over his name the day after Carlisle's great victory over Chicago." As an example of the falseness of the charges, he said that Samuel McClain—Afraid-of-a-Bear—came to Carlisle of his own accord, was not induced by money, and was enrolled at school in the junior class. The fact that all the major colleges in the East, from Penn to Navy, ignored the charges and had already signed up to play Carlisle in future seasons, that "the universities beg us for games," showed how petty the matter was, Mercer said, adding that if he was guilty of anything, it was of loving the football team too much. "I first saw the Carlisle team play in 1904, and made up my mind that if some few of the handicaps they were laboring under could be eliminated, they could win the championship of the United States," he wrote, "and I admit that in football matters I have strained the harness a little bit too enthusiastically in order to give the Indians, as nearly as possible, a fair test with their white brethren."

Left unsaid was the fact that the football team under Warner had been a moneymaking machine that benefited all officials involved. Receipts from the Chicago game alone brought more than $16,000 to the athletic fund, the largest chunk of the $50,000-plus share of gate receipts Carlisle received from its five major road games that year. The Carlisle Athletic Association was so far in the black that Superintendent Mercer felt guilty about it. "It is really embarrassing to have more money than we really need," he wrote in a letter to the Indian bureau, "but it has come without solicitation on our part, and dropped into our laps, as it were." It also dropped into the laps of the coach and his players. Some of the money was used to build a new two-story cottage on campus for Warner and his wife, while smaller funds were secretly if consistently doled out to the athletes in loans that were not expected to be repaid and direct cash payments, usually of $15 to $20 at a time. The player bonuses totaled nearly $10,000, including $500 to Jim Thorpe, before they were stopped in 1908, according to an investigation five years later that fully exposed Warner's reward system.

Several conclusions can be drawn from the Montezuma column and its aftermath that lead in different directions. There is no doubt that the attack on the football team was led by disillusioned former Carlisle officials motivated by their loyalty to Pratt. To Montezuma, Pratt represented something larger, a pan-Indian philosophy of survival through education that he thought was central to the rise of his people. In a letter to Thompson six weeks after the story broke, he was still pining for the founder's return. "You and I know that no one can fill the superintendency of Carlisle but R. H. Pratt," he wrote. "He is living, and I believe it is our duty to get him back there." The restoration never had a chance, but even if that misguided hope was what triggered Montezuma, it did not diminish the importance of the debate.

The controversy brought forward essential questions about the corrupting influence of big-time football in the nation's academic institutions that would resurface generation after generation. Carlisle's program was unique in some ways since the school was not a college and not beholden to college enrollment standards, but it was not an outlaw operation, or at least not much different from dozens of other schools in its under-the-table payments and recruitment methods. If the system was being manipulated, the blame fell heavily on administrators and coaches, not the players, especially not young Indian athletes who arrived from impoverished reservations to bring profits to a school gaining fame from an exotic heritage it was designed to erase.

ON THE MONDAY of Christmas week, when Jim and his classmates entered Room 10, they saw that Miss Scales, their teacher, had placed a miniature Christmas tree on her desk bedecked with "bright candles like stars." The next day, Christmas Eve, they joined the entire student body in the gymnasium for the annual presentation of gifts. Every boy and girl—"good, bad, or indifferent"—was handed a large bag of nuts, fruit, and candy and one individual gift. Jim's choices were a pocketknife or a new pair of skates that he could lace up for laps around frozen Conodoguinet Creek. "Uncle Sam is a good Santa Claus," proclaimed the *Arrow.* Among those celebrating was the youngest Carlisle Indian, four-year-old Richard Kesetta, whose family story was the bookend to that of *Wassaja,* the boy who became Carlos Montezuma. Richard's mother was an Apache like Montezuma, though a Lipan Apache from the Rio Grande Valley of Texas. Like Montezuma she had been separated from her people by force—seized by the U.S. Cavalry in 1877 after a raid in which nineteen of her people were killed.

Her Lipan name was *Kisseta.* When she arrived at Carlisle three years later as a member of Pratt's second class, she was given the name Kisetta Roosevelt. The entrance physical revealed three serious injuries to her head; when asked about them she said the welts were inflicted by her frightened mother, who beat her with a stone thinking it better to have her daughter dead than captured into the white world. Roosevelt was a popular student at Carlisle, and her face graced the middle of a postcard photograph featuring thirty healthy-looking students in 1881 captioned "Our Boys and Girls."

The story of what happened with Kisetta Roosevelt after that was mostly lost to history and shrouded in mystery, raising more questions than documents could later answer. She somehow remained connected to Carlisle for the quarter-century span that Pratt was there, by far its longest-tenured student. According to Carlisle records, she made a final Outing in

Baltimore in 1903 and it was while there that she became pregnant. Another possibility was that she got pregnant at Carlisle and was sent away for a year for that reason. The father was never named. Three years later, at age thirty-nine, she died, leaving her son as a ward of the school. He was given the first name Richard, after Carlisle's founder, and a surname from his mother's Indian name with a slightly different spelling, *Kesetta*.

In a photograph taken during the 1907 holiday season, the little orphan boy was dressed in Carlisle's full military outfit. He was the school's elfin mascot at the Christmas Eve gifting party.

Superintendent Mercer's gift was relief from his duties. He had announced his resignation from his post earlier that week, saying that after three years in charge at Carlisle the "daily annoying responsibilities" were more than he could stand. Pop Warner's gift was that he survived the turmoil relatively unscathed and could continue to build his program into a fearsome power.

6

The Newest Star

ONE MID-FEBRUARY NIGHT IN 1908, JIM THORPE AND SCORES of his classmates filed along the snow-cleared pathways at the Carlisle Indian Industrial School into the gymnasium for an Oklahoma Evening honoring the newest state, adding a forty-sixth star to the American flag.

The admittance of Oklahoma into the union in November 1907 seemed reason for great celebration at Carlisle, even though the school was more than twelve hundred miles from Guthrie, the first state capital. Among the Indian school's student body were a few hundred young men and women who had been sent east from reservations in Oklahoma, including Thorpe and many of Carlisle's finest athletes. They were Arapaho, Caddo, Cheyenne, Comanche, Delaware, Kickapoo, Kiowa, Osage, Pawnee, Peoria, Potawatomi, Quapaw, Sac and Fox, and Shawnee. The delegation would have been even greater, but Section 248 of federal Indian school rules mandated that many Cherokee, Seminole, Creek (Muscogee), Choctaw, and Chickasaw could not be enrolled in U.S. government schools unless they paid their own way. These Oklahoma-based nations were known as the Five Civilized Tribes, a description meant to delineate those who had adjusted to the American perception of civilization. No need, the government felt, to pay for acculturating Indians who had assimilated on their own.

Invitations to the Oklahoma Evening gala were composed by Jim's Sac and Fox friend Fannie Keokuk, a daughter in the first family of his tribe. His athletic mentor Albert Exendine, a Delaware, delivered "an eloquent address of welcome" on behalf of a reception committee of fellow football boys led by Michael Balenti and Pete Hauser of the Cheyenne, with Fritz

Hendricks of the Caddo in charge of decorations. After more speeches about the meaning of their Oklahoma homeland and a late snack, the room resounded with the singing of a new Oklahoma anthem, the lyrics set to the tune of "Tramp, Tramp, Tramp (the Boys Are Marching)," a popular Civil War anthem sung from the perspective of a Union soldier held in a Confederate prison. *And beneath the starry flag we shall breathe the air again / Of the free land in our own beloved home.*

Two weeks later, on February 27, Thorpe and the athletic boys gathered again with many of their classmates for what was called "the leading social function of the season devoted to pleasure pure and unadulterated"—the football banquet. Snow was turning to slush; just a few days earlier Pop Warner had been knocked to the ground by a snow-slide from a thawing roof. The cavernous gym was transformed into a "fairyland" by the coach's wife and a team of girls, with multicolored lights strung across the walls and the school colors of red and gold everywhere, from the posts to table candles. First came a meal of roast turkey and Waldorf salad and speeches by Wauseka and Exendine punctuated by shouts of *Minni wa ka, ka wa wi! Minni wa ka, ka wa wi!*—a school cheer first used at a football game in 1902. There are no recordings of the cheer, and it was transcribed phonetically in the student newspaper. Present-day Lakota linguists note that the first line is actually *mniwakhan*—"firewater" or "whiskey"—and the second phrase could be *kawewe* and mean "whip it up." It is doubtful that school authorities understood its meaning beyond the joy with which students shouted it.

Pop Warner was the last speaker, taking the stage for the presentation of varsity letters in football and track. Two went to Jim Thorpe, the school's "coming Indian star," as the *New York World* described him, the young man from Oklahoma whose potential gave his coach a "sweet smile."

A year earlier, when Thorpe in overalls made the casual leap over the high-jump bar that rocketed him onto the track team, few knew his name. Now he was emerging as potentially the finest athlete in the East. He had already shown all-around talent in track and field and untapped promise in football. Potential is a slippery concept to quantify. It is more aura than statistic, more glimmer and glimpse than full view, the mystery of the future more intoxicating than the reality of the present. Thorpe was twenty-one, entering the prime time when great athletes tend to mature year by year. His teammates could sense he was different. They had seen his easygoing nature, his lack of nerves, the resilience of his body and his resistance to pain, the rare combination of strength, speed, stubbornness, instinct, and agile grace, the hint of danger and spark of electricity.

Although Jim had been at Carlisle since 1904, that June marked the end of his first uninterrupted school year, with no Outings. He was an uneven student, and sometimes strayed from school. Still, the respect he had earned from his peers was evident. He was the star of the spring track season, setting several school records. In a dual meet against Syracuse in Elmira, New York, won by Carlisle on a cold and rainy Thursday afternoon, he scored nineteen points by himself, winning the two hurdles events, tying in the high jump, and finishing second in the shot put. "The Freshman class is certainly proud of their high jumper James Thorpe. He cleared six feet last Saturday in Philadelphia. What do you think of that?" the *Arrow* boasted after Thorpe took first place and broke the school high-jump record at the Penn Relays. In the classroom, when he was there, he emerged as a leader, even if not the keenest student. Once that spring, when the freshman class teacher, Mariette Wood, took a brief break to visit Washington and the Hampton Institute in Virginia, Thorpe filled in for her. How exactly is unclear, but one classmate said "he makes a fine teacher."

When the academic calendar ended, the school newspaper reported that "James Thorpe, one of our famous athletes, went to his house in Oklahoma." This marked the first time Jim had returned to the banks of the North Canadian since he had left in 1904. "I got homesick," he later wrote. "I had been away from the old stamping ground four years. I was thinking of my brothers and sisters." But he soon realized that while the river and ravines and horses were still there, life had changed and "things did not live up to the childhood memory I had retained of my early environment." His parents were dead. His older brother, George, had his own family and allotted land. His younger brother, Edward, was at the Sac and Fox boarding school, and younger sister, Adeline, was about to leave for the Chilocco

Indian School north of Ponca City. He stayed with his oldest half-brother, Frank, who had a wife and four children and farmed thirty acres of corn and cotton. He also spent time with his sister Mary, who was seventeen. Frank and Mary were quite a pair of Thorpes, as notorious in that pocket of Oklahoma as Jim was famous nationally. They shared characteristics with their old man.

Frank drank like Hiram, and Mary drank and fought like him. Jim was a little of both, but better at keeping his drinking and fighting under control at that stage in his life. He and Frank would "do some fishing," which was both a literal and a figurative term. They fished on the North Canadian and other streams, but as writer Jack Newcombe once noted, they also "fished" as in going out and drinking and raising hell. Mary was the most imposing person in the family. Known as Big Mary, she was six feet and a few hundred pounds of potent mystery. People thought she had supernatural powers, only one reason many were intimidated by her. She frequented the bars of Shawnee, drank and played football with the men, farmed her own patch of land, married young and badly, and fought her way through life, once punching out two Kickapoo girls who'd mocked her. Many people said she was deaf and dumb, but Big Mary could read and write. As a young girl, she'd fallen from a wagon onto a spear-like cornstalk, puncturing her throat, and thenceforth spoke in croaks and hoarse whispers. When she used English, few outside her family could follow. It was easier for her to communicate in Sauk, a more guttural language. Jim was one of the few people who understood her. They were comfortable in each other's company, neither particularly eager to talk much.

Thorpe's sinewy body filled out that summer to 175 pounds. Was it home cooking? Bill Newashe, his Sac and Fox pal and teammate, also fattened up during the home visit to the point where his sister Emma, another Carlisle student, said he was so blubbery she was embarrassed to stand next to him. Newashe was a second-string lineman. The weight that running back Thorpe added was all muscle. They returned to school together, catching the train in Oklahoma City for the trip east and the new season. "I look back on 1908 as the beginning of my career in football," Thorpe later reflected. "The work of the year before, when I had gone in as a substitute and had played out the season, was an apprenticeship which had prepared me for the games which awaited me from 1908 on."

THE FIRST ATTEMPT to adopt a commonly accepted way of playing American football had come in November 1876 when a group of young men from Harvard, Yale, Princeton, and Columbia formed the Intercollegiate Football Association. The rules had been changing year by year since then, moving the game further from its sporting roots in English rugby. From kicking to more running. From a free-for-all scrum to a line of scrimmage with one team possessing the ball. From team captains assessing penalties to the presence of judges and referees. From an endless back-and-forth of line plunges to the legal forward pass. From no sideline coaching to men like Amos Alonzo Stagg and Pop Warner who were paid to win games.

But football in 1908 remained far different from the game that would be played a century later. The pigskin had a twenty-seven-inch circumference, a full six inches rounder than later balls, making it harder to hold and much harder to throw in a spiral. The playing field was longer, 110 yards from goal line to goal line. It had both parallel and lateral lines, forming a pattern that explained the derivation of the term *gridiron.* If a player left the game, he could not return. The starting eleven played both offense and defense, often for the entire game, the length of which was negotiable and could be as short as twenty minutes for a first half and fifteen for a second to as long as seventy minutes total. Offensive linemen could take handoffs and catch and run with the ball. The goalposts were on the goal line, not at the back of the end zone. The team on offense had three downs, not four, to gain 10 yards. Teams often punted on first or second down. In a game between Carlisle and Minnesota that year, the teams punted for 753 yards. The kickoff was from midfield. And a touchdown was worth five points, not six, while a field goal garnered four points instead of three—explaining why a modern reader examining scores from that era might find them strange.

The team Pop Warner fielded that autumn was without Mt. Pleasant and Exendine, two leaders from the 1907 squad, but still seemed formidable. At left end was David Little Old Man, a Cheyenne from Montana who had entered Carlisle with Thorpe in 1904. At left tackle was Wauseka, the team captain, a Cheyenne from Oklahoma who preferred not to be called by his Anglo name, Emil Hauser. The left guard was Afraid-of-a-Bear, a Sioux from South Dakota also known as Samuel McClain. Napoleon Barril, a Chippewa from Minnesota, usually listed in press accounts as "Barrel," was at center. James Lyon, from the Onondaga nation in New York State, played right guard. The right tackle was Little Boy, another Chippewa from Minnesota, whose Carlisle records listed him as Scott Porter. At right end was William Gardner, a Chippewa from North Dakota. Michael Balenti, the Oklahoma Cheyenne, was the quarterback, sometimes replaced by Archie Libby, a Chippewa who first entered Carlisle in 1894 and had graduated in 1907 but was still playing. Fritz Hendricks, the Oklahoma Caddo, was at right halfback. Pete Hauser, Wauseka's brother and a brilliant holdover from the 1907 squad, was slotted at fullback but, subsequently injured for much of the year, was replaced by Harry Cries-for-Ribs, a Ponca from Oklahoma, and Albert Payne, the Umatilla from Oregon who had been moved to fullback to make room at left halfback for the team's new Sac and Fox star, Jim Thorpe.

Those were the rules and the players; what was the national landscape in 1908? The East Coast dominated the college game, especially Ivy League schools, plus Carlisle, Syracuse, Penn State, and the military academies. Yale's Walter Camp, from his perch in New Haven, was the football almighty, determining not only which players could be deemed All-Americans but which teams the sporting press should follow, which along with the preponderance of New York City scribes gave the sport a decidedly eastern tilt. Among the first- and second-team All-Americans that year, only two players out of twenty-two came from outside that eastern elite, quarterback Walter Steffen of Chicago and center Germany Schulz from Michigan. Fourteen were from the Ivy League.

The most prominent team in the South was Louisiana State, but when Grantland Rice accused it of paying players, his fellow sportswriters refused to acknowledge the school's unbeaten record. LSU was part of the Southern Collegiate Athletic Association, with many schools that later formed the football-mad Southeastern Conference, from Alabama and Auburn to Ole Miss and Mississippi State to Tennessee and Vanderbilt, but also including Mercer University and Sewanee, a tiny college in the Tennessee hills that placed three players on the All-South team in 1908. The Western Conference, then denoting the Midwest, included the University of Chicago and seven future Big Ten schools (minus Ohio State, Michigan State, and Michigan, a founding member that abandoned the conference in 1907 before rejoining a decade later). Notre Dame was an independent whose cupcake schedule included the Chicago School of Physicians and Surgeons, the Franklin (Indiana) Baptists, and St. Viator College. In the mountain states, the University of Denver Ministers were a power, along with Colorado and Colorado College. On the West Coast, Southern Cal's team was called the USC Methodists and their competition included Whittier, Pomona, Occidental, and Los Angeles High School.

Although newspaper coverage was extensive, stadiums were small and attendance spotty. A century later, LSU would pack 93,000 fans into Tiger Stadium for a game against Alabama; in 1908 its average attendance at State Field in Baton Rouge was 1,500. Rivalry games in the East and Midwest drew the largest crowds, reaching but rarely surpassing 30,000. The Carlisle team of Thorpe and his fellow Indians was so alluring it transcended rivalry and commonly attracted overflow crowds. Whatever the numbers, the fanaticism of that era was as intense as it would be for ensuing generations of college football hordes. When Chicago played Wisconsin for the Western Conference championship, four special trains carried a thousand Maroon fans north to Madison, including a deluxe special that charged what a *Chicago Inter Ocean* reporter considered the outrageous sum of eight bucks round-trip and jammed 200 "plutocrats" into a train designed to carry 150, provoking "a battle royal to get into the dining car." After Chicago prevailed for the conference title, the team and hundreds of fans trailed the marching band on a raucous march from Camp Randall Stadium up State Street to the Park Hotel on Capitol Square, where Coach

Stagg and his boys scrambled atop tables to lead the throng in cheers, though some players were "so overcome by the demonstration in their honor they were unable to speak."

Thorpe seized national attention by leading Carlisle through five straight wins to start the season. He scored six touchdowns against Conway Hall, Lebanon Valley, and Villanova, who were overmatched by a cumulative score of 102–0, then shared headlines with quarterback Balenti in closer wins over Penn State and Syracuse at the beginning of a challenging stretch of ten straight road games through the end of the year. His all-around talents were perfectly suited to football as it was then played. He could plow through the middle or race around one end, with knees high and stiff-arm extended, throw spirals when needed, catch the ball surely with his big mitts, intuit opposition plays and tackle ferociously on defense, thump booming punts, and—unless his right leg or ankle was injured—boot extra points and field goals equally effectively as place-kicks or drop-kicks. His head was a hard and massive boulder, his body firm and limber, and it was difficult to knock him out of the lineup, as much as opposing teams tried, though his intensity depended on his mood; there were times when Pop Warner felt he had to confront Jim to force him to concentrate. Jim wanted to win, but if victory seemed certain, he tended to relax.

At the Wednesday practice for game six, the rivalry match against Penn, Thorpe twisted his ankle so badly that Warner sent him to the indoor athletic cage for treatment. After two days of ice packs and massaging, he seemed improved by Friday, but center Barril was in the hospital, fullback Hauser was sidelined by injuries, Afraid-of-a-Bear and Gardner were banged up, and a backup end was booted from the team for breaking training rules (meaning he drank too much); bettors moved the line toward a Penn team that had been thrashed by Carlisle a year earlier.

"The Indians, they're here!" shouted the pregame story in the *Philadelphia Inquirer* that Saturday morning. For Penn and its fans, this was the match of the year, of such importance the Quakers team retreated to a hideaway in the remote Pine Barrens of New Jersey to prepare. When Pop Warner reached Philly with his team Friday night, he felt obliged to deny published reports that he had dispatched Indian spies to gather dope on the secret Quakers practices. "None were sent from Carlisle and I know of none being sent there," said Warner, a master of carefully worded non-denial denials. As was the case every year when Carlisle visited, the press focused not only on the Indian players but also on their female followers. When a headline in the *Inquirer* promised "Red Men's Football Squad Will Be Joined by Bevy of Maidens," it was playing to a centuries-old trope, the attraction of supposedly compliant Native American women. The lead photographic montage on the sports page the next day placed captain Wauseka amid five Carlisle coeds in capes and broad-brimmed hats holding pennants and megaphones.

The weather vacillated between radiant sunshine and sudden showers, as uneven as the play on the field, which was alternately thrilling and sloppy. Penn scored the only touchdown of the first half after recovering an onside kick, but in the second half Thorpe broke through the line and zigzagged his way forty-three yards, barely crossing the end zone for five points before Bill Hollenbeck, Penn's All-American backfield star, belatedly jumped on his back and brought him down. Thorpe then kicked the extra point to tie the score, 6–6. "Loud were the cheers of the Indian maidens and braves high up in the big stands, and great was the noise of the Indian band seated upon the field of play," an *Inquirer* correspondent reported. "The crowd was astonished."

Carlisle dominated the second half, frequently approaching the Penn goal line but unable to cross it again. Twice late in the game Thorpe's throbbing right foot failed him as he missed field goal attempts that might have brought victory to Carlisle. But his overall performance left a lasting impression. "His running in the open field was the greatest seen on Franklin Field in years," reported the *Washington Evening Star*. "He had the speed of a sprinter and the agility of a cat. He had numerous runs of twenty and thirty yards and his brilliant dash through the entire Penn team in the second half scored the only touchdown. He also kicked the [point after] from a difficult angle." (Another rule in that era: the ball for extra points was placed on a line directly back from where it crossed the goal.)

The tie against Penn was one Thorpe would not forget. "In all my twenty-two years of college and professional football this was the hardest fought game I ever played," he recalled after his retirement. "From the outset the game was a two-man fight between Hollenbeck and myself. A fight to stop each other. Word passed through the Penn eleven to 'get Thorpe—put him out of the game.' I'll say one thing for them—they did everything in the world to cripple me, but they didn't take into consideration the tough hide and stubborn constitution of the prairie Indian." If that sounded like an as-told-to writer putting words in his mouth, it nonetheless expressed his sentiments. Years later, when Thorpe encountered Hollenbeck in Europe, they reminisced about the game and how exhausting it was for both of them. Hollenbeck said he was so bruised afterward that he slipped off to Atlantic City to recuperate.

Considering that Penn was seeking revenge after its trouncing by Carlisle the year before, and that the Indians came in with more injuries, and that the Quakers had their best team in years (that tie would be the only blemish on their 1908 record), a headline describing the game in the *Evening Star* becomes more understandable: "CARLISLE INDIANS RIP PENN ASUNDER. Thorpe Plays Excellent Game for Uncle Sam's Wards." Ripped asunder by a 6–6 tie? It was an early variation of the famous description of an Ivy League game exactly sixty years later when an underdog Harvard squad scored sixteen points in the final minute to earn a tie. The result: "Harvard Beats Yale, 29–29."

Pop Warner came to feel that the Penn game and mounting injuries took so much out of his team that it could not reach its potential the rest of the season, which meant they were still better than average. As road warriors, they won five of their last seven games. One of the losses was to Harvard, the highest-rated team in the country, motivated as Penn was by a desire to avenge the previous year's loss to the Indians, and the other was to Minnesota during an exhausting five-game trip west that kept them away from Carlisle from November 14 to December 7. Pop had arranged the trip months earlier, before the arrival of the school's new superintendent, Moses Friedman, who tried to cut it short but failed, an early lesson in the lure of football and who had the real power at Carlisle.

• • •

FRIEDMAN WAS THE third superintendent in Carlisle's nearly thirty-year history, and unlike his predecessors Pratt and Mercer, he was no military man, but an Indian Service administrator recruited from an assistant's post at the Haskell Institute. Commissioner Leupp plucked him for the Carlisle job expecting him to continue Mercer's work turning the school away from Pratt's messianic kill-the-Indian-save-the-man notions to a more pragmatic and less idealistic if also misguided mission. While Pratt would say that he baptized his Indian students in white civilization, Friedman was a convert of a different sort. He was reared in a Jewish family in Cincinnati, and converted to Christianity after taking the Carlisle job. He was married to a Christian woman, Mary Buford Smith, the daughter of one of the most prominent figures in Kentucky. The career of Green Clay Smith, Mary's father, was a touchstone of political life in mid-nineteenth-century America. He volunteered for the Union army during the Civil War, rose to brigadier general, then resigned to run for Congress from his border state on the Unconditional Unionist ticket; he won and served until 1866 when he was appointed territorial governor of Montana, where he mediated tensions between white settlers and the Blackfoot nation, then returned to Washington and was ordained a Baptist minister, the "fighting pastor." A staunch prohibitionist and suffragist, he passed along those sentiments to his daughter, who brought them to Carlisle. Mary was only twenty-nine when she reached the Indian school and was something new for the place, a modern woman who rode horses and bicycles and held teas in support of the suffrage movement.

Moses was more introverted, and easily intimidated. His conversion to Christianity at the Carlisle Episcopal Church by some accounts was motivated not so much by his marriage to a gentile but by his need to survive and get along at Carlisle. Rabbi Charles Freund, writing in the *American Israelite,* asserted that Friedman had told him he was compelled to convert "by Christian ministers who said it was not fair for one to be the head of the Indian school who did not belong to the dominant faith." By the rabbi's account, Friedman regretted the conversion but admitted he was too weak to retract it. “I am not an active man, nor a prize fighter,” Friedman once said. “And any blackguard can come into my office and say anything he pleases.”

His devotion was to industrial education. He considered himself an efficiency expert, a progressive man of the new mechanical age. As Henry Ford was developing the manufacturing processes in Michigan that would churn out the first Model Ts that year, Friedman sought to modernize Carlisle in assembly-line fashion. He published pocket handbooks with schedules for students to follow hour by hour and throughout the year, documenting everything from the dates guest speakers would arrive to the hour football players would report for practice. First Pratt, then Mercer, now Friedman—all illuminated the various threads of progressive thought in that era when it came to what was called “the Indian problem.” All three believed they were acting from good intentions; all fell short in different ways.

Friedman’s superintendency provoked renewed animosity from founder Pratt, who viewed him as a Leupp lackey chosen to oversee the school’s demise. Pratt’s shadow remained so large that Leupp felt a need to answer him in a letter to the school newspaper refuting “any lies told about my treatment of Carlisle School.” The letter offered a halfhearted endorsement of the institution. While it was true that he opposed the existence of non-reservation Indian schools, Leupp argued, his appointment of someone of Friedman’s stature proved that he nonetheless would give the “industrial end of the school” his full support. “As long as Carlisle exists, I want it to be first-class,” he wrote. But first-class only in ways that he thought would be of practical help to the Indians, meaning less emphasis on academics and more “emphasis on skills that are marketable.” Football was not yet marketable in one sense: the organized professional game at which players could make a living was still years off. But it was marketable for everyone else, especially for colleges around the country who saw Carlisle as a means to fill their stadiums and athletic coffers.

• • •

THE FIRST STOP on the grinding train trip west was at Pitt, where a blizzard obliterated the yard markers and made spectators feel as though they were inside a giant flour sifter, unable to see much more than blurry blotches forming and reforming through the opaque whiteness. What was football like in 1908? Here was one of many scenes during the western trip. Both teams were chippy, ready to fight, and Pete Hauser of Carlisle, recently returned from the injured list, got so enraged by an official's call during the scoreless first half that he scooped up the ball between plays and punted it to the far end of the field, then sauntered to the sideline. "Go get it and bring it back," the official ordered. Hauser, arms folded, refused. When Thorpe and some teammates offered to be peacemakers and turned downfield toward the snow-slick ball, the official ordered them to stop and said he would penalize anyone on either team who touched it other than Hauser. If Hauser did not "personally return the ball inside a few minutes," he would be ejected from the game. Hauser finally relented, in his own style, wrapping a blanket around his shoulders and sashaying down to retrieve the pigskin, "returning in leisure." Carlisle came out angry in the second half and scored when the entire team massed around Little Old Man and pushed him over the goal line for the game's only touchdown. Thorpe, his ankle improved, booted the extra point.

Since the forward pass became legal in 1906, eastern sportswriters had portrayed Pop Warner as its master, if not inventor. In later decades, Warner defenders correctly refuted a contrary mythology that Notre Dame brought the pass into football in a 1913 game against Army when Gus Dorais completed fourteen of seventeen passes, mostly to end Knute Rockne. In fact, the pass was an offensive weapon for several midwestern teams in 1908 and earlier. Stagg had been using it in Chicago. Eddie Cochems, a former star at Wisconsin, had been drawing up cunning pass plays as soon as he began coaching at St. Louis University in 1906. And Minnesota coach Henry Williams, after watching his team fail to score a point in three consecutive games in 1908, decided to juice his offense with passes when Carlisle visited Northrop Field in Minneapolis on November 21. Minnesota threw the ball fifteen times, an inordinate number in those days, completing ten. As the *Star Tribune* explained after the Golden Gophers pulled off an 11–6 upset, "Minnesota completely outplayed Carlisle at their own game," using the forward pass "oftener and with greater effect than the Indians. It made several forward passes of forty yards and its two touchdowns were directly attributed to those plays." Thorpe was called the bright spot of the losing team, but mostly for his foot. He punted the ball a total of 490 yards.

A football frenzy seized the people of Minneapolis after the game. The home team was invited to attend a play at the Metropolitan Theater, which was awhirl with football fans "barring one or two couples who sat in deep gloom in the pit and wondered why so much more attention was given to the football team than the actors." A line formed outside the theater hours before the curtain went up, and people scrambled to the gallery with bags of confetti and colored paper, used later to shower upon their athletic heroes in the seats below. Between acts two and three, a chant rose for Minnesota's captain, Orrin Safford, who had been hidden from view under the balcony. He was snatched by teammates and dragged onstage "blushing like a schoolgirl" where he stood speechless, head bowed. At the nearby Bijou Theater, the college band was invited to join the regular orchestra. When both shows ended, "the merrymaking crowds piled into the streets and carefree fun began. . . . More than a thousand mobilized at the corner of Sixth and Nicolet as leaders danced and skipped down the avenue, the entire throng following pell mell." Such was the ecstatic effect of a game of college football in 1908.

When Carlisle had been defeated by Harvard, Pop Warner blamed his players, especially quarterback Balenti and captain Wauseka, saying they botched the plays. He was more gracious this time. His Indians were banged up, he said, but Minnesota deserved credit for beating Carlisle at its own game, the forward pass. "Their open style of play was certainly of a high order. It was no miracle that Minnesota won."

For Carlisle, the long road trip continued at seven fifteen the next night when the team boarded train No. 5 of the Minneapolis and St. Louis Railway for the overnight journey south to St. Louis, with stops along the way at Albert Lea, Mason City, Marshalltown, Grinnell, Oskaloosa, Albia,

Kirksville, Macon, and Moberly. Rolling six hundred miles at about forty miles an hour, the train arrived at Union Station in St. Louis at two the next afternoon. The M&StL featured all the modern trappings, with electric-lighted Pullman sleepers and library cars, and many of the Carlisle boys stayed up late into the night singing, arguing, playing cards, and jabbering. There were twenty-four players plus Pop Warner and his wife, the team doctor, and a manager on the trip. Thorpe stayed close to two second-string linemen: Newashe, his Sac and Fox friend, and Sampson Burd, who had been recruited to Carlisle the previous winter from the Piegan Blackfeet nation in Montana, near what would become Glacier National Park.

Thorpe and Burd were the same age, born six months apart. Burd came from a more stable family—his parents, Mattie Medicine Wolf and John Burd, were still alive—but the two twenty-two-year-olds shared a similar outlook, feeling caught between two worlds and looking for places of comfort and belonging. They became close friends talking about their frustrations and hopes. Sampson was the sharper student, Jim the superior athlete, both with a rebellious streak. Sampson called Jim by his school nickname, Libbling, the derivation of which is a mystery. They loved to hunt and fish, play pool, wrestle and monkey around, drink whiskey, ballroom dance with the girls in the Carlisle gymnasium, and talk football nonstop. "With him," Thorpe later recalled, "I often discussed my ambition to become a coach."

ON THE DAY before Thanksgiving, the nation's leaders assembled at a plaza at the corner of Massachusetts Avenue and Twenty-Third Street NW in Washington, D.C. Teddy Roosevelt, arriving from the White House, was met by most of his cabinet, a delegation from the diplomatic corps, Supreme Court justices, senators, and congressmen, plus a company of graybeard Union veterans of the Civil War there to honor one of their own. The army chief of staff led a military parade up the avenue and saluted the guests of honor, the son and widow of the legendary nineteenth-century soldier General Philip Henry Sheridan. After an address by the president, Mrs. Sheridan, who lived in a mansion across the street, pulled a cord and unveiled a bronze statue of the heroic general swiveled back on his beloved horse, Rienzi, summoning his troops into battle. The monument, ten feet high and twelve feet long, was sculpted by Gutzon Borglum, an artist whose works delineated the inconsistencies of American history from Sheridan in Washington to Confederate general Robert E. Lee at Stone Mountain in Georgia, and eventually to presidents Washington, Jefferson, Lincoln, and Teddy Roosevelt at the colossus of Mount Rushmore on South Dakota land sacred to the Lakota Sioux.

The main address at the Sheridan ceremony was delivered by Brigadier General Horace Porter, who spoke at length not only of Sheridan's actions during the Civil War but also of his later role in the 1870s as commander of federal troops during the western Indian wars. It was under Sheridan, head of the Military Division of the Missouri, that the army crushed uprisings by Comanche, Kiowa, Arapaho, Ute, and Sioux raiders desperately trying to keep their tribal homelands. And it was under Sheridan that professional white hunters littered the western flatlands with rotting bison carcasses, slaughtering millions in a calculated plan to deprive Plains Indians of a mainstay of their existence. The heralded Sheridan was a complicated figure whose military acumen helped hold the Union together and liberate the nation's enslaved blacks, yet whose "the-only-good-Indian-I-know-is-dead" formulation was the flip side of Richard Henry Pratt's founding motto at Carlisle, the Indian school whose football boys were heading to a practice field in St. Louis at the very time the general's bronze statue was being unveiled.

The coming of the Indians thrilled St. Louis football fans and sportswriters at the *Post-Dispatch*, who said the Thanksgiving Day matchup was "causing more interest than any football contest that has ever been scheduled in St. Louis." One called it the biggest event in St. Louis since the 1904 world's fair. On Thanksgiving eve, a thousand St. Louis University students marched behind the band out to Sportsman's Park to watch the final practice, yelling themselves hoarse, an unprecedented show of football fealty that even brought a smile to the dour mug of Billikens coach Eddie Cochems. Pop Warner ran his boys through a light practice at the nearby Washington University field. Thorpe, Balenti, and Hauser took turns punting and catching punts, and their coach, normally gloomy about his team when chatting with the press, was impressed, saying he had rarely seen his players show "such ginger and speed." On game day, an observer noted that "the entire St. Louis eleven seemed badly frightened before the game." It turned out that Carlisle was not as speedy or gingery as Warner might have wanted, but his boys dominated so thoroughly that he pulled Thorpe and other starters from the game at halftime.

The next day it was back to Union Station for a 450-mile train ride along the path of the Missouri River north and west from St. Louis to Omaha and across to Lincoln, the state capital and home of the University of Nebraska. The Carlisle squad had five days there before the midweek game on Wednesday afternoon, December 2. Knowing his boys were tired from having played eleven contests, more than most teams and with two more to go, Warner avoided scrimmaging and limited practice to an hour a day. The weather was rainy and turning more frigid by the day, so several practices were held in the Nebraska gym, and Thorpe and his pals spent much of their days and nights hanging out in the hotel lobby. They particularly enjoyed loitering near the cigar stand and flirting with the young women who worked there. Word spread around town about the "romantic members of the Carlisle team" who were telling tall tales about their exploits and how they were all descended from Indian chiefs, even Chief Pop.

Carlisle's team had two reputations, both inaccurate. One was that they played dirty; the other that they were choirboys off the field, tamed by years of admonishments from white administrators not to do anything that would embarrass the Indian race. A column in Lincoln's morning newspaper repeated a charge from a Minneapolis sportswriter that they used "urgentlemanly language" during the Minnesota game and that captain Wauseka had roughed up an official—behavior that prompted Minnesota to cut off all athletic associations with Carlisle. The truth was that the Indians swore less than most college boys and that by far the most foulmouthed person at Carlisle was their coach, whose salty language offended his players. And Minnesota did not cut off relations with Carlisle, but the other way around, for less sensational reasons that became apparent later that week. As for being choirboys off the field, the Carlisle players knew how to present themselves as dignified young men, but they also partied, drank, and chased girls when opportunities arose. Thorpe's popularity seemed to intensify week by week, and with it his opportunities. "His loving fans in each town or city began to toast him in the local saloons in post-game celebrations," Pop Warner recalled. "This new-found success and the many invitations for free drinks of whiskey or beer, however, would eventually begin to cause problems off the field for the Carlisle star."

The Indians were welcomed at every stop as performers in a traveling troupe that entertained the public and pumped money into the local economy, the football equivalent of Buffalo Bill Cody and his Wild West show. On game day in Lincoln, the university dismissed classes at two so students could reach Antelope Park for the two thirty kickoff. It was the coldest day of the season, a wind-whipped twenty degrees. A week of rain had forced the grounds crew to cover the field in straw, and when it was raked off, the ground was soggy and freezing fast. The stands filled early, all Nebraska rooters save for one section in the north bleachers that rocked with local Omaha and Winnebago Indians who rooted for Carlisle and took the field at halftime, dancing to the beat of an Omaha drummer. The game was well decided by then, and Thorpe's day was also done. In the first half, according to the *Nebraska State Journal*, Jim had "played a spectacular game for the Reds, his fast, dodging runs so dazing the Cornhuskers they were seldom able to bring him down." Soon after he scored on defense, scooping up a fumble and dashing forty-five yards for a touchdown, Pop decided to send in his second-string to play out the rest of the 37–6 victory, and Thorpe watched from the bench.

In the cold, crowded sidelines across the field, one face stood out. It was George Flippin, the leading physician in the town of Stromsburg and a former Cornhusker star from the early 1890s who had come to Lincoln to watch his alma mater take on the famous team of Indians from the East. Flippin was as much of a rarity as they were. He was an African American, the son of a freed slave who had fought in the Civil War with the Fourteenth U.S. Colored Infantry Regiment. The first and only black player on those early Nebraska teams, Flippin had faced his own civil wars. When his teammates voted him captain, the coach overruled them, saying the future doctor did not have the brains to lead. The Missouri squad chose to forfeit its game with Nebraska rather than take the same field as the star halfback. When Nebraska played a road game in Denver, the team's hotel said Flippin could not sleep there.

Denver was Carlisle's last stop on the 1908 road trip. There was no question about whether the Indians could find an accommodating hotel. Native American athletes were discriminated against and disparaged in various ways, but rarely as overtly as black athletes. They did not face the same color bars on the field or on the road. The concern was not whether Denver's people would reject Carlisle but whether Carlisle would reject them.

Weeks earlier, just as the team was leaving campus, Superintendent Friedman had declared that the western tour was excessive. He did not want to grant the players a three-week leave of absence. Drop the Denver game, he directed, and a telegram soon arrived at the University of Denver announcing that decision. It so happened that Henry A. Buchtel, the chancellor, was also the governor of Colorado, and a football fan. Buchtel immediately launched a lobbying campaign to save the game, which had been billed as a test of whether western football could compete with the game in the East. Not incidentally, it also would be a lucrative gate attraction for the school. Thomas M. Patterson, publisher of the *Rocky Mountain News* and former U.S. senator, wrote to Teddy Roosevelt that "all the state has become interested in the game" and that "we feel that if you say the word sufficient leave will be granted." Word went down from the White House to the Department of the Interior to Commissioner Leupp at the Indian bureau questioning why Carlisle dared to break a "binding football contract." Friedman explained that the contract had been signed before he took over at Carlisle, that he opposed such a long trip, and had asked Warner to cancel it. Only after Denver refused to go along, Friedman said, did he realize how much it meant to the western school, so he backed down. But from then on, with Leupp's approval, he instituted a new rule: no more than two western games, and none west of the Mississippi.

By the time Carlisle reached Denver, Friedman was busy trying to explain something else to Washington. The Interior Department had received copies of an article that made Carlisle sound like a prison. "Superintendent Friedman of the Carlisle Indian School has sent out a telegram to police in several cities asking for the arrest of an Indian couple who eloped from the school yesterday," the February 2 story reported. "The girl was a pupil at the institution, but her sweetheart came here from the west. The superintendent declined to permit the wedding without the consent of the girl's parents. Instead of waiting for the approval, the couple eloped. Their names are Joseph Twin and Lystia Wahoo."

Joseph Twin was a Winnebago from Nebraska, a friend of many of the Winnebago fans who had just seen the Carlisle game in Lincoln. He was also a former Carlisle student who had left school the previous summer and was well known to Thorpe and his teammates as an excellent athlete himself, a member of the baseball team for several years. It was commonplace for students at Carlisle to fall in love, and both Twin (age twenty-four) and Lystia Wahoo (almost twenty-one) were over the age of consent. The real reason Friedman did not want them to get married, he acknowledged, was that Lystia was a good student and he feared that Twin was "rather slow" and "did not have good job prospects." That was why he sent out an all-points bulletin to find them and arrest them. Indians who ran away from school were treated not all that differently from cons on the lam. As it turned out, the couple escaped south to Savannah, got married, and settled in Cherokee, North Carolina.

Back in Denver, Carlisle played a sluggish game against the Ministers, fatigued by the high altitude and long season. They managed to win 8–4, an oddity that in that era meant two field goals to one. It was enough of a contest to please Chancellor Buchtel, who wrote a note of thanks to Commissioner Leupp on his governor of Colorado stationery. "We had a great game on Saturday. . . . The Indians have played thirteen games this season and have crossed all goal lines except three, namely Harvard, Annapolis, and Denver. So we are feeling very comfortable, thank you, over the fact that we belong in the same class."

Thorpe returned to Carlisle in time to learn that he had been named third-team left halfback on Walter Camp's All-American squad, and second-team All-Eastern by Caspar Whitney in *Outing* magazine, the only Carlisle player to make either list. The players elected Little Boy captain for the following year, but Pop Warner and the Athletic Association had to nix the idea, acknowledging that new school rules put into place after the 1907 critique by Carlos Montezuma meant that no Carlisle athlete could play more than four years. Little Boy's four years were up, not even counting the time he had played earlier at Haskell. If Thorpe was the best player, his off-the-field actions seemed to be a problem for Superintendent Friedman. Twice that winter he and Sampson Burd slipped into town to play pool and drink for several hours, long enough for their records to include the notation "Ran." In one document, Friedman described Thorpe as "far from being a desirable student," a judgment that contradicted the assessment of the faculty. The record from the academic department listed Jim's scholarship as "very good" and his deportment as "good."

THE 1909 SPRING track season lasted barely a month, from the Penn Relays in Philadelphia to the State Intercollegiate Championship at Harrisburg, but it was enough time for Thorpe to enhance his growing national reputation. As he had the previous two years, he foreshadowed his all-around dominance at the annual Carlisle Field Day exhibition, where during an unrelenting rain he brought in twenty-six of his class's twenty-eight points, winning both hurdle events, the shot put, and the high jump, and finishing second in the broad jump and discus. For each victory he was given a watch fob by Warner, a gift in lieu of the cash bonuses the coach used to dole out to his most successful athletes. That meet was for local consumption; it was the dual meet in Elmira with Syracuse University on May 6, also in the rain and covered extensively by syndicated services, that spread Thorpe's name to a national audience. The contest itself could not have been closer as Carlisle upset the Orangemen 59–58. Thorpe was "the individual wonder of the meet," competing in eight of thirteen events and bringing in nearly half of Carlisle's points by finishing first in the two hurdles, the shot put, and the broad jump; tying for first in the high jump; and finishing in the top three in the hammer throw and the two sprints.

The most notable performance came when Thorpe defeated "Big Bill" Horr, Syracuse's gargantuan football tackle and track-and-field strongman, in the shot put. The winning throw of 42 feet 11 inches sounds meager in comparison with statistics from later generations, but in the context of the times—before more effective shot-putting techniques evolved and before the onset of diets, drugs, and sophisticated bodybuilding programs—it was enough to win most meets and only 6 feet off the world record. Horr had won the silver medal at the 1908 London Olympics in another field event, the discus. Soon he would take over as the head football coach at Northwestern. In a dizzying mix of metaphors, a wire service story that ran in papers around the country proclaimed that "Foxy Grandpa Warner" handed intercollegiate athletics "a jolt in the solar plexus" and "uncovered his ace" at the contest against Syracuse "when he turned loose Jas. Thorpe, the aborigine," who won "so easily that it was like taking a pap-bottle from the baby."

It was in Elmira that Foxy Grandpa Warner took his track and baseball teams to visit the Elmira Reform School, an institution that held fifteen hundred wayward boys. Carlisle's star pitcher, William Garlow, wrote of his impressions after the visit. Whatever the confinements of Carlisle, he thought, at least it was better than a reform school where boys were marched around from place to place in military formations, had to sleep in rooms that were "barely enough to lie down in," and answered not to their names but their assigned numbers. But if you tried to run away from either place, as Joseph Twin and Lystia Wahoo found out, there would be an all-points bulletin sent out for your arrest.

The culminating event of the season was the state intercollegiate meet at Harrisburg, on a beautiful Saturday in May when five thousand track fans, including several hundred pennant-waving Carlisle students, watched Carlisle take honors over Lafayette, Penn State, Dickinson, Swarthmore, Lehigh, and Washington & Jefferson. Thorpe was in "sensational form," winning the low hurdles, high jump, broad jump, and shot put, while Lewis Tewanima sprinted the last lap for a convincing victory in the two-mile run. With the big Sac and Fox and the little Hopi distance runner leading the way, Carlisle had gone two years without losing a match. When the undefeated track team returned from Harrisburg, Thorpe and his teammates fell in behind the school band and marched up from the athletic field to the bandstand holding high the championship silver cup.

During much of April and May, Thorpe had been playing two sports, not only track but also baseball. Before the season was out, he tossed a no-hitter against a Hagerstown team and a shutout against Millersville, and "covered first base like a veteran" against Dickinson. He fit right in with some of his old pals. The double-play combination featured two of his football teammates, fellow Oklahomans Balenti at shortstop and Newashe at second. Batting leadoff and playing centerfield was Jesse Youngdeer, a Cherokee from North Carolina, and playing left field and batting third was Joe Libby, a Chippewa from Minnesota. Unwittingly, their love of baseball and Thorpe's newfound affection for the game converged in a way that would affect him more than any of them could then understand.

7

Railroaded

THE PUBLISHER OF THE *ROCKY MOUNT RECORD* ONCE SAID that "a mule with blind staggers" could meander beyond the circulation area of his newspaper in fifteen minutes. Not quite, but it was an appropriately evocative colloquialism that reflected the self-deprecating humor in that part of North Carolina and helped explain the fabulist instructions given to the newspaper's cub reporter in the summer of 1909. A new character had ridden into town, someone who promised nothing but readers. Be sure to embellish every story about him, the publisher told Sam T. Mallison, his young sportswriter. Portray his baseball achievements in ever more spectacular terms and track his movements off the field in search of "pearls of wisdom from his lips which might edify or entertain the newspaper's pantingly expectant readers."

That was how Jim Thorpe was received when he reached town on June 15 to play for the Rocky Mount Railroaders, a first-year team in the new Eastern Carolina League. The fact that his arrival was hyped by the circulation-hungry local newspaper fit perfectly into the larger story of his experience as a minor league ballplayer in Rocky Mount. Why he left Carlisle, who knew he was in Rocky Mount, who lied about it, how he played on the field, how he performed off the field, and why any of that mattered were all part of the saga of Thorpe in the bush leagues. His two seasons there provoked exaggerations, prevarications, rationalizations, and occasional eruptions in a setting as unsavory as a loaded spitball, a raucous Class D league dripping with accusations of illegal trades, illicit betting, biased umpires, and thrown games.

The most important lie told about Thorpe's experience in Rocky

Mount came from Pop Warner, who described Jim's departure from school as a matter of routine that turned into an act of deception. "Jim's five-year term of enrollment at Carlisle concluded in the spring of 1909 and he returned to his home in Oklahoma," Warner wrote in his autobiography. "Or, at least, that is where the school administrators at Carlisle thought he had gone to."

Wrong in every respect. Although Thorpe had been at Carlisle since 1904, he still had years to go before he could graduate, and Superintendent Friedman, despite earlier run-ins with his star athlete over occasional absences, urged him to stay at school that summer. When Jim asked for a leave to play baseball, Friedman balked, saying Thorpe had exhausted his leaves the previous summer when he went home to Oklahoma and had promised then that he would continue at Carlisle until he graduated. In the end, the superintendent reluctantly granted a second leave, fully aware that Thorpe was heading south to play ball. In Carlisle records, if a student was gone for good the notation was "Departed." There was no such notation for Thorpe in 1909. Instead it read "On leave."

For Pop Warner to assert that he knew nothing about this strained credulity. By Thorpe's own account, he was recruited to play baseball that summer by one of Warner's athletic-world compatriots, Charlie Kelchner, the baseball coach at Albright College in nearby Reading, Pennsylvania, who coincidentally was also called Pop. Kelchner was among dozens of bird-dog scouts combing eastern colleges for talent to fill minor league rosters, and Carlisle was fertile territory. Scouts had been looking for promising Indian ballplayers since the discovery at Carlisle in 1902 of Charles Albert Bender, a Hall of Fame pitcher upon whom sportswriters inevitably bestowed the nickname "Chief." Bender was an Ojibwe from Minnesota who went from Carlisle, where he was an excellent student, setting the record for most books checked out of the school library, to become the ace pitcher for Connie Mack's championship Philadelphia Athletics, where he would set a record of nine consecutive complete games in the World Series. Year after year, other Carlisle Indians followed Bender into organized ball, though none approached his level of success.

The Carlisle diaspora in the summer of 1909 saw Bill Newashe playing in Atlantic City, Michael Balenti going off to St. Paul, and Joe Libby, Jesse Youngdeer, and Thorpe taking the twelve-hour train ride south to play in the Eastern Carolina League. They were all Pop's boys. Libby later claimed that it was their coach who arranged everything.

The lines between amateur and professional were blurry in that era and players frequently crossed between them. Thirty-five minor leagues slotted teams into hundreds of cities and towns throughout America, all thirsting for summer entertainment and in need of ballplayers. It was commonplace for college athletes to slip off to play in the minors as a means of summer employment, often using fake names to maintain their amateur status. One among the hundreds was a young West Point cadet named Dwight David Eisenhower who played in the Kansas State League under the alias Wilson. The joke among college boys was that they were joining the Pocahontas League because so many of them were named John Smith. Michael J. Finn, a longtime minor league manager and scout for the New York Giants, once recalled that players in the Eastern Carolina League "had as many aliases as the gunmen of New York."

Jim Thorpe was not among them. He came to Rocky Mount using his real name and never considered having an alias. Sportswriters throughout the Eastern Carolina League knew who he was and made certain their readers did as well. His name was in the box scores every time the Railroaders played the five other teams in the league, most located within convenient reach of the Atlantic Coast Line Railroad: the Wilson Tobacconists, the Goldsboro Giants, the Raleigh Red Birds, the Fayetteville Highlanders, and the Wilmington Sailors. At least once Thorpe made the front section of the *Raleigh News & Observer* for a "rampage" that had nothing to do with his work at the plate. He was usually referred to in the press by some variation of the appellation sportswriters gave Bender and every other Native American who achieved prominence. Jim "Big Chief" Thorpe was a gate attraction and good copy.

The excitement in Rocky Mount when Jim and his Carlisle teammates reached North Carolina "stemmed from the fact that these men were said to be full-blooded Indians," Mallison later wrote. "Few Rocky Mount citizens had ever seen one of these American originals." Original, yes; full-blooded, no. It was an expected part of the embellishment. A description using the terms "full-blood" or "pure-blood" was something Thorpe dealt with incessantly throughout his career, a notion in Anglo culture that an Indian untouched by white heritage was more mysterious, exotic, and perhaps dangerous.

Just being a ballplayer was exotic enough for young Rocky Mount boys awed by the Railroaders. Thorpe and many of his teammates kept rooms at the Cambridge Hotel across from the train depot, their room and board considered part of a salary that amounted to about $30 a month. On game days, local boys lined up outside the hotel, hoping to befriend a player and carry his bat or glove seven blocks north along unpaved Main Street to Falls Road and on to League Park just west of the intersection with Church. A boy named Tom McMillan got to carry Jim Thorpe's glove and would tell stories about it the rest of his life, saying the big Indian was a gentleman who liked children. There was no locker room at the field, so players usually emerged from the hotel in their uniforms and paraded through town like soldiers marching off to war.

Rocky Mount was mostly flat from end to end but drew its name from rock outcroppings on the nearby Tar River. It was a booming tobacco center in 1909, as were many towns situated along North Carolina's Inner Coastal Plain. Streets on the north end bustled with block-long tobacco warehouses, regional hubs for a cash crop of the New South, just now replacing cotton. The executives and their moneymen lived along a wealthy stretch of South Church Street in commodious Queen Anne–style homes with ornate friezes on their wraparound porches. To them, the coming of Jim Thorpe could not compare with the grandest event in town that month, the tobacco world's June German Festival sponsored by the Carolina Cotillion Club. "German" in that context was not about the nationality but described a formal dance. Thousands of Carolinians associated with the tobacco industry, men garbed in tuxes and tails, women in gowns, gathered in a cavernous Rocky Mount tobacco warehouse converted into a dining hall and ballroom for a celebratory midnight supper of ham and fried chicken followed by rounds of dancing that swirled until dawn. One tobacco warehouse participating in the event was, by chance, named

Thorpe and Ricks, so Thorpe was a familiar name in town long before the arrival of the Big Chief.

The Railroaders were on the road playing a three-game series against the Raleigh Red Birds when the three Carlisle boys got to Rocky Mount, but they joined the team in time for the second game. With Rocky Mount staggering at the start of the season near the bottom of the standings, two of the three Indians immediately cracked the starting lineup. Youngdeer was put in left and batted leadoff, Libby played right and batted seventh, while Thorpe sat on the bench until filling in at third base late in the game, the only time he played that position all year. Not much material there for anyone to embellish. But the next day Thorpe was sent out to pitch. "Warhoop Thorpe was on the firing line for the first time," reported the *Raleigh Times*. After giving up unearned runs in the first two frames, he threw seven shutout innings and finished with a complete-game 4–2 win in which he allowed only five hits, smacked two himself, and scored the go-ahead run. At the end of a game back in Rocky Mount three days later, the local reporter felt that embellishing Jim's performance would only be "gilding the lily." Before a standing-room-only crowd of fifteen hundred fans in the bandbox League Park, Thorpe pitched a twelve-inning 1–0 shutout against the Wilson Tobacconists, Rocky Mount's fierce neighbor and rival in baseball and tobacco.

That promising start did not lead to greatness. On a bad team destined to finish at the bottom, Jim was good enough to keep his spot in the rotation and play first base and the outfield slots most days he was not on the mound, faring better than his Carlisle mates Libby and Youngdeer, who left the club before season's end. But he was not as consistently spectacular as the *Rocky Mount Record* folks hoped. He finished the season with nine wins and ten losses and batted .253. That might seem like the definition of middling, but Jim was rarely average; he was either better or worse, flashes of brilliance followed by pitching sloughs and batting slumps when he seemed bored. He had the potential, a combination of speed, power, and a lively arm, but he had yet to acquire the intuitive instincts of a natural baseball player. In football, yes; hardball, no. And he suffered from a flaw common to otherwise brilliant athletes who struggled at the game, as the league's pitchers discovered. He had trouble with the curve.

THE YEAR THORPE came to play ball in Rocky Mount was the year North Carolina went dry. A statewide prohibition against the sale of alcohol took effect on the first of January 1909, after a decade-long campaign led by an odd coalition of Baptist and Methodist preachers, Temperance League activists, and white-supremacist Democratic politicians who considered taverns "Republican recruiting stations." That was the claim of Furnifold McLendel Simmons, the U.S. senator who used *Republican* as a code word for *black*. Simmons was the mastermind of a political machine that stoked a malevolent white-supremacist uprising in North Carolina in 1898 leading to the demise of the post–Civil War participation of black citizens in the democratic process and ushering in the Jim Crow era. In what was called an insurrection but amounted to a racial massacre, marauding gangs of white men roamed black sections of Wilmington murdering citizens, destroying property, and overthrowing the multiracial Reconstructionist city government by force. White-supremacist clubs sprang up in cities and towns throughout the state, including Rocky Mount, where during Jim's stay an unarmed black man named John Bootman was shot and killed by the chief of police, who was not charged with a crime or suspended from his job. The mission was to make North Carolina white again, by any means necessary. "North Carolina is a white man's state and white men will rule it," Simmons declared. "And they will crush the party of Negro domination beneath a majority so overwhelming that no other party will ever dare attempt to establish Negro rule here."

When the statewide referendum banning the sale of alcohol drew overwhelming white support on the 1908 ballot, it was seen as another step in assuring permanent white political dominance under the cover of religiosity and propriety. Not that any law could stop drinkers from drinking. Speakeasies and impromptu saloons known as "blind tigers" popped up in the backstreets, supplied by millions of dollars' worth of Richmond liquor bootlegged across the Virginia state line. There were also pseudo-legal establishments that sold "near beer" with minimal alcohol content, or at least claimed that was all they offered when authorities came around. Carousing young ballplayers in the Eastern Carolina League knew where the blind tigers were in every league town. The state liquor prohibition was not much of an impediment to Thorpe, who struggled with alcohol and came from a family of hard drinkers led by old man Hiram, who used to sell bootleg whiskey from the back of his wagon in supposedly dry Indian Territory.

Jim's behavior had always been mercurial. As a boy, that meant occasionally running from school and unpleasant situations, disobeying teachers and his father. As he grew older and started hanging out with his older brothers in Oklahoma or the football boys at Carlisle, his unpredictable disposition took on a physical aspect. When things were going well and he was not drinking, he was good company, kind, gentle, and easygoing. "But when something was unfair or he was drinking," Joe Libby said later, "all hell broke loose." In those situations, Libby was "scared to death of the man. That damned guy was crazy. He was an Indian's Indian." Once during their North Carolina sojourn, Libby and Thorpe were walking through town on the way to a game when a policeman tried to push them off the street. The cop might have been prejudiced against Indians; Libby did not make that clear. In any event, Thorpe turned to his friend and asked, "You like this guy?" and when Libby said no, Thorpe "just knocked the guy colder than hell." They spent that night in jail.

That was but one of many stories of Thorpe on the loose in Carolina. E. G. Johnston, the team secretary, recalled a time when he and H. L. Holden and his two daughters, Genevieve and Kewpie, traveled to Goldsboro for a series and Holden came running up to Johnston and said he had to get to the Hotel Kennon to intervene because "Thorpe was about to whip the Goldsboro police force." As Johnston told the story, when he arrived at the Kennon he learned that officers wanted to take Thorpe into custody on a minor charge and Thorpe had resisted. "When Thorpe recognized me the fury in his face disappeared," Johnston said. "He quieted down and explained that he thought they were trying to keep him out of the afternoon ball game and he wasn't going to let them do that and he would take orders from me and not them."

The final road series of the season was played in Raleigh. By then the Railroaders were cemented in the cellar, twenty-five games below .500, and when Thorpe pitched the first game there were no more than a hundred souls in the stands to watch him lose 3–2. After a defeat again the next day, Rocky Mount broke its losing streak on the final afternoon in Raleigh, and Thorpe's celebration that night made the local newspapers. In the Jim Crow world of North Carolina, Native American athletes, unlike African Americans, could play baseball with white teammates, stay in hotels with them, and party with them, but that did not mean they were treated exactly like them. In the press, it was Thorpe's Indianness that defined him. "Big Chief Goes on Warpath," read the headline in the *Raleigh Times* on August 26. "Big Chief on Rampage," blared the *News & Observer.*

The stories reported similar accounts, though in different languages, the *News & Observer* for the most part using typical newspaper jargon, the *Times* relying on hackneyed Indian stereotypes. "Overjoyed by finally winning a game after fourteen successive defeats 'Heap Big Chief Thorpe' eased an over-amount of firewater to his system last night and immediately started out upon the warpath. Ramping to and fro, giving war-whoops, the near beer and other stuff causing the old thirst of blood to return, the Red Skin . . . ," and the Indian stereotypes rolled on from there.

Taking into consideration the hyperbolic proclivities of the scribes, the events of the evening went something like this: After the game, several players from both teams ended up at one of the near-beer saloons on Exchange Street, an establishment that apparently surreptitiously sold "other exhilarants." The Railroaders were leaving for Rocky Mount later that night for a season-ending home series against the Wilson Tobacconists, while the Red Birds would board a predawn train to the coast to play the Wilmington Sailors. At some point in the evening, a group was out on the street and Thorpe got into a tussle with a teammate, Marvin O'Garra, the second baseman. "It is said that O'Garra tried to get [Thorpe] to go to his boarding place. Thorpe got angry with O'Garra and thumped him, there being a scuffle," reported the *News & Observer.* The other Raleigh paper propelled the story into more colorful language. "With a mighty swing he landed his huge colossal lunch-hook upon the cranium of the brave aforesaid O'Garra," reported the *Times.* "Reeling and rocking under the weight of the blow, O'Garra fell sprawling near the opposite side of the battle-ground—Exchange Street. Hearing the heart-rending cries of distress the boys in blue—two in number, with billets drawn, rushed to the rescue of the smitten one, hoping to avoid an impromptu scalping."

Thorpe was a handful for the two coppers, and it wasn't until a third, "the big Captain, Jack Beasley," came on the scene that they were able to subdue him, clasp snippers—handcuffs—on him, and haul him off to the station, where "he had to be dragged bodily down the steps, putting up a vigorous resistance. Thorpe is much of a man, having been on the Carlisle football team." O'Garra had slipped away by then, but another ballplayer, Reddy Rowe of the Red Birds, followed the officers and Thorpe back to the station, and insisted that he wanted to see Jim, calling for him through the sidewalk grating. The men in blue obliged by arresting Rowe and placing him in the same cell. After team officials interceded with the judge and minimum fines were agreed to, the players were released well after midnight. Jim's Railroaders were gone by then, and he missed the season-ending doubleheader against the Tobacconists.

Thorpe's night scuffling with teammates and cops in Raleigh seemed tame compared with the riotous events going on among executives in the Eastern Carolina League that week. In response to accusations by the Wilson management that Rocky Mount had thrown games in a spiteful effort to keep the Tobacconists from winning the pennant, representatives of the six clubs gathered in Goldsboro at ten o'clock on the Tuesday night of August 24 and talked, argued, heard charges, made motions, tabled motions, voted, rescinded votes, and argued some more until five thirty Wednesday morning.

R. B. Evans of Wilson came to the meeting armed with affidavits from seven witnesses to make his case. William Phoenix, after acknowledging that he played for Wilmington under the alias Lennox, swore before a notary public that his manager had told him Rocky Mount promised to throw all its games to Wilmington. Two Wilson players, John Cowell and Dick Miller, swore that during one game they told a Rocky Mount player that they had a good chance of winning the pennant, to which the Railroader replied, "Yes, if Wilmington doesn't beat you out," because Rocky Mount was going to "throw all games to that team." T. T. Fulghum certified that he heard "three or four" Rocky Mount players standing outside the New Briggs Hotel in Fayetteville saying they planned to throw all their games to Fayetteville, and one even boasted that he planned to bet five dollars the Highlanders would sweep the series. R. H. Howell's affidavit said that he was outside the New Briggs Hotel and heard Pat Krebs, the Rocky Mount centerfielder, say: "I swear I will do anything in my power to defeat Wilson for the pennant—lie down to any club to accomplish that purpose." G. D. Stanley, an agent for the Atlantic Coast Line, and J. L. Moody, a Wilson lawyer, swore they heard the director of the Rocky Mount club, J. M. Mason, threaten that Wilson "had to figure with Rocky Mount. I am in a position to know what I am talking about."

As the final point in his case, Evans accused the Railroaders' player-manager, catcher Joe Walsh, of trying to procure oil of mustard with toxic levels of erucic acid to smear on baseballs when facing Wilson's notorious spitballer, big Fred Anderson. According to Evans, the Rocky Mount skipper hoped that when Anderson applied saliva to the ball, fumes from the mustard oil would knock him from the game, if not permanently injure him. This charge was denied vehemently by Rocky Mount, though a previous episode involving Anderson and his loaded spitballs likely started the feud between the clubs. In a game at Wilson two weeks earlier, Walsh was behind the plate for Rocky Mount and Anderson was pitching for Wilson. Inning after inning, Walsh "pressed his olfactory organ into service" and detected great whiffs of resin and other substances on the balls Anderson had used the previous half-inning. Walsh ended up detecting so many doctored balls and having the umpire throw them out that the home team ran out of balls, and before the Tobacconists' batboy could round up another batch, Walsh pulled his team from the field in disgust and said they would play no more, forfeiting the game. It was after that game that word started to spread that Rocky Mount was determined not to let Wilson win the pennant. In the end, after all the contretemps and the overnight meetings, the Tobacconists came out on top.

WHEN THE SEASON ended, Thorpe did not return to Carlisle but instead made his way home to the banks of the North Canadian, where he left the impression that his school days were done. He asked the Sac and Fox agent, W. C. Kohlenberg, to arrange for his allotment royalty funds to be transferred back to Oklahoma so that he could buy equipment to use on the farm of his older half-sister, Minnie Rider, with whom he would stay. Kohlenberg dutifully sent off a letter to Carlisle in mid-October asking for the money and stating that "applicant intends to remain at his sister's place this winter and return to Carlisle in spring." The request infuriated Superintendent Friedman, who in a return letter on October 27 labeled Jim a deserter. "Referring to your letter of the 18th instant, relative to a request from James Thorpe that his money be forwarded to him, I beg leave to explain that James was granted a leave of absence for the summer of 1908 on the strength of his statement that he desired to return to complete his course," Friedman wrote.

Jim had deceived him, Friedman argued, adding that he erred in not getting Thorpe to make his promise in writing. "The mistake was made in having this statement a verbal one only. . . . He was granted leave to play ball in the south during the summer months. At the expiration of that leave he failed to return to school and under the circumstances he must be considered a deserter from this school. It is customary at this school, when students desert, that all funds to their credit are held until they return or until the matter is given special consideration after their original term of enrollment is expired. For the sake of discipline and in order that no precedent may be established it is necessary that James's money also should be withheld from him." Friedman did send Kohlenberg two government checks made out to Thorpe that had not yet been deposited. Along with what money he had left from Rocky Mount, it was enough for him to buy a team of farm horses and a supply of corn and hay, as though he were going to settle into the life of a farmer.

But Jim did not cut all ties to Carlisle. That November, Pop Warner and his football squad made a return trip to St. Louis. Friedman had forbade the team from playing west of the Mississippi, but St. Louis hugged the far side of the river and Pop had a personal reason to argue for putting the game on the schedule: his brother Bill Warner had taken over as coach at St. Louis University. Jim's many pals on the Carlisle team let him know about the trip, and he decided to take the train northeast to St. Louis to see them and watch the Thanksgiving Day game. It was the last contest of the season for the Indians, who without Thorpe had lost three games, to Penn, Pitt, and Brown, and tied Penn State. The captain of the team was none other than Joe Libby, Jim's erstwhile teammate on the Rocky Mount Railroaders. It stretches the imagination to assume that during that season Libby had never talked to Pop Warner about his experiences in the Eastern Carolina League with Jesse Youngdeer and Jim Thorpe.

After Carlisle smothered St. Louis 32–0, with Libby dashing eighty yards on one play, Jim joined the team for a Thanksgiving dinner at their hotel. Along with Libby, Jim's Sac and Fox pal Bill Newashe, now starting at left end, was there; as were Oklahomans Pete Hauser; the fullback, and his brother Wauseka, the left tackle; also Sampson Burd, Jim's road roomie from the past year, the right guard; and right tackle Lone Star Dietz, the assistant Carlisle art studio director and husband of artist Angel De Cora. They encouraged Jim to return to school. Newashe noted in a letter that he "saw James Thorpe and he was looking fine. He intends to come back [to Carlisle] next year." What Pop said is uncertain, but what he did next was curious. When his squad piled onto an eastbound train the next morning, Warner stayed behind and invited Thorpe to go hunting with him. Jim obliged, and he and his former coach spent several days tracking wild turkey and white-tailed deer in the wilds of eastern Oklahoma. Again, it is hard to imagine that during their days together Pop never asked his old halfback what he did the past summer. Jim was prone to exaggeration when talking about his exploits, but he was not a liar, nor in this instance was there any reason for him to fabricate a story.

One month after going on the hunt, Jim took the train to Carlisle for a Christmas week visit, escorting a group of younger Sac and Fox boys and girls who were enrolling. It promised to be a white Christmas, the campus grounds blanketed with snow, though warming temperatures meant there would be no ice skating on the pond. The new arch built at the school's west entrance was framed by incandescent lights. In the gymnasium, two large cedars sparkled with decorations and colored lights, a five-pointed star hanging on a rope between them. "James Thorpe, better known to his intimate classmates as Libbling, arrived here on Friday afternoon to spend Christmas with his many friends and former classmates," the *Arrow* reported. "It seems good to see our old star athlete with us and we hope he may remain a long time."

Perhaps Jim thought that as well. He played pool each day in the athletic dorm with Bill Newashe, who reported that his pal would "return home for another month before coming back and enroll for two more years." But Friedman thought differently, telling agent Kohlenberg in a telegram that Jim should not return until the following fall.

"As Thorpe has missed nearly half year in studies I do not think it advisable for him to return now," the superintendent wrote. Friedman and Thorpe seemed to be working at cross-purposes: when Friedman wanted him to stay, Jim wanted to go; if Jim wanted to come back, Friedman didn't want him. The writer Jack Newcombe described it as being like "a bad marriage."

The next year, 1910, was a lost year for Thorpe. He stayed in Oklahoma through the winter, hunting and helping around his sister's place, then on May 1 returned to Rocky Mount for a second season in the Eastern Carolina League. The shine seemed gone for this second coming of the Big Indian. After the dismal last-place finish the season before, the Railroaders had recruited a fresh batch of talent. Jim was the same ballplayer as the year before, pitching many strong games, winning ten, losing ten, and batting around .250, but there were no embellishments from the press this time, though occasionally he would add his own. The fans in the rickety wooden stands at League Park perked up whenever Thorpe rounded third on his way to the plate and shouted, "The Big Chief coming home!" The phrase became his calling card around town.

Until it was not. On August 11, as the Railroaders were making a run for the pennant, seeking to go from last to first in one year, they traded Jim to the Fayetteville Highlanders. In recalling that season later for an as-told-to biography, Thorpe was an unreliable narrator. He said that he strained a ligament early in the season pitching against Raleigh and from then on was consigned to playing first base or the outfield. He might have injured his arm, but it did not stop him from pitching throughout his three months with Rocky Mount and into his time with Fayetteville. He also recalled that he "stood in the pitcher's box" during the climactic moment of the season, when Fayetteville defeated his old team to win the league pennant. In fact, Jim had been hospitalized earlier that week after he was cut in the head while trying to steal second base. Fayetteville took the crown without him seeing action.

That cut at second base was one of many injuries to the head Jim suffered that summer. The most serious was largely of his own doing. At a restaurant in Fayetteville one morning, he boasted to his new teammates that he could run through the front window and land inside unbloodied. When he did just that, using the roll block and shoulder lurch that Pop Warner had taught him, someone put down five bucks that he could not do it again. They ended up at Clark's grocery down the street, but before Thorpe could launch himself, the groceryman coldcocked him with an ax handle, sending him to the hospital.

As it turned out, the physical harm Jim inflicted on himself was the least of the troubles that came to him because of his two seasons playing ball in eastern North Carolina.

8

Almost There

BY THE SUMMER OF 1911 THERE WERE NO ROCKY MOUNT Railroaders or Fayetteville Highlanders. The Eastern Carolina League was a thing of the past; two turbulent years and it was swept into the dustbin of forgotten minor leagues. But although Thorpe was better at football and track, he still saw baseball as his way out, largely because it was the sport that offered something more than glory—money in his pocket. Searching for another place to play, he signed with a team in Anadarko, a town on the far side of Oklahoma City, about a hundred miles southwest of his home turf. Anadarko was a hub of Indian life, located in the heart of the Caddo confederacy near what once were reservations for the Caddo, Delaware, and Wichita tribes, and it was familiar ground for Albert Exendine of the Delaware nation, the former Carlisle athlete who had been Jim's first mentor in football and track.

Ex was a man on the move, coaching football at Otterbein College in Ohio, studying law at Dickinson, scouting and doing some informal coaching for his old coach Pop Warner, and thinking about returning to Anadarko to set up a legal practice with his Dickinson classmate Emilio Marianelli, a young socialist from the mining region of Upper Michigan. In early July, he was in Anadarko for family business and while walking down Main Street saw a familiar face coming the other way. "I bumped into Thorpe on the street," Exendine recalled. "I was really surprised to see the change in him. He was big as a mule." They talked baseball, and when Jim said that he had just been dropped from the local team, Exendine saw an opportunity. Carlisle football had deteriorated in the two years since Thorpe left, losing an unheard-of six games in 1910. Pop was desperate for better players. The return of the gifted left halfback could make all the difference. "I felt Carlisle needed him on the team and I talked to him about returning," Exendine said later. "Jim doubted they would take him back."

Thorpe had reason to be skeptical. He and Superintendent Friedman were at odds, each feeling the other was duplicitous. The Carlisle records no longer considered Jim on leave. The last notation said that he was a deserter. But Ex had a clearer understanding of the Carlisle power structure, knowing that Warner usually got what he needed. "I phoned Pop and told him how Jim had filled out and how he looked to me." The coach wasted no time. His captain for the 1911 season was Jim's close friend Sampson Burd, and Warner enlisted the big Montana Blackfoot as a recruiting agent. He also wrote Jim a letter that made it sound as though his only concern was Jim's future, not his own future as a coach. If Jim came back to Carlisle, he could not only play football but also prepare for the 1912 Olympics along with Lewis Tewanima, the Hopi distance runner, who seemed certain to make the team.

"The personnel of the Olympic team was then under discussion, and I told Jim that he stood a good chance of being selected if he returned to Carlisle and went into hard training," Warner explained later. The sales pitch worked, especially since Jim had few other options, and from the other end Pop pressured Friedman into relenting as well.

Thorpe was still in Anadarko on July 23 when he wrote a letter to W. C. Kohlenberg at the Sac and Fox Agency, the federal official who controlled his finances.

> I would like you to send me 35 Dollars. I am not playing ball here any more. The mgr. said I was expensive and that he had a cheaper man to go in my place. It has been two weeks since I stopped. I need $35.00 to clear up and get home as I would like to go back to Carlisle on the first of Sept. If the check has to be signed by me first why not send check to Mr. Stacker Indian Agent here and I can go before him. Resp. James Thorpe, Anadarko, Okla.

Two years earlier, Jim had crossed the blurry line from amateur to professional to play baseball in Rocky Mount; this letter showed him crossing back to amateur to continue his football and track careers at Carlisle, at the urging of Pop Warner and with the consent, however grudging, of Friedman. There could be no clearer example of the thin line between fame and obscurity. Jim likely began his baseball journey with no intention of returning to Carlisle, thinking he was on a path that could lead to major league success, but instead it led him to a lonely pocket of Oklahoma, and that turned out to be for the better. Had he starred on the diamond during those two summers instead of being inconsistent if not average; had Ex not bumped into him on the Anadarko street; had Pop not pushed and Friedman not relented and Jim not agreed; he would now be lost to history. It was his first failure at baseball that led to all the success that followed.

During the first week of September, the Carlisle railroad depot hummed with students bound for the Indian school on the hill outside town. A superintendent's wife arrived from Oklahoma with seventeen boys and girls from the Potawatomi tribe, delighted by the admirable conduct of her charges during the long journey. A Sioux escort led eleven small boys from the Pine Ridge reservation in South Dakota. Robert Geronimo, son of the late Apache chief, made his way from Fort Sill, Oklahoma, to enroll for his first year at Carlisle at age eighteen. The Indian agent from the White Earth Agency in Minnesota accompanied fifteen new Chippewa students. Sampson Burd rode in from Montana with five new Blackfeet enrollees. Bill Newashe returned from Michigan where he had been playing baseball for the Jackson Convicts, an apt name in the town that housed the state prison, ready to take his place on Pop's starting line. From his home in Spooner, Wisconsin, came Gus Welch, who was not only president of the student body but a promising little quarterback whose classmates were "pleased to see him looking so strong and self-reliant." The student newspaper was also thrilled to see Welch's new roommate in the athletic quarters, "James Thorpe, all-around athlete," who "arrived last week to join our football team."

Pop Warner had spent the summer months vacationing with his wife in western New York, testing the "excellent state roads in regular automobile excursions into the countryside." It was from there that he wrote the letter luring Jim back to Carlisle, part of his extensive effort to reload the Carlisle football team, often in creative and rule-stretching ways. His linemen included Lone Star Dietz, the assistant art director, who by most records was already twenty-seven, and Henry Roberts, a twenty-three-year-old government clerk hired by Pop to run the gymnasium and serve as an assistant football coach while also playing football and basketball. Newashe, like Thorpe, was lured back after saying that he was done with Carlisle, and his friend and Jackson Convicts teammate William Garlow also returned, his school records noting that he was an intermittent student. That made at least three members of Pop's squad who had been playing for pay that summer and not making a secret of it. Garlow had sent a postcard to Carlisle that depicted a "Bird's-Eye View, Michigan State Prison." He thanked a school secretary for forwarding his letters to a boardinghouse in Jackson and reported there were "few other Indians in the league."

Pop had set the schedule in his customary manner: easy games to start the season. If that was a way to ease his wayward star into the violent sport after two years away, Thorpe needed none of that. Showing his best in every part of the game, running, punting, place-kicking, tackling, he led Carlisle to wins over Lebanon Valley, Muhlenberg College, and Dickinson by a cumulative score of 102 to zip. It was as though he had never left, only now he was bigger, faster, and more determined. He also seemed more relaxed and talkative in the classroom that fall, enjoying his status as a big man on campus. To Jim as to many students, Carlisle was a contradictory experience, at times alienating, but at other times comforting, a haven of order and friendship in a disorienting world. One of his daughters reflected decades later that her father once told her that "his happiest years were spent at Carlisle."

One afternoon as Thorpe and his teammates were practicing for the Dickinson game, they heard "unusual sounds coming to our ears from somewhere near the clouds." The players and students throughout the hillside campus looked skyward, transfixed as a biplane dipped low as if to land, then rose and looped and circled and dipped and looped overhead, "hanging in midair, apparently as much at home as the birds." Eight years after the first Wright brothers flight at Kitty Hawk, daredevil aviators were a national rage that fall, buzzing across the American landscape to perform their aerial stunts before crowds drawn by a sense of wonder and more than a hint of danger. By 1911 more than a hundred stunt pilots had died in crashes. Walter Johnson of Rochester, New York, was the aviator who flew into Carlisle to perform at the county fair. Fifteen thousand fair-goers watching nearby, he took off from the field of Colonel John Hays across from the fairgrounds on Spring Road at 5:22 p.m. and soared above the town and over to the Indian school, airborne for twelve minutes and reaching a height of two thousand feet before his gasoline gave out and he had to glide to a landing in a wheat field near Conodoguinet Creek.

Future and past both visited Carlisle that fall. Late on the Saturday afternoon after the Dickinson game, a band of Indians barnstorming with California Frank's Wild West show appeared at the school dressed in full regalia after performing in Lancaster in Pennsylvania Dutch Country. The star was a woman riding bareback outfitted in fringed tunic and Indian headdress who was said to be the Sioux sharpshooter Princess Wenona, daughter of Crazy Horse, born in a tepee. All hype. The princess was a poser—a hustling white girl named Lillian Smith, daughter of New England Quakers. Her appearance along with some more authentic Native Americans at the Indian school brought "great delight to some of the students," according to the *Arrow*. Maybe some students were pleased, but Superintendent Friedman had no use for the barnstorming shows and said efforts to "discourage employment of reservation Indians by Wild West shows and circuses should have the approval of all right-thinking men."

A week later Carlisle greeted another visage from the past: Luther Standing Bear, who had first arrived at Carlisle from the Pine Ridge reservation in 1879 as a frightened eleven-year-old thinking he had been sent east to prove his courage and die. Now he was forty-four and clerking at a dry goods store in Walthill, Nebraska. Soon he would leave for Hollywood to consult on cowboy and Indian westerns, but before that he had another mission. He was on his way to Washington, D.C., to persuade the government to grant him citizenship.

The students of 1911 were enthralled by Standing Bear's stories of how he and his Sioux classmates traveled east more than three decades earlier with their blankets and beads and long hair, taking secret delight in frightening the white people of Pennsylvania. Although Friedman might have disapproved, Standing Bear also talked of the years at the start of the new century when he joined a Wild West show and traveled the country and England with Buffalo Bill Cody as a chaperone and bareback rider. That lasted until a day in 1904 when a train carrying the barnstormers to New York collided with a mail train from the Chicago and Northwestern line and three young Indians—Phillip Irontail, Killed Head, and Thomas Come Last—were killed and twenty-seven more were injured, including Standing Bear, who broke his left arm, ribs, and nose.

Standing Bear knew that Friedman and other Indian reformers looked askance at the Wild West shows, finding them demeaning and counterproductive in the effort to lift Indians out of stereotypes, but he argued they were of some value. "The schools might not be in favor of the shows, but that is where I have seen and learned a good deal from, too," he said. "As the saying goes, experience is a good teacher, and during my travels I have been amongst good and bad." During his visit to Carlisle, Standing Bear spoke to the boys at a YMCA meeting, was serenaded by the band with marches and overtures, recalled that he had once been the school's lead trumpeter and marched his bandmates across the wondrous Brooklyn Bridge to celebrate its opening in 1883, and expressed his regret that the government still controlled the Indian people.

One improvement involved the football team, bringing the school national recognition once again. After trouncing St. Mary's College and Georgetown in the weeks after Standing Bear's visit, with Thorpe and his new backfield running mate, Possum Powell, leading the way, Carlisle with five wins and no losses faced its first test of the season in a road game against Pitt. A few days before the game, Pop wrote a letter to John Newhall, the coach at Cornell. "Pitt has a big heavy team—a lot of bruisers and ringers and if they would happen to put one over on the poor Indians you can bet Cornell [which was to play Pitt later] will have to watch out. While Pitt expects to trim us, I don't think they can do it as I have something of a team. But you can't always tell and they may make us take a fall." Warner, the master tactician, then filled the page with arrows and *x*'s and *o*'s, diagramming a trick play that involved a quarterback pass to a pulling guard, which was still legal.

At Pittsburgh that Saturday, Pop used his full bag of tricks, but he also had Thorpe, who exhausted the superlatives of local sportswriters. "To say Thorpe is the whole team would be fifty percent wrong, but he certainly is the most consistent performer trotted out on the Forbes gridiron in many a moon," exclaimed the *Pittsburgh Leader* after Carlisle shut out Pitt 17–0. "His returning punts, line-bucking, fake plays and other maneuvers getting him great applause. Thorpe carried the ball two out of every three times for the visitors."

The *Pittsburgh Post* matched that enthusiastic account. "It is safe to say that never in the history of the game in Pittsburgh has a more powerful and brainy aggregation appeared here against a local college team than the eleven which Warner sent against the Pitt team yesterday. The blazing first magnitude star of the whole game was the mighty Thorpe, who played halfback for Warner's machine. Those who thought the Indians had an irreplaceable backfield man in the doughty Pete Hauser [who had starred against Pitt in 1908] would forget there was such a player could they have seen Thorpe in action yesterday. Combined with great bodily strength and uncanny speed, this player displayed head work of high caliber."

And finally came the ecstatic appraisal of the *Pittsburgh Dispatch*: "This person Thorpe was a host in himself. Tall and sinewy, as quick as a flash and as powerful as a turbine engine, he appeared to be impervious to injury. Kicking from 50 to 70 yards every time his shoe crushed the ball, he seemed possessed of super human speed, for wherever the pigskin alighted there he was ready to grab it or to down the Pitt player who secured it." Strip away the purple prose and much of it was true. Thorpe's performance at Pitt was his finest yet.

ONE DAY THAT fall, Jim's friend Sampson Burd wanted him to meet a bright young woman in the senior class, Iva Margaret Miller. Iva already knew about him. "All the girls at Carlisle had heard that Jim Thorpe was returning after a two-year absence," she recalled. "He was reputed to be quite handsome and quite an athlete." Not that she cared or knew anything about football. At a Saturday-night dance in the school gym, Burd made the introductions and Jim asked Iva to dance.

"So, do you like my new hairdo?" she asked.

"Oh, you cute, kiddo," he responded.

His flippancy left her "a little put off," she said later. But Jim persisted. Dance after dance, there he was, asking for her hand. He was light on his feet and after that first wise-guy remark proved to be gentlemanly in manner. Gus Welch, the quarterback, also had his eye on Iva, and the two flipped a coin to see who could invite her to attend the rivalry game against Penn to be played in Philadelphia a few weeks later. Jim won.

Iva was six years younger than Jim, born in 1893 in Indian Territory, one of four children of schoolteachers at the Cherokee Seminary in Tahlequah. Her mother had died of pneumonia when she was five, and the father abandoned the children, essentially making them orphans and sending them off to a local mission school and then to the Chilocco Indian School north of Ponca City. Iva knew little about the family history and grew up in Indian culture, considering herself Cherokee. In the spring of 1904, before she had turned eleven, she traveled to St. Louis with the Chilocco superintendent and a hundred classmates to take part in the American Indian exhibit at the St. Louis World's Fair. The experience there shaped her perspective, though it almost changed her life even more dramatically. The Indian exhibit was built to resemble a large boarding school, with classrooms, dormitory rooms, and a large auditorium where visitors watched daily performances in which Iva took part, including the crowd favorite, a rendition of Longfellow's *Hiawatha.* Encircling the school building were little villages of various tribes: Sioux in wigwams, Pawnee in tepees, Pueblo in adobe huts.

One of many acquaintances Iva made at the exposition was Geronimo, the ancient Apache chief, who was used by the federal government as a mythic totem of vanquished rebellion, now at age seventy-five a tamed prisoner of war trotted out at fairs and exhibitions where he delighted curious audiences by dancing to a big drum and selling postcards with his signature for a dime apiece. Iva later said that she gave Geronimo the cards he sold and "then he'd get half-tight and give me four or five dollars." She also met Helen Miller Gould, a person as unlike Geronimo as humanly possible, the daughter of railroad tycoon and gold speculator Jay Gould, one of the most unscrupulous robber barons of the Gilded Age.

Helen Miller Gould, described as "the richest unmarried woman in the United States," was in St. Louis as one of the "Lady Managers" of the fair. She traveled between New York and St. Louis often during the many months the fair was in progress, arriving by private train car, holing up behind armed guards at the Washington Hotel, and riding to the fairgrounds in a carriage with curtains drawn. She had a special interest in the children of the world, and held a party at the fair to which she invited two girls each from Japan, Russia, Sweden, Norway, Holland, Italy, France, Germany, England, and Spain—and two American Indians, one of whom was Iva Miller. By one account, "Miss Gould became so interested in the bright little Cherokee maiden that she sought to adopt her." It almost happened, but Iva's father reentered her life briefly to prevent it. Iva greatly regretted that missed opportunity, she said later, not so much because of the wealth it would have provided but because she admired Gould's manners and elegant dress. "She was the motherless girl's idea of the very highest type of womanhood, the equal of whom she had never met since," reported an article in the *American Indian* magazine nearly a quarter century later.

Instead of living a luxurious life in Manhattan, Iva made her way to the Carlisle Indian Industrial School, arriving on campus at age sixteen in 1909 shortly after Jim had left to play baseball at Rocky Mount. Her records showed that she was five foot six, weighed 125 pounds, and had survived a mild case of smallpox in 1901. In the social parlance of the times, she was invariably called a Cherokee maiden. During her first two years at Carlisle, she was sent on two Outings, one of which was a disaster much like Jim's earlier experience at Arthur Buchholz's. It was at the home of Mrs. D. E. Maxfield in Moorestown, New Jersey, where Iva was paid $8 a week for performing housework and caring for the family's two-year-old. All seemed to go well at first, but when a Carlisle Outing field agent paid a second visit, Mrs. Maxfield declared that she was about to fire Iva for insubordination, claiming the young woman considered herself "above work, was bold and forward, and neither truthful nor trustworthy." Once, according to the patron, Iva had refused to help the toddler onto a streetcar because she did not want to sully her work dress.

It is probable that something else happened at the Maxfield home to cause unspoken tension. Judging from Iva's admiration for Helen Miller Gould, the part about not wanting to dirty her dress sounded believable, but her reputation was otherwise stellar and her report cards at Carlisle showed her deportment and academic performances rated from very good to excellent. She was a senior class official and one of the leading Susans, the nickname for girls in the Susan Longstreth Literary Society, named for a Quaker philanthropist from Philadelphia who was Carlisle's earliest and most generous benefactor under Richard Henry Pratt. With the Susans, Iva studied Longfellow, followed the inspirational writings of Orison Swett Marden, whose book *Pushing to the Front* taught her how to assert herself without seeming too pushy, and savored *The Rosary* by Florence Louisa Barclay, a novel about a woman who considers herself plain and does not trust the love of a dashing bachelor until he is blinded in a hunting accident and they can only see each other's inner beauty. The Susans had their own meeting room with a saying on the wall: LABOR CONQUERS ALL THINGS.

IF JIM WANTED to show that his labor on the football field could conquer Iva's doubts, he picked the wrong game. Playing against Lafayette in Easton, he badly injured his right leg and ankle and was on crutches by the time the team returned to Carlisle. Days before the Penn game, a story in the *Philadelphia Inquirer* noted that Captain Burd had a strained back, Newashe had just been released from the hospital after a bout with pneumonia, and "Thorpe, described as one of the greatest football players who ever lived, will be on crutches for several days." Jim was off crutches by Thursday, and took part in signal drills, but it remained uncertain that he would play. Penn assumed he would; Pop declined to say.

Carlisle students anticipated the Penn game not only for the rivalry on the field but because it offered the best chance for a large contingent of students to travel to the city. The team left for Philadelphia on Friday and spent the night dining and hanging out in the lobby of the Normandie, the grand hotel at Thirty-Sixth and Chestnut four blocks from Franklin Field. At 7:10 a.m. on Saturday, the Carlisle band and 160 students clambered aboard a train to Philly. The city greeted them with welcome signs in red and gold in store windows and flower barkers selling chrysanthemums in the Indian colors along the walk from the station to the stadium. Iva was among the girls sporting wide blue hats and waving Carlisle pennants as they entered through the south gate with the boys in military dress and marched to their seats in the temporary bleachers on the north end. "Carlisle Indians are always an attraction, wherever they go," the *Arrow* noted.

Down on the field before kickoff, Jim could be seen warming up. He practiced a few punts and sprinted along the sidelines, but that was it, too much pain in his leg and swollen ankle, and Pop put him on the bench rather than risk further injury. The Penn team had retreated to a hideaway in Wayne for two days of secret practices that week, and came in hoping to beat Carlisle, as they had the two years when Thorpe was gone. The Philadelphia press was less optimistic, although as patronizing as ever. A game-day cartoon in the *Inquirer* depicted an Indian in Carlisle headdress, his nose long and drooping with a nostril ring, scalps of past foes Pittsburgh and Lafayette hanging from a tomahawk in one hand, rifle in the other, making his way along a war path toward Philadelphia, where a helmeted and armed Penn Quaker stood guard in front of a statue of William Penn with a speech balloon overhead: "Wish I'd put something on that treaty about football."

Carlisle did fine without its star left halfback, winning 16–0. An early touchdown came on the trick double-pass to a lineman play that Pop had diagrammed in the letter to the Cornell coach earlier, and quarterback Welch also scored on a long and winding touchdown run of 85, 95, or 100 yards, depending on the newspaper. Being imprecise about statistics was a regular feature of sportswriting in that era. So were condescending stereotypes of Carlisle, few more egregious than the fabricated excitements of the *Inquirer* that day. "As the whistle blast of the referee finally signaled the end of hostilities, the Indians, with their bevy of winsome squaws, executed war dances and chanted in a dozen different Indian dialects the war songs of their tribes of the West. Does it pay to educate the Indian? queried a smiling alumnus of Pennsylvania. . . . No, no, no—not in football, chorused a half-score of undergraduates seated nearby who heard the remark."

Next came a trip to Massachusetts for a game against Harvard. Most football writers had called the Crimson the best team in the East through the first five games. Even after an upset loss to Princeton on the same Saturday that Carlisle thrashed Penn, the Harvard coach was so confident that he held most starters out of practice early in the week, intimating that he might play only three of them and instead rely on former players attending graduate school at Harvard. That changed as soon as he heard reports from Carlisle that while Captain Burd was still out, "the great Thorpe will likely be in shape to meet the Crimson." Suddenly all of Harvard's starters were scrimmaging and the coach was said to be anxious about facing "perhaps the craftiest team on the gridiron this year."

Earlier that week, as Dr. Charles William Eliot, president emeritus at Harvard, was preparing to sail for Asia on a worldwide peace mission sponsored by the Carnegie Endowment, a reporter asked him what he thought about the Harvard team's loss to Princeton. If the question was a deliberate attempt to provoke Eliot, it succeeded. He had been trying to ban college football because of its violent effects even before the reforms of 1905 and was still campaigning for its elimination. Football was more dangerous than prizefighting, Eliot said, and stunt aviation was the only entertainment more deadly. "Yes, aviation, that's demoralizing to the spectators. They don't go to see the aeronaut in flight, but with the anticipation of seeing him fall and perhaps be killed."

More than thirty-five thousand fans filled Harvard Stadium that Saturday, paying a dollar—or a dollar-fifty for prime seats—to see the Crimson take on the wounded Thorpe. In the crowd were eighteen Carlisle girls who had saved money since their summer breaks for the expensive trip. Emma Newashe, the Sac and Fox sister of the Carlisle lineman, organized the adventure, and Ella Johnson, a Seneca, kept a journal, describing their early-morning train ride through the fog to Philly and on to Jersey City; the ferry across the Hudson and the excitement of passing through Hell's Gate on the East River; their arrival at the United States Hotel in Boston at eight that night, tired and hungry; the *Boston American* photographer who awaited in the lobby to photograph the "picturesque Indian maids"; the tour the next morning in five automobiles through Boston's narrow streets to Bunker Hill, Faneuil Hall, Old South Church, the homes of Longfellow and Lowell, and on to Harvard, where they lunched at the university café and then walked to the stadium.

Jim stepped on the field gingerly, a weave of adhesive wrapping from toe to just below the right knee with padding up his leg. He told Pop he was ready—and stayed in the entire game. "Although every movement must have been agony, not once did he take himself out," Warner recalled. "Because of those injuries, and also because I knew that Harvard expected Jim to carry the ball on every play, I switched the plan of attack and used him only as interference through the entire first half." Carlisle trailed at halftime 9–6, with those six coming on two Thorpe field goals from thirteen and forty-three yards. In the second half, Thorpe was a whirlwind. "As Jim saw the day going against us, he forgot his wrenched leg and sprained ankle and called for the ball," Warner said. " 'And get out of my way,' he gritted. 'I mean to do some real running.' And how that Indian did run! After the game one of the Harvard men told me that trying to tackle the big Indian was like trying to stop a steam engine." Jim also kicked two field goals in that half, making all the difference in the 18–15 Carlisle upset.

After the game, the *Boston Globe* reported that although Harvard did some good things, "it was an Indian who was the center of all eyes. And most of the time it was the fleet-footed Jimmy Thorpe . . . who did more than anyone else to bring the splendid victory for the Indian school." A cartoon of the match carried the caption: "Imagine What Would Have Happened if Jimmy Thorpe Hadn't Been Lame." The *Boston Post* noted that Thorpe came to the stadium with a reputation as the best player ever turned out by Carlisle. "Even the most partisan Crimson supporter will gladly admit, through their admiration for his wonderful work against Harvard, that he not only upheld an already great reputation, but he has placed his name in the Hall of Fame, not only of Carlisle, but of the entire football world. It was indeed a pleasure to see a man not only live up to a great reputation but add to it through work beautifully accomplished."

Labor conquers all things, as Susan Longstreth said. Iva Miller missed the game, lacking the money to make the trip with her friends. But she was on the Carlisle campus that night when students flooded out of their rooms for an impromptu nightshirt parade, dancing in the moonlight as they carried a dummy of "Johnny Harvard" on a stretcher. And she was there again on Monday when the student body gathered around Thorpe and his teammates, returning heroes, and sang football songs late into the night. Iva was hooked, and by the end of the season, when asked to name her most thrilling experience, replied: "Watching a football game."

The only loss of the season came the following week, when Carlisle gave up a game played in the rain and mud at Syracuse. Pop always believed his Indians struggled on a sloppy field, and he feared they would be overconfident after the conquering of Harvard. He was frustrated with Jim during the first half and kept urging him to skirt the ends instead of banging up the middle to little avail, but Thorpe was nervous about slipping and reinjuring his ankle while making turns on the mushy field. Carlisle's nifty little quarterback Gus Welch, so beat up that he had stayed in bed most of the week with a bad back, watched the first half from the sidelines, but then suited up and almost led Carlisle to victory, falling one point short, 12–11. With the prospect of an undefeated season gone but Thorpe again at full speed, the Indians closed with two more wins, defeating Johns Hopkins and Brown on the road. On the way back from Providence after the final game, the team stopped in New York City and visited the Hippodrome on Sixth Avenue, then claiming to be the world's largest theater. Before the train reached Carlisle, the boys had elected their new captain for 1912—Jim Thorpe.

Thorpe's national reputation had grown game by game that year, and by the end it reached mythical proportions. He was portrayed as the avatar of Indians in America, for better or worse. A column in Pittsburgh's weekly newsmagazine the *Spectator,* said that Thorpe's success and that of his football team proved that "the Indian of today is coming into his own." But a wire service story carried in the *Louisville Courier-Journal* described Thorpe as the last bright flash of a fading people.

> Once in a while, across the vista of the passing years, a dying race startles those who are measuring it for the shroud by giving a kick that crabs the entire funeral proceedings. . . . The football season of 1911 has brought out prominently in the public eye another of these athletic marvels of a dying race, and the greatest of them all. This newest Indian marvel, who is just now the wonder of the athletic world and of professional trainers through the length and breadth of the United States, who without exception declare him to be the greatest all-around athletic marvel the world has ever seen, is Jim Thorpe, a redskin of the Sac and Fox tribe from Oklahoma.

Walter Camp, reigning monarch of college football, agreed with that last assessment, naming Thorpe the first-string left halfback on his All-America team. He was the only player chosen who was not from the Ivy League or one of the military academies.

TRACHOMA SWEPT THROUGH Carlisle late that fall of 1911. An insidious eye disease that could cause serious damage, including blindness, trachoma was not fatal but more contagious than tuberculosis and almost as common among Indian nations. In that era, it was also associated with impoverished populations in the shtetls of Eastern Europe, and as a manifestation of nativist anti-Semitism, a diagnosis of trachoma—or often a misdiagnosis of what was in fact only conjunctivitis—was sufficient to deny Jewish immigrants entry into America. Dr. Daniel W. White, a physician in the federal Indian Service, took an interest in trachoma in 1908 when he reported to the Indian school in Phoenix, where he found dozens of untreated cases. Within two years, he had persuaded the Indian bureau to undertake a campaign to combat the disease at Indian schools and reservations nationwide. Studies resulting from that campaign indicated that about 23 percent of the Native American population had trachoma, with the highest rate of 69 percent in Oklahoma.

At Carlisle in early December, White spent several days examining Carlisle students and found nearly a third, 190 of 586, with trachoma. The disease likely spread through dirty communal towels and washcloths. If untreated, it worsened by stages, first causing granules to grow on the inner surface of an upper eyelid, then making the eyelid thicken with secretions and turn inward, scarring the cornea and causing blurred vision. Of the 190 trachoma cases, White considered 94 serious enough to require operations. One of those, according to Carlisle records, was Jim Thorpe. White operated on Thorpe with what was called the expression technique. Cocaine was applied to his lids as a local anesthetic, roller forceps were used to squeeze out the granules, and boric acid was applied to clean out blood and debris. Then Jim rested in a darkened room during recovery with ice compresses on his eyes.

White left instructions with student nurses for postoperative treatment involving daily cleansing with boric acid, friction massage of the eyelids with a camel-hair brush, and the application of yellow oxide ointment to closed eyelids rubbed together for the time it took to count to one hundred. Jim's nurse was Rose DeNomie, a Chippewa from the Bad River band in northern Wisconsin who had arrived at Carlisle earlier that year. She described Jim as "either mischievous or just ornery," a contrast to Henry Roberts, an end on the Carlisle football team. Roberts had been knocked unconscious making a tackle during the loss to Syracuse and spent several days in the Carlisle infirmary recovering from the injury. As Roberts recalled the story, he awoke in a stupor one morning and the first thing he saw was "the pretty face of an Indian nurse." When he recovered, he courted Rose, and married her four months later at Superintendent Friedman's home, where Thorpe and the football team treated the couple to a four-course banquet. As the myth of Jim Thorpe grew in later decades, the story of DeNomie and Roberts was sometimes transposed to Jim and Iva, who was also a student nurse, but did not treat him at the hospital.

Jim's eyes recovered in time for the annual Susan-Invincible gala during the holiday season, a highlight of Carlisle's busy social calendar. Girls from the Susan Longstreth Literary Society invited boys from the Invincible Debating Society to a formal dance, the gymnasium swirling with three hundred celebrants, girls in gowns, boys in military uniforms. "The music was excellent and the refreshments dainty and palatable," reported the *Arrow.* Eight thespians among the Invincibles performed a rollicking comedy called "The Millionaire Janitor," and before the dance everyone lined up for a grand march "led by Miss Iva Miller and Mr. James Thorpe." They were a couple by then, the new king and queen of the student body. Jim considered himself lucky to find a girlfriend who was "sympathetic and understanding." Knowing her, he said later, "was a real inspiration in my life at that time." With her encouragement, he expanded his interests beyond sports, reading books with her, writing essays, and performing extemporaneous speeches at the Friday-night sessions of the Invincibles.

But he could not go long without a ball in his hands. When the basketball season started, he joined the team as a starter with Possum Powell and Henry Roberts. The team's sixth man was Wounded Eye, an appropriate name considering the medical troubles at school that year. Jim was also a graceful ice skater. He and Iva and their friends spent hours that winter skating on the frozen field just below Pop Warner's house and outside the school's front gate. There were two rinks side by side, with Garrison Lane running between them, both about the size of a football field and formed by water diverted from nearby Letort Creek. One side, known as Rubber Ice, was bumpy and uneven. It took its name from the rubber manufactured in town and was reserved for the white kids of Carlisle. Jim and Iva skated on the other side, the Indian Ice, which was as smooth as glass. Generations of Carlisle Indian Industrial School students, accustomed to being separated from the townsfolk, even at church, would take pleasure in this one situation where they got the better of it.

THE ROSTER OF employees at the Carlisle Indian Industrial School that year listed a superintendent and his assistant, twelve teachers under a principal teacher, seven clerks, three disciplinarians, two field agents under an Outing system manager, three matrons, three sewing room instructors, three cooks, two Indian art instructors, two carpenters, two farm instructors, two painting instructors, and two firemen, plus a librarian, a doctor, a quartermaster, an engineer, a storekeeper, a horticulturist, a baker, a blacksmith, a dairy instructor, a tailor, a carriagemaker, a shoemaker, a tinsmith, a teamster, and five temporary employees, including a business teacher. The others are long forgotten; the temporary business teacher was a young woman named Marianne Moore, who became one of the great poets of the twentieth century.

Miss Moore, as she was known at Carlisle, was Jim's age, born in 1887 in Kirkwood, Missouri, and had grown up without knowing her father, who had suffered a psychotic breakdown. With her mother and older brother, she'd moved to Carlisle when she was nine, living in a row house owned by a local judge on North Hanover Street about five blocks from the entrance to the Indian school. As an adolescent she knew the imposing Colonel Pratt and followed the first great Indian football teams, who were regarded as local heroes. After attending the college preparatory high school at Metzger, the local institution for the education of girls and women on the Dickinson campus, and then Bryn Mawr College near Philadelphia, where she was a mediocre English student, Marianne was uncertain what to do with her life. The Moore family was intensely private and literary, constantly writing long letters to one another and using nicknames drawn from the anthropomorphic children's novel *The Wind in the Willows.* Marianne was Rat, the character who spent time writing poetry and lazily rowing a boat on the river. She was reading Tolstoy and Henry James, and already writing poetry, but few outside her family and readers of the Bryn Mawr *Lantern* literary magazine knew it.

The opportunity to teach at Carlisle arose when she was not yet twenty-four, and she took it. "Why speculate on something of a literary sort when I could immediately take the place of a commercial teacher at the Indian school [who left] for work as a salesman I think of Smith typewriters in California?" she later wrote in the partial manuscript of an unpublished memoir. "The salary was $2000 a year and it seemed self-evident to accept it. With misgivings I did."

Teaching at the Indian school was demanding, not because of the students, who with few exceptions were well-behaved, but because of the hours. Moore rode her bicycle to school when weather allowed, arriving before her first class at eight thirty in a "large, airy, and unprepossessing" classroom, then left on her bike to eat lunch at Metzger, returned to Carlisle for afternoon classes, retraced her route to Metzger for supper, and then back to school to supervise an evening study hall, pedaling home well after dark. Moore was frail and slight, weighing ninety-eight pounds, and her eyes bothered her. Concerned about her health, her mother and brother urged her to quit after a few months. "The Study Hour business is an outrage," her brother wrote to her from Princeton, where he was studying. Marianne complained, especially about Superintendent Friedman, whom she thought of as an unimaginative bureaucrat. But she stuck it out and won the respect of her students in the bookkeeping, stenography, typing, commercial arithmetic, and commercial law classes. With few exceptions, she later recalled, "the Indians had great behavior and ceremony, and were exceedingly chivalrous and decent and cooperative and idealistic." She called them her salvation.

Among her students were Iva Miller and the football players Gus Welch, Alex Arcasa, and James Thorpe. Late in Moore's career, after she had established world fame, George Plimpton interviewed her by exchanged letters for *Harper's* magazine. Plimpton was fascinated by her years at Carlisle, pleased to find that she was a literary figure with a keen interest in sports, as he was, and curious about her encounters with Jim Thorpe. She wrote to Plimpton that as a student, Thorpe—or James, as she always called him, never Jim—was "a little laborious, but dependable—took time—head bent earnestly over the paper—wrote a fine even clerical hand, every character legible, every terminal curving up—consistent and generous." She never saw him be "irascible, sour, or primed for vengeance," but rather always courteous, recalling the time when they were walking to town to see the circus and she was carrying a heavy umbrella because rain threatened and James said to her, "Miss Moore, may I carry your parasol for you?" As to reports of his drinking, she wrote: "I don't mention trips away for I know nothing about them; but celebrations involving liquor (reputedly) can't be good for any athlete."

Late in the school day, after classes and before supper, she occasionally strolled down to the athletic fields. "I used to watch football practice after school sometimes; signals for passes, little starts with the ball, kicks for goal, and often watched sports in spring—throwing the hammer, at which James was adept, taking hurdles, the jump." Her eyes were riveted on Thorpe, and decades later she provided Plimpton with a description of him that surpassed in its precision any offered by the sportswriters who mythologized him. "He had a kind of ease in his gait that is hard to describe," she wrote. "Equilibrium with no stricture, but couched in the lineup in football he was the epitome of concentration, wary, with an effect of plenty in reserve."

Others besides Marianne Moore took pleasure in the way Jim moved. When springtime bloomed in the Cumberland Valley, Iva made a habit of stopping by the athletic fields after class let out at four o'clock to watch her boyfriend train for the Olympics. "This was naturally an incentive and in the light of her approving eyes, I would do my best work," he wrote later. As he trained for a variety of track-and-field events, Jim became obsessed with winning gold medals in Stockholm, where the games would be held, but his motivations were more practical than egotistical. "I wanted to win those events for one reason. It wasn't to be acclaimed the greatest all-around athlete in the world for the mere glory that accompanied that title. I wanted to win so that it might serve as a diploma to get me a job as an all-around coach in some university."

Pop Warner noticed a similar practicality in Thorpe in the spring of 1912, or at least a focus on money that threatened to distract him. Jim and Lewis Tewanima were the stars of the track team again. In a match against Lafayette, the duo scored more points than the entirety of the opposition. Early in the track season, before an indoor event at the Duquesne Gardens in Pittsburgh, Pop told the press that Jim was "doing everything he tries better now than ever before in his career," and predicted his star would win every event he entered. Thorpe proved him right, winning the high jump, shot put, dash, and hurdles against strong competition from Michigan, Ohio State, Cornell, and Penn. Still, there were times when Pop had to shake Jim from the notion that track and field and even football were dead ends and baseball, despite his uneven experiences in the minor leagues, was the only way out, the only way he could make money as a professional. "Many a time he moaned to me, 'What's the use of bothering with all this stuff? There's nothing in it,'" Warner later wrote. "And once as we were returning home from a meet, he came through the train smoking a big cigar. When I called him down, he exclaimed fretfully, 'Shucks, Pop, I'm through with track. It's baseball for me.' I pointed out the duty he owed to his school and his race and after a while he heaved a deep sigh and groaned, 'Oh, all right then, but I'd rather play baseball.'"

Just because those two ideas are contradictory does not mean that one has to be wrong and the other right—that either he was determined to win gold medals so he could become a coach, or he was tired of all that and just wanted to cash in by playing baseball. Jim was trying to sort out conflicting feelings, struggling to find the best way to take advantage of his athletic prowess.

If Jim was wondering what the use of it all was, he showed few outward signs beyond the occasional mutterings to Pop. As early as March 15 he sent a letter to the Sac and Fox Agency in Oklahoma asking that Agent Kohlenberg send him $100 from his federal lease allotment. "My chance on going abroad this summer is very bright, with the Olympic team. Please send money at once." Nor was there a hint of uncertainty in his training program. As the weather warmed, he played hooky from school whenever possible and devoted most of each day to training. He rose at dawn and headed out from the campus, running and walking twenty miles toward the Blue Ridge Mountains, building up his endurance. After a lunch of soup and salad and a brief nap back at the athletic dorm, he would run down to the track and work on the all-around program of the pentathlon and decathlon, the Olympic events he aimed to win. Most of the individual events came naturally to him, with his combination of speed and strength, but now for the first time he began practicing the pole vault, a decathlon event that at over 180 pounds he thought he was too heavy to perfect. The heights he reached that spring were modest, none higher than nine and a half feet; he thought he could go higher but was afraid he would break the ash pole and injure himself.

For the mile run, his training partner was Sylvester Long, known as Long Lance, an ambitious student from North Carolina who said he was a Cherokee, like Iva, and like Iva had interests far beyond athletics, serving as treasurer of the senior class. Emma Newashe, the class vice president, penned limericks about many seniors, and of Long Lance she wrote:

Among us is saintly Sylvester
Who we all know will be the world's master.
He is so free from guile
He'll meet life with a smile
And he's always be Carlisle's chief mester.

Sylvester Long would come in and out of Jim Thorpe's life for the next twenty years, a mystery man of many talents who was anything but free from guile.

THE CLASS OF 1912 was among the largest in school history. The class colors were tan and blue and the motto was Loyalty. Jim was supposed to be among them—before he dropped out for two years. As freshmen on Arbor Day 1908, "in the golden youth of the class of 1912," as the *Arrow* put it, they'd planted a horse chestnut tree across from the hospital. Now, four years later, it stood "strong and immovable . . . a worthy namesake of the athlete and gridiron hero whose name it bears, for the tree is known to Carlisle by the name of Thorpe."

Iva, chosen by her peers to be the class elocutionist, wrote an essay that described their senior classroom. "Room 14 is the goal which every ambitious student at Carlisle is striving with all his energies to reach," she wrote. "Where is this wonderful room of which I am writing? Imagine a large room situated in the extreme west end of the Academic Building, having outlooks toward north and south. Looking south, the beholder has an excellent bird's eye view of the eastern half of the city of Carlisle with its numerous spires and steeples, and the battlements of the county jail looming large in the foreground—a building that is the counterpart of the historic French Chateau d'If. [Iva had read *The Count of Monte Cristo.*] From the opposite windows, Nature spreads a gorgeous picture before the view—a well-kept road winding through the trees and cutting our beautiful campus, which is laid out in grass lawns, artistic flower-beds, and numerous walks."

The dimensions of the room, Iva wrote, were thirty feet wide and forty feet long, with high walls. On those walls hung "copies of masterpieces which are known and loved the world over: The Shepherdess by Millet, a Landscape Study by F. Leo Hunter, and a Study of Lions by Rosa Bonheur." She called Room 14 "a haunted room, full of sweet memories" of past classes. She hoped that over the years it would become "just a bit more precious because certain members of the Class of 1912 once sat here; that some of us may do something that shall make Carlisle proud of us and give us the privilege of haunting room No. 14." That would have been Jim, the horse chestnut, had he stayed in the class.

Iva's sentimental rendering avoided another way the school was haunted. On Memorial Day, Marianne Moore led her class to the Indian cemetery on the lower field behind the grandstands. They walked amid headstones bearing the names of scores of students who'd come to Carlisle and never left. Fanny Gibson, Shawnee; Della Aitkens, Shoshone; Robert Scott, Seneca; Sara Kirk, Kickapoo; Mary Paisano, Pueblo; George Bears Arm, Gros Ventre; Jemima Metoxen, Oneida; James Wolfe, Sac and Fox. Row upon row. "We cut the grass with sickles," Moore said.

In the days before graduation, Sylvester Long took a role as inquisitor for the traditional Character Book asking fellow students a series of twenty-seven questions about themselves. Iva said her Favorite Meals were scalloped oysters and cocoa. Her Nickname was Snookie. Her Wittiest Friend was "James Thorpe. U know him?" Her Most Thrilling Experience was watching a football game. Her Favorite Pastime was "watching someone on the athletic field. Who?" Her Ideal Man was "brave, courteous, true, and living up to his highest inclinations." And her Ambition was "at present to go home in June and be a good girl."

Jim wrote that his Favorite Author was Longfellow. His Favorite Dish and Beverage were strawberry shortcake and cream, and beer and wine. His Favorite Pastime was athletics. His Most Thrilling Experience was "while in North Carolina." His Worst Experience, "ditto, also in North Carolina"—answers indicating that he was not trying to keep his baseball days at Rocky Mount and Fayetteville secret. His Greatest Attraction was Iva, or "Cousin Miller," as he put it.

And his Ambition: "Almost there, the highest in athletics."

9

Stockholm

JUNE 14, 1912. EIGHT IN THE MORNING. THE YOUNG MEN mustered outside the YMCA at the corner of Sixth Avenue and Twenty-Third Street in New York City and lined up eight abreast in their blue blazers, white slacks, white shoes, and white straw boaters with black silk hatbands sporting the American shield. These were the finest of American athletics, 174 strong, selected to represent the United States at the Games of the Fifth Olympiad. More than a thousand well-wishers fell in behind the athletes, led by the Irish American Athletic Club band and its top-hatted Uncle Sam drum major, as they paraded eight blocks west to Pier 61 on the North River, where the SS *Finland* was berthed. At dockside, they merged with a waiting crowd of equal number to shout, wave miniature flags, and belt out "The Star-Spangled Banner" as the Olympians filed aboard the steamship for the sail across the ocean to Stockholm.

For several hours before the liner backed into the river for the long voyage, the bunting-strewn decks were aswarm with family and friends bidding farewells. The traveling party included, along with the athletes, two hundred officials and guests who had paid to accompany the team, plus a pack of big-city newspaper and wire service correspondents, assorted photographers, and a newsreel team. To satisfy requirements of the Bureau of Immigration and Naturalization, each passenger signed documents verifying he or she was an American. Three among them, as the Associated Press noted, "had a clearer title to the name Americans than any of their companions"—Jim Thorpe and Lewis Tewanima from the Carlisle Indian Industrial School and Andrew Sockalexis, a marathoner from the Penobscot nation in Maine.

Photographers and sportswriters worked the scene for pictures and good copy.

Click: Here was James E. Sullivan, overseer of American track and field, appointed by President Taft to lead the delegation, predicting that the American boys would sweep the medals in Stockholm. It was boys only as long as Sullivan had his way. Although women's swimming, diving, tennis, and gymnastics had been added to the Olympics for the first time and ten nations were sending women athletes, Sullivan would not allow them on the American team, considering competition "unfemale."

Click: There was Avery Brundage, a decathlete from the Chicago Athletic Association who had resigned from his job as an engineering construction superintendent to make the trip. A middling athlete who faced minimal competition in the midwestern qualifying tests, Brundage was overtaken by "unbounded emotion" when he received the letter announcing his selection, having "not the faintest idea of where this trip would lead and how it would effect" his future. He could not know then, in other words, that he would become the dominant figure in Olympic officialdom for a large swath of the twentieth century.

Click: Here was George S. Patton Jr., a young lieutenant in the Fifteenth Regiment, U.S. Cavalry, with an "unquenchable thirst for fame." The scion of a prominent southern California family, Patton carried with him noble visions of leading a heroic life amidst his daily leisure. At Fort Myer in northern Virginia, his last posting before leaving for Stockholm, Patton kept his own stable of ponies for polo and tally-ho fox hunting. Now he was huddling aboard ship with his proud mother and father and other family members who joined the trip to watch George Jr. compete in the modern pentathlon, a new event testing various military skills from fencing to sharpshooting to riding and running.

Click: There stood the massive weight-thrower Babe McDonald, whose usual beat on the New York City police force was the busy intersection of Forty-Third and Broadway. Now Babe was basking in the cheers of his fellow uniformed traffic cops who came aboard to present him with a floral horseshoe crafted in the blue and yellow colors of their department.

Click: Here was Duke Kahanamoku from the Territory of Hawaii, among the most popular and charismatic athletes aboard, star of the U.S. swim team, a waterborne wonder who'd spent his youth swimming and riding the waves of Waikiki on his *papa nui* surfboard.

Click: Here was Howard Drew, a lonely African American in a sea of white, the Springfield, Massachusetts, flash who began his sprinting career with gym shoes he transformed into cleats by pounding nails into them. Drew had won the dash tryouts decisively and seemed on his way to becoming the Olympic champion in an event dominated by Americans, but with his salary as a hotel bellhop could not afford to bring his wife and two children down to see him off.

Click: The photographers and scribes finally tracked down "the Indian trio, Jim Thorpe, the diminutive Tewanima, and Sockalexis, establishing camp near the promenade deck." For a time they were "not molested," reported the *New York Evening World*, "but eventually they too were discovered." At their side was Pop Warner, who paid their way with Carlisle Athletic Association funds after Olympic officials claimed they were out of transportation money and might have to leave them behind. For the two Carlisle Indians, all of this was a novel experience. Thorpe recalled that Tewanima was "a shy little fellow" who "stuck close to Pop and seldom mingled with the other athletes. He worshipped our coach and would not make a move without consulting Pop." As for himself, Jim had "never seen a boat as big as that before . . . nothing like that—walking on the boat, and all the cabins and the decks and eating and sleeping on it."

In the holds below, stevedores had loaded the foodstuffs it would take to sustain this hearty band of sporting men: 10,000 pounds of breakfast food, 650 gallons of fresh milk, 500 quarts of cream, 15,000 eggs, 200 barrels of flour, 25,000 pounds of beef, 600 pounds of mutton, 4,000 pounds of lamb chops, and sufficient fruits, vegetables, and spirits for the first ten-day leg to Antwerp, where provisions would be restocked before they continued on to Stockholm. There was no such thing as an Olympic Village in those days; the plan was to anchor the ship in port and use it as a floating hotel for the duration of the games. The athletes might eat like horses, but much of the apple and carrot stock, and all of the alfalfa, was meant for real horses, the gelding thoroughbreds Connie, Chiswell, Poppy, Deceive, and Fencing Girl who were also aboard ship to be ridden in the equestrian competitions.

The SS *Finland* was chartered from the Red Star Line for the occasion and retrofitted for its special mission, transformed into a floating gymnasium to accommodate daily practice sessions scheduled for the athletes. Workmen had installed a cork-padded running oval for the distance men, a hundred-meter straightaway for the sprinters on the starboard promenade, a canvas water tank measuring twenty by eight by four feet deep for the swimmers aft on the lower deck, and a pistol range for the marksmen with targets set at twenty-five meters, along with a reserved space for the fencers on the upper deck, a ten-foot backboard for the tennis player, stationary bikes for the cyclists, and mats for the high and long jumpers. The weight men would have the broad ocean itself as their playing field; the scheme was to tie the discus and hammer to ropes, heave and hurl them overboard, then retrieve them like fishermen hauling in a catch.

The excitement of the occasion included a tinge of fear. At the date of their departure, only two months had elapsed since the maiden voyage of the RMS *Titanic* had turned into an unimaginable horror. In the early-morning hours of April 15, the White Star Line's newest and largest ocean liner, on its way from the English port of Southampton to New York, struck an iceberg in the North Atlantic and sank, taking more than fifteen hundred lives with it into the frigid deep. The sinking of the *Titanic* had dominated the news ever since, with investigations on both sides of the Atlantic leading to new safety measures aboard big passenger ships, including an adequate number of lifeboats. The disaster had reverberated through the industry, with thousands of would-be passengers suddenly fearful of the transatlantic trip and changing plans. Fewer tourists signed up for the sail to Stockholm than anticipated, leading to a financial deficit that threatened the venture until Colonel Robert M. Thompson, the wealthy copper company mogul and president of the American Olympic Committee, advanced the necessary money.

To reassure skittish passengers, the committee vowed that everyone would be "well taken care of in the way of protection against any accident such as the *Titanic* met." The SS *Finland* was a smaller vessel, and its lifeboats and rafts could accommodate 947 people, while the crew and passengers for this trip totaled 631. Also, the steamship would chart a southerly route, steering clear of icebergs.

THE WATERS OF the Atlantic were smooth for the sail across, but the ship's rocking motion still made three athletes seasick, including two of the weight throwers, Ralph Rose and Jim Duncan, keeping them in quarters or at the rail for the first two days. Rose was a six-six 280-pound shot-putting behemoth from San Francisco whom photographers could not resist posing with Tewanima, who stood five three and weighed 112 pounds. It was said of Duncan, who threw the discus, that he was sick "only until meal times when he would suddenly recover and pack away enough for two men." As the team comic, Duncan particularly enjoyed hanging out with Thorpe and Tewanima and pretending he was an Indian, constantly urging them to do tribal dances and songs, with which he "materially assisted." The press thought this was funny; Jim and his Hopi pal played along, taking it as part of their condition.

Jim daydreamed about Iva, smart and sensitive with her shiny black hair and bright green eyes. He wrote to her nearly every day aboard ship and then from Stockholm, and she wrote back, though he would not see her letters until his return. "Jim could write nice letters," Iva recalled later. But she was the only member of her family eager to hear from him. After graduation, she had retreated first to Oklahoma and then to the southern outskirts of Los Angeles to live with her brother Robert Earl Miller. Earl, as he was known, was eleven years older than Iva and thought of himself as her guardian. He worried about her relationship with Jim and wanted her to stay away from his roustabout world of sports and drinking. If Earl could keep her thousands of miles away from Jim, he hoped, her feelings for the "uncivilized" Sac and Fox athlete eventually would subside.

There were two versions of the deportment of the athletes aboard ship—an official report written by James E. Sullivan, and more accurate accounts told by athletes and newspapermen. In the Sullivan version, his charges behaved with the decorum of Boy Scouts. "The boys were prohibited from sitting in the smoking room during the day and eating between meals was also under the ban," he reported. One fellow traveler remarked to him that the "gentlemanly conduct of the contestants was an example worth holding up to the youth of our land." Willie Kramer, a distance runner from Long Island, told a different story in a letter he mailed to the *Brooklyn Daily Eagle.* "With the exception of a few hours' workout each day, the members of the team had one long holiday on the trip over," according to the newspaper's recounting of Kramer's dispatch. "Little time was spent in the staterooms except for sleep and the general meeting place was the main saloon." Abel Kiviat, Thorpe's roommate aboard ship, a diminutive 1,500-meter whiz who was the delegation's lone Jewish athlete, seconded that version: "We trained all day on the deck, then we sat around at night, talking and drinking schooners of beer. Ten cents a liter."

Thorpe, who "would eat and drink anything," was "the best natured guy in the world . . . a big, overgrown country kid," according to Kiviat. He and other teammates noticed that Jim was not naturally talkative, but a few drinks loosened him up, and he loved to roughhouse. John P. Nicholson, a hurdler from the University of Missouri (and future track coach at Notre Dame), would say decades later that he was appointed Thorpe's "keeper" during the Olympic sojourn. As Nicholson told it, he learned that while Jim became rowdy while drinking at night, the next morning he would appear in good shape and raring to go. The second assertion about Jim's recuperative powers was established many times. That Nicholson was asked to watch over Thorpe might have been a bit of storytelling, as were so many anecdotes involving Thorpe over the decades, though it sounded like something Olympic trainer Mike Murphy, the longtime Ivy League track coach, first at Yale and lately at Penn, might have requested even if he already had Pop Warner along to chaperone Jim.

Silent Mike—the nickname given to Murphy because he was legally deaf, even though he could somehow hear most everything—was considered part psychiatrist, part evangelist, and he remained vigilant looking for ways to keep the boys sharp. He set the daily practice routines and the training table menus, even examining the morning egg supply during kitchen inspections and tossing rotten ones. Along with being the most innovative track man of his era, the first to develop the sprinter's crouch, Silent Mike was a disciplinarian who sought to control athletes through praise and intimidation. He knew Thorpe from the many times Carlisle had competed against Penn, giving him an intimate appreciation of the Indian star's physical talents, and he wanted to make sure Jim was in good condition for his Olympic events.

Whether Thorpe followed Murphy's training regimen aboard ship was uncertain, shrouded by unreliable reports of sportswriters who sought to portray him as a preternatural if lazy athlete who did not need to practice. Grantland Rice, who considered himself Thorpe's lifetime champion, was not on the trip but propagated the mythology by spinning his own version of stories he heard. "Francis Albertini, who covered the 1912 games for the [New York] *Evening Mail*, told me that going over on the old Red Star *Finland*, Thorpe would sit alone while the rest of the track squad pounded a stretch of cork laid down on the decks," Rice later wrote. " 'What are you doing, Jim,' asked Albertini one day, 'thinking of your Uncle Sitting Bull?' 'No, I'm just practicing the broad jump,' Thorpe replied. 'I've just jumped twenty-three feet eight inches. I think that can win it.' "

Aside from the casual ignorance and racism in that account (Sitting Bull was a Sioux, historic foes of the Sac and Fox), Rice was conflating the scene with another that might have happened in a different context, once the team reached Stockholm. The Rice version likely arose from the typical exchange of bunkum among sports-world pals; Rice worked at the *Evening Mail* in 1912 and Albertini happened to be his editor.

Evidence countering the Thorpe-didn't-practice theme included photographs of him aboard ship running laps in black track shoes and black cardigan sweater, and accounts of teammates like Ralph Craig, the sprint champion from the University of Michigan. "I can certainly remember running laps and doing calisthenics with Jim every day on the ship," Craig told Robert Wheeler, a Thorpe chronicler, decades later. "In fact, Jim and I nearly overdid it on one occasion because we were challenging one another in sprints." The reality seemed somewhere in the middle; Thorpe was a keen student of the games he played, and always prepared himself, if at his own pace. In one of many as-told-to remembrances, he said he was in "the best condition of my life" at the time of the Olympic journey. "I didn't work out strenuously, contenting myself with an occasional run or trot around the deck, as I felt ready for action and didn't want to become stale or over-trained."

Thorpe had more events to master than any teammate, a total of fifteen track-and-field specialties in the pentathlon and decathlon, although some were duplicative. It is safe to say he was not nearly as obsessive preparing for those events aboard ship as Lieutenant Patton was in trying to master his five events in the modern pentathlon, the entirely different event tailored to military pursuits. "My program on the *Finland* was as follows: Running on the deck with the cross country team at 6 AM, usually two miles; shooting with the revolver team from 10 to 12; fencing with the fencing team from 3 to 5; practicing swimming with the swimming team later in the afternoon," Patton wrote in a post-Olympic report to the adjutant general of the U.S. Army. "The method of practicing swimming was very ingenious. . . . The swimmer was placed in [the canvas tank] with a belt attached to which was a rope around his body. The rope was made fast and the swimmer worked against the rope remaining in one place but getting the full muscular exercise. In fact, it was much more distressing than ordinary swimming and we had to cut down the length of time we worked." Distress in this case meant rope burns.

After steaming through the English Channel past Dover and Calais, the *Finland* entered the North Sea and pulled into port for a forty-eight-hour stop at Antwerp on the Belgian coast to restock coal and food supplies. Silent Mike took advantage of the stopover to lead his boys through two-a-day drills on the grounds of the Beershot Athletic Club, and thousands of Belgians watched them practice through a steady rain. On the second day a party of history buffs paid a visit to the battlefield at Waterloo some sixty kilometers away—"appropriate enough for a team that expected victory," remarked Avery Brundage. When the ship prepared to leave at noon on July 26, another throng of a few thousand curious Belgians lined the quay. The departing Americans waved miniature flags from the decks, a band on shore played "The Star-Spangled Banner" (it would not officially become the national anthem for another four years), and the

SS *Finland* was off on her final leg up the coast of the Netherlands and Denmark, through the Skagerrak and Kattegat, then into the Baltic and north to Stockholm, where thousands of Swedes led by their Olympic officials waited to welcome them.

In the manuscript of his unpublished memoir, Brundage wrote that he was overcome by the glimmering splendor of their final passage.

> I shall never forget the two or three hour trip from the Baltic as the steamer picked its way cautiously through the alluring archipelago to the anchorage. It was approximately ten o'clock in the evening and the sun was about to set behind us. The myriad of beautiful, pine clad islands with neat and well cared for homes with flower gardens, the winding channels containing scores of boats of all sizes and shapes, the rosy glow of the setting sun, presented a picture of fairyland as I shall always remember. It was the first voyage abroad for nearly all of us and every impression in an unfamiliar and attractive country like Sweden is enchanting.

THE BIG SHIP docked in Stockholm Harbor snug against the center of Sweden's multi-island capital city, in the shadows of the royal palace and a few miles below the new Olympic stadium. The same quarters that seemed luxurious while at sea proved less than ideal as a stationary dormitory. The summer weather turned stifling hot, without sea breezes or air conditioning to provide relief, and night never seemed to fall, only relentless light along the 59th parallel—nineteen hours of daylight and another three-plus of twilight. All of this made sleeping difficult, and those who did nod off were often awakened at odd hours by returning teammates who "had celebrated with a night on the town." A select party of Olympic overlords found refuge aboard Colonel Thompson's yacht, *Katrina*, anchored nearby, where the president of the American committee kept quarters and a busy social calendar. George S. Patton also abandoned ship, taking a room at the Grand Hotel with his parents.

Jim spent the first few days mostly hanging around the *Finland*, venturing out only for training sessions at the Östermalm Athletic Grounds and two side trips to the stadium. On the morning of July 2, less than a week before the pentathlon, he wrenched his back while practicing the shot put, and American correspondents reacted with alarm. The wire services filed dispatches calling Thorpe's injury "the first setback for the Olympic team" that provoked "a distinct element of gloom among Mike Murphy and the other coaches." He had been showing spectacular form until then, they reported, but after Silent Mike and the team physicians examined his strained back muscles, they determined that he was "in bad shape" and needed treatment. Thorpe was less concerned. So often in football he had suffered what seemed like serious injuries that would have sidelined other athletes, but with his uncommon recuperative powers he quickly returned to the field of play. Within a day, Jim was healed enough to quiet all rumors of him being ruled out of the Olympics.

Shortly after that, Pop Warner moved his Carlisle stars to a camp for long-distance runners in Stocksund on the outskirts of Stockholm, where they could sleep in a private residence and train with fewer distractions. But to the Swedes, few things seemed more exotic than an American Indian. Most had never seen one, but many had read about Crazy Horse and Sitting Bull and Geronimo and powwows and tepees and sidesaddle riding and bows and arrows and scalps and drum dances. Jim realized this, "I stayed pretty close to camp as the Europeans looked upon a red man as a curiosity of some sort and I didn't want to be the object of their stares," he recalled.

Curious Swedes inevitably scouted him out. One day a group of girls stopped him near the training camp. They brought a picture of what they assumed Indians looked like, with feathered headdress and war paint, and there stood Jim in normal-looking civilian clothes. They did not speak English and he knew no Swedish, so they resorted to pantomime, pointing at him and then the photograph as if to ask, *Could you really be an Indian?* "I decided I would live up to their conception of an Indian, so I broke into a war-dance with an accompaniment of full-tone yells," Thorpe said later. The racket aroused all the athletes in the camp and brought them running. "But when I quieted down to explain that it was for the benefit of my feminine audience, the latter had disappeared. Evidently convinced that I was full kin to the war chief, they had fled and I never did see them again."

If there was a touch of exaggeration in that account, one thing rang true. Then and for the rest of his life, Thorpe would encounter people who expected him to look and act like the stereotype of an Indian, and for various reasons—to appease them, to show pride of ancestry, to make a buck, or all three at once—he often obliged.

It was at Stocksund that Johnny Hayes, a member of New York's Irish American Athletic Club contingent, marathon gold medalist in 1908 and marathon coach in 1912, witnessed something that he later turned into a story about Jim's easygoing training attitude. The Hayes account likely inspired Grantland Rice's fabulist tale of Thorpe's encounter with Francis Albertini aboard the SS *Finland*. "One day I looked out from our quarters in Stockholm and saw Jim get out of a hammock and walk to the sidewalk," Hayes recalled. "I saw him mark off about 23 feet. I thought he was going to do some jumping and was shocked at the idea he would try it on the pavement. He walked back to the hammock and climbed in, eyeing the two marks. For all I could see, that was the training he did for the broad jump."

There was more to it than that, as Thorpe later told his family. He was hoping to fall asleep in the hammock but was kept awake by a lingering fear that he would mess up in the broad jump during his first event for the pentathlon. Figuring he would need a jump of twenty-three feet or more to win the event, he paced off the distance, visualized the jump, realized he could do it, and returned to the hammock, anxiety eased. The notion that Thorpe was all brawn and little brains could not have been further from the truth. In his athletic endeavors, he had an uncommon ability to see and think his way through whatever he faced. Abel Kiviat, his shipboard roommate, recalled that Thorpe could watch another athlete do something once, think about the performance, and duplicate it.

The games opened in glorious weather on Saturday morning, July 6, presaging what became known in Sweden as "the Sunshine Olympic Games." Blue skies, the warmth of a northern sun. A city pulsing with festive pride, its people elevated by the occasion, a world celebration of la Belle Époque. The flittering of high-strung merchants, clerks, bankers, bureaucrats in three-piece suits and boater hats, and the strutting of aristocrats in frock coats and top hats; the women in elegant skirts and long white and yellow dresses with Edwardian hats bounteous with flowers and fruits, held in place by long hatpins over hair styled in the latest French-roll pompadour; earnest Boy Scouts in britches and campaign hats; gaily plumed horses, helmeted cavalry, sabers, lances, guidons, marching bands, carriages, trams, bicycles, open-air autos. All flowing down cobbled streets on the way to the two-tiered, four-towered, ring-walled brick castle of Olympic Stadium where King Gustav V and the Swedish royal family took plush-cushioned seats in the canopied royal box amid a standing-room-only crowd filling what one Swedish historian called "the most poetic arena for track and field in modern Olympic history." The 1908 Olympics in London had been loosely organized, provoked more disputes than goodwill, and were treated like a sideshow of little international importance; but the world seemed much more attuned to the games this fifth time around, with 445 accredited journalists on hand to record the competition among 2,541 athletes.

Most attention that first day was focused on the pageantry of the opening ceremony and the many heats of the hundred-meter dash. The athletes paraded through the tunnel and into the summer sunlight that morning behind their country flags and banners, the first time such overt nationalism infected the ceremonies. In establishing the modern Olympics in 1896, Pierre de Coubertin, the French baron and historian, had envisioned international athletic competition as a peaceful alternative to the endless wars that plagued humankind—yet most of the twenty-eight countries represented in Stockholm would be sending young men into the trenches to slaughter one another in a horrific world war only two years later. The German delegation stepping into the stadium in dark suits and ties was the most impressive among future Central Powers collaborators Austria, Hungary, and the Ottoman Empire (centered in Turkey), while Great Britain, France, the United States, the Russian Empire and its autonomous duchy of Finland, Canada, Australia, Italy, and Japan would align on the other side as the Allied Forces. Sweden was a serene meeting ground now for athletics and would remain neutral territory in the war soon to come.

For the heats in the dash that afternoon, there was one case of misfortune. Howard Drew, the swift black sprinter, won his heat by several yards but hit a soft spot on the cinder track, pulled a tendon in his left leg, and hopped uncomfortably at the finish line. He would try to run in the finals the next day, but the pain remained and he was forced to withdraw, crushing his Olympic hopes. Thorpe was focused those same two days on the pentathlon competition and did not witness the sprinter's injury, but he had befriended Drew during the trip over and was disheartened when he heard the news. "In my estimation he was the fastest human who ever put on a spiked shoe," Thorpe later wrote of Drew. "He had suffered a misfortune in the Olympics and was unable to show the lightning speed which directed his feet." Trainer Murphy expressed regrets with a mixture of sympathy and racial condescension. "It was unfortunate that the little colored boy broke down," he said.

Thorpe faced his own measure of condescension before and during the Olympics. He had already gained fame on the football field and had earned his way onto the Olympic team by winning three of five pentathlon events and finishing second in two others at the Olympic tryouts on May 18 at Celtic Park at Long Island City, New York. Yet many stories previewing the American squad mentioned him as an afterthought, used racial stereotypes in describing him, dismissed the decathlon as an odd event, and claimed the pentathlon was being held only to help the Swedes win points. As the *Chicago Inter Ocean* correspondent put it: "When this test was included in the Olympic games, conservative old timers both English and American who heretofore had dominated the field sports regarded it with suspicion as a trick of the newcomers to gain points which were not contemplated in the original program."

So much for that idea. Thorpe established his superiority over athletes from Sweden and everywhere else on the opening weekend. The press seemed confused about how the pentathlon scoring system worked, whether the winner should have the most points or the fewest. The correct system was documented in the Spalding athletic handbook Sullivan published shortly after the games, using the fewest-points method, with one point for first place in a given activity, two for second, and following in order from there. This system showed Thorpe three times better than his closest competitor.

Jim blistered the field, finishing with 7 total points compared to between 21 and 32 points for the next six finalists in what began as a twenty-five-man field. He started by winning the 200 meters in 22.9 seconds, nipping fellow American Jim Donahue at the tape and beating Brundage by a full second and a half. One event, 1 point. Then came the broad jump, always one of his strongest events, the one he had visualized in his hammock. Twenty-three feet would win, he had figured, and now he flew 23 feet 7/10 inches, surpassing Ferdinand Bie of Norway by seven inches and soaring nearly two feet farther than Brundage. Two events, 2 total points. For the next field event, he hurled the discus 116 feet 8⁴/10 inches. This was supposed to be Brundage's best event, but the Chicagoan finished second, outthrown by Thorpe by nearly three feet. Three events, 3 total points. Fourth up was the javelin, an event Jim had no expert training in and rarely practiced. This was the specialty of Sweden's Hugo Wieslander, who finished first by flinging the javelin 162 feet. Even without practice, Jim reached slightly more than 153 feet, good for third place. Four events, a total of 6 points. Finally came the 1,500 meters, a race Jim had prepared for during those spring mornings in the Cumberland Valley, running side by side with his Carlisle friend Sylvester Long. He ran it like an experienced miler, hanging back within reachable distance and thrusting into the lead by the bell lap, pushed on by the boisterous afternoon crowd. His time of 4 minutes 44 seconds outpaced the second-place finisher by five seconds.

Five events, seven points, athletic dominance, and a gold medal—a real one, the last year in Olympic history gold medals would be made from gold.

Many headlines categorized Thorpe only by race. "Indian Triumphs in the Pentathlon," said the *Chicago Inter Ocean* the next morning. "Indian Thorpe Stars," declared the *Buffalo Express.* "Oklahoma Indian Hero of Athletic Events," boasted the *Daily Oklahoman.* But now that he had won and compiled points for the U.S. team, more newspapers were inclined to embrace him patriotically simply as an American, the latest proof of the nation's athletic superiority alongside Ralph Craig, who sprinted to gold that same afternoon in the hundred-meter dash after Drew had to withdraw. “Craig and Thorpe Win for America,” was the headline in the *Daily Times* of Davenport, Iowa. “Craig and Thorpe Uphold Yankee Colors Brilliantly,” reported the *Washington Times.*

The next day was Lewis Tewanima’s turn. Pop Warner had persuaded American officials to enter his long-distance runner in the 10,000 meters, but thought that he was stronger in the marathon, which was to be run a week later. He had finished ninth in the Olympic marathon four years earlier in London, a remarkable effort considering the cultural distance he had already traveled in a short amount of time. It was only fifteen months earlier, on a snowy afternoon in February 1907, that eleven young Hopi men, including one named *Te-wan-i-i-ma,* arrived at the Carlisle railroad depot on the 12:27 train after a two-day trip from Arizona. They had never ridden a train before, never been to the eastern United States, never had much exposure to the world outside their insular nation. They were captives of the U.S. military who had been brought to the Carlisle Indian Industrial School for forced acculturation as part of a government effort to assimilate the resistant Hopi people. They arrived at Carlisle with looped silver earrings and long black hair rolled in a bun. When they were given Christian names, *Te-wan-i-i-ma* became Lewis Tewanima, his first name taken from the Lieutenant Lewis who brought them forcibly to Carlisle. Sportswriters often wrote it as Louis. It was Lieutenant Lewis who informed Carlisle officials that the Hopi were tireless runners, citing the story of a Hopi messenger who ran seventy-five miles from sunrise to sunset. As part of a religious rite, young Hopi men ran twenty-five miles as fast as they could.

On the Carlisle track team, Tewanima became a long-distance sensation, as well-regarded within track circles as his teammate Thorpe. After his performance in London, Mike Murphy declared him the “best man in America” at running between ten and fifteen miles. New York sportswriters took notice after watching him win a ten-mile race at Madison Square Garden the following spring at the Carnival of Sports meet. Lap after lap, he remained within distance of the two leaders. With five laps to go, he started challenging them with a series of intense dashes that pushed them to exhaustion. “But when the bell sounded for the last lap,” the *New York Herald* reported, “Tewanima lengthened his strides again and finished as though he had been jogging through a practice spin instead of fighting his way to the front in a race the likes of which had never been seen in New York." He dominated long-distance races from then through the 1912 tryouts.

Tewanima's chance for Olympic glory in Stockholm came on Monday, July 8, when he braced at the starting line with ten competitors for the gun that would send them twenty-five laps around the track. He was outfitted in white shorts, thin track shoes, and a white T-shirt with No. 293 on his chest, his thick black hair parted in the middle framing deep-socketed eyes, his skinny arms dangling down to short and spindly legs. He was born to run and run some more, but on this day in Stockholm he met his match, overtaken by a runner with equally inexhaustible stamina and a longer, smoother stride. This was Hannes Kolehmainen, the first of a long line of great Finnish long-distance runners immortalized as the Flying Finns. Tewanima ran flat-footed, and his maximum stride could not reach five feet. The Finn had his own style, touching down first on the balls of his feet, then heels, his arms circle-propelling forward as he glided along with effortless six-foot strides. He came to Stockholm with his own masseur, who worked on him so that his limber legs could "stretch like India rubber," and he maintained a strict diet of no meat, only fish, vegetables, eggs, and bread. Tewanima was the only runner in the field who could stay within sight of the Flying Finn after two miles, with six dropping out because of the grueling pace. The little Carlisle wonder kept pace as long as he could, but not long enough. Kolehmainen's relentless strides extended the lead in the final three laps so that by the end he was a quarter lap in front. After crossing the finish line, he took two deep breaths, smiled as though he had been out for a relaxing stroll, and turned back to watch Tewanima struggle his way in for second place.

Trainer Murphy, who supplemented his income by writing a column for newspapers back home, wrote that if Tewanima had only "saved himself more in his heat of ten thousand meters yesterday he would have been a more dangerous man in today's finals." Even so, Murphy said, Tewanima was "the only man in the same class with Kolehmainen." It was good enough for silver. The Carlisle boys had now won two early medals for the Americans. In St. Louis that day, a story ran in the *Post-Dispatch* that bragged about the American team's diversity while perpetuating outdated and unscientific racial categories. "Four races of men have thus far figured in the victories of the American Olympic team at Stockholm," the article began. "They are Caucasian, Ethiopian, Indian, and Mongolian." The Indians were Thorpe and Tewanima. The "Ethiopian" referred to was Howard Drew, the African American who had won his heat in the dash before an injury took him out of the finals. And the "Mongolian" was Duke Kahanamoku, who was flashing through the heats of the hundred-meter swimming freestyle on his way to winning the gold medal.

The modern pentathlon had started by then, with George S. Patton the sole American in the competition. Five events over five days, said to replicate the skills of a nineteenth-century cavalryman, the first time the event was held in the modern Olympics. In later accounts of that week, including his report to superiors, Patton exaggerated his performance in four events, provided an excuse in one that none of the judges bought, and for the fifth rationalized his collapse by confessing to the use of a performance-enhancing drug that was legal then but later outlawed.

In the first event, pistol shooting from 25 meters, Patton used his U.S. Army–issue .38 Colt Special. He fired twenty bullets; the judges found only seventeen holes in the target. He said that was because the other three bullets perfectly pierced existing holes. The judges said no. In later reports Patton said he scored eleven bull's-eyes while the official report said he had four, with eight near bull's-eyes. In any case, the first event found him in twentieth place. Next came a 300-meter swim. He finished seventh, so exhausted he had to be helped from the outdoor pool. For some reason he later said he came in sixth. The third event was fencing—one of his strengths—on the courts of the Royal Swedish Tennis Club. He finished fourth, but said later it was third, while also claiming he won his match against the eventual winner, Frenchman Georges Brulé. He did win that match, but Brulé in fact finished eighth. Why would Patton make this claim? Because he thought that would make him look better, according to Rusty Wilson, an Olympic historian at Ohio State. "He viewed the French as the best swordsmen." The fourth event was the 3,000-meter steeplechase. Patton was an expert rider. He had participated in several steeplechases that year and was a member of the Fort Myer polo team, but Fencing Girl, his horse, was injured so he had to ride a horse provided by the Swedes, and he came in fourth.

The final event was the 4,000-meter cross-country run, in which the competitors started in the stadium, lined up below the royal box, then ran a third of the way around the track and out the stadium tunnel onto a course that took them up a hill, into a forest, through a swamp, and back to the stadium. Of "our own Lt. George S. Patton Jr.," the *Los Angeles Herald Examiner* wrote: "This tall, slim, fair man took the regulation sprinter's start and undoubtedly took too much out of himself in the early going. He appeared well spent when he reentered the stadium and though he had a lead of fifty yards Lt. Patton stopped almost to a walk as [a] Swede brushed by, and when the American finished he dropped into a faint."

That account underplays what happened. Before the race, Patton was given a strong dose of hop by Coach Murphy. *Hop* was another word for opium. It was legal then, before the banning of performance-enhancing drugs, and was meant to get him to "run like hell," but it could also be dangerous, especially on a day as hot as July 12, when temperatures soared into the nineties. The scene of Patton reentering the stadium at race's end was startling as he came through the tunnel in the lead and then reeled, wobbled, staggered, almost fell, slowed to a walk, was passed by Swedish runner Gösta Åsbrink, and, utterly dehydrated, collapsed to the track as he crossed the finish line. As Patton later told the story: "The trainer gave me some hop before the start. I fainted after finishing the race and was out for some hours. Once I came to but could not move or open my eyes I felt them give me a shot of more hop. I feared that it would be an overdose and kill me. Then I heard Papa say in a calm voice, 'Will the boy live?' and Murphy reply 'I think he will but can't tell.' "

The claim that he was "out for some hours" is of uncertain accuracy. The aftermath of the race is not documented in the hours of film a Swedish newsreel company took for the Olympics. An article that appeared in the *St. Louis Post-Dispatch* and other newspapers the next day reported of Patton's collapse: "After a few minutes he was able to walk off, holding the arm of a friend." In the end, after all five events, Patton finished in fifth place, and all three medals went to Swedes.

THE SWEDISH ORGANIZING Committee assigned Svensk-Amerikanska Filmkompaniet to film everything—from the official opening of Olympic Stadium on June 1 to the bestowing of prizes and closing ceremonies a month and a half later. From that effort came twenty-five newsreels, one or two shot every day by SAF and a team of expert cameramen who worked for Pathé. Each night of the games, these newsreels were shown at movie theaters in Stockholm, attracting large numbers of sports fans who could not attend events during the day.

The newsreels were the television of that time, bringing action to life. After the Olympics, the Stockholm footage fell into disuse until the newsreels were restored and reconfigured into a two-hour-fifty-minute black-and-white documentary of extraordinary clarity in 2016 under the direction of documentarian Adrian Wood. "It is not that something is lost or no longer exists, we simply need to continue the search until we find it" was Wood's mantra. In Stockholm, his team found the original cellulose nitrate newsreels and duplicate acetate copies made in the early 1960s. They took both versions to a Warner Bros. division in Burbank, California, specializing in motion picture preservation and were stunned by what they saw in the original nitrate films. "People were amazed at the quality of cameras and emulsion used in 1912," said Wood, who was hired by the International Olympic Committee to produce restored documentaries for most of the games of the twentieth century. Using detailed records from the Stockholm archives and the IOC archives in Lausanne, Switzerland, his team realigned the newsreels into a coherent chronology that followed the games day by day, hour by hour, in life-giving detail. By calibrating between 12 and 16 frames per second, they rendered the movements of the athletes authentically, with none of the herky-jerky sped-up motion so common to old newsreel films of Babe Ruth running the bases.

Here is Duke Kahanamoku popping out of the Olympic pool at the outdoor swimming stadium in a saltwater sea bay on the city's southern shore, sporting his gap-toothed smile, victorious in the hundred meters; and fearless young-women divers from Sweden scooting to the top of the high wooden tower in their shoulder-to-knee one-piece swimsuits that snugly reveal the contours of their belly buttons; and steeplechase equestrians galloping and jumping in the Swedish countryside, one horse and rider barely avoiding a pesky white terrier who skitters upon the scene, the rocky soil and gentle fields of wildflowers ominously evoking the blood-soaked war soon to arrive; and eight-man teams of strongmen from Great Britain and Sweden digging deep into the soft pit in the middle of the stadium, hauling and straining in a bid for gold in the Olympic tug-of-war; and a nonchalant high jumper jauntily leaping, then rising and descending, with not only the bar but also his hat—why he wore it, who knows?—falling with him into the sandpit.

And here, in scene after scene, is King Gustav V standing atop a rostrum in the stadium infield in a gray frock coat, his goatee sharply cut, a cane dangling from one arm, his demeanor proud and sprightly if not a bit playful, as he breaks his regal stance and leans down, shakes hands, and sometimes utters a few words while energetically dishing out gold medals and plopping oak wreaths atop the heads of athletes, occasionally instructing an attendant to supplement a gold medalist's bounty by handing over an oversized trophy or challenge cup. Two of those latter scenes involve Jim Thorpe, who by then had swept his events.

The decathlon was held over three days, from Saturday, July 13, to Monday, July 15. Three events the first day, four the second, three the third. Jim had already competed in two individual events by then as a means of warming up for the decathlon, finishing strongly though out of medal range in the high jump and long jump. The first day for the decathlon brought the foulest weather of the games, a persistent rain that rendered the track slippery, the footing in the throwing rings tentative, the infield landing pits sticky with mud. Pop Warner came to the stadium anxious that morning, knowing from experience with his star athlete on the football field that Jim did not like to perform in bad weather. Jim was less concerned. "At no time during the competitions was I worried or nervous as to the outcome," he said later. "I had trained well and hard and had confidence in my ability. I felt that I would win."

At the start, there were twenty-nine all-around athletes in the decathlon field, so many that for the first event—the hundred-meter dash—the runners were divided into ten heats, each running against only two competitors. Thorpe finished second in his heat, but with a time of 11.2 seconds that put him tied for third place overall. As rain fell harder, spectators fled for shelter beneath overhangs and tower exits and a panoramic bloom of umbrellas protected those who remained in their seats. The athletes loitered in the drenched infield until the downpour subsided, then moved on to the next event, the running broad jump, where Pop Warner's fears about Jim underperforming in bad weather were almost realized. The slick push-off boards made him foul on his first two jumps, but his third and final attempt was clean if not spectacular, and his 22.3 feet was good enough for third in that event, leaving him in second place overall.

Before the next event, the shot put, Jim dashed into the locker room and switched from his drenched outfit to a dry warm-up suit. In that era, there were two shot competitions, two-hand (meaning first right, then left) and best-hand. The decathlon was best-hand only. This was where Thorpe began to separate himself. Though several competitors brought more bulk to the ring, none brought more coiled strength, and Jim won easily, topping his nearest competitor by nearly three feet, sending him into first place overall after the first day. Changing clothes was the key, he said to Pop in the dressing room later. The dry uniform helped him win. *Citius, Altius, Fortius* was the Olympic motto—"Faster, Higher, Stronger." Thorpe, after day one, was faster, longer, and stronger.

Day two of the decathlon, Sunday, July 14, broke clean and bright, the rains gone. The field was now down to twenty-three, with six competitors already dropping out. As he prepared for the first event that morning, the high jump, Jim had a problem. "I couldn't find my pet shoes," he recalled. What happened to them was unclear. He thought someone either stole them or went off with them accidentally. Perhaps he'd misplaced them himself. He and Pop reacted quickly, rounding up a pair of mismatched shoes. They were ill-fitting, different sizes, different laces. Here is where

Warner's many hours fiddling with equipment at the Carlisle shop proved invaluable. He jury-rigged temporary cleats and padded the heels and sent Jim into the stadium infield looking from the shins down like a ragtag interloper. The left shoe looked nothing like the right shoe, and he wore two socks on his left foot, a white sock over a black one, and a shorter, thicker sock on his right foot.

And then he went out and won the high jump, clearing the bar at six feet and one inch. A stunning photograph was taken of Jim standing on the stadium infield then. At first the viewer is drawn to the odd mix of socks and shoes, but soon the eyes move up to see his relaxed stance, hands on hips, left foot slightly forward, and then the majesty of his rugged face. Here is the beauty that poet Marianne Moore captured so well when she was his teacher back at Carlisle—Thorpe's "equilibrium with no stricture . . . the epitome of concentration, wary, with an effect of plenty in reserve." Now he was *Altius*, and after only four events seemed uncatchable, so far ahead that all he had to do was finish in the top six in the remaining events.

It was down to eighteen men now, with another five competitors dropping out before the running of the 400 meters. Six heats, three runners each. Thorpe, with a new and better-fitting pair of shoes, ran in the fifth heat and came in with a time of 52.2 seconds, good for fourth. Two of his American compatriots, Eugene Mercer and James Donahue, finished one-two, moving Mercer briefly into medal contention. He soon lost that position after the discus, an event dominated by another American, George Philbrook, but Thorpe took third with a hurl of 121.3 feet and extended his lead. The final event that Sunday was the 110-meter hurdles. Six heats, again three men each. Thorpe had been hurdling since his first season at Carlisle. Running at full speed with something in his way was second nature to him, whether on the football field or the track. He attacked the course with ferocious ease and sprinted away from the field with a winning time of 15.6 seconds. With three events to go and a night to sleep on it, Jim held a commanding 579-point lead, according to the abstruse decathlon scoring system.

Much of the Olympic attention was elsewhere that Sunday, focused on the marathon, still considered at least symbolically if not athletically the seminal event of the games. A South African, Ken McArthur, finished first, and Sockalexis, the Penobscot runner from Maine, finished fourth, but even their stellar runs could not grab headlines from what happened to Francisco Lázaro of Portugal and Shizo Kanakuri of Japan, one incident tragic, the other a potential tragedy that turned into mystery and farce.

By the start of the marathon, the sun was fierce, pushing the temperature past ninety degrees, dangerous weather for a long run. In the 1912 Olympics film restored by Adrian Wood and his team, there is a long section that shows marathoners funneling out of the stadium in an eager pack and picks them up later, strung out in ones and twos, as they pound their way up a dirt road—lined by trees, telephone poles, and well-dressed spectators—to the halfway point, where they loop around a marker with a giant *C* on it and stop briefly at a table in the shade providing water, tea, and lemonade, before heading back toward town and the stadium. As they run into view, some already seem to be struggling with the weather and terrain. Lewis Tewanima, fleet and tireless as he left the stadium, now knows he is nowhere near the lead and has zero chance of being a medalist. Then comes Lázaro, short and bowlegged, No. 518 in a painter's cap. He grabs a cup of refreshment, takes a gulp, spits it out, grabs another cup, repeats the process, and moves on past the scope of the camera.

Near the nineteen-mile marker on the return to the stadium, as Lázaro ascended the hill at Ofver-Jarfva, he staggered and fell, picked himself up, then reeled and fell again, losing consciousness. Boy Scouts assigned to patrol the course to aid runners found him and called for assistance. Three doctors soon arrived but were unable to revive Lázaro. After telephoning officials at the stadium, they placed him in a motorcar and transported him to Royal Seraphim Hospital, where, according to the official Olympic report, he was senseless, had violent cramps and body convulsions, was delirious, and had a temperature of 106.7. At six the next morning, Francisco Lázaro took his last breath, the first athlete to die during the modern Olympics. The cause was listed as sunstroke, although the fact that he had covered his body with wax before the race helped create an electrolytic imbalance.

Several other runners, including Tatu Kolehmainen, brother of Hannes, the Flying Finn, dropped out at about the same point that Lázaro collapsed. Tewanima kept pushing to the end and finished in sixteenth place. But what happened to Shizo Kanakuri? No one knew at the time. Kanakuri, who had reached the Olympics with great hopes as one of the marathon favorites after a ten-day train journey across Asia and Europe, failed to finish the race, but no Boy Scouts or official race-tenders saw him along the last third of the course. Only years later did the story come out. He had stumbled and collapsed near Tureberg, where a family holding a party found him, took him into their garden, revived him with orange juice, and sent him on his way. But Kanakuri was so embarrassed by his incomplete performance that instead of going back on the course he caught a train to Stockholm and left for Tokyo the next day without telling a soul. Eventually, he did return to the Stockholm marathon course, though by then many of those who had started the race with him were long gone. It was on March 20, 1967, when Swedish officials invited him back to finish the race, and he did just that, running the unfinished leg of the marathon at age seventy-five. His recorded time was 54 years, 246 days, 5 hours, 32 minutes, and 20.3 seconds.

The stadium crowd was buzzing with news of Lázaro's death on Monday morning when Thorpe returned for the final three events in the decathlon. Two more athletes had dropped out, the field now down to sixteen. The first test was the pole vault, the event Jim had practiced the least, fearful he might break the pole and injure himself. But with only his teammate Mercer specializing in the event, Thorpe's modest vault of 10.6 feet was good enough to tie for third, allowing him to lengthen his overall point lead, which was not endangered in any case. Next came the javelin, which none of the Americans had much experience throwing. While Mercer and Donahue dropped from medal contention with meager throws that were thirteenth- and fourteenth-best, Thorpe, in this case relying on pure unpracticed athletic skill, managed a fourth-place throw of 150 feet. Avery Brundage did not even try, dropping out before the javelin. In his unpublished memoir, he offered this explanation: "I was not quite ready for Olympic competition and did not do very well. Moreover, in the decathlon I committed an inexcusable error which I was to regret ever after. I was furious at my poor performance and did not even enter the final event, the 1500 meter run which I hated. This failure to finish the competition was unforgivable."

There is much to analyze in that self-assessment. Brundage got his own history wrong. The records show he dropped out before the javelin, not the 1,500. He was correct to say he performed poorly. After eight events he was in sixteenth place, almost two thousand points behind countryman Thorpe. His use of the words *inexcusable* and *unforgivable* reflected a sporting ethos he displayed later as an Olympic potentate, but only when assessing the deeds of others. With Brundage, it was all about moral posturing. He would write later that he came away from Stockholm with his conversion to Pierre de Coubertin's religion complete. He was now a believer in "Olympic noblesse oblige" where there was "no political chicanery," where "good sportsmanship and fair play prevailed," where "violations even of the spirit of the rules were followed by public disgrace." But there was more to it than that.

No political chicanery? Brundage also came away from Stockholm having made two important new friends in the German delegation, pentathlete Karl Ritter von Halt and fervent Olympic organizer Carl Diem, and would form an unholy alliance with them twenty-four years later in promoting the 1936 Nazi games in Berlin and spewing pro-Hitler and antisemitic propaganda. His notion of noblesse oblige had an autocratic stain. If he could not impose his will on competitors as an athlete, he would seek to control them, contain them, and judge them in other ways when he had the authority to do so. For decades thereafter, as he enriched himself and his aristocratic cronies through his Olympic connections, he portrayed himself as the symbol of athletic honor and arbiter of amateur purity, disparaging athletes of far lesser means who saw sports as a way up and out, not as a leisurely upper-class recreation. He was no match for Jim Thorpe inside the stadium in Stockholm. Thorpe was faster and stronger and could jump higher. But when they clashed decades later, off the field, over issues of fairness and honor, Brundage had all the power.

With the field down to twelve for the 1,500 meters, Thorpe held such a substantial lead that the only way he could lose was if he withdrew. Instead, he ran. There were three heats, four men each. As the *Olympic Games of Stockholm 1912 Official Report* described: "The third and last heat was Thorpe's, who ran the distance as good as alone, the rest of the field being a long way behind the leader." His time was the best of all the heats, 4 minutes 40.1 seconds. It could be said that Thorpe performed the entire decathlon as good as alone, the field being so far behind. Olympic officials, spectators, fellow athletes—all were stunned by what they had witnessed. "As Thorpe went from one strenuous event to another, never seeming to feel fatigue, the wonder and admiration of the onlooking athletes found expression in what came to be a stock phrase, 'Isn't he a horse!'" Pop Warner later recalled. Thorpe finished 700 points ahead of the nearest competitor with 8,412 points, a record score. With that win, Jim had provided the United States with six points, and when added with Lewis Tewanima's two points for the silver in the 10,000, Pop Warner's boys from the Carlisle Indian Industrial School—two athletes who were not recognized as citizens—provided more points for America than any other educational institution.

AT FIVE THAT afternoon, Thorpe took his place with the United States delegation as they marched into the stadium for the awarding of prizes and trophies. The top American officials, Colonel Thompson and James E. Sullivan, sated by two weeks of social functions on land and on the colonel's yacht, marched at the front in formal dress and silk hats, busting with pride that their American boys had bested all nations with a total of 85 points. The athletes behind them were a hodgepodge spectacle, most wearing their white hats, some in track uniforms or warm-up suits, others in finer outfits. Jim had found time to put on a black suit and vest with a white shirt and dark tie. The suit pants billowed in descent and bunched as they met his shoes, appearing a size too big. Once on the greensward infield, he joined gold medalists who formed a semicircle a respectable distance from the rostrum where King Gustav V handed out medals and trophies to the winners. The king looked jauntily regal in his frock coat, cane, and top hat. He was accompanied by four formally attired attendants who summoned the winners forward one by one for brief visitations and assisted with the handling of the precious merchandise.

Thorpe was brought forward twice, first for his win in the pentathlon. He approached from the left and met the king's extended arm for a handshake from above that was so enthusiastic it pulled Jim forward and almost off-balance. While the king stood firm, cane dangling from his left hand, Jim planted his right leg in the ground and bent his left leg, readjusting his balance as he had done countless times on the football field. With his hat in his left hand, he bent in a polite if awkward bow, almost a curtsy, before looking up to receive his gold medal. The king then patted an oak wreath snugly onto Thorpe's head before sending him away with a quick series of handclaps and a sly smile. Jim retreated with another humble half-bow without taking the Swedish King's Challenge Prize Trophy, a three-foot bronze bust so bulky it took two straining attendants to place it behind on the rostrum. It would reach Jim later.

Soon Thorpe was called back for decathlon honors, and the stadium came alive with whistles and cheers. The handing over of the gold medal came first this time, followed by a firm handshake from above and the placement of the oak wreath on Jim's head. An attendant stepped between them with the Emperor of Russia Challenge Prize Trophy, a thirty-pound silver replica of a Viking ship, more artfully designed than the pentathlon bust, but smaller and easier to handle. With his right hand touching the trophy, the king helped steer it toward Jim, pointed at him, and said a few words. There stood Jim, hat in one hand, gold medal in the other, neither hand free to take the trophy until he reacted quickly by casually stuffing the medal in his right coat pocket. He then switched his hat from left hand to right, took the trophy with his left hand while bracing it with the hat hand, retreated one step, nodded twice in appreciation, and said something in reply to the king, who pointed first at the trophy, then to his rear right, a gesture revealing the appropriate exit for Jim, who walked away carrying the Viking ship. All in about fifteen seconds.

What transpired between Thorpe and King Gustav V during those fifteen seconds would become a defining scene of Jim's life. The accepted story goes that the king greeted Thorpe in English by saying, "You, sir, are the most wonderful athlete in the world." Or, in a slightly revised version, "You, sir, are the greatest athlete in the world." To which Jim replied either "Thanks, King" or merely "Thank you." The world press—for understandable reasons, combining superlative praise with democratic jocularity—preferred the version that had Jim replying with the informal "Thanks, King." Thorpe himself in retelling the story later would insist that he was not flippant and responded only with "Thank you."

In any of those renditions, the essential message from the king was the same. Jim was the best athlete in the world. But the question arises: How is this conversation known to have happened? Was it a reasonable if slightly imprecise description of what was said—or was it myth?

There were no reporters within earshot, no audio recordings that captured the repartee of the medal transactions. Only newsreel, in this case silent film, and examinations of that film fail to provide conclusive evidence. The king and his court were not interviewed in the hours after the event, nor was Thorpe. Because of the time difference, evening newspapers ran stories about the ceremony that day, morning newspapers the following day. Thorpe was on the front page of some, the top of the sports page on most. In almost every report he was called the greatest athlete in the world or the greatest athlete the world had ever seen—but not in quotes from the king. The praising quote from the king did not appear in the *New York Times*, *New York Herald*, *Boston Globe*, *Chicago Tribune*, *Washington Post*, *St. Louis Post-Dispatch*, *Detroit Free Press*, or *Los Angeles Times*. One place it did appear was the *Brooklyn Times*, which wrote: "When Jim Thorpe stepped up to receive his prize, the King said: 'You, sir, are [the] most wonderful athlete in the world.' " The quote could have been taken from a wire report—but then, why was it nowhere to be found in hundreds of other papers that carried wire stories from Stockholm?

Within a week, the quote had made its way into the culture, repeated in newspapers throughout the country. Whether the conversation occurred is immaterial to the indisputable fact that Thorpe was the greatest and most wonderful athlete in the world. It is relevant in a different sense, in understanding the mystique that enshrouded him during his lifetime and after. He was now a mythic figure. As stories about him were shaped and reshaped in the public imagination, separating myth from fact became ever more difficult. The myth grew even as the reality of his life became rawer. Or maybe the myth grew precisely because of that reason.

Jim toted the Emperor of Russia chalice to the ship himself; the enormous bust also made it to the SS *Finland* unbroken, and both were put in the care of Pop Warner, who along with his Carlisle boys had returned to the floating dormitory. Although this was never explained to Thorpe, neither trophy was meant to be his forever; the Olympic plan was for them to be traveling trophies, staying with Jim for at least four years and then being handed off to whoever next won the events. The equivalent of how professional hockey later treated its Stanley Cup. Pop's plan was to put them on display at the Carlisle school, magnificent evidence of the world-class abilities of the Indians. He would place a $10,000 bond on their safekeeping. The scene aboard ship that night was raucous. With medal events over, Silent Mike Murphy's rigid training rules were relaxed. "And for the first time since they embarked in search of Olympic glory [the athletes] were allowed to eat what they pleased and smoke as many cigars and cigarettes as they desired," reported the Associated Press. Jim and his pals spent the night drinking and making merry aboard ship and at nearby bars.

The next day, for the enjoyment of Swedish fans, the Americans put on a baseball exhibition, splitting into western and eastern squads. Both sides put in claims for Jim, the West because he grew up in Oklahoma, the East because of his affiliation with Carlisle. He played outfield for the East and went one for two at the plate. Thorpe and his teammates might have been feeling the effects of a night on the town, but few noticed. The East won, 6 to 3. Curious athletes from other nations came to Östermalm field to watch the American national pastime, according to the AP. "The foreigners figured that in some mysterious way baseball must be accountable for the wonderful proficiency in athletics shown by the representatives of the Stars and Stripes in the stadium."

That night, their last in Stockholm, something happened that added to the Thorpe legend, a mythology that usually had two sides to it, one positive, one negative, or condescending and racist. What happened that night was that someone boarded the ship to invite Jim to a special gathering. For days thereafter, as Olympic officials and members of the press were sailing home aboard the SS *Finland*, and again after they had landed back in New York, they would weave the story into a negative and racist myth.

Version one was written by a reporter for the International News Service and appeared in Hearst newspapers throughout the United States. It said that on the day they were to leave:

> the king of Sweden sent an equerry aboard to take James Thorpe, the half-breed Indian who won the pentathlon and decathlon, to the Royal Palace and that Thorpe refused to go. This was probably the first time in history that an American or anyone else has refused a royal command of this character, especially as it was reported that the king wished to give Thorpe a decoration for his wonderful work winning both events, which stamped him as the greatest all-around athlete in the world. When the gold-braided and bedecked equerry boarded the ship to give Thorpe the royal summons, the Indian looked sheepish for a moment, tried to dig his toe into the deck, pondered the matter deeply and finally replied: "I guess I won't go." Commissioner Sullivan, who learned of the incident after the *Finland* sailed, was horrified at such a breach of etiquette and remarked regarding the Indian: "Let us hope his majesty has a sense of humor."

Version two was transmitted by the Associated Press several days later from New York, borrowing from and embellishing version one:

> An amusing incident of the Olympic games is being told at the athletic clubs here. It is said that shortly before the *Finland* was to leave Stockholm an equerry in uniform came aboard and demanded an interview with Thorpe, whose record at the stadium gave him the honor of being considered the best all-around athlete in the world. "The king has heard of your success," said the equerry, "and would like to see you at the palace in order to congratulate you" "Ugh! Ugh! I don't know much about kings," replied the big Indian, as he

grinned bashfully. "Offer him my regards and tell him I can't get away."

Both versions perpetuated the stereotype of Thorpe as an uncivilized Indian. The perpetrators took one thread of fact and wove it into a fabrication that fit their perceptions. In fact, King Gustav was preoccupied that night with a gala at the royal palace attended by foreign diplomats, the Swedish cabinet, and officials from the world's Olympic delegations. His guests dined in the great hall, then were ushered into a reception room where the walls were graced with Gobelins tapestries from Paris and the picture windows provided stunning views of the harbor, where lights from hundreds of small boats twinkled and a fireworks display illuminated the dusky sky. The king had other things on his mind than Jim Thorpe.

Ralph Craig, the Detroit sprinter and fellow double–gold medalist, later debunked the stories, telling Thorpe's first biographer and lifelong defender Robert W. Wheeler that when they returned to the ship that night there was "a man waiting at the gangplank with a message for Jim. It was an invitation from a Russian admiral requesting Jim's presence on his battleship. Since the hour was late, Jim declined the offer." Craig was closer to the truth, though inaccurate in a few particulars, according to Thorpe's version. "An American correspondent who had come over with us sent out a story that the King of Sweden had invited me to the palace and I had declined," Thorpe wrote. "This is not true. In the first place, the King didn't extend such an invitation and had he I would have been happy to have accepted. The newspaper apparently based his story on another invitation that I did refuse. A group of Swedish naval officers partying on a boat at anchor in the port sent word to me by courier in a small boat that they would like me to join them. I declined as I didn't want to be gazed upon as a curiosity."

That concern fit with Jim's sensibility, his shyness, and unease about how the world perceived him, but his newfound stature made one thing unavoidable. He would be gazed upon as a curiosity for the rest of his life.

10

Near Custer's Tomb

IT WAS ONLY FOOTBALL, NO ONE DIED, AND FOOTBALL PLAYers on game day rarely contemplate history or much of anything beyond blocking and tackling and a coach's barking and maybe a girlfriend in the stands. But the ghosts of history hovered. The date was November 9, 1912. The place was the United States Military Academy at West Point, high above the Hudson River sixty miles north of New York City. Army against Carlisle at the field on the Plain. Soldiers on one side, Indians on the other. In imagining the scene, N. Scott Momaday, the Native American novelist and playwright, said that it was like reinventing history. There was, he said, "something in the air that cold November day—something made of omens and prophesies. Some old imbalance was being set right."

Within walking distance of the field, among the former cadets buried at West Point Cemetery, stood the obelisk gravestone of the best-known Indian-fighter in American history: George Armstrong Custer, last in his class at the academy, first in his pursuit of Indians. Custer met his end along with all his men when encircled by Sioux and Cheyenne warriors at the Battle of the Little Bighorn in Montana in 1876, only three years before the Carlisle Indian Industrial School was founded. Its first students were the sons and daughters of some of the warriors who fought Custer. As momentous as that battle seemed in the dominant American culture, the last stand was a blip in the centuries-long history of whites dislocating, chasing, imprisoning, killing, and controlling resistant Indian peoples in their inexorable sweep across the continent. A football game could not set right the imbalance, but it gave the Indians something they rarely had, as Momaday explained: "Unlike their fathers and grandfathers, they were given an honest chance. . . . On the field at West Point, competing against the sons and grandsons of men who had devastated their people on the frontier, they were simply grateful for the chance to play on a level field."

Jim Thorpe was there that Saturday afternoon to face the Army eleven, four months after his triumph in Stockholm. Descendant of Black Hawk, member of the Thunder Clan of the Sac and Fox, he was not necessarily out to avenge what the army had done to his ancestors long ago when Black Hawk tried to reclaim territorial homelands in Illinois and Wisconsin. Jim was playing mostly because Pop Warner had persuaded him to return for one more season. As Pop made his case, it was all about the money. "I pulled Jim aside and told him that with the anticipated large gate ticket sales at Carlisle football games for the season, along with a fine performance by him that season and his recent Olympic victories, there was little doubt that his market value would substantially increase by season's end," Warner recalled. And with Army on the schedule, and the historical resonance that game would bring, the mythmaking sportswriters of New York would follow the star's every move, only elevating his already gloried status as the greatest athlete in the world.

That was enough to bring Jim back to Carlisle. "Well, Bud, I'm right in the game again, playing football," he wrote to his brother Frank as the school year began. "We have our first game next Saturday. . . . Frank, I have the chance to make a bunch of dough after leaving this school. Just started going today. God it's hard to go back again but it is for my good, so I will make the best of things."

JIM'S NEXT MOVE had been the subject of speculation and some confusion since the moment he stepped back on American soil after his Olympic triumph. On August 11, the same day that he was challenged to a sprint by Mayor John Francis "Honey Fitz" Fitzgerald in Boston, a story ran in the *Pittsburgh Press* with the opening sentence "JIM THORPE to be a Pirate!" Columnist Ralph S. Davis asserted that according to "the best information obtainable," Thorpe, after being made "an acceptable offer," had promised Pirates owner Barney Dreyfuss he would play major league baseball for Pittsburgh the following spring, once he had completed his final season at Carlisle. "Should Thorpe join the Pirates, he will from the start of his professional career be a splendid drawing card for the club," Davis wrote. "Should he make good he will be even more of an attraction. The American people love a hero, and in the realm of athletics there is none greater than Jim Thorpe."

Variations of that report spread across the country throughout August, sometimes saying that Thorpe would sign not with the Pirates but with the New York Giants. Many stories carried the caveat that he was a ward of the United States as a member of the "uncivilized" Sac and Fox tribe and needed the approval of the government before he could make the transaction. This caught the attention of the Brotherhood of North American Indians, a fledging organization founded in 1911 to lobby for Indian rights. Richard C. Adams, the Great Sachem of the organization, who like Thorpe was from Oklahoma, wrote to federal officials to protest. "He is probably as well able to care for himself as the Commissioner of Indian Affairs or any one of the numerous clerks in the Indian Office," Adams said of Thorpe. "Please inform me whether it is a fact that you require Mr. Thorpe to obtain permission from the Indian Office or the Indian Agent before he can sign the contract referred to and also what other restraints are put upon him in his business transactions with other people."

An official at the Indian Affairs office responded that they had no information on Thorpe's future plans and were confused as to how the issue arose. "James Thorpe is enrolled as a pupil at the Carlisle Indian School and while carried on the rolls is amenable to the same regulations in reference to outside activities as are other pupils," Adams was told. What Thorpe chose to do after he was dropped from the rolls was another matter. The Indian bureau then sent a telegram to Carlisle, asking Superintendent Friedman to explain what was going on. The relationship between Thorpe and Friedman had been tense for years and remained so now, even after Friedman showered praise on Jim at the homecoming celebration Carlisle had staged for his gold medal performances. Now a man of twenty-five, Thorpe did not need a guardian; yet Friedman's attitude toward him was a mix of concern and condescension, as though he knew best how to chart Jim's future. In his view, that future should not include professional sports.

"I respectfully inform the Office that Thorpe has had offers from a number of major league baseball teams . . . and that he has turned all these offers down," Friedman wrote in reply to Washington. "This he has done in order to continue with his schooling, and I have advised him personally that it was my opinion that this was the best thing for him to do. I informed him that he would find it in his interest to maintain his amateur standing, and not enter the ranks as a professional, and I pointed out to him how transient the successes of major league baseball were and how very few Indians had made a success of the game, and in most cases their success was of short duration. . . . I have advised him to finish up his schooling here this year and if possible go to a college to get a better general education. This would fit him to enter into some profitable, legitimate business which would enable him to maintain his amateur standing, and his renown as the world's greatest all-around athlete would be an asset to him in any business he took up."

The reality was that Friedman's advice carried little weight with Thorpe, who all along saw sports as his future vocation. Pop Warner, with a better understanding of the athlete, more effectively shaped his arguments around Jim's desire to make a living off his athletic skills, while also satisfying Pop's own needs as a coach who wanted to retain the best player in the country. Friedman, in arguing that Jim could best profit by maintaining his amateur standing, was conveniently forgetting that he not only knew about Thorpe's experience playing baseball in North Carolina but had put that knowledge in writing when arguing with Jim in the early summer of 1909 about his Carlisle status. And he was wrong about Indians and baseball. Albert Bender, the former Carlisle student, was then at the height of a long pitching career that eventually took him to the National Baseball Hall of Fame, leading the Philadelphia A's to three World Series championships in the four years from 1910 to 1913. At the same time, Zack Wheat, a Cherokee and another future Hall of Famer, was playing left field for the Brooklyn Robins (later renamed the Dodgers).

When Jim decided to return to Carlisle, he also tried to bring two of his younger siblings along from Oklahoma. Adeline Thorpe was seventeen and attending the Chilocco Indian School north of Ponca City; Edward Thorp was not quite fourteen and at the Sac and Fox Agency school near Stroud. They shared both parents with Jim, the youngest of Charlotte Thorpe's living children, which is to say they were orphans.

The requests were debated by federal officials in Oklahoma and Washington. The superintendent at Chilocco, Edgar Allen, who had been the deputy superintendent at Carlisle when Jim arrived in 1904, recommended against Adeline, citing financial and paternalistic reasons. "The objection I have to her transfer is based upon what seems to me the best interest of the girl herself and the discouraging tendency of Indian children to go from school to school, thus entailing additional expense upon the Government for transportation merely to gratify their desire to roam about." The Sac and Fox agent recommended against Edward, using the circuitous argument that the younger brother should not go to Carlisle because Jim would not be at the school much longer. Of Jim, he wrote: "In fact it is my opinion it is now time he should be out earning his living instead of attending school." Everyone had advice for what Jim should be doing. In the end, it was decided Edward could come, but the government would not pay his way.

THE 1912 FOOTBALL team was at least the equal of the mighty 1907 squad and might have been the most talented in Carlisle history. With Gus Welch at quarterback, Possum Powell at fullback, and Alex Arcasa and Thorpe at halfback, the backfield was so stocked that two extraordinary running backs, Pete Calac and Joe Guyon, a future All-American, could only find playing time as linemen. This was their first year on the squad. Guyon arrived from the White Earth Chippewa reservation in Minnesota as a five-ten 198-pound phenom with what the Carlisle doctor at his entrance physical called "the best heart I have ever examined." Calac, who crossed the continent by train from the Mission nation in southern California, had never played organized football before, but as soon as Pop and some of the boys saw his muscular and athletic physique they recruited him to join the team. He was awed to be on the same squad as the world-famous Thorpe and to see the Olympic trophies—the pentathlon bronze bust and decathlon silver Viking ship—shining inside a padlocked display case in the athletic dormitory. "He was my idol. I read about him in the Olympics," Calac said of Thorpe. "Jim took an interest in me and he taught me. Right off the bat we became good friends."

Pop always started the year with easy games at home or in nearby Harrisburg before he took his team on the road for the rest of the season to play eastern heavyweights in their stadiums. The first part of the schedule was to build the team's confidence; the second to make money while enhancing Carlisle's national reputation. In some ways the 1912 season marked another transition to what became known as the modern era, with the field shortened by ten yards, to an even one hundred, and the number of offensive downs increased from three to four. Carlisle took advantage of these new rules in its first four games by defeating Albright, Lebanon Valley, Dickinson, and Villanova by a combined score of 194 to 7. Thorpe captured the headlines after every game, making several dazzling runs while punting and place-kicking with skill, but Welch, Arcasa, and Powell were equally impressive, and the interior linemen dominated the line of scrimmage even though they were usually outweighed. They played for the fun of it and were fun to watch, fluid and unpressured; Thorpe was so confident that he often yelled out to the opposition from his backfield position what he was going to do before he did it, stop me if you can. And they most often could not.

For the fifth game, on October 5, the Indians took the train across Pennsylvania to play Washington & Jefferson, a private college thirty miles southwest of Pittsburgh. Sportswriters came down from Pittsburgh to cover the game in Washington, Pennsylvania, and were stunned by what they witnessed. Florent Gibson of the *Pittsburgh Post* began his story this way: "Joy in heaven that the Scriptures mention is a very mild variety compared with the kind that is fairly bubbling over the edges of the little city of Washington tonight. And there is good reason for it." The reason: a wholly unexpected tie game, 0 to 0. "Not only did the Washington and Jefferson gridders play the Carlisle Indians, captained by the famous Thorpe, to a scoreless tie this afternoon, but the struggle that resulted when Redskin and paleface came together was the big football game of local history. The English language has not adjectives strong enough to describe this contest. Even expressive American slang falls far short of the mark."

Washington & Jefferson was not a pushover, ending the season with an 8-3-1 record, tenth best among eastern teams, but what fell far short of the mark was the performance of Thorpe and his teammates. Twice they reached within a foot of the goal line without scoring, fumbling once and losing the ball on downs the other time. Thorpe did most of the running for Carlisle on a choppy field and made several large gains from Pop's tricky formations. But according to the *Pittsburgh Press* account, he "was tackled so hard and so often that toward the end of the contest he was nearly 'all in,' but Warner refused to take him out, fearing that a substitute would so weaken the eleven that it could not hold W&J." In the fourth quarter, Jim missed three field goals that would have won the game.

As deflating as the game was for Carlisle, what happened later that night could have been more troubling. While hundreds of Washington & Jefferson students, treating the tie like a victory, staged a celebratory snake dance around a towering bonfire on campus, the Carlisle team was stuck in Pittsburgh for several hours awaiting the train for the second leg of its trip home. Contemporaneous press accounts of what happened next differed in some details, but all reported that Thorpe had several beers and got drunk, resulting in a wrestling match or fisticuffs with the coach.

In the *New York Sun*, the headline read: "BIG JIM ON WARPATH, Coach Warner, However, Rescues Bottle and Chokes Off Yells." "It is said the world's greatest all-around athlete strayed from the path of prohibition and Warner caught him in the cigar stand with a bottle," the story reported. When Jim rebuffed Pop's demand to give him the bottle, according to this account, Warner put him in a clinch. A wire service story that ran in papers around the country said that "Big Jim" Thorpe was "nursing a few bruises which he did not get in Saturday's game with Washington and Jefferson." The bruises came instead, this story said, after "Thorpe broke training in the Seventh Avenue hotel. . . . Warner found him in the barroom, and a pretty fist fight followed, the coach winning in a knockout."

Years later, Thorpe and Warner gave their accounts of what happened. Warner said the press versions were largely fictitious, that no fists were thrown. "I've heard how I once bested the great Thorpe. There was nothing to it," he wrote. "We'd played a scoreless tie with W & J on a bad field and Jim was feeling low." When they reached Pittsburgh, many of the boys were bored waiting at the station and decided to go to a bar down the street. After an hour or so, a report reached Pop that Jim was "well tanked up—or drunk." Warner said he went to the saloon, grabbed Thorpe by the arm, said, "Jim, don't be such a damn fool," and marched him over to the Seventh Avenue Hotel, where Jim started shouting and yelling at him. "There was little doubt that he was mad at me for breaking up his post-game party," Warner recounted. A crowd gathered outside to see what was causing the commotion. Before the train arrived, Pop escorted Jim out a back door of the hotel and got him to the station safely and unnoticed. On the ride back to Carlisle, Jim apologized to Pop in front of the team.

Thorpe's account was briefer. "I felt badly after that game and went out," he explained. "I almost missed the train back [to Carlisle]. Pop didn't like my going on the town. He said it would hurt the team."

Disentangling fact from fiction in accounts of Thorpe's career was always complicated by the mythmaking of the sporting press, the fact that Jim at times was an unreliable narrator of his own life, and the tendency of Pop Warner to put the best light on his own actions, giving himself the role of white savior. In the case of the Seventh Avenue incident, it seemed clear that the press accounts were hyperbolic.

By the next weekend, all was forgiven. No troubles on the trains coming and going as the team traveled to Syracuse to meet the Orangemen. The game was played on a muddy field at Archbold Stadium, the sort that made Pop worry that his boys would play without their usual zest. Jim kept slipping as he tried to skirt the ends, leading to another scoreless game at halftime. Another confrontation between coach and his star running back ensued, but this one mild and only verbal and again won by Pop. " 'Jim,' I said, 'if you're going to do us any good, you'll have to bore straight ahead instead of sweeping everything wide,' " Warner recalled in an interview with Arthur Daley, a *New York Times* columnist. "He shook his head. 'Hell,

Pop,' he answered. 'Why run over 'em when you can run around 'em?' But I finally convinced him. So we scored 38 [33, actually] points in the second half. And from that time on Jim kinda liked to hit the line as well as run the ends."

Wins in the following weeks over Pitt, Georgetown, Toronto, and Lehigh gave Carlisle a record of nine wins and one tie going into its November 9 game at West Point, the battle near Custer's tomb.

THE MILITARY CULTURE at West Point was not alien to the Carlisle players. Their schooling was all about assimilation, and from the time of its founding by Richard Henry Pratt, the career army officer, a key part of Carlisle's acculturation process was to mimic the behavior of the American soldier. When Pop had his team watch the corps of cadets parade on the Plain that morning hours before kickoff, the scene was different only in size and grandeur but not in substance from the drills and parades Carlisle students performed in their snappy blue-striped military uniforms back on their campus field. All in the name of killing the Indian to save the man. But the attempts at transformation were superficial. They could never fully erase history or the reality of Native American experiences.

Always looking for an edge, Pop played on that history in the cramped locker room before the game. Pete Calac recalled the coach delivering a passionate pep talk, pacing back and forth as he reminded his boys of what the U.S. Army had done to their ancestors, then approaching each of them individually to give specific instructions. "Pop was anxious to make a good showing against Army," recalled Joe Guyon. In terms of national stature, this was the most important game on the schedule, more significant even than the annual rivalry against Penn. Pop knew the top writers from New York would be there and write about the game in detail. What made him especially anxious, he confessed earlier that week, was the "lack of interest shown in daily practice" by his players.

But it was not for nothing that Pop was called Foxy Grandpa Warner. His concern about his boys' commitment was for public consumption. What was happening in practice was something else: the refinement of a dazzling new offense. It was the double-wing formation, placing both halfbacks—in this case Arcasa and Thorpe—closer to the line and spreading them wide of the defensive tackles, with only the fullback in the backfield behind the quarterback. The offensive linemen were also spaced farther apart, which had the effect of opening the field and offering more blocking and running variations. With a gifted ball-handler like Gus Welch and two slicing, crisscrossing, elusive halfbacks coming at the point of attack from new angles, it would be difficult for any defense to adjust. Warner had been installing the double-wing step by step for weeks, waiting for the most propitious time to spring it on the opposition.

At game time, a cold diagonal wind sliced across the field; heavy gray clouds hung over the Hudson cliffs. The American flag was at half-staff honoring the recent death of James S. Sherman, vice president of the United States. The cadet corps, in long gray coats, watched from the west stands. Walter Camp, the dean of college football, observed from the sidelines. On the Army side, Ernest Graves, the head coach, sent his starting eleven to the south end for the opening kickoff, led by Leland Devore, their captain, a giant All-American tackle from Wheeling, West Virginia, whose nickname was Big 'Un, and a running posse that included seniors Leland Hobbs, Geoffrey Keyes, and an underclassman from Abilene, Kansas, named Dwight David Eisenhower. On the bench, one of the scrub linemen was Eisenhower's classmate Omar Nelson Bradley. Within the span of a few months, Jim Thorpe had encountered three men who would become the most famous American generals of World War II—on the Olympic team with Patton and on the football field against Eisenhower and Bradley. They were still unknown; he was world-famous.

Eisenhower arrived at West Point as a skinny 152-pound plebe, but after working out for a year had filled out to about Thorpe's size. Like all players of that era, he stayed on the field for both offense and defense, as a running back, end, and linebacker known more for aggressiveness than agility. Before the game, he and Hobbs and Charley Benedict had ruminated about Thorpe and plotted how they might team up on tackles with the goal of knocking him out of the game. On the other side, at Pop's instruction, Guyon and Thorpe were conspiring for a similar double-team disabling of Army's star, Big 'Un Devore. Even with all the innovations that football strategists like Warner had brought to the game, and with the rules changes that had eliminated violent acts like the flying wedge, it remained a riotous sport, not quite anything-goes, but close.

The first period was scoreless, marked by fumbles and punts. Thorpe and Arcasa broke off runs of ten, twenty, and thirty yards, befuddling Army with double-wing wizardry, and Jim out-punted his Army counterpart by ten or fifteen yards with every kick. But even though, as one sportswriter wrote, "the Indians outplayed the white folks," they could not get in the end zone. The first break in the second quarter went to Army when Possum Powell was ejected for decking Army's left guard, Charles Herrick, with an open-handed uppercut to the chin, and the referee decided to penalize Carlisle by moving the ball twenty-seven yards to the Indians' thirty-yard line, halfway to the goal. "The Indians lost heart because of the penalties against the team, a common trait of the team," wrote the correspondent for the *Washington Evening Star*, assigning to Carlisle the negative trope of Indians not responding well to trying circumstances. From there, Eisenhower, Hobbs, and Keyes carried the ball down to the four, then Hobbs swept left for a touchdown. The extra point scuttled under the crossbar, no good. Six to nothing Army.

After another exchange of punts, Carlisle took the ball near midfield. For the first twenty minutes of the game, Warner had been using Thorpe more than usual as a decoy, with Welch faking handoffs to him and giving the ball instead to Arcasa while Thorpe bulled into the Army wall and cleared a path for his backfield mate. Now the ball started going to Thorpe more, and all eyes were on him. He was showing the uncommon multiplicity of his running skills—his change of pace, stop-and-go, swivel hip swing, straight-arm, and burning speed, all with the power of a wild horse pounding the Oklahoma prairie. "At times the game itself was almost forgotten while spectators gazed on Thorpe, the individual, to wonder at his prowess," gushed the *New York Times* correspondent. After Thorpe's runs led the Indians inside the five-yard line, Welch called on Joe Bergie, who had been moved from center to replace the ousted Powell at fullback, and the Turtle Mountain Chippewa plunged in for the score. Thorpe kicked the extra point, giving Carlisle a 7–6 lead at the half.

The second half was bloodier than the first, with what one correspondent called "near rioting, rough work, slugging, and a general display of bitterness such as has seldom been seen on the gridiron." Army could not stop Thorpe and Arcasa, who combined to take Carlisle to three more scores before the day was done. At one point in the third quarter, Eisenhower and Benedict sensed their opportunity to hobble Jim during one of his end runs. "We gave him the old high-low, the old one-two, just like that," Eisenhower later said, recalling the play in a conversation with his brothers Milton and Earl. Ike plowed into Thorpe chest-high; Benedict hit his knees. Jim fumbled the ball and slumped to the ground, seemingly out cold. The two West Pointers lay nearby, groggy but conscious. By some accounts, Thorpe was out for more than a minute, and when the referee told Warner, who had run out to check on his star, that Carlisle had taken enough time and they had to get Jim off the field, Devore, speaking as the Army captain, said they did not stand on technicalities and urged the ref to give Jim all the time he needed. Eisenhower was certain Thorpe was done for the game. "But he managed to stagger to his feet in a minute or two and take his place behind the line. Even then we weren't worried because we were sure we'd ruined him for the rest of the day. But do you know what that Indian did? On the very next play he took the ball and went right through us for ten yards."

The next time Eisenhower and Hobbs tried to high-low Jim, they missed and smacked into each other. Eisenhower twisted his knee, and Graves took him out of the game. He watched from the sidelines, knee iced, anger rising, upset that his coach had yanked him, until he was so distraught that he trudged off to the locker room before the final whistle. It was the beginning of the end of Ike's football career. The knee was banged up again in a game against Tufts, and then wrenched further as he dismounted a horse, and he never played again. He was not the only Army starter who failed to play to the end. Devore, neutralized by the efficient blocking of Joe Guyon, who was outweighed by the Big 'Un by sixty pounds, became so enraged that on a kickoff he lumbered across the field to blindside an unsuspecting Guyon and then piled on him. As the crowd hissed, the Army captain was tossed from the game.

Thorpe made the most memorable run of the afternoon on a punt return, a run the *Times* correspondent declared "will go down in the Army gridiron annals as one of the greatest ever seen on the plains." It began with Army punting from its own end zone and Jim settling under the high kick at the Army forty-five-yard line. Surrounded by would-be tacklers, he fumbled the ball, scooped it up quickly, and with blocks from Welch and Calac began to twist and weave his way downfield. As described by the *Times*: "In and out, zigzagging first to one side and then to the other, while a flying Cadet went hurtling through space, Thorpe wormed his way through the entire Army team. Every Cadet in the game had his chance, and every one of them failed. . . . It was a dodging game in which Thorpe matched himself against an entire team and proved the master."

The run might have been the greatest ever seen at West Point, but it stood out in the annals of Thorpe mythology for two other reasons. *Reason 1*: Later descriptions of it were wildly exaggerated by Jim and his idolators, growing more hyperbolic through the decades. *Reason 2*: The run did not even count. The touchdown was wiped out by a penalty. Those two reasons were intertwined. In the fabricated retelling, the run was much longer than forty-five yards, and after it was called back Jim did it again, brilliantly returning the second kick for a longer touchdown. "Ninety-five yards this time. That was Jim's biggest thrill," claimed a 1952 *Esquire* article based on an interview with him. In fact, that never happened. The second punt was fielded by Gus Welch. Here was the essence of Jim Thorpe's career distilled into the reality and the fable of that one play, with its elements of magical athleticism, triumph, myth, hyperbole, and nullification.

As the game neared an end, the long gray coats in the west stands dissolved into the enveloping darkness. After the last of four Carlisle touchdowns, Jim missed an extra point, but it was hard to see and he was not wearing his kicking shoes and the eastern press corps was so awed by that stage that he could do nothing wrong. Indians versus soldiers turned out to be no contest. The final score: 27–6, Carlisle, what the correspondent for the *Brooklyn Daily Eagle* called "a massacre in every sense of the word." For this one afternoon, on the Plain of West Point within a short march of Custer's tomb, this was some payback, what Gus Welch later called "the rattling of the bones."

In the dejected Army locker room, Big 'Un Devore was still upset about his ejection. "When we were undressing after the game, [teammate Geoffrey] Keyes had a hard time keeping Devore quiet," recalled W. H. Britton, whose locker was nearby. "It was like restraining a madman." But once he calmed down, Devore had nothing but praise for Thorpe. "That Indian is the greatest player I have ever stacked up against," he said. "He is super-human, that's all. There is nothing he can't do. He kicks superbly, worms his way through a field like a combination greyhound, jackrabbit and eel. He is as cunning and strategic as a fox. He follows interference like the hangers-on follow an army." Eisenhower, sore and dispirited, encountered Jim outside the visitors' locker room. "This fellow seemed a very mild, nice mannered man," he said of the running back he had tried to knock out of the game. "Thorpe wasn't by any means tough [off the field]. Very quiet, retiring. But great at football. He could do everything anybody else could do and do it better."

The press corps agreed: Thorpe was the star. "His running with the ball was a revelation," wrote the *New York Herald* correspondent. "Starting like a streak, he shot through the line, scattering tacklers to all sides of him." From the *Times* came this ode to Carlisle's left halfback: "Standing out resplendent in a galaxy of Indian stars was Jim Thorpe, recently crowned the athletic marvel of the age. . . . To recount his notable performances in the complete overthrow of the Cadets would leave little space for other notable points of conflict. He simply ran wild, while the Cadets tried in vain to stop his progress. It was like trying to catch a shadow."

As the southbound train rolled through the Hudson Valley darkness that night on the way to New York City, Walter Camp sat in the same car with Warner and his players. The patriarch of American football said he was impressed by the Carlisle team, by Pop's offensive designs, and Jim's bold running. His one criticism was that their quarterback was too quick calling plays before studying the defense. As Gus Welch later told the story, Thorpe stood up for him by responding, "Mr. Camp, how can he study the defense when there isn't any defense?"

HOPES FOR AN undefeated season ended a week later, when Penn stunned Carlisle 34–26 in the annual rivalry game. The Indians made too many mistakes, fumbling and missing tackles. Warner blew up at Jim once when he seemed too nonchalant on the field, allowing a Penn player to slip behind him for a score. As Warner later described the scene: " 'Jim,' I said to him afterwards, 'couldn't you have intercepted that pass or knocked it down?' 'Certainly,' he answered, 'but I never thought he'd get under it.' " Thorpe was still the star of the game, breaking off an eighty-yard touchdown dash and piling up more than two hundred yards on the ground, but it was not enough. Army might have taken too much out of them, or maybe it was the pressure of going unbeaten for so long. But something more troubling bubbled below the surface. As brilliant a technician as Pop Warner was, his coaching demeanor was upsetting many of his players. Some openly despised him. Welch, the quarterback and a team leader, came to believe that Warner was a poor role model, an unprincipled huckster. The players saw him sell complimentary tickets in hotel lobbies and rake off the proceeds. They saw him bet on the games. Every day on the practice field he swore at them, called them *goddamn boneheads* and *sons of bitches.* Pop was a control freak losing control of his men.

Late in November, Warner took the squad to Massachusetts for a week. After defeating the Springfield YMCA Training School in an exhibition match, they set up training camp at the Leicester Inn near Worcester to prepare for a season-ending game against Brown on Thanksgiving Day. Thorpe made news in Worcester by announcing to the press that he was tired of the public limelight and intended to "drop out of the sporting world," as one account put it, the day after the Brown game. He might have been serious, or not, but it was a refrain that would become familiar for the rest of his long career. Every year or two, reliably, Jim would say he was going to chuck it all, and the press would blast out headlines about his imminent retirement, which never followed. His vacillation was understandable. The hoopla that surrounded the game made him uncomfortable, yet he loved to play.

Those sentiments overwhelmed him in the final game at Brown. "A feeling that is hard to describe came over me as I led my team out onto the soggy snow-laden field for the game which would be my last at Carlisle," he later wrote in "Red Son of Carlisle."

> Something cold, as cold as the biting particles of wind-blown snow and ice that filtered through the air, seemed to grip my heart. I was losing something I would never be able to regain. My body was bruised from the battering I had suffered in thirteen games through which I had been before walking onto the gridiron at Providence. But it didn't seem half as bruised as my heart while I stood poised to take the run for the kickoff. I felt as though I wanted to fling my arms about the field, the goal posts, and hold them tight, so that with their memories and traditions they might never escape me.

Jim captained his team to victory, 32–0, closing Carlisle's season with a 12-1-1 record. Walter Camp named him a first-team All-American for the second year in a row. From his two gold medals at the Olympics that summer to his brilliance on the football field that fall—where by the imprecise estimates of that era he scored more than twenty touchdowns and ran for nearly two thousand yards—it could be argued that Jim in 1912 had the single best athletic year in American history.

As much as he hated the spotlight, the spotlight unfailingly found him. He was always good copy for sportwriters, whether they were accurately reporting his deeds on the field, or turning them into myth, or looking for new ventures for the world's greatest all-around athlete. In the racist world of 1912, the rage among sportswriters was to find a Great White Hope to defeat heavyweight champion Jack Johnson, the dominant and fearless black boxer who had broken the race line to take the title. Robert Edgren, a syndicated columnist and sports editor of the *New York World,* dreamed up the idea of Thorpe as the answer, a Great Red Hope. "Wouldn't some searcher for a 'hope' like to get Jim Thorpe? Imagine what Jim would do if turned loose among the heavyweights?" Edgren wrote. "He is amazingly strong. He could fight a hundred rounds without breaking down, if necessary. This is shown by his phenomenal endurance in athletics, which enabled him to win both the pentathlon and decathlon at Stockholm. Moreover, Thorpe can take any amount of battering. He has never been 'laid out' in football [actually, he was, in the Army game], and there isn't a man in America more closely watched and eagerly attacked by all opposing players." Edgren tried to clinch his case by examining Thorpe's face. "You can see, unhidden by his massive chin and neck and the high cheek bones and keen eyes, unbounded good nature combined with unlimited courage and determination and aggressiveness."

Perhaps, to most of that, but the only sparring Jim Thorpe ever did was outside the ring.

In the final month of 1912, James E. Sullivan traveled the country expounding on the great success of American athletics that year, especially in Stockholm, boasting of how "Yankee speed, brawn, and endurance" was unsurpassed. He spoke of the sprinter Ralph Craig and the swimmer Duke Kahanamoku and the record-breaking American milers and pole vaulters and jumpers; then his speech would come around to the greatest athlete in the world. "It is difficult to properly estimate the relative importance of the new records," Sullivan said. "But one feat that seems to stand out at the head of the list is that of Jim Thorpe, the wonderful Carlisle Indian."

In the new year he would tell a different story.

11

Lo, the Poor Indian!

ROY RUGGLES JOHNSON WAS AT WORK AT THE *WORCESTER Telegram* on the Tuesday morning of January 21, 1913, when city editor Roland Friday approached his desk with a tip. As the county and country editor, Johnson was responsible for coordinating news coverage of the many Massachusetts towns and rural outposts in the paper's circulation area. One of those towns was Southbridge, southwest of Worcester near the Connecticut border, which was why Friday came to him.

He'd heard something that might develop into a good story, Friday told Johnson. The paper's baseball writer, Pat Dowd, had just been talking to Jesse Burkett, a former star big leaguer for the Cleveland Spiders who was now managing the Worcester Busters in the New England League. Dowd said that Burkett told him that Jim Thorpe, hero of the Stockholm Olympics, had once played minor league baseball.

Johnson quickly grasped the implication. That meant Thorpe was a professional, not an amateur, when he won his gold medals. "Looks like a pretty good story," he said, according to his later recollection. "Why doesn't Dowd write it?"

Friday explained how the tip arose. A man who'd once coached in North Carolina had dropped in to visit Burkett the other day and in the course of their conversation—two managers talking hot-stove ball in the offseason—casually mentioned that Thorpe had played for him, perhaps not realizing he was revealing "a whizzing story." As Dowd heard the account from Burkett and passed it along to Friday, the man's name was Carney, and he was staying with his sister in Southbridge. It could be gossip, the city editor said. It could be baloney like so many false claims concerning famous people. But best to check it out. Have your Southbridge correspondent snoop around and see what he can find.

Johnson realized that his Southbridge correspondent was inexperienced and "this story was too good and also too dangerous to trust to a novice." It was an assignment he had to take himself, a classic shoe-leather job in the January snow. He caught a streetcar on the old Worcester and Southbridge line for the fifteen-mile trip. First stop was the police department. *Heard of a guy named Carney?* he asked the police chief. No luck. Same with other town officials. He visited store after store in the business district. *Know a visitor named Carney, a baseball man staying with his sister?* Nobody had heard of him. He trudged out into the neighborhoods and started ringing doorbells. It was getting late and Johnson had not eaten since breakfast. Finally he talked to a man who ran a clothing store in town who said he didn't know anyone named *Carney* but there was a fellow named *Clancy* who fit that description—staying with his sister in a house off Elm Street. Johnson found the house off Elm Street. "I rang the bell and a man came to the door. I asked him if his name was Clancy and he said it was. I asked him if he managed a ball team and he said, 'Come in.' "

They sat down and talked baseball. They had a mutual friend, Pat Dowd, the *Telegram*'s sportswriter. Clancy said he managed in North Carolina in the summers and sometimes came north to Southbridge in the winters to stay with his sister. He talked about how he had visited with Jesse Burkett a few days earlier. What a ballplayer Burkett was back in the day! Twice for the Spiders in the 1890s he'd hit over .400. Johnson worked the conversation around to his key question: "Did Jim Thorpe the Indian ever play for you?"

Sure did, Clancy said, for better and worse. He told Johnson about how he'd played Thorpe as a pitcher and then at first base, that Jim's best quality as a baseball player was his speed on the bases, and that he had trouble hitting the curve. He said that Jim was lighter-complexioned than the Indians he knew, "showing the trace of Caucasian blood." Then he told a few stories about Thorpe's adventures off the field, including the time Jim "sauntered down the street with a jug" of liquor in one hand, and the time he dove through a restaurant window on a bet and "treated it like nothing more than a mosquito bite."

Johnson had his story. After fifteen minutes or so, he said thank you and good-bye and headed out into the snow for the streetcar to Worcester. Back at the office, he told the managing editor, Jim Estes, what he had. "Write it—and write it fast," Estes barked. As Johnson pecked away on his typewriter, Estes read over his shoulder, yanking copy page by page and slapping it into the hands of a copy editor, who wrote a headline that was "smeared all over the front page" the next morning: "THORPE WITH PROFESSIONAL BASEBALL TEAM SAYS CLANCY."

The first two paragraphs were set in bold type and boxed:

Southbridge, Jan. 21—That the great Jim Thorpe, the Sac and Fox Indian, world's amateur champion athlete, played professional baseball in the Carolina association for two years is the statement made by Charles Clancy, manager of the Winston-Salem team of the Carolina association, who is passing the winter in Southbridge.

The story then quoted Clancy:

"I signed Thorpe up as a pitcher. He would go along well for seven innings, perhaps, and then he would develop a lame arm. The arm would be all right next day. A few things of that sort decided me to switch him to first base, where he broke in pretty well. He was mighty fast on the bases. That was his best point. But all through his work on the Winston-Salem team he appeared to like a good time too well to ever become a successful player."

Note the team mentioned in that quote—Winston-Salem. Clancy in fact was the manager of a Winston-Salem team in the Carolina League when Johnson interviewed him in 1913, but when he managed Thorpe in 1910 they were in Fayetteville in the soon-to-be-defunct Eastern Carolina League. Johnson confused the two, a mistake others repeated after the story broke.

Word of the *Telegram* report spread up and down the East Coast, reaching Pop Warner at Carlisle, James E. Sullivan and the Amateur Athletic Union in New York, and sports desks at all the big-city newspapers along with the papers in North Carolina. Could it be that the great Jim Thorpe had broken Olympic rules and competed in Stockholm as an amateur when in fact he had been a professional? It was the biggest story in sports—and a question that produced a stream of obfuscations, misrepresentations, and feignings of innocence, along with valid debates about the meaning and future of amateurism. Jim was at the center of it all, his life and career on the line, yet in a sense he played a secondary role in the story; most of the lies and feignings of innocence involved officials trying to save their own reputations, not his.

In considering what happened over the ensuing weeks, it is important to remember the context. Unlike scores of other college athletes, Jim never tried to cover up his days in the Eastern Carolina League. He played for the Rocky Mount Railroaders and Fayetteville Highlanders in 1909 and 1910 under the name Jim Thorpe, not an alias. The preponderance of evidence indicated that he was recruited to play minor league baseball by close associates of Pop Warner. This was nothing new; Carlisle athletes had been playing summer ball for years and then returning to school to compete some more. If in the unlikely event Warner did not know what Jim was doing at first, it stretched common sense to think Thorpe failed to mention it when they went hunting together in the late fall of 1909 or during Jim's visit to Carlisle that Christmas season. Jim had no reason to hide anything at the time. He frequently talked to his teammates about his adventures in North Carolina after he returned to play at Carlisle in 1911 and 1912, again making it unlikely that Warner, who kept such close watch on his boys, did not hear about it. In the Character Book Jim filled out for his Carlisle friend Sylvester Long in spring 1912, he wrote that his most thrilling experience and his worst experience had both happened in North Carolina.

The evidence was equally strong that Moses Friedman knew. The Carlisle superintendent and his star athlete had been quarreling for years about Jim's status as a student. Jim did not slip off to Rocky Mount unnoticed: he specifically asked Friedman for a leave of absence from the school so he could play baseball. Friedman balked at first, but finally relented, fully aware that Jim was going south to play. Then Friedman tried to prevent Jim from returning to school in 1911 until Warner, in desperate need of his talent, prevailed and he was allowed to reenroll. The baseball program at Carlisle was dropped by Friedman and Warner in 1911 precisely because they were concerned that many of their athletes were being paid to play in the minors during the summer months.

Many others knew as well. At the Sac and Fox Agency in Oklahoma, W. C. Kohlenberg, representing the federal Indian bureau, had in his files documentation of Thorpe's professionalism—the letter Jim had sent him from Anadarko in the summer of 1911 asking for $35 of his royalty money that he needed after he was dropped from the local team because the manager "said I was expensive." That meant the manager at Anadarko knew, as did all Jim's teammates, and any team they played against. And in North Carolina, Clancy was just one of hundreds of people—players, managers, sportswriters, and attentive fans in Rocky Mount, Fayetteville, and the other cities in the league—who saw him play, wrote about him, and read about him. The *Charlotte Observer* knew. With a Fayetteville dateline, the largest newspaper in North Carolina published an article only three days after Jim's triumphant gold medal decathlon performance in Stockholm saying that "Jim Thorpe, who in the Olympic Games at Stockholm proved himself the greatest all-around athlete in the world, was once traded for Pete Boyle" when Boyle was playing in the Eastern Carolina League in 1910 under manager Charles Clancy. There was a general assumption in the Carolina baseball world that everyone knew Thorpe had played pro ball there, and an equal share of surprise when he was classified an amateur for the Olympics.

Then there was Warner's prominent friend on the Carlisle Athletic Association's advisory committee—none other than James E. Sullivan, the most powerful figure in amateur sports in America. As Carlisle's outside advisor, along with Walter Camp and a few other sports dignitaries, Sullivan had more familiarity with Warner's program than most officials, visiting Carlisle a few times a year. He would have known that the school's best football player and star trackman was gone for two years and then came back. And, given that he was the arbiter of what constituted amateurism in track and field, and the key voice in deciding which athletes would qualify for the Olympic team, it was curious that none of the stories from North Carolina crossed his desk and that he had no clue until the *Worcester Telegram* story broke.

All this—yet the story when it was published was considered a scoop, and the prevailing attitude was shock, concern, ignorance, denial.

The *Telegram* article reached Sullivan's desk the next morning. After reading it, he called in his secretary, Daniel Ferris, and dictated a letter to Superintendent Friedman at Carlisle telling him of the clipping from the New England newspaper and asking if it was accurate. There was no comment from Carlisle until the following day, when Warner denied the story with what he claimed was proof—a letter from Clancy denying particulars of what Johnson had written and a copy of an interview Clancy had provided to a Boston newspaper also refuting the *Telegram* story. In both letter and interview, Clancy chose his words carefully, walking a fine line of deception. "As a matter of fact and record Mr. Thorpe has never pitched a game for the Winston-Salem team or played any other position in that league," Clancy stated. "I have never paid Thorpe any money at any time for any purpose. The article in the Worcester paper is not founded on facts and was published without my authority."

It was true that Thorpe never pitched a game for Winston-Salem or played any other position in that league. Wrong team, wrong league. And Clancy was a manager, not an owner, so he would not have been the one to pay Thorpe. It was a lie built of small truths.

Warner and Sullivan, old friends with national reputations to protect, had a long telephone conversation on January 24. Later that day, Warner told the *New York Times* and other correspondents who had descended on Carlisle that Jim Thorpe was innocent. Charles Clancy had renounced the story, he said. In New York, Sullivan told the press about his conversation with Warner and how Warner had read him the letter from Clancy. "I don't believe there is any truth in the charges of professionalism against Thorpe," Sullivan said. "I have every confidence in his amateur status." The gossip in some pockets of the sports world at the time—a story that Warner helped propagate—was that the *Telegram* article was a put-up job by major league baseball scouts who wanted to force Thorpe into signing with a big league club. To that point Thorpe, at the center of the controversy, had not said a word in public.

JIM HAD RETURNED to Carlisle that January with his younger brother, Edward, at his side and the world in his hands. Winner of two gold medals, football All-American two years in a row, he was the best-known favorite son of Oklahoma (Will Rogers was still in the early traveling rope-trickster part of his career). He was an athletic icon, his name recognized throughout the world. He had spent the Christmas season and early January back in his home territory along the North Canadian, avoiding this newfound celebrity as much as possible. An article in the *Oklahoma Leader* said that he was being besieged with recruiting offers from vaudeville shows and various sports teams, not just in baseball but even the Toronto Tecumsehs in the National Hockey Association. That was mostly a publicity stunt—Jim had never played organized hockey, though he had proved a powerful and graceful skater on the creek at Carlisle. The story also said he was receiving about thirty letters a day from women who wanted to marry him. "Some girls must think I want to start a matrimonial bureau," the article quoted him as saying. Newspaper standards were loose in those days, when invented quotes were part of the culture. Maybe Thorpe said it, maybe not, but in any case his marriage ideas at that point were focused on one woman, Iva Miller, who was still in California, still under the watch of her concerned and domineering older brother Earl, though there were signs that, after Stockholm, Earl's opposition to Jim was weakening.

Jim had spent much of his time during that Christmas break hunting and fishing with his Sac and Fox pals and dreaming of becoming rich, and not through his athletic skills. There had been another rush of white men pouring into the old Indian Territory, much like when he was a young boy, but this time not for cultivating land but drilling far underneath. Oil had been discovered in central Oklahoma. The first gusher, Wheel No. 1, had been tapped in the Cushing-Drumright Field the previous March, not long after a man felicitously named Tom Slick discovered an oil seep on farmland east of Cushing. Now Cushing, Drumright, and Yale were boomtowns. Roughnecks, derrickmen, and wildcatters rode in daily on the Eastern Oklahoma and MK&T railway lines, filling rooming houses that struggled to keep pace with the exploding population. The overflow found quarters in boxcars and a tent community known as Ragtown. Dusty main streets popped with dance halls, gambling dens, and houses of prostitution. Could the oilfields stretch from Cushing toward the Thorpe allotments about twenty miles south near Prague and Bellemont? It was possible, Jim had thought, and so did a local newspaper correspondent who wrote that Thorpe "may yet become an oil king, or the Rockefeller among the Red Men."

No such luck. And now, after the *Worcester Telegram* story broke, no luck at all.

There was something curious in Pop Warner's account of events after his friend Sullivan inquired about the story. Jim had returned from Oklahoma by then and was at Carlisle. But before citing Clancy's letter to refute the story, did Pop ask Jim if it was true? In Warner's own autobiography, he later wrote: "After hearing the accusations I went to see Jim and asked him if the story was accurate. Without hesitation he told me, 'Yes, Pop. It's true.'" That means that either Warner did not ask Thorpe before denying the accuracy of the story to Sullivan and the press, or that he already knew the truth and was lying when he issued the denial. Given all the evidence establishing that Warner knew what Jim had done from the time his star player left for Rocky Mount, it is probable that he saw no need to ask Jim about it right away and was lying, trying to buy time to figure out what to do next.

By Thorpe's later account, he spent "two days and nights" deliberating how he should respond to the stories. "All my life I have laid cards face up on the table, but this was the biggest ordeal I had confronted up to that time," he recalled. He said he took long walks away from the hillside campus into the wintry Cumberland Valley countryside retracing the paths he had followed to train for the medals he was now in danger of losing. "Finally, I decided to write with cards up again and the decision lifted, as magic, a great load from my mind and shoulders."

By then, Clancy's second-day denial was disintegrating, and Warner's denial with it, as stories emerged from North Carolina quoting ballplayers who remembered playing with and against Thorpe in the Eastern Carolina League. Sam T. Mallison, the cub reporter who had been assigned to glorify the Indian Jim Thorpe's arrival in Rocky Mount in June 1909, said that "the Western Union office in Rocky Mount was inundated by telegrams from newspapers all over the country—Boston, New York, Philadelphia, Washington, Chicago, Cleveland, Detroit, San Francisco—asking that an unlimited number of words be filed with all possible speed giving details and colorful anecdotes of Thorpe's performance in the Eastern Carolina League." The telegrams reached Mallison at his desk in the *Record*'s second-floor office on Sunset Street. He had notebooks full of stories and anecdotes about Thorpe, he said. And "since the newspapers paid by the inch and since my exchequer was in its usual state of complete exhaustion, I gave them both barrels, around two full columns."

Thorpe had already decided to acknowledge his minor league past. The question now was how the school and Sullivan would handle it. If Warner and Friedman were to admit they knew about Jim's baseball days all along, it would harm their reputations if not cost them their jobs. Sullivan, whose entire career was built on his glorification of amateurism, would suffer even more if it came out that he also should have known or might have known. It was left for Jim to take the fall. He wrote a letter of confession to Sullivan. Or more accurately, according to Thorpe's roommate and close friend Gus Welch, Jim rewrote in his own hand a letter drafted by Warner as a means for the coach to absolve himself and place the entire onus on his player.

• • •

THE LETTER WAS addressed to James E. Sullivan, secretary of the Amateur Athletic Union, January 26, 1913. It was a piece of writing that reflected the thoughts and needs of Warner through the filter of Jim's life, and above Jim's signature:

Dear Mr. Sullivan,

When the interview with Mr. Clancy stating that I had played baseball on the Winston-Salem team was shown me I told Mr. Warner that it was not true, and in fact I did not play on that team. But so much has been said in the papers since then that I went to the school authorities this morning and told them just what there was in the stories.

This opening paragraph contradicted what Warner himself wrote later in his autobiography about how Thorpe acknowledged the truth as soon as the coach asked him. It also reinforced Warner's excuse for his initial denial—the *Telegram* story's mistake about Winston-Salem versus Rocky Mount.

I played baseball at Rocky Mount and at Fayetteville, N.C., in the summers of 1909 and 1910, under my own name. On the same team I played with were several college men from the North, who were earning money by ball playing during their vacations and who were regarded as amateurs at home. I did not play for the money there was in it, because my property brings me in enough money to live on, but because I liked to play ball. I was not very wise in the ways of the world and did not realize this was wrong, and it would make me a professional in track sports, although I learned from the other players that it would be better for me not to let any one know that I was playing, and for that reason I never told any one at school about it until today.

Here was a paragraph wending a downhill course from truth to stereotype to lie. Thorpe did play under his own name. There were many college players from the north on those teams who were being paid and played under aliases. Jim did play mostly because he loved the sport, but he also needed and wanted the money. Thirty bucks a week and free room and board might not have seemed like much, but it was the going rate in the lower minors then and more than enough to live on. His Oklahoma property did bring in some money, but it was neither prompt nor sufficient; he constantly had to beseech the Sac and Fox Agency in Stroud to send him small checks, and it was at the discretion of the federal agents whether to comply. The statement that he was not very wise in the ways of the world served as the introduction to the naïve Indian argument that would be made more explicitly in the next paragraph—the most egregious examples of Warner using a poor-Indian condescension in drafting the confession that placed Jim at the mercy of the court. The final sentence was an outright lie that made it even more apparent this was Pop, not Jim, making the case. To repeat, far from keeping his North Carolina days secret at Carlisle, he talked about them frequently.

> *In the fall of 1911 I applied for readmittance to this school and came back to continue my studies and take part in the school sports, and of course I wanted to get on the Olympic team and take the trip to Stockholm. I had Mr. Warner send in my application for registering in the AAU after I had answered the questions and signed it, and I received my card allowing me to compete in the winter meets and other track sports. I never realized until now what a big mistake I made by keeping it a secret about my ball playing and I am sorry I did so. I hope I will be partly excused by the fact that I was simply an Indian school boy and did not know all about such things. In fact, I did not know that I was doing wrong, because I was doing what I knew several other college men had done, except that they did not use their own names.*
>
> *I have always liked sport and only played or run races for the fun of the thing and never to earn money. I have received offers amounting to thousands of dollars since my victories last summer, but I have turned them all down because I did not care to make money from my athletic skill. I am*

very sorry, Mr. Sullivan, to have it all spoiled in this way and I hope the Amateur Athletic Union and the people will not be too hard in judging me. Yours truly

JAMES THORPE

The first sentence in this closing section had all the signs of being written by the coach, not the player. Jim did not think of himself as applying for readmittance but as being recruited by his teammates and Pop to come back. His studies were secondary to playing football, training for the Olympics, and further making an athletic name for himself in anticipation of a professional future. That he loved to play sports was true, but it did not mean that he did not want to make money playing. That was a nicety promoted mostly by upper-class sportsmen who felt no need to monetize their athletic skills. Most baseball players rose from the working class and played for both love and money. It was Warner himself who had quoted Jim a year earlier saying he was tired of playing for free and wanted to earn some money, and it was Warner who persuaded Jim to play one more year by saying another year of football would increase his fame and financial prospects. It seemed quite likely that Jim did not realize the consequences of his ball playing, especially given how common it was for college players to slip off to summer ball and then resume their amateur careers. It was notable that he was labeled *simply an Indian school boy* while the others were called *college men.* Jim was by now almost twenty-six—older than most collegians.

That full phrase—*I was simply an Indian school boy and did not know all about such things*—was the most telling part of the letter, and the most controversial. Native American scholars parsing it later could not help but focus on the emasculating resonance of those words, the stereotype of the poor Indian who was to be glorified and pitied at the same time, an instinctive creature who could not be held responsible for his ignorance. But this was not Jim's concession of Indian inferiority. It was Warner talking, not Thorpe, drawing on a way of thinking about Indians that was deeply ingrained in the white American culture of the early twentieth century.

One of the most common newspaper tropes of that period was to symbolize the plight of American Indians through a stanza in a poem written by Alexander Pope in 1734.

Lo, the poor Indian, whose untutor'd mind
Sees God in clouds, or hears him in the wind

What the British poet was evoking in those lines, the Indian's affinity for the natural world, was immaterial to the way it was reconfigured centuries later in the American press. In its revised popular usage, all but the first four words were dropped, and it came with an exclamation point at the end—*Lo, the poor Indian!* It became an all-purpose phrase. Feeling sorry for him? *Lo, the poor Indian!* Underestimating him? *Lo, the poor Indian!* Did the team you cover lose on the football field to Carlisle? *Lo, the poor Indian!* Did we whites steal their land? *Lo, the poor Indian!* What did L. C. Davis of the *St. Louis Post-Dispatch* think of what was happening to Jim? *"And now on his frame they're beginning to pile / Lo, the poor Injun, Jim Thorpe of Carlisle! / He played 'summer ball'!, well, if that were a crime / Full many an athlete would be doing time."* The phrase was so well-worn that at times a sportswriter could condense it to just *Lo!*—and readers would get the reference. The phrase had been applied to Carlisle and to Jim a few times before the medal controversy broke, but now it would follow him for the rest of his life. Whatever happened to him, good or bad, he was thought of as the embodiment of *Lo, the poor Indian!*

Along with the letter signed by Thorpe, Sullivan received a companion statement from Superintendent Friedman asserting that he knew nothing until Thorpe's confession, closing ranks with Warner. From the opening *My Dear Sir* to the closing *Very respectfully,* Friedman's letter dripped with feigned propriety.

Immediately upon hearing of the newspaper charges made against James Thorpe, a Sac and Fox Indian student of this school, to the effect that he played professional baseball previous to the Olympic Games last

July, the school authorities instituted a thorough investigation. I have just learned that Thorpe acknowledges having played with a Southern professional baseball team. It is with profound regret that this information is conveyed to you, and I hasten to assure your committee that the faculty of the school and the athletic director were without any knowledge of this fact until today. As this invalidates Thorpe's amateur standing at the time of the games in Stockholm, the trophies which are held here are subject to your disposition. Please inform me of your desires in the matter. It is a most unpleasant affair and has brought gloom on the entire institution.

The deal was done. Thorpe was cut loose as Warner and Friedman saved themselves.

The next day, January 27, after a hearing of the AAU's executive committee in New York, Sullivan wrote a letter to the Swedish Olympic Committee explaining the situation. The point of the letter, signed by Sullivan and officials at the Amateur Athletic Union and American Olympic Committee, was to apologize for allowing Thorpe to compete in the Stockholm games and to state that the AAU would do "everything in its power to secure the return of the prizes and the readjustment of points won by him, and will immediately eliminate his records from the books." So much for any hope of mercy, at least for Thorpe. The Sullivan letter was as manipulative and condescending as the confession Warner had drafted. Jim was the fall guy, again, and the poor Indian, again, and all officials were absolved.

The letter had nothing but praise for Pop Warner: "Mr. Glenn Warner, formerly of Cornell, a man whose reputation is of the highest and whose accuracy of statement has never been doubted." Why mention Cornell unless to imply that connection made him more credible than if his only attachment was to an Indian school?

It directed blame at the baseball people in North Carolina who unpatriotically failed to warn the world: "It seems strange that men having a knowledge of Mr. Thorpe's professional conduct did not at such time for the honor of their country come forward and place in the hands of the American Olympic Committee such information as they had."

It blamed the geography and population of the United States: "This country is of such tremendous territorial expanse and the athletes taking part therein are so numerous that it is sometimes extremely difficult to ascertain the history of an athlete's past." Perhaps, but this all happened on the East Coast, and as a member of the Carlisle Athletic Association board of advisors Sullivan himself should not have found it difficult to ascertain the history of Jim Thorpe's past.

It blamed baseball and the obscurity of the Eastern Carolina League—and even Thorpe's surname: "Thorpe's act of professionalism was in a sport over which the AAU has no direct control; it was as a member of a baseball team in a minor league and in games which were not reported in the major papers of the country. That he played under his own name would give no direct notice to any one concern as there are many of his name."

And then came the *Lo, the poor Indian* section: "The reason why he himself did not give notice of his acts is explained by him on the ground of ignorance. In some justification of his position, it should be noted that Mr. Thorpe is an Indian of limited experience and education in the way of other than his own people." A statement at once ignorant of Carlisle's mission and of Jim's life.

The first response from Swedish authorities was sympathy for Thorpe, and sorry-too-late for the rest. The *New York Times* correspondent in Stockholm, filing by Marconi transatlantic wireless telegraph on January 29, wrote that Thorpe's "disqualification awakened a unanimous sympathy for him here. All the men who took leading parts in the games think it impossible to take back the prizes he won." The reason? The rules of the Stockholm games "clearly prescribed that all protests against contestants on the grounds of professionalism must be filed within thirty days of the prizes." The *Times* correspondent was following a similar report that day in *Dagens Nyheter*, the largest daily in Stockholm, that put it this way: "A rule has now been inserted in the contest regulations which is of great importance in the case. The athletic organizations of the respective countries guarantee, its says, that the athletes who are registered for the events meet the requirements of the amateur rules; but in addition they also establish rules that reports against a contestant's amateur status shall, in order that they can be taken up, be sent to the Swedish Organizing Committee not later than one month from the windup of the Games."

By the end of January, 180 days had passed. According to the Swedes, this was all too late. If the Americans wanted to ignore the rule and have the prizes and medals recalled, they had to make that request to the International Olympic Committee in Lausanne, Switzerland.

But the trophies—that grand bronze pentathlon bust and silver decathlon Viking ship—had already been moved from the display case at Carlisle and had arrived at Sullivan's office on Warren Street in New York, where arrangements were being made by the transport company Davies Turner for them to be shipped to Sweden aboard the SS *New York* of the American Line on its next voyage across the Atlantic, leaving the following day. The decathlon medal was to be given to the Swede who'd finished second, Hugo Wieslander, who said that Jim Thorpe won it, not him, and that he neither deserved it nor wanted to accept it.

THORPE HAD LOST his trophies and soon would be stripped of his medals, his records erased from Olympic history, but the story reverberated for days, weeks, months, years, decades through the athletic world. While some sportswriters said stripping Thorpe of his medals was the proper course of action, the vast majority either expressed sympathy for him or denounced the hypocrisy of supposed amateurism.

Here was columnist Herbert Slater writing in the *Oakland Tribune*: "Was it an unpardonable offense for Thorpe to compete in the Olympic Games when he had accepted a few nickels for performing on a baseball field? Sullivan says it was. About 99 percent of the people not only in America but the world say no."

Here was a columnist writing in the *Daily Mail* of London: "If America really wants to know the true British feeling toward Thorpe, I think I can reduce the frenzied pace of Sullivan's outraged pulse. Is the secretary of the AAU satisfied that Thorpe ran straight and won straight when he carried off the decathlon and pentathlon prizes? If so Britain thinks none the worse of the Indian because of his baseball crime. Moreover, Britain thinks Thorpe's victory was above board even if Sullivan does not."

Here was Vilhelm Salchow writing in *Dagens Nyheter*: "What a scandal for the USA! To think that Thorpe is not an honest-to-goodness amateur! I am fed up with that eternal squabble about amateurism." After citing examples of athletes from many countries who in various ways were compensated for their skills, Salchow concluded: "I don't want to waste more words on this ridiculous business. *Praeterea censeo*; Let in all fairness sport remain what it mainly is: professional!"

As Leif Yttergren, an Olympic historian based in Stockholm, later pointed out, the Swedes themselves were no innocents. Six months before the opening of the 1912 games, the organizing committee in Sweden, hoping for a strong performance from the host nation, asked all employers to grant Swedish athletes leaves of absence, and the athletes "as a rule were compensated for the loss of income" by the committee. "The financial compensation must have been a violation of the amateur regulations and of a considerably more serious nature than the breach of the amateur regulations that Jim was disqualified for after the games," Yttergren noted.

The same could be said of all athletes who trained while in the employ of their country, including soldiers like Lieutenant George S. Patton of the United States team. Compare Thorpe and Patton. Thorpe was paid a minimal salary to play minor league baseball under his real name, not a pseudonym, for two summers in North Carolina, a sport that had nothing to do with his abilities in track and field. Patton was on the government payroll when he refined his skills in pistol shooting and steeplechase riding—and then used opium to enhance his performance during the games. Which man should be punished for what he did?

Here was Colonel William T. Chatland, the assistant attorney general of the United States, a former athlete at the University of Iowa, quoted in the *Pittsburgh Press*: "Why it's perfectly ridiculous to think that Jim Thorpe is the only man guilty of accepting an emolument in lieu of services rendered during his college career. Any person at all familiar with the situation today knows beyond any doubt that in nearly every amateur athletic association or club in the country is a system of proselytizing going on all the while, and that each and all of these organizations are offering to prominent athletes what is known as a 'better inducement.' Is the accepting of this inducement any better than what Thorpe did?"

Chatland's point bore deep into the diseased body of college athletics and offered another way of looking at Pop Warner's hypocrisy. The line between amateur and professional did not just involve athletes who played college football while also getting paid to play baseball in the summer. Football players often were also paid at school, including at Carlisle. Pop kept a ledger of funds he handed out to his boys over the years, often hundreds of dollars each, along with free clothing he had arranged for them at a haberdasher in town, practices that were common among big football programs then and always. The notion that payments of that sort disqualified any of those college players from Olympic or AAU competition was rarely considered.

The *Sporting News*, the bible of baseball, noted how easy it would have been for officials to check on Thorpe's amateur status beforehand: "It is no trouble to find Mr. Thorpe in spite of the protestations of ignorance and innocence on the part of amateur authorities. Turning to the T's in *The Sporting News* record, we find this card: Thorpe, James, Nationality Indian, Rocky Mount, 1909–1910 released July 1910 to Fayetteville. No record 1911. Under head of 'Remarks' there is a notation that Thorpe is a student at the Carlisle Indian School and holds title as all-around champion athlete." There was no love lost between the *Sporting News* and Pop Warner, who before the Thorpe story broke had disparaged organized baseball for making "bums" out of young men. Here was the publication's chance to fire back. Warner must have known, the paper said—"It was his business to know as one in charge of the government's Indian wards." Another editorial called Warner and company "a bunch of inconsistent fakirs" and said it was time for the arbiters of amateurism to allow college boys to play baseball in the summer. "It will permit college boys otherwise honest to come out in the open and play the game, not as they have been doing, under assumed names, but as a calling of which they need not be ashamed."

Thorpe emerged from the ordeal toughened but not ashamed. "While my castle fell about me, the American people, the student body of Carlisle, and my girl remained loyal," he wrote later. "I could ask for little more. Once I had made up my mind to face the world with the truth, I was no longer nervous or worried about the matter. I adopted a fatalistic viewpoint and considered the episode just another event in the red man's life of ups and downs."

12

Among the Giants

POP WARNER AND HIS CONTACTS IN MAJOR LEAGUE BASEball wasted no time. On January 31, 1913, the same day the bronze bust and silver chalice were loaded aboard the SS *New York* for their return to Stockholm, front offices of five major league teams sent representatives to Carlisle or were talking to Pop on the phone with the goal of signing his fallen star. If the amateurs wanted to erase Jim Thorpe, the professionals were eager to embrace him, and to do so they had to go through the Carlisle coach, who declared that Jim would sign with the highest bidder. Pop was working it both ways, cleansing himself of any guilty foreknowledge of Thorpe's playing for pay in the minors while at the same time looking out for his future in the big leagues. Their relationship was complicated but bound together by mutual need.

Pittsburgh had been recruiting Thorpe for months and the team's Pennsylvania scout was certain Jim had promised he would give the Pirates first consideration. The president of the Cincinnati club, August Herrmann—of whom Damon Runyon once wrote "his nose was bulbous, his complexion at all times as red as the sunset"—thought he had a "tacit understanding" that Thorpe would sign with the Reds. The Chicago White Sox and St. Louis Browns were also in pursuit. All had a chance, but then Warner arranged a call with John McGraw, manager of the New York Giants. McGraw and Warner were old friends, Jim liked New York City, and the Giants were the dominant team in the National League. "I got Thorpe on the long-distance telephone in Carlisle and he accepted my offer," McGraw recalled. It was not quite that simple.

First Thorpe told the Pirates that he would stand by his earlier word to consider Pittsburgh first. But owner Barney Dreyfuss, skeptical of Jim's baseball skills, gave him a weak offer, no more than a forty-five-day probationary contract. As Dreyfuss told the story, he was so impressed by Thorpe's integrity in keeping the earlier promise that he decided he could not in good conscience prevent Jim from getting a better deal. It might have been an effort by Dreyfuss to save face, or he might not have wanted Jim in the first place, but in either case his statement accentuated Thorpe's sense of honor at a time when it was being questioned. With the Pirates out of the way, Thorpe and Warner made a counteroffer to McGraw, who accepted it, raising the price to a salary of more than $5,000, with a bonus. There was speculation, never documented, that a finder's fee for Warner was also part of the deal. Late that night, a telegram reached the Giants confirming the verbal acceptance along with news that Warner and Thorpe would come to New York the next day for the formal signing.

The business office of the New York Baseball Club in the Fifth Avenue Building was the place to be on the afternoon of February 1. Sportswriters, photographers, newsreel cameramen, and Giants fans crammed into the room hours ahead of time awaiting the three o'clock event. One scribe said he had not seen such anticipation since Jack Johnson and Jim Jeffries, the so-called Great White Hope, huddled in the back room of a restaurant in Hoboken, New Jersey, to ink the contract for their world heavyweight boxing match in 1910. When Warner and Thorpe arrived, they eased through the crowd for a private huddle with McGraw before the public display. Jim was nattily dressed for the special occasion in a blue Norfolk jacket and purple fedora. McGraw knew Jim only by reputation. He had never seen him play baseball. Warner reassured him that Thorpe was a good teammate and had a knack for observing others do something on the track or playing field and then performing the same act "just a little bit better."

After the backroom meeting, the pact was consecrated with a staged signing ceremony as photographers posed Jim at various angles with pen in hand, McGraw smiling at his side. Jim was reluctant to say much about his previous experience as a pro. "That is something I don't want to talk about. The sooner it is dropped the better. I want to forget it all," he said when asked about his days in Rocky Mount. As cameras clicked, a Giants official asked Thorpe what his Indian name was. Jim paused, then said, "Drags-his-ropes." *C'mon, really.* But Jim kept the ruse going, gently mocking the question. No mention of his Sac and Fox birth name, *Wa-tho-Huk*, or Path Lit by Lightning. "Drags-his-ropes," he repeated, smiling. Not that he could control the way the press would play on his Indianness. The sober *New York Times* could not resist calling him "Chief Thorpe," while noting that in appearance despite "his swarthy face" there was "little about Indian Thorpe to suggest the redman of the forest. He looked more like a big college student who had just stepped out of a Broadway toggery shop."

The pressing question was whether Thorpe could make it as a major leaguer. McGraw expressed optimism based on Jim's physique and all-around skills, especially under the manager's expert tutelage. "He is a big, strong, clean-cut fellow and I think I can make a ballplayer out of him," McGraw said. "I know one thing, anyway: I've started with much rougher material than Thorpe and developed some stars. I can tell more about him when I see him on the diamond, but from all I can see now I think he has the makings of a good ballplayer." As the *New-York Tribune* put it, by signing with the Giants Thorpe had "graduated from the Glenn Warner school and matriculated into McGraw college."

Some were not convinced. "Thorpe a Joke on Ball Field," blared a headline in the *Boston Globe* the next morning. Five athletes who'd played against Thorpe in the Eastern Carolina League asserted that he was nothing more than a "fair minor league pitcher, a poor hitter and a worse fielder, and that his only asset was speed on the bases, which availed little as he seldom got on the bags." By giving him a "fancy" salary—and five grand was considered generous in that era for a player signed out of school—the Giants would end up feeling badly burned, the players said. A writer on the *Brooklyn Daily Eagle* was not expecting magic from Thorpe or wizardry from McGraw: "If he should prove a fizzle in the major leagues, Jim Thorpe will not be the first phenom who shriveled when he became a Giant."

Another reason for McGraw's gambit soon became apparent. Hours after meeting with Warner and Thorpe, McGraw had a final discussion with Ted Sullivan, personal agent for Charles Comiskey, owner of the Chicago White Sox, and finalized plans for the Giants and White Sox to embark on a world tour together at the end of the 1913 season. The idea of the tour had been hatched in December when McGraw was in Chicago as part of his offseason vaudeville routine, talking baseball onstage and taking questions from the audience for a thousand dollars a week. While there he met with Comiskey in the back room of Smiley Corbett's bar on Chicago's East Side. Here were the most colorful and controversial bosses in baseball. Two Irishmen. McGraw, a five-foot-six rooster as crafty and manipulative as his nicknames, the Little Napoleon and Muggsy. Comiskey, a portly and miserly owner known as the Old Roman and Commy. Each had been scheming separately to take his team around the globe. After meeting, they concluded it would be smart to make it a package deal with teams from America's two largest cities.

Now, on the same Sunday morning of February 2 that newspapers heralded McGraw's signing of the famous Jim Thorpe, companion articles announced that the Giants and White Sox would tour the world. This was no coincidence; the events were intertwined. McGraw and Comiskey were famous in the United States, as were their great players like Rube Marquard and Christy Mathewson and young Buck Weaver, but no one in Japan or China or Italy or England had heard of them. There was only one player who would be recognized wherever the White Sox and Giants went and prove to be a gate attraction for the entire trip around the world—the untested Giants rookie Jim Thorpe.

THERE WAS NO Grapefruit League in major league baseball then. Spring training was a movable feast, with teams relocating from one southern city to the next. Only one of eight National League teams, the Chicago Cubs, trained in Florida in 1913, and this was their first year in Tampa. Three teams warmed in Georgia—the Boston Braves in Athens, the Brooklyn Dodgers in Augusta, and the St. Louis Cardinals in Columbus. The Philadelphia Phillies set up camp in Southern Pines, North Carolina; the Pittsburgh Pirates were in Hot Springs, Arkansas, where the concept of spring training began in 1886; and the Cincinnati Reds trained in Mobile, Alabama. McGraw's Giants were hundreds of miles apart from the rest, in the hot-mineral-water resort of Marlin Springs, Texas, halfway between Dallas and Houston.

McGraw and crew traveled to Texas by train from New York, with several stops along the way, the longest in St. Louis, where players from other parts of the country assembled for the team's first roll call at the Planter's House Hotel. The Little Napoleon was flush with power granted him by Giants owner Harry Hempstead. He had just signed a five-year contract extension with a yearly salary of $20,000 and full control of his club. He was fully committed to baseball now, he said, after selling a billiard hall in New York and dropping his vaudeville routine. Although many had expected his newest recruit to board the train in Harrisburg, there was no sighting of Jim there, and he was not at the Planter's House either. What had happened? Speculation popped in the press that Thorpe was having second thoughts about baseball and had been enticed by promoters to become part of a traveling athletic show with wrestler Frank Gotch and boxer Luther McCarty. But rumors always hovered around him, and like most this one was bogus. Jim caught up with the train for the final leg from Arkansas to Texas.

Baseball fans and sportswriters greeted the train at station stops to grill McGraw about the team's prospects and seek a glimpse of the ballplayers. In Texarkana, some townsfolk demanded to see the player who "muffed the ball." That was a reference to Fred Snodgrass, the Giants centerfielder who had dropped a fly ball in the tenth inning of the decisive last game of the 1912 World Series against the Boston Red Sox, a play that became infamous as "the Snodgrass muff." "One of them had a lariat in his hand," reported the *Sporting News* about the inquiring fans. "But that might not have meant anything as lots of persons out here own a lariat. Perhaps it was just as well that Snodgrass wasn't along." At another stop a sheriff boarded the train and asked to see Thorpe. His teammates were leery of the request, wondering whether Jim was in trouble, and kept quiet, though it turned out the man just wanted to shake Jim's hand.

Team headquarters in Marlin Springs was at the Arlington Hotel, a spacious resort of red brick and white stone with its own billiard hall, reading room, barbershop, and underground passageway to the sanitarium bathhouse next door. The ballpark was two and half miles away, a trek the players made by foot every morning as part of McGraw's training regimen. Thorpe was assigned a room with the other Native American on the team, John Meyers, a good-hitting catcher who came out of the Cahuilla nation in California. In the baseball world, inevitably, he was known as Chief Meyers. An Associated Press account announcing that the two could be roommates overflowed with racial stereotypes, jocularly treating them like uncultured savages. "When John Tortes Meyers and James Thorpe meet in the Giants training camp there may be a clash between the tribe as to which will be entitled to the rank of chief of the clan of two, but nobody anticipates a scalp dance that is always preliminary to the digging up of the tomahawk. On the contrary, both Indians will bunk under the same tepee while here and be inseparable roommates when under the roofs of the white man's skyscraping hotels." Another paragraph in that same report was worse, reflecting a deeper strain of racism against black citizens. "Rain here today," it began. "Murphy [the groundskeeper] took a bunch of darkies out to Emerson Park yesterday when the weather looked a wee bit promising to drain the field. . . ." A reminder that unlike Native Americans, the only way African Americans could get on the ballfield was to tend the grounds.

Oscar Colquitt, the Texas governor, played hooky from his duties in Austin to take in the first day of Giants spring training. McGraw had two of his players, Larry Doyle and Harry McCormick, choose up sides for an exhibition game, and the governor, known as Little Oscar by his critics in the state legislature, threw out the first pitch, which got decent reviews from the New York press corps—"not one of those ladylike thrusts so common among the public officials." Doyle chose Thorpe for his team and played him at first base. Even the veterans stopped to watch Jim warm up. He was a curiosity, the main attraction in camp. At one point McGraw sidled up to Christy Mathewson and asked, "What do you think of him, Matty?" Looks like he has the natural ability, Mathewson responded, and the manager agreed. No regrets about signing him.

Mathewson—the Big Six—was the team's immortal, a brilliant veteran pitcher who had won at least twenty games each of the previous ten years and four times had won more than thirty, always with an earned run average under 3.00 and five times under 2.00. In 1905, he had led the Giants to the championship by pitching three shutouts within a six-day span in the World Series against the Philadelphia Athletics. Like many star athletes based in New York, he had his own newspaper column, or at least one written under his name. His ghost was John Neville Wheeler, who wrote for the *New-York Tribune* and the McClure Newspaper Syndicate and defined his job as "using other men's brains." With Mathewson's sharp insights as material, Wheeler had written his *Pitching in a Pinch*—an insider account of what it was like to pitch in the big leagues (and a book that later would be praised by none other than Thorpe's business teacher at Carlisle, the poet and intense baseball fan Marianne Moore). In Marlin Springs, he quickly set his sights on Thorpe.

"Well, I have had my first look at Jim Thorpe, the great Indian athlete, and he has impressed me favorably," Wheeler wrote under the Mathewson byline after the first ten days of practice. "I think he will make it as a big league ball player. McGraw has also been impressed by the Indian and is devoting a great deal of his time in watching him work and giving him tips." The column said that Thorpe seemed anxious to make good. "The first day that the boys were out on the field . . . he was throwing the ball around as if it were midseason. McGraw warned him about this. 'Be careful old boy, you may want to use that wing next week,' McGraw said. Thorpe responded, 'But I am in condition.' "

The Mathewson column described Jim as "big and wonderfully fast for his size—the fastest big man I ever saw, I think." He seemed humble and eager to learn. "He strikes me as being a typical Indian as I have always pictured the race in my mind," Mathewson told Wheeler. "He sits silent most of the time but by the keenness of his eyes you can tell that he is taking in every word that is being said." One advantage Thorpe had over other raw recruits, Mathewson thought, was that he already had experience playing before large crowds. What position McGraw would play him was still to be determined. "Thorpe handles himself pretty well in the outfield and his great speed should make him a valuable gardener, but it is still a question whether he would hit hard enough to be able to hold down that berth."

A few days later, the first picture of Thorpe in the violet-striped Giants uniform ran in the *Sporting News* under the caption: "THORPE IN GIANT WAR PAINT." His work in camp, the accompanying story said, was helping to dispel the notion that Jim would only be a "circus card" for the New York team. But there was more to baseball than that.

The essence of Jim Thorpe the athlete was that he could do it all. In football, he could run, block, throw, tackle, punt, and place-kick. In track and field, he could run fast, jump high or far, clear hurdles, put the shot, and hurl the discuss. He was great at everything from ballroom dancing to marbles, and there seemed an ease to him in most everything he did. Baseball was different. Being a natural athlete did not translate into being a natural ballplayer. The baseball writers came to Marlin Springs inclined to praise him, aware that the name Thorpe attracted readers; yet they also saw a rawness in his play during intrasquad games. On the afternoon of March 11, they watched in awe as he smacked a home run off Mathewson that sailed over the deep left-field fence and bounced onto a tennis court, eliciting a declaration from McGraw that they had all just witnessed "the longest hit in the world." Yet a few innings later they saw Jim make "a large fat muff" of a fly ball in the outfield. It was like that day after day, though long hits were less frequent than awkward swings and misses at curveballs.

As spring training neared an end, Jim and the Giants faced another problem from his bush league days. McGraw had scheduled two games against the Texas League team in Beaumont, but decided not to bring Thorpe, afraid "they might enjoin or even kidnap the Redskin and hold him for ransom." Beaumont management asserted that Jim belonged to them. It was a tenuous claim that went back to the brief period in 1911 when Jim played minor league ball in Oklahoma. According to Beaumont, it obtained Thorpe's contract from a financially desperate Oklahoma City team, which in turn had picked it up from Anadarko. Jim never played for Oklahoma City or Beaumont, and no one had mentioned any of this until now that he was a gate attraction as the greatest athlete in the world. When Sam Crane, a New York sportswriter and McGraw's close pal, heard about the claim, he asked Beaumont's manager what he wanted. "Six thousand iron men in cash and I want it quick," came the reply.

Beaumont "had about as much chance of collecting money on Thorpe as from the defunct Louisiana Lottery," Crane wrote. He was right, but just to be sure nothing funny happened, McGraw left Jim behind when he took the Giants to Beaumont.

Mathewson was not the only Giant with a syndicated newspaper column. McGraw also had one; his ghostwriter was Harry Cross, a Harvard man who worked for the *New York Times.* After setting the squad he would take north with him, McGraw, writing through Cross's typewriter, belittled members of the New York press corps for reporting that he was using Thorpe to sell tickets while privately believing he was not a major leaguer.

"I see they are panning me for keeping Indian Jim Thorpe," the column began. "Nobody has the authority for saying that Thorpe would be released at any time to anybody. And that is no April Fool's joke either." While acknowledging that Thorpe still had "a lot to learn about baseball," the column argued that so did most young players. Listing several of his established players, McGraw added: "Suppose I had cut Marquard loose after he failed me the first season? Suppose I had sent Hartley and Wilson back to the minors because I had no place for them the first year? Suppose I had canned Larry Doyle when he started off so badly in 1908? How about Merkle and Murray? Did Josh Devore look like a big leaguer his first year? Tesreau was of no use to me in 1911. . . . The hot stove leaguers are not giving me any orders. When I feel that I am incapable of looking after the Giants I will resign, but as long as I am here, I'll be the boss."

The Little Napoleon, indeed. McGraw, then eleven seasons into his reign in New York, would manage the Giants another twenty-two seasons.

THE 1913 SEASON was a frustrating one for Jim. The star gate attraction became the rookie ghost, visible briefly in batting practice and then vanishing into the shadows of the dugout before the first pitch, riding the pine. Of the 152 games the Giants played during the regular season, Jim took the field in only 19 with only 37 plate appearances. His statistics were anemic: 5 hits, 1 home run, 6 runs scored, 2 runs batted in, 2 stolen bases, .143 batting average, and a meager .167 on-base percentage. In the five-game World Series against the Philadelphia Athletics, won by Connie Mack's team four games to one, there was a great performance by a former student from the Carlisle Indian Industrial School, but it was not Thorpe. Albert "Chief" Bender, with a 21-10 record that year, won the opener and game four for the opposing American League club while Jim watched the entire series from the bench.

In "Red Son of Carlisle," Thorpe later praised McGraw, saying he "enjoyed every minute" he spent "under the keen and watchful eye of the Giants' mentor." But his relationship with McGraw was testier than Thorpe's with Pop Warner. In many respects McGraw and Warner were alike. Both were master strategists and innovators—McGraw was credited among other things with bringing the hit-and-run play to baseball. Both were chunky and cocksure men with outsize egos who thought they knew more about their sport than anyone. Both prided themselves on dealing with unruly athletes and molding them into a smooth-running and unstoppable machine. Both cursed at their players, expecting them to obey and follow a rigid system. Part of the difference certainly was that Jim was so much better at football than baseball, meaning there was never an issue about playing time during his Carlisle days. Part of it might have been that as Jim got older his carousing increased, along with his occasional stubbornness. But Pop better understood the extraordinary talent he had in Jim and was more selective and often more lenient in his treatment of him.

Jim's roommate, Chief Meyers, called him "an apt pupil" in McGraw's school of baseball and said he had never seen a raw player familiarize himself so quickly with methods that "must have struck home so strangely at first." But the pupil was impatient with the way McGraw critiqued his every move. Thorpe said he was upset with McGraw's "way of telling me when to swing and when to take one." Aside from Mathewson, the college boy sometimes referred to as the Christian Gentleman, the Giants of that era from the manager down were a rowdy band of drinkers and fighters, so Thorpe was no outlier, yet McGraw, far from an upright teetotaler himself, seemed to come down particularly hard on him. One oft repeated story was of the time Jim stayed out late drinking and McGraw blasted him, saying he should stay away from alcohol because firewater was the undoing of Indians. To which Thorpe reportedly replied, "What about the Irish?"

With Thorpe that season, all was conflicted and contradictory, including his coverage in the national sporting press. He was alternately regarded as a future star or a poor prospect soon to be cut. Sometimes papers looked desperately for a reason to promote his famous name. In mid-May the International News Service sent out a wirephoto from one of those rare games where Thorpe played. The picture showed him after being caught in a pickle between home and third and sliding safely back to third. The caption: "Indian Olympic Hero Proves Himself a Ball Player." When the Giants played the Cubs in early June, the *Inter Ocean* devoted a headline to the news, "Jim Thorpe Gets Into Game," with a paragraph in the story reading: "In the closing inning McGraw made several changes in his lineup, among others letting Jim Thorpe, the former Carlisle Indian school athletic marvel, break in. Jim pinch hit for Matty [Mathewson] and singled and then went to center field and caught a fly. Both performances aroused mad enthusiasm."

It was not until late September, after the Giants had clinched the National League pennant, that Thorpe appeared in the papers almost every day. By then McGraw was resting his regulars and playing his bench. Fully half of Jim's at-bats came during that stretch, and the papers took note when he hit a home run in Boston against the Braves, muffed a fly ball against the Phillies, lost to a Philly speedster named Hans Lobert in a pregame hundred-yard dash, but won an exhibition fungo hitting contest by tossing the ball in the air and smacking it 404 feet.

Then it was back to the bench for the World Series, where Thorpe was out of mind with a few exceptions outside the field of play. When the Giants arrived in New York after splitting the first two games in Philadelphia, several hundred fans stood in the rain to greet the team and watched as the players emerged from the station in twos and threes and disappeared into taxicabs. Here came Big Six sporting the smile of a pitching hero who had thrown a shutout in game two. And there was Chief Meyers, the catcher's injured wrist and thumb tightly bandaged. And look at Fred

Merkle, the first baseman, limping badly and leaning on the big shoulders of . . . *Jim Thorpe.* His first and only assist of the series.

Something of far more importance brought Jim back into the public spotlight that week.

After a fifteen-month long-distance courtship with Iva Miller, letters going back and forth almost daily, some read, some misplaced, some censored by Iva's older brother until she outflanked Earl by getting a PO box just for the love letters, some snooped on in the Giants locker room by Jim's friend and road roommate Chief Meyers . . . After Jim had twice won All-American honors at Carlisle and proved himself to be the greatest all-around athlete in the world at Stockholm . . . After he had found a way to earn a decent living as a professional . . . And after he told Iva that ballplayer wives were invited on a world tour that the Giants and White Sox were undertaking soon after the season ended . . . After all that, Iva said yes.

Big brother Earl and Pop Warner were both concerned, worried that she did not fully understand the rough life she was about to embark on. "My family and friends didn't want me to marry him," she said later. "But I was in love and it was going to happen. . . . I was determined to go with him on that trip around the world." Even with his doubts, Earl gave her the money to buy a wedding gown and several new outfits. She packed them in a traveling trunk and off she went, riding a train across the continent in time to sit in the stands at the Polo Grounds for game three of the World Series. The newspapers noted her arrival. "Thorpe's Fiancée Is Prettiest Indian Maid," read the caption atop a photo of "Miss Iva Margaret Miller, the bride-to-be of 'Big Jim' Thorpe."

The stories said the couple would be married soon after the World Series. *Lo, the poor Indian?* "Lo may have been a poor Indian but if all Jim Thorpe's plans work out, he'll be far from poor," noted one hyperbolic wire service account. "In fact, he will have taken quite a few steps toward cornering the money market. Every chance to make a dollar is eagerly seized by Jim and his latest hunch is a loo-loo. He's going to sell a moving picture concern the privilege of making a reel or two of him when he marries a little Cherokee maid at Carlisle."

13

Around the World

NINE MONTHS EARLIER, IN THE MIDWINTER DARKNESS, JIM had slipped out of Carlisle at the low point of his career—when the potentates of amateur athletics were stripping him of Olympic medals, trophies, and records, if not his honor. Now, on a bright Tuesday in autumn, he was back, huddling with eight groomsmen in anticipation of his midmorning wedding to Iva Miller. It was October 14, 1913. The event of the year in the Cumberland Valley. A cordon of uniformed Carlisle city policemen stood sentinel on the front steps of ivy-covered St. Patrick's Catholic Church to keep the entrance free and clear. Hundreds of townsfolk who could not get inside lined both sides of East Pomfret Street. Iva's wedding party—ring bearer, attendant, maid of honor, flower girls—flowed through the arched entrance into the nave and down the center aisle, passing friends, teachers, and dignitaries, every pew taken, latecomers standing in the back recesses of the old church.

The pipe organ resounded with the propulsive opening chords of the wedding march, and here came Iva in a lace gown of white charmeuse, her face graced by a veil of "cloud-like chiffon." She appeared, said one account, as the "laughing, dark-eyed princess of the Cherokee tribe, resembling in her dusky beauty the poet's conception of the storied Minnehaha." A caricature, to be sure, but apt if only in the sense that Longfellow and his *Song of Hiawatha* were among Jim and Iva's favorites. At her arm during the processional was not big brother Earl but Moses Friedman, the Carlisle superintendent, generously described in the local press as "a friend of both the bride and groom." Of the bride, perhaps; Iva had been an excellent student and never gave Friedman trouble. Groom, another matter;

the relationship, never smooth, seemed to rise and fall with Jim's fortunes. For this day, at least, it was rising again. The gloom that had descended over the school in those weeks after the bronze bust and silver chalice were removed from the display case had now lifted.

At the front of the sanctuary stood Jim and his groomsmen, all Carlisle students, including little brother Edward Thorp and former football teammates Pete Calac and Joe Guyon, Thorpe's successors as Pop's backfield stars. The previous afternoon, Jim had visited the practice field, where he reminisced with his coach and old pals and gave Calac and Guyon tips on how to get off a punt so quickly it could not be blocked. His best man was Gus Welch, the quarterback and 1913 team captain, who on a fall day two years earlier had flipped a coin with Jim to see who would first ask Iva for a date. Father Mark Stock, assistant pastor at St. Patrick's and chaplain at the Indian school, performed the ceremony, pronouncing Jim and Iva man and wife. High Mass followed, and Holy Communion. Jim grew up Catholic; Iva converted from Episcopalian. A full day of celebrations followed: wedding breakfast at St. Katharine's Hall next to the church, afternoon reception at the superintendent's house attended by two hundred students and the Carlisle band, and a joyous evening social in the school gymnasium. Iva and Jim were gone by then, catching a night train to New York to prepare for an all-expenses-paid honeymoon around the world with the New York Giants and Chicago White Sox. She was twenty; he was twenty-six. She lovingly called him "Snooks."

THE TRAIN DEPARTING Grand Central Terminal that Friday morning was called the Honeymoon Special. Jim and Iva, as it turned out, were not the only newlyweds aboard; Larry Doyle, the second baseman, and Jeff Tesreau, the big pitcher, also got hitched in time for the tour. A few hundred Giants fans flooded the station to bid the team farewell, a scene recorded by a movie crew that focused mostly on the three couples while not completely ignoring John McGraw, Christy Mathewson, Chief Meyers, and other players, aides, and newspapermen. "It's just a little treat for the boys and it will give us a chance we may never get again to see the world," said the Little Napoleon as he led his merry band into two reserved railcars. The interior was festooned with flowers, the dining car preparing for a bridal luncheon in honor of the honeymooners. All seemed joyous but for one irritation for Jim and Iva. He had sent their luggage from the hotel hours ahead, but the bags still had not arrived when the train left the station and would not reach them until the next morning in Cincinnati.

This was billed as a world tour of Giants and White Sox, but it was more than that. Before shipping out from the port of Seattle a month later, the road show would perform in twenty-nine cities in Ohio, Illinois, Iowa, Kansas, Missouri, Oklahoma, Texas, Arizona, California, Oregon, and Washington. And while billed as New York versus Chicago, some players were recruited from other teams to fill the rosters since some Giants and White Sox had offseason obligations or were wary of the roiling oceans. Ty Cobb and Nap Lajoie said no thanks to offers to become mercenaries, but the White Sox gained the firepower of two other future Hall of Famers, Wahoo Sam Crawford of the Tigers and Tris Speaker of the Red Sox, while the Giants snagged a few Phillies. They also brought along their own umpires, the demonstrative Bill Klem from the National League and Jack Sheridan of the American League.

Circus trains, traveling carnivals, Wild West shows, vaudeville troupes, magic acts, daredevil aviators, dramatic literary readings, fiddler caravans—the baseball barnstormers entered a picaresque American scene of itinerant entertainers crisscrossing the country that year. They drew exuberant crowds at every stop, starting on a blustery afternoon in Cincinnati when ten thousand fans filled Redland Field to watch the Giants, with Mathewson on the mound and Thorpe in center, open the tour with an 11 to 2 win. That Jim banged out three hits that day helped relieve months of tension after a season on the bench. Not only was he on an extended honeymoon, at last he was getting to play.

After another game the next day at Comiskey Park in Chicago, the two teams rode together on a chartered train for the remainder of the five-thousand-mile continental journey. The traveling press corps now included a band of Chicago scribes led by Bill Veeck Sr., writing under the pen name Bill Bailey, and Ring Lardner. There were five steel railcars, including three sleepers, one observation sleeper, and one combination buffet and baggage car. First stop, Springfield, Illinois, where it snowed and Jim hit a home run, then on to Peoria, followed by Ottumwa and Sioux City in Iowa, where hundreds of members of the Winnebago and Omaha nations crossed the river from Nebraska to watch their brethren, Thorpe and Meyers. "Polo Grounds fans who have delighted since Chief Meyers joined my club in giving those imitation war whoops when the Indian came to bat should have been with us today," McGraw noted. "They would have heard some whooping of the real variety."

The road show moved south from there, wending through Iowa into Kansas. Townspeople came out to see the train at station stops all along the route, often chanting for Christy Mathewson in hopes the great hurler would appear. But as McGraw explained, "Everybody knows that Big Six is bashful and he would generally refuse to go out on the platform. Germany Schaefer [recruited from the Washington Senators to play second base for the White Sox] would go out and pretend he was Matty and praise the people and the women and the streets."

The weather turned nasty again when the train reached Kansas City for a game on Sunday, October 26, but five thousand shivering fans filed into Association Park. By then, Bill Klem, the home-plate umpire, had refined his pitchman routine, bowing to the crowd and introducing the managers and batters with his operatic contrabass voice. "The greatest noise was provoked when he announced 'Jim Thorpe, the world's greatest athlete,' " reported the *Kansas City Times.* "Then the Indian cracked one for a clean single to right and showed what he had in the way of speed." Jim was proving his worth as a gate attraction even before the barnstormers went overseas. McGraw had said similar things before, and one could never be certain if he meant it, but here again he talked of Jim's promising baseball future. "I am going to play him regularly on the trip and it will be a great experience for him," he told the local press.

The marquee game of the American tour was held two days later in Tulsa when the best pitchers in the majors faced each other. Walter Johnson, with his 29-11 record and 1.14 earned run average, against Christy Mathewson, with a 25-11 record and 2.05 earned run average. The Big

Train versus the Big Six. Johnson, who played for the Washington Senators, was not part of the barnstorming troupe, but was so excited at the prospect of a matchup against Mathewson that he told Comiskey he would pitch for free and travel to Tulsa on his own from his hometown of Coffeyville, Kansas. All that and a chance to see the home-state hero Jim Thorpe. It was the event of the season in Tulsa, treated like a holiday.

Banks closed at noon and five thousand schoolchildren were let out for the day, many making their way to the stadium on the edge of town to watch through knotholes in the outfield fence. Oklahoma governor Lee Cruce arrived with his daughter. Oil magnate Ted Reese, who sponsored the contest, was there along with moneymen from the Tulsa Commercial Club and delegates in town for the International Dry-Farming Congress. At one o'clock, the teams gathered in uniform outside the Hotel Tulsa and paraded to the park behind a U.S. Infantry unit and band from Fort Logan H. Roots in Arkansas. A wonderful day for baseball, even if there was a biting north wind and the hint of snow.

Until . . . at two fifteen, as Company L of the Ninth Infantry marched under the right-field bleachers, the wooden stands collapsed, taking five hundred spectators down with them. "It came so suddenly that not even a scream was heard. It took a while for the awfulness to dawn on the crowd," reported the Tulsa paper. "For some minutes many of the more slightly injured lay prostrate upon the ground, many covered with wounds and bleeding. Frantic mothers searched the wreckage for children." Ambulances and private automobiles arrived carrying doctors to the scene and ferrying some of the injured back to the hospital for treatment. One woman carried her son, bleeding from the head, all the way to town. It turned out that the roofless stands were made of light and rotted wood, a combination that both caused the collapse and made it less catastrophic than it might have been. The lone fatality was one of the infantrymen marching underneath the bleachers, Private Chester Taylor.

The players had been warming up when the disaster unfolded and watched it all, some rushing to assist. What next? The powers that be decided the game must go on, so they played, and more than three thousand fans stayed around to watch "sorrowed by the sad accident that preceded the game." The Giants could not touch the Big Train's bullet fastball and deceptive sinker; Buck Weaver and ringers Sam Crawford and Tris Speaker had three hits apiece, knocking the Big Six out of the box in the fifth inning; and the White Sox prevailed 6 to 0. Jim played right field and went one for three.

On to Muskogee, Oklahoma, where the stands featured a few hundred hollering cowboys; and Houston, where Jim got hit in the arm and removed from the game; and Bisbee, Arizona, where he cracked a booming home run. Iva and the other wives were becoming good copy. G. W. (Gus) Axelson, a Chicago sportswriter, sat with Iva in the stands when they reached California and described how the "bride of a month" followed her husband's every move: "Oh you, dear boy. Hit it out. O, pshaw, he had to strike him out. O, well you just wait until next time. I know Jim can hit the ball." Axelson said that Iva and the wives of Larry Doyle and John Meyers "now and then take their regular practice, throwing and catching the ball. Mrs. Doyle has the distinction of being the only one knocked out during practice. The other day catching balls, she missed one and it hit her on the head. She was out for a couple of minutes. Now she sticks to the suffragette end of the game." Instructive that a sportswriter in 1913 would suppose that watching instead of playing was a matter of women's rights. Iva later put it differently: "Of course, all the ladies went to the game . . . and occasionally took the field in the smaller towns. We tossed the ball around and made a big hit with the fans. . . . We did not wear bloomers."

When they finally reached Seattle for the start of the ocean journey, McGraw's best player declared he would go no farther. "It was the water that scared the big fellow off the trip," McGraw said of Christy Mathewson. "We kept after him up to the end, but he declined. It was a great disappointment to me that he would not come along. 'No, nothing doing, Mac,' he said. 'I can't even stand the idea, let alone the reality, and you know I've tried.' " Bill Veeck Sr. wrote that Mathewson, when asked why he balked, explained that traveling over water disturbed him so much he almost got sick on a ferry from Manhattan to Brooklyn. That might have had nothing to do with the water but with the destination, Veeck joked, a reference to the rival borough. Losing Mathewson was unfortunate but far from fatal.

It was only an exhibition tour, there were other pitchers on the squad, and whatever McGraw lost in talent he and Comiskey made up for in profits. They basically got their players for free, paying each of them only $550 for the entire four-plus-month trip, plus expenses, and with Mathewson and Thorpe the main drawing cards in the States, they had been raking in money at every stop, earning more than $97,000 just in their last week on the West Coast.

IVA BROUGHT A travel journal and started making entries on November 19 in Vancouver, British Columbia, after a packet from Seattle took them to the *Empress of Japan*, the ship that would sail them across the Pacific to Yokohama, the first overseas stop. She wrote in fountain pen, in precise cursive script. Upon boarding at nine thirty that night, she and Jim visited the saloon, learned they had been assigned stateroom 215, and went to bed, exhausted. Sleep was no balm; rough seas. "Awoke very sick," she wrote on their first day at sea. "Jim was nauseated when he awoke but after breakfast was alright—but not his better half who only rolled and tumbled—and when on deck fed the fish too. . . ."

Day by day, the gale intensified. Frank McGlynn, who joined the sixty-seven-member troupe to produce a documentary, said riding through the storm was "the most appalling and awful it has ever been my lot to experience." The 485-foot-long ship "was tossed about like a small rowboat, and as the sea would strike her, a sound like the roar of artillery would accompany the blow." The captain estimated waves as high as 60 feet. For four days, when Iva wanted to leave their quarters, Jim carried her up to the deck. By the fifth day of roiling seas she could not move from their stateroom. She was not alone among the seasick. McGlynn noted that strong baseball skills did not equal strong stomachs. "Strange to say, some of the greatest athletes of the party [including Wahoo Sam Crawford and Tris Speaker] suffered more than mere mortals from this disagreeable and at times dangerous illness."

In an imperial suite befitting an Old Roman, Charles Comiskey had brought along seven Indestructo steamer trunks, but not an indestructible stomach, prompting his friend Charles C. Spink, publisher of the *Sporting News,* to pen a satirical poem titled "Commy Relates His Experience" in the fashion of Edgar Allan Poe's "The Raven":

And the undulating motion
Of that vessel on the ocean
In me started a commotion
I had never felt before
Suddenly there came a retching
And a straining and a stretching
From my commissary fetching
Things I'd eaten years before. . . .

Every sportswriter a poet in his own mind. The sports sections were chockful of corny doggerel and wise-guy limericks. One exception was Ring Lardner, who had an ear for the unschooled vernacular of ballplayers that he melded into an inimitable form of baseball literature. His observations of the traveling show as a columnist for the *Chicago Tribune* served as material for the final chapter of *You Know Me, Al,* a series of short stories in the form of letters written to a hometown friend named Al by the main character, Jack Keefe, a gullible hick who could pitch better than he could spell, which was not saying much. In that short story, "The Busher Beats It Hence," Keefe was recruited to join the tour. While the busher was a fictitious composite, Lardner used real names for the rest of his cast, including Comiskey, McGraw, [White Sox manager] James J. Callahan, and some of the other players.

The conceit of the story was that in his letters to Al during the train ride across the continent, Keefe kept claiming he would not make the overseas part of the trip, but McGraw and Callahan snowed him again and again and eventually persuaded him to go. One scene: "Callahan was talking about it to me to-day and he says he knowed that if I was to pitch for the giants on the trip his club would not have no chance of wining the most of the games on the trip but still and all he wisht I would go a long because he was scared the people over in Rome and Paris and Africa and them other country's would be awful sore if the 2 clubs come over there with out bringing none of there star pitchers along. He says we got Speaker and Crawford and Doyle and Thorp and some of them other real stars in all the positions except pitcher and it will make us look bad if you and Mathewson don't neither 1 of you come along."

Unlike author Lardner himself, who chose not to, his fictional busher Keefe in the end was persuaded to make the sail, boarding a ship he called the "Umpires of Japan."

Iva Miller Thorpe, the dulcet-voiced elocutionist of her Carlisle class, used better spelling in her travel journal. After five days of unease, her nausea cleared. "Sixth day awoke feeling excellent and we had a lot of pep—went to the dining hall for the first time and ate heartily. After so many days of fasting felt kind of hollowed. We (Jim and I) have a table in the saloon with Mr. and Mrs. Sam Crawford. Went to sleep on Tuesday Nov. 25 and woke up on Thursday Nov. 27, and Thanksgiving Day too. This was on account of crossing the 180 meridian." The traveling party celebrated Thanksgiving with speeches and songs, followed by a dinner feast and dancing late into the night. Jim and Iva, who had won dancing contests in the Carlisle gymnasium, swept around the ballroom with ease.

It was not easy for the ballplayers to stay in condition during the crossing, especially in rough weather, but Jim became the leader of indoor workouts. "He has shown the boys how to jump the rope, and a couple of days ago, before it was possible to do anything on deck, he showed a new wrestling game," manager McGraw recounted. "Perhaps the most novel stunt is the horse racing in the dining salon. The game is played with any number of horses and riders. The favorite horses are Thorpe, Schaefer, and Evans. The horses have to go on their hands and knees and the riders are not allowed to touch their feet on the floor. . . . Evans has won many races because his rider is usually six-year-old Dan Callahan, son of the Sox manager. Even under this handicap Jim Thorpe has won a good share of the contests because of his great strength and his ability to excel in the athletic exercises."

When the *Empress* reached port at Yokohama on December 6, the arriving party was greeted by an eager dockside crowd of Japanese baseball lovers and sportswriters who displayed a sophisticated appreciation of America's pastime. The delegation was taken by two-person rickshaws to the Grand Hotel. "Shopped in the morning with my hubby and Mr. and Mrs. McGraw. Then the crowd of us went to Tokio [by train] for the afternoon game," Iva noted in her journal. "—going from the depot to the diamond . . . Jim and I in a buggy the wheel of our buggy came off and Jim and I had a tumble into the street and were fortunate in not being injured." A buggy in their native Oklahoma was a rickshaw in Japan.

The first game of the world tour was played that afternoon at a bandbox stadium at Keio University before rabid fans that G. W. Axelson compared favorably with those at the Polo Grounds. Iva got caught up in the excitement. "My, such a funny sight—so many Japanese—with here and there a Caucasian face among them," she wrote. "The president of the university . . . pitched the first ball which was caught by the American counsel. After a lot of picture taking and hand shaking and practice, too—our boys played—White Sox beat the Giants. After the game returned to Yokohama where a big banquet was given in the evening—and an entertainment was given by the geisha girls—who proved to be very graceful."

THE SENTENCE IN that entry dealing with race and the rarity of Caucasians in the audience raised a larger question. Did the young woman described only two months earlier as a Cherokee princess consider herself one of those few Caucasians in the crowd? In her Descriptive and Historical Record file at the Carlisle Indian Industrial School she named her tribe as Cherokee and under *Deg. Indian Blood* she was listed as one-quarter. In other school records, including her original application, she wrote that her mother, Mattie Denton Miller, who died when Iva was five, was "½ Indian," born to the Cherokee band of North Carolina. In filling out the Character Book for her Cherokee classmate Sylvester Long in 1912, when asked which tribe she had written "same as yours." If the mission of Carlisle was to acculturate its students in the dominant white civilization, it also taught students like Iva Indian history and folklore and emphasized

Native American pride. Since she was a little girl, Iva had lived among Native Americans and presumed she was one.

"Mother grew up thinking she was part Cherokee," one of her daughters explained decades later. But as it turned out, that was a ruse concocted by Iva's older siblings, at least in terms of blood quantum. If she had an Indian ancestor on the Denton side, there was no indication of it in family genealogy records. Her father, Finas Miller, was of Scots-Irish descent. The notion of Indianness began after her mother died and Finas, an itinerant hotelier and stagecoach operator, wanted little to do with his children, sending four of them to the Chilocco Indian School, where the government would feed and clothe and teach them. It was then, Iva recalled later, that her older sister Grace "trained me to say who I was, with Indian background. It was all lies, but it was a way of getting an education. Others had done it."

Precisely when Iva learned of her real ancestry remains uncertain. One daughter said it did not happen until after she had married Jim. Others said she knew by the time she met Jim at Carlisle. Her journal entry about the few Caucasians at the ball game in Tokyo was far from expositive and might simply have been a reportorial observation that had nothing to do with her identity. Or it might have offered a hint. While at Chilocco and Carlisle, she embraced Indian history and culture; but once she finished her schooling, there are no indications she identified as Native American, and her older sister Grace was known at times to speak disparagingly of Indians. In either case, it did not matter to the young couple then, and it never seemed to matter to Jim.

FROM TOKYO THE players rode the train to Kobe outside Osaka, where they rejoined the women, who had gone ahead, missing the last two exhibition games. Then all aboard the *Empress* again to slalom through the island-filled inland sea to Nagasaki, where two of the honeymoon couples, the Thorpes and the Doyles, went Christmas shopping on December 10. Iva recorded in her journal that they "rode around town on Jinrikishas (oh! They're lot of fun)" and climbed the steps to a high temple. It was also in Nagasaki that she bought a delicate Japanese card. Addressing the envelope to "Miss Moore, Carlisle, Pa. USA," she wrote a note that later found its way into the archive of Marianne Moore: "A Merry Christmas and A Happy New Year. Best wishes from two of your pupils—Jim and Iva Thorpe."

From Nagasaki the *Empress* sailed across the East China Sea to Shanghai. Along the route, Comiskey, the tour impresario, received wireless reports that Shanghai was enveloped in rain and fog, causing concern that the baseball game would be washed out. The morning of arrival dawned gray and gloomy, reported documentarian McGlynn. "It rained as we swung into the mouth of the Hoang Ho River at Wu Sung; it rained as we slowly swung into anchorage, 14 miles below Shanghai, where we took a steam tender—a fast tug—for the city of Shanghai; it poured all the way up the river and a dense atmosphere overhung the river banks."

A colorful swell of umbrellas covered baseball-hungry ex-pats, formally attired Shanghai officials, and uniformed military crews as they greeted the American party at the pier and again outside the Astor House Hotel. Thorpe and the other players were honored with mahogany walking sticks, the silver handles inscribed "Shanghai 1913." An overflow crowd of twenty-five thousand was expected at the ballpark that afternoon, but the rain never stopped—game canceled. "So sorry it rained here—as the people were so nice and seemed so anxious to see our boys play," Iva recorded in her journal. "They gave us a real American welcome—a crowd met us at the wharf with a band and autos to escort us to the hotel. Of course, the game had to be postponed on account of rain. Mrs. Doyle and I went shopping with Mr. Allendessen [from the U.S. consulate]—and he certainly saved us a bit of money as he knew what we should pay. Returned to hotel where a reception was on." Jim and Iva hit the dance floor until the delegation left early that evening for the harbor, where the *Empress* prepared for the southern sail to Hong Kong.

Aboard ship the following night the Americans were guests at a commander's dinner; the captain was presented with a diamond pin and rounds of "For He's a Jolly Good Fellow" sung by the ballplayers in gratitude for the expert way he'd guided the tempest-tossed ship across the Pacific. But the jollity subsided when word came that a passenger who had boarded in Shanghai was infected with smallpox, forcing the *Empress* to ease into Hong Kong Harbor flying a yellow flag of quarantine and for all passengers to be checked for vaccinations before disembarking.

The Hong Kong stop was a cameo, barely six hours on land. Iva and Jim had the morning to look around town, but time was so short that the ballplayers had to warm up outside the hotel, flinging the ball around on the street, before hustling off to play a five-inning exhibition at the Happy Valley Recreation Grounds. No money for Comiskey and McGraw to be pocketed that Sunday afternoon—local law prohibited sporting events that charged admission on Sundays. Unlike the American leg of the tour, during which the women had attended every game, there was no such loyalty overseas. The sights in Hong Kong no doubt held more interest than those in Muskogee. Iva wrote that "in the afternoon we women instead of going to the game took a ride on a tramway up to the Peak—beautiful view shall never forget."

With her crew barred from shore leave because of the smallpox quarantine, the *Empress* was gone by the time the Americans returned to harbor late that afternoon. They were switching ships in any case to the *St. Albans*, a "tidy little steamer, most comfortable in every way," as McGlynn described it, that safely carried them through a violent if brief monsoon and then into the sunlight and pounding heat of the tropics on the voyage to the Philippines. Also aboard, huddled in steerage, was a covey of Russian émigré families, including political opponents of the tsarist regime and military defectors seeking refuge in Australia. On the main deck, the *St. Albans* featured a swimming tank lashed to the beams—larger than the one the Olympians had used aboard the SS *Finland* on the voyage to Stockholm a year and a half earlier.

Under the midnight stars of December 16, the ship eased into Manila Bay. The two-day stay in Manila was one social function after another from morning to midnight, including a tour of a national prison, a drive through the countryside to the neighboring city of Antipolo, a visit with American soldiers at Fort William McKinley where Olympic hero Jim Thorpe was besieged by autograph seekers, and a rooftop ball at the Manila Hotel. Iva said she and Jim had a special escort during their stay, Mr. S. E. Rhoades, and loved it all. She called the Philippines "the most interesting place we have been so far—seemed like the good old U.S. on account of it belongs to us and there are a lot of Americans there." But at the rooftop ball they were tired and adjourned early to their stateroom aboard ship.

Seven straight days at sea followed as the *St. Albans* sailed south, slicing between the islands of Indonesia and on toward Australia through the Arafura Sea. "Crossed the equator at 9:30 a.m. Didn't feel a bit different," Iva wrote on December 21. "Mr. Doyle played on the piano and a crowd of us sang. I tried to—Jim doing real well singing tunes—If he would only have more confidence in himself." They were still at sea on Christmas morning when they all gathered around a decorated tree in the ship library to exchange presents. Comiskey blessed his wife, Nan, with a silver spoon. McGraw gave his wife, Blanche, an embroidered handkerchief. "And my Snookie gave me a lovely gold-inlaid tortoise shell dressing set—Old Santa Claus was real good to us." Snookie, Snooki, Snook—all variations of her Jim. After Christmas dinner, the men smoked aromatic Manila cigars on the hurricane deck as strains of violin music played by the Old Roman's daughter-in-law wafted through the vents.

The first stop in Australia was at a Queensland seaport near Cairns. While some in the delegation took a special train to view Barron Falls, the Thorpes and Doyles visited downtown Cairns in the morning and went swimming that afternoon. Word quickly spread that the great Olympian Thorpe was in the water. "A large crowd of Australians swarmed around the plunge but pshaw—why would we worry—never see them again and if we did wouldn't remember them or them us," Iva wrote in her journal. "Jim and I bought a little canary—beautiful singer—named Ah Sing—shall take him to the states if we can."

The traveling party celebrated New Year's in Brisbane, where Jim and Iva received their first batch of mail, including Christmas greetings from Pop Warner and his wife, and Jim got a letter from a cousin. But Iva was distressed to hear nothing from her older siblings, Grace and Earl, who had never fully approved of her marriage to Jim. "My I wish my sister or brother would get a letter through to me," she wrote in the early-morning hours of January 1, after staying up past midnight to welcome in 1914. At the next stop in Sydney, Iva joined the women at the theater while Jim and the boys went to a prizefight. The sporting exhibitions included both the Giants and White Sox facing teams from New South Wales, and the Australians demonstrating the game of cricket. Iva attended both and found "cricket slower by far than baseball."

Melbourne, the next stop, delighted her. It was also the first time since they left the States that she reported on Jim's baseball performance. "Oh my such a wonderful place—well laid out in beautiful parks—wide clean streets—summer here you know so that everyone is enjoying the beaches like we do at home. Moving pictures taken of a crowd of we ladies at Zoological Gardens. Jim and I went motoring with a crowd of gentlemen—lovely drive—Mrs. D[oyle] and I after game went to a drug store and had ice cream sodas. My Snooks got two home runs and did some dandy good playing alright mighty proud of him." In three games there, the Giants defeated the White Sox twice and then whumped a Victoria team 18–0. The nightcap was a grand banquet, but Jim had grown tired of the social scene, and he and Iva skipped it, instead going out for a walk around town.

The overland train conveyed them five hundred miles across goldfields and wheat fields into South Australia and the port at Adelaide, where their next ship, the *Orontes*, awaited to sail the Indian Ocean to Ceylon. Iva was reluctant to leave Down Under. "Believe I should like to live in Australia—Jim seems much impressed, too," she wrote. Rough waters crossing the Great Australian Bight kept her in their stateroom at first, reading books. "Seasick kinda for two days although I didn't feel near as bad as when on the *Empress* [crossing the north Pacific]," she wrote. By January 12 she had recovered, ready to play games and dance. "Went up on deck with Snooks this afternoon—played follow your leader [with the group] and as Jim was our leader—he kissed Mr. Comiskey and hugged first this one and that one and of course we had to do the same."

On January 14, Iva took note of a special occasion. "Snooks and I have been married 3 months today—and we are still living together and as happy as can be." That night, a steward passed out sandwiches made of carrots, peppers, and onions. "While we were eating a Spanish couple started dancing on the upper deck," Iva later recalled. "It was the queerest thing, a combination of tango, hesitation, and maxixe. Of course, we were crazy to learn how, and Señor Matello obligingly taught us. After that we danced nothing else. I dubbed it the Onion Glide because it was part of the evening's entertainment to munch those sandwiches and do that dance on deck." Soon four bachelor ballplayers calling themselves the Tango Four—Tris Speaker, Germany Schaefer, Buck Weaver, and Fred Merkle—formed an Onion Club and chose the dance music for each night. The best dancers among the Americans were Jim and Iva, dazzling partners since their Carlisle days.

It was a Sunday when they reached Colombo, Ceylon's capital, and as in Hong Kong, another far-flung colony of the British Empire, local rules prohibited paid events that day, so again the Giants and White Sox played for free, using a portion of the Colombo racecourse to craft a diamond. The game drew a large crowd, with the great American Indian Jim Thorpe a major attraction. Documentarian McGlynn was engrossed by the spectacle in the stands: "Cingalese gentlemen with peculiar head dress and native robes, Hindoo Police with their individual costumes, Tamal natives and English soldiers together with the American and English residents, all combined in a picture that for color scheme would have been worthy of the brush of Remington." Their ship left Colombo at midnight with four hundred pounds of Ceylon tea aboard, a supply for every member of the touring party. Their names had been inscribed on wooden tea caddies, gifts from their solicitous host during the brief visit, Sir Thomas Lipton, the sporting Scotsman who founded Lipton Tea.

Then a weeklong voyage took them more than three thousand miles across the Indian Ocean, through the Gulf of Aden, and north on the Red Sea to the edge of the Suez Canal, where a train brought them the rest of the way to Cairo. After a "sumptuous breakfast" that morning at Heliopolis, the delegation went by taxi to view the pyramids and the Sphinx. "Rode on camels and donkeys out there. Very interesting," Iva reported.

The notion of the New York Giants baseball club visiting the Sphinx was strange enough to capture the fertile imagination of E. L. Doctorow, who decades later in his novel *Ragtime* placed one of his central characters, the financier Pierpont Morgan, at the monument at the same time. "As he passed the great Sphinx and looked back he saw men swarming all over her, like vermin. . . . The desecrators were wearing baseball suits," Doctorow wrote. Morgan asked his guides, "What in God's name is going on?" and word came back that it was the New York Giants on a world exhibition tour. "Running toward him was a squat ugly man in pin-striped knee-pants and a ribbed undershirt. His hand was outstretched. An absurd beanie was on his head. A cigar butt was in his mouth. His cleated shoes rang on the ancient stones. The manager, Mr. McGraw, to pay his respects, Morgan's aide said. Without a word, the old man kicked at the side of his camel and, knocking over his Arab guide, fled to his boat."

In fiction, Pierpont Morgan wanted nothing to do with the Little Napoleon and his ballplayers, but in real life the games played in Cairo were witnessed by Khedive Abbas II, the Ottoman viceroy of Egypt and Sudan. Olympian Jim Thorpe did not disappoint. "My Snooks played some ball both days in Cairo, getting one home run and two hits the first day (bringing in other runs) and four hits in four times at bat the second. Some ballplaying alright," Iva boasted.

Train to Alexandria . . . *Prinz Heinrich* liner across the Mediterranean to Naples . . . Jim and Iva studying French at sea . . . back on shore for tours of Pompeii and the National Gallery where, according to Iva, "Snooks bought three oil paintings, at the museum—statues found at Pompeii and Herculaneum" . . . and on to Rome, where the highlight was an audience with Pope Pius X on Wednesday morning, February 11. The men wore evening suits, the women dressed in black. They knelt as the pontiff entered. From Comiskey and Callahan to McGraw, from Thorpe and Doyle to McGlynn, most in the party were Roman Catholic, and as McGlynn put it, "the moment was fraught with the deepest import."

After the pontifical benediction, the papal secretary of state, Cardinal Rafael Merry del Val, approached. It was then that something else of deep import struck Iva: she realized the full measure of her husband's fame. The cardinal spoke to each of them individually, but the person he most wanted to meet was Jim Thorpe. "Everyone very anxious to meet my Snooks and they seem to know all about him," Iva gushed in her journal. As baseball historian James Elfers later explained: "For her husband to have fame among athletes and sports fans was not a surprise to Iva; after all, she had married the big man on campus. For him to be famous in as unathletic and cerebral environment as the Vatican gave Iva an entirely new perspective on her husband's fame."

A year had now elapsed since McGraw signed Thorpe to play for his Giants on the same day that plans for the world tour were announced. The presumption from the beginning was that McGraw's interest in Thorpe, aside from raw talent, centered on his world fame, that he would draw fans to the traveling show wherever it went. Now it seemed McGraw might be having the best of both worlds. In that first year with the Giants, Thorpe had barely played, but for the overseas games he was consistently in the Giants lineup and impressing his manager. McGraw wrote a letter to John B. Foster, secretary of the Giants, saying that Thorpe was "the most improved ball player imaginable." Foster then spread the word to baseball writers, and in mid-February newspapers around the country featured a report from syndicated columnist Hugh S. Fullerton asserting that Thorpe had made astounding advances and would be "the most sensational baseball player of 1914."

Chicago writer Gus Axelson had been observing Thorpe throughout the trip, taking note of how he was received and how he performed. Wherever they went, Axelson wrote, hosts knew about Thorpe's Olympic deeds and that he was an American Indian. Yet often he was not immediately recognized because he did not match presumptions of what he should look like. "Up to date, he has never been picked out first-hand by visitors, either to the ship or on land. Most all have painted Jim in advance dark of skin. And as for his wife, it is with considerable incredulity that the visitor accepts the statement that the light-complexioned, husky looking athlete is Jim Thorpe, and that the pretty and vivacious girl is Mrs. Thorpe. 'Why are no American Indians black?' is the usual query. At least they figure they must be of copper hue of the story books."

Once people realized which one was Thorpe, Axelson reported, "this great athlete becomes the attraction. He is pointed out in hotels, on the fields, and on the streets. Are they acquainted with his prowess on the athletic field? All that is necessary is to read the columns in native and English papers about the mighty deeds of James. His career is an open book in Japan, in the English possessions, and of course the Philippines. He is no stranger to China. On the baseball field, his every move has been watched. His speed, both in the field and on the bases, has been marveled at and apparently he has lived up to his advance notices."

Beyond being surprised by his appearance and impressed by his performance, the people of the world expressed a deep sympathy for Thorpe over the decision to strip him of his gold medals. "Although the Sox and Giants have visited countless countries where the spirit is high, the opinions have been unanimous that an injustice had been done to him. The very fact that such an action had been taken has undoubtedly increased Thorpe's popularity. In practically every formal speech of welcome and at the many banquets and receptions any allusion to Thorpe's prowess has been received with cheers."

AFTER A STOP in Nice where Jim threw the javelin and put the shot in a pregame exhibition (and lost seventeen bucks at Monte Carlo), the touring party reached Paris. Damon Runyon, then covering baseball for the Hearst newspaper chain, was waiting for them, ensconced in the lobby of the St. James Hotel, ready to follow them for the cushy Paris-London-and-home end of the journey. Runyon wrote in the style of the joyful wise guy in on life's joke. "Covered all over with foreign labels and all chattering away like Baedekers, the Giant White Sox party of sixty-seven—count them yourself—breezed into this sedate little village tonight with the firm determination of playing a five-night stand." All, that is, except the Old Roman. Charles Comiskey had arrived days earlier, scrambling to Paris ahead of his fellow travelers for treatment of a serious stomach ailment that now seemed repaired.

During five rainy days and nights in the City of Light, Parisians embraced Iva as the exotic belle of the delegation. "Hardly slept while we were in Paris. Some gay place," she wrote in her diary. Photographs of her appeared in papers on both sides of the Atlantic, with one caption reading: "Mrs. Jim Thorpe, the beautiful Indian bride of the Giants' star outfielder, has attracted more than her share of attention. Her classic style of beauty has evoked no end of compliments from connoisseurs of the City of Gayety." She and Jim were seen at the Olympia and Moulin Rouge ("the morals very low," she wrote), attended a luncheon at the luxurious quarters of George Kessler, a wealthy American wine merchant ("Never expect to see such magnificence again"), and joined the delegation for a visit to the grave of Napoleon Bonaparte at the Hôtel National des Invalides.

That scene was delicious material for Damon Runyon, who tagged along at the side of McGraw, the Little Napoleon himself. "M. Bonaparte probably felt high honored—though he did not say so," Runyon wrote. "After giving the coop where the great troublemaker is buried forever the 'once over,' McGraw said he knows just how old Nap felt about it all. 'I, too, met the Duke of Wellington,' said McGraw, 'only his name was Connie Mack instead of Arthur Wellesley.'"

McGraw in truth was facing another enemy besides the manager of the world champion Philadelphia Athletics. An upstart organization calling itself the Federal League was working to bust the major league monopoly and steal players from the Giants and other teams with lucrative offers. While McGraw was in Paris, the president of a new team in Brooklyn had wired Christy Mathewson with the message: "Will you manage the Brooklyn Federals? You may name your terms." The Big Six, whose fear of oceangoing had kept him from the world tour, had not yet signed a new contract, and Brooklyn's owner said he would be willing to double whatever the Giants offered. The players on the world tour knew what was going on. Many of them encountered surreptitious agents for the new league in the lobbies of their European hotels. "It appears that of late whenever our bold wayfarers . . . come up for air a shower of cablegrams from the Federal League promoters has sunk them immediately to the depths again. To date no casualties have been reported," wrote Runyon. The two best hitters on the tour, the mercenaries Tris Speaker and Sam Crawford, were especially coveted. James Gilmore, president of the new league, had formed a reception committee of owners from teams in St. Louis, Chicago, and Brooklyn who were planning to meet the ballplayers as soon as they docked in New York.

Last stop, London, and a performance for King George V of England, who had never visited the Chelsea football grounds. Now there he was amid thirty-five thousand other fans, comfortably seated in a Louis XV armchair upholstered in flowered silk in an enclosed royal box, derby hat on his head, pulling on his trim beard, receiving three hearty pregame hip-hip cheers from the visiting ballplayers, and nodding as the American ambassador explained the intricacies of the sport unfolding below him on the improvised field. Sportswriters were more interested in the king's reactions than in the game itself. The *New York Times* correspondent reported that he showed "keen amusement" at the mystifying shouts emanating from the stands—"Take him out!" "Get a new umpire!" "He's got a glass arm!"—but looked mystified "when someone called out 'There's a hole in the bat!' as Jim Thorpe swung wildly at a low one."

The next morning Iva was invited by Blanche McGraw to "go out for a spin with her—nice time—she sure is dear." Little did Iva know what Blanche really thought of the newlyweds. In *The Real McGraw*, a book about her husband she later wrote with Arthur Mann, Blanche called Iva "a sweet and pretty girl" but described Jim as "an unbridled Indian from the American plains." She portrayed him as an "uninhibited and gullible" character who created problems during the trip. "We were scarcely across the Pacific when John lost patience with carefree Jim's refusal to behave himself. 'If it weren't for your wife,' John scolded, 'I'd send you right back to your reservation by the next boat!' "

What to make of this harsh assessment? There was nothing in Iva's journal to hint at Jim's misbehavior. That does not mean it was not there; she was young and blinded by love. But none of the other numerous accounts of the trip singled out Jim as a problem. There were no descriptions of him embarrassing the delegation. Some accounts noted that he tended to leave social functions early with Iva and avoided many of the late-night shenanigans of the bachelors on the trip. There was no doubt that Jim could be uninhibited when drinking, and gullible at times, so Blanche McGraw's version was plausible. But it was just as likely that it reflected more on Jim's behavior after the world tour than during it, and also on the Little Napoleon's disposition. If John McGraw considered Thorpe an uncontrollable problem, why would he gush about his performance during the trip and about how he would be the sensation of the 1914 season? The book was written in 1953, after both men were dead, and long after McGraw had turned on Jim. Tour historian Elfers concluded that "McGraw was more of a jerk than I expected. The way he treated Jim Thorpe on the tour and at home was downright criminal. . . . He had a classic short man syndrome writ large."

An audience with the pope in Rome, five carefree nights in Paris, a ball game in front of the king in London—all seemed comfortable and sound in Europe on the last day of February 1914 as the world travelers boarded their ship at Liverpool for the voyage home across the Atlantic. But the ocean liner itself foretold a bleaker story. It was the RMS *Lusitania*, a British luxury steamship, queen of the seas. In a few months, the world would be at war, and the *Lusitania* would become a tragic casualty, sunk by a German U-boat as she crossed the other way from New York to Liverpool on May 7, 1915, with 123 Americans among the 1,195 passengers killed when it went down.

A future unknown to Iva and Jim and the rest of the troupe in the chilly evening mist of March 6 as the ship eased into New York Harbor, where "the sirens of harbor craft sounded a merry welcome" and "from every boat a hat or handkerchief waved glad tidings," including a crowd aboard the excursion boat *Niagara* comprising White Sox fans who had come from Chicago to greet their returning heroes. A larger throng, numbering in the thousands, awaited at the pier.

"Many of the players were brown from the tropical sun," reported the *New York Times*. "The Old Roman Comiskey, even after his serious illness, looked well and happy. . . . The honeymoon couples stood together and withstood the camera volleys. Jim Thorpe and his bride and Larry Doyle and his bride were surrounded by friends when they came down the gangplank." Another huddle engulfed Comiskey and McGraw, who proclaimed the tour a success in bringing baseball to the world. Comiskey could not stop talking about King George V, who kept a program with the batting order in front of him the entire game. "They all had so much to talk about that the crowded pier was soon as noisy as a suffragette meeting."

Early the next morning, as a crowd gathered outside tour headquarters at the Hotel Imperial at Broadway and Thirty-Second Street, Iva and Edith Doyle slipped away to the baggage room to examine their six trunks of clothes and souvenirs that had been released by customs agents overnight. Kimonos, teakwood vanity boxes, dresses, hats. "Mrs. Thorpe told about the trip," reported the *Times* correspondent as he watched the women examine their cache. " 'I guess we ate and tried on everything in the whole of Europe,' she began. 'All the boys are broke and there was the dearest parasol that I wanted Jim to buy when we were in Paris, but'—and here Mrs. Thorpe smiled—'even a player's wife can't have everything she wants.' "

14

The Reckoning

MARIANNE MOORE WAS STILL TEACHING BUSINESS COURSES at the Carlisle Indian Industrial School when she received the Christmas card postmarked Nagasaki from Jim and Iva Thorpe. She felt overworked and underpaid. Her mother and older brother, watching Marianne's mental and physical health decline, both urged her to resign. She despised her boss, Superintendent Friedman, or "the old Sourball" as the Moore family called him in their constant exchange of chatty letters. She found some salvation in her Native American students, whom she called "open-minded, also intelligent," but never felt at home at the school. "I felt myself to be an imposter there," she said later. "I was soldiering; it wasn't really my work."

Her disillusionment went deeper than feeling the job was not for her, that she needed to escape from the daily drudgery and write poetry. By her third year teaching in 1913 she was viewing Carlisle increasingly as a cruel and abusive place, what her mother called "a horrid, not even good, prison." She tried to keep a distance from the troubles, exhibiting a characteristically reserved approach. "All Moores were experts in deflection and diplomacy, and the Indian school offered [Marianne] much practice in those arts," noted Linda Leavell, her biographer. But there came a time when she had to speak, however softly. It involved the honor of one of her students, a young woman named Julia Hardin. What happened to Hardin was part of a dramatic unraveling at Carlisle that led to a congressional investigation, the firing of Friedman, the open rebellion of the football boys, the leaving under shady circumstances of Pop Warner, and the eventual closing of the school.

Hardin arrived at Carlisle in fall 1911, the same semester that Thorpe returned from his two-year adventure in the bush leagues. She was a Potawatomi from Shawnee, like Jim's late mother, Charlotte, and came to Carlisle from the Sacred Heart convent school, in whose graveyard Charlotte was buried. Like Jim, she was an orphan, her parents long since dead. She and her sister Maggie became interested in Carlisle when several girlfriends at Sacred Heart and from Shawnee went there.

By late spring 1913, Julia was excelling in the commercial department, taking classes in typewriting, law, shorthand, spelling, and arithmetic from Miss Moore. In monthly reports, she was listed as "excellent" in deportment and performance. She enjoyed the classroom work and had "no trouble whatsoever" with her teacher. Then, on June 2, 1913, the school's Outing department tried to compel her to leave for three months and live with a family in New Jersey. She did not want to go. Things deteriorated from there.

When Julia refused to sign a check that would pay for her railroad transportation to the Outing home, Superintendent Friedman directed Claude M. Stauffer, the music director at Carlisle, to help the matron in the Large Girls dorm coerce her into doing what they wished. Stauffer knew Julia well for her musical abilities; she had studied piano and was in the mandolin club. But that—and Julia's excellent behavior in Miss Moore's classes—mattered not at all when it came to dealing with the recalcitrant young woman, who the dorm matron said was acting "smart and impertinent and saying saucy things" while rebuffing efforts to get her to agree to the Outing.

"Julia, you are going to the country," Stauffer said. He ordered her into an office where the transportation check was on a desk for her to sign. Julia repeated that she did not want to go. She said that she did not have the right clothes nor a proper trunk to carry the clothes in. She also had a new boyfriend she did not want to leave. She refused to sign the check. Stauffer grabbed her, told her to sign, and slapped her face. They argued some more and, as Stauffer later recalled, he felt moved by a "sense of duty" to escalate the corporal punishment. As the matron locked the door and closed the curtains to the room, Stauffer picked up a board and thwacked Julia. She fell to her knees. He pushed her onto her hands and knees and then down to the ground. The matron and another female employee pinned Julia's arms and legs and Stauffer continued hitting her with the board. She put a hand over her face, trying to protect herself. "He struck me on the head and every place," she said later. He called the board a piece of kindling. He said he struck her eight or ten times. Julia said it was more like sixty times and he was using a thick two-and-a-half-foot board he had taken from the windowsill. Superintendent Friedman did not order the beating, nor did he condemn it. As he once acknowledged, he was easily intimidated and tended to let bullies have their way. He had instructed Stauffer to "handle the thing the way he found best."

The relationship between students and the Carlisle administration worsened quickly after that. The discipline was at once harsher and less effective as the school tried to control students speaking up or disobeying orders. The administration expressed alarm at an increase in drinking and of young Carlisle women being "ruined," the appalling term applied to those suspected of losing their virginity. Students were no longer cowed by authority but upset by what they saw as the hypocrisy and cruelty of the school's leaders. Friedman became a subject of ridicule and contempt. Finally, when leading members of the football team turned against Pop Warner, the schoolwide rebellion broke into the open and a congressional committee sent an inspector to Carlisle to investigate. The leader of the football revolt was Gus Welch, the quarterback and Jim's best man at his wedding, motivated in part by disillusionment over the way the school had abandoned Jim during the Olympic medals controversy.

ON JANUARY 7, 1914, Welch presented a petition to Arthur Ringwalt Rupley, the congressman from Carlisle, who filed it with the commissioner of Indian affairs. The petition was signed by 276 students and requested a thorough investigation of the school, citing misdeeds by Friedman and Warner and institutional inadequacies ranging from physical and mental abuse to poor food and lax morality. Twelve days later, E. B. Linnen, chief inspector for the Department of the Interior's Office of Indian Affairs, arrived on the Carlisle campus to undertake the investigation. Because many of the students pushing the petition, including footballers Welch and Alex Arcasa, were students in the commercial department, and because of the notoriety of the Julia Hardin beating, Friedman and his acolytes suspected that Marianne Moore was a behind-the-scenes instigator of the rebellion. She denied it, telling Friedman that she did not encourage "disrespect and rancor" and tried to give her students "as thorough a training in political honor as I can." A diplomatic denial, but not a refutation. Moore tried to keep her name out of the investigation, avoiding the inspectors "as if they were smallpox."

Linnen examined all aspects of life at Carlisle. He visited every department; interviewed scores of students, teachers, and staffers; and examined conditions in all the buildings, from the cafeteria to the hospital. It became apparent to him that "an open break and rebellion was imminent" upon his arrival and "the strained condition of affairs could not have much longer obtained." Much of what he discovered led back to Friedman's inept leadership, and the most sensational of his discoveries involved the beating of Julia Hardin, but his sharpest and most insistent focus was on Pop Warner's dominant position at a place where "everything was made to be subservient to athletics and football."

It had been nearly seven years since Dr. Carlos Montezuma first leveled charges against Warner's program, but this time, with Pop's own players turning against him and the government burrowing into his department, his position was less tenable. Linnen compiled critical affidavits from Welch and five other players and examined the books of the Carlisle Athletic Association looking for irregularities. Before finally capitulating to the inquiry, the secretary and treasurer of the athletic fund, W. H. Miller, following Warner's instructions, balked at turning over the books, claiming they were beyond Linnen's scope because the athletic association was a private enterprise that did not use federal funds.

It soon became apparent why Warner did not want a keen-eyed investigator probing his accounts. In examining checks written by the Carlisle Athletic Association since 1907, Inspector Linnen uncovered how Pop used the resources of the association to control the internal workings of the school and its public image. The lucrative gate receipts he took in when his exotic band of American Indian athletes played establishment teams like Harvard, Penn, and Army were craftily used to buy loyalty. Friedman, local newspaper correspondents, merchants, lawyers, ministers, law enforcement authorities—anyone who had influence and might help the program was getting money from Warner. The players were kept in line through the distribution of cash, free clothing, and jewelry—at least, they had been silenced until the rebellion.

Going over payments check by check, Linnen showed how Warner used the association to fund Friedman's travel expenses over the years, including hotel bills and theater tickets, often under the guise of the superintendent attending away games. This was one of the many ways that Warner, whose salary was higher than Friedman's, held more sway over the institution than his nominal boss.

Linnen's examination found that some of the association money went to good use, especially the construction of new facilities at the school. But the rest was questionable. The Carlisle police department and Cumberland County sheriff's office were paid by Warner's association for the arrest and detainment of runaway students. Local journalists Hugh Miller and J. I. Martin were paid hundreds of dollars to write "favorable reports" about the football team, the school, and Friedman and Warner. Several Carlisle lawyers and ministers were paid various sums from the athletic account—all of them, not coincidentally, offering to be character witnesses for Friedman and Warner as the investigation unfolded. Warner was also involved in various acts of self-dealing, from reimbursing himself extravagantly for road trip expenses to using athletic funds to buy food from the Springfield Canning Company, a canned goods firm in which he held a financial interest.

And then there were hundreds of checks to students who were "kept for the purpose of playing football." The list of players getting paid, Linnen found, included its top stars over the years—"James Thorpe, Frank Mount Pleasant, William Garlow, Gus Welch, Antonio Lubo, Peter and Frank Hauser"—and the track star Lewis Tewanima, all of whom received from $10 to $15 per month along with larger lump sums, loans, and free overcoats and watches from Carlisle merchants. Payments to Thorpe totaled more than $500. To put this in context, it should be kept in mind that many if not most major college programs found ways to get money to their top athletes. It could also be argued that athletes supplied the entertainment talent that made money for the schools and deserved some financial reward. What the Linnen findings established above all else was the hypocrisy and duplicity of Warner and Friedman claiming that they were amateur innocents and shocked to discover that Jim Thorpe was a professional before the Olympics because he had played minor league baseball. At the time, Pop had been operating the athletic program at Carlisle as a form of quasi-professionalism with Friedman's complicity.

While Linnen was at Carlisle, Warner and Friedman tried desperately to derail his investigation. Soon after Welch filed the petition, he received a telegram from home saying that one of his brothers was sick in Wisconsin. Another brother at Carlisle with Gus wanted to go home to check on the sick sibling, but Friedman and Warner insisted that only Gus could go. "They wanted to get rid of me during this investigation," Gus said he came to realize. The captain of the football team, Elmer Bush, and star running back Joe Guyon were then called over to Warner's house, where the coach asked them to launch a counterpetition in support of Friedman. They declined, and instead joined Welch and several other players in submitting affidavits critical of Warner to Inspector Linnen.

"I know he is kind of good to the football boys during the season and when he gets out of humor, he calls them all kinds of names," Bush said. "As long as they play football, he is their friend, but after they leave school he has nothing to do with them. After football season he has nothing to do with the football boys; in fact, he has nothing to do with the students who do not take part in athletics. I do not think he is honest. The boys have been displeased because they never know anything about the athletic receipts or disbursements. He has the say of the football boys whether they are to be sent home or to come back."

Gus Welch was harsher in his assessment of Pop, stating in his affidavit that "Mr. Warner is a good football coach but a man with no principle." He was a fair-weather mentor—"so long as he can use you, he is all right with you; but the moment you voice your own sentiments and speak up for them he abuses you." Warner constantly swore at his players, calling them "goddamn boneheads" and "sons of bitches" and once yelled at Roy Large, an end, that he would "knock his damn block off." During road trips, he sold dozens of complimentary tickets in hotel lobbies and pocketed the cash. Many of the football boys, Welch concluded, "were in favor of discontinuing athletics if Mr. Warner was retained as coach."

John Wallette, a Chippewa, said in his affidavit that Warner once came up from behind and lashed him with a switch when he was practicing with a sore shoulder. William Newashe, Thorpe's old teammate and Sac and Fox childhood friend, said he came back to play in 1910 and 1911 "at the request of Mr. Warner" and that it was "generally given out and supposed that he was a student during those years" when he was not enrolled. Edward Bracklin, another Chippewa, testified that Warner constantly abused the system to get his players. Pop, he said, "had full control of the football boys, makes them go and come to and from their homes as he sees it, and controls them." Joe Guyon agreed, stating that Warner had "full control of the boys who play football regardless of the superintendent."

It also came out during Linnen's investigation that Warner was present at the dank Guard House jail on campus one Saturday in the winter of 1913 when disciplinarian David Dickey ordered four boys to stoop over a washbowl and whipped them fifty lashes with a trunk strap. Bandmaster Stauffer was also there that winter night. Warner said the boys were being punished for "getting ahold of some liquor and raising cain" and that the corporal punishment was justified. "We felt it was a case where there was nothing else to do as good, and it did have a wholesome effect on the boys," he said. That was one of several occasions when authorities at Carlisle used whippings, spankings, and beatings to punish students, Linnen found.

Warner's rationalization for corporal punishment came during testimony before the Joint Commission to Investigate Indian Affairs chaired by Senator Joe T. Robinson of Arkansas. Following Linnen's initial investigation, the commission held field hearings at Carlisle, setting up shop in the YMCA hall at the school from Friday, February 6, to Sunday, February 8, 1914. They took testimony from sixty witnesses ranging from Warner to Friedman, from Stauffer to Julia Hardin. Marianne Moore, as she had hoped, successfully dodged the controversy, even as she sympathized with the Indian students and was dismayed by the school's prisonlike atmosphere. Many of the witnesses testified to Friedman's lack of control. It was learned that Friedman propped up his own image by writing articles about his brilliant stewardship of the school and its many success stories under his leadership, persuading newspapers to publish them without his byline, and then republishing them in the *Arrow* and *Red Man*, the Carlisle publications, citing them as praise from various newspapers around the state and nation.

Much of the anger directed at Friedman during the hearings might have seemed justifiable, but there was also an ugly side to it. It came out during the hearings that he was subjected to anti-Semitic abuse from rebellious students. Friedman was Jewish by birth, Christian by conversion. Linnen picked up reports of students snarling "Christ killer" and "pork dodger" when they saw him walking down the hall. In the end, the financial irregularities uncovered during the investigation, along with Friedman's inept leadership skills, prompted the commission to recommend that he be fired, and he was, soon after the hearings ended. Stauffer, who had inflicted the beating on Julia Hardin, was fired as well.

Linnen had also recommended the firing of Pop Warner, but that did not happen. Instead, Pop left on his own terms. He coached one last year at Carlisle and then became head coach at the University of Pittsburgh, his undeniable football wizardry leading Pitt to three national championships. He remained in the pantheon of football coaches, his name so illustrious that he eventually was inducted into the College Football Hall of Fame. The most popular youth football program in America would be named in his honor. Warner rewrote history, scrubbing the Carlisle scandal from his résumé. It barely warranted mentioning in his autobiography, where in a few paragraphs, almost as an aside, he blamed the investigation on a "Washington crowd" out to get Friedman and close the school, and said it was the investigation itself, rather than the conditions that led to it, that left Carlisle "in a rather demoralized condition." While praising the ingenuity of his Indian players, he also claimed they were "not fond of work" and exceedingly sensitive.

On May 29, 1914, nearly four months after the investigation, Carlisle expelled Julia Hardin and her sister Maggie, sending them home to Oklahoma. An Indian Service official in Shawnee lamented that "the Hardin girls should have appreciated the opportunity afforded them at Carlisle and have conducted themselves in such a manner as to have set a good example for girls of more Indian blood rather than a bad one."

Two weeks later, Julia got a strikingly different message from the government—a letter of praise from the Bureau of Indian Affairs:

My dear friend,

I take pleasure in transmitting herewith a letter from the Commissioner of Indian Affairs awarding you one of the third prizes that were given to students . . . during the past school year throughout the Indian School Service. I also enclose the emblem that represents the prize. Let me congratulate you, hoping that what you learned in gathering the material for your essay broadened your views about the duties and responsibilities of citizenship.

15

The Myth of a Vanishing Race

IN FOOTBALL AND TRACK AND FIELD, JIM THORPE'S TALents were obvious, his success assured. Not so in baseball. From his first season with the New York Giants into his third, it was the same uncertain adventure. Here scribes had John McGraw declaring that "Jim Thorpe has found himself." There they quoted Wahoo Sam Crawford, who had played against Jim from Tokyo to London, saying he was an unnatural hitter with a strange "little upward chop as he swings." Here was a headline announcing "Jim Thorpe Wins Place in Regular Lineup of Giants." Next came a story by Bozeman Bulger, famed sportswriter of the *New York World*, explaining how Thorpe proved that great athletes often failed at baseball. One month up, one month down, never fluid and easy, always a grind.

The Bulger story appeared in early May 1915, just after Thorpe had been demoted and dispatched across the Hudson River, farmed out to the Jersey City Skeeters of the International League. McGraw had threatened to send him down the year before, and the IL's Toronto Maple Leafs had been pining for him, but that never happened and instead he had endured a second unproductive season on the Giants bench, getting only thirty-one at-bats, hitting no home runs, stealing one base, compiling another batting average below .200. Bulger noted that Thorpe could run faster than any man on the club, defeat any teammate in a wrestling match, and outjump them all by many inches, but "he apparently lacked the baseball instinct, which strangely enough is possessed in large quantities by runts and weaklings who cannot run fast, who are not strong of muscle, and could not win an athletic prize to save their lives." Jim's baseball foray was a noble effort, but now it seemed to be over. Jersey City, Bulger thought, might be the end of the trail.

The end of the trail was a familiar theme that year. Across the continent at the 1915 San Francisco World's Fair, the phrase was being evoked in a larger context, a grand celebration of human progress. The official name of the fair told part of the story. It was called the Panama-Pacific International Exhibition. Panama because the Panama Canal connecting the oceans had been completed months earlier, Pacific marking the four hundredth anniversary of explorer Vasco Núñez de Balboa's encounter with the Pacific Ocean. In the words of ethnohistorian Abigail Markwyn, the exhibition was a spectacle of "expansionism, conquest, and progress." Manifest destiny accomplished, the western frontier conquered, progress inevitable.

The most popular attraction at the fair captured those ideas. It was sculptor James Earle Fraser's statue of an Indian on horseback, slumped in defeat, titled *The End of the Trail.* Eighteen million fair visitors who gazed upon the monumental figure near the fair's front entrance saw these words describing it: "The drooping, storm-beaten figure of the Indian on the spent pony symbolizes the end of the race which was once a mighty people." The statue and the idea behind it caught the fancy of the majority white population. It was photographed more than anything else at the fair and then copied in various statue versions throughout the country in years to come, displayed in places as diverse as the National Cowboy & Western Heritage Museum in Oklahoma City, the Metropolitan Museum of Art in New York City, and a city park in Waupun, Wisconsin.

Although Fraser conceived it out of sympathy, *The End of the Trail* became an icon of something more complex, a symbolic representation of what centuries of U.S. military might and decades of forced assimilation had wrought. Like the eighteen-foot-high figure on horseback, Indians by 1915 were romanticized as a vanishing race, once savage but now tamed and disappearing, overtaken not by oppression but by the scientific progress of the modern world. It was history written from a comfortable distance by the winners. It was also simplistic and ultimately wrong.

The precise number of indigenous people in the United States before

Europeans arrived remains uncertain, estimates varying widely. In an essay in the seminal 2017 anthology *The Great Vanishing Act: Blood Quantum and the Future of Native Nations,* Russell Thornton, an Oklahoma Cherokee and UCLA anthropologist who studied Native American populations, put the figure in the middle range of estimates, at about seven million. Through the genocidal combination of war, disease, and government neglect, the population diminished exponentially from the sixteenth century through the end of the nineteenth century, reaching a low of about 248,000 by the 1890s and the massacre at Wounded Knee, the last major act of military violence against the Indian people. But a quarter century later, as *The End of the Trail* arose at the San Francisco World's Fair, the numbers were slowly rising. Thornton noted that the 1910 census counted 265,683 Indians in the continental U.S. plus another 25,331 in the territory of Alaska, marking "the first increase in the Indian population since European contact." The indigenous nations did not vanish but kept moving, adjusting, and finding ways to survive against the odds.

The same could be said of Jim Thorpe. Here he was in May 1915, approaching his twenty-seventh birthday. He had already lost much in his life—much of the land and freedom of his Sac and Fox heritage, a beloved twin brother, both parents, the magnificent trophies and gold medals of the Stockholm Olympics, and now, perhaps, his hopes of succeeding as a major league baseball player. More losses were yet to come, year after year, some inflicted on him by society, others of his own doing as a talented but flawed human being. From that perspective, his story could be viewed as tragedy, the decline and fall of a once mighty figure, ennobled in his weakness. But Thorpe's life might best be understood not as tragic dissolution but as gritty perseverance. With all the obstacles the world and his own failings put in his way, from the duplicity of powerful men to his personal struggle with alcohol, Jim kept going. Rarely demonstrative, more introvert than showman, lonelier than he ever showed the public, he endured nonetheless as the itinerant entertainer, the athlete, the Olympian, the Indian in constant motion, moving from one city to the next across America, fueled by a combination of willpower and often desperate financial need, searching for ways to adjust and survive.

• • •

MCGRAW'S DECISION TO send him to the minors did not disillusion Jim. To the contrary, he had wanted the move. Being a scrub on the bench was "a pretty tough business," he said. He would rather play every day somewhere else than "sit around and watch the other fellow do the work." So off to the minors he went. He and Iva, nine months pregnant, maintained their apartment near the Polo Grounds after he was demoted, and he commuted across the river to Jersey City. He played well immediately, starring in the first home series against the Toronto Maple Leafs where he batted third, played right field, and scored both runs in the first game. It was the start of a bountiful week of multi-hit games. As was often the case with Jim, from his earliest days at Rocky Mount to his spring training performances at Marlin Springs, he made a good first impression.

His life took another turn for the better on May 8 when Iva delivered a ten-pound baby boy. Jim was overjoyed, passing out cigars to teammates and writing letters to friends and relatives, including one to Iva's sister, Grace, and brother-in-law, Charles Morris, in Arkansas City, Kansas, just across the border from Ponca City, Oklahoma. "In that husky little fellow who I was told was a chip off the old block I placed my dreams and ambitions for the future," he later wrote. "I was building my own monument, I thought." The christening of James Francis Thorpe Jr. took place at St. Aloysius Roman Catholic Church in Harlem.

Soon Jim was off on a road trip with the Skeeters—and the main gate attraction again. Upstate New York was gray and frigid when the Rochester Hustlers held their home opener on May 17. The sports columnist for the *Rochester Democrat and Chronicle* found Thorpe an easy subject for hackneyed sarcasm, combining Indian stereotypes with his Olympic misfortune. "By noon we had exhausted all our expletives regarding the weather and had half a mind to go up and ask Jim Thorpe, Olympic champion and right fielder for the Jersey City club, what he thought about it, thus: 'Ugh, big chief. Do wintry chills send redman's thoughts leaping backward to when ice crusted Thorpe wigwam?' And then we thought better of it, remembering that Thorpe was still healthy and that our life insurance hadn't been paid. But Jim Thorpe, just the same, probably knows a heap about cold weather. The AAU decision about his medals probably gave Mr. Thorpe quite a working knowledge of chills."

Although the Skeeters were dwelling in the International League cellar, Jim's stellar play at the plate and in right field continued through midsummer. The cycle of Thorpe the player of great potential and Thorpe the disappointment seemed back at the positive end of the perpetual loop. The Associated Press declared again that Jim was "destined to develop after all into a major league star of the first magnitude" and criticized McGraw for not sending him to the minors earlier so that he could develop with regular playing time. The *Brooklyn Daily Times* wrote that Thorpe was showing "flashes of brilliant playing ability" and would "undoubtedly wear a Giants uniform" soon.

Then his luck turned. During a home game against the first-place Buffalo Bisons in July, thieves broke into the dressing room at Skeeters Park on West Side Avenue and stole Jim's diamond ring, valued at $400. His tenure on the Skeeters ended a few days later, when he was transferred to another team in the International League, the Harrisburg Indians. Many accounts said Thorpe requested the transfer, which brought him close to his old turf in Carlisle, twenty miles to the southwest, but that makes less sense when one considers how the move took him farther from New York City and his wife and infant son. Some stories said the Skeeters, managed by Hooks Wiltse, a former Giants teammate who had traveled around the world with him, had tired of Thorpe, although no reasons were cited. One disparaging nugget made its way into sports pages around the country, asserting that with Jim ending up in lowly Harrisburg, "the AAU ought to be convinced he never was a professional." In any event, Harrisburg wanted and needed him after a starting outfielder broke his leg.

Jim was received as a hometown hero. Additional bleachers went up in Island Park's right-field section to accommodate the largest crowd of the season. He did not disappoint, clouting a home run to center that was described as "one of the longest ever made on the Harrisburg field." He stayed hot well into August at the plate and on the basepaths, with several multi-hit performances and twice stealing three bases in a game, though he still had trouble hitting the curve from right-handed pitchers and was uneven in the field. The *Buffalo Courier,* calling Jim "a fairly well known Indian," described a typical game in which he "showed he is human like the rest of us." He dropped an easy fly ball in left but also got three hits and three steals and "did more damage to the Bison cause than to Harrisburg."

His best friend on the team—and roommate on the road—was Al Schacht, a jovial little pitcher from New York's Lower East Side later known as "the clown prince of baseball" for his comedy routines on the field and as the proprietor of a Manhattan steakhouse. Schacht was five years younger than Jim and as a teenager had idolized the All-American football player at Carlisle. "He called me 'little Injun,'" Schacht recalled. "Said I looked like a Jewish Indian." When Schacht asked him about the Olympics and how Jim felt losing the medals, he could not elicit much of a response. "I mentioned it twice to him about the medals, he wouldn't answer me, wouldn't say yes or no. Just say, 'Ooooh'—much like that." He considered Thorpe "a good-natured fellow [who] wouldn't hurt anybody," yet said he remembered a time when Jim "cleaned out a saloon."

Alcohol and insults formed the combustible mix. The incident had happened earlier in the season, when Jim was still with Jersey City and Schacht was on the Indians, then still located in Newark. As Schacht recounted it, after a game between the two teams, both men were heading to their homes in New York and stopped at a bar near the train depot before catching the commuter line into the city. Three "real tough mugs" in the bar started riding Jim from a nearby table, ridiculing him for the error he had made in left that day when he charged a ball and it bounced up from his glove, splitting his lip. "A guy comes in with a beer in his hand to join these three fellows and sees Jim and starts ribbing him. Jim is getting a little firewater and I know it's bad." The heckler says Jim "will get his brains knocked out some day going after a fly ball," Schacht recalled. "And Jim says, 'You little boys better keep quiet there or I'm gonna go over and spank you.'" With no interest in getting caught up in a bar brawl, Schacht said, he went to the bartender to urge him to quiet the hecklers before they got hurt. "And I hear, boom, boom, and two guys are out, and another is against the wall. . . . That was Jim Thorpe."

Schact's memory was imprecise. There was more—or less—to the story than that. Thorpe and the catcher for the Jersey City team, William Reynolds, were arrested during a brawl that night, charged with beating a young man named Edward La Forge. According to a complaint sworn out by La Forge's mother, Reynolds kicked the young man in the head. What Thorpe did was unclear. The charges were dropped when La Forge told authorities he could not remember the brawl, and years later Jim claimed the story libeled him.

Harrisburg took advantage of his popularity by staging a Thorpe Day at the ballpark on August 17. More than two hundred students of the Carlisle Indian Industrial School came to honor their famous alumnus at a doubleheader against the Providence Grays. John DeHuff, acting superintendent after Moses Friedman's ouster, arranged for the Cumberland Valley Railroad to carry students and guests at a bargain seventy-five-cent round-trip rate to and from Harrisburg. Before the game, the Carlisle students presented Jim with a baseball bat in the red and gold school colors, then marched across the diamond to take seats in the centerfield bleachers, all waving pennants, the young women in their traditional broad-brimmed hats. "Cheers greeted the big Indian at his every appearance and play," reported the *Carlisle Evening Herald*, adding that Jim "played a good consistent game and figured strongly in the credit end of the box score."

What was daily existence like for the greatest athlete in the world playing baseball in the International League in 1915? It was several calibers higher than the Rocky Mount Railroaders team Jim had played for six years earlier, but still it was the bushes, rough and haphazard. Crowds in Harrisburg that summer were so unruly that Edward G. Barrow, the league president, said the "rowdyism must cease" or he would transfer the team next season. The fans were like riotous vaudeville theater audiences, but instead of rotten tomatoes they heaved more dangerous projectiles. "Part of the enjoyment of a ball game is vested in the good-natured roasting that the fans can give an umpire, but when it goes to such a limit as throwing pop bottles and other missiles, it will not be tolerated," Barrow said. Umpires were not the only ones taking cover. Players and teams were flying around like tossed pop bottles, moving from one team and city to another.

Harrisburg, now ordered to behave or else, had a team that year only because the Indians had suffered from miserable attendance figures in Newark, where they were losing fans to the upstart Federal League, and fled to Pennsylvania's capital city. The Orioles moved from Baltimore to Rochester for the same reason.

Although it boasted a worldly title because of its teams in Toronto and Montreal, the International League's daily milieu was closer to the sticks. The day after Thorpe Day, the Harrisburg team drove to the hamlet of Chambersburg for an exhibition against a local squad in the lowest rung of the minors. Thorpe was part of a traveling crew that included the team president, three local sportswriters, manager Eddie Zimmerman, and seventeen players. They left Harrisburg at midmorning in a six-car caravan, five men to a car; meandered through the fruit orchards of Cumberland and York Counties; stopped in Mount Holly Springs for a Farmers Picnic where the players danced "with the fair country maidens"; and then rumbled on to Gettysburg for a two-hour tour of the Civil War battlefield. The roads were unpaved and rugged, the automobiles unreliable. One car caught fire on the last leg between Gettysburg and Chambersburg, and several others had flat tires along the way, but they arrived in time for the five o'clock start at a lumpy and potholed ballyard on the edge of a cornfield.

Thorpe was the main attraction, according to Wellington G. Jones, a correspondent accompanying the team. "When he stepped from his automobile and walked across the field there was prolonged cheering until he lifted his cap." In left field, Jim had to dodge holes as he chased fly balls and listened in bewilderment as local fans shouted "Horseshoes!" after every good play. His roommate Al Schacht came in as a reliever to win the game, and they all retreated to the Hotel Washington for a turkey dinner before piling into the six autos for the return ride through the darkness to Harrisburg.

A few days later, Iva took the train to Harrisburg with Jim Jr. in tow, arriving late on the afternoon of August 25. It was their first trip out of the city, although earlier they had tooted around the streets of Manhattan in Mrs. McGraw's car. The plan was to stay a week with Jim at the team hotel during a long Indians home stand. A photograph of Jim holding Junior ran in the *Harrisburg Telegraph* and went out on the wires for newspaper display across the country. Jim was sitting down, dressed in a striped shirt and tie, a white porkpie hat with black band atop his head, gazing proudly at his son, alert and chunky in a sleeping gown. "If Jim Thorpe Jr. isn't a 'bear' of an athlete in days to come, then this picture belies the truth you surely will agree," the caption read. "Don't you think the little papoose is the image of his 'pap'?" The father's ambitions for his namesake went beyond athletics; he said he hoped the boy would be more like his mother. "Jim will get the best education that can be had. There's nothing too good for the boy, I can tell you," he said.

Iva and Junior had no sooner settled in than the situation changed. Jim's days with the Indians were done. " 'JIM' THORPE GETS HIS RELEASE," announced the *Harrisburg Courier.* "Harrisburg Cans Thorpe," blared a headline in the *Chicago Tribune.* "Jim Thorpe Bounced by Harrisburg Club," declared the *New-York Tribune.* The stories blamed Thorpe in various ways. "The big Indian was released because he has been practically worthless to the Harrisburg team, it is said," wrote the New York paper. The *Carlisle Evening Herald* said Jim's release "caused a sensation in the city" but was not a surprise because he "had been benched early last week" following "the remarkable work of William Tamm in the left garden." The Chicago paper said it was "understood that Thorpe has been a disturbing influence in the camp of the Indians."

In truth, Jim behaved no worse than most players on the team, a typical collection of baseball roustabouts. And although developing a sore arm, he continued playing well until two days before his release, making no errors in left, stealing two bases, and going eight for fifteen at the plate in his final games. Harrisburg dumped him for other reasons, mainly because they wanted to keep Tamm, who was younger and thought to have more baseball skills (wrongly as it turned out). What the stories revealed was how willingly and inaccurately the press would turn on Thorpe—a pattern that would haunt him the rest of his career.

• • •

EARLIER THAT YEAR, a rumor had flitted through New York that Thorpe would be the next football coach at Columbia University. It sounded plausible, at least from Jim's perspective. Going back to his earliest days as a player, he had thought that someday he would coach. Hal Sheridan, lead sportswriter for United Press, filed a story in May, just after Jim was shipped to Jersey City, that used vague wording to imply that Thorpe was bound for Columbia, fudging the notion by saying that college sports fans were excited by the prospect and that school officials would neither confirm nor deny the rumor. The only thing that could prevent the hiring, Sheridan wrote, was money. Columbia would have to "revise their figures upward about four times" to match the salary Jim was getting from the Giants. That made it sound like Jim had planted the story himself, which was likely. The hiring did not happen.

But Jim did not stop looking, and in early September, after Harrisburg cut him loose and sent him back to New York to sit on McGraw's bench, he landed his first coaching job. The offer came from Clarence C. Childs, head coach at Indiana University, who had been Jim's teammate at the 1912 Olympics, winning a bronze medal in the hammer throw in Stockholm. Jim would coach the kickers and backfield men, Childs said, and would join the team in Bloomington when the baseball season ended. One year, four jobs, four cities, nowhere near the end of the trail.

16

Never Look Up

WHEN CLARENCE CHILDS COACHED THE INDIANA UNIVERSITY football team, he spent much of his downtime in the lobby of the Hotel Bowles at the corner of Sixth and College Avenue plotting and reminiscing in a huddle dubbed the Coaches Corner. Bloomington sportswriters in search of inside dope knew that was the place to go. One reporter wrote in the town's *Daily Telephone* that "more football battles have been fought in the corner between Coach Childs and his friends than have ever been played on Jordan Field." On the morning of October 8, 1915, the lobby filled with curious Hoosiers looking for something more—the appearance of a newly hired assistant coach. His arrival was awaited with such anticipation that journalists had estimated the time it would take him to reach Bloomington from New York. They were off by a half day. Jim Thorpe and his wife, Iva, came through the hotel entrance with their infant son at exactly 10:10 a.m.

No time to waste. After reconnecting with his former Olympic teammate in the lobby, Jim situated his young family in a suite upstairs, and by midafternoon he was at the University's Jordan Field sporting an Indiana sweatshirt and cap, putting in the first day of work for the $2,078.69 he was being paid for the season. It was a Friday, and there was a home game the next day against Miami of Ohio. The students were so ecstatic to have a famous athlete on their sidelines that several hundred attended practice, with yell leader Chick Griffith organizing a nine-rah cheer for Jim. He "seemed greatly pleased with his reception and, with a broad grin on his face, bowed in acknowledgment of the cheers directed at him," reported the correspondent for the *Indianapolis Star*, who interviewed him on the field. Thorpe said he wished he could have reached Bloomington sooner but was looking forward to coaching the running backs and kickers. It had been three years since he last starred for Carlisle. He dearly missed football and loved it as much as ever, he said.

The next day offered a promising start to his new career. Indiana tried only one forward pass all game, and that was incomplete, but ran the ball efficiently in swamping Miami 41–0, and Thorpe deserved at least some credit, according to Ralston Goss, sports editor of the *Star.* "Thorpe, by the way, has taken hold with a vim and, in a quiet way, has done much to instill confidence in the players," he reported. Along with the confidence boost, Jim was also expected to work wonders with the Indiana punters and place-kickers after he had more time to teach them his tricks.

Thorpe was now the latest branch of a blossoming Pop Warner coaching tree. Pop himself had just escaped Carlisle, relatively unscathed from the 1914 scandal, and was reinventing himself at Pitt, where he would lead the Panthers to an undefeated season. Six of his old players followed him into the coaching ranks. Albert Exendine and Frank Mt. Pleasant—two of his sharpest former players, stars of the 1906 and 1907 squads—were now also head coaches, Exendine at Georgetown and Mt. Pleasant at Buffalo. Bill Gardner, a star end on those teams, had coached at Manuel High in Louisville and Sewanee in Tennessee. Lone Star Dietz, the grizzled lineman and assistant art director at Carlisle, had just traveled cross-country to begin his coaching career at Washington State. William Garlow had been hired to coach at West Virginia Wesleyan, and Mike Balenti, whose best sport was baseball, had dipped briefly into the football coaching ranks the previous season for a one-year stint at Chattanooga.

When a conversation went to subjects that Jim did not care about, it was hard to get more than a *yes* or *no* or *not sure* out of him. But as a tutor of kickers he knew what he was talking about and had much to say. The first trait he looked for was the ease with which a punter could drop the ball and swiftly raise the leg to meet it. If that did not come naturally, little else could help. The next thing he looked for was build. He thought a punter should be at least average height if not taller; a short punter was a rarity, his kicks more prone to being blocked. Even though Jim was adept at all forms of kicking, he thought of himself as the exception to the rule and urged his punters not to place-kick or drop-kick because the different motions developed different muscles. The place-kick demanded a straight-leg movement, while raising the leg for a punt required strong thighs and loose hamstrings.

Starting in practice the week after the Miami game, he began imparting his ideas to the Indiana kickers. He taught them that, much like a batter in baseball, it was essential for a punter to keep his eye on the ball throughout the kick. They should choose their direction first, which side of the field they would aim the punt toward, and then never look up. He told them to "hold the ball as far away from the body as possible, directly in front of the kicking foot, with one hand on each side of it and the outer point of the ball slightly lower than the end nearest the body." Then drop the ball so that it fell toward the leg without turning. Extend the kicking foot and swing the leg mostly from the hip, bending only slightly at the knee, meeting the ball about two and a half feet from the ground. To get the most power in the kick, bend the body backward slightly while following through with the kicking leg as high as possible. Much like a baseball pitcher, an effective punter needed good control and should be able to put juice on the ball, he said. Striking the pigskin at a slightly different point of the foot could produce various results. If the ball was not caught by the punt returner, subtleties in the kick could make it bounce left or right, forward or backward, or drop flat as if it were deflated.

This was a living legend standing there telling them how to punt, and the Indiana boys were anxious to hear about his experiences at Carlisle. He told them about the time he kicked the ball so high and far he was able to run down and field it himself. He remembered a game against Princeton when his boot went the entire length of the field, end zone to end zone. And then he demonstrated how he did it. One afternoon as he was coaching the kickers, a group of boys from nearby Margaret McCalla elementary school—the Skirvin brothers and a friend—walked over to watch football practice after school let out.

"We lingered in the grass, close to the eastern goal post, and looked on as the kickers did their stuff," Herbert H. Skirvin recalled. "Taking turns, five backfielders got off some pretty good punts traveling about forty yards in the air on average. The big stranger talked with them a few minutes and then put on a demonstration of his own. He punted four balls all of them sailing downfield from 45 to 55 yards in the air. Several gridders came over for a closer look and we asked one, 'Who is that guy?' The player replied, 'That's the great Jim Thorpe. He's one of our assistant coaches.' The name did not mean anything to us then. But having heard the word great, seeing the man kick and noticing he looked like an Indian, we wedged in as near as possible. From this vantage point we heard one of the backfielders ask Thorpe, 'What was the longest punt you ever got off, coach?' In so many words, Thorpe answered, 'I'll try to give you a show,' and he told the center to heave him another ball. Catching the ball at the goal line he took a couple of strides forward and gave the pigskin a terrific smash with his foot. As the plunk reverberated over the area, the ball soared through the air landing seventy-five yards away then bouncing over the goal line. . . . It was almost unbelievable. . . ."

Quite a story—but like many Jim Thorpe stories, this one should be received with a degree of caution. It came from an older man recalling a moment in his childhood, and it was told long after Thorpe had become immortalized. In describing the encounter, Skirvin joined the multitudes who saw Thorpe do something extraordinary on a football field or track and later transformed a memory into a Homeric ode to otherworldly prowess. Sometimes the memories were accurate, sometimes not. That is how athletic myths are made, by the desire to rise above life's ordinariness and associate with the transcendent. Myths at once distort a specific reality and fill a human need, revealing a larger truth.

Indiana was a state institution with a large student body to draw from and was part of the prestigious Western Conference comprising the big land-grant colleges of the Midwest plus two private schools, Northwestern and Chicago. But Jim soon learned that the talent in Bloomington was inferior to what he was accustomed to at Carlisle. After the easy win against Miami of Ohio, Indiana lost three games, tied one, and won one, finishing the season with a 3-3-1 overall record, 1-3-1 in conference play. There was only so much he could do as an assistant coach; he could not put himself in at left halfback or as the kicker. But fans expected more, demanded more, and Jim tried to accommodate them. In one of the defeats, a 10–9 loss to Ohio State at Columbus, he performed at halftime, setting "the crowd wild with exhibition punts of 85 yards and perfect dropkicks from the center of the field." The halftime performance became part of his routine through much of the rest of his career, showing off either his powerful leg or his Indian heritage, or both.

Not long after the loss to Ohio State, one of Jim's former teammates from Carlisle visited him in Bloomington. It was Bill Gardner, the star end on the 1907 Indians who was now supplementing his income playing football for pay on Sundays in Canton, Ohio. Gardner had been assigned by Jack Cusack, owner of the Canton Bulldogs, to persuade Thorpe to join the team for its final games of the season. The Bulldogs were part of a loosely affiliated network of teams competing in what was known as the Ohio League, considered the incubator of professional football (although some city clubs had slipped money to players now and then going back to the 1890s).

Cusack sent Gardner to Bloomington with an enticement that meant more than old school sentiment: a promise of $250 per game. It was an offer Jim would not refuse. That was nearly twice as much as the league's best players were making, and Cusack, then only twenty-four, the chief clerk at a gas company, understood the risk. "Some of my business advisers frankly predicted that I was leading the Bulldogs into bankruptcy by paying Jim the enormous sum," he said later.

There were ample reasons to believe they were right. Pro football ranked near the bottom of sporting attractions, far below college football, major league baseball, boxing, tennis, golf, and horse racing. There was little professional about the Ohio League except the modest salaries. No team was on sure financial footing. Every year for a decade, the league had been shape-shifting, with teams folding, moving, and being born again. Cleveland, Toledo, Columbus, Dayton, Akron, Cincinnati, Canton, and Massillon were among the Ohio cities that at one time had teams in the league. Games rarely drew more than a few thousand fans, and often only a few hundred, even for the most competitive contests. The atmosphere was freewheeling and rife with deceit. The free agency of the National Football League a century later would look restrictive compared with the movement of players in 1915, when it was not uncommon for talented ringers to switch teams game by game, ignoring a gentlemen's agreement among owners against raiding the opposition. Much like the baseball minor leagues Jim had played in earlier in his career, the football teams in the Ohio League were stocked with college players—even college coaches—using aliases to avoid being declared ineligible at their schools.

All of that made Cusack's $250-a-game offer seem chancy. On the other hand, Thorpe was a proven gate attraction and always a favorite subject for the national press. The economy in Ohio was on the upswing in 1915, in part because the war in Europe brought more business to manufacturers in the industrial Midwest. Maybe it was the right name at the right time, Cusack thought, when people with more disposable income would spend some of that to see the famous Indian athlete. He considered it worth the gamble, and he was right. Bob Carroll, the noted football historian, called Cusack's hiring of Thorpe in early November 1915 "the single most important pro football action ever taken up to then." The creation of the NFL was still five years away, Carroll said, "but its beginnings were in 1915" when Thorpe came to Canton.

Not that Thorpe immediately decamped from Bloomington to take up the life of a pro in Canton. He kept his day job at Indiana and came to Canton only for the final two games, with little time to practice with the team. On November 13, after helping coach Indiana to a win over Northwestern in a Western Conference road game, Thorpe left the squad in Chicago and traveled four hundred miles east to Canton for his first game the next day against their main rival in the nearby Ohio town of Massillon. In some ways, it was an inauspicious start. Thorpe's name drew an uncommonly large crowd, at least six thousand, and Jim played well when he was in the game, once breaking off a forty-yard run before slipping in the mud; but the Bulldogs coach, Harry Hazlett, refused to start Thorpe and played him only sparingly. The Massillon Tigers, led by former Notre Dame quarterback Gus Dorais, a passing wizard, and his college teammate and receiver Knute Rockne, won 16–0.

Some said Hazlett declined to play Thorpe more because he was upset by the salary. Some said it was because Thorpe had not been able to practice with the team beforehand. One sportswriter attributed it to the fact that "the famous Indian athlete lacked the necessary wind to carry him through the entire contest." In any case, the reaction was the same. Fans roared when Jim had the ball and were angry that they did not see more of him. Cusack was upset too, so much so that he fired Hazlett and installed Thorpe as the player-coach for the rematch in Canton two weeks later.

Town and team rivalries held special importance then, as always. When Jim returned to Bloomington after Canton's loss, he began preparing for another rivalry game, the intrastate contest between Indiana and Purdue. It was the last game of the season for both teams, the last ever to be played at Jordan Field (which was being replaced by a new stadium), and a special homecoming to which every living Indiana U. athlete had been invited—all of that plus Jim Thorpe on the sidelines and the brotherly competitiveness between major state schools brought the largest crowd of the year. To steer clear of the hubbub, Childs and Thorpe moved their players to a sanitarium in nearby Martinsville to stay the night before the game. Nearly fifteen hundred Purdue fans paid $1.50 round-trip to ride special trains along the Monon Route between West Lafayette and Bloomington on game day, arriving at the station in time to see a parade of hundreds of IU old boys marching through downtown behind the band on the way to the field.

Three days of rain and snow had rendered the field a sloppy mess, which described the game as well, not only disappointing for Indiana, which lost 7–0, but dreary for Jim, who was criticized by fans and sportswriters for the lackluster offense. The feeling was that if Thorpe was so spectacular, he should have found a way to keep his running backs on their feet, as if he were responsible for the muddy field. "Perhaps the greatest disappointment was the inability of the Indiana backfield to come across with what was expected," reported the *Indianapolis News.* "Every one of the players behind the Crimson line had a world of speed, but when the play had hardly started it was the same story over and over, slip, bang! Down they went." When it was over, "gloom pervaded the atmosphere" on the Indiana campus while Purdue fans celebrated with a snake dance around the county courthouse before piling back on the train.

Jim was discouraged by the final loss in a mediocre season, stung by the criticism he and Childs were getting, and looking for another chance. The college season was over, but there were still games to be played, and not only with Canton. Jim found a pro match on Thanksgiving Day that would perfectly serve his needs. On one side was a University All Stars squad composed largely of Purdue alumni, including a few Boilermakers who had just concluded their amateur eligibility, along with Eddie Hart, an All-American tackle from Princeton who'd gained notoriety by enduring an entire season wearing a headguard that supposedly protected his broken neck. On the other side was a team ostensibly representing Pine Village, a tiny town between Lafayette and the Illinois border. In the murky world of early pro football, Pine Village, a hamlet of 217 residents, managed to hold its own by paying enough to attract talented ringers. For this game, the key ringer was Jim Thorpe, who would bring along several Indiana seniors who had played their final college game against Purdue. Jim was not breaking a contract with Canton to play, in part because Pine Village was not in the Ohio League and in part because his agreement with Jack Cusack was as loose as the league itself.

"Jimmie Thorpe is on the warpath and out for revenge," reported the *Bloomington Evening Star*, noting how the lineups simulated Indiana versus Purdue. "Thorpe believes he is going to have a chance to even up in the game Thursday." The article then quoted Thorpe, though the formal language sounded more like a paraphrase of what Jim might have said: "It is seldom that I am beaten and when I am beaten I am always looking for a chance to even the score. I think that I will play about the best game I have played in many years against those Purdue players. I have kept in good condition and should be up to my old form."

The game, held at Red Sox Park in Lafayette, drew a crowd twenty times larger than the population of Pine Village and coverage in all the Indiana papers. Thorpe on the field again, as player not coach, and playing on Thanksgiving Day—that was the attraction, and the *Star*'s Ralston Goss could not resist noting the significance, interestingly ignoring the traditional holiday gloss of Indian and Puritan harmony for the more gruesome reality of American history:

In days of old
Red Injuns bold
Our forebears sought to slay
But now we pay
To see them play
Upon Thanksgiving Day

Revenge in all forms, then. Flashing the all-around skills that had made him an All-American at Carlisle, Thorpe dominated—running, passing, tackling, and punting. The press called him the clear "star of the game" and "the main factor of the Pine Village teamwork both offensively and defensively." It was clear from the second play—an eighty-yard touchdown gallop called back because of a penalty—that Jim was the best player on the field. He scored two more touchdowns that counted, one on a fifty-five-yard run, and boomed an eighty-five-yard punt in leading Pine Village to a 29–0 win. The little town got its 250 bucks' worth.

The next day Thorpe traveled to Canton again for the Bulldogs' rematch with Massillon, a season-ending contest that in the ambitious subculture of the Ohio League claimed to be for the world championship of pro football. Both teams stacked their lineups for the game. Massillon featured not only Dorais and Rockne, but also four other former Notre Dame players. Canton recruited two star tackles, Bob Butler from Wisconsin and Gideon Smith, the first black player at Michigan State. A mile-long caravan of Tiger boosters jammed the roads for the sixteen-mile journey from Massillon to Canton to become part of an overflow crowd at League Park that filled the bleachers and sidelines and spilled ten-deep into the end zones.

Jim was primed this time and, as the team leader with a jealous coach out of the way, did not have to worry about playing time. His all-around brilliance shone again. On defense, his sure tackling kept Massillon in check, and on offense, he consistently broke the line and rounded the ends for effective runs, frustrating Knute Rockne, the Fighting Irishman who had been assigned to shadow him. The matchup against Rockne inspired another Thorpe legend enhanced later by both men. As they would tell the story, Thorpe chided Rockne after a tackle, saying the fans were there to see only one thing and that he should "let ol' Jim run." Later in the game, after the big Indian bowled over him "like a ten-ton truck rambling over the remains," Rockne recalled, Thorpe patted him on the back and clucked, "That's a good boy, Knute, you let ol' Jim run, didn't you." Perhaps there was a shred of truth to the story, but it was mostly laugh-line material for delivery at athletic banquets on the chicken dinner circuit.

It was Jim's kicking, not running or tackling, that won the game. His two field goals—a twenty-one-yard drop-kick in the first quarter and a thirty-seven-yard place-kick in the third—accounted for all the points in a 6–0 Canton victory. At least officially. Nothing was that clear and easy in the Ohio League. A decisive play near the end of the game encapsulated the competition in all its wild and messy wonder.

With three minutes to go, the Massillon Tigers had the ball and were moving downfield. Dorais completed a pass to Windy Briggs, a halfback from Ohio State, who broke clear at the fifteen and sprinted toward the end zone for what looked to be a touchdown that would at least tie the game and win it if the extra point was good. But as Briggs neared the goal line, the frenzied end zone crowd surged forward and engulfed him. The ball popped loose and Gideon Smith of Canton fell on it. Touchback, not touchdown, ruled the referee. Bulldogs' ball. What had happened? Briggs was furious, claiming that a Canton fan, not a player, punched the pigskin free, causing the fumble. He made one unfortunate mistake in presenting his case, claiming that a uniformed policeman committed the underhanded punch, even describing the brass buttons on the uniform. Impossible, he was quickly told. Canton had no uniformed cops. Fans on both sides stormed the field by the hundreds. Dazed and fearful and unable to restore order, the officials declared the game over. Massillon partisans would not stand for it. Surrounding the refs, they demanded a reconsideration of the call and an explanation of how it was made.

Okay, said the intimidated officials, we will write down our decision, place it in an envelope, and not allow it to be read until half past midnight at the Courtland Hotel. Most Massillon fans had returned home by the time the hotel manager opened the envelope and announced that Canton had won. No one would ever know for sure, but a Canton fan years later confided that he was the culprit who punched the ball free, motivated by his desire to win a thirty-dollar bet.

FOOTBALL SEASON DONE, Jim returned to Bloomington to pick up Iva and Jim Jr. at the Hotel Bowles. The local reporters greeted him in the hotel lobby, just as they had when he first arrived two months earlier. He told reporters that he had enjoyed his time there and hoped to return to coach for the 1916 season. No chance of that; Childs was about to be fired.

Iva was a sociable person and had made many friends in the college town, but she was eager to get back to Oklahoma, and so was Jim, who still dreamed of getting rich from an oil strike. The triptych of his life was being etched: baseball in spring and summer, football in fall, Oklahoma in winter. It was in the old territory that Jim could get back to what he always said were his favorite pastimes, hunting and fishing. And it was there that he could try yet another sport, the game of golf. During a warm February, taking the advice of his Giants teammate Christy Mathewson, Jim spent his afternoons at the Oklahoma City Golf & Country Club hacking away at a dimpled little ball. The Big Six, still rooting for Jim to make it in the big leagues, told him that golf could improve his hand-eye coordination and help him hit a baseball, a skill he was still determined to master.

17

Gains

AT THE END OF 1916, AFTER ANOTHER YEAR OF SEASONAL athletic migration, Jim gained a home, a deed, and citizenship. He and Iva and Jim Jr. moved to Yale, a town in north-central Oklahoma halfway between Oklahoma City and Tulsa. Yale arose on land that was once part of the Pawnee reservation, and more recently had been at the center of an oil boom, but the Pawnee were mostly gone and oil was drying up. What drew the Thorpes to Yale was the presence of Iva's sister Grace Morris and her family. They moved in next door at 706 East Boston Avenue on the east side of town one block from State Highway 51. It was a two-bedroom Craftsman bungalow, gray with white trim, an asphalt roof, weatherboard walls, and a fenced backyard where Jim kept a kennel of coonhounds who howled when the moon was full.

Ten days before Christmas, a letter arrived there from Horace J. Johnson, chief agent at the Sac and Fox Agency in Stroud. One document inside proclaimed that James Francis Thorpe had qualified to be deemed a United States citizen. He was twenty-nine. He had lived his entire life on American soil. He was educated at government schools. He could read and write. He had brought glory to the United States as the greatest athlete at the Olympics in 1912, praised by President Taft for representing "the best type of American citizen." His income as a professional baseball and football player exceeded the $3,000-a-year minimum that required him to pay federal taxes. All of that, yet only now was he granted citizenship.

A second document inside the envelope was what was known as a fee simple patent—a deed signed by the current president, Woodrow Wilson, that finally granted Jim full control of the land allotment near the North

Canadian River that he was assigned when the Sac and Fox reservation was carved up in 1891 as a consequence of the Dawes Act. He'd had to wait a quarter century for that outright deed to his own land as a stipulation in the federal act. Until then, because of his Sac and Fox heritage, he was not considered competent to handle his own property affairs and required the guardianship of the government.

Soon after, another package arrived containing a purse, an arrow, and a citizenship pin with an eagle emblem. These talismans were meant to be symbols of his new status. "The secretary requests that you keep the arrow always," Jim was instructed. "It will be to you a symbol of your noble race and of the pride you feel that you come from the first of all Americans. The Emblem of Citizenship is to be worn in the button-hole of your coat. Wear this badge always; and may the eagle on it never see you do aught of which the flag will not be proud."

Here was another action shaped and warped by the power of the federal government over the indigenous community. Some Native Americans, especially those like Thorpe who were educated at government boarding schools, wanted citizenship, but others did not, viewing it as another form of forced assimilation. In either case, citizenship was a complex issue, as Patty Loew, director of the Center for Native American and Indigenous Research at Northwestern University, later noted. While the government characterized it as an earned gift, it was also something that enhanced federal control and "ignored and circumvented tribal sovereignty." And enough had been done to Jim already, more than he could ever do to the American flag. An arrow and a buttonhole pin could not replace the gold medals, bronze bust, and silver chalice taken from him after his triumph in Stockholm nearly four years earlier, nor restore all the land seized from his Sac and Fox people for centuries before.

The past year had been uneven for Jim professionally, but more positive than not. Once again McGraw had brought him to spring training with the Giants, and this time even had him try swinging his heavy black bat left-handed to see if that would help him hit the curveball from right-handed pitchers, but once again the manager bailed on Jim before giving him a chance. In mid-April, McGraw had sent him down to play in the American Association with the Milwaukee Brewers. Rather than give up, Jim excelled, showing himself to be the best regular on a miserable club that lost a hundred games and finished eighteen and a half games out of first place. It was in Milwaukee that Jim showed glimpses of his full promise as a multitool ballplayer, leading the league in stolen bases with 48, along with 10 home runs, 85 runs batted in, and a solid .274 batting average.

Had the Little Napoleon given up too soon? At the time, many sportswriters believed the opposite, that McGraw had been coddling Jim for years, providing him with more chances than he deserved only because of contract obligations and Jim's public fame. Even though baseball was full of rough characters, Jim seemed less polished than most, on and off the field. His way of releasing pent-up energy was to wrestle teammates. One day during spring training in 1916 he went on "a happy rampage" and took on most of the team, prompting a writer to call him "as gentle as a wild African water buffalo." One reason McGraw sent him to Milwaukee, it was said, was out of fear that he would injure one of the Giants stars.

But in retrospect, a growing number of baseball mavens and Thorpe friends concluded that the Giants manager mishandled the situation from start to finish, that he failed Jim more than the other way around. In the press, McGraw rarely had anything but positive things to say about Thorpe, but in their day-to-day dealings at the ballpark he was more often foulmouthed and dismissive. Pop Warner came to believe that McGraw misunderstood Jim. "I've often thought that John McGraw never handled him properly when Thorpe played baseball for the Giants," Warner reflected decades later. "Jim was a horse for work and McGraw didn't give him that work."

In football, Thorpe's talents were indisputable, and never more on display. As the left halfback and captain-coach of the 1916 Canton Bulldogs, he had led the red-and-white to an undefeated season. They allowed only 7 points all year while scoring a total of 258—including consecutive midseason drubbings of the Buffalo All Stars 77–0 and New York All Stars 68–0—and captured the "world championship" with a convincing season-ending 24–0 defeat of the rival Massillon Tigers. Thorpe was "a veritable demon in his playing," declared the *Akron Beacon Journal.* It seemed almost like the old days when he was with the Carlisle Indians; in fact, by then he had recruited several former Carlisle teammates to join the Bulldogs for some games that year, including quarterback Gus Welch and running back Pete Calac.

So here was Jim in the first days of 1917. He had a house, a wife, a son, some land, proof of citizenship, hunting dogs, and jobs in baseball and football. He was in his prime, among the most famous people in America, newspaper copy wherever he went and whatever he did. In those ways his life was quantifiable. What was inside him, what drove him and explained him, was not so easy to discern.

Friends came away with conflicting impressions. Some thought the defining force in his life was what happened to him after Stockholm, that he was changed by an undoing that had to be redone. Others said he seemed unbothered by his fate. These were casual observations more than definitive conclusions. Jim was reserved, rarely showing his deepest feelings. It was not that he was inarticulate, more that he was brief. Albert Exendine, his teammate and mentor at Carlisle, once reflected that it was only in white society that Jim was considered shy. "Introverted is not the way I knew him. In comparison with other whites he might have been. Among Indians, he was one of the most talkative," Exendine said. "But whites, you know, they talk a lot." Jim wrote letters and little poems and sketched animals. He referred to himself self-deprecatingly as "that ole Injun." Seven years later, his letters would reveal his interior life more deeply, but not yet.

He was a big man, "the Big Indian," the press called him, but in fact he seemed bigger than he was. He measured six feet at most, and was still under two hundred pounds, yet people thought of him as a mountain of a man. Partly because his head was oversized and heavy, like the bronze bust they took away from him. Partly because he stood erect. He was straight up, even when he ran. Partly it was his charismatic aura. His face was mesmerizing. When he smiled, recalled one relative, he grinned so hard his eyes would close. "And you'd feel that, you'd feel that warmth and magnetism. He didn't have to talk—you'd feel it."

Jack Cusack, the Canton owner, grew close to Thorpe, so close he invited Jim along for his honeymoon in Oklahoma City later in 1917. He thought Jim was good-natured and likable and had many friends but few intimate ones. "I loved him and I say that from the bottom of my heart," Cusack recalled. "*Buddy*, he used to call me. He was big-hearted, full of pranks. He'd give you the shirt off his back—and that was what was wrong with him. If he had $500 and someone needed it more, he'd give it to him."

Generosity was not a fault; it reflected the noblest part of his character. He was a person without pretenses or guile, "as natural as a fresh stream of water," as Cecilia Blanchard, a lifelong friend from the Shawnee nation in Oklahoma, once said. But his willingness to help people and take them at their word created problems for Jim in that he rarely saved money no matter how much he earned and was constantly struggling to stay afloat financially, a precarious condition that kept him on the road and often away from his family.

A trait of more dire consequence was his drinking. He was drawn to liquor and changed by it. His easygoing sensibility vanished; he could become ferocious when aroused. "Jim needed a lot of looking after and a lot of care, but he never drank the night before or the day of a game," said Cusack, who occasionally roomed with him on the road. "Four drinks and he was gone. He'd get sick and want to die." Iva had not seen that side of Jim before their wedding and was not listening when Pop Warner and her siblings tried to warn her before she married him. "I'd never seen him drunk. Then I learned," she said. The problem grew apparent to her after they reached Yale. He rarely drank in her presence, and there is no evidence that he harmed her when drunk, but she felt the aftereffects. During her youth at Indian schools, she'd become a practicing Methodist and grew up believing that "drinking and smoking were strictly forbidden and were things that ladies and gentlemen in her generation did not do, at least to excess."

But Jim and his pals behaved differently. In the offseason, Pete Calac visited their house so the two Carlisle pals could go hunting. They would stay up through the night, then head out before dawn to track raccoons and shoot squirrels out of the pecan trees. "I remember making huge breakfasts for them after they would come in—six eggs each," Iva said later. Full and exhausted, Jim and Pete would doze off. "Then I'd be horrified to find the closets full of bottles. If you didn't drink, you didn't know. They were out there working up a huge appetite."

ON APRIL 16, 1917, ten days after the United States entered the Great War in Europe, Bozeman Bulger of the *New York World*, the same columnist who two years earlier had declared that Thorpe had reached the end of the trail, offered a more optimistic assessment. At spring training with the Giants, Bozeman reported that Jim had "an excellent chance" of making the major league squad as the fourth outfielder. "If the big Indian does come through it will show what determination really can do," he wrote. "Every man who knows Thorpe is pulling for him to land."

But the cycle of loss and recovery continued. The season had barely begun when Thorpe was again dropped from the fickle McGraw's plans, though what happened was a boon for him. He landed a job as a regular in the major leagues, just not with the Giants. He was sold outright to the Cincinnati Reds with a contingency in the agreement that McGraw had an option to take him back if the Reds later wanted to release or trade him. His manager now was his old teammate Christy Mathewson, who had retired from the Giants at midseason the previous year to take the Reds job.

Jim made his way to Cincinnati with Iva, who was three months pregnant, and Jim Jr., now a two-year-old. In a letter, Iva described her son as "a big, strong youngster. He looks like his Daddy, only has blue eyes, light hair and the fairest skin imaginable." The Thorpes found an apartment on Northern Avenue a few blocks from the Cincinnati Zoo. As they were settling in, a syndicated column under Mathewson's byline went out on the wires. While not directly criticizing McGraw for his handling of Thorpe, Mathewson presented a strong case for Jim as a bona fide major leaguer.

The Reds manager explained that his best outfielder, Edd Roush, was injured, and another regular had a sore arm, and without them he was in desperate shape. "I was up against it, so I wired McGraw for Jim Thorpe. Mac sold him to me." The timing seemed right for everyone. Mathewson had heard that McGraw was ready to cut Jim loose again. He also heard that Jim was so frustrated "he even discussed quitting baseball and entering the oil business in Oklahoma City." Then came the need in Cincinnati, and the encouragement of a manager whose personality could not have been more different from the old boss—from McGraw, the Little Napoleon, to Mathewson, the Christian Gentleman. Chief Meyers, Jim's old teammate, thought that might make all the difference, saying that if "Jim ever got under a proper manager, he would make good."

According to Mathewson, McGraw once told him that Thorpe was a great athlete and a good ballplayer, "but as Hughie Keough, who was on the *Chicago Tribune* before he died, once said, 'The helluvit is he ain't hittin.' " Now that Jim had the chance to play regularly, Mathewson thought he would prove he could hit, just as he had done with the Milwaukee Brewers the year before, although that was against minor league pitching. "He is that type of player who will keep plugging at a weakness until he has overcome it—and he knows his batting has kept him out of the regular order. Thorpe has all the qualities of a real sticker—a good eye, a nice position at the plate, and the ability to swing from either side. He stands up well to all kinds of pitching and does not stick his foot in the water pail when a twirler ropes through a fast one in the vicinity of his neck," Mathewson noted. "When a man of Thorpe's type gets his chance only once in a while, he is under quite a strain, for he feels he must make good then or he may never have another opportunity. He therefore presses, as we say in golf, and does not show his best."

The change seemed promising at first. Mathewson gave Jim a place in the Cincinnati outfield, where he contributed regularly. He made headlines in Chicago on May 2 at the end of one of the most remarkable games in major league history. For nine innings, each team was held without a hit by the opposing pitcher, Fred Toney for the Reds and Hippo Vaughn for the Cubs. In the tenth, Reds shortstop Larry Kopf broke up Vaughn's no-hitter with a single. After advancing to third on an outfield error, he scored when Thorpe nicked a slow bounder between the mound and first and legged it out for an infield hit, bringing home Kopf for what proved to be the winning run as Toney completed his extra-innings no-hitter in the bottom of the tenth.

But by mid-June, just as the team's outfield roster returned to full strength, Jim's average started declining, and Mathewson worried that the words of Hugh Keough were ringing true again—*the helluvit is he ain't hittin.* Jim found himself on the short end of an outfield platoon with Greasy Neale, another two-sport star who also played and coached football. Neale was in the lineup against righty pitchers and Jim against lefties. Most pitchers hurled from the right side, so Greasy played more. Baseball writers still looked for any chance to get Thorpe's name in print. On July 18, newspapers around the country carried a story about Jim in Philadelphia accomplishing something at the Baker Bowl "that no other ball player has ever succeeded in doing during the thirty years the park has been in use." What did Jim do? He hit a ball so far over the left-field fence that it landed on Lehigh Avenue, a "tremendous feat" that elicited "most vigorous recognition" from the fans. Only one problem: his momentous home run came during batting practice, not in the game.

When he did something notable in a game, the press was still prone to using stereotypes to describe his feats. That same week the *Philadelphia Public Ledger* ran a banner headline across the sports page that recycled General Sheridan's violent old phrase: "THE ONLY GOOD INDIAN IS A DEAD INDIAN, AND THIS APPLIES TO JIM THORPE, OF REDS." The story described Thorpe as "a real Redskin" and implied that he deserved the death penalty for driving a home run into the centerfield stands and bringing home another run with a single in a win over the Phillies. It also pointed out that Neale was hitting over .300 and "Big Jim Thorpe cannot show anything like this in the averages."

In August, as the gap between the batting averages of Neale and Thorpe widened and Jim's playing time decreased, reports surfaced that other clubs were interested in him. The Yankees assigned Joe Kelly, one of their top scouts, to sit in the stands at Crosley Field during a Reds home stand and compile a report on Thorpe. The assumption was that the Yankees would make a deal for him before Kelly left town. Then Jack Hendricks, manager of the Indianapolis Indians in the American Association, came to Cincinnati to talk to Mathewson about acquiring one of his outfielders, preferably Thorpe. Before any move could be made, Mathewson called McGraw, who had first rights. Concerned that two of his outfielders might be drafted into the war, McGraw decided to pull the string one more time and yank Jim back to the Giants for the stretch run. Five seasons now of this on-again, off-again relationship between the Little Napoleon and Jim, a perpetual yo-yo loop from potential and hope to inertia and dysfunction.

BEFORE THE TRANSACTION sending Jim back to New York from Cincinnati was announced, Iva wrote a letter from their Northern Avenue apartment to the superintendent at Carlisle. The school had gone through two leaders since Moses Friedman was discharged. The new man was John Francis Jr., a Kansas native who had worked at the Indian bureau in Washington for much of his career, rising from clerk to run the land office and then the education division. Francis must have suspected before he arrived that he was being sent to oversee the last days of Carlisle, and it became obvious soon enough, as he began sending dispatches back to the home office seeking advice on how to best manage demise and decay.

Iva knew none of this. In her letter, she wanted to know if Carlisle might enroll her younger brother, Clyde, who at age nineteen had been working for the Santa Fe railroad in Needles, California, sweltering in the summer heat of the Mojave Desert. Iva had not seen Clyde in four years, she wrote, "but he seems to be a bright, ambitious boy" who wanted to improve his education. Carlisle would be good for him, she assumed, just as it was for her. Her fondness for the school had not diminished since she graduated in 1912 as class elocutionist. "If Mr. Thorpe plays on an eastern team next year I am going to come to the commencement at Carlisle," she wrote. "There is nothing I would enjoy more than to see the dear old place and my many friends there." Just as Iva was unaware of the deteriorating condition of her alma mater, Clyde was unaware of how Jim's drinking was ripping the fabric of his sister's marriage. Unlike Iva's older siblings, Earl Miller and Grace Morris, all Clyde could see was his brother-in-law's fame and he assumed all was well. "Jim certainly is doing fine, isn't he?" he wrote to Iva. "Tell him I congratulate him and wish him the utmost success in anything that he endeavors."

Clyde never became a student at Carlisle and Iva never returned for a commencement there, even though she was on her way east again with Jim within days of writing her letter. With the Yanks now joined in the world war, pressure was mounting on the school to close and allow the campus to revert to its original military use. More and more Carlisle boys were leaving to enlist. One day that summer the AP listed the names of Carlisle athletes who were joining the armed forces, "and in a short time Germany will most likely hear their war whoop: Enoch Owl, Earl Wilber, George Kaquatosh, David Crow, and Edward Thorp, a brother of the famous Jim." Edward became a bugler in the U.S. Navy, where he learned to call out Reveille, Mess Call, Evening Colors, Taps, Man Overboard, and Abandon Ship.

At age thirty, married with one child and another on the way, Jim registered for the first draft that summer but was not called and did not enlist. Other Carlisle alumni were already in the armed services, including Gus Welch, Jim and Iva's close friend and best man at their wedding. Welch took leave from law school at neighboring Dickinson College when the U.S. entered the war and was now at Fort Niagara in New York training to be an officer. His commanding officer praised Welch as a "natural soldier" who was so tireless that "no amount of work dulled his enthusiasm."

Another Carlisle friend, Sylvester Long, who'd interviewed Jim and Iva during the 1912 graduation period for the class Character Book and helped Jim train for the Olympics by going on long runs with him through the countryside, was already engaged in trench warfare overseas. He now went by the name Sylvester Chahuska Long Lance. Not waiting for the American entry, he enlisted with Princess Patricia's Canadian Light Infantry and was in France in April 1917 when they faced the German Sixth Army at the gruesome Battle of Vimy Ridge. In a letter to Welch at Fort Niagara, a Carlisle official wrote that he had heard Long Lance "had been wounded in the head with a shell fragment but is getting along very nicely." This came at about the same time that the *Washington Post* published a long feature story on Long Lance that said he had "gone through the terrible battle of Vimy Ridge unscratched and emerged the only surviving officer of his rank in his battalion."

The headline and subhead of the *Post* story portrayed Long Lance as the most interesting man in the world. "SYLVESTER CHAHUSKA LONG LANCE, FULL-BLOOD AMERICAN INDIAN, FOUGHT BRAVELY AT VIMY RIDGE. Trick Rider, Fistic 'Meeter of all Comers,' All-Round College Athlete, Essayist, Musician, Movie Hero, Carlisle and St. John's Graduate, President Wilson's Appointee to West Point Cadetship, He Now Turns Up as First Lieutenant of Princess Pat's Crack Canadian Unit." A breakout quote said that he "Defeated Thorpe in three-mile run." The story also said he was born into the Eastern Cherokee tribe of North Carolina and had traveled with a Wild West show when he was thirteen.

Sylvester Long was indisputably intelligent and talented. Over his lifetime he awed people with the variety of his skills. But what he was more than anything else was a master of deception, one exaggeration or fabrication after another, Long Lance a concoction of his own imagination. The wound in France came when he broke his nose falling on his face. He never rose above the rank of sergeant. While it was true that he won an appointment to West Point, he never enrolled there. He might have been a better distance runner than Thorpe, but they never competed officially in a three-mile run.

JIM FINISHED THE Giants season in his usual spot, on the bench, watching as his team clinched the National League pennant and then lost to the White Sox four games to two in the 1917 World Series. The national pastime was not a national obsession that fall as the press and public focused on a more important team fighting overseas. The Giants and Sox had traveled the world together four years earlier, but Jim was among only a handful of players from that trip still around either club. He almost got into one World Series game, the fifth at Comiskey Park, when he was listed in the starting lineup playing right field but was removed for a pinch hitter in the top of the first—perhaps a fitting coda to his playing days under McGraw.

By the time he reached Canton for the football season, the Bulldogs had already played two games, including an 80–0 thumping of the Altoona Indians. His teammates again included some Carlisle athletes, this time Pete Calac and William Garlow, along with his outfield platoon partner in Cincinnati, Greasy Neale, who coached West Virginia Wesleyan on Saturdays and played for Canton on Sundays under various aliases. Neale was talented in all three of his athletic iterations, as an outfielder in baseball and as an end and then a coach in football, eventually leading to his enshrinement in the College Football Hall of Fame. He was also a virulent bigot.

Baseball was segregated, so Neale did not face black players when he played with the Reds, but there were a few African Americans in college football then, most notably Paul Robeson, the multitalented All-American end at Rutgers, and Neale as coach at West Virginia Wesleyan refused to play against him or any team that fielded a black player. There were also a few blacks in professional football in 1917, a half decade before the race curtain fell on that sport. In the fourth game of the season, Canton played at home against a team from New York, the Rochester Jeffersons, whose star left halfback, Henry C. McDonald, was black. After one play, Neale tried to rough up McDonald and snarled at him, "Black is black and white is white where I come from and the two don't mix." A fight seemed imminent when Thorpe pulled his belligerent teammate away from McDonald and shouted, "We're here to play football!" As McDonald recalled the scene, Thorpe effectively put a stop to Neale's racial aggressions for the rest of the game.

Pro football in its infancy was violent enough without the extra component of prejudice, and Jim was as rough-and-ready as anyone in the league, an equal-opportunity pain inflictor. He used his shoulders as weapons, lowering and then uppercutting them into would-be tacklers with a ferocity so sharp some insisted he must have lined his pads with sheet metal, which was not true. They were made of hard sole leather.

Unless he had too much to drink, Jim was gentle off the field. On the field he was a different character. "The dirtier the football got, the meaner Jim got," Pete Calac once recalled. "The pros would gouge your eyes, knee you on every play and just outright slug you time and again. With Jim, they would just pile on. But he wore longer cleats and when they got him on his back he would double up and start kicking his way out of the pile. He was provoked . . . but he answered them, too. He would stand out there at halfback and yell across the line to tell them where he was going to run. We'd open a hole in the line and Jim would run over anyone else who got in his way." Joe Guyon, another of his Carlisle teammates who turned pro, said Jim perfected a technique they were taught by Pop Warner: fake a defender, make him stop, then charge right at him and hit him with a hip or a stiff-arm and crush him. Warner called it "unexpected contact."

Jack Cusack recalled that Jim would kid him before a game by making a face and saying he planned to eat a few raw steaks so he could go out and kill the opposition. "Then he'd laugh and say, 'Aw, Jack, I don't need steaks to do that,' " said the Bulldogs owner. "And he didn't. He was so fast that before you knew it he'd stiff-arm the linebacker and give the safety the hip and be gone. I guess the thing I remember most about him is the fear other players had of tackling him. The particular way he had of holding his hips out and using that stiff-arm they don't use anymore."

Most of the world had no clue about American football, much of the country knew little about the professional game, attendance was spotty, lineups were as fluid as the names or pseudonyms of players—all of that, and yet it seemed every week there was a matchup in the Ohio League billed as a world championship. The Bulldogs played four such games in 1917. "Indian Jim Thorpe, alias Canton football team, limped back to Canton Sunday afternoon still retaining the championship of the earth," declared the *Akron Beacon Journal* after the Bulldogs defeated the Akron Pros 14–0 on November 14. When they went on to twice defeat the Youngstown Patricians, the papers called it a sweep of a "home and home football series for the professional championship." And finally came the two games against rival Massillon. The first game was played in the late-afternoon darkness and a blizzard so blinding that few fans could see the field by the fourth quarter. Thorpe dominated the game, leading his team to another world championship 14–3. But the next week, Massillon, now led by Charles Brickley, the former All-American halfback at Harvard, won

6–0 and claimed the world title for themselves. By that measure, Thorpe and his Bulldogs had won three world championships and lost one in a span of five weeks.

But what stuck with Jim was the one they lost. He was said to be so depressed losing to Brickley's squad that he declared he would quit the pro game. Cusack said Thorpe had confided in him that he did not plan to return to Canton in 1918. Jim said maybe he was through with baseball too; he didn't think he got the best out of himself in baseball, though he did not think it was all his fault. Maybe he would just devote his time to the oil wells in Oklahoma. Newspapers dutifully carried the stories, but few believed them. That was just Jim; every year it seemed he would say that his athletic career was over, but he always came back for more.

That winter he was back in his Oklahoma homeland, at the little house on Boston Avenue in Yale with the coon dogs howling at the moon and a new member of the family bawling inside. He arrived home from the football season several weeks after Iva gave birth to a baby girl, Gail Margaret, on Halloween night, October 31. The family was growing, and Iva had filled the house with new furniture she and a friend had bought in Oklahoma City. Jim ended a year of gains with a home, a deed, a country, and what he called "my little family" of four. He was not a perfect husband or father, but he took comfort in his family that winter. It was, in some ways, his last fine time.

18

Losses

THE DECLINE AND FALL OF THE CARLISLE INDIAN INDUSTRIAL School had seemed probable since 1904, when Richard Henry Pratt, its founder and truest believer, was removed from the institution he had led for a quarter century. After that, it became increasingly apparent that the Indian bureau in Washington was turning against the idea of a national school for indigenous students, and Carlisle's closing was only a matter of when. The reasons were more financial and practical than ideological. It was not that enlightened minds came to regret the degrading racism inherent in a policy of forced assimilation that attempted to whitewash native culture, language, dress, and attitudes out of the students. To many politicians and bureaucrats in Washington, it just seemed that maintaining Carlisle was too expensive and that Indians were not worth the effort.

All the fame the school garnered during the Thorpe years—especially 1912 with the brilliance of the Olympic gold medals and the defeat of Army on the football field at West Point—only delayed the inevitable. Soon after that came the congressional investigation and scandals of 1914, and by 1916 opposition to the school's annual appropriation was so intense it became obvious the end was near. That end came in the summer of 1918. How appropriate that Carlisle died then. Nineteen-eighteen was the Grim Reaper of years, the deadliest of the early twentieth century, a year when the world was ravaged by war and disease and millions of families were scarred forever, including the family of the Indian school's most famous former students, Jim and Iva Thorpe.

The history of Carlisle was saturated in war. Before the Indian school was located there, the site had been a military post going back to the Revolutionary War. When Pratt founded the school in 1879, he saw it as a less violent alternative to the Indian Wars of that century, yet he maintained a military regimen by outfitting his Indian students in mock cavalry uniforms. Now, with the Great War raging in Europe and more than a million American doughboys engaged in the fighting in France, the post was returning to a version of its original purpose, reclaimed by the War Department for use as a convalescent hospital for wounded soldiers.

Before Carlisle faded into history that troubled summer, the students, teachers, and administrators joined city leaders and townspeople for a closing ceremony held on the night of August 26. The evening began with an assembly in downtown Carlisle followed by a parade out to the school, the same route followed six Augusts earlier when Thorpe, Tewanima, and Pop Warner returned victorious from Stockholm, though this time the procession was more funereal than celebratory. A platoon of Home Defense Police led the way, followed by fifty veterans of the Spanish-American War and a blocks-long cavalcade of marchers and automobile passengers, all eventually gathering outside the superintendent's house on the hill. "A spirit of solemnity marked the occasion, an entirely different spirit than has attended any event at the school in the past," reported the *Carlisle Evening Herald*. "United States Army officers in full uniform at various points through the audience gave the scene a martial air. Far and wide over the beautiful campus buildings blazed forth myriads of lights, and on the band stand in their brilliant red uniforms were the members of the Carlisle Band."

Jim and Iva Thorpe might have been honored guests, but Jim was in St. Louis in the middle of a long road trip with the Giants, nearing the end of his final unproductive year in a New York uniform. Pop Warner was there, arriving from Pittsburgh, where he was preparing for another season coaching Pitt, a team he had led to an undefeated record the previous year. Pop was showered in applause when announced to the crowd. He strode to the rostrum as students serenaded him with the school song, an anthem whose lyrics he had written. *Remembering thee we'll never fail / We'll weather every storm and gale / While o'er life's troubled sea we sail / Old Carlisle, our dear Carlisle.* The school, Warner declared, had fulfilled the mission General Pratt set out for it. Recalling his great football teams—from the days of Mt. Pleasant and Exendine to those of Thorpe and Welch—he likened their will to win to the boys fighting overseas. "We have the greatest team today we have ever had, and it will not be beaten," he said.

Pratt was there in words and spirit, if not in body. An organizer of the event read a telegram the seventy-eight-year-old retired general sent from his home in Williamson, New York. He made clear that his belief in his school and its methods of "civilizing" Indians had not diminished, nor had his affinity for flowery language.

> MY PHYSICAL CONDITION IS NOT FAVORABLE TO TRAVEL AT THIS HEATED SEASON," Pratt's telegram began. "THE ABANDONED MILITARY BARRACKS OF 1879, REHABILITATED AND GROWN THROUGH THIRTY-NINE YEARS INTO THE BENEFICENT GREAT PLANT WHICH HAS TRANSFORMED YOUNG INDIANS FROM ALL TRIBES FROM THEIR ABORIGINAL IDEA OF LIVING INTO THE ABILITY AND COURAGE OF AMERICAN CITIZEN LIFE, IS NOW TO BE FURTHER HONORED AND EVER GLORIOUS BY BEING FIRST SELECTED FOR THE MOST WONDERFUL NEW USES EVER EVOLVED TO SAVE MANKIND IN THIS OUR GREATEST NATIONAL EMERGENCY.

More speeches followed from Carlisle's mayor and an army major in charge of transforming the campus into a hospital complex for two thousand wounded soldiers. All talking done, the band struck up "The Star-Spangled Banner" and guests retired to the school gymnasium for ice cream and cookies and a round of dancing. At 10:54 that night, a train pulled into the Carlisle station carrying a medical corps unit from Fort Hamilton, New York, that would be stationed at the hospital.

The next morning, the corps went to work, joining a vanguard battalion of officers and enlisted men reconfiguring buildings and preparing for the arrival of cots and medical equipment. The last group of Indian students left for the station that same morning, bound for new homes as transfer students at the Chilocco Indian School in Oklahoma, the Haskell

Institute in Kansas, and a scattering of smaller boarding schools in Oregon, Nebraska, Minnesota, Michigan, South Dakota, North Carolina, Wisconsin, California, New Mexico, and Arizona. A skeleton crew of federal workers remained into September to clear Carlisle of four decades of accumulated stuff and ship it off for storage or reuse.

Here were the remnants of a lost civilization. To the Indian Warehouse in St. Louis went whisk brooms, union suits, shovel handles, ladies' vests, sewing needles, uniform coats, scout hats, white duck coats, pillow slips, flannel shirts, basting spoons, tablecloths, boys' knee pants, carving sets, scrub brushes, leather boots, bunting, gym shoes, clothes baskets, and a school bell with clappers. The Cherokee School in North Carolina received 50 folding chairs, 2 volleyball nets, 3 basketballs, 4 checkerboards, 100 barbells, and 9 mats. To the Haskell Institute went 41 cup and saucer sets, 42 salad plates, 2 pickle dishes, 57 forks, 2 double sinks, an electric iron, and a porch swing. The Indian bureau headquarters in Washington was sent a beaded buckskin coat, an old gun, and a model battleship. And the Susan Longstreth Literary Society, a club that had once included Iva Miller among its avid readers, was shipping its library of several hundred books overseas to the camps of American soldiers in France. "One cannot think without a thrill of pride and admiration of the patriotic impulse which prompted this gift," wrote a local columnist. "And what soldier will not be touched when he realizes as he opens one of these volumes that some Indian girl has done her best to bring comfort and cheer into his life at the front?"

"TAKING JIM THORPE to Texas is a disease with McGraw." So wrote Jack Veiock, sports editor for the Hearst Newspapers syndicate that March when Jim reported to Marlin Springs for his sixth spring training. In a bit of sports page doggerel, Veiock explained why:

Who spurns the pitcher's cunning wing
And slams the pill with might and main,
When bats are cracking in the spring

As big league teams begin to train?
Jim Thorpe.
But when at last the team returns
With sluggers eager for the fray,
Who envies Benny Kauff and Burns
While sitting on the bench all day?
Jim Thorpe.

True to form, Jim played well enough that spring to make the team, then rarely saw action as a utility outfielder playing mostly behind three men with superior batting averages: Benny Kauff, George Burns, and rookie Ross Youngs. He stayed with the team all year but played in only fifty-eight games, and then often only as a pinch hitter or pinch runner. Another frustrating year from all sides—Jim frustrated again with his minimal playing time; the Giants management and fans frustrated again with his struggles at the plate. If there was anything surprising about how seldom Thorpe made the starting lineup, it was that it happened even though the league was depleted by war and disease.

When the military began drafting men into the war, baseball players were classified as productive workers and exempted from service unless they chose to enlist. The national pastime was considered essential for public morale, part of a symbiotic relationship developing between sports and the military. For soldiers fighting overseas, baseball evoked American normality amid death and chaos, and more than seventy leagues were formed by army units in France. At ballparks back home, the game became infused with military pomp. Players went through marching drills as if they were in military units and paraded onto the field in formation shouldering wooden bats like rifles, a signifier of national pride that soon led to the playing of an anthem before games. But as combat persisted into the summer of 1918, the War Department, in need of more men, changed course with a "work or fight" order that reclassified ballplayers as unproductive—no different from restaurant workers, store clerks, and elevator operators. Athletes could either be drafted or work at shipyards and other war industry plants. In many jurisdictions, law enforcement authorities were instructed to root out "idleness and loafing of able-bodied persons" as one public poster put it: "GO TO WAR—GO TO WORK—OR GO TO JAIL."

Before the war ended later in 1918, 227 major leaguers found a way to serve, and 8 players or former players were killed in combat or died of disease while in uniform. The Red Sox batting order was so depleted that pitcher Babe Ruth was inserted into the everyday lineup against right-handed hurlers, launching his legendary rise as a power hitter. Branch Rickey, in a break between stints as general manager of the St. Louis Browns, became an officer in the Chemical Warfare Service, eventually recruiting Hall of Famers Ty Cobb and Christy Mathewson to serve with him in the Gas and Flame Division. That mission took them to the Allied Expeditionary Force Headquarters in Chaumont, France, where a gas drill mishap left Cobb and Mathewson exposed to a "good dose of the stuff," an accident that might have contributed to Cobb's retirement from baseball a decade later and to the tuberculosis that killed Mathewson seven years later. The White Sox, defending World Series champions, fell to sixth place in the American League after five key players went into service or took jobs in war industries, including Shoeless Joe Jackson, their sweet-swinging outfielder. The Giants, defending National League pennant winners, lost two pitchers and outfielder Kauff, who departed after playing only sixty-seven games. That left a hole in the outfield that Thorpe might have filled, but McGraw played him only sporadically.

Even when Thorpe was not playing, he remained a popular figure at the Polo Grounds, radiating goodwill to the fans and roughhousing in the clubhouse with teammates, often accompanied by his namesake son, a delightful three-year-old miniature version of his famous dad who came to the park in his own Giants uniform and pranced on the diamond before games with a bat and glove and the same wide grin. Once the games started, Jim might have fit the wartime definition of idleness as he rode the bench, though as a married man with two children he kept his deferment and was not derided as a slacker. Ty Cobb was the same age and had three children, but said he felt guilty every time he saw a casualty list and decided to enlist. If Jim harbored similar guilt, he never remarked on it, but a clue to the answer might have come a quarter century later when he was an old man of whom little was expected and chose to enlist in the merchant marine to support the troops during World War II.

WAR AND DISEASE were lethally intertwined in 1918. They shrank the major league player pool and eventually shrank the season. The disease became known as the Spanish flu, but it might more accurately have been called the Kansas flu, for it was in Kansas that the deadliest pandemic of the twentieth century might have begun. Some historians trace the influenza that killed at least 50 million people worldwide and 670,000 Americans to a rural stretch of southwest Kansas, not to Spain, a nation that had its name misapplied to the disease because of an outbreak there months later. China, France, and Vietnam were other possibilities for origin points. Haskell County, Kansas, boasted more hogs than people and happened to be along a migratory flyway for seventeen bird species. Birds, pigs, humans, and submicroscopic infectious viruses formed a deadly quartet. Evidence suggested that a bird virus infected the hogs of Haskell County and combined with a human strain to create an H1N1 influenza that in January 1918 began making farmers and townspeople sick with aches and fever. The local paper called the ailment "la grippe."

When a passel of young men from Haskell County was inducted into the army, the virus accompanied them along the Union Pacific Railroad line across the state to Camp Funston, a massive cantonment training camp constructed in a meadow near Junction City. The first flu case there was reported on March 4, and soon the camp, with fifty thousand soldiers who bunked in close quarters in row after row of barracks, became ground zero for the disease. By the end of March more than eleven hundred men were being treated in the base hospital. From spring to summer to fall, the virus mutated and traveled from Camp Funston to the East Coast and across the Atlantic to Europe and the world, then back again on ships carrying infected soldiers and sailors into the ports of New York, Boston, New London, New Orleans, and Philadelphia. This brought the second influenza wave, a far more lethal strain. Public health officials were outmatched, failing to grasp the science behind the disease and how to combat it. Many newspapers and politicians worsened the situation with misleading statements minimizing the danger. In the end, no place, profession, or family could escape the contagion.

In the battle trenches of France and then camps back in the States, the virus spread with alarming speed and attacked the lungs with brutal aggression, leading to the deaths of 45,000 American soldiers. As the influenza wave washed back to the American mainland, the largest forts became death traps. At Fort Devens in Massachusetts, 14,000 soldiers fell sick and 757 died. At Camp Funston, where it all began, more than a thousand men were killed by the flu and one of every four soldiers was sent to sickbed. One of the dead was David Larabee from the Sioux nation, known on the divisional football team as Big Chief. Accounts of his death said he played football at Carlisle with Jim Thorpe and "won a backfield position on Walter Camp's All-American second team in 1911." That appeared to be inaccurate. According to Carlisle records, David Larvie, occasionally spelled Larabee, arrived at Carlisle near the end of Jim's final 1912 season and left before the 1913 season began, meaning he played no varsity football there. The exaggerated obituary said less about the young man's veracity than about the mythology of Jim Thorpe and how throughout his life other people wanted to be attached to his greatness.

From the Philadelphia Naval Shipyard and Camp Dix in nearby New Jersey, the virus flashed across Pennsylvania, eventually killing more than 60,000 statewide. In the center of the path sat the town of Carlisle, so overwhelmed with cases that an elementary school was reconfigured into an emergency hospital. Epidemiologists determined that an early contributing factor to the spread there might have been the closing ceremony of the Carlisle Indian Industrial School that brought hundreds of visitors and soldiers into town. While some cities imposed strict social distancing edicts, Philadelphia did not, and its citizens paid a morbid price. Here again, war and disease danced a haunting pas de deux. The catalyst for a deadly outbreak in the city was a Liberty Loan campaign rally that brought more than 200,000 people into the downtown streets. In New York, when troop ships from Rotterdam and Le Havre carried the disease into New

York Harbor, the city health department started requiring quarantine for all those infected, but within weeks that city was dealing with more than a thousand cases a day.

The baseball world was not immune. Babe Ruth caught what was called the flu in mid-May after swimming at Revere Beach just north of Boston. If this was the flu, it was a less lethal early strain. It sent Ruth to the hospital where hyperbolic reports said he was on his deathbed before recovering. Several teammates had been infected earlier during spring training in Hot Springs, Arkansas, either because of conditions in the public baths or a trip the team made to play at an army base in Little Rock. Among baseball people who died from the influenza were Silk O'Loughlin, a popular major league umpire; sportswriters Eddie Martin of the *Boston Globe* and Chandler Richter of the *Philadelphia Evening Public Record*; and several minor leaguers. There was another less significant but fascinating baseball victim. The contagion marked the beginning of the end of the spitball, which for sanitary reasons was banned temporarily for the World Series that year and outlawed entirely a few seasons later. That World Series, in which Ruth's Boston Red Sox defeated the Chicago Cubs, was played nearly a month ahead of schedule after war and disease forced major league baseball to shorten the regular season, ending it on the second day of September. Though series crowds during three games at Fenway Park were smaller than usual, they only contributed to a citywide spread that killed nearly five thousand Bostonians by the end of the year.

THE NORMAL MIGRATORY pattern for Jim was to leave for Ohio and football when the baseball season ended, but 1918 was not a normal year. There was no football for the Bulldogs or any professional team that fall, all games canceled because of war and influenza. Jim and Iva remained in New York for three weeks before packing their belongings on September 21 and starting the long drive home to Yale with Jim Jr. and infant Gail. The second flu wave had reached Oklahoma by then and was starting to ravage Indian Country, especially Tahlequah, capital of the Cherokee nation, where more than a hundred people would die in a town of two thousand. On the journey southwest from New York, Jim noticed something was wrong with Jim Jr. "The bright fire had suddenly begun to grow dim in his dark eyes," he recalled. "His ankles began swelling and he seemed listless. His little hands clung tight to mine." By the time they reached Yale, the boy had a high fever and his arms and legs ached and throbbed with pain.

On the evening of September 27, as Jim Jr.'s situation worsened, Dr. E. G. Newell was called in. He stayed with Jim and Iva at the little house on East Boston Avenue through the night. They were in the living room near the fireplace, Jim and Iva holding Junior and trying to comfort him, Dr. Newell reaching the dire diagnosis: the three-year-old's heart was fatally inflamed. Jim was not one to show emotions readily; now they overwhelmed him. He "begged and pleaded and cried." A Sac and Fox and a Catholic, he beseeched his people's ancient spirits and the "white man's God"—anything to save his boy. At four in the morning of September 28, Jim Jr. died. "I held him in my arms for a long time," Thorpe said. For the second time in his life, he had lost the one person in the world he saw as part of himself. First it was Charlie, his twin brother, who died at age nine of typhoid fever early on a March morning in 1897. Now, twenty-one years later, it was his son. Junior had lived three years, four months, and twenty-one days.

The Oklahoma State Board of Health death certificate filed in Payne County stated that James Francis Thorpe Jr. had been ill for ten days, implying he was starting to flag before the family left New York. Dr. Newell listed the cause of death as endocarditis with rheumatism as a secondary cause. Endocarditis, an inflammation of the heart's inner lining usually caused by bacterial infection, is not common in children. A related affliction, myocarditis, an inflammation of the heart muscle usually caused by viral infection, is more common, and a known complication of influenza. Iva believed her son died of the flu, and that became the accepted family story. This was well before the era of sophisticated scanning technology, no X-rays were taken, and there was no autopsy, so it would be difficult to establish certainty about the cause of death. But according to a leading expert in the field a century later, Iva's assumption had merit.

"I would think it would be more likely that he died from some complication of influenza, of the Spanish flu, rather than something rheumatic and endocarditis," said Dr. Stuart Berger, the head of cardiology at the Lurie Children's Hospital in Chicago. Doctors knew little about myocarditis in 1918, Berger said, but it could develop suddenly from the flu and kill someone within a matter of days. Jim Jr.'s other symptoms were also consistent with a virulent strain of influenza. While not ruling it out, Berger said that if the boy had endocarditis and inflammatory rheumatism, he likely would have had an abnormal heart from birth. There appeared to be no other evidence of that.

The day after Jim Jr. died, he was buried at the Harrell Cemetery in the nearby town of Cushing. The memory of looking into the grave as her "darling son" was laid into the ground would haunt Iva the rest of her life.

"We went home then and packed up the little fellow's baseball suit, balls, and toys," Thorpe later recalled. "Gail, bless her little heart, missed her brother, too." He then sent a telegram to New York in care of John B. Foster, the Giants' secretary, informing the club of his son's death, and from there the news spread to newspapers and the wire services. The "little Indian lad" was recalled as a "great favorite" of players and fans, who enjoyed watching him toddle around the field with his pop. It had been six years since Jim had been stripped of his Olympic medals and trophies, but this was far worse. "The most precious trophy I had ever been awarded in my life had been taken from me," he said. Iva, in her grief, could see that his heart was broken. In a year of loss, this was the loss from which he would never fully recover.

Jim Thorpe was an archetype—the great athlete—and a stereotype—the romanticized noble Indian. During the 1912 Stockholm Olympics, he competed in mismatched shoes after his track cleats disappeared.

2

Thorpe's paternal grandmother, *No-ten-o-quah,* from the Thunder Clan of the Sac and Fox nation and possible descendant of Black Hawk.

3

Jim's father, Hiram, a big man with an outsized reputation in Indian Territory, a ruffian in a rough land.

4

Jim (l) and twin brother, Charlie, who died of typhoid fever at age nine. "No two brothers were ever closer."

5

"Kill the Indian, save the man," said Richard Henry Pratt, founder of the Carlisle Indian Industrial School. Pratt viewed assimilation as the answer to earlier exterminationist policies.

6

Carlisle opened in 1879. Student Luther Standing Bear thought "white people wanted little Lakota people there for no other reason than to kill them."

7

Jim arrived at Carlisle on February 6, 1904, not yet seventeen years old. The school ledger said he was five foot five and a half inches tall and weighed 115 pounds.

8

Before 1906, football seemed a case of unnecessary roughness in which helmets were optional and serious injuries routine.

9

Thorpe became an All-American halfback with a rare combination of strength, speed, stubbornness, instinct, and agility, exuding a hint of danger and a spark of electricity.

10

Thorpe (third from right, second row) became a sensation in 1911 when he kicked four field goals on an injured leg and ran "like a steam engine" in an 18-15 upset of Harvard. Coach Glenn (Pop) Warner stands behind him.

11 Warner was an innovative coach, but at the time of Thorpe's greatest peril, he lied and feigned ignorance to save his reputation.

12

Moses Friedman, Indian school superintendent during Jim's rise to stardom, was once described as "the old Sourball" by the poet Marianne Moore, who taught business classes at Carlisle.

13

Thorpe (fourth from right), with teammates standing in front of a billboard for Tutti Frutti chewing gum, a sponsor of the 1912 U.S. Olympics team soon bound for Stockholm.

One of many Thorpe myths was that he never trained on the ship crossing the Atlantic. Here he runs on the cork-padded oval of the SS *Finland*.

14

15

Lewis Tewanima, Thorpe's Carlisle teammate, a brilliant Hopi distance runner who won a silver medal in Stockholm.

16

Thorpe (left, holding hat, with laurels atop his head) won gold in the pentathlon and decathlon and was honored by Sweden's King Gustav V as the greatest athlete in the world.

17

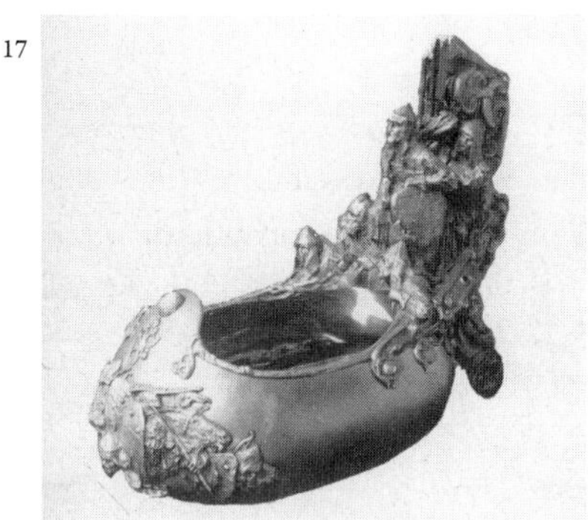

18

The Viking ship chalice awarded to Thorpe for his victory in the decathlon and King of Sweden bronze bust bestowed for his pentathlon win.

19

Thorpe's gold medals, later taken from him when it was revealed that he had played bush league baseball in the Eastern Carolina League in 1909 and 1910.

When Thorpe returned from his Olympic triumph, he was celebrated at parades in New York City (above), Philadelphia, and Carlisle.

The business office of the New York Baseball Club in the Fifth Avenue Building was the place to be on the afternoon of February 1, 1913. Before an off-camera throng of sportswriters and fans, the world-famous Thorpe signed a contract to play in the National League for John McGraw's Giants.

22

Jim married Iva Miller, a Carlisle student described as a "dark-eyed princess of the Cherokee tribe," although it was later learned she was not Native American. The marriage lasted a decade before Iva tired of his excessive drinking and divorced him.

23

McGraw signed Thorpe in part to use him as a featured attraction on a world tour staged by the Giants and White Sox after the 1913 season.

24

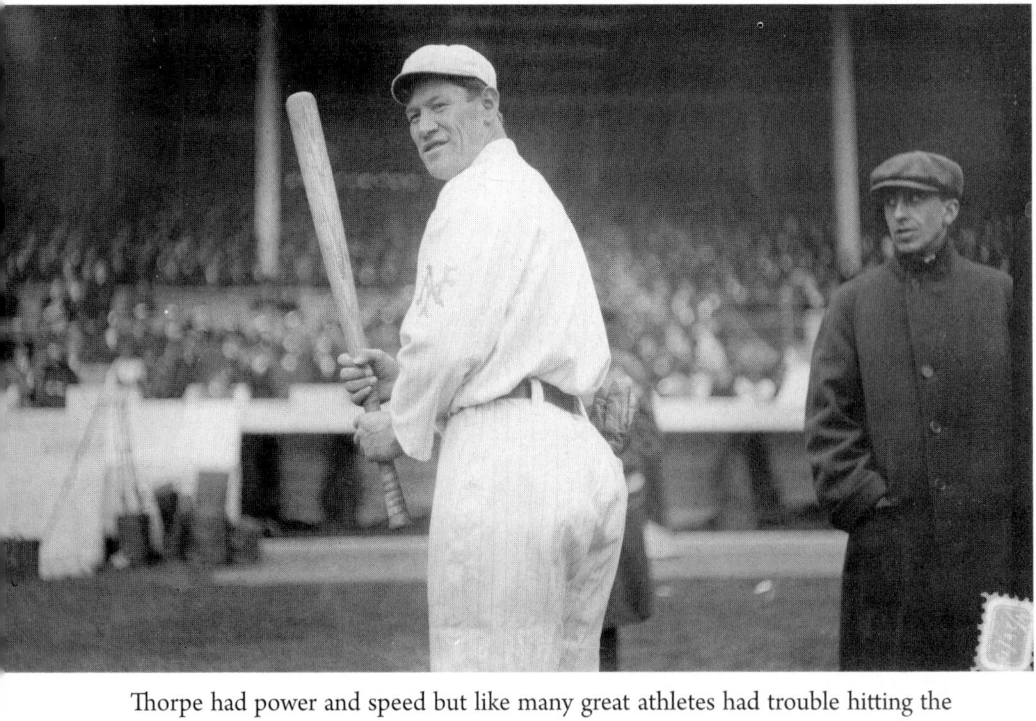

Thorpe had power and speed but like many great athletes had trouble hitting the curveball. He was also misused by McGraw and spent most of his time on the bench.

25

A brilliant runner, placekicker, and punter for the Canton Bull-dogs, Thorpe was also the first president of what became the NFL and star of the first class of the Pro Football Hall of Fame.

26

"There's nothing too good for the boy, I can tell you," Thorpe said of Jim Jr., but his first son died at age three during the 1918 influenza pandemic.

27

28

Jim (top row, center) became player-coach of the Oorang Indians, an NFL team comprised entirely of Native Americans and named after a breed of Airedales. The players trained the hunting dogs at the Oorang Kennels in LaRue, Ohio.

29

Grace Thorpe, youngest of three daughters, saw little of Jim in her early years. “A lump bigger than a football came into my throat when I had to tell her who I was,” he recalled after visiting her at the Haskell Indian School.

30

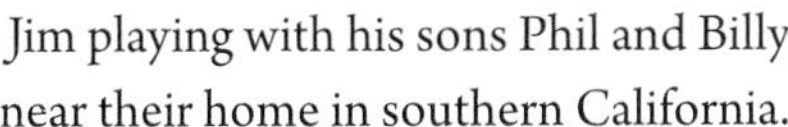
Jim playing with his sons Phil and Billy near their home in southern California.

31

Desperate for work during the Depression, Jim took a job as a laborer with a pick and shovel at the construction site of a Los Angeles hospital.

32

"A man has to keep hustling," Thorpe said when he became player-coach of Harjo's Indians at age forty-six.

33

When columnist Grace Wilcox visited Thorpe and his second wife, Freeda, and their three boys in the mid-1930s, she described "a world in which simplicity, charm, and love make a home fit for a king." The reality was different.

34

Thorpe's favorite sport was not football, baseball, or track and field, but hunting racoons and squirrels with his hounds.

35

36

During his Hollywood years, Thorpe became a leader of Native Americans lobbying for roles at a time when the studios often hired white actors to play Indians. Jim had bit parts in more than seventy films.

37

Thorpe (far left) and cast members assume formation during a break on the set of *Under Pressure,* a film about laborers known as sandhogs who dug the tunnels under the Hudson River.

 38

The Chicago Park District hired Jim as youth director in 1948. The press ran photographs above the caption, "Great Athlete Back on Track," but his attendance was spotty and he was let go within a year.

 39

Jim consults with star Burt Lancaster and director Michael Curtiz on the set of *Jim Thorpe, All-American*. The 1951 movie was empathetic but misguided in some important ways.

 40

"The Chief is really something. What a wonder he must have been in his prime," said Ted Williams, who appeared with Jim at autograph sessions in New York and Boston in 1952.

41

In an AP poll, Thorpe was voted the greatest athlete of the first half of the twentieth century. At a Touchdown Club banquet in 1951, he huddled with a team of all-time All-Americans. Back row, from left: Alex Wojciechowicz from Fordham, Thorpe, Pudge Heffelfinger of Yale, Don Hutson from Alabama, Sammy Baugh from Texas Christian, and Ernie Nevers from Stanford. Front row, from left: Bennie Ooseterbaan from Michigan, Bob Suffridge from Tennessee, and Ki Aldrich of TCU.

42

Avery Brundage, who had lost to Thorpe in the 1912 decathlon, refused throughout his later career as Olympics potentate to restore Jim's rescinded medals. They posed for a cool handshake in Los Angeles in 1952.

Jim with third wife, Patsy, his chief promoter and business manager. His sons viewed her as a slick manipulator while his three daughters considered her a melodramatic woman devoted to getting Jim his due. There was some truth in both perspectives.

44

After Thorpe died of a heart attack in a trailer park at age sixty-five, his casket was taken from Los Angeles to Oklahoma for a burial that never happened when Patsy thought the state's plans for his memorial were inadequate.

46

Patsy cut a deal with Mauch Chunk and East Mauch Chunk to change their names to Jim Thorpe, Pennsylvania, and build a mausoleum park in his honor. His sons' legal efforts to return his bones to Oklahoma failed.

45

47

48

At least 186 children were buried at Carlisle after dying at school. Their bones, like Thorpe's, are in Pennsylvania soil far from home, but, at least for some, repatriation is finally underway.

Six of Thorpe's children were in Los Angeles in 1983 when IOC president Juan Antonio Samaranch (center) presented them with copies of the medals taken from Jim seventy years earlier. It was a hollow victory in the fight for full restoration.

50

For all his troubles, whether caused by outside forces or of his own doing, Jim Thorpe persevered. The man survived, complications and all, and so did the myth.

19

Gamblers

JOHN MCGRAW WAS A WIN-AT-ALL-COSTS MANAGER, BUT going into the 1919 season he had won only one National League pennant in five years, the other times finishing eighth, fourth, and second twice, a record that left him dissatisfied and looking for new ballplayers to take the Giants back to the top. He became what one sportswriter called "a trading fool" trying to resurrect his team, orchestrating a total of eleven transactions with the Pirates, Cubs, Cardinals, Phillies, Reds, and most of all the Boston Braves, whose manager, George Stallings, was said to owe his job to the outsize influence of the Little Napoleon. Some trades worked in his favor, some failed, and one drew the most attention.

With the influenza pandemic fading, the war in Europe concluded, and the season not yet a month old on May 21, McGraw traded Jim Thorpe to the Braves for cash and a player to be named later, who turned out to be Pat Ragan, a journeyman pitcher near the end of his career. The "great aborigine," as the *New York Herald* called Jim, was considered dispensable after McGraw's earlier trades stocked the team with an excess of outfielders. Going back seven seasons, since he'd signed with the Giants in 1913, Thorpe had been sent away to other teams three times, but always with strings that McGraw eventually pulled to bring him back. This time there were no strings. He was gone for good on the eve of his thirty-second birthday. The only American Indian on a team of Braves.

Jim traveled to Boston by train the day after the trade as a pounding rainstorm and thick fog swept to sea, his presence welcomed but drawing less attention than the sight at Boston Harbor, where an armada of twenty-four submarine chasers churned in through the Cape Cod Canal after hunting German U-boats across the Atlantic. Jim donned a Braves uniform in time that Saturday to witness war and baseball honored together at the ballpark for Hank Gowdy Day.

Gowdy, the gifted catcher who had led the "Miracle Braves" to a World Series championship in 1914, became the first big league ballplayer, and the first of fourteen Braves, to volunteer to fight against the Germans. He left the team abruptly one day in late June 1917 with the words "So long, boys, I'll meet you in Paris," and was off to Europe with the Forty-Second "Rainbow" Division, surviving combat at Saint-Mihiel and the Argonne. Now, after two years with the army overseas, here he was at Braves Field, ready to strap on the tools of ignorance, as catchers' gear was called, and take on the visiting Reds. His teammates, led by shortstop Rabbit Maranville, presented him with an odd trunkful of clothes, and Boston's mayor gave him a gold watch and a cigar cutter. In his first at-bat, Gowdy singled to right. Jim watched from the bench. He was back in his familiar perch, though not for long.

When Stallings inserted Thorpe into the lineup, he started hitting and kept hitting. The weekly batting average statistics showed him leading the league through June and July, at one point rapping out thirty-three hits in thirty-four games. His name appeared on the sports page almost as often as that of Babe Ruth of the crosstown Red Sox. On July 26, he was in heady company. Ruth led the majors with fourteen home runs, Ty Cobb was the top hitter in the American League with a .350 average, and Thorpe was best in the National League at .375. Under a photo montage ("Where Did They Steal Those Bats?") of Thorpe and two other players whose averages had vastly improved from past years, Newspaper Enterprise Association sportswriter Fred Turbyville wrote: "Jim Thorpe, who never could hit with the Giants, is heading the procession in the National. Maybe a change in pastures helped." Jim tailed off somewhat after that, slowed by a lingering leg injury incurred while scratching out an infield hit, and played sporadically in September, finishing with a .327 average, still by far his best performance in the majors. There were several positive events in his life that September. The month started with Jim deciding that he was not through with football, as he had earlier proclaimed. On Labor

Day, he mailed a signed contract to Ralph E. Hay, new owner of the Canton Bulldogs, agreeing to coach and captain the team again that season. A few weeks later on the afternoon of September 16, as Jim went two for four and drove in two runs in a home game against St. Louis, Iva was in the hospital giving birth. One year after they lost Jim Jr., along came a second girl. They named her Charlotte in memory of Jim's late mother.

That same day, the Reds defeated the Giants and clinched the pennant in Cincinnati. All of McGraw's trading was not enough as the Giants finished second, nine games out.

DAMON RUNYON, VERNACULAR poet of America's sporting underbelly, assigned himself a chair in the lobby of a Cincinnati hotel and observed the passing scene before the first game of the 1919 World Series. "Fans looking for rooms. Fans looking for drinks. Fans who have found drinks. Yes, indeed, this is Cincinnati. And just before the battle, Mommer," he wrote. "Dope favors the White Sox. That gives the Reds a great chance. Baseball dope is about as safe as a sure thing over at the Lavonia track. Ask any lads how sure that is."

As it turned out, Runyon was right. The fix was already in. Arnold Rothstein, gambling mastermind, sat in the lobby of the Ansonia Hotel in Manhattan as the opening game was about to get underway, waiting for an announcer to begin reporting play-by-play relayed to him by telegraph. He had bet $270,000 against the heavily favored White Sox. One of Rothstein's partners in crime took a prime seat in the lower stands near the White Sox bench. When knuckleballer Eddie Cicotte, winner of twenty-nine games that year, hit Reds leadoff man Morrie Rath in the back, the gamblers understood the signal. It meant the illicit deal with Cicotte and seven White Sox teammates was in motion, an agreement that had been consummated with $5,000 cash bribes. *Plunk*, the players would throw the series and let the Reds win.

In the long and gloried history of American baseball, the 1919 World Series would rank among the most memorable, but for all the wrong reasons. What became known as the Black Sox scandal led to the lifetime ban of eight players, including Shoeless Joe Jackson, who took the money yet led both teams with a .375 average during the series, and Buck Weaver, who knew about the conspiracy but did not take the bribe. Jim Thorpe was nowhere near any of this. He was on the other side of Ohio by then playing football for the Bulldogs. But how he dealt with the corruptible milieu around him was instructive, at times revealing a double standard in terms of behavior that he faced throughout his career.

Consider McGraw, the man who brought Thorpe into the sport. McGraw had two nicknames that applied to different parts of his life. On the field, he was the Little Napoleon, strategizing and bossing others around. Off the field, he was Muggsy, a character straight out of Damon Runyon's imagination, and not just because of the traveling vaudeville show he was part of in the winter of 1912. Other winters he could be found in Havana down in Cuba, where he had shares in a racetrack and casino controlled by gangsters. In New York, from his apartment on 109th Street, he moved easily between the highbrow and lowbrow subcultures of the city, bouncing around town full of whiskey and vinegar, looking for fights while belting out "When Irish Eyes Are Smiling." His fame got him into the Lambs Club, a prestigious men's dining fraternity comprising mostly theater and arts people, including Cecil B. DeMille and John Philip Sousa. *Floreant Agni*—May the Lambs Flourish. But his orneriness eventually led to his suspension from the Lambs for getting into a fistfight with British actor William H. Boyd. As the story went, Muggsy strutted into the club late one evening before closing time and roamed from table to table passing around whiskey he had purchased from the doorman. When Boyd took exception to the foul language McGraw was using, a larger argument ensued about the relative merits of British versus American actors, a dispute that was resolved with thrown water bottles, chairs, and fists.

McGraw was more often found in grittier quarters. Since 1908, he had owned a pool hall downstairs in the Marbridge Building on Herald Square next to the *New York Herald*, whose thundering press runs would shake Muggsy's twenty-seven billiard tables at night. His hall was a hangout for newspaper hacks, pool sharks (including Willie Hoppe, the national champ), and gamblers. One of the silent partners in the joint was none other than Arnold Rothstein, the World Series fixer.

Early in his career managing the Giants, McGraw had placed and won a $400 bet on his team to win the 1905 World Series, an act that if it had happened later would have led to his banishment from the game. For the 1919 season, he acquired the same Hal Chase who had been suspended years earlier by Mathewson in Cincinnati, and before the season was out Chase took part in another game-fixing cabal with Heinie Zimmerman, a veteran Giants infielder. Zimmerman ended up being suspended, but Chase survived through the end of that season and then used his gambling connections to win $40,000 betting against the White Sox in the World Series.

The worlds of pro baseball and football were domains of great athletic feats and desperate personal lives. The men played in fear, without financial security, their existence determined by fickle and often penny-pinching bosses. Any history of the Black Sox scandal and why the players did what they did invariably leads back to the dismissive and penurious actions of Charles Comiskey, the owner. To some extent, the players saw the bribe as both an act of survival and anti-owner retribution. But it was more than one cheapskate mogul. Sports were riddled with betting and fixing in Jim Thorpe's era. Newspapers routinely cited the gambling odds in college football games and their stories reported how the outcomes affected bettors. In the pro ranks, gambling was rampant. Remember that incident in 1915 when a Canton Bulldogs fan emerged from the end zone and knocked the ball out of the Massillon runner's hands just as he was about to score the winning touchdown on the game's final play? That was unusual only in how it was done, not why—to preserve a bet.

There were unfounded rumors that Thorpe bet on football at Canton, and that once he put down a couple thousand dollars on a game against Massillon. It was another of the many myths about Thorpe. "Pure fiction!" said Jack Cusack, the owner who had lured him into the pro ranks and had good reason to know about his star and betting. "At his request, I kept all of his money until the end of the season." As for baseball, Thorpe was not the most obvious target for the gamblers and fixers, since he was rarely a starter in the majors, but he said they did approach him once and he rebuffed them.

"This bribery of athletes is a terrible thing. I don't think the athletes themselves work it the right way," he said decades later, as another national bribery scandal unfolded. "While I was playing outfield for the Giants, a couple of gamblers came up to my hotel room. That was before the Black Sox scandal. They started making me a proposition and I didn't want to hear the end. I bashed their heads together two or three times and threw them out in the hall."

The Jim Thorpe who emerged from this was an honest man, and one whose behavior, while at times rowdy, was no more so than that of many who played with him, managed him, or judged him.

JACK CUSACK HAD ceded ownership of the Canton football team a year and a half earlier and left for Oklahoma in search of oil riches, going from Bulldog to wildcatter. The new owner was Ralph Hay, who made his money in the automobile business. Hay was a gregarious young man in his late twenties, a "live wire" who flitted about his hometown in spiffy bespoke suits and shined shoes, puffing on a cigar. He had a fast rise from salesman to boss with his own dealership, the Ralph E. Hay Motor Company, at the corner of Cleveland Avenue and Second Street in downtown Canton. His fortune was tied to the popularity of the Hupmobile, a Detroit line of steel-bodied touring cars and runabouts named for founder Robert Hupp, just as the Oldsmobile was named for company founder Ransom Olds.

Hay bought the Bulldogs to promote his Hupmobiles, but that was forestalled when war and influenza forced the cancelation of the 1918 football season. His first chance to field a team was 1919, not the most propitious time to enter pro football. The weekly wages for a team roster—reaching $2,000 a week—often exceeded gate receipts. Only teams with stars could draw crowds, creating a wild-west bidding war among teams, with some players as mercenaries moving from one high bidder to the next week by week. In the scrape for talent, owners could not stop themselves from spending more than they could afford. This was a variation of a lament voiced by billionaire owners generations later, although by then they were flush with cash, making it less a matter of what could be afforded than how much management was willing to share with labor. In that sense, even if pro football was not the most lucrative endeavor for athletes in its early days, the lack of league organization and agreed-upon rules gave players a freedom they would lack for decades thereafter.

Two months before the 1919 season opened, Hay met at Canton's Courtland Hotel with the owners of the Bulldogs' nearby rivals, the Massillon Tigers, to discuss these issues. While failing to agree on a salary cap, they did vow not to steal each other's players. Someone had already attempted to lure Thorpe away from Canton, and the maneuver came from a most unexpected source. Jim's former manager, Muggsy McGraw, who was done with him as a baseball player, led a group forming a professional Giants football team that would play at the Polo Grounds, and he tried to talk Thorpe into being the face of the franchise. Jim declined, saying he had already signed his contract with Ralph Hay.

Here again, Thorpe demonstrated a basic integrity, reminiscent of 1913 when he was reluctant to join McGraw's baseball team because he had made an earlier promise to the Pittsburgh Pirates, and only signed with the Giants after the Pirates' owner released him from his informal commitment. Compare that with the heralded Knute Rockne, glorified later as the legendary coach of Notre Dame's Four Horsemen teams, who was Thorpe's contemporary in the cutthroat world of early pro football. In *Pigskin: The Early Years of Pro Football,* sports historian Robert W. Peterson recalled that the Nesser boys, a band of six brothers who played for the Columbus Panhandles, claimed they faced Rockne on five different teams.

Thorpe's Bulldogs played ten games in 1919 with nine wins, no losses, and one tie as the only blemish on their record, a 3–3 draw with the Hammond All-Stars. That game was played at the Indiana team's home gridiron, which happened to be not in Indiana but in Chicago at a stadium later named Wrigley Field, and was notable mostly for something that happened before the visitors reached the game. Their bus broke down on the way into Chicago and could not be fixed in time, so the twenty-five

Canton players grabbed their equipment bags, trudged to the nearest station, and rode the El up to the park.

Sportswriters at the game did not hold back on superlatives, one calling it "the greatest professional football game ever played in Chicago." They agreed that if not for Thorpe's kicking and tackling, the underdog Hammond team would have won. Covering the game for the *Munster Times*, a local Hammond-area paper, a columnist using the pen name Wring Lardner, mimicking the celebrated *Tribune* writer, described Thorpe's play in the *You Know Me, Al* dialect. "Well, Al, James Thorpe, the Indian which I shall name Jim Thorpe was in the box for Canton and from where I was sitting he also filled most of the other positions on the nine plus two. I have kind of got an idear that if the Hammonds team had any sence they would paid Jim his jack before the game started and let him go back to the reservation in Canton."

The All-Stars were stocked with players who came out of midwestern football schools, including four from Notre Dame, three from Minnesota, and a six-foot 180-pound right end from Illinois named George Halas, who dropped at least two key passes during the game. It was the first of many meetings between Thorpe and Halas, the two most important figures at the dawn of pro football. One year after that first encounter, Halas founded the Decatur Staleys. Within three years he was leading the Chicago Bears, a team Papa Bear would symbolize for the next half century. From Jim Thorpe at the start of his career to Vince Lombardi at the end, Halas was the thread that ran through the sport.

In moving through the schedule without a loss, winning six games by shutouts and outscoring their opponents 195 to 20, the Bulldogs had the look and feel of the finest old Carlisle teams, especially the backfield, where Hay hired Joe Guyon to run alongside Pete Calac and Thorpe, all starters on the 1912 Carlisle Indians squad that trounced Army. Because of Carlisle's peculiar situation as an institution that was well below colleges academically but fielded sports teams at that level, Guyon had a bifurcated career. After leaving Carlisle, he endured a three-year hiatus at prep institutions before qualifying to enroll at Georgia Tech, where he starred in 1917 and 1918 as the best halfback in the South, once running for 344 yards in a rout of Vanderbilt. Like several other pro players, he also had a job in the college ranks the same year he signed with the Bulldogs, coaching Union University in Tennessee on Saturdays.

Among other Ohio League players who also coached in college was a halfback for Akron, Frederick Douglass Pollard, head coach at Lincoln University, a historically black college in Pennsylvania. Known familiarly as Fritz, Pollard had graduated from Brown University with a degree in chemistry after leading his team to the 1916 Rose Bowl, where it lost to an undefeated Washington State squad coached by Thorpe's Carlisle teammate Lone Star Dietz. Pollard made history wherever he went. He was the first black player at Brown, the first to make Walter Camp's All-American team, and now the first black player in the Ohio League. When his team faced the Bulldogs, the *Akron Beacon Journal* promoted it as a match between "the two greatest backfield men in pro football." In the rain, mud, and snow, the game was less than the hype. Pollard ran well, but Canton controlled the game so thoroughly that Thorpe saw no need to enter the contest until the fourth quarter of a 14–0 win.

In football, running backs often have the shortest careers at peak performance, their bodies worn down by tacklers hurtling at them and slamming into them at full force game after game, season after season. That wear and tear was doubled in the era when they played both offense and defense, never leaving the field, a full game of being tackled and tackling others. Thorpe once boasted that he never worried about getting hurt playing the game, but at thirty-two he was past the age when most running backs decline, and as a player-coach was more judicious about how much he played. One reason he put himself in for only one quarter in the game against Fritz Pollard's Akron squad was because of how he had extended himself a week earlier in the rivalry game against Massillon. It was another of those so-called world championship games, and Thorpe the colossus dominated in a 23–0 shutout.

"The game was another demonstration of the fact that there is only one Jim Thorpe," wrote a *Canton Repository* reporter afterward. "At the age which sees most athletes willing to rest on laurels gathered in the past, this great Indian seems just as good as ever, still the superman of football."

His old Carlisle mates Calac and Guyon were impressive as well, forming "the greatest backfield that football has ever seen, a backfield which yesterday worked with the precision of a clock and the effectiveness of a Yankee tank."

When the season ended, Jim went home to the bungalow house on East Boston Avenue in Yale. Around him, the nearby oil boom was long gone. Farmers struggled as wheat and cotton prices declined precipitously from the heights they had reached from the demands of war. Most of the land was tilled by tenant farmers who did not own it. Some were leaving for California and new lives in the West. Oklahoma swirled with the political crosscurrents of super-patriotism and socialism, populism and racism. The Knights of the Ku Klux Klan were infiltrating the state. Sixteen Klansmen in white hoods and robes rode on horseback in a Liberty Loan parade in Skiatook, a town sixty miles northeast of Yale, early in 1919 and threatened to lynch three men who did not buy bonds. Months later, to the southwest in Oklahoma City, the Klan held a membership meeting at Sifer's candy store. Soon enough, the violent secret society would sweep through Yale and across the state.

Iva was home with two little girls under age two. Jim played basketball with a local team, shot pool at a hangout on Main Street, and went hunting with his coon dogs. "They'd say he'd run those dogs all night and stay right with them, jumping creeks or brush or fences like nothing you ever saw," recalled Tex Brown, a Yale resident. "When he was coon hunting he'd say goodbye at sundown and hello at sunup." When one of his dogs was killed accidentally, Jim cradled it in his arms, heartbroken again. Even though the winters in Yale offered a respite from the nomadic life, lately the time at home did not improve his marriage. Iva's sister Grace, their next-door neighbor, had never liked Jim. She was strict and prudish and looked askance at his Indianness and his roughhouse lifestyle, and her attitude influenced Iva. One of Jim's daughters recalled decades later in an interview that a coon dog in Jim's kennel was named Grace. It was not unwittingly, but with some enjoyment, that at feeding time Jim would go into the backyard and boom out loudly enough so that his sister-in-law might hear, "Come here, Grace, you old bitch."

20

Start to Finish

THE SPORTING WORLDS OF JIM THORPE CONVERGED ON September 17, 1920. In the afternoon, playing right field for the Akron Numatics in the International League, he went two for three against the Toronto Maple Leafs in the opener of the final series of the season. The ball game was inconsequential except as a marker in the curious course of his baseball career. After playing for the Boston Braves in 1919 and excelling by batting .327, Thorpe had been traded that winter to Akron, a Triple-A club where he stayed in his hitting groove and was now finishing with a .360 average, sixteen home runs, and thirty-two stolen bases. Year by year he got better at baseball, but baseball did not get better for him. His demotion to the minors at age thirty-three was final; never again would he see a major league roster.

A few hours after the game ended in Akron, a business meeting was called to order at the Odd Fellows Building in downtown Canton twenty-three miles to the south by Ralph E. Hay, the car dealer and owner of the Bulldogs football team on which Jim was the main attraction as player and coach. Fifteen people arrived for the gathering, too many to fit into Hay's office, so they moved to the auto floor, where some found seats on the running boards of new Hupmobiles. It could be said that what happened that night in Ralph Hay's showroom was the most consequential event in the history of pro football, the beginning of what would become the National Football League. It was Thorpe's fame that made it possible.

Before that meeting, pro football had been a haphazard free-for-all, players coming and going at will to the highest bidder, sometimes week by week, teams rising and falling and folding, sportswriters reluctant to pay much attention outside the hometowns, the game mostly played on fields with bare bleachers rather than inside stadiums, most owners losing money due to paltry gate receipts. Canton had played for years in what was called the Ohio League, but it was a league only in the loosest sense, an appellation attached to it despite there being no common rules, no commissioner or league office, not even an understanding of what teams were in or out.

The meeting that night in the Hupmobile showroom was intended to organize a strong league with all the elements the Ohio League lacked. Representatives from eleven clubs were there at the creation, extending the scope beyond the confines of Ohio. Team officials from Hammond and Muncie in Indiana; Rock Island, Decatur, and Chicago in Illinois; and Rochester in New York joined Canton, Akron, Dayton, Massillon, and Cleveland, though financially bereft Massillon was then withdrawing from the professional ranks, ending its historic rivalry with Canton.

There were no reporters at the meeting. Accounts of what happened relied on abbreviated minutes kept by Frank Nied of Akron and the recollections of participants, including George Halas, who had arrived by train from Chicago to represent his new team, the Decatur Staleys, named for the central Illinois food-starch manufacturing plant where he worked and coached. Hay's grandson, James Francis King, a physician named after Thorpe, recalled before he died in 2018 that he often heard stories from his mother, Virginia King, and great-uncle Lester Higgins, who was secretary of the Bulldogs, that the room was filled with cigar smoke and there were ice buckets of beer on the floor.

No doubt about the cigars. If there was beer, it was most likely Cascade beer from the Canton Brewing Company, sponsor of the Bulldogs in 1919, meaning the businessmen in the showroom were skirting the law. Prohibition had gone into effect in January 1920, making it illegal to sell, buy, or manufacture alcoholic beverages, but not to drink them. Hay might have kept some old cases of Cascade around after the Eighteenth Amendment was enacted. Or it might have been the bootleg variety. Although local beermakers were selling nonalcoholic cereal beverages in public, they were also brewing illicit beer on the side, with little interference from local lawmen. Not for nothing did Canton claim the nickname Little Chicago. It was a mob-friendly town, a cozy hangout for gangsters at the halfway point along the Lincoln Highway between Chicago and New York offering gambling dens, prostitution houses, speakeasies, even its own crime boss, Jumbo Crowley.

Various studies indicated that alcohol consumption in Ohio during the early days of Prohibition was about one-third of what it had been before, but for Jim, as for millions of Americans who struggled with excessive drinking, the ban seemed to have little effect, and not just because of Canton's loose ways. Drinking in places that were legally dry was part of the Thorpe family history. Alcohol was banned in Indian Territory when Jim's father, Hiram, sold jugs of bootleg liquor from the back of his wagon. Although Oklahoma had been dry since it became a state in 1907, the prohibition written into its constitution, Jim never had trouble finding alcohol when he was home hunting and drinking with his pals during the winter months.

When the organizational meeting began at eight fifteen that night, Hay told the others about a preliminary session held in August at which four Ohio members had discussed the formation of a new league. The original plan was to call it a conference. With the expanded group this time, it was changed to association—the American Professional Football Association, or APFA. Columbus, Buffalo, and Detroit were also brought in, rounding out the league at fourteen teams. After the name was approved, a motion was passed that made Thorpe president. Then, according to the minutes, Thorpe appointed Dr. A. A. Young, part-owner of the Hammond team, to chair an executive committee that would draft a league constitution laying out rules and regulations. That this notation is in the minutes is noteworthy for one historical reason. In George Halas's autobiography, published more than half a century later, he wrote that Thorpe was absent. The minutes indicated he was there, which meant he drove down from Akron after playing baseball earlier that day.

Also according to Nied's minutes, the representatives set a $100 league entry fee and directed each team to print stationery reading "Member of American Professional Football Association." The Brunswick-Balke-Collender Company, a manufacturing conglomerate that made everything from billiard tables to automobile tires, donated a trophy to be awarded to the league champion. It was a silver loving cup, forgotten ancestor of the modern Lombardi Trophy given to Super Bowl winners, although in 1920 the winner was decided by a vote of league officers and the cup somehow vanished after the inaugural season.

If there was an agreement to ban the practice of luring college athletes playing under aliases, or to prevent players from skipping from team to team, no such decisions were cited in the minutes, although several stories the next day mentioned those issues, and the stories emanated from officials at the meeting, so they likely were discussed. The lone personnel issue recorded in the minutes was that at the end of the 1920 season each team should give the league secretary a list of players it had used that year "so that each team would have first choice in services [of those players]" for 1921. The first modest move in a century-long effort by football management to control labor.

Thorpe's obligations as league president were not delineated in the minutes, nor was there documentation detailing any actions he took as president. He was not the paper-pusher type. His role was essential only as a revered public figure whose name gave the league stature. Few had heard of George Halas yet. Knute Rockne had left pro ball to coach at Notre Dame. There were other good players, but only one Jim Thorpe. He was being used, in other words, but not unwillingly. "J. Thorpe Heads Pro Grid Teams in New League," declared the headline in the *Akron Evening Times.* "Jim Thorpe Heads Circuit of Eleven Mid-West Cities," noted the *Fort Wayne Sentinel.* In newspapers around the country, articles about the meeting mentioned Thorpe in the first paragraph.

Canton began its inaugural season in the APFA two weeks later with characteristic dominance, winning the first three games by a combined score of 97 to nothing, but Jim at thirty-three was not the player he once was. He could still amaze in small bursts but had lost speed and stamina and was unable to sustain excellence game by game or through four quarters, often remaining on the sidelines for the first half. In the fourth game, Canton showed signs of deterioration, allowing the underdog Dayton Triangles to escape with a twenty-all tie. Next came the Akron Pros, the rising team led by Fritz Pollard that viewed the match at Canton's League Field as a prime opportunity to claim supremacy and hand Thorpe's squad its first loss in three years.

Interest in the matchup was so intense that Akron's owners met with Thorpe on the Thursday before the game and pleaded for the release of more tickets. Bettors and gamblers flooded into Little Chicago from Cleveland, Youngstown, and Pittsburgh and buzzed around the Courtland Hotel lobby Saturday night and Sunday morning putting down odds. The Northern Ohio Traction and Light Company added special cars on its streetcar line to carry fans to and from the game at the field out near Meyers Lake Park. The papers predicted a crowd "which will rival the World Series"—hyperbolic for a field that accommodated ten thousand, but reflective of the game's importance. Most of the pregame focus was on a battle of the stars, Thorpe versus Pollard.

The *Akron Beacon Journal* called Thorpe "probably the most famous gridder who ever donned the moleskins" and "the example set before would-be stars by the best coaches in the game." Acknowledging that Jim was not expected to start, the article added that "anyone who has studied the man knows that he could no more keep out of the battle, especially if his team is losing, than he could fly." Pollard had hurt his shoulder a week earlier in Akron's match against Cleveland, but sent a telegram to his coach a few days before the game. "You may be able to take me out of a game with Cleveland but nothing on earth can drag me out of the game with those Thorpe fellows," Pollard cabled from Philadelphia, where he lived while studying dentistry and coaching at nearby Lincoln University.

Pro football was not as blatantly segregated as major league baseball, at least not yet. Pollard played for Akron at a time when great black baseball players were kept out of the whites-only majors and consigned to the Negro Leagues. But through the first half of the 1920s, there were only at most two or three black players in pro football in any season, Pollard the most prominent among them. Later, an unofficial policy among team owners kept all African Americans out of the league from 1934 to the end of World War II. Just as sportswriters invariably described Thorpe as "the big Indian" or "the great Redskin," virtually every reference to Pollard included a casually racist phrase that categorized him by skin color. He was called "the dusky backfield man" and "the colored star from Brown" and "the dark-skinned one" and "the little colored boy."

These came from reporters who admired him, or at least his skills on the field of play. Here is how the *Beacon Journal* scribe described Pollard when comparing him to Thorpe: "The next man who will be called for by the fans will likely be the Akron colored star, Fritz Pollard. This particular black chap weighs just 145 pounds but judging from the testimony of those who have played against him he must tip the beams to at least the 250 mark. Tis said he hits the line like a submarine destroyer although no one seems to be able to solve his method of attack. . . . He sidesteps, he straight-arms, he jumps, in fact he just naturally works thru the opposition like a snake in the grass. He is the original exponent of the true wiggling style of football."

The game proved to be more than a two-star struggle. As expected, Coach Thorpe did not send player Thorpe onto the field until the third period, when Canton was trailing 10–0, and though the hometown crowd roared when they saw him enter, and though he was able to complete a few long passes to Guyon, his former Carlisle teammate, Jim could not prevent the shutout loss. But there was one notable on-field encounter, or near-encounter, between Thorpe and Pollard. It happened in the fourth quarter, Thorpe on defense, Pollard skirting around the end with the ball. "He dived for the little colored boy but Fritz cleverly sidestepped and as the Indian dove over Pollard's head and went crashing into the ground, Fritz stopped just long enough to give Thorpe the 'merry razz.' "

That description came from an Akron sportswriter who might have been sensationalizing the struggle between the two stars. His story claimed that when Pollard was late arriving at the field after a long drive from eastern Pennsylvania, Thorpe had disparaged him as being "yellow." That did not sound like Thorpe. He was a rough-and-tumble player, but not verbally provocative and not racist. At the Stockholm Olympics he had been the strongest ally of the lone black athlete on the U.S. team, Howard Drew, and in a pro game a few years earlier he had stepped in to prevent racist teammate Greasy Neale from picking a fight with a black player at a game against Rochester.

In the event, Pollard got the best of Thorpe twice in 1920, leading the Pros to a 7-0 victory in a Thanksgiving Day rematch in Akron. Canton finished the season with a 6-4-2 record. By a vote of owners, the APFA silver trophy went to Akron (eight wins, no losses, and three ties), an action disputed by other teams with similar records. It was an inauspicious start for the league, but still a start. What would become of the APFA remained uncertain. Even the most optimistic predictions were cautious. "There is a tendency for development of the game, and possibly some day we may see a national league with representatives in the big cities," wrote one New York–based sportswriter. "But that era seems quite a distance away. . . . Professional football may pay in places where there is not the lure of big college contests, but it will never rival the amateur brand."

IN THE FRATERNITY of twentieth-century sportswriters, Ring Lardner represented one distinct style, Grantland Rice another—Lardner with his affinity for busher dialogue and sarcasm bordering on knowing cynicism, Rice with his affinity for glorifying odes and an optimism overflowing into mythology and schmaltz. "He was the evangelist of fun, the bringer of good news about games," a friend said at Rice's funeral. "He was forever seeking out young men of athletic talent, lending them a hand and building them up; and sharing them with the rest of us as our heroes." One of those heroes was Jim Thorpe.

Even as he perpetuated Indian stereotypes and advanced the dubious claim that Jim was such a natural athlete he did not have to practice, Rice was nonetheless an ardent Thorpe believer throughout his career. In churning out six columns a week for more than a half a century, an estimated twenty-two thousand columns comprising sixty-seven million words before he was done, along with more articles in national magazines, Rice occasionally returned to a favorite standard, picking various all-time athletic teams. Near the end of the 1920 season, writing in *Leslie's Weekly*, Rice named the first of his all-time college football teams with the help of four noted college football men: Fielding "Hurry Up" Yost, the coach at Michigan; John W. Heisman, then coaching at Penn; Big Bill Edwards, a former star at Princeton who had written *Football Days*, a popular book about the sport; and Pop Warner, still coaching at Pitt.

Rice noted that Jim was the only player cited by all four. "Thorpe could do everything," Yost exclaimed. Heisman said he was "almost as fast in football togs as in a track suit" and "strong in every department." Edwards considered him "good enough for any backfield." And Warner called him "the greatest halfback in all football history." In all, Rice wrote, this meant Thorpe was "the greatest star in grid history." Football experts had been saying much the same for the past decade, but what was important was its perpetuation now. Just as his talents on the field were diminishing, Jim Thorpe's permanent place in the national consciousness was solidifying. Grantland Rice was making sure of that.

JIM WAS AN all-around athlete all around the year. Even home with his family he could not turn away. Football season over, baseball season not yet begun, he turned to basketball and played for the local American Legion team. He was not the best player on the hoops team—George McCool, a hot-shooting forward, scored most of the points—but he was a tenacious defender and the main gate attraction. "It was a rare opportunity to see Jim Thorpe, world famous athlete, in action," declared a story in the *Yale Record* after a game against the Oklahoma City Ramblers filled the high school gymnasium one cold Wednesday night in late January 1921. He did not play for cash this time. The proceeds went to needy war veterans.

He was in Oklahoma that winter when he learned that his baseball peregrinations would take him to yet another city. At that point he had already played baseball in Rocky Mount, Fayetteville, Anadarko, New York,

Jersey City, Harrisburg, Newark, Milwaukee, Cincinnati, Boston, and Akron. Next stop: Toledo to play with the Mud Hens, who were owned by Roger Bresnahan, a former catcher who had once played for McGraw and the Giants. Toledo paid Akron $1,500 for the rights to Thorpe in a transaction that briefly passed Jim through Ty Cobb's Tigers on the way to the minor league affiliate. Hitting .360 for Akron failed to increase Thorpe's monetary value. His purchase price this time was half that of a year earlier, when Boston sold him to the Numatics.

The migratory life was not easy on the family, but Iva, with two little girls in tow, tried to follow Jim whenever she could. At the start of their marriage, when she rode the honeymoon train across the continent with the barnstorming Giants and White Sox, and then sailed the seas on the world tour, she'd delighted in being part of the action with her "Snooks." Now the thrill was gone. Her motive was to hold the marriage together. On to Toledo.

The American Association of 1921 was a top-flight minor league, the teams stocked with future and former major leaguers and piloted by rising managers. The player-manager of the Louisville Colonels, Joe McCarthy, was on his way to a stellar quarter-century career managing in the majors, most of them with the New York Yankees, who won seven World Series championships during his reign. His winning ways were evident at Louisville, where he led the Colonels to the pennant, while the Mud Hens struggled and finished seventh in an eight-team league. But Jim did not struggle. He put together another outstanding season, his third in a row, this time batting .358 with 36 doubles, 13 triples, 9 home runs, and 34 stolen bases. Three of those homers came on one prolific day, July 13, at Borchert Field in Milwaukee against the Brewers. "He is in Toledo, and there are outfielders in the big leagues who would be better in Toledo and Jim in the majors," noted a sportswriter for the *Washington Evening Star.* Not to happen.

While Thorpe played for the Mud Hens that spring and summer, several changes were made in the American Professional Football Association. League officials replaced Jim as president with Joe Carr of the Columbus Panhandles. Thorpe's visibility was essential for publicity that first year, but the owners now felt they needed a businessman at the top. On the field, the league would now follow college rules. Off the field, the owners would tighten control over players, among other things agreeing to territorial rights in which teams had claim to players who lived or went to college in their region. More teams were added, expanding the league to a bulky twenty-one franchises, though several proved financially untenable and folded during or after the season.

The Staleys of George Halas moved from Decatur to Chicago, and by the end of the year changed their name to the Bears. The largest city fielding a new team was New York, with the Brickley Giants. The smallest was Green Bay, Wisconsin, with a team called the Packers. The New York team lasted one year. The Packers survived and thrived, staying in the league even as all other teams except the Chicago Cardinals and Decatur Staleys eventually folded. Even those two teams had to move to stay viable. Only the Packers kept at it while playing with the same name in the same city, tiny Green Bay. Not owned by a wealthy benefactor but publicly held by the people, the Packers went on to win a record thirteen championships and sport the best won-lost percentage of any pro football team over a century of games.

When the 1921 season began, Thorpe was not only no longer the league president, he was no longer in Canton. The Bulldogs had moved on from their aging star, and he from them. Along with his Carlisle running buddies Pete Calac and Joe Guyon, he switched allegiances to the Cleveland Indians. Also joining him in Cleveland was his longtime friend Jack Cusack, the founder of the Bulldogs who had returned temporarily from the Oklahoma oil business. "While assisting in the building of a refinery in Arkansas, I developed a severe case of malaria and found it necessary to leave that locality for a while, so I decided to go back to Canton until I recovered," Cusack recalled. "Jim Thorpe had transferred his interests to the Cleveland Indians, and the old warhorse asked me to come to the Ohio metropolis and look after his financial affairs. His contract called for a guaranteed amount for each game or a percentage of the gate, whichever was greater."

Even with Thorpe and the new recruits, the Indians struggled on the field and at the gate. They won three and lost five, although all but their loss to Halas's Chicago squad were close games. In looking after Jim's interests, Cusack determined that he was being shorted after many games as owners manipulated the gate receipts through various deceptions, including inflating the number of complimentary tickets. Twice he found discrepancies where the receipts were about a thousand dollars less than they should have been, considering ticket sales, and in both cases the supposed complimentary tickets were far in excess of what they should have been. "In both instances, after strong and vivid argument, I succeeded in collecting our share of the deficiencies," Cusack later wrote.

The last scheduled game of the season was at the Polo Grounds in New York against the Brickley Giants, led by Charles Brickley, a former All-American from Harvard who had been on the 1912 Olympic team with Thorpe (competing in the hop, step, and jump) and had played against him in the Ohio League as a member of the Massillon Tigers. Now they were two grand old men in a young man's sport. Brickley was thirty, four years younger than Thorpe, but looked the older of the two, balding and pudgy around the middle. Jim played while Brickley remained on the sidelines. Cleveland ended up winning 17–0 in a game contested in the mud before a disappointing crowd of five thousand fans. Jim kicked a field goal and an extra point and pulled off one exciting run recounted excitedly by syndicated columnist Sid Mercer. It started with Jim running one direction and then changing course, looping the other way from ten yards behind the line of scrimmage. Then:

> He plunged right into a group of five or six Brickley huskies all intent on tackling him. The way *Jeems* went through those boys carried us back to the day when he raced up and down the plains of West Point with cadet tacklers clinging to him but not impeding his progress. That was some ten years ago, and if Thorpe has since forgotten anything about gaining through a broken field he recalled it. . . . It was a broken field indeed after he finished with it. The first tackler to dive at Thorpe was strong armed and spilled in a mud puddle. The second fared worse. Thorpe's left shoulder encoun-

tered the tackler's chest and knocked him flat on his back. A third man grabbed the Indian around the legs and slipped off. By this time they had slowed Jim up, but they hadn't stopped him. He still had a trick or two. By revolving his body Thorpe shook off one or two tacklers who had now fastened themselves to him. All the time he was making progress toward the enemy's goal. At last he stumbled, just as two more of Brickley's players loomed in front of him. As he fell, he rolled over and advanced the ball a little farther. He was down, and several of his opponents were out.

All of this for a ten yard gain.

Other than Thorpe's run, the contest offered little drama. The Brickley Giants gained one first down for the afternoon. But if the game itself was forgettable, what happened at halftime and then after the game at the Hotel Imperial and Penn Station were memorable. The halftime featured what the game did not, a one-on-one duel between Thorpe and Brickley, competing in the dying art of the drop-kick. When the football was rounder, more like a rugby ball than the sharply conical shape it would become, extra points and field goals were often drop-kicked—that is, there was no holder; the kicker merely dropped the ball and booted it just as it hit the ground. Thorpe was known for his powerful leg, as was Brickley, who at Harvard had booted thirty-four field goals, including many with the drop-kick. Their contest began at the twenty-five-yard line and moved back from there to midfield and beyond. As was often the case in that era, when all statistics depended on the eyes of fallible sportswriters, accounts differed on the results. Although it was agreed that each man made six of twelve attempts, some credited Brickley with a long drop-kick of fifty yards and Thorpe of forty-five, while others insisted that Thorpe connected from fifty-five yards while Brickley's boot from there struck the crossbar.

After the game, the Cleveland team returned to the Hotel Imperial at Broadway and Thirty-Second Street. The same routine after every road game: they would wait at a hotel until management representatives came by with the check for proceeds from the game. This time they expected to split $3,750 among the players. Thorpe and Cusack, who shared a room, became suspicious early that evening when a bellhop stopped by with a statement covering hotel expenses. Cusack guessed what that meant: the team treasurer and his lawyer were trying to skip town without paying the men. Pro football was a money hustle of one sort or another in those days, and here was a classic case. Cusack and Jim raced over to Penn Station a few blocks away and found the treasurer and lawyer waiting for the next train to Cleveland, set to leave in a half hour. Cusack described what happened next, which sounded like material for Damon Runyon:

"I demanded that he return to the hotel and pay the players, but he refused, saying they would receive expenses only. Getting nowhere, and with time running out, I sought out two detectives stationed in the lobby and explained the situation, whereupon they decided—for a certain sum—to help us. . . . When the train was announced and the gates opened for boarding, the two men reached for their [traveling bags], but at that juncture the detectives grabbed them and we all went down to a precinct station in a taxicab. The two frustrated birds of passage were not long in deciding they did not care for the atmosphere of the police station and agreed to return with Thorpe and me to the hotel. There, with several big gridsters giving me silent support, I succeeded in convincing the treasurer that the time for settling accounts was at hand."

A second game between the same two teams had been scheduled for Ebbets Field in Brooklyn, but that was canceled after the first game drew so poorly. Cusack instead arranged more exhibition matches for the Indians, including one against the Richmond Athletic Club on December 10 that ended in a scoreless tie. While that game was being played, Iva was back in Yale delivering the third Thorpe girl, Grace Frances. Nine days later, Jim finally made it back to Oklahoma, off the road at last, if only briefly.

In what had become an annual tradition, word spread during the winter that he was through with sports and would enter the business world. Newspapers around the country ran a column by Cleveland-based syndicated columnist Norman Edgar Brown asserting that Thorpe's football days were done and "it is a good bet that he will not return to baseball.

Time has taken its toll." Time's toll was indisputable, the rest premature. For all his strength on the fields of play, Jim's interior dialogue was a churning river of uncertainty and longing for something just out of reach—and occasionally his angst burst into the open as a declaration that he was retiring. And then, inevitably, he would return to what he knew, to the world of sports.

THE RELATIONSHIP BETWEEN Jim and money was an endless cycle of generosity and need. Throughout his life he was selfless with money and scrambling for it. He was anything but avaricious, yet money was rarely far from his mind. He was known for giving it away to people who were disadvantaged, yet he worried endlessly about his financial condition. For all his athletic accomplishments, he felt underappreciated, never duly rewarded, and often battled with owners offering him less than he deserved. *Lo, the poor Indian.* It was happening again in early 1922.

On February 9, William Klepper, president of the Portland Beavers in the Pacific Coast League, announced that after two months of negotiations he had purchased Thorpe from Toledo and had wired terms of the salary to Jim's home in Yale. Another baseball town for the itinerant athlete, his eleventh. Portland fans and baseball scribes were exhilarated. For a "very handsome price of $5,000," the *Oregon Journal* noted, Portland had landed "the greatest all-around athlete ever" whose "presence in the Beaver lineup will be a drawing card."

But the negotiations were with Toledo, not Jim, who did not consider the salary so handsome. He asked for more than five thousand, which prompted Klepper to complain that he had offered a fair amount and that despite Thorpe's impressive performance at Toledo he was no cinch to win a starting outfield slot. The *Journal* did Klepper's bidding with a headline that blared "Indian Outfielder Wants Exorbitant Salary." Management had the power, while Jim had a family to support and no alternatives; two weeks later he relented and signed. The Beavers were training in the warmer climate of Los Angeles, and Jim arrived in time for the opening of camp on March 13. Iva stayed home with the girls; they would join him later after he had settled in Portland. Jim traveled west with an Airedale terrier he had received from the Oorang kennels in LaRue, Ohio, run by Walter Lingo, a hunting pal who had an affinity for dogs and Native Americans.

With the Beavers, characteristically for Jim, he made a dazzling first impression. "Jim Thorpe is a great big good-natured fellow with a smile for everybody. The big fellow made an instant hit with the other players on the squad the minute he appeared in camp," wrote George Bertz, the *Journal's* sports editor. "Thorpe, with the exception of the Indian face characteristics, is real light. He has black hair. He looks much bigger than he really is, although he weighs but 190 pounds. Run, he has all the speed in the world and if he gets the pepper that the rest of the players have, watch out for Jim."

His value to the team was immediately evident. With Thorpe as the new attraction, attendance at Portland's Vaughn Street Park for the first homestand of the season was the largest in years, capped off with a Saturday doubleheader against the Oakland Oaks that filled all fourteen thousand seats in the stadium while hundreds of fans crammed into the aisles at the top of the grandstand. In the second game, Jim clouted a home run into the left-field bleachers, the first at the ballyard that season, provoking a roar from the overflow crowd and earning him a week's worth of free haircuts at the Corbett Building barbershop and a free suit from Hart Schaffner & Marx.

Life in the Northwest seemed to suit Jim. He celebrated his hot start at the plate—a .414 batting average in his first seven games—by heading out on a Wednesday morning expedition to fish for salmon at the invitation of E. C. McFarland, a prominent dentist and state legislator regarded as one of the better anglers on the Willamette River. "Thorpe did not have much to say—he's a man of few words," a witness reported, but he hauled in a sixteen-pounder and "from his actions it readily could be seen that he enjoyed himself and will be a frequent visitor" to the river. Then his luck turned again. He twisted a knee and was out of the lineup more than in it. By the time Iva and the girls reached Portland after an exhausting train ride in mid-May, Jim was playing irregularly, only against left-handers.

And by June 1 it was all over. The manager decided to go with younger outfielders; owner Klepper announced that he had given Thorpe his unconditional release.

Iva had been through this before, when she had left New York with their infant son in 1915 to live with Jim in Harrisburg, only to see the club cut her husband soon after she arrived. The fabric of the marriage had been torn by his drinking, his long absences from the family, the constant moving. Now what? Jim was down, but his name still drew attention, and two new offers came in, from Salt Lake City and Hartford, Connecticut. It was Iva who announced to reporters that he preferred the Hartford offer, which might have included a bonus. "I think Jim will take it," she told the press. He did, and on they went across the continent to another baseball town, where Jim would play for the Hartford Senators of the Eastern League.

JIM AND IVA and their three girls arrived in Hartford on June 13 and settled into the Highland Court Hotel: six dollars a day for two rooms plus breakfast, lunch, and dinner at the five-story red-brick lodge with "the atmosphere of an old English inn and the comfort and convenience of an American home of the best class." The locals hoped Jim would suit up for the game that day, but he still had to shake off "some kinks" from the long trip east. He awoke the next morning ready to play and opened one local newspaper to see an illustrated spread that welcomed him by depicting an Indian in headdress beating a drum and dancing under the headline "Welcome Big Chief to the Local Wigwam!"

The *Hartford Courant* greeted Thorpe's arrival more coolly, mostly because of the paper's running feud with Senators owner James H. Clarkin, a contentious and pompous busybody who'd named the ballfield after himself and was constantly trying to manage the team from the stands, an early version of George Steinbrenner of the Yankees. The *Courant*'s disdain for Clarkin was so intense that it printed letters critiquing his moves almost daily. While suspecting that Clarkin had hired Thorpe only as another promotional scheme, the editors said they would give Jim a fair shake but not immortalize him just to feed the owner's bank account. "It is better to be a Great Has-Been than a Never-was. If Thorpe makes good, the *Courant* will say so. . . . If Thorpe is merely a sideshow the *Courant* will not make a second Babe Ruth out of him."

During his first month with the Senators, Jim played as though he were some version of Ruth and Ty Cobb. In his first game, he rapped out five hits in six at-bats. Days later, during a weekend doubleheader, he thrilled the fans with a "clean steal" of home plate, a dash into the right-field corner to haul in a line drive, and a home run that cleared the scoreboard in left center. On the road, Thorpe drew the largest crowds of the season wherever the Senators went, from Bridgeport, Connecticut, to Albany. At Albany he smacked two home runs, one that "was still in the clouds as it cleared the barrier" and another that rose on a hard line from home plate to the fence. At Pittsfield, Massachusetts, he clouted "a real Babe Ruth wallop . . . the only gleam in a sad day for the Senators who lost both games."

Jim seemed on his way to becoming a Hartford folk hero, popular with fans and local businesses. The most coveted auction item at a West Side Athletic Club carnival was a baseball autographed by Thorpe. The Black and White Taxi Service placed a large advertisement in the *Courant* as an open letter to the athlete. "Dear Jim: We like the way you hit the ball for Hartford, the way you're helping Hartford to get the pennant this year." To show their appreciation, the cab company said it would haul Jim or his wife around town anytime they wished. "It will cost you nothing. . . . Just say Jim Thorpe is calling and we'll do the rest." The Thorpes called many times.

Not to be outdone, Dave Roberts of the Hartford Buick Company brought one of his red Buick Roadsters over to the Highland Court Hotel and handed the keys to Jim to let him drive around town. "The famous man consented to give the car the once-over," wrote a reporter covering the scene. "As everyone knows who has ever seen this big Indian in action, he has a squint and when those fathomless eyes turn on anything they generally go right to the bottom and see all there is to be seen. Jim liked the Buick and said so without reservation. 'Nifty little car' was his terse report as he climbed in, took the wheel with a practiced hand, adjusted his body comfortably to the seat and felt the pedals with feet that have carried him to many a record performance."

Big crowds, Ruthian home runs, good press, joyrides in a roadster, free taxi trips around town—all of that could ease Jim's mind and make him feel comfortable. He and Iva and the girls had moved out of the hotel and settled into a well-appointed apartment at 34 Lancaster Road in West Hartford. Then it fell apart, again. Jim's drinking was becoming more troublesome.

It all started on the road in Waterbury when Jim, suffering from a foot injury, declined to compete in a pregame footrace around the bases against Joe Cosgrove, the fastest man on the opposing Brasscos team. A buoyant Sunday crowd had filed into the stadium eager to witness the race and reacted in anger at the cancelation, booing Jim heartily all game long. He responded smartly on the field, banging out three hits, but the hostile reception depressed him and apparently triggered a night of drinking. Bootleg liquor was no harder to find in Connecticut than in Ohio. The next day, when the Senators took the field at New Haven for the start of a Monday doubleheader, Jim showed up "indisposed," as one sportswriter politely wrote. The New Haven press could see that he was in no condition to play. At the plate, his swings were lame and late; on the field, he looked lost chasing fly balls "like a wooden Indian." The Hartford manager, Jack Coffey, yanked him from the first game. Jim changed into his civilian clothes and was about to leave the park, then returned and was put in the second game, where his play was equally sloppy. Boos cascaded down from the stands. Jim had to be restrained from going after his tormenters. Headlines the next day described the ballpark scene as a near riot.

Thorpe's Hartford demise came quickly thereafter. Between games of a doubleheader with Waterbury, Clarkin appeared in the dugout and accused Thorpe of "lying down." Jim was still hitting well and was outraged by the accusation. "I came to the conclusion that Clarkin wanted to dispense with me," he said later. The team was losing and out of the pennant race. Jim had the highest salary on the team. It seemed to him that Clarkin's "butting-in tactics" were motivated by a desire to cut him and save money.

A few days later, during a doubleheader against Springfield, Massachusetts, Jim provided Clarkin with all the reasons he needed. He had lost heart by then, worn down by the criticism, aware of Clarkin's intent. "And I was foolish enough to stray right into the trap," he said. Or stumble into it. He arrived at the game late, after the Senators had taken their first at-bats, and staggered to his place in center for the bottom of the first. He was the first man up in the second, and according to a *Courant* account, "the crowd and manager Coffey caught notice that the Indian was not himself and the latter proceeded to bear out that impression by his actions." He missed the first pitch by a foot, choked up halfway up the bat handle for the second and missed the pitch, then "fanned on a perfect strike, waist high and right across the middle."

Any player can strike out; it was his fielding that gave away his condition. One ball went through his legs and rolled to the wall; another bounced off his mitt. His indifference was so obvious that Coffey yanked him, sent in a replacement, and ordered Jim to leave the dugout and return to the hotel. He walked off with his bat in one hand and his glove in the other and never played for Hartford again. He had been suspended for the rest of the season, Coffey announced between games.

The next night, a reporter drove to 34 Lancaster Road and rapped on the door. Thorpe answered. His hair was a mess, his bright pink shirt unbuttoned, his eyes "mere slits in his bronzed face." Before Jim could speak, another man identifying himself as "Dr. Hodges" emerged and ushered Jim into a back room before returning and declaring that "Mr. Thorpe has retired for the night." Iva then appeared, and she and the doctor answered the reporter's questions. Hodges did not make clear where he practiced but said he came to Hartford after Jim was pulled from the Springfield game and that he was the Thorpe family physician. In a story describing the scene, the reporter wrote that the doctor "seemed to make himself entirely at home in the pretty little West Hartford apartment with its bookcases and mahogany tables and chairs, rushing around the rooms with his cap pulled down over his forehead and leaning comfortably against the door while Mrs. Thorpe stood talking to the reporter." When the doctor joined the conservation, the reporter said, he "discussed Thorpe's case with unprofessional frankness."

Iva and the doctor said Jim wanted to continue playing, and even pleaded with them to let him attend the Senators game that day to make his case, but "his physical condition had been such that he had not been allowed to do so." He'd stayed in bed most of the day, and earlier in the evening he and Iva had gone for a drive. Jim had been "under a tremendous strain," Dr. Hodges said. He was constantly being built up as an athletic superman, then torn down in the papers. Yes, Jim was thirty-five, acknowledged the doctor, but "his mind is like that of a child and criticism hurts him deeply." He was as temperamental as any great artist, according to the doctor. He was like Fritzi Scheff, the high-strung opera soprano.

Sensitive and temperamental, yes; the mind of a child, no. Here was a variation of the letter that Pop Warner had ghostwritten and had Jim sign back in January 1913 when his Olympic medals were rescinded. The line then was "I was not very wise in the ways of the world." *Lo, the poor Indian,* again. Iva insisted that owner Clarkin would bring Jim back onto the team.

For Iva, it was another desperate attempt to hold things together, but it did not work. Clarkin refused to reconsider, and instead sold Jim to the Worcester Boosters in Massachusetts for a thousand dollars. Another city, another team, another hot start, more promises, all ending in nothing. How strangely fitting that the unsettling season ended in Worcester, the very place where nine years earlier a story unfolded that led to Thorpe's loss of Olympic honors.

The first games Jim played for Worcester came in a doubleheader against Hartford. He won the first with a double and had three hits in the second. "It was Thorpe's way of paying his respects to James H. Clarkin, Hartford's baseball wizard," wrote a scribe for the *Courant,* delighting in the payback against the paper's nemesis. A few days later, Jim told the press that a former Carlisle teammate, now a priest, had sent him a telegram telling him that he was the greatest representative of his race, that his only enemy was liquor, and that he had to stop drinking. Jim said he took the pledge and would abstain from alcohol "for good."

In her effort to keep the marriage together, Iva had bounced around one too many times, heard his promises to reform too often to believe them anymore. Yet she stayed in New England as Jim played out the season in Worcester, then piled the girls into their Pierce-Arrow and rode out to Ohio with him for the next adventure in football. "We had friends who were priests and they talked to Jim," she said later. "Jim used to say, 'How can you put up with me?' and I'd say we had a family and friends and I'd put up with him until he finally fell by the wayside."

21

Oorang Indians

BEFORE THE 1922 SEASON BEGAN, THE AMERICAN PROFESsional Football Association changed its name. From then on it would be called the National Football League. As usual, some teams had dropped out and new teams were added. One new team was the Oorang Indians, based in LaRue, Ohio, a dot on the map known for its world-class dog kennels and proximity to Marion, hometown of Warren G. Harding, a newspaper publisher and Republican pol who had been elected president of the United States after a campaign that took him no farther than the front porch of his dark green house.

The Oorang part of the Oorang Indians name derived from a hunting dog, a terrier breed first imported from England that became known as the Oorang Airedale, with its noble exemplar, King Oorang II, whelped from a long line of champions. As for the Indian part of the name, sports teams the country over called themselves Indians, but few claimed authenticity like the Oorang Indians. Every member of the team, led by Jim Thorpe, the player-coach, was an American Indian. The dogs and Native Americans were brought together in a promotional scheme conceived by the owner of both enterprises, Walter Lingo, who grew up in LaRue absorbing Horatio Alger stories of bootstrap capitalism and accounts of Indians in the Wild West with equal passion.

Lingo's Oorang Airedales business, billed as the world's largest dog kennels, brought outdoorsmen of all sorts to tiny LaRue. Coon hunters, duck hunters, deer hunters, bear hunters, possum hunters. Lawyers, doctors, farmers, laborers, merchants, athletes, industrialists—they all wanted to see Lingo's dogs, which sold for an average price of $150. Gary Cooper, the movie star, visited Lingo's kennels, as did baseball greats Ty Cobb and Tris Speaker, and boxing champ Jack Dempsey, who left a lasting impression when his limo got stuck in the mud and he handed out silver dollars to local boys to push it out. President Harding entered the White House with an Oorang Airedale named Laddie Boy.

It was perhaps inevitable that Thorpe, during his many years playing football and baseball in Ohio, became familiar with Lingo and his Airedales, and that Lingo in turn took an interest in Jim, the world-famous Indian who had an affinity for dogs and loved to hunt. The concept of a football team named for the kennels and featuring Thorpe and other Indians had taken hold one day the previous winter when Jim and Pete Calac came to LaRue to go possum hunting with Lingo, not long after the Cleveland football team they had played for in 1921 folded. A few months later, before Jim left for baseball in Portland, Lingo visited him in Oklahoma, finalized the deal, and headed off to the Upper Midwest to scout for Indians who might fill out a roster featuring the trio of Thorpe, Calac, and Joe Guyon, plus a few old Carlisle teammates.

The price of admission into the NFL was cheaper than Lingo's dogs, a $100 entry fee he paid into league coffers that summer, but it was Thorpe's name that made other owners eager to embrace the Oorang Indians. And it was the resonance of Jim's celebrity and Indianness, more than his diminished football skills, that made Lingo willing to pay him the sizable salary of $500 a week. The owner viewed his star and the rest of the Oorang Indians as an all-in-one package, not just football players but advertisements for his Airedale empire. The plan was that players and dogs would travel together from one NFL town to the next, performing Wild West Indian skits and dog tricks at halftime, while at home in LaRue the players would run the dogs and train them. "Indians are real trackers and hunters and I knew my dogs could learn something from them that they could not acquire from the best white hunters," Lingo once explained.

IN A TWO-TONE Pierce-Arrow sedan with front headlights that bulged like a big-eyed bug, the Thorpe family reached LaRue from New England on the Wednesday evening of September 27, Jim and Iva with Gail, Charlotte, and baby Grace, weary travelers looking for a new home. In five months, they had moved from Portland to Hartford, and now back into the continent's middle. LaRue was about the size of Yale, Oklahoma, with a population well under a thousand souls, sliced by State Route 37 on the north-south axis between Columbus and Toledo. The Thorpes found a place to stay at the Coon Paw Inn. For Iva, still shaken by Jim's troubles in Hartford, this would be her last stand.

Most other Oorang players reached LaRue before Jim. The first to arrive was Nick Lassa, a kinetic 210-pound lineman and irrepressible entertainer from the Flathead Nation in Montana who enjoyed wrestling carnival strongmen and trained bears. More as a sales shtick than an expression of racial pride, Lassa and other players on the Oorang team were identified by English translations of native names in the game programs and publicity blurbs. His was Long Time Sleep. On his first day in LaRue, he found a kennel for the pet coyote he brought with him, jogged the road to Marion, took a dip in the Crystal Lake bathing pool, and found a room for longtime sleeps above Cook's Meat Market.

Then came Big Bear and Lone Wolf and Woodchuck, Strong Eagle and War Eagle and Eagle Feather, Running Deer and White Cloud, Little Twig and Tomahawk. Cherokee, Chippewa, Iroquois, Tuscarora, Mission, Flathead, Mohican, Sac and Fox. The oldest among them was Thomas St. Germaine, known at LaRue as Chief St. Germaine, a forty-three-year-old Chippewa from northern Wisconsin who had attended Carlisle and the University of Wisconsin—where he played baseball and water polo, swam, and wrestled—before earning a law degree at Yale. A few, like Thorpe and Guyon, came with wives and children in tow; most were single and bunked in a converted clubhouse near the kennels on the south bank of the Scioto River.

Delayed by the Eastern League baseball season, Thorpe reached LaRue only a few days before the first game. He ran his charges through practice on a field they shared with the local high school team. William Guthery, one of the high school players, later remembered Thorpe as "a nice guy" who took time out from working with his team to teach the youngsters how to tackle, block, straight-arm, and kick. "He had a policy, that was always tackle. Don't jump on a guy, get him off his feet," Guthery recalled. A sportswriter who watched the Indians' practices described a chaotic scene of "warhoops, hound dog howls, bear growls, coyote yowls." The *Dayton Daily News,* scouting the Oorang Indians for the game against the Dayton Triangles, reported that Thorpe had installed new plays for his squad and was "confident his aggregation will give the Triangles a great battle in the season opener."

Hardly a great battle, more like a thorough thumping. Dayton won 36 to nothing, and the game was more lopsided than the score. Thorpe's men seemed baffled as Dayton's running backs consistently sliced through the line for long gains and scored in every quarter. The result revealed more than a lack of preparation due to Coach Thorpe's late arrival in LaRue. The Oorang Indians were not an imposing team. They had evocative names and a few skilled players, but barely enough talent to compete in the NFL and certainly not enough to win consistently. More than half the players had been Carlisle scrubs or never played above the amateur town level.

Thorpe, Calac, and Guyon, the prized triumvirate of Carlisle backfield stars, still excelled in spurts but were all past their prime. Jim did not even send himself in to play against Dayton or the following week against Columbus and entered games after that only because road crowds demanded it or he felt his team would be humiliated without his presence. For the season, the Indians won three, lost seven, and were shut out four times, including one shellacking in which a mediocre Akron Pros team amassed 62 points.

In the short and peculiar history of the Oorang Indians, however, what happened during the football games was secondary to the spectacle of the all-indigenous squad. Sportswriters never tired of the hackneyed literary possibilities of this posse of Indians and hunting dogs. Stereotypes they had applied to Thorpe could now be used for an entire team. No story was more egregious than a pregame setup in the *Akron Beacon Journal* before the loss to the Pros. "Remember in the days when your mother used to tell Indian stories?" the piece began. "Remember the creepy feeling that used to come over you, when your mother told you how the tribe raced down on the white settlements, abducted fair Priscilla, and just for pastime added another scalp to their list, much to the discomfiture of Priscilla's dad? Hard guys, those. Modern version of the Indian story will be enacted at Elks Park Sunday afternoon. From Marion O a band of redskins are coming—coming in Pullman coaches and dressed not with feathers in their head but fashion's latest gray derby. Out to do a little scalping . . ."

The halftime shows played into this white vision of the Indian world much as traveling Wild West shows did. As historian Philip Deloria put it: "Indian athletes were expected to display white cultural understandings of Indianness to their predominantly white audiences." This involved Thorpe's men donning war bonnets and feathers at intermission, dancing to the beat of big drums, tossing tomahawks and long knives and lariats, reenacting battle scenes, and then putting the Oorang Airedales through various tricks, including retrieving targets and reenacting how they treed bears and delivered first aid to wounded Indian scouts during battles against the Germans in the Great War.

The players understood that they were being asked to pander to the expectations of a white world. It was something they had been dealing with all their lives—*Lo, the poor Indian!* Daily experiences had taught them to accommodate without acquiescing, using expectations for their own purposes. "White people had this misconception about Indians," said Leon Boutwell, an Oorang quarterback and Carlisle alumnus whose nickname was Lo. "They thought we were all wild men, even though most of us had been to college and were generally more civilized than they were. Well, it was a dandy excuse to raise hell and get away with it when the mood struck us. Since we were Indians, we could get away with things that whites couldn't. Don't think we didn't take advantage of it."

Two days after the opening loss to Dayton, Thorpe and his Oorang mates were called into action of a different sort. They became actors in a local drama that proved to be much ado about nothing but for one tense week accentuated their hunting and tracking skills while also propagating

Indian stereotypes. It began when a farmer claimed that a lion was on the loose a few miles west of LaRue in the fields and woods between Kenton and Mount Victory. Such a thrilling rumor, touched with danger, led to the mobilization of search parties accompanied by reporters who sensed a story with nothing but readers. A United Press reporter filed his first account with a dateline that was the envy of his peers: "WITH THE LION HUNTING POSSES, Kenton, Ohio." Airline pilots circled the woods, a police sharpshooter arrived from Toledo, and residents were said to be "in a state of terror and siege." The main attraction for reporters, aside from the elusive lion (or by some accounts two lions), was the posse of Oorang Indians led by Thorpe, Calac, and Long Time Sleep, who headed out from their camp at eight at night to track the woods near the Nave farm along the LaRue–Mount Victory road with a pack of a dozen Oorang Airedales. Thorpe was quoted as saying that his men did not need rifles, that "tackling the lions will give them a good workout." He was joking. They carried rifles.

"Using all the cunning and woodcraft of their skilled ancestors, the redskins conducted their search systematically," reported a *Marion Star* correspondent who followed them. "Two miles out they turned south into the thickly wooded country. At this point the dogs were let loose and immediately picked up a trail that led to a rail fence separating two farms. They followed the trail back to the Mt. Victory Pike and went west about 200 yards again turning off into the woods. In wild Indian style several war whoops were let out by the hunters, who surrounded the woods expecting to trap the animals."

Tension built, at least in the retelling. "Building fires in several places around the woods, the Indians started closing in. The redskins had been taught by forefathers that no wild animals run toward fire. For 30 minutes not a sound could be heard with the exception of footstep on dry leaves and the occasional bark of the dogs. Suddenly a shot rang out from the gun of Running Deer and with another array of war whoops the Indians came in closer, meeting at a stream in the center of the woods they came upon two red foxes."

Two red foxes, that was all. The lion on the loose story turned out to be a ruse concocted by a farmer because too many city folks were driving into the countryside to abscond with prized hickory nuts in his woods, and he wanted to scare them away.

LATE ON HALLOWEEN afternoon, Iva hosted a gaggle of twenty children at the Coon Paw Inn to celebrate Gail's fifth birthday: carved jack-o'-lanterns, cutouts of black cats, miniature pumpkin faces filled with candy for the guests, a birthday cake with five candles. Jim left early to join his team at a performance by a quartet of Indian entertainers who had stopped in LaRue on their way through the Midwest. Princess Madonis, an Ojibwe poet, recited her poetry in full dress. Chief White Eagle, her husband, demonstrated various war dances and scalp dances and talked about his Winnebago tribe. Frances Red Wing sang to the accompaniment of Edith Wildflower. The travelers were surprised to be welcomed by the football players. They recognized Thorpe and agreed to come to the Oorang clubhouse afterward for a Halloween masquerade party organized by Long Time Sleep.

The home field for the Indians was in nearby Marion, but games there were rare, only one league game and one exhibition all year. The team was built for the road, much like the Carlisle Indians team Jim had played on a decade earlier. It was the novelty that made them gate attractions. For Pop Warner and Carlisle, the goal was to bring money to the Indian school by sharing road receipts with big institutions like Harvard and Penn and Syracuse. For Walter Lingo and his Oorang squad, the goal was to spread the word about his prized Airedales. This meant Jim was away from Iva and the girls for weeks at a time, first during a November road trip to Minneapolis, Chicago, and Milwaukee.

The night before the Chicago game against the Bears, the Oorang men partied in a way that reinforced Lo Boutwell's observation that as Indians they could raise hell and get away with it. As the story went, they were drinking at a speakeasy when the bartender made a last call at two in the morning because he wanted to go home, and the players responded by stuffing him in a telephone booth, turning it upside down, and pouring drinks for themselves until dawn. At Cub Field against George Halas's squad the next day, the effects were apparent as the Indians lost 33–6.

Thorpe did not enter the game until late in the third quarter, but even then, in the rain and slop of a muddy Cub field, with the game well out of reach, sportswriters seemed awed by the old man's remaining talent and were eager to advance the legend. The *Chicago Tribune* said the Indians "looked like a real football team when Jim was in." Bert Collyer, who ran a popular sports gambling and stock market tip sheet that had helped reveal the Black Sox scandal three years earlier, was hardly prone to a rosy view of athletes, but he could not resist when it came to Thorpe: "It was an inspiring sight to see him race out on the football field. . . . The performance was worthy of an epic. It was unfortunate that the inclement weather dissuaded many from being present to witness the spectacle of an athlete from almost another generation defying what has come to be accepted as the laws of nature and emerging from the battle a heroic figure."

Scoring a touchdown in a lost game is a low bar for an epic, but this paean to Thorpe revealed something beyond statistics and written accounts. Thorpe in the flesh, in action on the field, thrilled observers in a way only the most charismatic athletes could, not as an agent in the quotidian act of winning and losing games, but as a work of art. Even long after his prime, even after joining his mates in stuffing a bartender into a telephone booth and drinking the night away, even as he was gaining weight and losing speed, there was some magic to him that now and then could flicker into view and leave a cool-eyed skeptic like Bert Collyer in awe.

Something more epic occurred the next week in Milwaukee, though none of the 7,500 fans who came out to see the Oorang Indians play the Milwaukee Badgers could fully appreciate the history they were watching. Its luminescence became apparent only in retrospect. The Indians came in with a record of one win and six losses, while the Badgers had won one, lost one, and tied three, including two successive 0–0 games against Green Bay and Hammond, so neither team was in contention for the league title. The resonance of that day had to do with the confluence of two monumental lives: Jim Thorpe and Paul Robeson.

In the course of his long career in track, football, and baseball, Jim had competed with and against many famous people. He had traveled to Stockholm on an American team with George S. Patton and Duke Kahanamoku and Avery Brundage. He had run over Knute Rockne in a game at Canton and been tackled hard by Dwight D. Eisenhower on the Plain at West Point, with Omar Bradley watching from the bench. He had tried to get a hit off the Big Train, Walter Johnson, at an exhibition in Tulsa and played with and for the Big Six, Christy Mathewson, in New York and Cincinnati.

All impressive in various ways. But imagine being a fan who happened to be there on November 19, 1922, when Jim Thorpe and Paul Robeson played against one another. Native American colossus against African American colossus. Heroes for their mistreated people, struggling against the odds in a white country. One considered the greatest athlete the nation had yet produced. The other a man of manifold talents who, along with being an All-American end at Rutgers, also later played Othello on Broadway, sang "Ol' Man River" in *Show Boat*, organized a committee to fight lynching in the American South, supported the antifascist troops in the Spanish Civil War, and was labeled un-American and stripped of his passport when his fight against American racism made him sympathetic to communism.

Robeson was in Milwaukee that fall to earn money playing professional football while also taking law classes at Marquette University. It was a temporary hiatus from his legal studies at Columbia in New York, where he would get his law degree in the same class with William O. Douglas, the future Supreme Court justice. He was recruited to play with the Badgers by his friend Fritz Pollard, who had left Akron for Milwaukee. Two pioneer black athletes, running back and end, in an overwhelmingly white NFL that within years would bar men of their skin color. In the sporting press of that time, Pollard was often referred to as "the little colored boy," and Robeson as "the Negro giant." And then there was Thorpe, "the big Indian."

The game was not billed as a match between Thorpe and Robeson or Thorpe and Pollard. The Badgers' star was supposed to be Bo McMillin, an All-American quarterback from Centre College in Kentucky. McMillin was a darling of the press, a golden boy much like Notre Dame's triple-threat quarterback of a later era, Paul Hornung, and like Hornung he had a propensity for wagering, leaving college with a substantial gambling debt that he was now paying off in the pros. For the Indians, Thorpe played the entire game, a rarity during his Oorang tenure, and acquitted himself well, breaking a few runs and excelling on defense "backing up the Indian line effectively throughout and making nearly half the tackles behind the scrimmage wall." But it was Robeson who dominated, scoring both touchdowns as Milwaukee won 13–0. On defense, he recovered a Lo Boutwell fumble at the Oorang ten-yard line and rolled in for a score. And on offense he scored on a fifty-yard touchdown pass. It was the finest of the fifteen games he played in the pro ranks. The *Milwaukee Journal* said he "stood out head and shoulders over every lineman in the game."

The Indians traveled the country by train, with their own reserved sleeping car and diner. Billy Ellis, who worked for Lingo at the kennels, served as advance man, moving from town to town ahead of the team to drum up interest. When he reached Baltimore on a Friday night in early December to promote an exhibition match against the Baltimore Pros, he promised that Thorpe would play that Sunday at Venable Stadium despite reports that he was injured. The crowd was disappointing and disappointed. Fewer than five thousand fans came, and those who were there expressed "much adverse criticism" when they saw Jim standing on the sidelines in his street clothes, never to appear in a contest the Indians lost 7–0. In other words, they booed him.

Some reports said the team would make various stops in the South from there and end up in Havana, but that did not happen. Jim did head south with Walter Lingo after the game, but only as far as Washington, where he talked with officials at the Indian bureau about his royalties in Oklahoma. Lingo suggested they also visit the White House to meet an old Marion associate, Dr. Charles Sawyer, who was President Harding's personal physician. As Lingo later told the story, he and Jim and the doctor were chatting about the president's dog, Laddie Boy, when the president approached and invited them out to the porch, where the four men talked "dog talk for half an hour." Here again, Jim was retracing the route of his Sac and Fox ancestor Black Hawk, who had visited Andrew Jackson at the White House ninety years earlier.

BARNSTORMING WAS A regular part of life for professional athletes during that era, although in 1921 the powers that be in major league baseball temporarily tried to put a stop to it, fining and suspending Babe Ruth when he organized a tour in late October after the World Series. Pro baseball by then had the power, money, and popularity to circumscribe the actions of its players in a way the NFL did not. Pro football needed all the public notice it could get and encouraged players to take the game around the country in the offseason.

When the Oorang Indians' plans to barnstorm in the South and Havana fell through, Thorpe joined forces with another team, the Toledo Maroons, for a series of exhibition games in Texas and Oklahoma. He won one game against a collection of recent college All-Stars with a forty-yard drop-kick field goal. One of the college All-Stars was Steve Owen, a lineman from Enid who went on to become a Hall of Fame coach for the New York Giants. Owen later recalled that whenever he saw Thorpe after that game he would accuse him of illegally punting the field goal because it seemed impossible for anyone to drop-kick effectively on a muddy field. "Thorpe has never replied except with a laugh," Owen said. "Maybe he could drop-kick a spiral in the mud. He could do nearly everything else."

In the first of two games in Tulsa, Owen said, he was "overawed by the great man," and on defense whenever he came in contact with Thorpe used his hands "very gently." But in the second game, he concluded that Thorpe "was getting old and didn't care" so he decided he did not need to pay attention to him. "First thing I knew I was on my back on the ground, with the wind knocked out of me," Owen recalled. "Thorpe had hit me, and the ball-carrier had gained about fifteen yards through my position. The Indian had shown me a real professional mousetrap."

When the barnstorming ended after another round of games in Texas, Jim picked up Iva and the girls in Yale, where they had been staying for two months, and returned to Ohio. The family stayed at the home of Carl Hoffmire, a Marion-area businessman who enjoyed coon hunting with Jim and later inducted him into the Mount Gilead Fraternal Order of Eagles as its only Native American member. Jim worked at the kennels that spring and summer, training the dogs and representing the Oorang Airedales at fairs and farm exhibits. He felt at home in this world of dogs, tracking raccoons and deer, an experience that reminded him of childhood hunts with his father near the North Canadian River in Oklahoma. Walter Lingo sought to enhance the legend of his famous employee by writing a series about Thorpe's life that appeared in the *Athletic World* magazine and was syndicated to several Ohio newspapers. The series began, predictably, with the words "You, sir, are the most wonderful athlete in the world"—the quote attributed to King Gustav V when presenting Jim with his decathlon gold medal in Sweden, the foundation story of the Thorpe athletic legend.

Even after his disappointments in Portland and Hartford, Jim could not get baseball out of his system, and signed up to play first base for a semipro baseball team in nearby Bucyrus sponsored by the Ohio Locomotive Crane Company. When Lingo decided to keep the Oorang Indians going for another year, Jim returned to coach, but he rarely played and the team was an embarrassment, losing its first nine games by a combined score of 235 to 12, prompting one scribe to write: "Had Sitting Bull's braves applied themselves in battle with the same tenacity that Thorpe's team applied to its games, General Custer might still be alive today." With the Carlisle pipeline now dry since the school had closed five years earlier, and all the best former Carlisle players now well into their thirties, they could not compete against the influx of top-flight college players flooding the league. Jim tried to recruit new blood, including his younger brother Jack, but Jack had no experience in football and though athletic proved little help.

Many of the players had injuries but kept playing because they were paid by the game, not by seasonal salary. The more pathetic their play, the rowdier they became, raising hell at home and on the road. Game promoters still emphasized their exoticism and the fame of Jim Thorpe, but attendance at road games diminished and Lingo sensed that his concept of using Indians to sell his dogs was losing its shine. By season's end, so had Jim's marriage.

It had been ten years since the bright Tuesday in October when "the laughing, dark-eyed princess of the Cherokee tribe, resembling in her dusky beauty the poet's conception of the storied Minnehaha," as the local press described Iva, walked down the aisle of Carlisle's St. Patrick's Catholic Church and married the best athlete in the world. So many myths shattered. She was not the Indian people thought she was. Being the wife of a famous man was not what she'd hoped. Month by month after the troubles in Hartford, Iva had felt the marriage dissolving. Now, at the end of another football season, when she and Jim talked about the decade they had spent together, they reached the same conclusion.

"Incompatibility, we confessed, stared us in the face," he recalled. "Athletics, to which I had devoted my life, perhaps was in some measure responsible for the gulf that had come between us. It seemed I was doomed for the road and its itinerant engagements." From Iva's perspective, there was more to it than the fact that he was rarely home. His drinking, she said, "went from bad to worse, to bad to worse." Not just on the road, but also at home. One of daughter Gail's early memories was of entering the bedroom one afternoon. The shades were drawn, her father sprawled in bed. "Evidently, he must have been out and my mother came in there and caught me, and she picked me up and she said, 'You can't stay here; your father's very sick' . . . and I'm sure it must have been drinking because I'm sure he wasn't sick."

Iva told Jim she was taking the girls back to Yale, that she would not follow him anymore. She left open the possibility that if he stopped drinking they might reconcile. She would wait in Yale and see, but he would have to come to her and prove it. He never did. "Maybe," she said, "he had found someone else."

That someone was a young woman named Freeda Kirkpatrick, known as Libby, who worked as a secretary at the Oorang Airedale kennels. She was still in her teens, just out of high school and overwhelmed that a famous older man was interested in her. Her father had moved the family from West Virginia to a farm outside LaRue around 1910, but when his farm failed, he became groundskeeper at the Marion golf club. Freeda was a shy, attractive redhead who loved to read. After Iva left, Freeda's flirting friendship with Jim turned into a sexual relationship. They were brought together by the Oorang dogs, but Jim called her his "Krazy Kitten."

22

Letters 1

A BATCH OF LETTERS WRITTEN IN THE SUMMER OF 1924. The first postmarked July 6, the last dated August 16. All penned in neatly looped cursive handwriting by Jim Thorpe to his girlfriend Freeda Kirkpatrick, known familiarly as Libby. She was nineteen; he was thirty-seven.

He was in Massachusetts, playing baseball for the Lawrence Independents, a semipro team in the regional Twilight League in the vicinity of Boston. In his eleven-year descent from the New York Giants to the lower rungs of baseball, this was the bottom. The Twilight League derived its name from the tradition of starting at 5:45 so men could play ball after a day's work in the mills. It was not unusual for games to be called on account of darkness. But it was still money—the Independents paid him $3,500 for the season—and it was still baseball. There were some talented players in the league, and he was among the best. He batted .403 for the season, showing that he could even hit the curveball.

Jim was staying at a lake cabin on the outskirts of Lawrence with his dog Dempsey—named for the heavyweight champ, one of Walter Lingo's regular Airedale customers—and Joe Little Twig, his Carlisle and Oorang Indians teammate. He and Iva were separated but not divorced. She had gone to California briefly after leaving him in Ohio, but was now back in Oklahoma, soon to move from Yale to Tulsa to take a job as a hotel mail clerk. Freeda was in LaRue, Ohio, still working at the Oorang kennels. She had traveled east with Jim when he was on his way to join the Lawrence team and they had spent a few days at the Duck Inn on Martha's Vineyard. Jim called it their first honeymoon and from then on reminded her that they were "engaged."

In the days when he was playing football at Carlisle and competing at the Olympics at Stockholm, he'd written scores of letters to Iva, but those were thrown away or burned after their separation and eventual divorce. Iva even cut his face out of photographs of their trip around the world. The letters to Freeda survived. In conversations with journalists, Jim rarely revealed all that was churning inside. This led him to be characterized as the wooden Indian, stoic and one-dimensional. His letters to Freeda revealed something more: his yearning, turmoil, promise, sexual desire, loneliness, fear, sappiness, hope, pride, vulnerability.

The letters were addressed to: *My dear Libby. My own Libby. My Own Little Girl. My Own Libby & "Krazy Kitten." Dearest Kitty.* He signed off: *Little Boy. Your Lonesome Indian Jim. Your faithful Injun Jim. Your only true blue Injun Jim. Still your lonesome and faithful Injun the true blue type. Still your lonesome Injun, faithful to the end, Jim. Faithful Injun, also lonesome wants my girl, Jim T.*

FIRST LETTER. JIM was sitting on the cabin porch on an off day. He and Little Twig were back from the lake. Libby had returned to Ohio only a few days earlier, and he'd hated to see her go. He said he came close to breaking down after she left. He was glad she got home safely but knew how much she feared her parents' reaction to their daughter running off to visit this still-married older man. Jim had promised Libby he would refrain from drinking and would get a divorce:

Honey, talk about being lonely I miss you so much and can hear you talking at times which only makes things worst for me . . . Honey do be careful and keep your promises every one, don't give up hope . . . I mean to be what I said and intend to carry out everything—I know it will take "time" . . . I have not heard from Oklahoma yet.

The letter continued the next day, after he had received one from Libby. He had just played one of his best games of the year—home run, triple, single in four at-bats. The Independents were in first place:

Oh what a joy . . . and everything going so good working towards my end honey . . . Sure is fine your mother took the side of things . . . now keeping in good condition—shall do that for you . . . be careful and not let the folks read my letters . . . but Libby remember I am lonesome for my little "Krazy Kitten" . . . P.S. Don't forget we're engaged.

The next day at camp:

I think of you day and night—then between times. Well dear the Lawrence ball club won the first half of the league pennant winning 19 games and losing but the 3 games when you were here . . . also I have made 12 home runs and still leading the team with my hitting . . . have plenty of write ups in the Boston papers and shall send you one . . . sorry you had a cut in your salary . . . your little boy is feeling fine and am playing great base ball although we lost yesterday to Dilboy . . . better be a good little girl and my "Krazy Kitten" . . . Dempsey has returned to the hospital seems he was breaking out more with that mange or whatever it was I know he will be all right soon . . . between Dempsey and Joe shall have company all the time . . . God knows dear that I miss you most of all and would be so tickled to see you hug and kiss you then have you rock me to sleep—could you do that? Gee I wish this baseball season was all over and I was on my way to Ohio and sweet memories.

Another letter arrived from Libby on July 8. He wrote back:

My dear Libby, Your letters make me feel so good and try to do better in everything I under take to do—you know what I mean, don't you honey? . . . You say you're never taking a bath since you left here—better look out they will be planting potatoes or making garden around your neck and ears, ha! ha! Yes dear I wish you were here too so we could [go swimming] in altogether just you and me and we had lots of fun . . . So the folks will let you do most any thing be careful and not take advantage of since don't want to lose my "Krazy Kitten" not for the world . . . I have written to Mrs. T and am still looking for the wanted answer not even a word from the lawyers at Pawhuska [Oklahoma]. She is wanting to come east but nothing doing—as I wrote her that I didn't want to live near or with her, so this should stop all proceedings of wanting to come.

The implication is that he had heard from Iva, who by his account wanted to visit him with the girls. In his usual explanations of the dissolution of his first marriage, he made it sound as though the breakup was all her doing and left him despondent. The letters to Libby indicated otherwise. And in all the letters, the names of Gail, Charlotte, and Grace were never mentioned. His single-minded focus was on the wooing of Libby:

I wants my Honey and "Krazy Kitten" that's all. Then the world is mine. Yes Libby I'm always lonesome for you, them Hugs & Kisses could really cry for them, want you so bad dear . . . The dreams of you are of the best type, some I laugh about and others make me fear some thing the unseen as it may be. Had a dream of a small snake, played and had a great time with it. And then took it to the lake, where I lost it in the water, some dream. Don't think this was of you, the dream I mean—ha ha. Oh God honey thinking of those arms around me why I pray for them to return.

An article on the Twilight League appeared in the *Boston Globe* the next day. "Jim Thorpe, the famous Indian who has been playing center field, is always a big drawing card around the circuit," wrote Albert J. Woodlock. "His hitting has been timely and heavy and he is a dangerous man in the pinches." Jim's next letter—addressed to LaRue, Ohio, with a two-cent stamp attached—came a week later. Libby had written him that one of the Oorang Indians players had been jailed in Marion for drunkenness. Jim told her the player better reform or he would be cut from the team. But would there be a third Oorang season in the NFL? No word from Walter Lingo. After being hit by a pitch and sitting out two games with a sore wrist, Jim was back in action. Lawrence had lost the last game to North Cambridge:

But oh what a crowd something like 10 thousand people, lots of fun also . . . the umpire was knocked cold by one of the spectators after the game . . . Yes honey dear I do love you with all heart and soul and will do everything in my power to win you . . . can I sweet mamo?

He expected the season to be over by September 15 so that he could be back in Ohio by the twentieth:

Honey I think of the times we have had and spent together bathing, huntin' and all the moonlight rides. They must come back to us for I was in my glory when with you Libby . . . Honey trust me I am not thinking of anyone but you. How could I do otherwise dear . . . and besides we are engaged, get me "Krazy Kitten" . . . Oklahoma news seems to be scarce and have not had returns from my last missive west . . . wonder what they are framing to do, in our favor I hope . . . Do you remember the two pictures hanging here in camp, one of the

Indian buck calling across the lake to his sweetheart and she is answering—but what—come on over I think.

Jim and Joe Little Twig went swimming in the lake every morning. They were both excellent swimmers and took on the duty of becoming unofficial lifeguards. July 21:

Must have my morning dip dear. What a nice bright morning but still cloudy to me for . . . your Injun wants his little girl . . . Joe saved another girl yesterday, age 10 to 11 years, so we are even at two a piece . . . Wish you were here to enjoy my pleasures with me would really treat you nice and let you have your way. How nice of me don't you think honey? Remember the Duck Inn. Am sending you a post card of it . . . Well I haven't heard from Mr. Lingo yet and am writing for the news . . . Honey I had a wonderful dream of you last night, heard you laugh and call to me. You should of seen me get out of bed. One step and I was on the floor looking around for you even thought you had hidden and looked, turned on the lights, lonesome now . . . Oh yes had another dream of you seems we were living in some home where we had a great big fire place and you were sitting where the red fire flow would show you up and in your lap was a baby, wonder who's Injun.

Jim was seeing his name in the local paper for more than his baseball, he wrote in a letter to Libby the next day:

Going to send clipping telling what life savers Joe and self are—it will tell you all but did mention your little boy saving Kennedy, the fellow who runs the store in town so this makes two for me . . . I have been swimming a lot lately and can do my stuff pretty good. Also have been playing great ball now hitting around .430, trying to stay above the 400 mark, can do it I'll say so . . . Send me lots of love in your letters dear and I will be the boy of "true blueness." Yes, I'm your Injun and will always be, tell the world if you wish . . . Still no news from the west [Iva in Oklahoma] and wondering what is going on. Hope for the best, do you?

That same day Jim received a letter from Libby, apparently telling him about her dreams. They had exchanged thoughts about when they would see one another again. In his next letter, he enclosed the clipping of his lifesaving exploits on the lake:

God knows I want you at any time, now, tomorrow or any time you see fit . . . I know how things would be if you ever returned to "me" and your folks would go wild, maybe do things they would be sorry for . . . Can I be your rescuer and life saver . . . Now dear try not to be so lonesome for it won't be long until I have you in my manly arms o what a thought, but to go crazy thinking of such a thing.

On July 24, a letter arrived from Walter Lingo that expressed reservations about sponsoring the Oorang Indians football team for the 1924 season. Jim told Libby that he had another plan for his future if his days with Lingo came to an end:

Hope to receive better news in a couple of days from him, but if not dear shall try to be in Bucyrus with Mr. Michael at the factory working for at least ninety days before taking up an office somewhere in the East—New York most likely. This would stop all my athletic work and into a business life. No more hunting or outdoor life only on vacation time.

Charles F. Michael was the richest man in Bucyrus, the industrialist who owned the Ohio Locomotive Crane Company, sponsors of the semipro baseball team Jim had played for briefly the previous summer.

Honey between you and I don't care much if Mr. Lingo decides not to continue in football for I really believe a change in life would do me much better. Would mean more to me. I shall write to the factory asking to go to work Oct. 1 so by the first of the year I can take up my new duty as manager and of course want your help as my right hand lady. I really did think Mr. Lingo would not go through with football as money was not to be had or gotten . . . Honey if you leave it up to me the words "all over" shall never be spoken or put down in black and white . . . Honey your dear mother would never have to fear of you not being happy with me, for that would be my only thought for you . . . As to visiting [your] home would think along twice before going for they have said plenty against me, but mostly in anger.

On the last Sunday in July, Jim and his teammates were invited guests at services at the West Boxford Congregational Church. The sermon was delivered by Reverend Harold C. Cutbill, a recent theology school graduate better known as the Flying Parson, the leading middle-distance runner in New England. "The true athlete, like the true man, is the fellow who comes through for God and righteousness when he is 'all in,'" Reverend

Cutbill proclaimed. An athlete, he said, must live a clean life and have regular habits to succeed. Then again, he also once said that Babe Ruth would make a good pastor because he could provide a wallop. No one ever accused Ruth of living a clean life, nor Thorpe or most athletes, for that matter. But Jim was trying. His next letter to Libby followed a road trip to play two games in Portland, Maine:

We all stayed at the Old Orchard Resorts and what a time we all had . . . Talk about fun, lots of it . . . We played the Cornets of Lynn from a league team and two of the boys were carried off the field by the police . . . honey no "lovins" up there . . . tried the saltwater gee but it was cold Joe couldn't take it and came out while our Injun took a long swim supposed about a mile and back but nearly froze after coming out. Chilled through. Well dear honey I haven't heard from the west yet and can't write you anything about it, being in hopes of our second "honeymoon" . . . Oh God Libby can't you be here to go with me, bed I mean . . . promises couldn't be kept tonight honey for I am wild right now thinking of you.

What this meant is unstated. Likely it meant he broke his promise not to drink:

I know Libby you will think one thing but I want you now and for always—come to me if possible dear . . . I want to fulfill all and take you "whif" me wherever I may travel which takes me to many pleasant spots. Xoxoxox Honest Injun.

No more mentions of plans to work for Mr. Michael in Bucyrus or of New York. In his next letter Jim wrote of going on a second honeymoon after the next football season. Maybe he would play in Cleveland if the Oorang team folded. Maybe they would go south for the winter. He was worried she would fall in love with someone else while he was out there playing ball and swimming:

Honey the lake water sure is great—have been staying in the lake for two or three hours every day and can sure put on my stuff real good now. Lots of people coming to the pond these days. Joe and self are always helping someone from the water. Lots of "thank yous." They call us the two "water dogs" and sometimes "Joe and Jim the Indians."

When Jim next wrote on the morning of August 11, it was raining, meaning the game that day against Malden would be called off. He had been sick for a few days—food poisoning, he thought—but now was feeling better and buoyed by the return of his dog from the hospital. And he was proud that he had resisted temptation:

Oh yes Dempsey our boy is back with us again and looks all right. But the disease left him lame in his left leg . . . Your boy spent the day watching the drunks put on their stuff. Must have been a dozen fellows having one great time but I refused every one that tried to give me a drink, told me that I was a big stiff and no good for not drinking with them. I only laughed and had a good time "kidding" them. Don't you think me fine and need encouragement. No honey dear you're the world to me and am doing all this for you. My love is too great that's all.

He worried that she doubted his love. She had said she did not want to live if that were so:

Talk of you eating lots of worms and die, why you little darling of course I care and life would mean nothing to me either . . . yes Libby I would love and love you so much that I'm afraid you would get tired of me and just go off to sleep and me still hanging on to you . . . Dear do you doubt me in my love . . . You write of second honeymoon and say will it ever come true—that's my only thought and pray everything works out so you can be mine for ever and ever never to part. "Buddies." I always knew we were mated—nature has proven that for us.

The final letter was postmarked August 16. Joe Little Twig was soon to leave for Ohio. Jim was still trying to entice Libby to come to Massachusetts. He said he would send her money in the next letter, a promise he often made. If she came out, he wrote, they could have the cabin to themselves and then drive back to Ohio together and maybe stop at Niagara Falls. Instead, he came back to Ohio alone.

His options were closing, as it turned out. The Oorang Indians folded. Cleveland did not seek his services. Mr. Michael and the Ohio Locomotive Crane Company did not hire him. There was no word yet from Oklahoma about a divorce. He was still married, though he had not seen Iva or the girls for a year. He was still in love with Freeda, Libby, his "Krazy Kitten." But he did not stay in Ohio. He rounded up Joe Little Twig and they left for another season in the NFL, this time for the Rock Island Independents.

Jim's arrival in Rock Island, across from Iowa on the Illinois side of the Mississippi River, was hailed by the local football fans. His reputation brought status to the town and the team, which perhaps inevitably was referred to in the press as "Thorpe's Independents." He was thirty-seven now, long past his prime, and his performance along the Mississippi was uneventful athletically. He scored only seven points that season on two field goals and an extra point. But his presence here had a far deeper emotional significance, closing a circle for the Thunder Clan. The team played at Douglas Park, a field built near the very spot where the village of Saukenuk once stood, the ancestral home of the Sac and Fox people before the white man pushed them out. *Wa-tho-Huk*, Path Lit by Lightning, the boy his mother believed to be the reincarnation of Black Hawk, was running on sacred tribal ground. He played there for parts of two seasons.

23

Letters 2

SIXTEEN MONTHS LATER, JIM'S TRAVELING HAD NOT stopped. From football to baseball, with a little basketball in between, he was always on the move. Now came a second batch of letters to Freeda, postmarked from December 21, 1925, to March 1, 1926. He wrote one from Cincinnati on his way south, the others from Tampa, Florida. He called her Freeda now more than Libby, sometimes *My Dear Honey* or *Sweetheart* or *Dear Little Woman*, but no more *"Krazy Kitten."* And no more sign-offs as *Your Lonesome and faithful Injun of the true blue type.* He was as lonely as ever, but the pleading in his letters was not to win her love but to prove they could have a stable life together.

Jim remained the itinerant athlete, still trying to earn a living as a migrant worker chasing the seasons, still on the road more than home with a wife, but now the wife was Freeda, not Iva. Freeda Thorpe. He and Freeda had been married in late October 1925 in New York City. No wedding ceremony, just a civil union. Her parents, as dubious of Jim as Iva's siblings had been, learned of the marriage in a telegram that began "HAVE JOINED OUR HANDS AS ONE" and said more details would be forthcoming.

Brief notices of the marriage appeared at the bottom of wire dispatches combining it with a less joyous event. Jim had just been cut by the New York Football Giants, the NFL's newest team, owned by Tim Mara, a former bookmaker. Having pro football in America's largest city was considered essential to the league's future, and Mara was determined to succeed in his inaugural season. He tried to sign Red Grange, the Galloping Ghost who at the University of Illinois had captured the nation's imagination as the most exciting running back since Carlisle's Jim Thorpe; failing that, the Giants turned instead to old man Thorpe, who lumbered on heavy legs and banged-up knees. After one uneventful season playing for Rock Island near his ancestral homeland, Jim thought New York might reinvigorate him. The tryout did not go well.

One game with the Giants and that was the end of it. With a brace on his left knee, he played in a contest against the Frankfort Yellowjackets, but he was sore, out of shape, and ineffective. "Jim Thorpe Fired from Grid Team" blared the headline in the *New York Post*. There was speculation that this would mark the end of his football career, but Jim could not let go. He returned to Rock Island to finish out the season, his second with the Independents, then organized a group of Rock Island players and old Carlisle teammates for a barnstorming tour in Florida. That was what brought him to Tampa just before Christmas, leaving Freeda home alone in Ohio.

Thorpe had been divorced from Iva since the previous April. Tulsa attorney Elden J. Dick, representing Iva, charged that Jim had abandoned and deserted his wife, but did not make specific charges of adultery. Iva won full custody of the girls and a payment of $125 a month in child support, money she needed but doubted she would ever see. As difficult as her life with Jim had been, her financial situation worsened without him. With no means to care for her girls and work at the same time, she first had them stay with her sister in Yale, then shipped them off to a convent school, and finally got them enrolled at the government Indian schools, Haskell in Kansas and Chilocco in Oklahoma, another generation following the path of the parents. Jim had seen the girls only once since he and Iva parted ways; he had gone to Oklahoma after receiving a telegram informing him that Charlotte was seriously ill, though by the time he arrived she was better.

Jim's southern adventure began with a mishap. He expected to meet his newly assembled barnstorming team in Cincinnati, and waited for them at the Grand Hotel, only to learn that they had already gone ahead. "I certainly have had my share of hard luck this fall," he wrote to Freeda.

Feeling lonesome, he drew a bath and took a nap, but sleep would not come as his mind raced "thinking of everything in the world." He wired Archie Bowlby, business manager of the Rock Island team, urging him to wire more money. The Pullman train car to Florida would run $46.47 and he also needed to eat.

He reached the Hotel Tampa Terrace on the night of December 23 as the town clock struck eight. He shared a room with Pete Calac on the tenth floor. Looking out through windows facing west, he saw "the wonderful sun setting behind clouds." Although he and Freeda would be apart for Christmas, he hoped he could earn enough money to pay for her to join him in the sunshine. An optimistic thought. But his hard-luck autumn lapsed into a harder-luck winter. He had always been an outsider trying to figure out the white materialist world, but until recently his sheer talent had eased the way. Now the greatest athlete in the world seemed to resemble a different American archetype, the bewildered and lost man.

In his letters from the sunshine, Jim deluded himself about his remaining football skills and those of his ragtag team. He was deceived in turn by promoters promising crowds and gate shares that never materialized. He attempted to reassure Freeda about his plans for a life after sports, mentioning various job offers in booming Florida, but each dream quickly dissolved in the warm gulf breeze.

On December 27, 1925, he wrote on Hotel Tampa Terrace stationery provided in his room. It was four days until the first exhibition game on New Year's Day against Red Grange and the Chicago Bears. Grange was hailed as the second coming of Jim Thorpe, only sixteen years younger. It made Jim feel he still had something to prove:

The Chicago Bears arrived in town yesterday and they are all surprised to find the Rock Island club intact here and they all know that they must play real football to win . . . I expect to beat Red Grange and his football outfit . . . I am going to show that Red Grange has nothing on me in the line of football.

Thorpe's Rock Island crew, now called the Tampa Cardinals, were practicing, but to call them intact stretched the meaning of the word, as Jim noted later in the letter:

I had a duck hunt the other night but had no luck for the two fellows I went with got full [drunk] or were that way before going and one of them fell overboard and I did my stuff getting him out.

Jim also had things other than football on his mind, maybe a career in Florida real estate. Anything seemed possible; the place was wide open, all speed and land and bootleg whiskey:

Things are sure booming, people talking thousands instead of dollars and after my football enchantment shall turn to my job and expect to make this our home. Have two or three propositions that I must consider in the next week . . . Honey the old bankroll is gone but I should worry as all my expenses are paid even meals . . . Florida sure is having its day rushing, hustling, grafting like that of the old days in Oklahoma when the oil fields first opened up. Can expect most anything here, one has to be might careful what he does. Autos from all over the country are sailing around—speed is no question. Cops have their hands full. The old wagon is busy, all the night long everything is wide open like Lawrence, Mass was as you well remember.

Next report. Maybe he was trying too hard:

This year sure is a rotten one if I may use that expression . . . honey dear I sure was sick but feel so much better. I had hard luck in practice this afternoon, had been working too much I suppose and my right calf either tore a muscle or just went lame . . . wanted to be right for this game so bad but don't know what the outcome will be may not be able to do my stuff . . . It's three days before the game shall take the greatest care and will stay off some.

Better for him to think of things other than besting Red Grange:

It's tuff to be away like this hope I get a job right away so you can leave the old cold and join me here where everything is so great . . . This real estate co is suppose to give me a job after the first of the year, salesman and a commission on all sale eight percent—everything is sold in thousands so I should make some real dough.

The *South Bend Tribune* reported from Bears camp: "When the boys awoke today on their private car they thought they were back in Chicago for the thermometer showed 28 degrees. Red Grange poked his head out between his berth curtains and cried loudly for his ice tongs. After the practice session the players scattered for motor, golf, and fishing expeditions. Many of the Bears were at ringside last night to see Gene Tunney and Dan O'Dowd in their boxing match. The squad is in fine shape for the game."

Grange spent most of his days at the Temple Golf and Country Club or speeding down country roads in a big Packard. The showdown with Thorpe almost collapsed before it happened. The promoter could not come up with the $15,000 guarantee, and it took a last-minute infusion of money from Dr. H. E. Opre, a Chicago surgeon striking it rich in Florida land speculation, to keep it going.

Jim wrote Freeda on the eve of the game:

Honey how's everything at home, tell the folks that I am in great shape, my leg turned out right as it was only muscle soreness from hard work getting in shape so Red Grange will have the time of his young life with the old boy . . .

The game did not turn out the way Jim hoped. In reporting the Bears' 17–3 victory over Thorpe's team, the *Tampa Tribune* wrote: "It was literally over the prostrate forms of the Tampa Cardinals that Red Grange yesterday afternoon tacked a touchdown on the totem pole he snatched from Jim Thorpe, Little Twig, Calac, and the rest of the Cardinal tribe. When Red had finished a 70-yard run at Plant Field he left a veritable furrow of fallen bodies. . . . Cold analysis cannot tell of the feelings of old Jim Thorpe, who is to football what Christy Mathewson was to baseball, as he realized he is not as young as he used to be."

After the disappointing match against Grange, Jim moved from the Hotel Tampa Terrace to cheaper lodging at the Park View Motel. He kept hustling games and looking for opportunities. The next letter to Freeda was not until January 7:

My dear little Sweetheart . . . I must confess that I have been undecided as to my plans. Have been trying for a few games so that I can make some money . . . there is nothing doing up there or nothing that I can do or see so I will just stay here—and get a job. Some of the gang is still sticking around. They played today at Winter Haven, didn't get much for their work only forty & expenses—wanted me too but that wasn't enough cash so I drove the bunch down in a Lincoln car which a friend let me use while in Tampa . . . this is a great country and a fellow with some get up should make plenty of cash. . . . Honey dear don't worry for things will come out all right . . .

The next day he started making plans for games in St. Petersburg and Fort Myers. He had it figured out, he said. If he charged $2.20 for general admission and he drew a crowd of about 2,500 and his expenses ran a thousand, he could make at least a thousand or more and sitting pretty. Better than real estate, it seemed:

Things are not so good in real estate as everybody wants to buy it all, but they can't keep a good man down . . . Honey dear I intend staying here in the South at least until spring—please dear don't think me selfish it's getting the cash if possible. Think I can send you fifty dollars [for a car payment] in my next letter just rest easy and be careful of yourself. I would send it [now] but have no money to do so unless things break as I expect. I will have to buy a car down here in order to get around also if I intend selling real estate can't do a thing without it. Have to show them customers around. Plenty of money here if handled right and I'm going to do my best to do so. I know I make lots of promises. My intentions are good but something always turns up.

Good intentions, great expectations, desperate means. On January 10, he wrote:

Well dear the game I wrote about playing at St. Petersburg is on and I expect to make a killing, I mean by this to get plenty as my end. Anyone that promotes a game and can't figure enough for his self is crazy—so that's what I'm doing, might as well take advantage of things. I'm not being crooked by any means but just getting the cash . . . The game at Ft. Myers that I wrote about is off for [the promoter] failed to tie it up. If I am to get along suppose it is up to me and will push on taking advantage of things and keep quiet about it . . . I am to make arrangements to take two clubs to Cuba, that is if I can get expenses for both teams, shall try to cover fares over and back . . . I want about five thousand to make the deal which I think I can make in St. Petersburg. I've made a friend here with a Mr. Cahill who promises me a job in Cuba making all arrangements for big sports events as prize fighting, football, baseball . . . How does this sound to you?

But there was another matter Jim knew he had to deal with before he could get Freeda to follow along with his dreams:

Oh say I forgot to tell you about my scrape that I had. I know you read about same in the papers. Where Widerquist and I were put in jail, which was true, but listen dear it was not my fault. Widerquist was so drunk and I was trying to take care of him, he yelled like a wild Indian in my room at the Tampa Terrace, so some people in the next room called the cops [who said] I should go along and only stayed there a short time. Po Lo the Redskin is always the blame.

Thorpe and tackle Chet Widerquist were charged with public intoxication late on the Saturday night after the game against the Bears for "allegedly disturbing other guests" at the hotel. They were released on $20 bond after spending a few hours in jail. In his letter to Freeda, when Jim wrote "Po Lo the Redskin is always the blame," he was using a shorthand version of *Lo, the poor Indian!* As his athletic talents faded, he became increasingly conscious of the ways his Indianness was being viewed in the dominant white society. He explained to Freeda:

I can live with it and everybody here thinks a big joke, so don't feel mean at me, will you dearie. Give me kiss and forgive . . . If I can only get some real money how tickled your boy will be, want to send for you, but must be sure I have a job or a place for you, at least an income . . . so I'll never leave my love so long again.

Lo, the poor Indian! He had said he expected to make a killing in the contest against St. Pete, but hardly anyone showed up for the game. January 14 to Freeda:

Life is such a guess, you can never tell what will happen. Certainly is a blue one at present. The game played today a hard fought battle, the score 0 to 0. The split of the gate was $160 giving each man $13.30 as his share, nearly broke my heart to think how I worked in the advertising end and paid out twice as much money thinking it would be a knock-out. Well such is life . . . We are playing at Sarasota this Saturday and have guarantee of 5 hundred dollars in expenses so this will help some and maybe we will get a break before long . . . I guess I should never look for the best in things, have sure gone wrong in my last few years.

Jim kept trying to arrange exhibition games, kept looking for other employment. On Sunday morning, January 24, he awoke early, unable to sleep, and went for a long walk. His mental state plummeted:

Ed Terry of Mt. Gilead [Ohio, near LaRue] has a son living here and might be that I will work for his Realty Corp. that is if the inducement is good might be that I can get a room with them just for a while until I can find something for ourselves . . . This might be an opening until I can find something much better. What say honey? They are to take me out and see the land lots and whatever they have to sell . . . I can live here so just as easy for I have nothing to do up there . . . I've never been so unsettled in my life as this last year. Honey I need you to help me and keep my nerves right, so uneasy . . . where there's a will there's a way—that is if you wish.

More than two weeks without writing, and by then his situation had worsened. His teammates returned north without him. The promise of a job with Ed Terry's son fell through. Overtaken by the blues, trying to resist the temptation of booze:

Well my trip to St. Pete was not what I expected and things look pretty blue. Have a bad check on a man at Winter Haven Florida, which was returned. This I found on my come back from the outing which I had left with the rest now. God honey I'm here with a week's hotel bill and nothing to pay out with. I am wiring the world over to find money. Don't I have a great time trying to stay out of jail. I am a good boy, too, makes a man feel like going on a big drunk . . . Honey if you ever hear me getting drunk just take out papers for a divorce, which I know would certainly hurt me more than anything that could happen. Never again dear.

Jim said he had to get up to Rock Island and get some more money from Archie Bowlby. The man owed him for four games, he said. He knew he had to change and live up to his promises. So much for those earlier notions of making crazy money in the sunshine:

Don't I write like I had the blues. A man is a fool with easy money and that I've had, now it's look for real happiness, love first of all and the rest will come, don't you think sweetheart? I am sorry that things didn't go through but dear there is lots of time. I thought that athletics, baseball, football was out of my life, but I guess that is what I am made for and the last thing I do here, we'll see.

What next? He'd heard that Rube Marquard, the old pitcher, once his teammate on the Giants, was managing up in Providence, Rhode Island. Maybe Jim could play there or help coach. He kept telling himself that things would turn brighter, sunshine tomorrow. On February 18 he wrote to Freeda that a company wanted him to sell cars. But he had had enough. He wanted to return north:

Just as soon as I get some cash on hand you can look for me back for I don't like the idea of being away from you any longer. I really think that you believe I don't "loves" you now—get that out of your sweet little soul I loves you heaps.

MARCH 1926. HIS two months in Florida ended like this: Jim did not sell real estate in Tampa. He did not become a sports promoter in Cuba. He did not sell cars in St. Pete. He did not play baseball in Providence. Almost penniless, owed money that he would never get, he returned to Marion, but not for long. The athletic migrant worker kept moving. Another season, another game, another state. He had played professional sports for teams in New York, New Jersey, Connecticut, Massachusetts, Pennsylvania, Ohio, Indiana, Illinois, Wisconsin, Oklahoma, Texas, North Carolina, Oregon, and Florida. Next stop: Shelby, Montana, to play for the Drillers. The *Great Falls Tribune* announced his imminent arrival: "Jim Thorpe, one of the greatest, if not the very greatest, Indians of all time since the earliest American settlers gave up tossing spears 'n arrows for heaving javelins, pigskins, and baseballs, will be seen here when the Northern Montana Baseball League opens its season May 2."

24

World Famous Indians

BASEBALL SEASON IN MONTANA WAS SHORT AND WILD. ITS constricted length, from early May to Labor Day, was determined by the rugged northern weather; its character shaped by a collection of outcasts who came in search of another chance, along with money, good times, and bootleg liquor, if not salvation. The state was booming, from the powerful dams and electric power plants of Great Falls to the vast copper mines near Butte to the thriving small towns that traced the Great Northern Railway route across the top of the state, a horizontal stretch known as the Hi-Line bracketed by wheat fields in the east and mountain peaks in the west.

Jim Thorpe's 1926 season in Montana was even shorter. He lasted two months, playing for a team first called the Shelby Drillers and then, when the club relocated soon after he arrived, the Havre Hillers. Considered the crown jewel of the Hi-Line, Havre was named after the French city but pronounced in a purely American way: "have-er." Shelby, farther west along the Hi-Line, was in territory familiar to Jim for its proximity to the Blackfeet reservation, home to Sampson Burd, his close friend and captain of the majestic 1911 Carlisle team that upset Penn and Harvard.

In the decade and a half since they were teammates, Thorpe had been in constant motion, his athletic odyssey taking him around the world and to every corner of America, while Burd returned to Montana and stayed, building a family and a ranch on the edge of Glacier National Park, sacred ground to the Blackfeet. He was talented enough to be elected to the American Indian Athletic Hall of Fame, but life on the ranch was sufficient; he saw no need to play on as a Canton Bulldog, Oorang Indian, or Havre Hiller. Jim often dreamed of settling down to be a rancher in

Oklahoma or a hunting and fishing guide in the South or West, but he never did, propelled by financial need, restlessness, and the burdensome expectations of fame.

Freeda accompanied Jim to Montana. It was not a honeymoon; they had already been apart too long in their brief marriage because of his barnstorming in Florida. A rocky start, but Freeda believed in him the way Iva had thirteen years earlier when she walked down the aisle of St. Patrick's Church. With his most productive athletic days behind him, Thorpe thirsted for that affirmation. Freeda, he later wrote, "brought hope and confidence and an encouragement which made possible my dreams of beginning again." The dreams were always short-lived. His life now consisted of beginnings followed by quick endings.

Flush with Roaring Twenties cash, every town in Montana seemed to be looking for athletes who could give them an edge. Thorpe, who signed for $600 a month plus expenses, was the best known of the ballplayers who found their way to Montana, but not the best. The team in Plentywood, tucked into the northeast corner of the state, brought in John Wesley Donaldson, one of the great pitchers of his era, who stood out because of his entertaining presence as a mound wizard and the fact that he was the rare black man playing for a white team at a time when organized baseball banned blacks. Donaldson was as peripatetic as Thorpe; by the time he reached Montana he had already played for white teams in Minnesota, South Dakota, and Saskatchewan as well as the Tennessee Rats, World's All Nations, Los Angeles White Sox, Brooklyn Royal Giants, Indianapolis ABCs, Detroit Stars, Chicago American Giants, and Kansas City Monarchs. His Montana stop came during the middle of a legendary thirty-year career in which it was said he won more than four hundred games and influenced the style of young Satchel Paige.

To compete against Donaldson and Plentywood, the team in nearby Scobey, a small town with a big reputation as the largest wheat shipping center in the nation, strengthened its club by recruiting two former major leaguers, Swede Risberg and Happy Felsch, who found liberation in Montana after receiving lifetime bans from organized ball for their role in the infamous 1919 Black Sox scandal. Although opposing fans enjoyed heckling them for their plummet "from the big leagues to a cow pasture," the Montana milieu suited their personalities. Much of the state was in wide-open defiance of Prohibition; Al Capone was a frequent visitor to examine his mob's business smuggling bootleg liquor over the line from Canada. Swede and Happy were known for their heroic appetites for the state's three b's—brawling, booze, and broads.

During his career, Jim had been known to brawl occasionally and drink often, but with Freeda by his side he seemed to be on good behavior during this brief spell in Montana. It was trying too hard on the field, rather than lapses off it, that shortened his stay. Characteristically, he started strong, batting over .400 and driving in key runs in several early games against the Great Falls Electrics and Anaconda Mining. And, much as he had done in the years since his breakout 1919 season with the Boston Braves, he sustained his pace as one of the league's leading hitters. Even acknowledging that the competition grew weaker as he descended into lower leagues, it nonetheless seems apparent when examining Thorpe's baseball career that it was played upside down. He likely would have had a better chance at success had he started with several years in the minors, playing every day, instead of spending five unproductive early years mostly riding the bench in the majors, there because of his fame, not his still-undeveloped skills.

Before the end of May, the club left Shelby for Havre. The local paper promoted the move as though Buffalo Bill's Wild West show or the Barnum and Bailey Circus were coming to town: "THEY'RE ON THE WAY—OLD HERB HESTER AND THE FASTEST PLAYING BALL TEAM ON EARTH—STARRING JIM THORPE WORLD FAMOUS ATHLETE—THEY'RE THE CHAMPION REPRESENTATIVES OF ALL NORTHERN MONTANA AND THEY ALL OFFICIALLY SIGN THE HOTEL REGISTER 'HAVRE.'"

The pennant race in June was "as tight as a shoemaker's stitch," but then Havre started losing, through no fault of Thorpe's. On June 11 he "brought a thousand spectators howling to their feet" by hitting the longest home run of the year, deep over the center-field fence. Three days later, in a loss to Anaconda Mining, he strained a leg muscle while legging out an infield hit, leaping "ten feet for the first sack, stumbling as he crossed the bag." He sat out an exhibition series against the Happy Felsch–led Scobey team, then returned to lead the Hillers on a winning streak. By June 20 he was fourth in league batting with a .404 average, tied for fifth in runs, leading the league in doubles, and second in total bases. When his leg tightened, Havre announced that he was taking a "leave of absence" while the team traveled north for a three-game series across the border in Climax, Saskatchewan. An anticlimax: Jim never played for the Hillers again. The manager figured there was no use paying him to sit on the bench. By the Fourth of July he and Freeda had returned to Ohio. They found a house in Marion near her father's not far from the golf club. By August, Freeda was pregnant.

THEY WERE BACK in Ohio, but Jim did not settle down. He was thirty-nine, an age when most athletes have retired. "My best deeds had been done, my greatest victories won," he later reflected. But he could not quit. When his leg improved, he finished the late summer playing baseball with old Oorang teammates, finding games where they could. Then he rejoined his first pro football team, the Canton Bulldogs, a once-dominant squad now in as much decline as he was. Even after the discouraging one-game tryout with the Giants a year earlier and the drubbing his Florida barnstormers had taken from Red Grange and the Bears, the fire was not extinguished. The NFL had grown to twenty-two teams by 1926, and Canton finished in twentieth place, winning only one and tying three of thirteen games. Jim started at his traditional left halfback position, but as the season wore on he switched to the line, where he was still feared for his sure and violent tackles. Not through quite yet.

When the NFL season ended in late November, Jim did not rest. He organized a barnstorming basketball team called the World Famous Indians. The squad's composition changed month by month. It started with a few Oorang teammates including Long Time Sleep. Then, briefly, after an unsuccessful tour of Indiana, Jim took on a few white players from an Indiana industrial league, and for the third iteration he recruited a group of talented players from Haskell, the national Indian school still thriving nearly a decade after Carlisle's demise. Jim suited up but played intermittently, always a fan favorite, never the star, better at passing and defense than scoring.

The inaugural barnstorming tour of Indiana took the World Famous Indians—or WFI, as they were identified on their uniforms above the logo of a brave in headdress—to Indianapolis, Rushville, Muncie, New Castle, Portland, Spiceland, and Richmond through much of December. They lost those games, or as local newspapers could not refrain from declaring, got scalped. The Indians, at least one of them, might be famous, but they could not compete in territory where basketball was the state religion. Fans turned out to see Thorpe and cheered heartily when he entered a game, but that was often not until the second half, by which time the contests were out of reach. "It's rather doubtful whether the Indians could cope with the class of basketball played by any of Indiana's better known high school teams," noted the *Muncie Evening Press.*

At New Castle, it was the World Famous Indians against a company team from the Chrysler auto plant. After losing again, most of the Indian players were so disheartened they quit and went home, leaving only Jess Parton, a Delaware known as Swift Deer, and Thorpe, who played under the name Bright Path, a concise translation of his Sac and Fox name. Scrambling to keep his tour going, Thorpe recruited the coach and several members of the Chrysler team to join him for the next leg in West Virginia. "When is an Indian not an Indian?" asked a columnist in the *Richmond (IN) Item.* "When he is a white man, of course. It seems that the World Famous Indians . . . successfully read five automakers and paleface basketball players out of the white and into the red race by securing them to play with the great Jim Thorpe and his Indians who are trekking eastward where football is football and basketball is not basketball as she is played in Indiana."

The use of faux Indians was temporary. They were soon replaced by young stars from Haskell as the WFI swept victorious through West Virginia. The new players included former hoops captain Raymond West, known as Light Foot, a Cheyenne from Oklahoma and relative of the famed chief White Buffalo who was born with white hair; Dennis Hildebrand, or Eagle Feather, a Cherokee from North Carolina and descendant of Chief Sequoyah, inventor of the Cherokee alphabet; and Leo Wapp, Running Hawk, a Sac and Fox whose grandfather was a scout for Union troops during the Civil War.

Nearing the third trimester of her pregnancy, Freeda stayed home in Marion. Jim saw her for only a few days when he stopped on the way from West Virginia to another leg of the tour in Michigan, and then again for a few more days between Michigan and a final barnstorming tour of Pennsylvania. If he wrote letters to her on the road, as he had from Massachusetts and Florida, Freeda did not keep them.

When the team reached the Penn-Harris hotel in Harrisburg, a reporter found Jim in the lobby and peppered him with questions.

"Do you think that the highly developed social life of the present day is having a deleterious effect upon present day athletics?" the reporter asked.

Sportswriters always seemed preoccupied with variations on the theme that athletes were not what they used to be, the fallacy of the innocent past. It was that way in 1927; it would be that way every generation thereafter. Jim had perhaps the perfect terse response. "I never noticed," he said.

The reporter persisted. Here was Thorpe, about to turn forty, looking to the observer "as though he lived on cup custards in his oversize striped shirt." So came the question: "How do you account for the fact that you can still stand the gaff of professional athletics?"

"Well," said Jim. "I smoke and I might take a drink, but I don't keep late hours."

At the end of that week, Jim and his World Famous Indians took a short train ride south from Harrisburg to Carlisle for a game against the U.S. Army Medical Field School team, quartered in buildings on the campus that once housed the old Indian boarding school.

It had been fifteen years since Thorpe's incandescent final year at Carlisle, the year he became world-famous and had a prolific twelve months unmatched in athletic history. After the 1912 Olympics that summer, when he had returned to Carlisle with Pop Warner and Lewis Tewanima, an exuberant crowd had greeted them at the train station and accompanied them in a parade out to the school on the edge of town, where a day of speeches included the reading of a telegram from President Taft. Now, after a decade and a half as the journeyman pro, the gap between his fame and his daily existence growing wider by the year, Jim was astonished to see a crowd similar in size and enthusiasm awaiting him and his World Famous Indians that afternoon when the 4:15 train from Harrisburg reached the Carlisle station. No parade this time, but a warm reception and a reminder of what once had been, explaining why Jim would say, despite the culture-killing callousness of Indian school education, that his days at Carlisle were the best of his life.

Friday night in the army barracks gymnasium, the same gym where Thorpe and Welch and Mt. Pleasant and Exendine and Hauser and Calac and Guyon and Burd had played games and danced and held celebrations, the World Famous Indians prevailed over Army once again. Jim's "play at guard was brilliant," according to one observer. He scored only three points, but his basket came on the first shot of the game, and once again he heard the roar of an adoring crowd. He might have lost "the punch and drive of youth," noted the *Carlisle Sentinel*, "but he still retains much of the elusive something that made him a star."

The roundball barnstorming continued into early April, ending with a game in East Liverpool, Ohio, on the way back to Marion. One month later, Jim and Freeda's first child was born, a son they named Carl Phillip Thorpe, the middle name the same as Jim's father, Hiram Phillip Thorpe. The boy most often went by Phil.

For the remainder of 1927, closer to home but still on the move, Jim followed the Scioto River south to find athletic work. He played baseball that summer for the Columbus Collegians, sixty miles from his wife and infant son in Marion, and when baseball season concluded he traveled another ninety miles farther south to coach and play football in Portsmouth, a town in the foothills of Appalachia across the Ohio River from Kentucky. Jim had signed a contract to play ten games for the Shoe-Steels, sponsored by the Shelby Shoe Company and Whitaker Glessner Steel Mills, and he recruited enough talent to turn them into winners; but after those ten games, when an eleventh was added to the schedule, he went home to check on his family and dog kennels and never returned.

ONCE AGAIN CAME a tale of the vanishing Indian. This time it was not the decline of all indigenous people, but of the athletes among them. "The Indians are losing their grip in athletics. Is it because they lack the psychological quality that enables anybody to keep his feet on the ground? Or are they equipped with excess mental baggage?" So asked a column in the *Hartford Courant*, reflecting a popular perspective of the time. "The Red Men, up to ten years ago, were penetrating sports very formidably. Some of them were wonderful athletes. However, it is revealed that virtually all of them were unable to withstand the temptations of prosperity. Physically they were on an even plane with the whites. Psychologically, they didn't keep up."

The column was a litany of derogatory Indian stereotypes condemning indigenous athletes to eventual failure. It mentioned Louis Sockalexis from the Penobscot nation, a former major league ballplayer for the Cleveland Spiders who was said to be "no more amenable to discipline than a schoolboy." And Tom Longboat, an Onondaga from the Six Nations Reserve in Canada who once won the Boston Marathon before owning and then losing a tobacco shop in Toronto. And Clay Turner, a light-heavyweight boxer "who collapsed because of the Indian philosophy and faded out of the picture." Jim Thorpe was used as Example A.

The editorial was inspired by Lawrence Perry, a Princeton graduate who wrote about college football and yachting in a prominent column syndicated nationally by the Consolidated Press. Lately, Perry wrote, he had been hearing "a persistent story that Jim Thorpe has gone back to his tribe and resumed the blanket." Perry was using the false rumors as a means of making another point. "The chances are that Jim is still living among the palefaces. . . . But today Jim Thorpe, athletically, had as well be back with his tribe. For today he is merely a brave memory."

Were Jim and these other men alone in struggling when their playing days ended? It would have taken no effort to find thousands of examples of white athletes who could not withstand the temptations of prosperity, who faded along with their athletic skills, or who drank too much and frittered away their money. And little effort to track the lives of Native Americans like Gus Welch and Albert Exendine who later found success as lawyers and coaches. Were there fewer noted Native American athletes in the 1920s than in the first two decades of the century? If so, one obvious reason was the demise of Carlisle, the school that nurtured and produced indigenous athletes as part of its mission and had one of the most effective coaches in the country in Pop Warner, whatever his flaws. The pervasive view of the debilitated Indian athletes failed to consider the corrosive effects of a dominant culture that left them straddling two worlds, constantly fighting against the odds, romanticized and dehumanized at the same time.

Weeks before those stories appeared, Jim had played his final professional football game. It was Thanksgiving Day 1928, the Chicago Bears against the Chicago Cardinals at Wrigley Field. Last game of the season. The NFL had winnowed to ten teams, six of them in the big cities of Chicago, New York, Philadelphia, and Detroit. The Cardinals were finishing one of the bleakest offensive seasons in NFL annals with an offense that scored zero points all year; their lone touchdown had come on an interception return. Feeling he had nothing to lose and looking for a reason for fans to show up for the city rivalry, Cardinals owner Chris O'Brien signed Thorpe on the eve of the game. Jim was forty-one and overweight but jumped at the chance, citing a need "to make one last charge down a football field." It was important to him, he said, because the only time he felt "the great spirit" in his heart was when he was carrying a football toward the goalposts.

Things did not go well. Jim never got near the goalposts. The Bears overwhelmed the Cardinals, 34–0, and the mismatch was worse than the score. Jim did not start, and when he came in as a substitute, he was ineffective and looked "a mere shadow of his former self." Newspapers around the country ran a brief AP dispatch, many with headlines that noted Thorpe's "failure." Early versions of the wire story misidentified him as a "former Haskell Indian star." The *Chicago Tribune* game story did not mention him at all.

Jim and Freeda had two sons by then. The second, William, had been born that August. Freeda left them both behind with her parents to witness the game in Chicago. "I couldn't help but wish she had seen me play back two decades ago," Jim later said. "After the game we returned home. If it had not been for my wonderful and new little family, I probably would have felt pretty blue."

CHARLES CASSIUS PYLE was the smooth-tongued sports impresario who'd persuaded Red Grange to drop out of the University of Illinois and turn pro by signing with the Chicago Bears during the 1925 season and then organized the postseason barnstorming tour that had young phenom Grange face off against old man Thorpe in Tampa. He went by C.C., and those who knew him said the initials stood for Cold Cash. Pyle believed in the glitter of celebrity more than the magic of sports. He usually had a moneymaking scheme in motion, none as audacious as the Grand Continental Footrace he staged in 1928 and 1929. Sportswriters dubbed it the Bunion Derby and one called it "one of the most heroic, if one of the most absurd, athletic contests ever held."

The first year of the Bunion Derby was inspired by the opening of U.S. Route 66 stretching from Los Angeles to Chicago. Pyle's idea was to recruit a global collection of long-distance runners and have them follow the route of the new highway, then continue eastward to New York—3,400 miles of running over three months, 30 to 50 miles at a time, with the winner collecting $25,000 in prize money out of a total pot of $60,000. The enterprise would be supported by businesses and chambers of commerce in cities and towns at stops along the way, who in return for tourism promotion were to provide housing, food, and money.

The 1928 race drew 275 runners, including one outfitted in biblical robes and another who jogged along with two hound dogs at his heels. Pyle hired his client Red Grange to send the runners off from the starting line at Ascot Speedway in Los Angeles. When the derby trudged through Oklahoma, the appearance of the runners stirred such excitement that a thousand-car caravan escorted them into Oklahoma City. While C.C. and the press traveled in comfortable sleeping coaches, the runners were not so lucky. "Pyle was supposed to provide accommodations but often did not," noted Bill Crawford in *Oklahoma Today.* "The runners slept in tents, chicken houses, granaries, stables with dirty blankets." By the time they reached New York, only 55 entrants remained in the competition, and no one in the big city cared.

C.C. lost cold cash on the venture that first year, but decided to try again, this time reversing the continental route, starting in New York and ending in Los Angeles. He enhanced the 1929 event with a road show of celebrities, actors, comics, radio personalities, and chorus girls who would perform vaudeville-style revues along the way in the "Cross Country Follies." The derby had not quite reached the halfway point when Pyle announced that he had hired Jim Thorpe to serve as the master of ceremonies. The mood was bleak at that point, the race on the verge of collapse. The runners had just struggled through a lonely fifty-two-mile stretch in southern Illinois in bitter winds and pelting rain. Pete Gavuzzi, a waiter from Southampton, England, was in the lead, nearly four hours ahead of Johnny Salo, a New Jersey cop. News of the world-famous Indian joining the troupe gave the traveling press corps some good copy.

A few days later, as the derby reached Springfield, Missouri, Thorpe made news of a larger sort. His athletic days were essentially done, and he had started thinking more about all that had happened to him. In conversations with the Bunion Derby publicist, Lon Scott, Jim indicated that the full weight of how he lost his Olympic medals had hit him. Scott was fond of Jim and realized he could promote the race and Thorpe's cause at the same time. He drafted a release for the wire services in which he quoted Jim challenging the authority of amateur officials to take away his medals and trophies. The release served its purpose: the story moved on the AP wire and reached newspapers as far away as Copenhagen, Berlin, and Rome. It was the opening move in a struggle for reparations that would persist for decades.

The response in 1929 came from Daniel J. Ferris, then national secretary of the Amateur Athletic Union, who had been James E. Sullivan's assistant when the medals were stripped from Thorpe in early 1913. The answer was one that Jim and his family would become all too familiar with over the ensuing years: nothing doing. Thorpe had "no chance of recovering his old medals or trophies," Ferris said. "This looks like just a little ballyhoo."

When the derby caravan reached Oklahoma, the state again embraced the show. For many towns, the coming of the runners and celebrities led by Thorpe was the big event of the year. In Holdenville, Jim and some runners dined at Price's Lunch and told the manager, Mrs. H. L. Price, that "from New York to Holdenville they had never been treated any nicer." The first five runners into town were given free meals at the Manhattan Café. Jim and the traveling troupe were greeted with freshly cleaned clothes that the owner of the Holdenville Laundry Company had washed, dried, and folded for them. When Jim introduced the follies at the Grand Theater he looked out on a raucous full house.

The trip west offered Jim a chance to reconnect with old friends and associates he had not seen in years. In Tulsa he spent time with Albert Exendine, fellow Oklahoman and former Carlisle teammate. Exendine had played a central role in Thorpe's rise to fame, serving as his mentor in both football and track; and at a low point in Jim's life, it was Ex who encountered him on a street in Anadarko and helped persuade him to return to school, a decision that propelled Jim to global fame. In the years since, while Jim was playing pro baseball and football, Ex had practiced law and developed into an excellent college football coach. When they met in Tulsa, he had just agreed to be Pappy Waldorf's top assistant at Oklahoma A&M after successful stints as head coach at Georgetown, Washington State, Occidental, and Northeastern State Teachers' College in Tahlequah. Jim had tried to land several college coaching jobs during that period, without success. Both men had itinerant sports careers, yet they were heading in different directions.

When the derby reached Texas, it diverted south to Dallas and Fort Worth and then west to Odessa, and from then on zigzagged on and off

Route 66 as it moved west so Pyle could sell his shows in the more populous areas around El Paso and Phoenix. In Odessa, Jim huddled with Jack Cusack, the former Canton Bulldogs owner who was now in the Texas oil business, based in Fort Worth but with fields in the Permian Basin. Cusack had taken care of Jim's money and roomed with him on the road during their football days together. He understood Jim in full: his fearlessness on the football field and insecurities off it, his generosity and carelessness with money, his inability to avoid alcohol and the ways liquor stunted his relationships and professional ambitions. Now here was the great athlete, his playing days over, desperate if not quite destitute, reduced to bouncing along the highway flacking for Cold Cash Pyle's traveling vaudeville show. Cusack gave Jim $100. "He was broke except for a $1.25 suitcase," Cusack recalled.

The caravan left Mesa, Arizona, on the morning of June 6 with nineteen runners still in the race after three thousand miles. Johnny Salo, now known as the Flying Cop, was in the lead, but was slowed by stomach troubles. The car carrying Thorpe and four officials broke down on the road, so a local dealer furnished a Studebaker to take them through Phoenix to the next rest station in Buckeye. Things deteriorated from there. It became apparent that Pyle was grifting the runners and entertainers, promising money he did not have.

At the end of the road, stranded in Los Angeles without financial reward, the runners and Thorpe organized a final marathon at the American Legion Speedway. They called it the Bunion Derby "consolation race." As if running across the continent was not torture enough, a group led by Bunion Derby winner Johnny Salo formed two-man teams to run continuously day and night for six days. Thorpe was named the event's supervisor. It was a running version of the dance marathons that had started a decade earlier and would become a means of survival for desperate citizens during the Great Depression. When Jim oversaw the six-day marathon, Black Friday, the day the stock market crashed and the economy fell with it, was only three months away.

The consolation marathon was not worth the effort. It brought in little money, and Thorpe and others who had been duped by Pyle's transcontinental scam were left to file claims with the California Labor Commission. Being pursued by creditors was nothing new for Pyle, who "has had as many suits as a tailor," in the words of the *Washington Evening Star.* Jim filed claims for $259.83 and then $1,000—two among many. When Pyle, after hiding out in Santa Rosa, finally emerged under threat of arrest at the Labor Commission offices, he was "greeted by a milling crowd of claimants," Jim among them, before he disappeared behind a door with M. E. Richardson, the deputy labor commissioner. When they came out it was clear no claims would be met. Cold Cash had none. "It is no use," explained Richardson. "Pyle said he didn't have a thin dime." This was not the first time Thorpe had been taken, nor would it be the last.

JIM EMERGED FROM the Bunion Derby bamboozled and broke, but not dispirited. Once in the promised land of California, like thousands of migrants before him, he saw it as a place where he could reinvent himself and raise his family. In August he found a house in the countryside between Hawthorne and Inglewood on the southwest rim of Los Angeles and arranged for Freeda and the boys to join him. "We took a little house at the end of a blind street that faces a rolling, open prairie," he wrote. "Perhaps it is in my blood, but I like to live, and I want my boys to live, where they can gaze across the sloping plain and see the sun go down."

He had all he needed for a new life except a job, meaning that once again he had to try to survive by being the world-famous Indian, an increasingly dehumanizing task. One Saturday morning in early September he made money by giving a punting and drop-kicking exhibition at the Rancho Country Club before a golf match between Cyril Tolley and three other world-class amateur golfers. In early October he drove up the coast to Pebble Beach to serve as a bodyguard for the president of the California Golf Writers' Association at the national amateur championship. A reporter noticed that when Jim walked through the crowded dining room of the tournament hotel, "not a head turned to look at him. He stopped at a table where newspapermen were seated and shook hands with a few who remembered his football exploits and his marvelous record in the

Olympic games at Stockholm in 1912. Seventeen years makes a whale of a difference."

When writers remembered him, it was mostly out of sadness, with only a lingering touch of awe. Speed Evans wrote in the San Pedro newspaper about seeing him at a welterweight bout between Bobby LaSalle and Tommy Elks at the Wilmington Bowl in early November. "Preceding the main event, Jim Thorpe, the greatest athlete the world has known, was introduced. The great Indian did not get the hand he deserved, and it was apparent that the customers, sad to relate, didn't know the man. Jim is getting old. Many wrinkles have formed on his noble brow and his waistline has become flabby. The world hasn't been as kind to Jim as it should have been. In his old age the great warrior is deserving of better treatment than the fates have meted out. He was a man!"

Drawn to the struggles of this once great figure, syndicated columnists started knocking on the door of his countryside home. After recounting the story of how he was shorted by C. C. Pyle, Frank Getty, sports editor of United Press, wrote that Jim was "ready to trade the remnants of his athletic fame for steady work whereby he can support his wife and family." But what could that be? Maybe managing a winter league baseball team in California, Getty thought. Or: "If anyone wants an athletic director, the Indian is the man!" Even in decline, something about Jim seemed to inspire exclamation points, if not job offers.

None of his temporary gigs kept Jim afloat as he sought permanent employment. Bereft of money, he reached out to old acquaintances for loans, just as he had done with Jack Cusack on the road in Odessa. One of his most successful friends was Sylvester Long, the Carlisle classmate who had accompanied him on training runs through the Cumberland County countryside in the spring before the Stockholm Olympics. Over the years, the fabulist life story Sylvester Long had concocted for himself had reached new levels. To get into Carlisle, he had portrayed himself as a member of the Cherokee nation of North Carolina. After serving with a Canadian unit in the Great War, he told people falsely that he had been awarded the Croix de Guerre and suffered many war wounds and was a “Cherokee from Oklahoma.” Now he was identifying as a member of the Blackfeet confederacy from Montana.

Here was a man of as many talents as deceptions. While Jim was struggling to stay in pro sports, his former classmate thrived as a journalist, author, speaker, actor, and entrepreneur. He had become a popular orator on the national lecture circuit, expert on all things Indian. His autobiography was a bestseller in America and had been translated into Dutch and German. And just as Jim was reaching California in 1929, Long Lance took a starring role in his first Hollywood movie. Producer Douglas Burden, praising him as a “full-blooded Blackfeet,” cast him as the lead in a Paramount Pictures film titled *The Silent Enemy*, in which he portrayed an Ojibwe brave in eighteenth-century Quebec. The silent enemy was hunger. Long Lance's character, Baluk, was about to be burned to death on a sacrificial pyre to appease the spirits, when a caribou herd came into view and he was saved. The performance earned rave reviews. *Screenland* magazine, after asserting that Long Lance “was born out in the cottonwoods of Montana, in the neighborhood of the sweetgrass,” said he had “New York right in his pocket.” *Variety* said he presented “an ideal portrait of the Indian because he is purebred.”

Chief Buffalo Child Long Lance was living the high life, popular in New York intellectual circles, residing at the new quarters of the elite Explorers Club on Cathedral Parkway. He was, in many ways, the world-famous Indian. He heard about Jim's financial struggles and sent him money. In the week between Christmas 1929 and New Year's, Jim was with his family in Las Vegas, staying at the Overland Hotel. On December 30, he addressed a letter to *Chief B. C. Long Lance, Explorers Club, New York City, N.Y.* “Dear Chief Long Lance, the jack received and sure was a help,” he began, *jack* being vernacular for money. “This sure is one tuff country to make ends meet. The family is with me and things have turned around ok.”

When Jim had gone to Las Vegas looking for work after hearing that the federal government might build a dam nearby, he wrote, “but things are not ready in the plans for the Boulder Dam, have not been passed on from Washington. Everybody here expects the good news most any time and then an athletic club would be in the makings." The letter's tone of naïve optimism mirrored the way he wrote to Freeda during his months in Florida. One possible job after another, just out of reach. He said he had "been running the country over trying to locate a coaching position" and now thought he might land one at Loyola University in Los Angeles. "Should hear from it real soon but can't as you know touch firewater. . . ." Maybe, he proposed, Long Lance could come west and they could write stories together. In any case, he was thankful "from the very bottom of my heart" that Long Lance had helped him out. "Mrs. Thorpe joins me in sending very best of love. . . . Your old Injun friend, Jim Thorpe."

Four days later, Jim was back in southern California. He had received a letter from Long Lance that apparently mentioned the moviemaking business and suggested Jim could get a film job playing an Indian. On January 3, Jim wrote to say he had received the letter and signed a check. Las Vegas was still on his mind. He thought of it much as he thought of Florida earlier. "I returned from Las Vegas last night but expect to return by Monday or later. There sure is a great chance for some one to make plenty of jack, the town is wide open. . . . If you can arrange that movie picture, let me know at once, for I will be tied up soon."

If Jim knew the truth about Sylvester Long, he never mentioned it. But as it turned out, Long Lance's starring role in *The Silent Enemy* marked the start of his unraveling. During the shoot, several Native Americans on the set, including Chief Yellow Robe, a Sioux descendant of Sitting Bull, became suspicious of his lineage. A member of the Blackfeet nation challenged his knowledge of tribal history and customs. Slowly but inevitably the real story started to emerge. Sylvester Long had been born not in the sweetgrass of Montana but in Winston-Salem. He was neither a member of the Blackfeet nation nor a Cherokee from North Carolina or Oklahoma. His parents were African Americans, descendants of slaves, treated as second-class citizens in the Jim Crow South. There might have been an ancestor on his mother's side of Croatan Indian descent, which was common in an area where oppressed blacks and Indians often mixed, but that was it. Sylvester Long had reinvented himself as Long Lance and Chief Long Lance and Chief Buffalo Child Long Lance as a means of surviving as a black man in a hostile world. It was how he got into Carlisle, how he made his name and fame, how he was hired in Hollywood and welcomed into the haughty Explorers Club. His skin was too dark for him to try to pass as white, but he could fool people into thinking he looked like an Indian and was talented enough to pull it off for two decades.

The fates of the two men reversed quickly. Two years after Long Lance helped his old friend Jim by loaning him money, he fled the New York social scene and tried to reinvent himself again in California, working as a bodyguard and personal secretary for Anita Baldwin, heiress to one of the state's wealthiest real estate families. He was depressed and drinking too much, haunted by his exposure as an imposter. One Sunday morning, he retreated to Baldwin's library and shot a bullet through his head.

IN THE YEARS since he and Iva divorced, Jim had not seen his three daughters. He had only memories; they could not remember what he looked like. Iva had not seen much of the girls herself, though her absence was more of necessity than neglect. She was trying to survive as a mail clerk at a Tulsa hotel, lacking the means to support her family, and felt Charlotte, Gail, and Grace would be better off in Indian boarding schools. "I could understand why," Charlotte said later. "There was no room for a bunch of kids."

Grace was at Haskell Institute in Lawrence, Kansas. Charlotte started there before transferring to Chilocco in Oklahoma to join Gail. The girls grew up thirsting for a secure family, searching for home. When Grace wrote letters to her mother from Haskell, addressing them to *Mrs. Iva Thorpe, 720 South Denver, Tulsa, Oklahoma, Apartment B4,* she invariably included a plea for her mother to please visit at Christmas, at Easter, on summer break. Often Iva could not come. Then, in the fall of 1930, Grace heard that Jim Thorpe was coming to visit as part of the school's homecoming weekend. It was announced that he would perform at halftime of the game against the University of Kansas under the lights on Friday night, October 10. She knew little about her father, except that he was famous. Her mother had kept his medals after the divorce—except, of course, the

Olympic ones taken from him—and one of Grace's earliest memories was of people in Yale asking her to show them one. "He had two or three trunks filled with nothing but medals and I didn't know any better," she recalled. A few weeks before his planned visit to Haskell came another reminder that she was the daughter of a famous man: newspapers around the country ran an Acme Photo of her with the caption: "Among the little girls enrolled at Haskell Institute is Grace Thorpe, eight-year-old daughter of Jim Thorpe, America's greatest Indian athlete of all time."

The American economy was collapsing and jobs were scarce, but after Jim's search for work in Las Vegas came up dry he'd managed to find employment as a painter's assistant at the Standard Oil Refinery in El Segundo six miles from his Hawthorne home. But when Haskell invited him to participate in its homecoming, he put aside his "bucket of paint," as he described it, to make the trip to the school he had left thirty years earlier. He arrived in Lawrence as two thousand Indians from around the country were setting up a makeshift village in a field on the edge of campus. They were there for the Haskell powwow, an intertribal bonding that drew alumni and friends from the Osage, Otoe, Cheyenne, Kickapoo, Delaware, Sac and Fox, Potawatomi, Sioux, Caddo, Iowa, Comanche, Arapaho, Blackfeet, and Kiowa to the school grounds for days of storytelling, dancing, cooking, and eating—some of them might even attend the homecoming football game.

In the autumn afternoon, the field transformed into a landscape from an earlier century, tents and tepees in a great circle, campfires flickering, smoke rising with the scent of buffalo meat, the hum of a hundred conversations, war bonnets, jangling bells, drums beating late into the night. This was not a reenactment, but a cultural celebration, a remembrance of what was lost and what survived. And it was more than nostalgia. The white population, noted historian Kim Cary Warren, "tended to point to the powwow . . . to accentuate contrasts between older Native Americans and Haskell Institute students." But this was a misreading of a sensibility that had gained momentum among young leaders in Indian Country that "did not require a divorce from the past," Warren said. "They did not feel forced to choose between Native American culture and white culture as mutually exclusive entities. Rather, they developed strategies enabling them to shift between worlds and to navigate terrains of language and customs in both white and Native American societies as if they were ambassadors in each."

Some of the visiting Indians arrived in wagons and on horseback, but most came by automobile, a few with trailers attached that carried comfortable living room sets. Bacon Rind, an old Osage chief, hired young Haskell students to set up his three-tent campsite, one for cooking, one for entertaining, and one for sleeping, complete with an ornate brass bedstead. Bacon Rind was no poor Indian. He was among the Osages who had acquired wealth when oil was discovered on their land. Once, in testimony at a congressional hearing, the chief noted the irony that whites had forced his people to move to a godforsaken region of Oklahoma "thinking we will drive these Indians down to where there is a big pile of rocks and put them there in that corner." But when that supposedly useless land turned out to be worth millions, Bacon Rind said, "everybody wants to get in here and get some of the money."

The oldest and most revered chief among those attending the Haskell powwow was Chief Magpie of the Cheyenne, whose life traced the arc of trauma and survival for indigenous peoples in the American West. As a teenager in 1868, he had survived what became known as the Washita Massacre, when the U.S. Seventh Cavalry led by Lieutenant Colonel George Armstrong Custer conducted a devastatingly bloody early morning raid of Chief Black Kettle's encampment along the Washita River in Oklahoma. Eight years later, after his people had joined the Northern Cheyenne in the Powder River country of Montana, Magpie was among the warriors who surrounded and killed Custer and his troops at the Battle of the Little Bighorn. He later became a scout for the U.S. Army, then moved back to Oklahoma, joined a motorcycle club, and converted to Christianity, once saying that he forgave Custer for the Washita Massacre. "I pray that God will forgive Custer," he added.

By the time of the Haskell powwow, Chief Magpie was nearing eighty and one of only two Cheyenne warriors still alive who had fought at the Little Bighorn. He did not speak English but was accompanied by a son-in-law who served as interpreter. He brought with him a letter that said he was interested in the education of his people and urged all young Indian men and women to go to school. When a reporter asked him if he had come to watch Haskell play Kansas on Friday night, he replied that he was eager to see his first football game, then asked, "How much does it cost?"

Haskell had held its own against Kansas and other big universities in recent years. Its head coach was none other than Lone Star Dietz, Jim's old teammate at Carlisle, who had landed in Lawrence in the middle of a career that took him from Washington State to Purdue to Louisiana Tech to Wyoming to Haskell and eventually on to the NFL as head coach of the Boston Redskins just before they moved to Washington. It was Dietz, the artist, who designed the Redskins logo and might have inspired the nickname itself as the team changed from the Braves to the Redskins shortly after he was hired in 1933.

This—even though Lone Star Dietz in truth was no more of an Indian than Sylvester Long. He claimed before reaching Carlisle and during his years coaching that he was an Oglala Sioux reared by white parents in northern Wisconsin, the product of a secret tryst between his father and a Sioux woman. He said his father took him home to Wisconsin after his wife lost a child in stillbirth. But Lone Star could not speak the language, his supposed Sioux half-sister said she had never heard of him, and historian Linda Waggoner later documented that the story was fabricated. Life is full of curiosities: here was a white man passing through life as a Native American.

Jim's main concern was passing as a father. He performed at halftime of the game (Haskell lost 33–7), punting, drop-kicking, and passing the ball in an exhibition with Haskell's former star John Levi. Before stepping out on the field, he asked to see Grace. "A lump bigger than a football came into my throat when I had to tell her who I was," he recalled. Grace remembered watching her father and Levi compete, standing at opposite ends of the field and trying to boot the ball from one goal line to the other. In his prime, Jim could punt the ball a hundred yards, but on this day he could not boot it past eighty. He felt disappointed, but the crowd did not care, and Grace certainly did not.

"I can still hear the noise from the crowd, they went crazy—I wasn't impressed," she said later. "I remember asking if my daddy was finished because he had promised to take me to town for ice cream and candy and I wanted him to come right now. I was growing impatient waiting for him, not realizing then that he had to change his clothes and that people in the crowd all wanted to say hello and shake his hand. I got so frustrated that I started to cry and I was cold and someone caught his attention. . . ."

Jim saw the disappointment on his daughter's face and went to comfort her. He felt gentle and warm, she thought. He wrapped his jacket around her and lifted her up to his shoulders so that she would not be trampled by the crowd and could look around and see how these people, his people, just wanted to be near the world-famous Indian.

25

Pick and Shovel

WHEN THE AMERICAN FOOTBALL COACHES ASSOCIATION convened at the Hotel Astor on West Forty-Fifth Street in Manhattan during the week after Christmas 1930, its members spent their mornings networking in the lobby, their afternoons debating new rules and familiar criticisms of their sport, and their evenings in the banquet hall telling tall tales.

This was their first meeting after a blistering report from the Carnegie Foundation charged that collegiate athletics were overcommercialized and urged school presidents to reform their programs, deemphasizing big-time sports. As might be expected, that did not go over well with the coaches, who took no direct action in response but spent a lot of time "blowing steam." The most-discussed rules change was to eliminate the point after touchdown, an idea voted down later by the newly formed National Collegiate Athletic Association. The coaches found the most freedom doing what they did best off the field, celebrating their hail-fellow brotherhood at a banquet where they told the football equivalent of war stories. There was even a prize for the best yarn, an iron hat called the Brown Derby. Jim Thorpe was not there, but his former classmate and former best man Gus Welch was, and he left New York with the Brown Derby by telling a story of their Carlisle days together.

There was stiff competition. Sleepy Jim Crowley, the Michigan State coach who had been immortalized by Grantland Rice as one of the Four Horsemen of Notre Dame, told a story about his glory days. It had something to do with coach Knute Rockne inspiring his team with a stirring pep talk before the 1924 Army game where Rice first used the horsemen metaphor. Sleepy Jim was a fine storyteller, but his performance was sandwiched between entertainment acts and the coaches were yakking away and "the crowd wasn't quiet enough to let him finish." Rockne could not be there in person because he was at the Mayo Clinic getting an old leg injury examined, but he sent a telegram that was read to his colleagues: "Happy New Year to all coaches. Suggest for air-minded mentors removal of all goal posts and substitution instead of baskets and backboards. . . . Regards, Rock."

After a few more entrants, along came Gus Welch, then assistant football coach and head lacrosse coach at the University of Virginia. He set the scene. A game against Cornell. Thorpe had just scored a touchdown to put the Indians ahead, but Cornell was moving the ball and seemed about to score. Gus and Jim were frustrated because their beefiest lineman, a 220-pound guard, was "laying down on the job."

Welch waved an unlit cigar as he spun the tale to his coaching brethren at the banquet tables below. "I was thinking hard and I had an idea. I was playing safety, but I called Jim back and went up to the line. Then I went over to the referee and told him, 'If you see me slug somebody it won't be a Cornell man. It will be one of these Indians.' The play came through [our] big guard. I ran up and there was a big pileup with this guard on the bottom and his face showing on one side. I reached down and with my flat hand—like this [*thwap*]—I slapped him. The pile heaved and up he came, a nice rosy mark on his cheek. He rushed over and said to the referee, 'Did you see that? Cornell slugged me!' The referee laughed and said, 'That's all right, I'll get him next time.' Well on the next play this big bird went through and nailed them for a two-yard loss. On the next play he nailed them three yards behind the line."

There are different ways to motivate players, Welch said, and he and Thorpe had figured out how to get their big galoot to play angry. Once, he said, Jim even bit the guard in the side to make him play harder. Finally, after the last game of the 1912 season against Brown, Gus and Jim told their teammate what they had done. "He looked at me for a minute and then said: 'Why, I've said a lot of mean things to those referees. I must write them all a letter and apologize.' "

Roars from the crowd. Some of what Welch said might even have been close to the truth, though Carlisle did not play Cornell during the years Thorpe was there. Not that it mattered. "Here's the Brown Derby," said the presiding officer, Frank Cavanaugh, the coach at Fordham, handing him the hat.

Jim had spent much of his post-playing career yearning to be among these men, to join Gus and Ex and Lone Star and so many other Carlisle Indians who became Pop Warner coaching disciples. Even when he was the star left halfback at Carlisle, he wrote that he saw college coaching as his future. He had applied for many college coaching jobs, including at Mississippi State and Dickinson College back in Carlisle, and talked about applying at many others, but the only one he ever got was as an assistant at Indiana in 1915. He thought college coaching would be a way for him to settle down to a stable existence. But the college coaching life was never as free and easy as it appeared when the boys were telling tales in the banquet room of the Hotel Astor. Consider the case of the presiding officer that night, Frank Cavanaugh, known as the Iron Major. During his career, he coached at Cincinnati, Holy Cross, Dartmouth, Boston College, and Fordham. All of that, and then he died blind and forgotten at age fifty-seven in Marshfield, Massachusetts.

The Iron Major's advice before he died: "Get out of coaching while you can. The end of every coaching career is a disaster."

WHEN JIM LEFT Kansas after the Haskell powwow and the visit with Grace, he dropped down to Oklahoma to see Gail and Charlotte at the Chilocco school before returning west. They felt much as Grace had, experiencing both their father's warmth and his distance. He called Charlotte "daughter," in a way that made her unsure he knew her name. The press found him in Ponca City during that visit and quoted him saying that his kicking exhibition on the Haskell field convinced him he was finally done with football. "I was rotten," he said. "I'm through. Getting old and stiff, you know. I can't punt over eighty-five yards now."

His athletic career seemed distant, set in bronze. He was the toy statue in a Carlisle uniform for sale in the Favorite Heroes display at McAlpin's department store in Cincinnati. He was the left halfback in the all-time old-school backfield named by Knute Rockne in a radio interview with sports editors for the Hearst newspapers in Los Angeles and Chicago. He was the twin portraits in a *Then and Now* photography layout that ran in newspapers from Hagerstown to Eau Claire with the caption: "Jim Thorpe, left, as the great Indian athlete looked when he was with the New York Giants in 1913. Jim Thorpe, top, today, grown too heavy and old for much sport activity."

The job as a painter's assistant at the oil refinery in El Segundo was gone when Jim got home. Scrapping around for another way to feed his family, he talked to an old acquaintance, George Capron, a wealthy real estate broker in Long Beach. Jim had first met Capron when Carlisle played Minnesota in football in 1907; Jim was a young substitute on that Indians team while Capron was an elite quarterback and drop-kicker, good enough to be named a third-team All-American by Walter Camp. Now, nearly a quarter century later, they talked about organizing a professional football league on the West Coast. Thorpe said he thought California was "ripe for pro ball," and Capron agreed. They were approaching owners of baseball's Pacific Coast League to see if they might support a football version in their cities, led by a team based at Wrigley Field in Los Angeles.

Thorpe had fame but no money; Capron had money but less fame. In that sense the situation seemed similar to when the owners of the American Professional Football Association in 1920 chose Jim to be their first president of the precursor to the NFL. This time, though, the scheme went nowhere, like so many of Jim's dreams in recent years. It was a smart concept ahead of its time. The first West Coast pro football team was established in Los Angeles, and even took the name of Thorpe's first pro team, the Bulldogs, but not until 1936, and without his participation.

Jim's next job was trying to sell oil leases near the beach areas around Venice. "This venture wasn't very profitable," he reflected later. An understatement, but some in the press inflated it into Jim's being an oil baron. Which made his next job only that much more poignant. In early 1931, an acquaintance in the Los Angeles County Forestry Department told him he should take any entry-level job for the county and work toward a promotion to a better slot in the recreation or forestry department. With that in mind, he signed up as a laborer working on the construction of the new county hospital.

"I took a shovel and went to work . . . loading dirt into trucks," he recalled. "I was paid $4 a day. It helped. I was listed on the payroll as J. Thorpe, a nonentity among a motley crew of men tearing a bare living from the soil. I had worked there only a few weeks when [the newspapers] found me. They posed me with a pick and shovel and the papers carried the picture—a far cry from the day I stood beside King Gustav of Sweden with my arms loaded with trophies."

Photographers swarmed the construction site, snapping away, and their pictures ran in scores of newspapers: Jim leaning against a shovel, wiping his brow. Jim holding the shovel in his gloved hands, the long sleeves of his shirt rolled up his muscled forearms. The inevitable caption: "Jim Thorpe, acclaimed as the greatest football player of all time, found recently with pick and shovel as day laborer in Los Angeles."

Soon the news service feature writers were again finding their way to his home. The first to arrive was Jean Bosquiet of the AP. Jim invited him in and tried to put a positive spin on his situation. He was not looking for pity. He had a job and would find his way to something better. The writer evoked the scene inside as a remembrance of things past: "After work Jim goes home to a very small cottage where Mrs. Thorpe also can smile still, and Phillip 4 and Billy 2 wait for him. Sometimes at night Jim opens a big book and the little Thorpes look properly awed, as though understanding it all. The book contains many clippings and some photographs. The photographs include snapshots of Jim being handed something by the king of Sweden, and there are pictures of what the king gave him. . . . It's hard to find a reason for the present state of affairs of the smiling former athletic kingpin."

Jim provided an answer. "Guess it's an old story," he said.

Next came a reporter for the Newspaper Enterprise Association. Again, Jim did not want the world to feel sorry for him. His luck didn't last forever, he said, and he had no money saved, so he took to the pick and shovel. Four dollars a day was far less than he used to make, but it kept his family going during these hard times. "Take a look at the kids if you don't believe it," he said. "Did you ever see kids any huskier?" Then he scooped up his boys and hoisted them, one on each shoulder, smiling as he started to run.

POP WARNER WAS also on the West Coast in 1931, at age sixty still the football master. After leaving Carlisle, he had coached at Pitt for nine seasons, and was now in his eighth year at Stanford, where he continued his winning ways, his teams there going 65-13-6. And he was back with the Indians, or at least the faux variety. A year earlier, after a recommendation by the Executive Committee of the Associated Students, the school officially adopted the Indian mascot and nickname. Not that there were any Native Americans on the Stanford University teams.

As for the real Indians he once coached at Carlisle, Pop looked back on those days nostalgically in a three-part series he wrote for *Collier's* magazine. The headline of parts one and two reflected the racial mores of that era. Meant to highlight Warner's sympathetic perspective on his Native American charges, the titles were "Red Menaces" and "Heap Big Run-Most-Fast." There were no more than a thousand students at Carlisle, and half were girls, Warner said, yet "out of this little group of so-called savages came some of the greatest athletes that ever took part in competitive sports . . . closer to being athletes in the real meaning of the word than any other group I ever knew." He named Jim Thorpe first—"the most remarkable physical machine in the annals of athletics"—but also mentioned Lewis Tewanima, Frank Mt. Pleasant, Albert Bender, and many others, including Sundown, a Tuscarora pole vaulter, and Schenandore, an Onondaga hurdler.

Pop had been duplicitous in dealing with his greatest star's Olympic medal controversy, and by his final years at Carlisle he had alienated many of the school's athletes, including the redoubtable Gus Welch, but now he was presenting himself as someone who understood the plight of indigenous people, their defender and friend—which, compared to many of his contemporaries, he was. "Our treatment of the Indian is a dark chapter in the history of the United States, which is perhaps the reason the white man has never made any honest effort to understand the red man," he wrote in "Heap Big Run-Most-Fast." "Having driven him from his lands, breaking treaty after treaty, and subjecting him to every known spoilation, it soothed our consciences to rate the Indian as a lower order of human life putting him in the same class as the beaver, the buffalo and other wild creatures compelled to give way before the march of civilization."

THE LAST TIME the Olympics had been held in the United States was 1904. They were in St. Louis that year, part of the world's fair at which young Iva Miller, then a Chilocco student working at the exposition's Indian exhibit, befriended the famous old Apache Geronimo. Then came London 1908, Stockholm 1912, no Olympics during the world war in 1916, Antwerp 1920, Paris 1924, and Amsterdam 1928. A thoroughly European affair until the games returned to America in 1932, the track and field events to be held at the Coliseum in Los Angeles, sixteen miles from where Jim Thorpe now lived.

Here was the paradox. In the years since Stockholm, because he had broken amateur rules and in so doing exposed the hypocrisy of a system designed and run by plutocrats, Thorpe's name meant decidedly different things to the populace and to Olympic officials. To the people, he was the symbol of Olympian greatness. To the potentates of amateurism, he was a reminder of something they would rather ignore.

In the days leading up to the Los Angeles games, Jim was frequently in the press. Here he was making an appearance in the book section on the ground floor of J. W. Robinson's department store to hawk *A History of the Olympics*, a book to which he'd contributed his insights and his name as the coauthor with Thomas F. Collison. There he was on radio station KHJ starring in *Heroes of the Olympiads*, a dramatization of his performances in Stockholm. Now he was posing for wire service photographers with Josephine McKim, champion swimmer at the LA Athletic Club, before she embarked on a cross-country tour of sixteen cities promoting the games.

("'Lo, the poor Indian' is familiar to all of us," read the cutline about Jim and his "shapely" partner. "But apparently Jim Thorpe is one redskin who doesn't need any sympathy.")

Jim even ventured over to the Olympic village before the games began and visited the Swedish delegation. Swedish sports journalist Glokar Well later recalled that Thorpe appeared good-natured but "made a very unsophisticated impression in his cheap ready-made suit." He carried himself like an athlete, but "his face had become bloated and he looked flabby. He was marked for life, and it was rather depressing to think that this was the great hero of the sunny Olympics in Stockholm."

A book, a radio show, newspaper stories—and yet on the morning after the opening ceremonies, the *Los Angeles Times* reported that the Olympic organizers had shut Jim out. "The tragedy of these Olympics isn't . . . athletes who will try and fail. Jim Thorpe hasn't a ticket to these games. The greatest athlete in the world is forgotten and alone as the trumpets blare forth for the opening of the Tenth Olympics. The famous Indian was cornered on the eve of the grand opening that he might recall the glory of other games. He said: 'It's a wonderful show. It's great—but, well, I won't be there.'"

Charles Curtis, the vice president of the United States under Herbert Hoover, was in Los Angeles to attend the opening of the games. He stayed as a guest at the beach house of Louis B. Mayer, the founder of MGM studios and vice chairman of the State Republican Committee in California. On Saturday, he served in President Hoover's place as the head of state declaring the games open. The next morning, at the start of a day that took him on a social call at the home of *Times* publisher Harry Chandler, a drop-by at the Olympic village, and a reception at the Mayer mansion attended by the Hollywood A-list and every major political figure in the state, Curtis read in the Sunday paper that Thorpe did not have a pass to the games.

Curtis, a Kansan, claimed Indian heritage. His mother was a member of the Kaw nation, a descendant of Chief White Plume. He grew up learning Kansa as his first language. As a teenager he was known as Indian Charlie. He worshipped Jim Thorpe, the great Indian athlete. "I was not only surprised, I actually felt almost tearful when I read the story," Curtis told the gathering of glitterati at the Mayer mansion on St. Cloud Road. "If I had known that Jim Thorpe was here and had not been made an honored guest at the games, I'd have invited him to ride to the stadium with me yesterday and sit right next to me throughout the opening ceremony. I'd have felt honored, too, because Jim Thorpe is the greatest athlete the world has ever seen and I'm proud to think that he and I are descended from the American Indian race."

Later that Sunday night, Curtis boarded the Santa Fe Limited for the train ride back to his home in Topeka, where he would cast a vote in the Kansas presidential primary. But before leaving, he instructed his movie mogul host to find Jim Thorpe and give him passes so that he and his boys could attend the games. Mayer assured Curtis that tickets would be in Thorpe's hands the next day.

When he got the pass, Jim considered the initial snub an insult not to him but to all Indians. "It had to be another Indian who finally got me the invitation," he said.

26

"A Man Has to Keep Hustling"

TO GET HOME FROM DOWNTOWN LOS ANGELES, JIM DROVE southwest toward Mines Field, the airport that later became LAX. Two miles before reaching the ocean, he turned down a series of dirt roads that cut through acres of barley and lima beans to reach a lonely stretch on the outskirts of Hawthorne. His closest neighbors were all named Miller, though unrelated. The Millers on one side were Clyde and Emza. Clyde was Jim's former brother-in-law, Iva's younger brother. He revered Jim, unlike his suspicious older brother Earl, and his wife had taken a liking to Freeda and the boys. The Millers on the other side were Frank and Kate, who'd moved there for work in the aerospace industry. Frank and Jim had much in common. Both struggled with alcohol, loved to hunt and fish, and kept packs of dogs. Jim's beloved kennel of eighteen hounds, including Sonny Boy, Beezer, Bolger, and old Geronimo, were for the trail; some of Frank's were for racing at the track in Culver City.

Clyde and Emza were childless. Frank and Kate's daughter, Margie, was in the same age cohort as the Thorpe boys. She later remembered Mr. Thorpe as an affable man who was rarely home but enjoyed roughhousing and joshing with the kids when he was around. He once distributed pieces of chocolate and started "laughing uproariously," teasing them by saying it was really a laxative. Most of the time, the children had little adult supervision and "pretty much ran free and got in all kinds of trouble."

Jim wanted it that way; at least to have his boys live unencumbered, as he and his twin, Charlie, had during childhood along the banks of the North Canadian. Whatever discipline was administered came from Freeda, now home with three sons, including baby Dickie, born in

December 1932. It was far from the life she'd expected in the summer of 1924 when she was nineteen and Jim wooed her with love letters to his "Krazy Kitten."

After more than three years in California, still scratching for employment, finding work only occasionally as an extra in movies, Jim came out of athletic retirement and resumed his life as the itinerant ballplayer and exotic Indian curiosity. The lure was to be manager and occasional player for a semipro team named Harjo's Indians. These Indians were based in Holdenville in the Creek and Seminole country of Oklahoma, familiar turf to Jim about forty miles south of his Sac and Fox homeland.

Leaving his dogs in the care of neighbor Frank Miller, Jim returned to his home state in May 1933, reversing the path along Route 66 that had taken him west with the Bunion Derby four years earlier. He had been recruited by Ben Harjo, owner of the all-Indian squad, who financed the team with money his wife, Susey, accumulated when oil was discovered on her allotment. At one point her field was pumping ten thousand barrels a day. "Ben Harjo's oil wells spout gold into his pockets and thence to the pockets of scores of baseball players, a perfect double play," read his team's promotional brochure. Harjo claimed that his team included "several wealthy Indians" who had turned down offers from organized baseball to play with friends and neighbors. In truth, he was not as rich as he seemed, and his men played for money, some needing it more than others. Thorpe, who had never struck oil on his Oklahoma allotment, was decidedly in the latter category.

Here was the third iteration of Jim as the main attraction in an all-Indian traveling athletic show, the trifecta of ball sports: first in football with the Oorang Indians, then in basketball with the World Famous Indians, now in baseball with Harjo's Indians. This was an ambitious enterprise. The Indians scheduled games from Oklahoma north into the Midwest and across to the East Coast, traveling by Pullman bus to fulfill a schedule of 138 games from May into September. At times they played two or three games in different towns on the same day: one at noon, another in late afternoon, and a third after sundown. Two years before the first major league night game was staged at Crosley Field in Cincinnati, Harjo's Indians illuminated the night on ballfields across the mid-American landscape during the depths of the Depression, hauling portable light stands with their luggage in the belly of the bus.

Baseball was only part of the show. Along with bats, mitts, cleats, uniforms, and portable lights, Jim and his players brought along eagle-feathered headdresses, moccasins, drums, and tomahawks—all the paraphernalia necessary for them to entertain white audiences with traditional Indian dances before and after games. The indigenous ballplayers understood the contradiction of performances that helped them survive financially and to some extent celebrated their history while also serving as a form of minstrelsy accentuating dominant stereotypes of the American Indian. Finding it necessary to perform for white audiences, to redeploy a phrase Jim used fatalistically after his Olympic medals were yanked, was viewed as "just another event in the red man's life of ups and downs."

This dichotomy was also evident in how the players were presented. In their daily lives in Oklahoma—and in the box scores—they were Thorpe, Frohman, Cussins, Bailey, Honea, York, Wilson, Bowden, Collins, Mallery, McCurtain, Ryington, Jones, Hart. But in the player introductions before games they were Bright Path, Jack Rabbit, Lone Wolf, Little Buffalo, Snake Hide, Bear Hide, Big Heart, Roaring Thunder, Scatter Cloud, White Eagle. Which represented the truer selves? A question tangled in generations of cultural conflict.

The ball games were a dizzying mixture of high and low athletic theater. Following the popular traveling show model of the House of David, a team of bearded baseball wizards from a Christian sect in Benton Harbor, Michigan, Harjo's Indians would take on anyone who wanted to play them, some games staked by local businessmen at stops along the way, others booked by national promoters. The competition varied from town teams with no professionals to Negro League teams with some of the best players on the planet. Along the way, Jim sat in the dugout at Yankee Stadium chatting with Babe Ruth and played a four-game set against Ruth's power-hitting equal from the Negro Leagues, Josh Gibson of the Pittsburgh Crawfords.

There was another remarkable thing about Jim's baseball days with

Harjo's Indians. He was forty-six, more than twice the age of the youngest player on the team, Izzy Wilson, his nephew and a former football star from Prague High in Oklahoma. Thorpe was not a paragon of good health. He smoked and drank and ate fried foods. With extra girth around the middle and a massive head and chest, he appeared more top-heavy than ever. At one stop in Pittsburgh, a local newspaper headline described him as "Fat Old Man." But he not only managed the team, he also played, and more than adequately, running out infield hits and swatting home runs. Long past his prime, in a sport that was never his best, Jim kept going. Throughout his career, coaches and sportswriters remarked on his inconsistency of habit and mind, but in truth it was persistence that defined his life.

THE FIRST GAME was on May 21 in Emporia, Kansas, where the biggest crowd of the season came out to Soden's field on the outskirts of town. The fans had been promised that along with traditional dances, Thorpe would demonstrate his football kicking and passing skills before the game, but with a brisk wind flashing across the Flint Hills he canceled the exhibition, saying he would hold off until warmer weather. Whatever disappointment that caused dissipated in the fourth inning. Two men on base. A writer for the *Emporia Gazette* watched as Thorpe "strode to the plate, grabbed a handful of dust for his bat handle and his eyes seemed to twinkle as he surveyed the situation. He put every ounce of his 220 [not quite, but well over 200] pounds behind a swing [and] there was a veritable explosion when his bat met the ball." The field was without outfield fences. The ball soared over the left fielder's head, bounded on a dirt road, and rolled out of sight into the cornfield beyond. Jim had touched home plate before a fielder made his way through the stalks and retrieved the ball.

After a game in Topeka, Jim bought a postcard showing the field house at Washburn College and penned a brief note to Frank Miller. No mention of family, just a reference to the dogs: "High old Tap, Howza things going out there. Shall write you later and send some dog feed, Jim." Then a yo-yo route south to Tulsa and back north to St. Joseph, Missouri, tag-teaming with another exotic independent traveling team, the all-black Kansas City

Monarchs. Jim had not played baseball in Tulsa in twenty years, since the tragic incident in 1913 when the wooden bleachers collapsed and a soldier was killed before a barnstorming game featuring Christy Mathewson versus Walter Johnson. The Monarchs now were managed by another Hall of Fame pitcher nearing the twilight of his brilliant career, Bullet Joe Rogan. Advertisements promoting the Tulsa doubleheader noted that "One large section of the fairgrounds will be reserved for Negro patrons." It was another reminder of the distinction between two races that were discriminated against in different ways by white society. Native American fans customarily sat together but were not always forced to assemble in a segregated section.

The Monarchs swept the Indians at Tulsa and St. Joseph, but the games were competitive; the Indians did not seem embarrassingly overmatched. Pinch-hitting in the ninth inning of the nightcap in Tulsa, Jim cracked a clean single to left "to the intense delight of several hundred Indians in the grandstands." At City Stadium in St. Joseph, he started in right alongside his nephew in center. He drove in one run and scored another with a double off Hooks Beverley, an ace Monarchs pitcher. On to Kansas City and Council Bluffs and through the towns of Iowa; then the bus turned east toward Ohio and more familiar territory for Jim, first in Canton, where his football career had begun with the Bulldogs, then Akron, where he had played baseball for the Numatics.

In Ohio and western Pennsylvania the Indians again faced an all-black club, this time the Pittsburgh Crawfords, who took their name from the Crawford Bath House, a recreation center in Pittsburgh's Hill District. The Crawfords were then the best team in the nascent Negro National League and stocked with baseball immortals. The players on the 1933 Craws included not only Josh Gibson, the home-run hitter known as "the black Babe Ruth" (or alternatively, Ruth was "the white Josh Gibson"), but also future Hall of Famers Oscar Charleston, Judy Johnson, Cool Papa Bell, and Satchel Paige. This talented ensemble routed Harjo's Indians in Canton and Akron, then played them again in McKeesport, Pennsylvania, and Pittsburgh.

When Jim reached Pittsburgh, he was interviewed by Claire Burcky of the *Pittsburgh Press.* Burcky had watched the barnstormers play at Cycler's Park in McKeesport, and said Jim was easy to recognize as the biggest man on the field, a more polite description than the "Fat Old Man" headline accompanying his story. "First time I've been in Pittsburgh for ten years or more," Thorpe told Burcky. He recalled games from the old Carlisle days: how they beat Pitt handily in 1911 and 1912 but had a scoreless tie with Washington and Jefferson in 1912. "I still remember that W and J tackle Henry," Thorpe said, speaking of Fats Henry, a prodigious lineman who was now the school's athletic director. Jim failed to mention the darker story surrounding that game—that he had played poorly and drank too much at a hotel bar near the Pittsburgh train station afterward, causing Pop Warner to arm-lasso him and frog-march him back to the depot.

The Harjo's bus rolled across Pennsylvania, the Indians playing twice a day along the way, with several games in metropolitan Philadelphia interspersed with a visit to a Phillies game against the Cubs. A reporter for the *Inquirer* cornered Jim at the game and they chatted briefly. Thorpe said he played occasionally but spent most of his time "bossing" his players. Why was he still on the road after all these years? "A man has to keep hustling when he has a family," Jim answered. There were now three boys back in California, and though he rarely saw the three older girls from the marriage to Iva, he included them in the comment, saying he had six youngsters to feed.

Any of them athletes? he was asked. "All of them. One of my girls is a crack basketball player and the boys, even though they are young, show plenty of ability. I put a football and baseball in their hands when they were old enough to walk." His frequent absences did not stop Jim from investing his hopes in them just as he had with his first son, the adorable Junior who died at age three during the great influenza of 1918.

THE DAUGHTER JIM mentioned was Gail, then a sixteen-year-old star of the Chilocco Indian School basketball team. He was not around to see her play, nor was her mother. She and her sisters in boarding school were as bereft of parental guidance as the Thorpe boys running wild in the California countryside.

Iva had remarried and taken the name of her second husband. She was Mrs. Harrison Gray Davies, wife of the president of Tulsa's Superior Oil and Gas Company. This was the Depression, and Davies's title made him sound wealthier than he was, but still Iva's new life was more comfortable than it had ever been. She no longer had to work as the night mail clerk at a downtown hotel and share a one-bedroom apartment with another woman. Once, long before, Iva had glimpsed the leisure of the upper class. She was a schoolgirl then working at the Indian exhibition at the 1904 world's fair in St. Louis, where Helen Miller Gould, among the richest women in the world as the daughter of Gilded Age gold speculator Jay Gould, took a liking to her and almost adopted her.

Harrison Davies was far from that status, but he provided Iva financial security. The orphaned white girl who grew up thinking she was a Cherokee was shedding much of her old life. She now had the resources to bring Gail, Charlotte, and Grace home, but Davies, the stepfather they called "Daddy Harry," was not keen on having three teenagers around, so Iva relented and kept them at school. She rarely saw them on holiday breaks. "Everybody else went home, except for us and maybe one or two others who didn't have any parents," Charlotte recalled. "The poorest kids in the world would go home for Christmas, and we'd have to stay there." When Iva saw them at school, the visits were short and awkward. "Mother would come to visit in a great big shiny Packard car with chrome covers on the wheels—great big flashy beautiful looking car. Mother would come in and Daddy Harry would stay in the car. He never would come into the dormitory. She'd go like this with my hair—'eeaahh'—because I had smoothed my hair with Vaseline to make it straight so I would look like an Indian. Then she'd leave and I'd cry my eyes out."

In 1933, as Jim rumbled from town to town in the Harjo's Indians bus, Mr. and Mrs. Harrison Gray Davies packed their shiny Packard and moved from Tulsa to Chicago, where he took a management job at Socony Vacuum Paint Products. She was done thinking about Oklahoma, except for one image she could not erase: standing in a graveyard on a late September morning in 1918 and watching the casket of her little boy descend into the dark red loam of Oklahoma.

THE HEART OF the season came in July, as the Indians reached New York. Nat C. Strong, a promoter and owner who ran a vast baseball enterprise from his skyscraper office in the World Building in Manhattan, had booked the team for a rasher of games on the East Coast, from New Jersey to Maine, centered on a series of contests against two noted semipro teams, the Bay Parkways and the Bushwicks of Brooklyn. Strong was part-owner of both, along with controlling several Negro League teams. White-haired and blue-eyed, driving a big Cadillac from his manse in New Rochelle to work on Park Row, Strong seemed to have a dictator's grip on eastern semipro baseball. It was said that no games could be played within the New York metropolitan area without his approval, or his 10 percent cut in the gate. He was all about the money, and the entertainment value, and he saw a team led by the world-famous Indian Jim Thorpe promising both.

"The Indians are coming!" breathlessly declared the *Brooklyn Daily Eagle.* "Half-way across the continent, from the far plains of Oklahoma, doubly tanned by wind and sun, keen-eyed and clean-limbed, they come. This time they are 20th Century Redskins. They have abandoned the wiry mustang for a steel bus. . . ." The story line might never change: scalps, tomahawks, chiefs, war paint. Sportswriters invariably in the thrall of mythic Americana. The games themselves drained much of the romance. Thorpe's men seemed daring in print, but on the field they were outmatched by both the Bushwicks and the Bay Parkways. Another inevitable depiction: "Lo, This Poor Indian," read a headline after they were clobbered 13–2 by the Bushwicks. The biggest workout Jim got was before the game "arm-weary signing autographs."

During a break in the schedule, Thorpe visited Yankee Stadium and mingled on the bench with the players before the game. He and Babe Ruth had met in Boston in 1919 when both played in the city, Babe on the Red Sox, Jim on the Braves. According to a reporter who witnessed the scene,

Babe and Jim greeted one another as old friends in an elite club of all-time great athletes, both past their prime. Babe was thirty-eight, in his penultimate year in pinstripes.

"Hello, Jim!"

"Hiya, Babe. See you're still pasting that ball."

Art Fletcher, a Yankees coach and former shortstop who had played with Jim on Muggsy McGraw's old Giants teams, started the dugout razzing. "Hey, Jim," he yelled. "You still chasing that curveball?"

"Chased it right out of the league," Jim responded with a laugh.

Jim asked Babe how his legs were holding up.

"Great. I tape them before every game and they feel fine. I figure that taping the ankles will keep me going another year."

"Not gonna retire, then?" Jim asked.

"I'm still hitting those homers."

"Taping the legs is great," Jim said. "I had my ankle hurt in the Lafayette game in 1911 but two weeks later taped from ankle to knee I kicked four goals against Harvard."

"That was before Harvard perfected the defense against field goals," joked Harvard grad Charley Devens, a young Yankees pitcher just called up from Newark.

"There was no defense when I kicked them," said Thorpe.

This clubhouse bonhomie was what Jim missed, what most old athletes missed, almost as much as the money.

The next day, a letter addressed to Jim was delivered to Nat Strong's office in the World Building. It was from Frank Miller, who among other matters, based on Thorpe's response, must have asked when he would get paid back for taking care of the dogs all those months Jim was away. Jim wrote in reply on July 22:

Dear Friend Frank,

Your letter rec'd and I was more than glad to hear from you again.

Well the season is coming to a close and will have plenty of money this fall if only I get it. I have twelve hundred 50 buck coming soon on this year's salary but seems rather hard to get—that is from the owner.

I am glad to know that all the dogs are going good—how was Geronimo doing can he still run or has the old heart bothered him.

Frank I sure miss the chasing and look forward to doing it again. If things turn as I want them we can take a few dogs on the track.

Mrs. Thorpe has not written very much, wish you would write and tell me what's going on. See the boys are in good health—how's your family?

Have sent money to Mrs. Thorpe now and then but was up against it for awhile. Regards old boy with best of luck to all,

Same old pal
Jim Thorpe

In truth, Jim's time on the road was far from over. This was midsummer and he would not get back to California until late September. He was trying to keep things together, but with money and marriage troubles, life seemed precarious. Would Ben Harjo pay him? Would Freeda grow tired of his disappearances? A man has to keep hustling. Across the Hudson to New Jersey, up the Hudson to Red Hook, New York, on to Hartford in August for a five-game series against the Savitt Gems, a talented semipro team owned and promoted by Bill Savitt, a prominent local jeweler. The Gems played in the local twilight league, but Savitt also booked Sunday doubleheaders against the most entertaining traveling clubs: Harjo's Indians, House of David, the Homestead Grays, the Georgia Chain Gang, and the Brooklyn Royal Giants, who that year had a promising first baseman named Buck Leonard, a ferocious power hitter who later combined with Josh Gibson to form the most dynamic duo in the Negro Leagues when they played for the Grays. Leonard was connected to Thorpe by geography as well as baseball. He came from Rocky Mount, the North Carolina town where Jim got his professional start. Buck was only two years old when Jim played for the Railroaders, but he grew up knowing Thorpe as a local legend.

Hartford had been another station of the cross for Jim. Eleven years earlier, in the summer of 1922, he had starred for the Hartford Senators of the Eastern League and was the toast of the town until toward season's end he drank too much, clashed with the owner, tested the patience of Iva, and suffered what some thought was a nervous breakdown. Something about Hartford haunted him, and this time was no different.

In the first game of a doubleheader, Jim yanked his team off the field over a disputed call on a ball slashed down the right-field line. He was playing right and barely missed catching the ball as his momentum sent him crashing into the grandstand fence, leaving him slightly dazed. What dazed him more was that the home-plate umpire, hundreds of feet from the scene, called fair ball. Jim erupted, certain it was foul. The raucous Sunday crowd jeered the ump. The ump was blind, they said, missing calls for both sides. They chanted for their thirty-five cents back. Thorpe raged in protest, but the ump refused to budge and quit on the spot. The game eventually continued with players on both clubs calling balls and strikes.

On a return trip to Hartford later in August, after games in Massachusetts and Maine, Jim sat down for an interview with Albert W. Keane, sports editor of the *Hartford Courant.* Keane described himself as the cross-examiner with Jim on the stand. The first question broached the subject of Jim's drinking and the trouble that had brought when he played for the Senators. "No, you cannot class me as a drinking man now," Keane quoted Thorpe telling him between sips of an amber-colored three-two beer, a brew whose low alcohol content eluded Prohibition laws. "I can handle this stuff but the harder stuff handles me. Took me a long time to find it out. Once I thought I could master that stuff. Now I know better."

They hashed over his days with the Senators, and how owner Jim Clarkin mistreated Jim, and his version of why he quit playing for the team after Clarkin chewed him out in the dugout, unfairly Jim thought, when a ball got by him in the outfield because of a bad bounce and he was accused of loafing. They went over the athletic origin story of Pop Warner discovering him in the Carlisle Indian Industrial School high jump pit in the spring of 1907, and the fall from grace beginning when Charlie Kelchner, baseball coach at Albright College and bird-dog minor league scout, lured him into playing pro ball in the Eastern Carolina League in 1909. Jim reminisced about playing in the big leagues for Little Napoleon and his regrets that he never made it the way he had hoped even though his batting statistics improved markedly over the years and even now at age forty-six he was a leading hitter on Harjo's Indians.

Keane asked Jim which sport he preferred, football or baseball. Jim said he liked hunting and fishing better than either of those. It was in his blood, he said. He wished he could go back to the days of his forefathers and provide for his family by hunting deer with his bow and arrow.

AFTER A FINAL swing south through Brooklyn and Baltimore in early September, Harjo's Indians made it home to Oklahoma by the middle of the month. Fourteen weeks on the road, fifteen states, an average of nine games a week, winning eighty-seven, losing forty-one. There had been plans for more. A few final games in the Kansas City area were canceled and the notion of taking the team to Cuba and Mexico collapsed. All for the same reason: Ben Harjo, despite the supposed family wealth, had no money. Jim was still waiting for the money he'd told Frank Miller he expected to be receiving in late July. The amount he was owed had grown since then from $1,250 to $2,050. It was the Bunion Derby situation all over again, Jim spending months on the road and getting stiffed in the end.

The reasons now were more complicated than what had happened to him at the end of Route 66. This time he was the victim not just of an untrustworthy promoter but also of the federal government. He became collateral damage in another case of the Bureau of Indian Affairs' paternalistic treatment of Native Americans. The problem was that Ben and Susey Harjo (Seminole Roll No. 1578) were classified by the government as "restricted" Indians, meaning they did not have full control of their own financial affairs but needed the approval of the Seminole agent in Oklahoma before spending from their allotment account. The Harjos had been under intense scrutiny since oil was discovered in 1927. "It is the conviction of this office that expenditures from this account are running higher than the needs of the family justify," Acting Field Clerk C. L. Ellis wrote, calling Susey "a free spender" who after buying two new cars and a truck was asking to purchase a new Lincoln.

Ben Harjo told Thorpe that the road show had lost money and he needed to tap Susey's account to pay him and settle other debts from the baseball enterprise. Of the $15,000 the oil property was earning every month, the Harjos were granted only $500. When the government denied Harjo's request for more, asserting that he and Susey had been wasting the funds, Jim took up the cause on his own behalf. He said the government policy was demeaning and "makes the Indian feeble minded." He wrote to the commissioner of Indian affairs, to U.S. Senator William McAdoo of California, to Oklahoma Governor E. W. Marland, to the U.S. Department of Justice, and eventually to President Franklin D. Roosevelt. "I've stood for the Indian and represented him before the world in the Olympic Games and stand very high in public opinion," Thorpe told the president. "All I want is justice and pay for my endeavor—yours truly, James Thorpe."

For various reasons, including both the reluctance of the government and the eventual stubbornness of the Harjos, Jim never got the money.

But he kept hustling. During his time touring with the baseball team, he occasionally boasted that any day he might be called back to California to work as a technical director for MGM, which had bought the rights to "Red Son of Carlisle," his life story. Hollywood might make him a star.

27

Akapamata in Hollywood

FOR THE RIGHTS TO "RED SON OF CARLISLE," METRO-Goldwyn-Mayer paid $5,000 but Jim got only one-third of that, the rest going to Russell J. Birdwell, the Hollywood publicist who wrote the life story in Thorpe's voice. Early promotions indicated that Clark Gable would play Jim. Gable was in his early thirties, just starting to make his reputation as "all man . . . and then some," as *Life* magazine once called him. He was six-one, dark-haired, and rugged enough to once work as an oil wildcatter in Oklahoma, but his athletic career had ended with ninth-grade baseball and he was not Native American. No matter; MGM did not give the movie a green light. And no matter, at least to Hollywood, about Gable's race; it was all too common for the studios to cast non-Indians to play Indians.

That did matter to Jim. From the time he reached southern California, he had hoped to make a living in the movie industry, and his point of entry was as an Indian playing an Indian. He landed his first credited role in late 1931 as Swift Arrow, a Cheyenne warrior, in *Battling with Buffalo Bill*, a serial western based on a book by William F. Cody, the iconic Wild West showman. The Indians were foils in the movie. Buffalo Bill was the hero; a sinister, gold-thirsty gambler named Jim Rodney was the villain; and Swift Arrow and his warriors were there only to scare white audiences with pounding drums, wild circle dances, and occasional war-whooping attacks on a nearby town.

For the rest of the 1930s and into the next decade, Jim performed on the edges of the studio system, landing bit roles, credited and uncredited, in more than seventy films. Studios sometimes flaunted his famous name in the movie billing, but he was never the star, rarely called on to deliver more than a line or two, hired as a pieceworker a day or week at a time. Westerns dominated his filmography, most of them lost in the dust. *White Eagle. The Red Rider. The Golden West. Wild Horse Mesa. The Rustlers of Red Dog. The Wanderer of the Wasteland. Treachery Rides the Range. The Phantom Rider. Trailin' West. Wildcat Trooper.* He played Swift Arrow, Black Cloud, Chief Scarface, Eagle Feather, Charlie Jim, Red Smoke, Big George, Gray Cloud, and dozens of unnamed Indians.

He was also a native dancer in *King Kong* with Fay Wray and a pirate in *Captain Blood* with Errol Flynn, and was directed by John Ford in *Air Mail* and *Wagon Master*, Howard Hawks in *Barbary Coast*, and Frank Capra in *Meet John Doe.* Among the extras, he was the most notable face in the crowd, working with and often befriending a who's who of Hollywood stars. Jim drank and roughhoused with Flynn, regaled Bob Hope with stories of his sporting exploits, and partied late into the night with Buster Crabbe, a fellow Olympic gold medalist who launched his acting career after swimming his way to fame at the 1932 Los Angeles games. He also appeared on movie sets with Mickey Rooney, Betty Grable, Ward Bond, Ralph Bellamy, Buster Keaton, Helen Gahagan, Randolph Scott, Henry Fonda, Andy Devine, James Arness, Claudette Colbert, Spencer Tracy, Jimmy Durante, Broderick Crawford, the Three Stooges, Joan Fontaine, Tex Ritter, Pat O'Brien, Ronald Reagan, Gary Cooper, Barbara Stanwyck, Bing Crosby, Dorothy Lamour, Edward G. Robinson, and James Cagney.

Thorpe's career in movies was a frustrating grind. He earned between $7.50 and $11 a day as an extra and perhaps twice that for a minor spoken part. He spent his time roaming the studio circuit, pleading for work, with countless hours of sitting around punctuated by brief moments of trauma. Once his car was stolen from outside the RKO lot on Gower Street. During a western shoot, while riding without a saddle, he was bucked from the horse and fell backward onto a rocky trail, sending him to the emergency room. Another time, trying out for a scene in *Too Hot to Handle* that required extras to jump fully clothed from a burning ship, he suffered a leg cramp and needed a lifeguard to pull him from the chilly waters off the Hermosa Beach pier. With all that, Jim could not rely on acting alone to support his family. He sold cars and gave speeches and occasionally borrowed money (Bob Hope was a generous benefactor). Freeda worked in a stationery shop and sold handmade dresses when she could find time.

But those Hollywood years were affirming for Jim in essential ways. Even while battling his human frailties, he grew as a leader, fighting for fair treatment for his people, doggedly looking after his rights and those of hundreds of other Indians trying to eke out livings in an industry where they were considered superfluous. Who needed authentic red men when war paint and long hair on a grunting white guy could suffice? Jim spoke out, organized, and helped create a sense of community among the diverse Indians in Los Angeles, an important urban center for indigenous people. He became known to some as *Akapamata*, the Sac and Fox word for "caregiver."

CONCERNS ABOUT HOW Hollywood treated Indians stretched back decades into the silent film era. As early as 1911, soon after the industry settled in Hollywood and westerns became a movie staple, a delegation of Native Americans petitioned Washington for redress, arguing that studios "have used white men costumed as Indians in depicting scenes that are not true pictures of Indians and are in fact grossly libelous."

Luther Standing Bear, the most prominent member of Richard Henry Pratt's inaugural class at Carlisle, who came east as an eleven-year-old thinking he had to die to prove his bravery to his father, a Sioux chief, arrived in Los Angeles at age forty-four in 1912 to serve as a consultant on silent westerns where Indians were routinely portrayed as the enemy. After a few years in Hollywood, Standing Bear began appearing in films himself and joined the Screen Actors Guild. His first movie action was an uncredited role in *Ramona*, a film that represented a partial victory. While the Indians were portrayed sympathetically as victims of land-hungry white settlers, the title role of Ramona and her Native American suitors Alessandro and Felipe were all played by white actors.

Standing Bear went on to take small roles in scores of films alongside Douglas Fairbanks and Tom Mix, Hollywood's first star cowboy, and emerged as a leading voice for Indian rights. He was the author of the acclaimed memoir *My People the Sioux* and a founder of the War Paint Club, an organization that provided studios with a pool of Native American actors, demanded more accurate portrayals, and pushed Hollywood to hire real Indians. Echoing the words of the 1911 petition to Washington, the War Paint Club sought to "keep the Indian character from defamation or ridicule . . . as often is the case when white men, who don't know what it's all about, are dressed up to represent Indians."

When Jim Thorpe arrived on the Hollywood scene in the 1930s, Standing Bear was still there, and they became connected in a network of well-known Indians—among them another former Carlisle student, William Hazlett, known as Chief Many Treaties. They served as organizers and spokesmen for their Indian brethren, at times as allies, at times as competitors. They were called Hollywood Indians—Lakota, Sac and Fox, Blackfeet, and a score of other tribes joined in the common cause of struggling to make it in Hollywood far from reservation life.

The stereotypes Thorpe and the others confronted were encrusted in American culture. Even while reporting on their protests, the movie press often reflexively resorted to derogatory language and images. "The Indians are on the warpath," began a March 1934 AP report on demands for fair treatment made by Thorpe and Chief Many Treaties. A few paragraphs later, the dispatch noted that both men "learned perfect English at Carlisle University" and were now "dusting off their war bonnets." This construct came easily in the dominant white society: educated and urbane Indians could be time-traveled back to a primitive past with the stroke of a few words as surely as with the flickering of a few celluloid frames. Perhaps it was assumed that because Indians called themselves the War Paint Club any similar language was acceptable, misjudging how minorities used words as ironic shields.

The Indian club members also found themselves competing for acting scraps not only against white extras but with other powerless groups, a familiar condition in the American socioeconomic system. "This business of motion picture companies casting Mexicans, Hawaiians, Arabs, Negroes, and Chinese as American Indians in their productions has got to stop," Chief Many Treaties said. The industry response was striking: if this happened, it was only to meet visual expectations. The average Indian seeking a job in Hollywood "does not look like the Indian the motion picture public expects to see," one director argued, adding that the film audience "likes his Indian tall, husky, and well-proportioned."

Thorpe had those characteristics, though his skin was light and often darkened by makeup departments. One film in which he was an extra, shot late in 1934, had nothing to do with westerns and Indians but explored forced competition within the working class. Directed by Raoul Walsh, *Under Pressure* involved two teams of laborers known as sandhogs digging a traffic tunnel under New York's East River, grueling and dangerous work. The teams started from opposite sides of the river, with the one that reached the halfway point first picking up bonus money. While the lead roles went to Edmund Lowe and Victor McLaglen, who built their acting careers as intense if ultimately friendly on-screen rivals, their sandhog teams were filled mostly by imposing ex-athletes on the fringes of Hollywood. Thorpe was joined by several one time Southern Cal football stars and black actors Sam Baker and John Lester Johnson, a former boxer who once broke Jack Dempsey's ribs.

For Baker and Johnson, as for Thorpe, Luther Standing Bear, and Chief Many Treaties, getting jobs in Hollywood meant striving to maintain a sense of identity while accommodating demeaning stereotypes. Baker was cast most often as a black convict or an African chieftain in jungle pictures. Johnson's best-known role came a year before *Under Pressure* when he played Bumbo, the "Wild Man from Borneo," in an Our Gang film. It was a spoken part in which Bumbo shouted "Yum Yum, eat 'em up!" whenever he saw candy. Their characterizations in *Under Pressure* were equally demeaning; at the first sign of trouble in the tunnel, they were directed to clownishly bug out their eyes and flee in fear, a classic racist trope. Thorpe, for his part, was such an anonymous extra that movie viewers would have difficulty picking him out of the crowd, even with his distinctive face.

The filming of *Under Pressure,* originally titled *East River,* was of particular interest to a U.S. senator from California, William G. McAdoo, a son-in-law of former president Woodrow Wilson, a former secretary of the

Treasury, and an engineer who had started his career as a New York–based railroad executive promoting the construction of tunnels leading into Manhattan. One day while Thorpe was there, McAdoo visited the set with his daughter. There had been an accident a day earlier when a gantry cage elevator built to take the sandhogs down into the bore broke loose and six extras were injured, an incident that mimicked the dangerous nature of the real job. McAdoo made a point of taking out a wrench and testing the nuts and bolts himself before descending in the elevator. Afterward, he chatted with Thorpe, one of his sporting heroes. They talked football mostly, but Jim was also lobbying the senator as an FDR ally to pressure the Bureau of Indian Affairs to release funds so that Ben Harjo could pay him the money he was still owed as manager of the traveling Indian baseball team.

The tunnel film was still being edited when *Behold My Wife!* was released, with Jim playing an Indian chief. It was not a classic western, but a modern melodrama involving a young man from an aristocratic New York family who wooed a young Apache woman named Tonita Storm Cloud as a means of gaining revenge against his snobbish parents. Suicides, car wrecks, the authentic primitive versus cultured artifice, unrequited love, stormy breakups, and murder accusations all came into play in a story that concluded happily with the lead couple finally in love.

Produced by B. P. Schulberg, an ardent supporter of the New Deal and progressive causes, *Behold My Wife!* nonetheless relied on the degrading stereotypes and inequities that Thorpe and his Indian allies campaigned against. Tonita Storm Cloud was played by a white actress, Sylvia Sidney, and the white actor Dean Jagger took the role of her Apache friend Pete. Eleanor Barnes, drama editor of the *Los Angeles Daily News,* noted that "Miss Sidney didn't look Indian to the writer" and feared that a committee of angry Native Americans might come "trotting out to Paramount with Indian clubs and protest." Another reviewer said the story was "founded on society's strictest taboo—miscegenation." Newspaper promotions for the film played to those prejudices: "She exchanged her beads for pearls, moccasins for French slippers, buckskin dresses for silk . . . but she could not exchange her savage heart for that of a white girl."

As Jim became more of a presence in Hollywood, the press came calling. Whether he was down on his luck or on the rebound, sooner or later they found him to be good copy. George Kirksey, sportswriter for UPI, visited Thorpe on the set of a movie eventually titled *The Daring Young Man*, starring James Dunn and Mae Clark. The story was of a newspaperman who on the eve of marrying a woman reporter from a rival paper accepted an assignment to go undercover in jail to expose violent gangs behind bars. Thorpe played convict No. 13,111. When Kirksey arrived, director William Seiter was on one end of the set working a scene while prison-clad extras gathered around a table at the other end shooting dice. Thorpe, he observed, "looked on amusedly at the game but didn't shake when his turn came." At a break for lunch, they talked.

Kirksey asked about football. Jim had not played since that disappointing game with the Chicago Cardinals on Thanksgiving Day 1928. He said he rarely paid attention to the sport anymore. The NFL had not yet reached the West Coast and he seldom went to the Coliseum or Rose Bowl to watch Southern Cal or UCLA. No fat-man verbiage from this writer; he thought Jim looked in "fairly good condition." Jim said he was "out kicking the ball around the other day" with his boys and some other kids from the neighborhood. "I can still kick it and pass it but I guess I'm too old to play," he said. Jim's boys Phil, Billy, and Dick were eight, six, and two. He was almost forty-eight.

The outdoor track and field season in 1935 got Jim ruminating about his Olympic experience in Stockholm nearly a quarter century earlier—and the new generation of American athletes preparing to compete on the world stage at the 1936 Olympics in Berlin. What had happened to the trophies from the tsar of Russia and king of Sweden that Jim had been forced to return? Someone had told him they were in the king's palace in Stockholm. Over the years his belief that he was unfairly punished and deserved the trophies intensified. He had started a campaign on his own behalf during the Bunion Derby that took him to Los Angeles in 1929, but soon dropped the effort; now he revived it, paying a visit to P. N. Engblom, vice consul of Sweden at the consulate in Los Angeles, to ask how he might retrieve the trophies. An investigation requested by the Swedes discovered that the trophies had been offered to the second-place finishers in the pentathlon and decathlon, F. R. Bie of Norway and Hugo Wieslander of Sweden, who had declined to take them, saying only that they belonged to Thorpe.

Nothing reminded Jim of his glory days in Stockholm more than the emergence of Jesse Owens of Ohio State, an incandescent all-around track and field star in the sprints and broad jump. At the Big Ten championship meet at Ann Arbor that spring, Owens broke three world records and tied another within less than an hour, an unprecedented feat for which the press pronounced him the greatest ever.

The accolades made Jim take notice. He was being supplanted in the public imagination, a situation that brought out his competitiveness. Owens was "a marvelous athlete," Thorpe said, acknowledging that the young black man's marks in the sprints and broad jump were superior to his best. But Jim insisted that in his prime, if he were "twenty years younger and fifty pounds lighter," he could win a two-man meet. "I'll tell you why," he said. "In my day we didn't think about records. We ran or jumped or threw weights to win. When somebody pressed me, I set a record. When they didn't, I just won." There was some truth to that; throughout his career, Jim calibrated his effort to what it would take to win. And if the matchup were a true all-around contest, he would prevail in the weight events. But it was wishful thinking that he could outrun or outjump Jesse Owens.

If only. But Jim was not twenty years younger and fifty pounds lighter. A wirephoto in newspapers around the nation showed Thorpe on the set of the movie *She* with stars Randolph Scott and Helen Gahagan (the future Democratic politician Helen Gahagan Douglas, defeated by Richard Nixon in his red-baiting 1950 U.S. Senate race in California). The film, a bizarre allegory about the fallacy of eternal life, taking place in a fantastical ice palace in the frozen north, was supposed to be a breakthrough for Jim. Press reports boasted that he would have a leading role. In fact, his few lines as captain of the guards of "the ancient civilization of Kor" were unintelligible, his tribal costume and severe makeup rendered him virtually unrecognizable, and the press focused instead on his girth. The caption: "JIM THORPE'S MISSING NO MEALS. That rather portly gent in the rear is Jim Thorpe, though you might not recognize the super-husky once greatest all-round athlete, with that extra *om-bom-pwom*, as the French have it, added to his mighty frame."

The debate over whether the United States should participate in the Summer Olympics in Nazi Germany had begun by then. Jewish organizations demanded a boycott on the grounds that the racist and antisemitic policies of Hitler's government were unconscionable and contradicted the expressed ideals of the Olympic movement. But in opposing the boycott, Hitler found a strong ally in Avery Brundage, president of the U.S. Olympic Committee. While arguing publicly that the Olympics should transcend politics, Brundage worked diligently behind the scenes spreading Nazi propaganda and claiming that the American press was sensationalizing Hitler's atrocities.

This was the Avery Brundage who had competed against Thorpe in the decathlon in Stockholm—and was trounced by him before withdrawing prematurely—and who since rising to power in the Olympics movement had thwarted Jim's efforts to get his records restored and medals returned, a stance he would take for the rest of his career. Thorpe and Brundage were teammates in Stockholm but never close. When Brundage wrote about the friendships he made during the 1912 Olympics, his favorites were the German athletes Carl Diem and Karl Ritter von Halt, who went on to become influential Nazis and leaders of the organizing committee for the Berlin games.

Thorpe's position on whether America should take part in the games evolved. In a story tilting heavily to Brundage's side, a correspondent for the *New York Daily News* wrote that Thorpe "has no sympathy to waste on those who would have the United States refuse to participate in the 1936 Olympics in Nazi Germany." Jim's reasoning had more to do with what he saw as American tolerance than German intolerance, though he seemed naïve about Nazi antisemitism, quoted as calling it a "religious controversy." Americans should disregard any differences, he said, "just as we have always disregarded the race, color, religion, or local affiliation of any and all athletes we have sent to the Olympics in the past."

Some of the statements attributed to Thorpe in the news article seemed concocted by the author. There was no byline on the story, but it was likely Sidney Skolsky, the Hollywood reporter for the *Daily News,* who had included a tidbit about Thorpe in a separate gossip column after visiting him on the set of *Barbary Coast,* a film in which Jim was an uncredited extra playing an Indian janitor toting mop and pail. The concluding quote from Thorpe in the Olympics piece sounded as if it could have been written by Brundage: "Probably there were differences of opinion and politics among the ancient Greeks in those days. But such periods pass. The games go on. This period will pass. When it has passed followers of sport and fair play will be glad nothing interrupted the games this time. Let's keep out of the Old World affairs, especially out of affairs that might lead to bad feeling."

"The games must go on" would become Brundage's trademark phrase, one he uttered most unforgettably thirty-six years later after eleven Israeli athletes were murdered by Arab terrorists at the 1972 Summer Olympic Games in Munich. Considering what had happened to Thorpe after Stockholm, "fair play" was not the first thought that came to his mind when the subject was the Olympics. In the event, his position seemed to change—or was soon clarified. "Our athletes should not be exposed to whatever may develop in Berlin," Thorpe said when he was asked again months later.

After seeing Jim's name in Skolsky's column, Grace Wilcox paid a visit to the Thorpe home in July 1935. Wilcox was the newly minted Hollywood bureau chief for *Screen and Radio Weekly,* a nationally syndicated supplement published by the *Detroit Free Press.* She was trying to establish her credentials against Skolsky and Hedda Hopper, both of whom had just arrived on the Hollywood writing scene, along with the reigning queen of movieland gossip, Louella Parsons.

"The other day I went out to see Jim Thorpe . . ." Wilcox told her readers. Jim and Freeda were gracious hosts, the three boys on best behavior. "It was like being transported to a new and different world—a world in which simplicity, charm and love make a home fit for a king. Their small, neat cottage and the sandwiches, tea and cake served us as a gesture of true hospitality gave me a sense of satisfaction that no elaborate dinner in a palace has ever done. Jim Thorpe and his lovely little wife have found true happiness. They joke with each other, have their own private stock of wisecracks which they bring forward on the slightest provocation, and their three little boys live in an atmosphere of gentle gayety."

When Wilcox asked Jim if he missed the athletic life, he laughed and pointed to a photograph of him playing with his sons. "They keep me athletic answering their questions," he said. "Besides, I have to feed them."

"And I have to feed all of them," said Freeda, also laughing.

Wilcox noted Jim's role as a leader for many of the Indians seeking employment in Hollywood. "Chief of the tribe," she called him. She said Jim told her that many of the Indians were "fairly contented" with how they were treated in Hollywood—when in fact he and they were constantly pushing for better pay and equitable treatment. She noted that he had "an important role" in *Barbary Coast*—when in truth it was uncredited. She was struck by how Jim explained his place in society by telling the story of one friend asking him if he'd married an American girl. "No," he replied. "A girl of the United States consented to marry me—an American."

Were Jim and Freeda role-playing to impress a visitor? Their marriage had strains that a guest could not see, from Jim's absences to his financial struggles to his occasional bouts of drinking that would render him useless for days, and the boys often went weeks and even months without him. They suffered from his uneven parenting. Phil later told the writer Paul Zimmerman about a time their father took the boys fishing at the Redondo Beach pier. When they bragged that they could swim twenty miles out to Catalina Island, Jim responded to their boasting by throwing them off the pier. "Actually, we couldn't swim worth a damn," Phil recalled, but when they screamed for help their father ignored them. "The beach is that way," he said, pointing, and they barely struggled back to shore.

Nothing idyllic in any of that. But the Wilcox column was nonetheless a reminder that family relationships were a complicated mix of love and disappointment, endearment and dysfunction. The private language Jim and Freeda used went back to the days of their long-distance courtship when he was playing baseball in the twilight league in Massachusetts and writing letters home to his "Krazy Kitten." If it was spoken less often inside the home, the argot was not forgotten. But Freeda, who'd entered the relationship as a teenager worshipping a sports idol, also understood the importance of maintaining Jim's public image, especially when it came to writers from the movie industry. Hollywood was essential to the family's survival. Sometimes Jim found work there for all of them as extras portraying an Indian family. In such cases he did not complain when Freeda was made up to look Native American.

After a trip to the Midwest during that period, Jim returned with the youngest of his daughters, Grace, who felt increasingly out of place in the home of her mother and stepfather, Mr. and Mrs. Davies. She asked to join Jim in California and finish high school there. Jim met her in Oklahoma. They stopped first to see Jim's sister Big Mary, who lived in a cabin near the original family homestead along the North Canadian. No running water or electricity, an outhouse and water pump in back, light provided by kerosene lamps, clothes washed in No. 10 tubs. Mary cooked them a fried squirrel breakfast before they began the long drive west. "You have to understand the Indian people don't stop overnight; we don't have the money," Grace later recalled. At sunrise after Jim had been at the wheel through the night, he turned to Grace and announced that this was the perfect time for her to learn to drive. "I was fourteen at the time and eagerly said, 'Okay.' He showed me where the brake was and how to hold the steering wheel and give it the gas. Then he put it in gear and watched me for a few minutes to see if I was all right with a car coming and climbed into the back seat and went to sleep."

MAYBE THE END of the trail was instead an endless loop. Consider that once, when Jim's first love, Iva Miller, was eleven years old, she spent a summer at the world's fair in St. Louis entertaining white people at the American Indian exhibit by pretending she lived in a wigwam and taking part in daily performances of Longfellow's *Hiawatha.* Nearby the ancient and broken-down Indian prisoner of war Geronimo danced to the beat of a big drum and sold postcards with his signature for a dime apiece. That was in 1904. Eleven years later, in San Francisco, came the unveiling of the most popular exhibit at the Panama-Pacific International Exhibition, sculptor James Earle Fraser's *The End of the Trail*, an eighteen-foot-high statue of an Indian on horseback slumped in defeat, meant to establish the inevitability of manifest destiny while romanticizing the vanishing of America's indigenous people.

Now came a third variation on the theme in 1935 as San Diego hosted the California Pacific International Exposition. The world was on display across the three-hundred-acre fairgrounds, with exhibits replicating almost anything that could be imagined. Here was Spain's El Moro Gardens. There was a House of Charm where the "beauty of woman is on an imaginary pedestal and unconsciously you bow down and worship before the shrine." Across the way crowds enjoyed a sprawling version of New York's Coney Island amusement park. Then they could gawk at a village populated by midgets imported from overseas. Finally, in the middle of it all, stood an Indian village whose entrance proclaimed THE END OF THE TRAIL.

Enticed by the pounding of big drums, visitors encountered "150 [Native Americans] of almost twenty different tribes." The Indians, a mix of authentic artisans and reenactors, wove rugs, blankets, and baskets, threw pottery, and knapped arrowheads. "From time to time," noted one report, "the village will be the abode of Indians whose names are linked with the romance of America." One played the role of Black Hawk, the great Sac and Fox warrior from a century earlier. And for a few days, when tourists reached "The End of the Trail," they could see Black Hawk's most famous descendant, Jim Thorpe, playing the role of Jim Thorpe. Or at least a Wild West version of him. Jim was not there to exhibit his athletic prowess. He was paid to don a headdress and moccasins and other accoutrements of the Thunder Clan and perform the Eagle Dance and sign autographs, a spectacle not all that different from old man Geronimo's in 1904.

The duality of honoring his ancestry while performing as a white man's version of an Indian was a situation Jim had dealt with all his adult life. From his earliest days playing football at Carlisle, the white press had described Thorpe in the violent imagery of tomahawks and scalpings and portrayed the school's coeds as "winsome squaws"—aware or not that the latter word was a derogatory and condescending label. Indians connoted the wild and exotic. Those Swedish girls who encountered Jim near the practice grounds in Stockholm would not believe he was an Indian until he scared them off with wild war whoops. Oorang Indians, World Famous Indians, Harjo's Indians, Hollywood Indians—all performances that mixed indigenous tradition with white expectations and financial opportunity. It was that combination of factors that also led Jim and Chief Many Treaties to participate in a Fourth of July Wild West show in Southern California where they came as "feather-plumed" Indians to hang out with an aging group of former outlaws, including Emmett Dalton from Oklahoma's Dalton Gang and bank robber Al Jennings. And it was what motivated Jim to help organize a three-day powwow that drew hundreds of Indians from scores of tribes to Broadway Park near his home in Hawthorne, where they camped and celebrated with parades and beauty contests and traditional games and dances.

"LO, THE POOR Indian, he can't even play himself in the movies, mournfully complained Jim Thorpe. . . ."

So began a United Press account of the day Jim visited the offices of the U.S. attorney in Los Angeles in 1936 to seek legal help in his long-running fight with the studios. He and Cecilia Blanchard, an Oklahoma Shawnee friend who lived near him in Hawthorne, were running a loosely organized casting agency representing a few hundred Hollywood Indians. At the meeting with Pierson M. Hall, the federal prosecutor, Jim noted a survey conducted by the Labor Department establishing that only four in ten people hired to play Indians were Native Americans. Hall was partially sympathetic, saying he thought Thorpe had a justified complaint, but he believed there was nothing he could do because the studios were not breaking federal law. Translating Hall's response into the white version of Indian-speak, the wire service said he told Thorpe he would refer the issue to "the Great White Father" in Washington.

The problem involved more than who was hired for Indian roles. Studio executives seemed to be turning away from cowboy and Indian movies, deeming them passé. "There are only a few pictures each year we can work in, and when they use white men it means we can't make a living," Thorpe said. The second assertion was more accurate than the first, but the number of western films was shrinking. One major production bucking the trend was *The Plainsman,* an extravaganza directed by Cecil B. DeMille that tapped into the hoary myths of the West with a fictionalized story that intermingled Wild Bill Hickok, Buffalo Bill Cody, Calamity Jane, and General George Armstrong Custer. The film starred Gary Cooper, Jean Arthur, and Charles Bickford, with young Anthony Quinn, in his first year as an actor, playing an Indian.

In this case, it was not just the hiring of the Mexican American Quinn for an Indian role that bothered Jim, but something more complicated—the fact that DeMille bypassed Thorpe and his troupe of Hollywood Indians and instead used a band of Cheyenne on location in Montana. Apparently without appreciating the paradox, DeMille said he "wanted Indians that looked like real Indians, not the Hollywood variety." Jim found that argument disingenuous, noting that the Hollywood Indians depended on the work as their livelihood, while the Cheyenne did not, and he and most of his troupe could speak tribal languages and ride bareback.

Enraged by it all, Thorpe dispatched letters to the two most powerful people he could think of: President Roosevelt in Washington and Louella Parsons in Hollywood. When Parsons received the letter from "Indian Jim," she took note of it in her syndicated column. "Lady luck hasn't smiled very generously on him lately, but Jim has never wavered in his interest to his people, and he enclosed a letter of protest to President Roosevelt against *The Last of the Mohicans* and *The Plainsman,*" she wrote. "Whether Jim is right or wrong, he's really sincere in his feeling that only bona fide Indians should be permitted to portray Indian tribes on the screen, and not the proverbial Hollywood extras."

Variety, the Hollywood trade publication, blended its own peculiar lexicon with the usual Indian stereotypes in describing the same scene: "Hollywood's 250 Po Lo's Making Tepee: Allege Films Go-By. Producers of sagebrush symphonies have the Indian sign on poor lo's who make a living out of pictures, and their spokesman, Jim Thorpe, wants something done about it. Jim's squawk is that palefaces are getting jobs that should go to McCoy Indians. There are 250 of the vanishing Americans around and Jim kinda looks after their studio welfare."

EVERY FEW YEARS, Grantland Rice wrote a column about the greatest football players of all time. New names would be added to the list, but the one at the top stayed the same. In the 1936 version he said he talked to a dozen of his buddies, most of them coaches, a few fellow scribes. They mentioned Ernie Nevers of Stanford and the Chicago Cardinals, Red Grange of Illinois and the Chicago Bears, Dutch Clarke of Colorado and the Detroit Lions, and Bronko Nagurski of Minnesota and the Bears. But "the vote for number one was practically unanimous—Jim Thorpe, ball carrier and blocker, linebacker and broken-field star, passer and pass receiver, punter, drop kicker and placekicker, defense wrecker, a half dozen recalled the practically impossible things they had seen him do."

Thorpe the athlete was man and myth. Grantland Rice saw the first and helped create the second. In the age before television, sports columnists spun images that shaped the public imagination, none more than Rice, who worked in prose and doggerel. He was fifty-six now, eight years older than Jim, and determined to keep the two old-timers alive. "We've left a lot of years behind us," he wrote in an ode to Thorpe:

But reading mem-ry's slate
You still can play for me, big red man,
And let the others wait.
Yes I've seen other guys who had it.
Guys with a double share:
They knew their way above the scramble,
With something else to spare:
But when I start in to remember
Lost years that knew their flame,
I'll ride with you till hell starts freezing—
The red ace of the game.

Rice wrote his ode not long after the 1936 Olympics ended that August in Berlin, where Jesse Owens won three gold medals in the sprints and another in long jump, putting on a display of all-around skill that embarrassed the Aryan supremacist Hitler and had sportswriters harkening back to Thorpe's performance in Stockholm. The question of whether Owens was better than Thorpe resumed. In an editorial, the *New York Daily News* called it "an argument we won't undertake to settle," but noted that Owens competed against specialists to win his medals, while Thorpe competed against other all-rounders.

Along with the American press corps' disdain for Hitler—"It probably galls Hitler to see his racial theories, as they relate to physical superiority, conspicuously disproved," wrote the *Daily News*—they also spoke disparagingly of Avery Brundage, the U.S. Olympic potentate who had championed the Hitler games. It was not just his coddling of Hitler and the Nazis that bothered them, but the prudish and dictatorial way he lorded over athletes, a behavior they connected back to how Thorpe was treated when his medals were stripped after the 1912 Olympics. The Olympic bosses were "old maidish" then just as Brundage was now. Then it was imposing aristocratic standards of amateurism against Thorpe. Now it was kicking Eleanor Holm Jarrett off the team because the brilliant swimmer, who also happened to be a gregarious nightclub performer, was seen drinking champagne and shooting craps late into the night with scribes in the bar of the SS *Manhattan* carrying the American contingent across the Atlantic. Some suspected that Brundage, a notorious womanizer, was motivated by sexism, hypocrisy, and jealousy more than prudishness, just as jealousy and hypocrisy seemed to be factors in his refusal to restore Thorpe's medals.

It was left to Damon Runyon, the inimitable chronicler of rakes and rogues, to put this incident in perspective. Eleanor Holm Jarrett, he reported, after being "heaved off the Olympic team for doing a bit of guzzling one evening of the old sparkling, was now Telling All. She says that not only was elbow-bending somewhat profuse on the *Manhattan*, but that the Olympic officials themselves cut up no little."

The incident, Runyon wrote, reminded him of "teapot tempests" in past Olympics. "We saw a movie short the other night in which a fat Indian had a small part, and the appearance of the Indian brought back memories of another tumultuous Olympic year marked by species of scandal. It was the Stockholm year of 1912 and the Indian in the movie short was then the greatest athlete that ever lived. He was Jim Thorpe, of the Sac and Fox tribe, who grabbed all the honors of the Olympic Games, then had to give up his medals when it was discovered afterwards that he had played a bit of professional baseball down south before going to the Games. Of course, his Olympic disqualification didn't keep Jim out of the unofficial title as the greatest athlete, but it caused a rumpus beside which the Jarrett incident is just a mild zephyr. And to this day, Jim Thorpe's place in athletic history is undisputed, which may be some consolation to the pretty Mrs. Jarrett."

THE FIRST WEEK of a new year, January 1937. Ernie Pyle had left his job as managing editor of the *Washington* D.C. *Daily News* to work as a roving reporter for the Scripps-Howard newspaper chain. He drove across America, often accompanied by his wife, Jerry, known in his popular six-days-a-week column as "that girl who rides with me." His columns were called the "Hoosier Vagabond," an homage to his small-town Indiana roots, or "Rambling Reporter." Living out of suitcases and a satchel, steering his Ford coupe along the back roads, Pyle wrote about "anything interesting I bump into along the way"—from the midnight shift of a Pittsburgh steel mill to the "nation's best soda jerk" in Evansville, Indiana. Most of his subjects were salt of the earth types; only a few had known fame.

When Pyle reached southern California, he put out word that he wanted to see Jim Thorpe. Jim, alerted by a friend that Pyle was on his way, stayed home from the studios that day. Following a twenty-mile drive from downtown Los Angeles to the bungalow on the edge of Hawthorne, Pyle arrived to find Jim burning trash in the backyard. The clapboard house seemed a bit shambled, the vines overgrown. An old four-cylinder Ford sedan was parked out front. When Jim invited Ernie inside, Pyle searched for clues to the man he was about to interview. Small rooms. Modest furniture. A few photos of the athlete in his prime hanging on the walls. The home of a workingman, Pyle thought. About as well off as the average husky longshoreman, like the men who worked at the Port of Long Beach thirty miles down the road.

Jim told Pyle the story of how he got to Los Angeles. By coincidence, it was another Pyle of a different disposition, Cold Cash Pyle, who led him to the coast by getting him to serve as the master of ceremonies for the 1929 Bunion Derby. "The Bunion Derby promoter left him stranded here, and he has been here ever since," Ernie Pyle wrote. "He says [C. C.] Pyle still owes him the money." And that was not the only time. Jim recalled how he played baseball for Harjo's Indians in 1933, traveling from town to town across America sort of like Ernie was doing. "He didn't get all his pay from that, either. He seems to have bad luck collecting."

Pyle observed that Jim liked newspapermen and that he was a good conversationalist who enjoyed talking. That depended on the company; Ernie had a way of making him relax. Jim confessed that he had stopped taking regular exercise and his weight was up to about 225 and he wished it were 190. Ernie noticed his stomach. "But he's still a fine figure of a man."

"How do you feel about getting old and being out of the sports limelight?" Pyle asked.

"Why, I'm not old," Jim said, though he was now fifty. "I'm as good as almost any man at thirty and I don't feel old. If I'd take off some of this meat and limber up a little, I'd be good as ever." Probably not. It was characteristic of Jim to believe in his restorative powers. True, he had hit remarkably well for a forty-six-year-old playing for Harjo's Indians four years earlier, but his last feeble effort on the football field was nearly a decade past, and no amount of lost weight could restore his football prowess.

Pyle was a practiced listener burdened with his own level of naïveté in describing his subject. "Thorpe is a Sauk and Fox from Oklahoma. He says he's about five-eighths Indian. He has an Indian face but speaks without an accent. He can speak Sauk and Fox fluently, and a little of three or four other dialects. He separated from his first wife and married again 11 years ago. He has three boys ranging from 4 to 9. Mrs. Thorpe has no Indian blood, but all three boys have slight Indian features. The whole family works in the movies—Mrs. Thorpe just a little, the boys fairly often, and Jim all the time he can get work."

His work in the movie business had disillusioned Jim in two ways, he told Pyle. First, it took the magic out of it. "It has killed going to theaters for me. I go to sleep watching movies now," he said. "A movie is all pretending to be somebody else. It spoils the illusion when you realize that. Indians aren't good actors anyway. An actor has to exaggerate. It's against an Indian's nature to exaggerate or be emotional." Second, though he still helped fellow Indians, he'd given up his casting agency because it was draining him financially, he said. So many Indians were calling him collect to inquire about studio work that it cost him about $25 a month. That explained why Pyle could not call to say he was coming but had to rely on one of Jim's friends. To save money, he had had his house phone disconnected.

Pyle approached his subjects with empathy but did not romanticize Jim as Grace Wilcox had a year earlier. He assessed Thorpe as a man struggling to find a secure place in his post-athletic life. Like many retired athletes talking about the good old days, Jim disparaged the modern style of football and said he rarely watched it. When not hustling for studio jobs, he told Pyle, he read magazines, fished off the nearby ocean piers, and went coon hunting alone late into the night. He still wanted to be a coach but regretted that he had not polished his coaching skills more instead of continuing to play baseball and football after his prime. He'd applied to be an umpire in the Pacific Coast League but did not get the job. Money was harder to make than it had been during his playing days, Jim said. "But you know how it is. Easy come, easy go. I thought it would last forever, I guess." One reason he welcomed Pyle's visit was that he was starting to feel isolated. It was so arduous to get down to Hawthorne from LA that people were no longer coming to see him. "Jim sits around the house or goes on his daily search for movie work, just as though he never were a world-famous figure."

Easy come, easy go. A popular movie dealing with an Indian football star was produced in Hollywood that year, but it was not about Jim Thorpe. It was a musical comedy titled *Life Begins in College*, starring the

Ritz brothers, a zany variation of the Marx brothers. In this fictional account, the actor Nat Pendleton, who was white, played Little Black Cloud, also known as George Black, the only Native American enrolled at Lombardy College, an institution that was said to have been founded in the mid-1800s to give Indians access to higher education. It was as though Carlisle still existed but now catered to white students. Through various inane plot twists, Little Black Cloud leaves the football team after an embarrassing hazing ritual but then returns and leads the team to a series of victories, until . . . it is discovered that he once played football for money and is booted from the team.

Perhaps the idea came from elsewhere, but the most likely origin was the story of what had happened to Jim. He had nothing to do with the movie, not even as an extra. Two of the musical numbers were "Big Chief Swing It" and "Our Team Is on the Warpath."

FOR THE FIRST half century of Jim Thorpe's life, the central issue in the relationship between Native Americans and the federal government involved how Indians were to be assimilated into the dominant white culture once they were no longer being tracked down and killed by the U.S. Army. In 1887, the year Jim was born, the legislative answer came in the Dawes Act, which broke up and privatized communal lands as a means of forcing Indians to dissolve into society as individual farmers. The effect over fifty years was devastating. Tribes lost an estimated ninety million reservation acres to white settlers, dropped further into poverty, and were in danger of losing their traditional cultures along with their land. Land and the traditional ceremonies and ways of life were inextricably linked; when one was taken away, the other was endangered.

With the New Deal administration of President Franklin Roosevelt and his progressive commissioner of Indian affairs, John Collier, there was an attempt to reverse that trend, though in many ways it was still a case of white authorities telling Indian nations what they should or could do. The Indian Reorganization Act, also known as the Indian New Deal, was meant to return land to the tribes, promising them more representation within the Indian bureau and granting them more autonomy in running local affairs through tribal constitutions and governments. But the tribal governments were defined by Washington, imposing the language of "chairman" instead of "chief" or "sachem." And even though there was a superficial expression of democracy, with tribes voting on whether to adopt new constitutions, the end result was often new governments dominated by puppets for Washington, which still controlled most of the finances.

Jim Thorpe opposed part of this new deal as it would be applied to his Sac and Fox people in Oklahoma and was recruited by elders to campaign against it. His reasoning went back to his acculturation at the Carlisle Indian Industrial School and the lasting influence of its founder, Richard Henry Pratt. Like Pratt, Thorpe had negative feelings about reservation life and believed that a return to any system that separated Indians from the economic mainstream was a step backward. Also like Pratt, he distrusted the Indian bureau and wanted nothing to do with it even as it proposed reforms. There was one important area where Jim's thinking diverged from the Pratt philosophy: Carlisle's foundational motto *Kill the Indian, save the man.* Jim honored traditional Indian culture and never bought into the school's attempts to drain the Indianness from his people. He wanted to be judged and accepted on his own terms.

Jim returned to Oklahoma on December 5, 1937, two days before the Sac and Fox tribe vote on reorganization and a new constitution. He came to tribal headquarters in Shawnee as a favorite son, the most illustrious member of the Sac and Fox Nation since Black Hawk. When he spoke, the press listened, and the measure's opponents considered his voice the best way to make their case. Jim acknowledged that his role was as front man, not campaign manager.

"It would put Indians back to the blanket days," he told reporters tailing him before the vote. "What is the use of educating an Indian and training him for citizenship and then forcing him to live under a separate constitution?" When a reporter pressed him on what was intrinsically wrong with a new constitution, he said his real issue was with the federal government. "The government insists on special legislation for the Indian. It is all done under the guise of . . . offering him protection. But that's a lot of hooey.

There are poor down-and-out Indians, sure there are. But there are poor down-and-out Irishmen, Scotsmen, and Germans, too, aren't there? And listen, there hasn't been a single poor Indian helped by any of this legislation. The Indian who has the money is the Indian the government is always trying to protect."

Among those who disagreed with Thorpe was Pauline Lewis, a member of the Sac and Fox election board who happened to be Jim's cousin. Lewis was a prominent figure in her own right, a craftswoman whose "character dolls" of famous tribal leaders, including a Ponca medicine man and Chief Bacon Rind of the Osage, were coveted by collectors of Native American art, including First Lady Eleanor Roosevelt. However popular Thorpe was, he did not have the clout to prevail. The new constitution and tribal reorganization passed by a 210 to 120 vote. Jim's involvement was a sideshow, but nonetheless became the main focus of the press.

"SIC TRANSIT JIM THORPE," read a headline in the *Kansas City Times,* and the story was a familiar chronicle of a fallen star. "By a large majority the Sac and Fox tribe of Indians has voted to change its tribal constitution. . . . This would not deserve much comment were it not for the fact that the leader—on the losing side of the election—was Jim Thorpe. Jim Thorpe? You remember him. . . . At the height of his power, he not only was a national hero, but among the people of his tribe he was almost a God. Today not even the Sac and Fox are so humble as to do him reverence."

The press accounts only worsened when Jim returned later in the month in an unsuccessful attempt to reverse the Sac and Fox decision. "Jim waddles his 235 pounds in and out of offices of local bigwigs, quotes theories and impressive sounding figures and teases off jokes like a professional baby-kisser," wrote Arthur Edson for the North American Newspaper Alliance. "He's fat and fiftyish now, his jowls flapping lazily when he walks. For it has been 30 years now since this wild young Oklahoma buck was picked up and ran east to Carlisle for taming."

• • •

FROM HIS TIME at Carlisle to now, Jim had been negotiating different worlds in his own way. If he had an aversion to reservation life, he had no resistance to being around fellow Indians. Finding jobs for his Hollywood brethren was frustrating, and their collect calls were draining his meager income, but Jim was a generous man who enjoyed their companionship. His fondest memory of childhood, when his mother, Charlotte, was still alive, was when his family would gather with neighbors for an evening of games, music, and storytelling in the warmth of a communal feast. His Indian compatriots on the outskirts of Los Angeles re-created that atmosphere as best they could. On Saturday evenings, after Jim and others had spent the day hunting for rabbits and fowl, they would gather around an open fire in a country field near Hawthorne. Men preparing the game for the women to cook, a kettle of Cecilia Blanchard's corn soup bubbling on the open fire, children scampering about, adults telling stories about the old days in Oklahoma and Montana and South Dakota, every now and then a bit of advice from *Akapamata* to newcomers on how to apply for jobs in the movie industry. There are tidal pools of calm even in the most turbulent public lives, and this was one for Jim.

28

Never Forgotten

KNUTE ROCKNE AND JIM THORPE CAME INTO THE WORLD one year apart and rose from unlikely circumstances to become sporting legends. Rockne, born in 1888 in Norway, was five when his family emigrated to the United States and settled in the Logan Park neighborhood of Chicago. He played football in high school but then worked in the post office for several years and was twenty-two when he enrolled at Notre Dame, where he majored in chemistry and starred as an end on the football team. His gridiron days with the Irish overlapped with Jim's last two colossal seasons at Carlisle, 1911 and 1912, but the teams never met. The first encounter came three years later when they were both professionals in the sketchy Ohio League, Thorpe for the Canton Bulldogs, Rockne for the Massillon Tigers. Jim was the bigger name and superior player. He ran over Rockne "like a ten-ton truck" during their first match.

In 1918, the year of the great influenza pandemic, Rockne became head football coach at Notre Dame. His first win, against Case Tech in Cleveland, with Curly Lambeau and George Gipp in his backfield, came at the end of the same week that Thorpe's beloved namesake son died at age three, probably from the flu. The arcs of their lives diverged further from there. Rockne went on to coach Notre Dame during its most illustrious era, winning three national championships and compiling a record of 105 wins against 12 losses and 5 ties over thirteen seasons. He was a brilliant promoter as well as an innovative and inspiring coach, and his teams became a national sensation, assisted by the mystique of Notre Dame and the mythmaking of golden age sportswriters.

As much as Grantland Rice strove to further Thorpe's glory, his words did even more to immortalize Rockne and his men at Notre Dame. It was at the Polo Grounds in New York in 1924, when Rockne's Irish were running over Army, that Rice wrote the most famous opening in college football history: *"Outlined against a blue-gray October sky, the Four Horsemen rode again. In dramatic lore they are known as Famine, Pestilence, Destruction, and Death. These are only aliases. Their real names are Stuhldreher, Miller, Crowley, and Layden. . . ."*

Nothing gilds a legend like premature death. Rockne died at the peak of his coaching career at age forty-three. He was on his way to Los Angeles to meet movie executives, when the Fokker Trimotor plane he was flying in crashed into a field in Kansas on March 31, 1931. The nation mourned; Rockne was transformed from man to myth.

In 1940, Warner Bros. turned his life story into a movie, *Knute Rockne, All American.* The cast included Pat O'Brien as Rockne, or Rock, as he was called; Ronald Reagan as George Gipp, Rockne's ill-fated first star player, known as the Gipper; and Gale Page as Rockne's wife, Bonnie, who helped shape the screenplay as "one of the most tender love stories ever known." While actors took the roles of the famed Four Horsemen, coaching legends Pop Warner and Amos Alonzo Stagg played themselves in a scene where they defended big-time college football against its critics. There were also two Thorpe sightings. First, Jim's eldest son, Phil, was among a group of boys playing football with young Rockne in a Chicago alley, and later Jim came on-screen as an official in coat and tie who poked his head into the Notre Dame locker room at halftime of a game against Army to inform the coach that the second half was soon to begin.

It was a speaking part of three words: "Two minutes, Rock," he said.

At the time the Rockne movie was released, a screenplay depicting Thorpe's life and career had been around for a decade but was no closer to being made than when MGM first bought the rights. Why Rockne and not Thorpe? Both stories offered the drama of an underdog achieving great success against the odds, the American Indian and the immigrant American, the greatest athlete and the greatest coach. Both stories were shaped by tragedy—Jim losing his twin brother and then the Olympic medals and trophies, Rockne losing first the Gipper and then his own life.

But Jim's was the story of an outsider who remained an outsider, no matter what he accomplished, a stranger in a now-strange land that had once belonged to his people. Rockne's was a journey more familiar and comforting to mainstream America, that of a European immigrant in the melting-pot nation, one family among the "millions like themselves, simple hard-working people from the old countries following the new road of equality and opportunity"—as a scroll near the film's opening declares. Football eases Rock's assimilation as a boy. "Papa, don't talk Norwegian," he says to his father in the film. "We're all Americans now, especially me. I'm left end." Jim, on the other hand, the left halfback, never fully bought into the Carlisle pedagogy attempting to drain him of his Indianness. And while the Indian school was long gone, lost in the past, Notre Dame football still transfixed the sporting public with its stirring fight song and an accompaniment of exaggeration about Rockne, the Four Horsemen, and George Gipp. All were used to dramatic advantage in a Hollywood movie propagating an "only in America" theme at a time when the nation's values were being threatened on the brink of war.

Yet Jim Thorpe's ghost haunts the Rockne movie in ways that extend beyond his fleeting appearance at the locker room door.

George Gipp is presented as the white version of Thorpe. At the beginning of Rockne's first season as Notre Dame's coach, he is seen talking to his players and lamenting that he lacks a game-changing left halfback who can run, pass, and kick. He would give an arm for a player like that, he says. "Somebody on the order of—on the order of *Jim Thorpe!* I know a player like that comes along only once in a lifetime. . . ."

To which a player responds: "A guy like that would never come to a little school like Notre Dame."

A little school like Notre Dame. The best-known Catholic institution of higher learning in America. Already on its way to becoming a football powerhouse. The public was to believe that a guy like Jim Thorpe would never go there because it was so insignificant, but he would go to a little Indian school in the hills of Pennsylvania.

Then comes the origin story of Gipp making his way onto Rockne's football team, a tale with striking parallels to Thorpe's own origin story with Pop Warner. The Thorpe story: Jim in overalls, pausing beside the high jump pit and stunning the veteran trackmen; Pop summoning him to put on a uniform; Jim's first football drill when he sprinted through the defense, leaving players sprawled in his wake.

Here is how it happens in *Knute Rockne, All American.* Gipper, as played by Reagan, is seen on a field wearing street clothes, mitt in hand, tossing a baseball in the air. Baseball is his sport. The football team is practicing nearby, and when a stray football lands at his feet, Gipp picks it up and nonchalantly punts it high and far until it disappears over the wooden bleachers. Rockne is stunned. When Gipp repeats the feat, the coach orders him to go find a uniform. He is part of the team. Later, at a practice, Rockne lets him try out in the backfield. The coach and other players are skeptical, but just like Thorpe, Gipp weaves through the defense unstoppable, making it look easy. A star is born.

The decisive football moments in the Rockne movie involve Notre Dame in games against Army. In dramatizing these scenes, the past is revised, effectively airbrushing the accomplishments of Carlisle from history. The first comes in 1913, when Rockne is still a player and he and his roommate, quarterback Gus Dorais, are credited with revolutionizing the game by emphasizing the forward pass in pulling off a 35–13 upset of Army. The viewer is left with the impression that no college football team had ever before employed a passing game and that it was Rockne's novel idea, conceived before the season began while he and Dorais were serving as lifeguards at a beach in Ohio. That was how Notre Dame publicists portrayed it then and how Hollywood publicists wrote it later, claiming that Rockne "becomes the star of a hitherto undistinguished football team and invents the forward pass. . . ." In fact, for the previous seven years, the passing game had been essential to the offenses of several teams, including St. Louis U., Minnesota, and the University of Chicago—but none more than Pop Warner's Carlisle Indians, from the days of Frank Mt. Pleasant and Michael Balenti to Gus Welch and Jim Thorpe.

Why Rockne and not Thorpe? The question arises again in the film's depiction of the 1924 Notre Dame game against Army and the immortalizing of the Four Horsemen. In this case the movie was playing on mythology already written by Grantland Rice and advanced by the Notre Dame publicists, including Rockne himself. But Notre Dame's 13–7 defeat of Army "outlined against a blue-gray October sky" was by no means the most dramatic or meaningful upset of Army. It could not compare with what had happened on the Plain at West Point twelve years earlier, when it was Indians versus soldiers for the first time, and the Indians won 27–6, a peaceful act of revenge against the institution that had spent much of the previous century tracking down and killing indigenous Americans. The Four Horsemen were fine football players, but not the equal of the Carlisle backfield of Jim Thorpe, Gus Welch, Possum Powell, and Alex Arcasa, with Joe Guyon and Pete Calac in reserve.

Then there is the matter of how football shapes character, or the mythology of that idea. The most famous scene in the Rockne movie is so bathed in melodramatic pathos that it made Ronald Reagan famous and became the motto of his later political career. It takes place in a hospital room, with Gipp on his deathbed, succumbing to a streptococcus infection only months after playing his final game at Notre Dame. Rockne leans over to inform him that he has been named a Walter Camp All-American. Gipp responds with his final plea: "Rock, someday when the team's up against it—breaks are beating the boys—ask them to go in there with all they've got—win just one for the Gipper. I don't know where I'll be then, but I'll know about it. I'll be happy."

The dying words of a hero, or so it seemed. But Gipp likely never said them. The evidence suggests that Rockne contrived the "Win just one for the Gipper" line ten years later during a pep talk to a lackluster Notre Dame squad trailing Army at halftime, inspiring his boys to an upset victory. Even without that famous phrase, the movie's portrayal of Gipp is gauzy fiction. "We'd like our boys to grow up and be just like you," Bonnie Rockne says to him earlier in the movie. The Gipper responds by saying Rockne "gave me something clean and simple." The truth was different. Gipp rarely attended class. He dropped out once, was expelled once, and spent much of his time playing poker and pool in the back room of Hullie and Mike's restaurant on Michigan Street and other speakeasies in South Bend. During football season, he often missed practice. In all those ways, he outdid Thorpe in roguishness. In Rockne's autobiography, the coach claimed he knew none of this, and it goes unmentioned in the movie. Patrick Chelland, a sympathetic biographer, and *Sports Illustrated* writer Coles Phinizy later documented that Rockne was aware of Gipp's waywardness but tolerated it because of his talent.

Although circumstances differed, Rockne's claims of innocence about Gipp echoed Pop Warner's insistence that, despite all evidence to the contrary, he knew nothing about Thorpe's playing summer baseball for money and was as surprised as anyone when that was uncovered, prompting American Olympic officials to strip Jim of his Olympic medals and trophies. That reality would also be glossed over by Hollywood—when the time came.

IN EARLY 1940, as the Rockne movie was being filmed, Jim signed a contract with the W. Colston Leigh Bureau in New York, a speakers' agency that also represented Eleanor Roosevelt. He had given speeches before, but this was the first time he treated the lecture circuit as his primary occupation. Publicity letters went out to schools and service clubs attempting to reclaim the Thorpe magic: "Twenty-five years ago this man was the world-acclaimed hero: he was the present day conception of Lindbergh, Babe Ruth, Jack Dempsey, Joe DiMaggio and all of the rest of them, rolled into one." With the agency's guidance, Jim worked up four distinct speeches, and depending on the topic would show up either in suit and tie or full Indian regalia.

In one speech he talked about the expectations for that season—football in late summer and fall, basketball and hockey in winter, baseball in spring and summer. A more popular speech was titled "Thirty Years an Athlete," with Jim recounting his years at Carlisle, his "never-to-be-forgotten success" at the Stockholm Olympics, and his experiences in professional baseball and football. A third, intended for youth groups, was meant to be inspirational. In "An Hour with Jim Thorpe," he reflected "on the significance of sports in modern life and the true meaning of sportsmanship," centering it on examples from his own life. "The American Indian Today" was the topic of his fourth speech. "As one of the most outstanding members of his race," as the agency described him, Jim "surveys the position of the Indian in America today and discusses his future. He tells of the Indian's ancient culture, his legends, his traditions, and his present-day attainments." Jim dressed the part for that speech and cared the most about it.

With slight variations at each engagement, this was the core of what he said about the American Indian:

> I came from the Sac and Fox tribe in Oklahoma and I have never forgotten that I am an Indian. No Indian can ever forget it. Indians, you know, are misnamed. We aren't Indians. We are Red Men and we settled this country long before the white people ever came to these shores. Why then should we be deprived of citizenship until we can qualify with a written examination? None of you here is a government ward. You are citizens because that heritage has been passed on to you. But Red men are wards of the government. There were thirty thousand Indian volunteers in the last war. They fought for this country. Many gave their lives for its people and its resources. In return the Indians should be given full citizenship with all the rights and privileges that go with it. . . . I have four sons who want to be loyal Americans. So that's what I'm working for, that and better athletic training for all American youth. I would like to ask every one of you here to work for the improvement of Indian conditions. They can be bettered with your help. Perhaps some day another Abraham Lincoln will come along to free the Red Men of this country.

When the tour took Jim to New York early in 1941, Stanley Woodward, sports editor of the *Herald Tribune*, paid him a visit. Woodward wanted to talk about sports; Jim was more interested in discussing the plight of his people. "It is pretty hard to pump up much popular interest in the lot of the Redskin in these times, no doubt," Woodward wrote. "But the matter is of vital moment to old Jim and is the subject about which he likes to talk the most. As a matter of fact, it's pretty hard to keep him on sports for more than a few minutes at a time." Thorpe showed Woodward a pamphlet on his desk that promoted two congressional measures he supported to "straighten out the legal status" of Native Americans. One called for full citizenship of all Indians plus minor reparations of $3,000 per person. The issues were outside Woodward's comfort zone—"Indian affairs is not in your agent's repertory of well-grasped subjects"—so after expressing his general concern, he guided the conversation back to sports.

Although Woodward found Thorpe to be "a pleasant kind of fellow . . . inclined to laugh" about his troubles, Jim was no more reluctant in sports than in the civic arena to stand up for his rights and express his displeasure with men in power. In this case his anger was directed at his longtime nemeses, the overseers of amateurism.

A collegiate All-Star football game scheduled to be played in January at the Los Angeles Coliseum had been scrapped after "almost insurmountable interference" from the Amateur Athletic Union. AAU officials declared that Tom Harmon, the University of Michigan All-American and Heisman Trophy winner, and all his fellow college stars would be classified as professionals and lose amateur status if they took part in the game, even though it was a benefit for the British War Relief Association of Southern California. The decision infuriated Thorpe, and reopened old wounds. It was another case, he thought, of wealthy men imposing their own self-righteous standards on athletes.

If the AAU were made up of officials who understood what it took for working-class athletes to survive, Thorpe said, "then there probably wouldn't have been any trouble about Harmon, or about Eleanor Holm in the last Olympics, or about me. There isn't much sense in the Harmon case in view of some of the other rulings of the organization. Take the west coast football players. Whenever the movies want football scenes, they put them to work. They're the type. Nothing is ever said about it." Jim was speaking from experience; he had worked as an extra with many Southern Cal and UCLA athletes on movies ranging from *Under Pressure* to *Knute*

Rockne, All American. Years earlier, one of those USC players who got his start as an extra on the studio lots was a guard named Marion Morrison, who later became known as John Wayne.

Jim saw little of his family in 1941. Freeda was left in California with four sons—the youngest, Jack, born in 1938, was now three. Phil had just reached his teenage years, Bill was twelve, and Dick eight. Their father was on the road most weeks, the constant traveler piling up thousands of miles, just as he had done during his long athletic career. But now his performances were in high school auditoriums and city athletic clubs and gatherings of Rotarians and Elks and Eagles. *A man has to keep hustling when he has a family,* Jim had once explained. He was still hustling, but how much his hustling was paying off, and how much it was helping his family, were other matters.

One summer night during his eastern lecture tour he wrote a letter detailing his desperate financial situation to C. D. Russell of the Newark Athletic Club in New Jersey. Newark had become one of his home bases on the East Coast. "Dear Friend Russell," it began. "Rec'd the magazines then left Newark Thursday evening—had to check out of the hotel because of lack of funds to pay up or give some borrowed account so thought I had to take off. Had a 5 spot to my name, but was enough to get me to Jersey Shore, where I am staying with a friend on the dear old farm. Sure is a great place to think and rest. . . . I sure don't know just what I should do as you know cash is scarce as hens teeth. . . . Wonder if you wouldn't loan me a ten spot for awhile. See me dropping back that way before long." Whether the Newark Athletic Club had paid him for a speech is unclear. It had declared bankruptcy that year and was in receivership.

That letter was written on August 6. Less than a week later, Jim was back in his old haunts in Ohio, and acting as though he was without troubles. He gave a speech at the Fraternal Order of Eagles hall at Mount Gilead, not far from LaRue and Marion. Jim had many friends in the club and had been inducted as a member five years earlier, "the only Indian ever to be accorded that honor," according to club historians. Wherever he lived after his Oorang Indians days, he returned to the area once or twice a year to go coon hunting with pals and a pack of Airedales. He once told an interviewer that he thought it was the most beautiful place he had ever lived. During this visit to the Eagles lodge, he sat at dinner next to Charles Hostetler, sports editor of the *Marion Star.* Not a hint of financial worries. Hostetler noted that Jim's career had been a series of peaks and valleys but "just now he's astride the second pinnacle of success after a comeback from nowhere that's almost as sensational as his first climb to prominence."

Thorpe told Hostetler about his movie appearances and his many stops on the lecture circuit. He talked about his glory days, but said he was as puzzled as anyone trying to explain his athletic prowess. "My youth was just like that of any other country boy," he said. "Like a wild horse, I was allowed to roam, run, shoot, swim and compete with other boys my age." He loved his sporting life, but what meant most to him now, he said, was gaining full rights for all Indians.

When he was on the road, Jim often stayed with old friends and teammates. In Mount Gilead, he was put up by Carl Hoffmire, a hunting buddy he had known since his days with the Oorang Indians. Hoffmire's wife, Luella, remembered Thorpe's occasional visits. She described one the previous winter as an idyllic family scene.

"We spent the evening chatting and enjoying ourselves. Jim always enjoyed our children and they looked forward to seeing him," she recalled. "On this particular visit Jim was up the next day before the children. He wanted to get something from the car, what I don't remember. Anyway, he didn't take the time to put on his shoes. The next thing we knew Jim was running around the [outside of the] house barefooted in the snow. When the children got up, Jim met them with an exaggerated story about the world's biggest Indian who was dancing outside last night. To verify his story, he showed them the tracks. . . . I'm sure he missed his own children because of the lecture tour he was on. Maybe that's why he enjoyed mine so much. Jim would sit at our piano with my four children. He would pick a bass note and pound the piano as if it were a drum. At the appropriate time that only Jim and the kids would know, they'd let out a war whoop, and I'd about go through the ceiling, but my how the children loved it."

Jim no doubt missed his children, as Luella suggested. But one of the paradoxes of his life was that he loved children even though he was rarely around his seven. Often, it seemed, he did better with other families, other children.

FREEDA HAD DEFINITIVELY reached that conclusion a few months later. On October 29, 1941, while Jim was on a lecture tour in New Jersey, she appeared before Superior Court Judge John Gee Clark and sought a divorce. She and Jim had been married sixteen years, almost half her life. She was now thirty-five, Jim fifty-four. According to her complaint, they had been separated since Jim left on his speaking tour, but his long absences were not the only reason she wanted to end the marriage.

"He used liquor to excess for some time before our separation," she told Judge Clark. "And he stayed away from home for long periods of time."

Her attorney, W. H. Hodges, asked her to tell the court about Jim's attitude toward their children.

"He was very indifferent," Freeda replied. "He didn't seem to care how we got along. It's now more than a year since he left home the last time."

From Freeda's perspective, it was an understandable judgment. To some degree, Jim was a more easygoing version of his wayward father, prone to drinking sprees, bursts of unpredictable behavior, and coming and going at will. But what to Freeda seemed like indifference might also have arisen from other factors, including his inveterate inclination to be on the road and embarrassment over his inability to provide a more secure financial situation for his family.

The Los Angeles newspapers and wire services were in the courtroom the day Freeda appeared. "JIM THORPE DIVORCED IN FIREWATER CHARGES," blared the headline in the *Los Angeles Times*. "Wife Freed from Indian Who Won Fame in Athletics." The story took note of the irony that Freeda was divorcing Jim because of his drinking at the same time that he was on the other coast "lecturing on health and physical culture." The INS wire service chose to send out a photograph of Jim in Indian headdress along with a cutline that began: "Although he once was the sports idol of America, Jim Thorpe, Indian athlete, proved a neglectful husband, overly fond of the cup that cheers."

Looking back on the situation decades later when she was living in Washington State, Freeda said she stayed in the marriage as long as she could, but eventually it wore her out. "I was losing my health over it, and I didn't think it was a good idea to be there with the children," she told the *Yakima Herald-Republic.* "I was practically a nervous wreck." When Iva divorced Jim a decade and a half earlier, she was so angry she tore out all his photos. Now it was Freeda's turn. "After we divorced, I didn't want to see him or talk to him," she said. "I didn't even want to think about him, and I lost all interest in sports."

Much like Iva before her, Freeda went into the marriage hoping Jim would change. She was wowed by him and thought he was gentle and funny. "I learned a lot about alcoholism living with one," she said. "I thought at first they could quit any time they wanted to. I was always hoping he would. There isn't much you can do for them. . . . I never have come to terms with it. Sometimes I'll still sit and shake when I start talking about it. It's funny. I was very bitter, but at the same time I had been warned. People tried to tell me, but I wasn't experienced because I'd been raised in a church. And that is no training for marriage to a famous person."

Jim stayed on the road. Annapolis, Baltimore, Newark, Rochester, Detroit. The way he was identified in newspaper accounts marked the change in his status. He used to be "the Big Indian." Now he was "Old Jim Thorpe." The day before Thanksgiving, using the Leigh Bureau offices as his return address but stationery from the Hotel Fordson in Dearborn, Michigan, he wrote a letter to his old Carlisle pal Gus Welch, who then lived in Washington, D.C., where he had coached football at a high school and ran a football camp on a farm in the Shenandoah Valley of Virginia. Jim sounded alone and bereft:

> *Dear Friend Gus—your letter was forwarded to me while on the tour as you know glad to hear from you.*
>
> *I have been on the road since October 1 and have covered thousands of miles to date, so you can see the old Injun is going places. . . . All of*

my earnings seem to be burning up on the road. Gas, oil, and other expenses—like hotel and eats, pressing, laundry, and God knows what else. I am getting damn disgusted with the whole thing and am trying to land something else since Mrs. Thorpe has her divorce and I am free and 21 again. I don't know what the court set or anything about it, so all I can do is sit tight and wait. There can't be anything left for them to do or take. A woman is hell when they get started in the courts. . . . Well if she wanted it that bad, more power to her. I do feel sorry for the boys and I love them more than people think. They'll be coming to me before very long. They think the world of their Daddy and can't believe anything will hold them back.

Gus, I'll try my best to get that way and see you—it's hell to be alone without friends. A good old fashioned meeting would buck a fellow up, don't you think. Sorry to hear your camp wasn't a success this year. All a man can do is keep trying. Keep your chin up. Well Gus, if I ever get around Washington will certainly give you a ring—in the meantime keep battling. Regards to you and Mrs. And a lot of luck old boy.

Freeda was not "hell" in the courts. She did not ask for alimony. She just wanted out. She was exhausted by the chaos and uncertainty of her life and on the verge of a nervous breakdown.

TEN DAYS AFTER Jim wrote his despairing letter, the Japanese bombed Pearl Harbor and the United States entered World War II. In his lectures on the plight of the red man, Jim had emphasized the number of Native Americans who fought in the First World War and how he and his indigenous brethren displayed a strong loyalty to the nation and deserved full rights in return. With America at war again, he wanted to be a part of it. During a stop in Washington, D.C., he inquired about enlisting in the Marine Corps. "They told me I was too old," he said. "To me that sounds silly. I can shoot today as accurately as I could when I was a boy. Maybe I'm a little heavier, but I can still move around pretty quick on my feet." If he was too old for combat, he thought, maybe the military would use him in other ways. "I could help the boys in the Army, the Marines and Navy a lot—you know, just by going around from camp to camp and saying a little something."

The military expressed no interest in bringing on a hefty fifty-five-year-old. What else? He applied for a job coaching at the University of Oregon. No response. He applied for a post with the New Jersey highway department. No follow-up. He spoke at a father-son banquet for high school athletes in Bernardsville, New Jersey, and then headed back to Ohio and spent several weeks near Marion living with Chic Skelly, who had once played baseball and basketball with him. Finally, in March 1942, he landed a job tangentially related to the war effort, working security at the massive River Rouge auto plant of the Ford Motor Company in Dearborn, Michigan, on the outskirts of Detroit.

It was an adrenalized but difficult time for the Detroit auto industry. As the military started its massive buildup to supply material for a two-fronted war in Europe and the Pacific, Detroit's plants became known as the Arsenal of Democracy, manufacturing everything from B-24 bombers to gas masks. The assembly lines at the Rouge plant pumped out aircraft engines, armor plates, tractors, and military jeeps. But along with the war effort came clashes of race and economics. As black laborers streamed in from the South and white workers from Appalachia, racial tensions intensified over housing and jobs, a combustible mix that eventually led to a deadly riot in 1943. Only months before the U.S. entered the war, the United Auto Workers had successfully organized the Ford plants and were now in constant battle against efforts to quash the union by founder Henry Ford and Harry Bennett, the Ford Service Department chief of labor relations who operated a squad of enforcement goons for what was described as "the toughest private police force in the world."

For Thorpe, the connection to Ford went back to the Carlisle days. For the last decade of the school's existence, groups of young men from Carlisle were sent to Ford on their Outings to learn the automotive and manufacturing trades. Jim never went, but many of his friends and fellow football players did, including Pete Calac. That was long before the days of Harry Bennett; the pipeline now was of a different sort. Bennett and his top lieutenant, Stanley Fay, a former star halfback at the University of Michigan, were recruiting "a lot of tough bastards" for the protective force—Bennett sought boxers, bouncers, ex-cops, and lowlife thugs, while Fay brought in old athletes. They wanted men who were strong but pliable to the command and control of Bennett, one of the nastiest autocrats in American business. Jim needed the money and thought he was helping the war effort. When he signed up to be a foot soldier in Bennett's army, he did so unmindful of the politics involved but drawn by the pay—$180 a month at first. He was used for show, not for strong-arming. They gave him an assignment in Protective Security as a guard working the eight-to-four shift six days a week at Gate No. 4, the main entrance, only yards from the overpass where Bennett's toughs had beaten up labor leader Walter Reuther in 1937.

Jim's tenure at Ford was sporadic. According to company records, his first stint there lasted only fifteen days, from March 10 to March 25, 1942, while he lived alone at the Hotel Dearborn. Then he left for Ohio, where he tried to join the Army Air Corps at Wright Field in Dayton (he was rebuffed) and spent the next six weeks before returning to Detroit and Ford. On May 4, writing on Hotel Fordson stationery, he recounted his time in Ohio for a friend, saying that after Dayton he went on to Canton, his old football stamping grounds, where he had car trouble. And he acknowledged that he had taken to liquor again. "Also fell off the wagon," he wrote. "Guess I can't stay off the hard stuff."

The next day he went back to work at Gate 4.

On one shift that summer, Bennett's henchmen gave Jim political nominating petitions and ordered him to have autoworkers sign them as they came through the gate. The petitions were for Gerald L. K. Smith, one of Bennett's favorite right-wing politicians, a virulent antisemite and Nazi sympathizer seeking to run as a Republican for the U.S. Senate from Michigan that year. According to an FBI report from the Michigan field office to director J. Edgar Hoover filed on July 17, "Smith had considerable assistance in getting his nominating petitions filed from employees of the Ford Motor Company. The former football player, JIM THORPE, filled one complete petition during one eight-hour shift." Jim was an unwitting pawn in the game. When Smith failed to get the nomination, he blamed it on "the Jews."

It was also that summer of 1942 that Jim learned that the situation was deteriorating in Hawthorne. Freeda, who had custody of the four boys, was near collapse. She could not handle them and go on with her life. Seeking a break, she agreed that they should live with their father in Detroit. From Phil at fifteen down to Jack at five, they were thrown from one uneasy family situation to another. Jim rented a house in nearby Romulus and got the boys enrolled in local schools, and somehow the motley crew survived. At the start of the new academic year, Jim headed off to work before his sons left for school, with the older boys shepherding the younger ones most of the time. Grace, the youngest of Jim's three girls at age twenty-two, also arrived to work at the Ford plant for several months before enrolling in the Women's Army Corps.

As Jim later wrote to a friend, "being a father, mother, nurse, and housekeeper for my 4 boys takes up a lot of a man's time." More than taking up time, it took a toll on his health. On the morning of February 11, 1943, while at his station at the Rouge's Gate 4, Jim collapsed and was taken to the hospital. Doctors determined he had suffered a heart attack. Jim downplayed it, insisting it was just "a cold-flu with nerves shot" and all he needed was rest. He stayed in Henry Ford Hospital for a week before being released in satisfactory condition.

What happened next is unclear. The press reported that he went to Oklahoma to recuperate, staying with his sister Big Mary in Shawnee. If he did, he stayed only briefly and made it seem later that he had not been there recently. In one letter from Detroit early that spring, he said to a friend in Tulsa: "Well old top, how's Oklahoma? Would sure like to be out there if only had the right setup . . . shall expect some news from the old home state. . . ." It was a curious question and comment if he had just been there, but that was typical Jim. He could confound friends with his imprecision and indecision, the way he seemed to be on the move in different directions and end up nowhere, stalled by some combination of unease, uncertainty, politeness, and reserve.

When news of Jim's heart attack flashed on the wires, sports columnists and radio announcers lamented the decline of the once-great athlete and urged readers and listeners to cheer him up. In Raleigh, North Carolina, a young man named Ben Templeton was listening to NBC radio broadcaster Bill Stern's *Colgate Sports Newsreel* ("Bill Stern the Colgate shave man is on the air / Bill Stern the Colgate shave man with stories rare"). He immediately followed the announcer's instructions. "Dear Mr. Thorpe," Templeton wrote. "I was listening to the radio tonight when Bill Stern said something about you. He said something about America's greatest athlete being sick. I knew right away he was talking about you. He said you had a heart attack, Mr. Thorpe. He said that Knute Rockne once said you couldn't be stopped and I know that you won't be stopped now."

In Tulsa's afternoon newspaper, the *Tribune*, an editorial took note of Thorpe's troubles and suggested the time had come for him to move home. The piece drew the attention of Tulsan Lon Scott, who had befriended Jim in 1929 when they traveled together on the Bunion Derby, Scott as publicist, Jim as emcee. It was during that cross-country trip that Scott first took up Jim's cause, sending releases to the wire services demanding the return of his Olympic medals. Now, fourteen years later, Scott worked as a salesman for D. W. Haering, a national chemical company, and his sympathy for Thorpe had not diminished. He reached out while Jim was recuperating at Henry Ford Hospital, offering to find him a job in Oklahoma. Jim wrote back several weeks later. He reassured Scott about his health, fibbing that the flu had caused his collapse and that "the old Injun is feeling great." It was the beginning of a pen-pal relationship that revealed Scott's uncommon devotion and Jim's warm but often exasperating responses to his friend's attempts to help.

In a June 4 letter, Jim told Scott that he could not care for the four boys in Detroit and hoped to place them at Chilocco or one of the other Indian boarding schools. He already would have driven them to Oklahoma, he said, but for "trouble in transportation—meaning my car couldn't make the trip out there." Then he said he had to work as a plant guard for a few more months to get the financial means to make the trip. Were these explanations or excuses? Scott kept getting mixed messages but persisted in writing letters to schools to find placements for the boys.

He also contacted government officials to find Jim suitable employment. In a letter to Oklahoma Governor Robert S. Kerr, Scott noted Thorpe's "marvelous athletic record" and wondered if the state could hire him as a guard or guide at the state capitol building. He also broached the idea that Jim could be hired at the Oklahoma Ordnance Works in Tulsa, where the commander, Colonel L. E. Angle, had expressed interest in him, and told the governor about the need to place the Thorpe boys in Indian schools. The governor responded positively. "I think the plan for returning this world-famous Oklahoma athlete to our state is a splendid one," Kerr told Scott. If the ordnance job did not work, he added, "I will be glad to discuss the matter of his employment with you and other interested friends in an effort to secure him a job. With reference to his four boys, I am confident we will have no difficulty in placing them in one of the Indian schools referred to."

Even with the state's leadership committed to assisting Jim, it was easier said than done. To place the boys in boarding schools, Scott contacted officials in the Bureau of Indian Affairs and at the Gilcrease Foundation, a wealthy oilman's charity in Tulsa that provided scholarships for Indian students. Scott advised Jim on how to proceed, but Jim was slow to act. And there was another question: whether he had custody rights allowing him to make decisions about his boys. Emmett Brown of the Indian bureau was assigned to find out. "Had some trouble getting the call past St. Louis and when we got thru to Dearborn Jim was away from the gate," Brown wrote in an August 10 memo. "On second try an hour later we got thru alright. Jim explained that his divorced wife did get custody of children but since she did not care for them, he brought them all to Detroit with him and has not heard from out there in more than a year. Does not know whether court order has changed or not to permit him to have the boys."

Brown also reported that Burton Logan of the Gilcrease Foundation had traveled to Shawnee to talk to Jim's sister Big Mary. "He did not find her but heard she had turned deaf and dumb. He finally found one of Jim's brothers, George, [who] lived in a shack by the river, but he was gone. His wife told Logan they thought Jim was still living in Detroit, didn't know he was divorced from his second wife in Los Angeles or even had any children." George's wife likely was hedging with the official, wary of his intentions.

Most of the problems were resolved by summer's end. Jim's car was repaired, he had enough money to make the trip to Oklahoma, and the boys were admitted to Indian schools—Phil at Chilocco and the younger three at Pawnee. Whether Jim would take a job nearby and stay in the state remained uncertain. On the morning of September 15, he and the boys packed up the green Plymouth coupe and left Detroit. They headed south into Ohio to stay with friends for a day, then drove nonstop through the next day and night from Marion to Tulsa, arriving on the afternoon of September 17. Lon Scott greeted them, and as an inveterate publicist made sure the local press was there as well. A photo in the *Tulsa Daily World* showed Jim kneeling at the back of the Plymouth with "the gang consisting of his 4 husky sons" who had packed into the coupe for the long trip "like the great Injun football player used to pack the fans wherever he played."

There were some inaccuracies in the story. Jim left the impression that his wife "remained in Detroit." He said he had the flu the previous winter and "when he went to a doctor to ask about dizzy spells he was told his heart was at fault." No matter. "Jim looked hale and hearty and not a gray hair on his head." All seemed promising. He would visit Big Mary in Shawnee, meet with a Sac and Fox agent to secure the enrollment for his sons, drop them off at school, and return to Tulsa for a longer stay to pursue employment. He wanted to live in Oklahoma, he said, but one thing could change that—Hollywood. If the Knute Rockne story could make the silver screen, why not Jim Thorpe's? Plans were being made, he said, to film a picture of his life.

29

Road to Utopia

THE PAWNEE INDIAN SCHOOL WAS SIXTY MILES WEST AND slightly north of Tulsa, separated from the town of Pawnee by Black Bear Creek. It opened on reservation land in 1878 after the Pawnee had been removed from their homeland in Nebraska and relocated to Indian Territory. But the coed student body included more than Pawnee. There were also Ponca, Kickapoo, Kaw, Shawnee, Otoe, Tonkawa, and Sac and Fox. By the time Jim's sons arrived in the fall of 1943, the school had been operating for sixty-five years. To students and alumni, it was known as Gravy U, a nickname inspired by the chipped-beef gravy served in the cafeteria for breakfast. The Thorpe boys hated the place. They knew they were sent there because of their father's heart attack and thought he probably assumed that if Indian school was good enough for him it was good enough for them. It also lessened his financial burden, since the government would pay for their room, board, and education.

Jack, the youngest of the Thorpes, was not yet six when he was sent to Pawnee with his brothers. His life had been chaotic enough already, first separated from his mother and shipped off from sunny California to gritty Detroit to live with his father, and now separated from both parents to live the regimented Indian boarding school life. The boys' dormitory had a leaky roof. It was drafty in the winter and always overcrowded. Some boys were housed in a sleeping porch built in the rear. To get to the toilets and baths you entered a stone annex connected to the porch. Little Jack was asthmatic, and when he caught a cold or flu his asthma worsened and he had trouble breathing. One day that first winter he fell so sick he fouled his bed. An older boy pulled him out of bed, discovered the accident, found a razor strop and started beating him, then dragged him off to the shower. One more trauma in a young life. One of his older brothers ran away briefly and hid out at Aunt Mary's cabin in the countryside near Prague until an Indian agent tracked him down.

Jim was long gone from Oklahoma by then, despite the efforts of Lon Scott and others to find him a job. Scott was so devoted to Thorpe that he paid off a parking ticket Jim received in Tulsa one day after walking in circles, unable to remember where he had left his car. Scott also concocted a plan for the two of them to go into business when the war ended "making swell looking, great big cowboy type western hats which we will call the Jim Thorpe hat." After hard lobbying, he even landed a solid job offer for Jim. The state highway department would hire Thorpe to travel across Oklahoma, delivering inspirational speeches to schools and civic clubs, tossing in a few lines about roads along the way. Jim declined, saying his heart was in sports. Half his heart, at least. He knew that friends in Holdenville had circulated a statewide petition asking the University of Oklahoma regents to appoint him to a position with the athletic department in Norman. That job, he said, would be "the finest thing I could hope for." The petition drive failed; the offer never came.

Telling only his sister, Jim left for California, a departure that Scott discovered by reading the newspapers. On November 9, 1943, the Shawnee paper ran an article under the headline: "JIM THORPE DREAM FADES; HEADS WEST." The wire service piece said Jim had been "keenly disappointed" not to be hired by the state university and intended to work at a war plant in southern California. But that did not happen either. He ended up in Los Angeles, working as an extra in movies again and living with Chief Many Treaties and another friend in a house on Seventh Street.

"Well, Xmas is over, thank God, and had just a little 'cheer'—handled it better than former years," Thorpe wrote in a letter to Scott on December 27. He said he had been invited to a sports award banquet that night where he would see Bob Hope and Bing Crosby, along with his former coach Pop Warner and Amos Alonzo Stagg. That got him thinking about his own movie again. "Oh well . . . I honestly believe my life story is going to be made but every Tom, Dick, and Harry wants the story for nothing.

Have had propositions running around 20 grand mark feel that is my last stand . . . so I am sitting tight signing nothing until the right time and plenty of dough behind it."

The banquet was the first annual *Los Angeles Times* National Sports Award Dinner, a gathering of eight hundred members of the sports tribe at the Biltmore Bowl, the grand ballroom of the Biltmore Hotel. Hope and Crosby cracked jokes; Bing sang "White Christmas;" Sergeant Joe DiMaggio, gone from the New York Yankees to play for the Army Air Forces during the war, came from his station at Santa Ana to sit at the head table; and fifteen athletes were honored with sterling silver medallions as the best in their fields that year. They included Byron Nelson in golf, bantamweight Manuel Ortiz in boxing, national champion Pauline Betz in women's tennis, Ann Curtis in women's swimming, quarterback Sammy Baugh in pro football, and Heisman Trophy winner Angelo Bertelli, the quarterback at Notre Dame, in the college game. Jim was asked to accept the trophy for Bertelli, who could not attend.

The opportunity to rub shoulders again in 1944 with Bob Hope connected Jim to another movie opportunity. It was an uncredited role in *Road to Utopia*, one of the "Road to" musical comedies, starring Hope and Crosby. This time the traveling duo played vaudeville charlatans who called themselves Professor Zambini and Ghost-O and ended up skedaddling out of San Francisco on a ship to Alaska, where they discovered a map leading to a secret gold mine. Jim is one of the passengers on the ship. He can be seen standing near Hope and Crosby in winter garb as the vessel docks in the frozen north. The men disembark one by one, each stating his name to a customs clerk at the bottom of the gangplank. Jim's speaking part consists of one word, his last name. "Collins," he says.

Road to Utopia did not show in theaters until after the war was over. By then, Jim had sailed around the world for the second time in his life and gotten married for a third time.

THE MARRIAGE CAME first, but only two weeks before he began his journey, and Jim's new bride did not sail away with him. It was common then for couples to take vows shortly before one shipped off to war, but not many involved a man who had just turned fifty-eight. Phil Thorpe, now eighteen, had enlisted in the navy, and Jim wanted to do his part as the war dragged on into 1945. Although the navy made it clear it would not take him, he obtained a seaman's certificate and signed up with the United States Merchant Marine for the maiden voyage of the Liberty ship SS *Southwestern Victory.*

His third wife was different from the first two. Both Iva Miller and Freeda Kirkpatrick were young and naïve, smart but unworldly when they met and were wowed by the great athlete. They had been warned about his bouts with drinking but thought he would reform or that they could change him. Patricia Gladys Woodbury Askew was a well-traveled woman of forty-seven when she became Mrs. Patsy Thorpe, and was on a third marriage of her own. Born in Joplin, Missouri, she had followed a meandering path around the country, travels brought about by her marriages and her career as a husky-voiced, piano-playing bandleader in cocktail bars in a group called the Patricians. She lived for a stretch in Louisville, Kentucky, and a shorter spell in Rock Island, Illinois. That was in 1926 and 1927, when Jim, at the end of his football career, was playing for the Rock Island Independents on land where his ancestor Black Hawk had once stood. Patsy met Jim there, and admired him thereafter, but as she put it in a letter to an acquaintance, "the romantic angle did not develop until the past year," meaning 1944, after Jim had returned to California from Detroit and Oklahoma and she was living in Lomita not far from him.

They originally met in a bar. They got married in Tijuana on the second of June, 1945, full of liquor. She was a hard drinker herself. As his wife, but also his business manager with full power of attorney, she did not want to change how Jim dealt with the world so much as how the world dealt with him.

Jim had received his seaman's certificate two weeks before the quickie marriage. The U.S. Coast Guard issued it on May 19, with Jim posing for the photo on the ID card tieless in a wide-collared white shirt. He listed his address as 26208 Belle Porte Avenue, where Patsy lived. He said he was born on May 28, 1888, a date he often gave though in fact he was born on May 22 a year earlier. Under the category *Color*, the card said *White*, though his proof of citizenship was a 1939 registration paper from the Sac and Fox Census Rolls as a full-blood Sac and Fox Indian. His height was listed as 6' 1½" and weight 215. Brown hair, brown eyes. Next of kin: Mrs. Patricia G. Askew, relationship—friend.

At four on the afternoon of May 23,. *Southwestern Victory* was degaussed at the California Shipbuilding Company at San Pedro, reducing the magnetic field in the hull to make it less detectable, and moved to Pier 1 at Long Beach, where she was outfitted with a Zig Zag Clock used to plot swerving courses to confuse the enemy, a vital timepiece for a ship traveling across threatening seas to India without convoy or escort. Eleven days later, the ship was moved to Victory dock for loading army explosives—drums of 100 octane aviation fuel and racks of 500-pound bombs. Volcanic hell tucked into the belly of the beast. Another four-day break before the full crew reported: fifty-three merchant seamen and an Armed Guard detachment of twenty-five sailors from the Naval Reserves. Jim was ship carpenter and oldest of the crewmen. They called him Pop.

On June 13 they pushed out to sea. The first leg was across the Pacific from Long Beach to Australia, 7,081 miles in 21 days, 5 hours, and 37 minutes. Along the way, they tested the Zig Zag; fired four practice rounds of the 20 mm guns on the aft, midships, and forward decks; suffered boiler trouble; sighted two other Liberty ships and a Norwegian steamer but no enemy vessels; and gathered for nightly bull sessions on deck or in the mess hall. Jim was friendly but quiet during that first leg, and some mates seemed not to know they were traveling with a man who once was the greatest athlete in the world. He was not an old salt, but he had traveled these waters once before, on the world tour with the Giants and White Sox in 1913, so he helped initiate first-timers into the ritual when they crossed the equator. In later years, one seaman vaguely remembered that Jim might have played King Neptune in the ceremony. He certainly had the necessary look for the part.

When they anchored at the Gellibrand pier in Melbourne, the Naval Armed Guard were given shore leave. One guardsman was picked up and put in the brig for drunkenness, and another failed to report back to the ship and was found the next day by an Aussie civilian who said the sailor had been struck over the head and knocked unconscious while drunk. No such trouble with Jim.

With the boiler fully repaired, the ship set off on the second leg from Melbourne to Calcutta, 5,565 miles over fifteen days. Along the way they took evasive Zig Zag action when an unidentified steamer was noticed four miles to port. The crew held more evening bull sessions, with Jim now the star attraction after someone had notified *Stars and Stripes* about his history and whereabouts. "He had lots of tales to tell and kept everyone's interest," recalled Wesley A. Nimtz, a third engineer who worked belowdecks. He could tell tales about Oorang Airedales and hunting coons and playing football against Ike at Army and Knute Rockne in the pros and sailing around the world with Little Napoleon and trying to get a hit off Walter Johnson.

By the time *Southwestern Victory* slipped into King George Docks in Calcutta on the afternoon of July 24 to pick up censored mail and unload the aviation fuel and 500-pound bombs, word had reached the port commander at the army base station that Jim Thorpe was aboard. That commander was Brigadier General Robert R. Neyland, who likely knew more about Thorpe and his athletic significance than any general in the army this side of George Patton, who had been a 1912 Olympian with Thorpe, and Dwight Eisenhower, who had faced him in the Army vs. Carlisle Indians football game on the Plain.

Neyland had been an Army plebe in 1912 and did not take the field against Thorpe, but sat in the stands and watched Jim blast through the Black Knights defense in leading Carlisle to its historic upset. Thorpe was gone into pro baseball by the time Neyland starred as an Army football end and baseball pitcher in 1914 and 1915. They might have been teammates on the New York Giants after that, except that Neyland turned down McGraw's contract offer and devoted his life to generalships of two sorts: in football and the military. From 1926 to 1952, with two military interruptions, he served as head football coach at the University of Tennessee, leading the Vols to two national titles and becoming such a legend that they named the stadium in Knoxville after him. The second interruption was for five years, when he returned to the army for service in the war that eventually took him to the posting in Calcutta.

And so it was that a commanding general summoned not the captain but the lowly carpenter of the offloading Liberty ship to be his special guest on shore. "The captain of our ship . . . could not understand why a brigadier general and people like that would be glad to see someone who was as far down in the ship as I was," Thorpe recalled. There was something larger than chain of command at play here. An army reporter noted that when "Big Jim" and General Neyland met, "tales of olden times" flowed forth. Tall tales, no doubt; football stories were like war stories.

Also eager to meet Thorpe was the athletic officer of the Calcutta base, Captain Chester A. Chesney, who had played center for George Halas and the Bears before entering the service. Chesney escorted Jim on a tour of installations, including Rest Camp No. 1, the 142nd General Hospital, and a place they called Monsoon Square Garden, a boxing pavilion named after the famed New York arena, where the Liberty ship carpenter was greeted like royalty when he addressed the Indian Burma Theater Invitational Volleyball Tournament.

For the return trip, fuel and bombs were replaced by tea, 346 tons of it loaded at Berth 5 on August 2. They left the next day and were one day out of Colombo, Ceylon, when the Yanks dropped the atomic bomb over Hiroshima. Eight days later, as they were crossing the Indian Ocean, the Armed Guard celebrated the announcement of Japanese surrender by firing the 20 mm guns. Then into the Red Sea and through the Suez Canal to Port Said, another place Jim had been thirty-two years earlier with Iva and McGraw and the baseball boys.

That same day in California, Patsy Thorpe was combing through her new husband's files and found letters Lon Scott had written him. She was looking for ways Jim could benefit financially from his fame. Scott might be of help, she thought, so she wrote him. She told him about how she and Jim were married in Mexico in June and had been inseparable until he decided to enlist in the merchant marine. "As you know, Jim has in the past been exploited unmercifully and was beginning to eye this exploitation resentfully," she wrote. "But to our war effort he has given himself unstintingly." Then she started laying out her ideas. "Now that the war is over, it is my earnest wish to have something lined up for him upon his return." If she had read Scott's letters, she did so with rose-colored glasses, seeing only Scott's devotion to Jim and not the frustration he and Governor Kerr had trying to work out a job for him in Oklahoma. In that respect, she was like her husband.

> *I have several irons in the fire at this time to bring him back into the public eye with constructive publicity. It would be most fitting for Oklahoma to offer something so as to relocate their native son.*
>
> *I have completed a story sketching his athletic achievements etc. and bringing his life up to the present time. This story is now placed with* Sports Digest *at Hollywood, Calif. For publication.*
>
> *Your gov Robert Kerr was in Los Angeles a short time past. It was my misfortune not to have contacted him at that time, due to have been suffering with a painful mastoid and taking penicillin to the extent I was not alert.*
>
> *Do you still entertain the hat manufacturing plan? As I had Jim's power of attorney and I am his self-designated business manager I should like very much hearing from you. If there is anything you have in mind which will benefit Jim's future we will be most happy to cooperate in every way.*
>
> *I have in mind collaborating with a cartoonist for a syndicated strip on Jim's life from time of birth. . . . Jim has expressed his wish in one of his recent letters, to play one more football game. Fantastic as it sounds (Jim is forty-seven years of age) I'm sure he could do it. He was in super excellent physical condition when he left and after all there is only one Jim Thorpe.*
>
> *May I hear from you soon, Mr. Scott. Due to your great personal interest . . . I should like to have your opinion regarding my ideas of promoting publicity. The possibilities are endless as is the interest of the athletic world.*
>
> *Patricia G. Thorpe*

The letter revealed that Patsy Thorpe was all-in trying to help restore Jim but also seemed as unmoored from reality as he was at his weakest moments. That she misreported his age by eleven years may have been a careless typo, or not.

The merchant ship passed into the Mediterranean on August 20, sailed through the Strait of Gibraltar four days later, and was one day from American soil when the Japanese formally signed the instrument of surrender aboard the battleship USS *Missouri.* At 11:45, September 3, *Southwestern Victory* arrived at the entrance to New York Harbor. Jim had been gone three months. He flew home to a new wife but mostly the same old life. He kept on hustling.

LATER THAT SEPTEMBER, a young man named William Thourlby, fresh from the navy, strolled into an establishment on the San Pedro waterfront at the southern tip of Los Angeles due south of Lomita. The Bank Café was a sleepy joint, dark and empty but for the bartender and one man seated alone. It was Jim Thorpe. He and Patsy had bought the café with money he saved from the merchant marine. The name derived from the building's previous life as a financial institution. A vault that once held stacks of bills now stored liquor, and some male customers came in looking not for prime interest rates but procured sex.

Decades later, this same William Thourlby would author a book titled *You Are What You Wear.* By then he would be living in Atlanta, operating a fine men's haberdashery and writing a nationally syndicated column advising businessmen on how to dress, sporting his own dapper outfit of blue blazer, white shirt, dress slacks, shined shoes, and pocket square. First impressions were everything, he would write. People can size you up in fifteen seconds, judging everything about you from your socioeconomic status to your moral character. All in your appearance. But in 1945 he was just a twenty-one-year-old kid from the sparsely populated Thumb of Michigan who had completed his wartime naval service and was doing odd jobs and hoping he could take his six-three frame and rugged good looks to Hollywood.

When he stepped into the Bank Café, Thourlby could not know how the random encounter would affect both their lives. Jim looked as beaten-down as the establishment he ran, a fifty-eight-year-old with an expanding torso and double chin, mushrooming nose and heavily lidded eyes defining a broad face creased from years of smoking and drinking. Yet here was the exception to the rule of first impressions and dressing for success. From that first meeting, as unalike as they were in appearance and demeanor, Thourlby and Thorpe felt an immediate bond, so much so that they soon became de facto family, with the young man taking the stage name Buddy Thorpe and the old guy introducing him to people as "Buddy" or "my buddy"—his adopted son. Jim had seven children of his own, and though they were not estranged from him, their time with him had been minimal and they were scattered. For now, at least, he seemed closer to this faux offspring Buddy Thorpe than to Gail, Charlotte, Grace, Phil, Bill, Dick, or Jack.

Soon after their first meeting, Thourlby decided to help Jim out by investing in the bar and changing its name to Jim Thorpe's All American Supper Club. He had some family money; his father was a sales executive for Standard Products, a company that made plastic parts for automobiles. But the investment in the supper club was ill-timed and short-lived. "It was something neither of us needed," Thourlby explained later to Furman Bisher, sports columnist for the *Atlanta Constitution*, during the days when he was selling men's apparel on Peachtree Street. "One of us who didn't drink and one of us who couldn't. Every broken-down athlete would come in needing a free meal and a drink, and Jim saw that they got it. It wasn't long before we were closed down."

Thourlby had been a decent athlete at Castle Heights Military Academy in Lebanon, Tennessee, where his parents had sent him as a teenager, but Jim told people his Buddy was more than that, almost a second coming of Jim Thorpe himself. Over the years the line between real and imagined became so blurred that much of the public did not know the difference, especially after Thourlby's acting career took off. The most extreme example came after Jim died when Earl Wilson, the New York gossip columnist, dropped a three-dot item stating ". . . Buddy Thorpe, son of the late athlete, changed his name to William Thourlby . . ."

One thing Thorpe and Thourlby had in common was an interest in the movie industry. Jim knew the studios and stars, Thourlby was handsome and had acting talent, and their friendship grew as Jim took him on his rounds. After being delayed for two years, *Road to Utopia* was finally about to be released in early 1946 when Jim and Thourlby visited Paramount, where they met with Bob Hope. As Thourlby later told the story, they found the actor in his bungalow on the studio lot, and at the end of a pleasant conversation Hope asked Jim to repair to his back room with him. When they emerged, Hope said, "Buddy, take care of this guy, he's the best." Later, Jim explained to Buddy that Hope had lent him some money. "He helped us out a little, Bob is one of the good guys," he said. It was handled in private so as not to embarrass Jim.

Thourlby recounted that story to biographer Kate Buford on February 5, 2003, ten years before he died. He was seventy-nine then and living in Room 811 at the New York Athletic Club at Central Park South and Seventh Avenue, where he had been a longtime resident. The once-all-male club had a resonance concerning Jim that Buddy might not have appreciated. One of its most distinguished members a century earlier had been James E. Sullivan, founder of the Amateur Athletic Union and the man most responsible for stripping Thorpe of his Olympic medals, trophies, and records. It was at the NYAC every year since 1930 that the AAU presented an annual award to the best amateur athlete, an honor known as the James E. Sullivan Award. Sullivan was the patriarch of old-school amateurism, but he was also part of the official sham when Jim lost his medals.

In his old age, Thourlby's devotion to Jim had not waned, nor had his sense of taste. Buford later recalled that on the day she met him at the athletic club, he was "handsome still, erect and graceful, with salt-and-pepper hair and wearing a soft, white expensive-looking pullover sweater." At one point in his career he had been a model as well as an actor, and was an original Marlboro man, though he was not a smoker and had the role before the ad agency costumed Marlboro men to look like cowboys. Jim, to him, was still more than what he wore.

He said that Thorpe was uncommonly generous—"generous to a fault"—loaning money to people who were down on their luck even if he had to borrow the money himself to do so, and that he had an "incredible capacity to treat everyone exactly the same," regardless of their status. Thourlby also had a fondness for Patsy that Jim's sons did not share. To them, she became the manipulative stepmother who was using their father. Buddy saw her differently. He called her Mom and described her as Jim's strongest defender, fighting "like a lion" to get him what he deserved.

BY EARLY 1946, Jim and Patsy had left the café and southern California. They bought a trailer and with their dog Butch drove east across the continent, their mobile home stuffed with fishing gear, hunting equipment, and golf clubs, retirement toys Jim enjoyed during the leisurely trip east along Route 66 to his Oklahoma homeland before they dipped down through Arkansas, Mississippi, Alabama, Georgia, and Florida to the end of the road in another Hollywood, the town just north of Miami. He was a big man maneuvering in cramped quarters, and before the adventure was done he said that he had "knots all over my head from living in a trailer."

But Jim and Patsy had not come to Florida to live out their days as snowbirds in the tropical sunshine. He was still hustling to earn a living, searching for an occupation and lifestyle that could satisfy him, pushed on by a wife who not only accommodated his restlessness but encouraged it. Patsy's life had been as nomadic as his; she understood both the urge not to be tied down and the need to capitalize on whatever opportunities were out there. Their plan in Miami was to open a sports camp where he could train young athletes and coaches in a variety of sports, from baseball to football to track and field to golf. He told one reporter that in golf, the game he first took up at the urging of Christy Mathewson, he was now shooting in the mid-seventies. "I've had a lot of fun," he said. "Now I'd like to teach."

That idea went the way of most Thorpe projects—raised and soon abandoned. So was the life in Florida, a brief stay made more chaotic by a visit from Jim's son Dick, who of late had been at the Sherman Institute, an Indian school in Riverside, California. Rather than take him on for the holiday season, Freeda put Dick on a bus to ride across the country penniless to cram into the trailer with his dad and stepmother. He stayed with them off and on for the next few years. It did not go well. The one success the Thorpes had in Florida was fulfillment of the plan Patsy had laid out in her letter to Lon Scott while Jim was at sea—to write the story of his career and plant it in newspapers to rekindle interest in him. The *Miami News* ran a multipart series on Jim's life largely drawn from Patsy's account. But by the end of 1946 they had moved on, briefly to South Carolina and then to Chicago, and the endless effort to keep afloat continued. Jim tried to get a job as a wrestling referee but was denied a license by the Illinois Athletic Commission because he had not been a state resident for a year. While looking for other possibilities, he revived his public speaking career, taking any offer that came his way. Patsy tried to enforce a rule that he would ask for $500 and accept nothing less than $100, but the fees were flexible and the requests were scattershot.

Jim spoke to the Loyal Order of Moose in Cicero, Illinois; the Rotary in Kenosha, Wisconsin; the Kiwanis in the Bloomington High School cafeteria in Indiana. Not exactly the road to utopia. He enjoyed telling stories about the old days during his speeches, a past that alternately evoked nostalgia and bitterness. In Chicago, he paid several visits to Joe Farrell, then the public relations man for the Chicago Blackhawks ice hockey team, who in 1913 had accompanied Comiskey's White Sox and McGraw's Giants to publicize their world tour, a trip on which by far the best known of the American travelers was Olympic champion Thorpe. From the tragic collapse of the stands in Tulsa to the ball game played in the shadows of the Great Pyramid to the one performed in front of the king of England, Joe and Jim had many memories to relive.

When summer arrived Jim and Patsy were on the move again, back in South Carolina, landing a gig at the Beachcomber Club near Charleston, where Jim appeared nightly to tell stories and emcee the evening's entertainment with Al Stewart and his orchestra. When Eddie Allen of North Carolina's *Charlotte Observer* heard that Thorpe was nearby, he tried to track him down, checking with friends down in Dorchester County. "From the inevitable cowboy-crazy period of my childhood when I saw old Jim playing the part of some stolid Indian chief in a woolly western, I have been a professed member of the Thorpe fan club," Allen wrote. His efforts to find Jim reached Patsy at Folly Beach. Never missing an opportunity to promote her husband, she quickly wrote to him as though he were another booking agent.

> The enclosed will acquaint you with what Jim is doing in Charleston. I am Jim's business manager and have booked him here until August 11. Therefore his time is fully occupied until that date, except Sundays, when we go fishing or just relax. When Jim's engagement ends here, we may come to Charlotte. He has been making personal appearances at clubs, schools, lecturing etc. for the past five years. The minimum fee for one appearance is $500 a week. . . . Jim sleeps most all day and as I wrote he likes his Sundays with his family.

Patsy sent letters to sports editors and columnists at dozens of newspapers about his latest endeavors. While in Charleston, she saw that Dan Parker, sports editor of the *New York Daily Mirror*, had championed Jim in his syndicated "Broadway Bugle" column. Parker quoted one of Thorpe's former Carlisle classmates, Leon Miller, the lacrosse coach at New York's City College, saying that "in light of modern practices in so-called amateur sports, Jim Thorpe was the victim of a terrible injustice that should be righted while there is still time." It had been almost thirty-five years since Moses Friedman "crated the trophies presented to Jim by King Gustav as reward for his remarkable performances at Stockholm," Parker noted, but "from that day to this, no one has found out what happened to the trophies."

Soon after the column appeared, Parker received a letter from Patsy. He informed his readers: "Mrs. Patricia Thorpe writes me from Charleston, S.C., where her heap big Indian chief, Jim, has just closed a month's engagement at the Beachcomber Supper Club, that Jim's Olympic trophies, which were the subject of discussion in this pillar, are on permanent display in Lucerne, Switzerland. She adds: 'Jim is in excellent health and all things look good for the immediate future.' "

If the trophies were in Switzerland, they were not in Lucerne but Lausanne, headquarters of the International Olympic Committee, an understandable confusion, given the similarity of the names. Whatever her other faults, whether she was motivated more by money or honor, Patsy was then the most persistent voice calling for the restoration of Jim's Olympic prizes.

After a brief return to Chicago, where Jim joined fellow legend Red Grange in promoting a youth football league, he and Patsy headed south again for speaking engagements in Jackson, Mississippi, where he addressed the Touchdown Club at the Heidelberg Hotel, and then Atlanta, where he was interviewed by the AP. Patsy had arranged the meeting with the wire service, hoping for national attention. The reporter asked Jim how he liked football these days, with teams able to substitute almost at will, compared with his era when he and his teammates were sixty-minute men who never left the field.

"Jim says it's sissy," said Patsy when Jim paused before answering. "Oh, I know he doesn't want to appear critical or in the role of one of those old-timers, but . . ."

The resulting headline was provocative if inaccurate. "Modern Football Is 'Sissy' Game, Says Jim Thorpe."

By the holiday season of 1947, Jim was being paid to make appearances at Morrie Mages' Southtown Sport Store in Chicago, just one attraction among the many on hand including duck callers, bowlers, and wildlife photographers. He also took a job as the greeter at a saloon on West Madison Street in the Loop. Harman W. Nichols of United Press met him there one day in November and watched Jim shake hands with customers who came in to buy a highball or martini. Nothing distasteful about the work, Nichols noted, and Jim was not complaining, but it was not what he envisioned himself doing at age sixty. "I'm not broke and I won't ever be broke," Jim said. "It's just that I want to settle down with something I know how to do—and there doesn't seem to be anything in sports for me."

It was his familiar lament. He and Patsy were living in a trailer park at the corner of Indianapolis Avenue and 106th Street on the far South Side of Chicago, the Calumet River and belching steel mills on one side, the grinding terminus of the Indiana Toll Road on the other. The day Nichols met him at the bar, Jim took out a dog-eared scrapbook that showed all the extraordinary things he had done in his life. But memories alone could not satisfy him. He had to keep moving in an unceasing search for something right, a quest that seemed to keep taking him around in circles and leading to places like the dreary industrial rim of Chicago. "I'm not through. Don't put that down," he told Nichols. "Another guy and I are planning on starting a hunting and fishing lodge down in Florida on the Indian River. Me as a glad-hander and maybe as head guide."

What happens to a dream deferred? Jim's sagged like a heavy load, as the poet said.

Three weeks before Christmas, thieves broke into his car and stole five hundred dollars' worth of his clothing. When he reported the theft to the Chicago police, a desk sergeant asked if he would have chased down the culprits if he had caught them in the act. "I couldn't have done anything but yell," said Jim Thorpe.

30

Thunderbirds

ON SATURDAY MORNING, MARCH 20, 1948, JIM AND PATSY left Chicago to spend the weekend in New York City. They stayed at the Pennsylvania Hotel across from Penn Station, where Patsy set up shop working the angles of her twin causes of the moment. Her usual focus was on three interrelated pursuits, but one of them, Jim's employment, had been temporarily resolved when the Chicago Parks District hired him as a youth athletics coach earlier that week. The trip to New York was to negotiate with executives interested in the movie about her husband's life, and to entice the big-city press into writing more stories about Jim, particularly the restoration of the medals and trophies that had been taken from him thirty-five years earlier.

That campaign now focused more than ever on the one man Jim and his advocates considered the story's villain: Avery Brundage. While Jim struggled to earn a decent living after his athletic career, Brundage had become a multimillionaire developer and Asian art collector, operating his construction business from offices in the La Salle Hotel, his prized piece of real estate in Chicago's Loop only blocks from the bar where Jim had worked as a greeter. Brundage also dominated the Olympic movement, both nationally as president of the U.S. Olympic Committee and globally as the first vice president of the International Olympic Committee. In both positions, he consistently dismissed the idea that Thorpe deserved to have his medals and trophies returned.

When Jim confronted him directly, Brundage responded by restating his philosophy of amateur purity and asserting that what had happened to Jim was no big deal in any case because the entire world recognized

Thorpe as the world's greatest athlete. That argument was his means of deflection. When a reporter in Dallas asked Brundage about the Thorpe situation, his answer diverted into praise of Thorpe the athlete, saying that he was one of the great natural athletes of all time and with modern training techniques and facilities would be "as big a sensation [today] as he was in his day." It was hollow praise that required no hint of corrective action, and it was not enough to satisfy Jim.

At the hotel in New York, Patsy announced that she and Jim hoped to talk to Brundage soon, though she also expressed fear about how such a meeting might go. "I'm sort of afraid Jim will hang one on him," she said. To Thorpe it was a matter of pride and justice. He wanted the trophies so he could put them on display in Oklahoma. He wanted his decathlon and pentathlon records back on the books because he felt they had been unfairly erased from history. He called Brundage "stubborn and opinionated" and suggested he should retire from his Olympics positions, but added: "To give him a break, however, I think he's followed his convictions."

While disparaging Brundage, Jim held no grudge against the Olympics. On the contrary, he was a vocal supporter of the amateur games. As part of his job in Chicago, he had been appointed to a committee seeking to bring the 1952 summer games to the city. He also proposed that Soldier Field host a national junior Olympics, with young athletes converging from around the country to compete in track and field events. "We could have short distances and light weights for boys between ten and the junior high school age and other divisions for high school and military academy athletes," Thorpe said. It was a "one-man proposition," he acknowledged, but one that officials might adopt as part of the federal effort to combat juvenile delinquency. While the national event never happened, a local variation was sponsored by a local Amvets post, with eight parochial and public school teams competing and Jim shepherding the event as referee.

But here was a case where Jim talked a better game than he played. His position with the Chicago Parks District lasted only that summer. His city personnel records are incomplete—some were destroyed in 1972—but point to the probability that he was fired after receiving F marks for efficiency from his supervisor for the second and third quarters, at least in part because he was gone so often. When he was on the job, he produced several good publicity shots and some lifetime thrills for the Chicago youngsters who met him. In May, a photograph went out on the wire showing Jim in a white Chicago Park District sweatshirt and black cap running in the lead of a pack of boys and girls from the Kilbourn Park track club. The caption: "GREAT ATHLETE BACK ON TRACK." One picture in June showed him in the same uniform teaching a relay team how to pass the baton correctly, and another found him surrounded by children in white T-shirts seeking autographs. And there he was in July with a group of children taking the Freedom Pledge near the Freedom Train, an exhibit of historic documents including the Constitution and the Emancipation Proclamation being transported by rail from city to city to promote the concept of American liberty.

"I am an American," Thorpe and the youngsters said. "A free American. Free to worship God in my own way. Free to stand for what I think is right. Free to oppose what I believe wrong. . . ." The red-white-and-blue train sponsored by the American Heritage Foundation rolled into Chicago at a time when President Truman was feeling intense anticommunist pressure as the nation was in the grip of the Red Scare. A grand jury in New York had just indicted the twelve leading members of the Communist Party USA on charges of conspiring to violently overthrow the government. "Free to choose those who govern my country," Thorpe and the children continued. "This heritage of freedom I pledge to uphold for myself and all of mankind."

By mid-August, the Chicago Parks District freed Jim from his job, and he and Patsy, with Dick in tow, left Chicago for New York. He had been paid $337 a month for the past five months. Dick would later say that Patsy spent much of it on clothes and jewelry.

ED SULLIVAN BEGAN his television career during that summer of 1948 as the host of a Sunday night variety show on CBS, but he was already well known for his "Little Old New York" entertainment column that ran in the *Daily News* and was syndicated nationally. On August 19, after teasing his readers with items about private dicks tailing several misbehaving Yankees and comedian Milton Berle preparing for his gig at the Latin Quarter, Sullivan offered this sighting: "In front of the Hotel Belvedere, Indian colossus Jim Thorpe shaking his head as he reads the Babe Ruth story."

Sullivan had spotted Jim on the morning of the eighteenth, when the city's newspapers overflowed with articles about George Herman Ruth's death from cancer two days earlier. Front-page photos captured the scene at Yankee Stadium, where tens of thousands of mourners filed past the mahogany casket two hundred feet from home plate in the lobby of the House that Ruth Built. Babe was fifty-three when he died; Jim was sixty-one when he stood outside the hotel on West Forty-Eighth Street and read of his death. One giant of twentieth-century sports lamenting the passing of another. Ruth and Thorpe were outsiders who came from troubled backgrounds to forge their singular paths to fame. They were naturals who set the standard as the best ever at what they did. Imposing men with boyish hearts who were light on their feet. The Big Fella and the Big Indian. They had played baseball in the same city for one year, 1919, when Thorpe had his best season in the majors for the Boston Braves and Ruth was playing his last year for the Red Sox before being traded to the Yankees. Through the years they ran into each other occasionally at offseason banquets, and once, when Jim was traveling with the Harjo's Indians club in 1933, they sat in the dugout at Yankee Stadium before a game and traded good-natured barbs, two old warriors past their prime. In retirement, each suffered a similar fate, largely spurned by the sports to which they brought priceless glory, unable to land management jobs they coveted.

After reading stories about Ruth's death, Harry Keck, sports editor of the *Sun-Telegraph*, the Hearst paper in Pittsburgh, ruminated about the post-career fates of Ruth and Thorpe. "Baseball has been falling all over itself the last week or so in paying tribute to Babe Ruth now that he is dead. For years the Babe was eating his heart out to get back into the major league picture in some capacity, and everybody was looking the other way. Which of course is the way life happens to be," Keck wrote. "People always send flowers for the dead, rarely for the living."

This line of reasoning led Keck directly to Thorpe. He had recently received a postcard from one of Jim's former Carlisle teammates asking why "some professional football team doesn't give Jim a job." The postcard was unsigned, but likely came from Gus Welch, the quarterback and best man at Jim's first wedding, who had taken up Jim's cause with renewed vigor. Earlier that year, Welch had gone to the American Football Coaches Association meeting at the NCAA convention in New York to campaign for his old friend. "It's a black mark on sports that such action hasn't been taken before this," he told his coaching colleagues there. His defense of Jim even elicited a mild endorsement from Pop Warner, ten years retired from his final coaching job at Temple, who told the press he thought Jim got "a rough deal." Time had healed some wounds that went back to the congressional investigation of 1914, when Welch had led the player revolt against Warner in part because of his anger over the way Pop and the Carlisle administration abandoned Jim to save their reputations.

To the question of why some football team would not give Thorpe a job, Keck responded, "Why not indeed. . . . True enough, Jim was a wild one in his early days, but he's mellowed with age and, far from being a problem man, he could be quite helpful in teaching some of these young 'uns the tricks of the trade in the capacity of an assistant coach, and he would be good publicity copy." Thorpe's sin, playing summer baseball for little money, was "something almost any college player does with impunity these days," Keck argued. He urged the powers that be to act before it was too late, as they'd failed to do with Ruth. "If we're going to shed a lot of tears for Jim Thorpe when he's lying in his casket, why not make them mean something by doing something substantial for him while he's alive?" That meant restoring the medals and giving Jim a job. "Professional football is a good spot to do that for him," Keck wrote. "It might even make him curator of the Hall of Fame which it is planning."

A month after his Thorpe column ran, Keck was in New York to cover a boxing match and spotted Jim crossing the street near Madison Square Garden. It was a serendipitous encounter; he had been trying to find Thorpe's address. Jim told him that he and his family—meaning Patsy and Dick—were putting up at the Hotel Belvedere and planned to stay in New York into the holiday season. Professional football had not sought him out for a job as Keck had suggested, but he was finding interesting sports-related piecework here and there, Jim said. Metro-Goldwyn-Mayer had hired him to give some baseball tips to Jimmy Stewart for his role in *The Stratton Story*, a movie about Monty Stratton, a star pitcher for the White Sox who tried to make a comeback after having his leg amputated following a hunting accident on his farm in Texas. Stewart was disarming as usual in the role, but even with expert tutelage he looked no more a ballplayer than a spunky young June Allyson pounding a catcher's mitt as his wife, or old Frank Morgan, who went from being the wizard in *The Wizard of Oz* to portraying Barney Wile, a vagabond bird-dog scout who discovered Stratton and brought him to the majors.

On September 21, Jim was in the welcoming party at Idlewild Airport when the national soccer team from the newly formed state of Israel arrived from Belgium to prepare for matches against the U.S. team, which had been eliminated from the 1948 Summer Olympics in London that July, trounced by Italy 9–0. The Israeli team, formed too late to compete in London, had hired Thorpe to help coach Egon Pollak train his players for a series of friendly matches in New York and Philadelphia to benefit the United Jewish Appeal. Jim knew conditioning drills better than he knew the sport of soccer, but hoped he could show the players "some tricks about kicking and running that they didn't know existed." His main contribution might have been as a drawing card. At halftime of the first match at the Polo Grounds, he trotted onto the field in full football uniform, with high-top black cleats, white padded pants, a round strapless leather helmet, and a jersey sporting the number 68, the same uniform he had worn earlier that year at an exhibition at Kezar Stadium in San Francisco. Still, at age sixty-one, he had the leg power to put on a drop-kick and punt exhibition. "MIGHTY REDMAN," read the wirephoto caption.

That same week, Jim and Patsy heard some positive news on the movie front. MGM had hired a new batch of writers to adapt *Red Son of Carlisle* from the as-told-to manuscript written by Russell Birdwell. The writers were Doug Morrow and Vincent X. Flaherty. Morrow had credentials in the sports biopic field; he had written the screenplay for *The Stratton Story*, for which he would later win an Academy Award. Flaherty was a well-known sportswriter for the *Los Angeles Herald Examiner* who socialized with the Hollywood crowd and earlier that year had completed a screenplay about Walter Johnson, the Hall of Fame pitcher for the Washington Senators, a gentle man with a big heart who had struggled after his playing days. When Bob Considine, a fellow Hearst journalist, heard about Flaherty's Johnson script, he wrote in his "On the Line" column: "There is material for a great sports epic in Johnson's life. He was perhaps the most exploited athlete of them all, with the exception of . . . Jim Thorpe."

Morrow and Flaherty had little use for the Birdwell manuscript. They started instead with Thorpe material compiled by Flaherty's brother Edmund, known as Pat, a former athlete and an actor who had been Jim's friend for decades. Pat and Jim had played against each other in the minor leagues and for one year in the NFL when Thorpe was with the Oorang Indians and Pat was with the Chicago Bears. They also had encountered each other in Hollywood and were on the set together for *Knute Rockne, All American* and for Frank Capra's 1941 film *Meet John Doe,* where Flaherty had a bit part and Jim was an uncredited extra in a courtroom scene. Vincent was the writer in the Flaherty family and became as obsessed with the Thorpe story as his brother Pat. He would figure out the story arc; Morrow would work on dialogue. There was no director yet, and no movie star to play Thorpe, but the project that had been dormant for nearly two decades now seemed like it might happen.

BY THE START of 1949, Jim and Patsy had abandoned their migrations on the East Coast and around Chicago and returned to southern California. In the yin and yang of Jim's life, the closer he thought he was to having the movie made, the more stress fractures showed in his relationship with Patsy. This time, unlike his marriages with Iva and Freeda, the blame was not mostly his. Jim was passive by nature, unless he was fueled by alcohol, and felt he needed an aggressive person like Patsy to champion him, but it came at a cost. It was not only her propensity to hang out in bars and play the piano and drink. In dealing with Jim, she could be supportive and loving but also condescending, verbally abusive, and cruel. And in pushing Jim's cause to others as his self-assigned business manager, she often seemed unrealistically demanding and unpredictable, helping and hurting him with equal force.

Her negotiations with MGM were as counterproductive as they were Machiavellian. When it was mentioned that perhaps the four sons could have minor roles in the movie, Patsy brought the youngest, Jack, back from his latest boarding school, the Chemawa Indian School in Salem, Oregon, and moved to take custody of him from Freeda, who was a remote parent. She then assumed the role of agent for him and the other sons, but MGM became so tired of her money demands that the studio decided to drop the biography project entirely rather than deal with her. What seemed like a disastrous situation was saved when Flaherty bought the rights for $8,000 and scrambled to find a new home for the movie. Warner Bros. bought it for $35,000, though that price did not involve Patsy, meaning the studio still had to deal with her demands.

So did young Jack Thorpe. After he was no longer of monetary value, Patsy shipped him back to Chemawa. He felt lost: unwanted at home, unhappy at school. The people most concerned about him were Frank Hardy and his wife, who worked at Chemawa as the plumbing instructor and office secretary. With no children of their own, the Hardys would take Jack home from school on weekends and eventually said they wanted to adopt him. As Jack later recounted the story, they contacted Patsy to work out an adoption. "Patsy wanted ten thousand dollars to sell me to the Hardys," he recalled. "Once they told me what was taking place I refused to be adopted or sold. The Hardys were sure nice people and it broke their hearts when I refused to be adopted. Even though I hated the Indian school system and wanted to be out of there I would rather stay at boarding school than to be sold."

The return to Los Angeles had done nothing to stabilize Jim's uncertain existence. Among the traits he and Patsy shared, they were perpetual dreamers, concocting one scheme after another that might make them comfortable, if not rich. Jim was better at the dreaming, Patsy at the scheming. How, beyond the movie, could they dream and scheme their way to the promised land? Patsy suggested they sponsor a women's basketball team, but it proved too difficult to organize. What else? Softball was the rage on the West Coast, and professional women's baseball had been on the rise since the World War II years, when an all-female pro league was formed to fill the void left by the depleted major leagues. Putting those two trends together, the Thorpes decided to own and manage an all-female professional softball team. They called it Jim Thorpe's Hollywood Thunderbirds. Thunderbird was his favorite name. If he owned a fishing camp, he said he would call it Jim Thorpe's Thunderbird Fishing Camp. It went back to his Sac and Fox roots, his allegiance to Black Hawk and the Thunder Clan.

Patsy went to work, talking up the idea with prospective sponsors and local reporters. She said that Tex Oldham, manager of Joe DiMaggio's restaurant in San Francisco, might chip in $10,000. She claimed that the possibility of "sharing in fabulous profits" also elicited interest from comedian Lou Costello's youth foundation. She said that a new five-thousand-seat ballpark was being constructed at an amusement park in Venice that would serve as the team's home field. The plan was for the Thunderbirds to roam the country from California to Florida, playing as many as two hundred games between April and October. It was the latest variation on a familiar Thorpe theme, another traveling show, much like the World Famous Indians in basketball and Harjo's Indians in baseball, only this time the world-famous athlete would stay in the background and shine the spotlight on a talented group of women athletes wearing short skirts six inches above the knee.

All unmet dreams, as it turned out, although Jim was able to recruit a formidable squad of local and national talent, including shortstop Snooky Harrell and pitcher Betty Luna, two stars of the Rockford Peaches, the All-American Girls Professional Baseball League team portrayed a half-century later in Penny Marshall's fictionalized movie *A League of Their Own.* After putting his players through several practices at Hollywood High, Jim left for Phoenix to arrange a series of home and away games with the Phoenix A-1 Queens, a powerhouse squad that had finished second to the Jax Brewers of New Orleans in the National Softball Congress tournament the year before. Thorpe seemed engaged and energized. He knew the position of every young woman who tried out, and showed no uncertainty about names, never resorting to calling any of them "kid" or "daughter"—as he once did with his own daughter Gail. "I like this venture," he said. "Girls play a fast game. They must be good athletes."

The home opener was played at Gilmore Stadium not far from the La Brea Tar Pits, a venue that had been used for pro football, baseball, midget car racing, and political rallies. Within two years, Gilmore would be torn down for the construction of CBS Television City. The appearance of the Thunderbirds did nothing to slow the stadium's demise. They split a pair of well-played, close games during a weekend series with the Phoenix Queens in late April, but few fans came out to the eighteen-thousand-seat park to watch them. In a column about the rising popularity of softball in southern California, Paul Zimmerman of the *Los Angeles Times* took note of the small crowd and explained it in blatantly sexist terms: "Jim Thorpe is fronting for another outfit which opened with a game at Gilmore Field yesterday but there wasn't anything about the crowd that indicated the sports public is going to find softball gals in shorts irresistible. P.S. With the weather like it is, the beaches are cluttered with better pristine pulchritude."

The dream deteriorated from there. Lacking the funds for their own bus, Thorpe's Thunderbirds traveled to Phoenix by car caravan, but one of the cars broke down along the route and arrived too late. Two starters missed the opener, another stayed home sick, and the rest barely made it in time, exhausted by the long same-day drive. They were humiliated by the Queens, 20–1. When Patsy was unable to come up with enough money to pay for hotel rooms, several players threatened to quit. The Arizona promoters were also furious that the Thorpes had already pocketed the $500 guarantee yet were unable to field a team for the second game. They threatened to call the police. Finally, the company that sponsored the Queens, the popular A-1 Beer, contributed enough money to handle the bills and satisfy the rebellious Thunderbird players. A second game the next day was more competitive, with Betty Luna pitching a masterpiece until the Queens finally prevailed in thirteen innings, 2–1.

That was the end of the line for the Thunderbirds. No money, no way to travel, no more games.

Soon after Jim and Patsy arrived back in LA, they moved into a room at the Hollywood Melrose Hotel. A friend owned it, and hired Patsy as night manager. Another friend gave Jim a job as the front-door greeter at a dimly lit downtown bar and grill with a bright neon sign in front flashing SPORTS CLUB. The friend and proprietor was Stephen H. Welch, who went by Suey, the nickname he'd picked up hitching rides on the back of a Chinese laundry truck as a boy. It was in Akron in 1916 that Jim and Suey first met as football players in the Ohio League, Welch for the Akron Indians, Jim for the Canton Bulldogs. Their friendship rekindled when they both ended up in Los Angeles. Suey established the steadier career, emerging as southern California's leading fight promoter at the Olympic Auditorium and manager of several boxers, most prominent among them William Landon Jones, a black middleweight champ. Welch eventually left the boxing business after facing charges for tax evasion, but remained a popular figure in the sports world, and writers and athletes flocked to his bar and grill near Pershing Square.

One night not long after Jim's sixty-second birthday that May, Suey staged a party at his Sports Club to introduce Jim to his regulars. Paul Zimmerman, the *LA Times* journalist who had been skeptical about the Thunderbirds enterprise, handled the formal welcome and said he hoped Jim would hang around for a long time. "I can use it," Jim said of the job. He was always being invited to sports banquets, and felt honored to attend them, he said, but he could not eat honors. As a stream of well-wishers visited Jim's corner table and patted him on the back, Al Stump of *Sport* magazine took note of his appearance: the clean white shirt and thick arms, the reserved nature and "huge prognathous jaw." Viewing him was not like going to a freak show, Stump thought, but there was "still a touch of sadness" to the scene.

The party ebbed, the crowd filtered out, and Bob Myers of the AP sat alone with Jim. "Then was when he told of his dearest dream, his last dream, it seems," Myers wrote. "His life story, the story of a great athlete named Jim Thorpe, had been tied up in Hollywood film factories for 17 years. He wishes that story would be filmed. . . . His story and its reward is about all he has to leave as a heritage to his four sons. 'It would mean a lot,' he said, and looked into space. Only Jim knew whether he was looking into the future or the past." It was typical during that era for stories on Jim to omit mention of his three daughters.

GRANTLAND RICE DID not need much motivation to take up Jim's cause. Thorpe was a central part of his sports pantheon, the bond between them so strong that when Ralph Edwards chose Rice as the subject of his *This Is Your Life* show on NBC radio the week after Christmas 1948, Jim showed up as one of the surprise guests, along with the Four Horsemen of Notre Dame. A few months into 1949, Rice was back on the case. Perhaps he had received a letter from Patsy, or it might have been at the instigation of publicists at Warner Bros., or perhaps both. On June 21, 1949—after the collapse of the Thunderbirds and while the studio was trying to work out a new agreement with Jim and Patsy—Rice decided to assist Thorpe not only through his column but through private letters. From his office in midtown Manhattan, he wrote to Avery Brundage connecting the Thorpe movie to the fight for his Olympic restoration:

> *Dear Mr. Brundage,*
>
> *Warner Brothers is going to start shortly a story on Jim Thorpe's athletic career. I think the title of the picture is to be* The Red Son of Carlisle.
>
> *As part of the picture they are going to use the fact that Jim has always been so keenly interested in kids—in helping them, advising them etc. in their athletic work. This will be part of the theme of the story.*
>
> *It would, of course, be wonderful for old Jim if he could get those trophies back that he lost at Stockholm. I have talked with him and he seems to be more interested in that than anything else.*
>
> *I would appreciate it if you could let me know if there is any chance of having those trophies returned to him after this long spell of time, which*

as I recall, was over 35 years ago. I think it would be a very, very popular move of the AAU or the Olympic committee and I know what it would mean to Jim.

I would appreciate it if you would let me hear from you.

Grantland Rice

Brundage responded as he always did. Thorpe was a splendid athlete but had committed an Olympic sin that could not be rectified, he said. But this time Brundage offered a twist. He said the American Olympic Committee, the International Olympic Committee, and the Amateur Athletic Union all had no relevant standing to accede to Thorpe's request. It was up to the Swedish Organizing Committee, he said. "And I am very doubtful that they would have any interest in the subject." That would be news to the Swedes, who had been sympathetic to Jim's cause since the controversy first broke in January 1913, when they said the statute of limitations had passed and they had no intention of stripping Jim of his medals and trophies. That, the Swedes maintained, was for the Americans and IOC officials in Lausanne to decide.

It had been thirty-six years since Pop Warner essentially wrote Thorpe's confession letter to James E. Sullivan. Now Jim had another ghostwriter—his wife. Patsy was persistent in seeking absolution for her husband, always looking for a new angle and a new base of support. One day after Rice, Patsy typed a letter under his name to Jeremiah T. Mahoney, a long-standing member of the American Olympic Committee. She tried to hit every note in the emotional scale. As Warner did, Patsy had Jim play the naïve Indian role. The letter described him as "a simple Indian boy unversed as I was in the ways of the white man." It said he was "now an old man" who for decades had "brooded and wondered about my public disgrace." It said he wanted the vindication not for himself but for his "sons of which there are four." If Mahoney helped return the trophies, it would make "an old American Indian a happy man and when I go to the happy hunting ground my blessings will be upon you."

Patsy had no more luck than Grantland Rice.

At the time of the Rice-Brundage exchange, filming had just finished for *White Heat,* a gangster movie starring James Cagney as the murderous gang leader Cody Jarrett, who in the end is shot and dies in a conflagration atop one of those gas tanks that look like a giant golf ball on a tee. It was a Warner Bros. film, and the studio gave Jim an uncredited extra role as an inmate relaying a verbal message down a prison chow line. That did little to satisfy him—or Patsy, who seemed to the studio as combustible as that orb full of gasoline. Jim lamented to the Hollywood press that he was on the soundstage for *White Heat* when he read in a trade paper that Flaherty and Morrow had completed the screenplay for his movie. He was in the dark before that, he said. "Then the producer came to the set to offer me a technical advisor's job at $150 a week. I said no. I want to be in the picture reminiscing about my life, and for more than $150."

When Aline Mosby of the United Press came to interview Thorpe at the Sports Club one night, he sounded unenthusiastic about the latest movie news. "I hear they want Burt Lancaster for the picture," Jim said, glancing at a baseball game on the television set above the bar. "I don't think any Hollywood actor could play me." If Warner Bros. wanted a realistic portrayal, he suggested, they should hire Jack Jacobs for the part. Jacobs was an Oklahoma friend of Jim's, a Creek Indian from Holdenville who was a quarterback and kicker for the Green Bay Packers and had a cameo role in the 1948 football movie *Triple Threat.* If not Jacobs, Thorpe said, maybe Glenn Morris, who had won the decathlon gold medal at the 1936 Berlin Olympics and once played Tarzan in the movies.

"I'd like to be on hand to be sure every scene is correct," Jim said. "*The Babe Ruth Story* was awful. And *Pride of the Yankees,* well, Gary Cooper couldn't play baseball, could he?" As a film critic, Thorpe was on the mark. The Ruth movie, released a month before the Babe died, consistently landed on lists of the worst movies ever made, and although Cooper captured the essence of Lou Gehrig off the field, he knew nothing about baseball before he took the role in *Pride of the Yankees,* and it showed. Still, Jim underestimated the athleticism of Lancaster, who was in excellent shape and had once been a circus acrobat.

The movie was going forward now with or without him. On August 3, one day after Jim played film critic at Suey Welch's Sports Club, Major

P. L. McPherran, the public information officer at the Carlisle Barracks, caught a cross-country training flight with his assistant and several albums of old Carlisle Indian Industrial School photographs. The material was bound for Hollywood at the request of the head of the Warner Bros. research department. At the end of that same week, Everett Freeman, slated as producer and cowriter, announced in a memo to the studio bosses that Jim—meaning with Patsy's okay—had finally agreed to serve as a consultant for a price that "was quite a comedown from what the Thorpes were asking." It was, Freeman said, "a very difficult and trying procedure to reach any sort of agreement with the current Mrs. T and quite frankly I came close to shelving the whole project in exasperation. In any event, the matters have adjusted themselves and I hope all goes smoothly in the making of what should be an exciting and colorful picture."

Patsy never shied away from her role as the difficult wife demanding fair treatment for her husband. She fought hard for Jim, but in the end the Thorpes were overmatched by studio might. They had to take what they could get. It was Jim's life, but Warner's movie. Jim was paid $12,500—far less than Patsy demanded but more than the studio's original offer. It was not part of the deal, but as soon as Thorpe was in the fold, Warner publicists pushed the effort to restore his records, medals, and trophies. Playing off his fame was one thing; taking advice from him was another. He would be technical advisor in name only.

THORPE HAD A soft voice, throaty but not deep. When answering questions, his words eased out nasal and friendly, slow and hesitant, usually opening with a drawn-out "Well . . ." It was the plainspoken voice of the Plains. There was a touch of Will Rogers to it, and Dwight Eisenhower.

In the fall of 1949, radio listeners tuned to the CBS network could hear an evening show called *Mystery Voice.* Asking the public to identify a mystery guest through the sound of his or her voice was the latest national fad. From the Cactus Drive-In Theatre in Odessa, Texas, to the Berkshire Industrial Farm in Canaan, New York, companies and nonprofit enterprises were using mystery voice contests to attract audiences and customers and raise money. On the national show, the guests were public figures who offered obscure clues in their statements. One week it was Alf Landon, the former Republican presidential candidate. Another week it turned out to be Tommy Henrich, nearing the end of his career as first baseman for the New York Yankees. In late October, Walter Winchell had the scoop on the latest unidentified voice in his three-dots Broadway gossip column. ". . . Isn't the mystery voice—Jim Thorpe, famed Indian athlete?" And so it was.

One of Jim's clues led to the revelation that his eldest son, Phil, was stationed at Fort Monmouth, New Jersey, and playing on the army post's football team, the Signalmen, after returning from service overseas in Korea and Okinawa. At 174 pounds, Phil was less muscular than his father in his prime but looked like him and was the most athletic of the sons. He had played halfback at the Chilocco Indian School in 1942 and 1943 and briefly later at Northeastern State Teachers' College in Oklahoma before entering the army. At Fort Monmouth, he was so wary of receiving special treatment becuse of his lineage that he told coaches and teammates that he was only a distant relative of Jim's—until *Mystery Voice* blew his cover.

Like his father before him, Phil hoped to become a coach. At Okinawa, he had been the player-coach for the Signal Corps team, and on his way to Fort Monmouth he had stopped in Los Angeles to see his family. While there, he talked to his father about the game. Jim passed along some of the lessons he had learned from Pop Warner. Speed and power were important, but so too was deception. The way to become polished and proficient was to practice every phase of the game. The best athletes were all-arounders. For Phil, that meant joining the post's basketball team when the football season ended. And then moving on to his next assignment, a place with special resonance in the Thorpe family. Nearly fifty years after his father had first stepped foot there, Phil was going to train at Carlisle Barracks.

The past circled back to Jim Thorpe as the first half of the twentieth century ended. Who had been the best athlete over that span? The answer was Thorpe, again and again. First the Touchdown Club in Washington, D.C., presented Jim a scroll at its annual winter banquet naming him America's Greatest Athlete. Then the Associated Press, after polling 391 sportswriter and broadcasters, declared Thorpe "the No. 1 gridiron performer of the last 50 years," as he far outpaced Red Grange and Bronko Nagurski, the only other players in double figures in the voting, followed by Ernie Nevers, Sammy Baugh, Don Hutson, and George Gipp (who had four votes). When the same electorate chose the greatest track athlete of the half-century, Thorpe finished second behind Jesse Owens. More bests were named in succession in baseball, boxing, basketball, golf, tennis, swimming, and horse racing—until on February 11, 1950, the AP announced the ultimate crown.

The group of fifty-six athletes who received at least one vote as Greatest Athlete of the Half-Century included Willie Hoppe in billiards and Dave Freeman in badminton, but the top eleven formed a gallery of major sports legends. At eleventh came the electric Jackie Robinson, in his third year as the pioneer of black players in the major leagues, with 2 first-place votes and 24 total points. Next, counting down, came Nagurski at tenth, then Lou Gehrig, Owens, Grange, Joe Louis, and Bobby Jones, none of whom reached a hundred votes. For the top four, the numbers jumped exponentially. Ty Cobb had 11 first-place votes and 148 points for fourth. Jack Dempsey claimed 19 first-place votes and 246 total points for third. Babe Ruth had 86 first-place votes and 539 total points for second.

All overshadowed by the colossus. Jim Thorpe finished with 252 first-place votes and 875 total points.

It was a remarkable run, and Jim was "polite and patient" as he accepted the honor and his deeds were recounted: All-American football player. Olympic track champion. Major leaguer. Founding president of the NFL. But as he once said, banquets and honors could not pay the rent. "My wife and I live wherever we find a nail to hang our clothes," he told reporters at the Touchdown Club. Maybe the notice would help him get back his Olympic medals, he said, but he still had trouble persuading the man who mattered most. "That Avery Brundage . . . is just a stuffed shirt. He acknowledges that I was the greatest American athlete, so he says why do I need the medals to prove it?"

Patsy was with him on the East Coast when the other honors came his way as greatest ever at football and all-around. Jim called her his business manager, secretary, and treasurer. "She's sometimes too aggressive for me," he said. "But she had been good for me. We Indians have never been known for our business ability. She has that."

For her part, Patsy said she knew Jim better than anyone. They had been married for only five years, but she had first met him in a bar in Illinois, more than two decades earlier when he was playing football in Rock Island. Back then, she said, she thought: " 'He's the ugliest man I've ever seen. He walks like an ape.' Now, I'm his wife and you better not tell me he's ugly. Not pretty, maybe, but handsome, in a mannish sort of way." Her mission now was to transform all the midcentury honors into money. She said her new goal was to make Jim a million dollars. "Jim is the greatest athlete in the world, but he needs someone to talk for him and see that he gets what is coming to him," she told reporters in early March 1950, when she and Jim, always looking for that nail on which to hang their clothes, were making the Belvedere Hotel their New York headquarters. "From now on, I'm doing the talking."

Jim sat back and smiled as she explained that he was overly generous and needed her toughness. "The other day he got a call from a person he has known for years. He wanted Jim to come to his town and tell of some of his experiences. Jim said he would be glad to do it. Then I got on the phone. I asked how much they planned to pay Jim. The reply was, all expenses of course. I said Jim's fee is five hundred dollars and expenses and that was as low as that only because of Jim's friendship with him. Anyone who now wants Jim Thorpe to give a talk will have to meet a thousand dollar fee and expenses. He's worth every penny."

As Patsy issued that edict, Jim took out a red matchbook that read "Jim Thorpe, World's Greatest Athlete," and autographed it for a fan named Elwood C. Waters of Erie, Pennsylvania.

Over the years, journalists often portrayed Thorpe as down and out, a shadow of his once grand self, working his way back to a better life from the bottom he hit digging ditches in Los Angeles during the depths of the Depression. It was an understandable if inadequate depiction. The arc of his life after his prime athletic years was less a series of jagged ups and downs than an unceasing exertion against the tide. He had launched so many endeavors, in and out of sports, always temporary, always on the move. Hollywood extra. Indian organizer. Seaman. Bar greeter. Banquet speaker. Parks employee. Sports entrepreneur with the Tampa Cardinals in football, the World Famous Indians in basketball, Harjo's Indians in baseball, Jim Thorpe's Thunderbirds in women's softball. Patsy had many more plans for Jim, ranging from a national television show to an agreement to return to pro football with the Philadelphia Eagles to serving as a pro wrestling manager—all, they hoped, leading to the ultimate goal of fulfilling Jim's long-held dream of running the Thunderbird fishing and hunting lodge along Florida's Indian River. As usual, most of it would never happen.

In the first step of her "make a million" campaign, Patsy signed a three-month contract for Jim to make personal appearances while serving as manager for Suni (or Sunny) War Cloud, a 225-pound professional wrestler from the Blackfeet nation who at age twenty-five had just won an all-Indian tournament in Montana and was known for his strong legs and "Indian deathlock." War Cloud's other name was Joe Chorre, and his mother, Marie Chorre, was an actress who had worked with Thorpe pushing for Indian rights in Hollywood. The deal—Patsy said it was considerable, a guarantee of $500 a week, plus expenses—was consummated in Buffalo with matchmaker Ed Don George, a former world champ who now ran the National Wrestling Federation. With Thorpe appearing at his side, if not in the ring, "Chief" War Cloud would wrestle at arenas and temples from Buffalo to Syracuse to Binghamton to Albany as the good guy in Virtue versus Villainy affairs with fellow grapplers Ali Baba, Goon Henry, Farmer Jake, Laverne Baxter, Kay Bell, Seely Samara, the Green Hornet, and Sky High Lee. War Cloud was usually in the undercard, but he and Thorpe were hard to miss as they made their walk to the ring in headdresses and full Indian regalia, with War Cloud entering with a whooping war dance.

Jim and War Cloud traveled by train from town to town. One night in late March, when they reached Union Station in Albany for a match in nearby Troy the next day against Winnipeg's Tex McLarty, a man approached and was about to introduce himself. No need.

"Why, Mike Regan, you old so and so," Thorpe said, recognizing him immediately.

"I didn't think you'd remember me," said Regan. "Thirty-two years is a long time."

Regan had recently retired from General Electric. In 1917, he and Jim had been teammates on the Cincinnati Reds and roomed together on the road. He'd won eleven games that year, while Jim batted .247 before Christy Mathewson shipped him back to the Giants near the end of the season.

"Us bushers never forget each other," said Jim.

Among his talents, he had a knack for remembering names and faces from the past. With his life, there were a lot of them.

ON MARCH 23, while Patsy and Jim were in Buffalo, a letter reached them from Japan. The envelope said it was from Mrs. FW Seely, Hdqrs, 8th Army Engineer SHC, APO 343 Carte Postmaster, SF, California. This was Grace, the youngest of the three Thorpe daughters. Now almost thirty, Grace had last spent any significant time with her father in 1943, when they both held jobs at the Ford plant in Detroit. After that, she had enlisted in the Women's Army Corps and served overseas in New Guinea, the Philippines, and Japan before receiving an honorable discharge and staying in Japan to work as a civilian recruiter at General Douglas MacArthur's headquarters. While in Tokyo, in 1946, she married Fred W. Seely, an army lieutenant. They now had two young children, Jim's grandchildren, Dagmar and Paul. Grace's letter said the family was returning to the States in April by way of San Francisco, on their way to settle down in Pearl River, New York.

When the letter arrived, Jim was in Syracuse with War Cloud, so Patsy wrote the response. She had never met Grace, but the relationship felt like a clean slate, with none of the evil-stepmother sensibility of her dealings with Jim's sons. Time and distance made the difference. For Grace, Patsy was one stepmother removed. She had already gone through the Freeda period, and her mother had long since remarried. Patsy's letter was newsy and revealing, as though they were old friends. She was eager, she wrote, "to know you and your lovely family."

She said she had returned to southern California briefly in February but "had no sooner gotten a deep breath when Warner Bros. sent me east to obtain releases for them." As part of the movie deal, Jim was supposed to get releases from old Carlisle friends and teammates who might be portrayed in the picture—all, that is, except Iva, who was approached separately by the studio and signed the release on the condition that she would be identified as Margaret.

Gus Welch, Albert Exendine, Bill Newashe, Frank Mt. Pleasant, Pete Calac, Joe Guyon—she had them all, Patsy said, except Lewis Tewanima, the Hopi runner and Jim's 1912 Olympic teammate. "I located him by long distance after calling all over the country, in the Hopi Indian reservation at Keams Canyon Arizona just outside Ludlow. The poor guy is up there herding sheep and cannot speak English," Patsy wrote. "I tried to talk through an interpreter but that was no good, so I sent him the releases in care of the Indian office. He refuses to sign. He is afraid of the white man's legal terms I suppose, and I do not blame him. So I must on my return trip get off the train at Ludlow, hire a taxi and go up in to the reservation, run him down and try to make him understand what it is all about. Pray for me."

She talked about Jim's job managing War Cloud and that they had also lined up a position in public relations for the NFL's Eagles. "I have been determined to get Jim back in the limelight and damned if I haven't made it," Patsy boasted. "But I work on it 24 hours a day. I have literally kicked doors in all over the country and Jim Thorpe will be the greatest thing in the sports world from now on. Of course, you know how lazy he is. I have to dynamite him every so often and ride herd on him constantly." Sometimes, she admitted, she was too aggressive for her own good. "I made the statement, idly, that I was going to make a million dollars for Jim, to an AP man in Manhattan, the so and so put it over an AP release and it went all over the country. Now I've got to do it."

Patsy said she would stay in Buffalo through a March of Champions banquet honoring Jim at the end of March, then take the train west to find Tewanima and settle a few things in Los Angeles. Grace could reach Jim by writing to the Bellevue Stratford Hotel in Philadelphia or the Hollywood Melrose Hotel. That was their permanent address, or the closest thing to one, although she did not think she and Jim would return there permanently. "I wouldn't live in California again if they gave me the entire state," she wrote. "I detest the phonies out there."

Especially at the movie studio. "I have been fighting with Warner Bros. almost a year, just about the time I feel a little good toward them they pull another phony on me and I blow my cork again."

Still, the movie was on track. On the first of June, Patsy told Grace, Jim would return to Hollywood to serve as technical advisor for the story of his life.

31

"Have You Seen the Movie?"

FOR TWENTY YEARS, JIM THORPE WAITED ANXIOUSLY FOR Hollywood to make a movie about his life. When it finally happened, the film offered a largely sympathetic story, star power, decent acting, and several evocative scenes of his rise, fall, and attempt at resurrection. Biographical pictures are fictionalized accounts, not documentaries, and should be regarded on those terms, even if they try to hew closely to facts and chronology, which this film did not. But along with its conflations, omissions, and inaccuracies of detail, *Jim Thorpe—All-American* was misguided in a more important way, reinforcing the stereotypes of a white perspective on an Indian's life. Thorpe was the main character, the fallen hero, but the story was told not through his eyes but from the perspective of the wise narrator, Pop Warner, Jim's old coach and supposed savior. The implication was that if only Thorpe had taken Pop's advice, stopped brooding about his fate, and fully integrated himself into white society, he would not have suffered the way he did. *Lo, the poor Indian!*

The first mistake was the glorification of Warner, glossing over Pop's self-serving cover-up when Jim lost the Olympic medals, the fact that as football coach he professionalized his supposedly amateur Carlisle team, and the student rebellion against his coaching methods that led to his departure from the Indian school. Veteran supporting actor Charles Bickford captured Pop as the character was presented to him; the problem was not in his performance but in the impressions the screenplay had him convey. The real-life Warner would not allow the film to use his character as the storyteller until he saw the script, and he would have declined had it made him out to be less than a noble figure. The portrayal also reflected a larger issue: what happens when a film about an American Indian, even if well-intentioned, is filtered through the comprehensive whiteness of its creative team and cast.

Thorpe was listed twice in the credits. The Russell Birdwell as-told-to autobiography was credited as source material "in collaboration with Jim Thorpe." And Jim was credited separately as technical advisor. In the end, the Birdwell material was largely ignored and Jim's technical advice was rarely called upon. He spent several weeks gathering material he hoped might be used in the movie, but little if any of it was. He was treated more as a nuisance than a helpful guide into his own life, and at one point was kept away from the set.

The screenwriters, Doug Morrow and Everett Freeman, who was also the producer, and the director, Michael Curtiz, struggled with the central themes of the movie. Was the story tragic or uplifting? Jim performed many heroic athletic feats, but what should they do with the rest of his difficult life? Some members of the production team were dismissive of him, turned off by his and Patsy's demands. Were they ennobling a figure who did not deserve the hero's treatment? In an internal memo to Steve Trilling, a top Warner Bros. official, Morrow addressed those feelings and described how he dealt with his own ambivalence.

> You said something yesterday about Jim still being a bum. Maybe he is. I don't know. All I know is that from the beginning in my approach to this picture I have tried to keep as uncynical about Jim as possible and have kept my mind free of the thought that he might still be a bum. The audience doesn't know what we know concerning his intimate personal life. They will only know what we tell them. And we can only tell them something effectively if we ourselves assume even temporarily a greater sincerity of feeling regarding the fictitious construction in the second part of the story. We must make ourselves believe if we have any hope of making the audience believe it. After all, we are making a motion picture, not writing history.

Morrow was on the sympathetic side of that debate. But during a time when Hollywood was accustomed to appropriating Indianness, little consideration was given to the idea that Thorpe's tribulations might be dealt with more honestly if his life were considered from an Indian point of view. The result was an uneven mix of harsh reality and overwrought sentimentalism—all variations of the vanishing Indian overtaken by the modern world.

Thorpe spent years lobbying for Native American rights in Hollywood, pushing the studios to hire Indians to play Indians. Now, for his own movie, he was portrayed by two white actors. As a boy in the opening scenes, Jim was played by Billy Gray, a prolific child actor who a few years later would be cast as the son, Bud, in television's *Father Knows Best.* For the rest of the movie, playing Thorpe from age seventeen on was Burt Lancaster, a silver screen star since his breakout role in 1946 as Swede, the troubled boxer executed by mobsters in *The Killers.* Gray had high cheekbones and Lancaster had deep-set eyes, but that was the extent of their Indianness. For their roles as Jim Thorpe, their faces were darkened with greasepaint and Max Factor's Pan-Cake makeup and their hair dyed black.

Jim wanted a Native American to play him, even proposing his eldest son, Phil, who looked like his father and was athletic but whose acting experience was limited to a few parts as an extra. In that era of dominant studios and a star system, without an actor of marquee stature the movie would never be made. As a New Yorker, Lancaster did not attempt to assume Thorpe's soft Oklahoma drawl, and even with makeup looked nothing like Jim, his body too angular, his face too sharp, his hair too curly despite efforts to straighten it for the filming. But he was well cast in other respects. Even at age thirty-six, he was fit and athletic enough to be believable in the football and track-and-field scenes, and Lancaster wisely maintained that "a faithful interpretation of Thorpe's life is much more important than being a facial copy of him." He infused the part with his liberal sensibility, sympathetic to minorities, underdogs, and outcasts. In his brief scenes as young Jim, Billy Gray was not required to consider the social context. He had never heard of Jim Thorpe when he got the part and was told nothing about him during the production. "I was just playing an Indian kid," he said.

The third central character, Jim's sweetheart and first wife, Iva, was played by actress Phyllis Thaxter, who made a career in the role of a loving, patient wife. In the film, at the real Iva's insistence, the character was identified only as Margaret Miller, not Iva, and everything about her relationship with Jim was wildly off chronologically, including when she discovered that she was white, not Indian. The movie also used three composites as Jim's friends at the Carlisle Indian Industrial School, and two of the three were played by white actors. A character named Peter Allendine, meant to resemble Albert Exendine, was played by Steve Cochran, a handsomely slick actor and Wyoming cowboy who was often cast as a villain, including as a psychotic mobster in *White Heat*, the Cagney film in which Thorpe was an extra. Dick Wesson, a comedian from Boston, was cast in the role of Ed Guyac, a name that merged Pete Calac and Joe Guyon, although the fictitious Guyac was a bookish water boy rather than a star football player, as Calac and Guyon were.

The third Carlisle student role, as Little Boy Who Walk Like Bear, went to Jack Bighead, a twenty-year-old Yuchi Indian from Oklahoma who was playing football at Pepperdine University. In the film, he was asked to portray Little Boy in dime story Indian fashion, speaking in broken sentences and saying "How" as a greeting. The screenwriters did give him the most pro-Indian statement in the movie. In his dorm room with Thorpe and Guyac, he was reading a history book and found it interesting that "when white man licks Indian it is great battle; Indian licks white man it's a massacre." One other Native American had a brief speaking role. Joe Chorre, also known as Suni War Cloud, the professional wrestler Jim had been managing, was cast as Wally Denny of the Oneida Nation, a Carlisle alumnus who served as Pop Warner's assistant. Patsy Thorpe, who brought Jim and War Cloud together for their wrestling enterprise, likely orchestrated that casting and took a cut.

• • •

IN EARLY AUGUST 1950, the word rippled through Muskogee, Oklahoma: Hollywood was coming to shoot a movie. Even before the news was announced, the front desk at the ten-story Severs Hotel on North State Street deduced what was up when Warner Bros. called to reserve eighty rooms from August 24 to September 7. Bacone College, located on the edge of town along the old King's Trail cattle route running from Texas to Canada, had been chosen as the site for the Carlisle scenes. Soon the studio was rearranging things at Bacone, moving the goalposts at the stadium from north-south to east-west for better shots and constructing an old-style track to resemble Indian Field at Carlisle. The local chamber of commerce announced that Warner Bros. needed as many as a thousand local Indians, students and townsfolk, to serve as extras and was also looking for four old-fashioned buggies.

In preparation for the location shoot, a caravan of five trucks arrived from Los Angeles hauling a portable costume department with two thousand outfits, from Carlisle cadet uniforms to feathered Indian headdresses and moccasins to track and football uniforms. Rawlings Sporting Goods made throwback uniforms to fit Thorpe's era. The company had records of Jim's baseball history going back to his first minor league days with the Rocky Mount Railroaders, and even had his measurements: size 44 shirt, 31-inch waist, number 10 shoe, and 7⅜ths cap size. It was easier to round up the buggies from the local citizenry than authentic Indian dress. Many of the students had never worn moccasins; some young women would complain that the soft shoes hurt their feet. "I'm not Pocahontas," one said. "I'm used to high heels."

Bacone College (pronounced "bay-cone") was almost as old as Carlisle, founded in 1880 as a private Christian school for Indian students from the Cherokee nation whose families had been forced from North Carolina to Oklahoma decades earlier along the Trail of Tears. By 1950 its student population was diverse, representing forty tribes, and it was more of a college academically than Carlisle had ever been. The school was chosen for the Thorpe movie after an intense lobbying campaign by its president, Dr. Francis Thompson, and the Muskogee business community. An advance team led by director Curtiz visited Oklahoma and decided on the school because of its classic campus feel, with neocolonial architecture and verdant landscape.

Curtiz was a veteran director who had emigrated from Hungary in 1926 at age thirty-nine and had a prolific if underrated career at Warner Bros. Of the scores of films he directed, many were forgotten but some ranked among Hollywood's most honored classics, notably *Casablanca* for which he won the Oscar for best director in 1944. His brusque personality combined with his heavy Eastern European accent often frustrated actors. "Do what I meant, not what I said," Billy Gray remembered the director instructing him, repeating a phrase often heard on any Curtiz set. But while other directors had no interest in Thorpe, Curtiz was attracted to the story of an underdog. As British film historian Peter Wollen wrote, Curtiz films often dealt with "injustice, oppression, entrapment, displacement, and exile." In various ways during his life, Thorpe dealt with all of those as well.

Whether Curtiz and Thorpe had ever spoken before is unclear, but Jim had been on his set as an extra at least once—fifteen years earlier in *Captain Blood,* the 1935 action drama starring Errol Flynn. In promoting the Thorpe production, studio publicists concocted a story that the relationship between director and subject went back to the 1912 Olympics and that Curtiz had been in Stockholm as a member of the Hungarian fencing team. Not true. Hungary had an excellent fencing team that year that won three gold medals, but Curtiz was not on it, although he became such an exercise fanatic that he was called Iron Mike.

The cast and crew descended on Muskogee in time for the location shoot to begin on Friday, August 25. A stickler for preparation, Curtiz was already there when a chartered plane brought in most of the ensemble a day earlier. Lancaster arrived separately on a commercial airliner and Bickford rode in by train. "This will be one of the big pictures of the year because it has a good story and good script and sports is a subject that everyone is interested in," Bickford declared as photographers snapped him unpacking his suitcase at the Severs Hotel. Of his own role he added: "Pop Warner was a great gentleman. It will be a fine part."

To absorb the role of Thorpe, the demands on Lancaster were as physical as emotional. He had a posse of trainers: Jess Hill, the track coach at Southern Cal for track sequences; Bill Spaulding, a former UCLA football coach for football scenes; and Mushy Callahan, a stuntman and boxing trainer with his ever-present diamond-studded belt, to help work the star into fighting shape. Al Lawrence, an all-around track star at USC, came in as a double for a few difficult events, including the pole vault, but the rest was Lancaster. "I was in really wonderful condition in those days," he said later. "I did roadwork every single day for three solid weeks. I learned to run, learned to hurdle, not that I was particularly good, but I mean I was able to put the shot, the discus and the javelin very well, that is, with form. You know, we could trick the distances. All I had to do was look pretty good doing it. . . ."

Thorpe was also on hand part of the time to offer pointers on how to perform a drop-kick, though Curtiz and his crew found him a nuisance and arranged for him to leave early. At Patsy's urging, Jim came to Bacone with a slightly rejiggered mug after undergoing facial surgery at the hands of Dr. Robert Alan Franklyn, one of Hollywood's busiest plastic surgeons. It was said to be a refreshing up in preparation for movie publicity. Unlike a woman named Bunny, another of Franklyn's customers, Jim did not "storm in demanding an Ingrid Bergman nose," though it would take another operation before Patsy was satisfied with the results.

Lancaster had been training since six thirty on the morning filming began, running laps on the Bacone track and rounding the bases of the school ballfield. Callahan, prone to the hyperbole of the boxing world, called him "one of the finest natural-born athletes I've ever seen." By the time the star reached the set, a throng of goggle-eyed fans was cataloguing his every move. Between scenes, he reclined on the grass, trying to find a cool spot away from the blazing Oklahoma sun. A murmur of delight passed through the crowd every time he agreed to rise from the shadows to pose for photos. That was easy compared to the athletic scenes, an arduous enough assignment made more difficult by the fact that he and the director rarely seemed in sync. For the action scenes, Curtiz often ordered Lancaster to race down the track one more time for a better shot and once had him repeat a football run fourteen times. For the emotional scenes,

Lancaster was the one asking for another take with the director arguing that what they had was sufficient. In both cases, the one who wanted more takes won the argument.

More than half the faculty members at Bacone were new that year, arriving at the same time as the Hollywood contingent. Mrs. Dwight D. Saunders, wife of a new history professor, described the scene in a letter that made its way to the college archives: "Our first impression of the campus was a hubbub of activity—Indians in native dress, tepees, tom-toms, and young braves dancing in many rhythms. If we were to prepare these young aborigines for life in a white man's world, we'd have, we felt, a job on our hands. Imagine our surprise to learn the tepees, costumes and tom-toms were all imported from Hollywood. The film *Jim Thorpe—All-American* was being made on the Bacone campus. Our students, we discovered, dress and behave like college students everywhere."

Among those watching the filming were Lancaster's father, James, a retired postal worker, and Thorpe's old Carlisle teammate Albert Exendine. In many ways, Exendine had lived the life to which Jim aspired. He was sixty-six now, settled in Stillwell after a long coaching career that had taken him from Otterbein to Georgetown, Washington State, Occidental, Northeast Oklahoma, and Oklahoma A&M. With his law degree, he had also worked on indigenous issues for the Bureau of Indian Affairs. He was in Muskogee partly as a fan, but also to see how the movie presented a modern Indian. The character supposedly based on him, Pete Allendine, was portrayed by Steve Cochran more as a Southern Cal frat boy than as a son of the Delaware nation from Indian Territory. Cochran, a notorious carouser, cut a wide swath through Muskogee but failed to make as deep an impression as his dog, Tchaikovsky, a stringy-haired mutt who was on the loose during the location shoot, roaming backstreets into the night.

As the Thorpe movie was being filmed in Oklahoma, the National Congress of American Indians convened in Bellingham, Washington. This was the seventh convention of the congress, formed in 1944 to lobby the federal government for tribal and reservation rights. Like the Society of American Indians earlier in the century, the NCAI was a pan-Indian organization comprising mostly professionals who had been educated at Indian boarding schools, but the congress was more activist-oriented, shifting the focus from surviving through assimilation to preserving indigenous cultures and gaining power through unity.

The first secretary-treasurer of the congress was one of Jim's strongest proponents, D. M. Madrano, a Caddo chief who during two terms in the Oklahoma legislature had sponsored bills calling for the restoration of Thorpe's Olympic medals and trophies. In Bellingham, he pushed the same cause, leading the way for passage of a resolution to be sent to Avery Brundage on Jim's behalf. Also during that convention, the congress called for the reworking of high school history books to present Indians in a more favorable light and condemned Hollywood films that pictured Indians as villains. Those stereotypes were so imbedded in white culture that an Associated Press account of the convention opened with the phrase "The Indians are going on the warpath today. . . ."

As the location shooting in Muskogee neared an end, the cast and crew took up a collection to fund six scholarships for Bacone College. Curtiz said he was impressed by the "quiet, spiritual" approach at the school and described its sensibility as "truly an American one." He also said that before returning to Hollywood he would take an hour's drive north to Claremore to examine the home turf of Will Rogers, the humorist who was to be the subject of his next biographical film. Lancaster was taking his family on a vacation to Italy. Jim, back in Los Angeles with his new face, appeared at the annual fall pigskin preview luncheon of the LA Press Club as the guest of Warner Bros. publicist Ralph Huston "to take a bow as ballyhoo for his film."

JIM THORPE—ALL AMERICAN opens newsreel-style in the grainy black-and-white of a packed banquet room in Oklahoma City. The state's elite are gathered to pay tribute to an Oklahoma native son. Roy Turner, the governor, is speaking at the dais. It really is Roy Turner, not an actor, and he really is governor, placing the scene in the present, meaning 1950. In what for a politician would be considered an uncommon moment of modesty, the governor says he is not the right person to complete the introduction and hands it off to "one of the immortals in the world of sports—Pop Warner." Pop then strides to the microphone. Documentary fades, movie-making begins. It is Charles Bickford playing Pop. In his deep narrator's voice, he tells the audience of a boy who roamed the woods and didn't like school—"that frightening institution of the white man's world." The rhythmic minor chords of what is meant to be Indian music rise behind his words.

Pop the narrator recounts one of the original Thorpe fables: the time his father took him by horse and wagon to school fifteen miles from home and Jim, rather than going inside the school, turned and ran homeward, taking a shortcut and beating his father to their cabin. As Warner talks of a boy who ran "with the grace of a wild deer," we see Jim sprinting through the countryside, leaping ditches and hurdling fences. Billy Gray plays young Jim, but this is not him. "I thought I was a pretty good runner, but they hired a double for that," Gray said more than seventy years later. "I took offense at that. I think they were afraid I'd get hurt." As Jim reaches his family ranch, the shot requires a willing suspension of disbelief. This is supposed to be the cabin above the banks of the North Canadian River in central Oklahoma, but there is a mountain range in the background. There are no mountains in central Oklahoma. It was filmed at a movie ranch in the foothills of the Santa Susana Mountains on the northwest rim of Los Angeles.

Before viewers see the cabin, Jim encounters his stoic grandmother sitting outside a tepee in the dirt yard. The Sac and Fox were Algonquin Woodland Indians, not Plains Indians. Tepees were not part of their culture. A Thorpe grandmother in the old days might have lived in a lodge or wigwam, but not a tepee.

Jim's parents then discuss the proper punishment for his running from school. His mother, Charlotte, hands Hiram a belt and directs him to whip Jim, but Hiram is softhearted and cannot do it. The real Hiram was a tough-talking, hard-drinking Indian hombre. The screenwriters make him out to a be an Indian version of their Pop Warner, offering sage advice, telling Jim he can either sit around wrapped in a blanket or he can try to make something of himself. "You must change for your own good," Hiram says. Suddenly Jim is off to the Carlisle Indian School.

In fact, Charlotte was dead by the time Jim left for Carlisle and he was sent there in part because Hiram's new wife didn't want him around.

In the first scene at Carlisle, here comes Burt Lancaster, age thirty-six, playing seventeen-year-old Jim, dressed in a business suit and toting a suitcase amid a throng of Indians making the pilgrimage on foot and in wagons. As they move toward the school's front gate, Warner the narrator proclaims them "all eager to prepare themselves for a new life." A harmonizing chorus of "Carlisle, Our Carlisle" plays in the background, the school song whose lyrics were penned by Pop Warner. It is a rosy perspective. In fact, not all students came eagerly or voluntarily; a few were kidnapped and shipped there, while many were compelled to attend as part of the government's effort to drain the Indianness out of them. And Jim arrived not at the start of a fall semester but alone by train on a drizzly February night. In the movie, his first encounter on campus is with a huddle of cocky upperclassmen wearing big C letter sweaters, looking like old chaps, fraternity boys out of the Ivy League or Southern Cal. The Peter Allendine character asks Jim if he speaks Indian, and if so whether he can recite the Gettysburg Address in Indian. Jim's answer—no—is met with approval. "Good, we only speak English here," Allendine says, an exchange meant to accentuate the benefits of immersive assimilation.

Jim is introduced as a freshman who struggles to study, doesn't want to be at school, and is so restless he finds comfort only in running. The most preposterous scene in the film has him rousing from bed and fleeing from his dormitory room in wingtips, dress pants, and white shirt, sprinting like a madman down the school paths and out to the athletic track, where Pop is timing a practice heat in the 220-yard dash—and here comes Jim in street clothes joining the field, whizzing past the rest of the runners, and racing beyond the finish line and out of the frame. "Either I need a new watch or we need a new runner," Warner exclaims in disbelief.

Everything that happens at Carlisle after that is a mix of compression, hyperbole, and myth. Jim is the athletic superman, but Pop Warner is hero and wise man. When Jim complains that things don't go his way because he is an Indian, Pop says that's just another hurdle to get over. When Jim is about to lose his Olympic medals because of his experience playing in the Eastern Carolina League (a period barely hinted at and not shown), it is Pop who rises fearlessly to his defense. "You mustn't take these medals away from him. You mustn't," Warner is seen telling a ruling body of amateur officials. When one says ignorance is no excuse, Pop replies that in this case "ignorance *is* an excuse." The Indian athletes at Carlisle have all expenses paid at school, he argues, but does that make them pros? Jim played one year of summer baseball for expenses, does that make him a pro? An interesting argument, but not one Warner raised at the time. It was Pop who feigned ignorance then, not just for Thorpe but more pressingly for himself, claiming he was clueless about what Jim was doing in Rocky Mount and Fayetteville (for two summers, not one).

His major league career is defined by one short scene in which the Giants' manager, McGraw, chews him out for not following a sign and rapping out a base hit instead of bunting as he was supposed to. "It's a team game," the Little Napoleon tells Thorpe, as though the team concept was alien to an Indian and more illustrative of his up-and-down baseball career than McGraw's reluctance to play him or Jim's troubles hitting the curveball.

Jim heads to Ohio to play pro football, bringing along his wife and young son, Jim Jr. He is a football whirlwind, a pioneer of the pro game, but Warner the narrator explains that "even football took second place to his son." No doubt Jim cherished his son; there is no evidence he would leave practices to be with him, as the movie implies. This uncommon devotion is presented for a reason—as the movie's Rosebud moment that would explain Jim's decline and fall after Junior's death.

The death scene is fabricated. In real life, Jim Jr. was three years old in 1918 when he fell ill as the family, which by then included a baby sister, Gail, was driving to Oklahoma from New York after the baseball season had been curtailed due to the influenza pandemic. At their home in Yale, Jim and Iva held their son through the night until he died, likely from the flu. But the movie makes Jim Jr. out to be seven or eight. There is no Gail, just as there would be no other Thorpe daughters, sons, or new wives in the entire film. The movie family is limited to Jim, Margaret, and the one ill-fated son. When Junior dies, Jim is placed far from the scene. The movie has him in Chicago, happily posing for the press as he leaves the team hotel for the stadium, and then after the game click-cleating into the locker room, where he is handed a telegram. He looks at it in shock, crumples it, and throws it to the floor, just before the team's irate coach enters and chews out the team, including Jim, for playing poorly. In a rage, Jim attacks the coach until a teammate unfolds the telegram. GOD TOOK YOUR SON THIS EVENING, it reads.

As Jim's life tumbles downward, Pop reemerges in the role of savior. He finds Jim in the dank basement dressing room of a decrepit ballroom taking off the greasepaint makeup of an Indian chief. So inept at life he couldn't even play that role, he has just been fired as the Indian emcee of a Depression-era dance marathon. Pop is there to lift him out of self-pity. Warner is now head coach at Stanford and offers Jim a job as an assistant. "Forget it, Pop," Jim says, too proud to take help from his mentor. He wants Pop to leave. "Nice seeing you," he says. Frustrated, Pop responds that it was not nice seeing Jim, then delivers a lecture of tough love. "Somewhere along the line you went completely haywire, picked up the idea that the world owed you something," he tells Jim. "Well, it doesn't owe you anything. So you've had some tough ones. You've been kicked around. They took your medals away from you. So what? All I can say is that when the real battle sounded, the great Jim Thorpe turned out to be a powder puff!"

Before leaving, Pop hands Jim a ticket to the opening ceremonies of the 1932 Summer Olympics in Los Angeles. Jim rips the ticket and throws it to the floor, but later tapes the torn pieces together and shows up at the Coliseum, settling in the seat next to Pop. When the U.S. team marches in, Warner joins the crowd in enthusiastic applause. Jim sits stone-faced. The movie switches to newsreel briefly as Vice President Charles Curtis officially opens the games. Pop turns to Jim and says, "The announcer forgot to announce one thing, or maybe didn't find it necessary. Charles Curtis, Indian."

In fact, it was Vice President Curtis who provided the tickets for Jim to attend the games. Pop had nothing to do with it. But altering the reality allows the film to deliver Pop's message: There is an Indian, Curtis, who so successfully integrated into the highest rungs of white society that his race need not be mentioned. You could have accomplished the same, so quit feeling sorry for yourself and your people. The scene ends with Jim sitting alone in the Coliseum, pondering his life as words of wisdom from his father and Pop come back to him. If only Jim had listened. What happened to him was all his fault. One final pounding home of the theme of self-responsibility and the fallacy of structural unfairness.

The movie's two final scenes yank Jim back from the abyss. In the first, he is a truck driver hauling freight down a road in the gritty industrial edge of Los Angeles. Several boys are playing football in a nearby railyard, huge gas storage tanks looming behind them. Their football rolls into the road and under Jim's truck, and is flattened. The boys are lamenting its demise, when Jim appears with a new football. He gives them instructions on how to tackle. They have no idea who he is but are impressed that he knows so much about the game. They ask him to coach. *Coach.* He likes the sound of it, steps back, and boots the ball; the camera follows it soaring into the air, then pans back to look down at him from high above.

The story could have ended there. Curtiz considered it a poetic closing shot. Lancaster thought it was too sappy, what he later called "a cockamamie idea" that unnecessarily romanticized Jim when "his accomplishments [spoke] for themselves." But the studio bosses wanted even one more scene to wrap up a happy ending. It went back to the beginning, to the banquet hall in Oklahoma City with the elite gathered to honor the state's favorite son. The last words are given not to Jim, but to Pop Warner, speaking from the dais: "And so Jim found himself and was again on the true path, the bright path, teaching and helping young people everywhere. This was his greatest victory."

BEFORE THE MOVIE came out, Jim underwent his second facelift. He was back to his itinerant ways, traveling the country delivering speeches and signing autographs. When he was in New York, he stayed with William Thourlby, his quasi-son Buddy Thorpe, in a cold-water flat on West Fifty-Eighth Street. Thourlby later said that Jim was no longer drinking and that one of his favorite pastimes was watching cowboy and Indian movies on television. The Indians always lost.

On April 29, 1951, Jim was back in Hollywood, staying with Patsy on Highland Avenue, when he wrote a letter to his daughter Grace in Pearl River, New York, mentioning his second round of plastic surgery:

> *I look about twenty years younger and feel much better. Patsy is writing a book on my life and she is doing a good job of it—She certainly is a go getter and I love her very much. . . .*
>
> *My life story has been made by Warner Br's studio and I get to travel with the picture when it is released so I guess that I'll be in New York City around the August period when the picture is shown there. Burt Lancaster—who played my part in the Film—did a very good job of it and the picture should go over with a bang. I'll give you a ring while there and try to see you and the kiddies. Do give them my love and that I'll be expecting to see them. I guess I've said all that I can think of so I'll close with love from us both—your loving father, Jim Thorpe. Ps Patsy said to give her love and that she is anxious to see the children—Love Daddy.*

Patsy was hoping that her story of Jim's life could serve as a companion book to the movie. She was also still fighting with Warner Bros., now about how much the studio should pay Jim for his publicity appearances. Using her many contacts in newspaper sports departments, she placed another round of calls to argue her case. On the morning of May 5, she talked long-distance with Bus Ham, sports editor at the *Washington Post,* who was inviting Jim to play again in the *Post*'s National Celebrities Golf Tournament that June raising money to combat juvenile delinquency. Ham had known Jim since his days as sports editor at the *Daily Oklahoman* in Oklahoma City. He told Patsy that he thought Warner Bros. was "ready to deal" with her demands, eager to get the Thorpes in line before the movie was released.

Two weeks later, Patsy was in Manhattan, staying again at the Belvedere Hotel. Her feelings about the studio had soured again. "We are getting no place fast with Warner Bros. and I am about to tell them to go to and stay put," she wrote to Grace. "They have treated your Dad very badly, and if they will not come to my way of thinking, which is fair, I am in favor of trying to ruin the picture or something. The methods they employ would make a saint a devil. Damn all of them."

Among Patsy's skills was an uncanny ability to get her views planted in the press. This time she used Dorothy Kilgallen, who wrote the "Voice of Broadway" gossip column syndicated by Hearst and was developing national recognition as a panelist on the new television show *What's My Line?* After relating a story about Milton Berle paying thousands of dollars of medical bills for his chauffeur, who had suffered a stroke, Kilgallen wrote, ". . . Mrs. Jim Thorpe, wife of the sports hero of another era, is reported to be none too pleased with the film version of his life story. Thinks it's 'the usual Hollywood treatment,' they say, and would rather Jim didn't pitch in on the publicity stunts when the flicker has its premiere."

WHEN JIM REACHED Washington for the celebrity golf tournament, he conducted a long telephone conversation with Bob Wolff, a local sportscaster for WOL radio. Wolff began by noting that Thorpe had been chosen the top athlete of the half-century.

Wolff: Jim, what sort of golfer are you? I know you're a great man at other sports.

Thorpe: Well, I used to be a pretty good golfer but now here lately I haven't been playing any and I guess I'm not so hot.

Wolff: I know you've been a star in everything you've competed in, but what's your favorite sport?

Thorpe: Fish and hunting.

Wolff: [*laughing*] Fishing and hunting! Well, they're not quite as competitive as some of the other sports you've been in, are they?

Thorpe: Well, you can relax at least.

The interview then entered the realm of myth, with Jim the mythmaker. Some of the hyperbolic stories of his athletic career had been repeated so often for so long that perhaps Jim came to believe them.

Wolff: Well, Jim, I'd like to ask you some of your top thrills in sports. First of all, I know you were a great baseball player. Some folks seem to overlook that you were a star major leaguer with all of your football prowess and track ability, but in baseball what was your top thrill?

Thorpe: Well, when I hit three home runs into three different states in one ball game. Down in Texas. Texarkana.

Wolff: Three different states? How'd you do that?

Thorpe: Well, over the right-field fence was Arkansas and over the left-field fence was Oklahoma and the ballpark was in Texas. So I hit one in the ballpark past the outfielders and one over the right-field fence into Arkansas and one over to Oklahoma over the left-field fence.

(Quite a feat—impossible, in fact. The Oklahoma border was forty miles beyond the left-field fence.)

Later, Wolff asked him about any thrills that stood out in his football career. He repeated the myth of the great Carlisle versus Army game of 1912. Thorpe was magnificent that day, no need to exaggerate, but the fable had persisted nearly four decades and Jim told it one more time—how he returned a punt for a touchdown but there was a penalty on the play, so "it's kicked to me again and I carried it right back through for another touchdown."

Wolff: Boy, that is quite something, huh? Lightning can strike twice when Jim Thorpe is running with the ball.

Thorpe: [*laughing*] I guess so.

It was ninety-five degrees the next day when the tournament got underway at the Army-Navy Country Club. Before the first golfers teed off, members of the All-Time All-American football team were awarded silver trays. The group included Bennie Oosterbaan, Don Hutson, Sammy Baugh, Alex Wojciechowicz, Ernie Nevers, and Jim Thorpe. "The first tee was torture for the self-conscious, with a semicircle of thousands of curious eyes on the contestants, a deep gully directly in front and uncharted wilderness on the left of the fairway beckoning wayward balls," reported Whitney Martin, covering the event for the AP. "Jim Thorpe never did make that canyon after six attempts."

LATER THAT MONTH, Jim and Patsy moved their traveling show to Milwaukee. Patsy had lined up some gigs for Jim as a celebrity emcee. "The church bells are ringing," she reported in a letter to Grace on June 15. "This is a nice down to earth town, not so many phonies and chiselers, such as I refused to become accustomed to in California. It is my hope that I shall never have to return there."

Jim was not home, she said, but out on Lake Michigan taking part in a telecast for the sailboat races. Otherwise, he would be writing himself, thanking Grace's children for a card they had sent to their grandpa. "Poor Jim, he is inarticulate, but you know he loves you dear and is really sorry for his past mistakes. This damned typewriter is in the same condition I am, worn out. According to the doctors, there is just about everything wrong with me that could be. . . . The weather here has been almost cold, a lot of rain etc, which is doing my sinus and mastoids exactly no good. Gall bladder, liver, kidneys, heart and whatnot. If I could jack up the old chassis and run a new one under it, all would be well."

Jim and Patsy lasted in Milwaukee six weeks. Bookings were not as plentiful as Patsy had hoped. Thorpe's biggest event was presenting a torch to Don Gehrmann, Milwaukee's "magnificent miler," and firing the starting gun as Gehrmann loped up a mile stretch of Wisconsin Avenue to mark the thoroughfare's reopening after a yearlong reconstruction project. By late August, the Thorpes had left town.

That was when the movie was released. Premieres were scheduled for

Los Angeles, Carlisle, and Oklahoma City, but the first was a daylong celebration on August 20, 1951, in Muskogee for what a poster advertised as "The Colorful World Premier of Warner Bros. Greatest Indian Production of all Time . . . There'll be Movie Stars galore and a galaxy of FREE ATTRACTIONS to entertain every member of the family." First a press conference at the Severs Hotel. Then a parade through town and a benefit luncheon at Bacone College. Then movie stars visiting the hospital and signing autographs at the Jones department store for the benefit of the Milk and Ice Fund. Then a five-mile Indian race, and finally a showing of *Jim Thorpe—All-American* at the Ritz Theater.

Virginia Parlin, a Dickinson College student recently crowned as Miss Carlisle, flew in from Pennsylvania to represent the state. Phyllis Thaxter came back to town and rode at the head of the parade in an old open-air Ford, followed by brightly festooned Indian dancers. Thousands of townspeople lined the streets as the parade passed. Jimmy Brown, a rising cowboy star for Warner Bros., filled in for Lancaster, who was filming in Italy. Billy Jo Harjo of the Creek nation was given a trophy for winning the footrace. A huge throng gathered outside the theater and every seat was filled inside when the projector started rolling.

It was a fine time had by all, with one exception. Thorpe was a no-show. He and Patsy asked for $42,000 to promote the film, but Warner Bros. and the local chamber balked and paid him nothing. He didn't show up at another grand opening in Oklahoma City the next night either, disappointing a large crowd that awaited him, though he had appeared at a Rotary luncheon with Governor Turner earlier that day. The press called it "a mutually disagreeable disagreement." Thorpe called the studio "a bunch of stinkers." A Warner Bros. official responded by saying that "Thorpe better hadn't show up." As he prepared to skip town, Thorpe declared: "There's no money here, so I'm going to Carlisle where they appreciate me."

The Carlisle event that Thursday was a bittersweet homecoming. Jim returned to the scene of his happiest days still sore at Warner Bros. for what he believed was unfair financial treatment and with mixed feelings about how the movie portrayed him. But he was showered with praise and surrounded by admirers all day. His son Phil, a corporal stationed at Fort Devens, Massachusetts, was there in dress uniform to greet his father, along with Brigadier General Arthur Trudeau, acting commandant of the Army War College. Friends from his Carlisle football days included Pete Calac and Lone Star Dietz. Bo McMillin, who had often competed against Jim in the early NFL days and was now coaching the Eagles, came over from Philadelphia, and Governor John S. Fine arrived with his two sports-loving sons, Jackie and Donald. Phyllis Thaxter, his movie wife, stood next to Jim and looked at him adoringly as a marker was unveiled on the courthouse square recognizing his Carlisle achievements. One witness later claimed that Jim had been drinking and staggered his way onto the courthouse lawn. Probable, though there is no other evidence of that. He was in the public eye all day, moving from a reception at the home of Leslie V. Bentley, owner of the Molly Pitcher Hotel, to the marker ceremony in a ten-car caravan, to a dinner banquet at the Dickinson College gymnasium attended by five hundred guests, and on to the Carlisle Theater, where Thaxter, "a sweet, demure actress," paid another tribute to Jim as "a real All-American" before introducing the film, which ran until midnight.

What next? Jim and Patsy kept moving. Milwaukee had been disappointing, the movie premieres had not gone the way they hoped, but there was always a new city, a new plan. By the end of the month, they were living in Memphis, where a veteran publicist named Early Maxwell, who had toured with Bob Hope and managed golfers Cary Middlecoff and Sam Snead, said he could help rekindle interest in Jim and bring them some money. Patricia announced the move in a September 6 letter to Grace.

"We have rented a beautiful old place, six miles out of Memphis proper. A huge yard with many fine old trees (which I love) in which birds, crickets, and locusts serenade us. It is tranquil & I am truly enjoying it fully. This is the nearest to having a home we have had since I sold my place at Lomita California in 1945. What are we doing in Memphis? The agents at Milwaukee were a complete fizzle. Early Maxwell of this city is a terrific publicist and booking man. . . . He tells us he can get $2,000 per week for Jim. Let us pray and I'm 150% in favor of it."

Patsy expressed mixed feelings about *Jim Thorpe—All-American.* "Have you seen the movie? It missed the boat and where, in my opinion, it is an above average picture—it missed being great. However, Lancaster, although he is a conceited ass and a communist, did a good job. The locker room was magnificent. Iva should have had herself several thousand dollars for the release—but that is water under the bridge."

But what was most on Patsy's mind was Jim's loneliness and separation from his children. Especially the girls from his first marriage. The wounds still seemed too fresh for Patsy to accommodate the boys, who despised her. "If I am permitted to remain in this place for a period of time (I pray) I think it would be very nice if you and the children can spend the holidays with us. An old fashioned Xmas with your Dad, who Xmas times have been all too lacking, for a long time. Gail and her girls, too, if possible. Jim is 63—it is possible he has not too many years left. Just once, before it is all over I should like to see him with all of his children around him."

Patsy urged Grace to write often. Their relationship showed the better side of Patsy. She was tough and could be manipulative, but there also at times was a resigned sweetness to her, and a longing for family love. "I like you. You are genuine and worth knowing," she told Grace. "The best of everything in your new endeavor. [Grace had started work with the Pearl River Welcome Wagon.] Doing for others is a sure way of filling that empty void in all of us. Your new mom, Patricia."

Before stuffing the letter into an envelope, she got Jim to add a few words. "Well here we are in Memphis Tenn and the Sunny South," he wrote. "It was very hot here but somewhat cooler now. I am to sign up with Early Maxwell today or tomorrow—said he could make me around two thousand per week—which is not hay—let's hope & pray he can do it. I do hope you come down for Xmas with Gail and the kiddies too—this is all I can think of at this time, Your Dad. Give the kiddies my love and that this Grand Daddy loves them very much."

When the film came to Pearl River, Grace organized a Saturday afternoon outing to the theater, taking her two young children, Dagmar and Paul, and a carload of their friends. "We waited in a long line to buy tickets," Grace recalled. "It was kinda fun looking up to see Dad's name on the marquee—wish the kids had been old enough to read and remember. Anyway, we bought the usual candy bars and the noise moved from the kids to the screen. When Burt Lancaster playing my Dad's role first bounded on the screen, my son looked at him, mouth agape, shook his head and said, very seriously and very slowly, 'That's not my grandpa.'"

32

Waving Good-Bye

MEMPHIS PROVED TO BE AS MUCH OF A BUST AS SO MANY towns before. A tranquil life in a big house in the countryside graced with red maples and songbirds, the family gathering for the holidays around Granddaddy Jim—all another unrealized dream, along with the prospect of earning two thousand dollars a week. The film about his life was receiving positive reviews and doing well at the box office, featured at hundreds of theaters across the country. But that was fiction, celluloid fantasy. Burt Lancaster fared better than Jim Thorpe, who was on the road again, this time with another variation of thunderbirds, not a softball team but a song and dance revue featuring Jim and six Native American entertainers billed as Jim Thorpe's All America Thunderbirds.

That venture was cut short in early November 1951 when Patsy discovered an unsightly growth on Jim's lower lip. They were in Philadelphia then, and Patsy sent him to the doctor. It turned out to be a tumor—lip cancer. Jim was operated on at Lankenau Hospital in suburban Wynnewood on November 9, after which the hospital reported: "It was possible to remove the tumor radically by surgery. The defect was closed by plastic surgery and a deformity will be avoided." That marked the third facial surgery for Jim within a year. He was instructed not to talk or eat solid food for a few days but take liquids through a straw.

Photographers snapped pictures of him a day later waving from his hospital bed, a large bandage covering his lower lip and jaw. Patsy, hovering nearby, broke into tears, lamenting their plight and thanking the surgeon for not charging for the operation. "We're broke," she said. "Jim has nothing but his name and his memories. He has spent money on his own people and has given it away. He has often been exploited." The nightclub act was already struggling, but now it would have to be abandoned. Patsy lamented that they had "no plans, no money, no definite place to go." She hoped the sporting world would come to Jim's aid. Maybe the National Football League would hold a Jim Thorpe Day or his old baseball team would sponsor a benefit for him. Newspaper headlines called him "flat broke" and "destitute." The Associated Press said he was "bulky, fat, and aging with thin graying hair and heavy wrinkles in his face"—a description that enraged Patsy.

One week later, Jim was out of the hospital, and he and Patsy had moved on to New York, where they reconnected with William Thourlby, a.k.a. Buddy Thorpe. Patsy and Buddy saw a way to serve their mutual interests by inviting the press to a news conference where Jim would talk about his operation and his future actor Buddy would promote his next movie. Patsy orchestrated the event, intent on undoing the AP image of Jim as fat and old. For the public to stay interested in him, she figured, he had to be regarded as the athletic marvel he once was.

"Don't smile too much honey. Hold your lip still," she said, rubbing Jim's back in a room at the Roosevelt Hotel as photographers snapped pictures of him holding a certificate proclaiming him the best athlete of the half-century. "Look at that physique—at 63," Patsy gushed. "The doctors said he had the blood pressure of a man of twenty. He weighs only two pounds more than he did at the 1912 Olympics." Jim likely had lost some weight but was still well over two hundred pounds. Some scribes seemed willing to go along. "At age of 63 this remarkable man weighs only 190, about five pounds above his best playing weight," reported Arthur Daley in the *New York Times.*

Daley lamented that Thorpe was "being used as a shill" to promote the picture for Buddy. "Not that Old Jim objects," he wrote. "He is much too good-natured for that. That's been his trouble most of his life." The sports columnist chose to ignore the movie promotion and focus on Jim. He said there was one embarrassing question he had to ask. The life story of Thorpe had been filmed and was making scads of money. Then why was Jim flat broke? Wasn't he cutting in handsomely on the gate receipts?

Jim shook his head before answering. He explained how he had first sold the rights to MGM in 1931 and received only fifteen hundred dollars then, and that MGM sold the rights to Warner Bros., who never paid him what he deserved. "I've received nothing," Jim said. Not true—he had been paid as a technical consultant, but he and Patsy had already spent that money. Presumably, Jim was referring to Warner's reluctance to meet the requests for more money to promote the film.

The cancer surgery, followed by the stories from New York, sparked a national response of sympathy over the great athlete's physical and financial health. Funds to raise money for Jim were organized by the Green Bay Packers of the NFL and the Pittsburgh Pirates of the National League. Another fund was established by George Trautman, president of the National Association of Professional Baseball Leagues, overseeing the minors. An Ohio-based company, General Tire and Rubber, also set up a medical fund for him. The *American Weekly*, the Sunday supplement of Hearst Newspapers, urged readers to send get-well messages to Jim with wishes for a brighter Christmas and New Year, as did NBC radio sportscaster Bill Stern.

Leigh Montville was a sports-loving eight-year-old, the only child of older parents living in an apartment in New Haven, Connecticut, who at night in his bedroom listened to Stern's *Colgate Sports Newsreel.* He knew about Thorpe because he had seen the movie with Burt Lancaster. Stern "went into a long, sad story about how America's greatest athlete now was very sick and living in the Roosevelt Hotel in New York City, broke and despondent and if you could, please send him some money," Montville recalled. "I was really bothered. I took whatever money I had—I bet it was $1.53 or something, all in change—and sent it to the address Stern read. I added a note asking Jim to send me his autograph in a self-enclosed envelope. . . . He sent me his autograph—'Thanks Pal, Jim Thorpe'—on one piece of stationery and a letter on another piece. Being a kid, I kept the autograph of course and threw away the letter."

After reading Arthur Daley's column, a twenty-six-year-old Justice Department lawyer who earlier that year had earned a degree from the University of Virginia School of Law dispatched a sharp letter to Warner

Bros. criticizing the studio for mistreating Thorpe. "I wanted you to know how shocked I, and all those with whom I have talked of the matter were at your disrespectful treatment of Jim Thorpe," wrote Robert F. Kennedy, whose older brother John was a congressman from Massachusetts and whose grandfather had once raced against Thorpe at an Elks Club picnic in 1912. "As related in the nation's newspapers and magazines and commented on particularly by Arthur Daley in the *New York Times*, we feel that your monetary arrangements with Mr. Thorpe were as an extreme case of exploitation as we have ever heard. To put it bluntly—it is disgusting. We feel your company is a natural disgrace and we are urging all our friends to boycott your movies."

Attempting to defuse the negative publicity while *Jim Thorpe—All-American* was still drawing moviegoers, a studio publicist announced that he had donated $2,500 to a fund set up for contributions from the movie industry. Jim's response to fans like young Leigh Montville would prove easier to document than how much money found its way to Thorpe and how that money was used. Trautman of the minor leagues reported that by Thanksgiving his fund had raised $1,268.80. If the other funds neared that amount, the total might have approached $6,000. Jim's sons would say that Patsy spent much of the money on herself. Patsy would say that Jim gave much of it away to friends or strangers who seemed needier than he was. There was some truth to both, but in either case, despite the efforts to lift Jim out of his hole, there were no apparent changes to his daily struggle.

A man has to keep hustling. Thorpe traveled on to Marlin, Texas, where he had once trained with the New York Giants, to be the guest of honor at the third annual Milk Bowl featuring peewee football players. Then up to Philadelphia for the 140th anniversary meeting of the Union Society for Detection of Horse Thieves and Recovery of Stolen Property, where in a mock trial Thorpe was brought before an elite jury that included the governor and two judges—and convicted and hanged. "The group hangs a well-known personality at each annual get-together as a throwback to the days when horse thieves were an actual menace in these parts," one account explained. All in good fun, it was said, even or especially the part where the jocular crowd led the victim to the scaffold before attending a luncheon feast. Jim had been hanged enough in his life.

IN THE MONTHS since the movie had been released in late August, all through the fall of 1951 and into the new year of 1952, the powers that be in amateur athletics worried that public sympathy engendered by the film would intensify the pressure to restore Jim's Olympic trophies and medals. Although studio publicists promoted the push for redemption, the movie's depiction of the Olympic controversy was brief and presented both sides equally, much to the relief of amateur officials.

Before the film reached larger audiences in the Midwest, Marion H. Miller, an AAU official in Kansas City, issued a positive scouting report to Avery Brundage. "I had the opportunity last evening of previewing the new Warner Bros. picture on the life of Jim Thorpe," he wrote. "As you probably know, Burt Lancaster plays the role of Thorpe and I thought that it was a very credible picture. I was interested, of course, in how they handled the situation regarding the Olympic medals and in my opinion this was also portrayed in a manner that reflected credit rather than discredit on the Olympic organization and officials. All in all, the picture coming out at this time will serve to create considerable interest in the '52 games [to be held in Helsinki] since a considerable portion of it is devoted to past games and particularly those in 1932."

Brundage's rise through the Olympic ranks was nearly complete. Within a year his athletic domain would include not just America but the world as fifth president of the International Olympic Committee. He had not yet seen the film but had heard much about it. "Thanks for sending the information on the Thorpe movie," he responded to Miller. "I have been somewhat apprehensive of the treatment the Olympic movement might receive in this film, since whenever they wanted publicity Thorpe called me a stuffed shirt for not returning his medals, as if I had anything to do with it. I am glad to learn that it is reasonably innocuous."

But the issue would not die. Sportswriters and Thorpe proponents forced the AAU to take up the Thorpe case at its annual convention that December 1 and 2 in Daytona Beach. The delegates would not budge, passing a resolution that said "no facts have been presented to cause a reversal of the decision" made in early 1913. After the convention, the organization's magazine, the *Amateur Athlete,* noted the rise in public sympathy for Jim after his lip operation. But "restoring Thorpe's amateur standing is, of course, out of the question," the magazine asserted, arguing among other things that the issue was too far in the past. "Few of the people who were active in amateur sports in 1912–13 and had some part in the action taken by the American Olympic Committee and the AAU in the Jim Thorpe case are still alive. Moreover, one cannot trust to his memory of some happenings of forty years ago."

The decision provoked an intense public backlash from diverse perspectives. Some thought it was discrimination against a Native American. Others saw it as a hypocritical act of overkill that lacked common sense. And then there were boosterish types who loved college football and thought the treatment of Thorpe was part of a larger conspiracy by Brundage and college presidents to diminish big-time college sports. The Spokane Athletic Round Table issued a vitriolic broadside against amateur officials and invited Thorpe to be its guest when the AAU held its 1952 convention there. "Members, are we going to let 'em kill football? No! The game belongs to the kids, not to the school boards and kill-joys. Come in, Scrooge! Jim Thorpe will be our guest. . . . We hope the AAU gives Jim back the medals he won in Sweden for being the world's best athlete. We hope to see the best football player that ever lived. We want Jim to accept our belated Board, Room and Tuition."

Jim's two strongest proponents remained his wife Patsy and sportswriter Grantland Rice, who combined forces in December when Rice let Patsy write his syndicated column. "Just what happened to Jim Thorpe's stolen, lost, or confiscated medals and trophies? What is the real truth behind the AAU and the Olympic committee? We have asked Mrs. Jim Thorpe, his wife, to tell us the true story of this world-wide scandal. Here it is—from Patricia Thorpe," Rice wrote, turning the rest of his space over to her. Patsy offered a brimming stew of arguments, diminishing and honoring her husband at the same time.

She described Jim as "an ignorant Indian boy from the reservation. . . . Ignorant, that is in the ways of the so-called white man." It was the same argument Pop Warner had used when he ghostwrote Jim's letter of confession back in January 1913. She claimed "every newspaper in the country" had printed stories about Jim's exploits in Rocky Mount. An exaggeration, but certainly there were enough stories in the North Carolina papers, including the *Charlotte Observer*, about what he was doing that it was not a secret. She placed Jim's response in a sociological context, saying "the demand that his Olympic honors be stripped from him stunned and bewildered him. Keep in mind all of the time the Indian's nature, the denial of rights as citizens, relegation to reservations etc."

Finally, in arguing for the return of the King Gustav V trophy for his pentathlon win and Emperor of Russia trophy for the decathlon, Patsy said the trophies were "personal gifts to Jim Thorpe" and that they were returned "without Jim's knowledge or consent." The truth here is complicated. Jim did know they were returned. He was at Carlisle when Pop Warner sent them to New York, where they were loaded onto the SS *New York* bound for Sweden. But what happened to them after that was unclear and it seemed the IOC did not mind leaving everyone confused about their whereabouts.

In closing Rice's column, Patsy asked: "Where are Jim's Olympic trophies? No one has any legal right to them but Jim Thorpe."

Brundage and his compatriots were outraged by the column. "You know Grantland Rice better than I do, I believe. How could he print such tripe?" Brundage wrote to Gustavus T. Kirby, who had been president of the AAU when Thorpe lost his medals and trophies and was now in his mid-seventies and living in retirement in Bedford Hills, New York. "Don't you think you should write him a letter about it so he won't harbor such ideas?"

Kirby did as Brundage asked, sending off a letter to Rice on January 24, 1952. "My dear Grant," it began, "The heading of your article, Jim Thorpe and the Stolen Trophies, is untrue, unfortunate, and entirely unfitting for one of your great name and fame, who should not be, and seldom is, swayed by prejudice or otherwise, and who, in my judgment, has always endeavored to and generally does speak 'the truth, the whole truth, and nothing but the truth.' The whole article is filled with unwise, uncalled for, and in general untruthful statements and innuendo."

Kirby concluded his letter with a contradiction, repeating the argument that the trophies were not personal gifts to Thorpe, but adding: "Personally, I do not believe that these trophies were of any great value but even if they were, after Thorpe's disbarment, they belonged not to him but to the IOC, whose privilege it was to either hand them down to others or to do as has been done, keep them in their archives."

That at least answered one pressing question. For years, Thorpe and others had wondered what had happened to the trophies. It turned out they never traveled at all but were squirreled away by the IOC at its headquarters in Lausanne, Switzerland. But then another question arises: If they were meant to be traveling trophies, why were they not then passed along to the next pentathlon and decathlon gold medalists? The Olympics were not held in 1916 during World War I, but at the 1920 Olympics in Antwerp, Belgium, there was no effort to retrieve the Emperor of Russia trophy and give it to that year's gold medal decathlete, Helge Lovland of Norway. Nor did the trophy resurface to be given to American Harold Osborn in 1924, Paavo Yrjola of Finland in 1928, or Americans Jim Bausch in 1932, Glenn Morris in 1936, or Bob Mathias in 1948. That history renders the IOC argument specious.

From his winter perch at the Beverly Wilshire Hotel in Beverly Hills, Rice was diplomatic in response. "The Thorpe situation seems to be beyond everybody's grasp," he wrote to Kirby. "I've had more quests to see that he got his trophies back than I ever had from anything else in sport. The column you referred to was written by Mrs. Thorpe. Some time back I wrote Avery Brundage about Thorpe's trophies. He wrote a vague letter back to the effect that Thorpe was a pro. And he didn't know where the trophies were. . . . Thousands, or I could say millions—would like to see Thorpe get his medals or other prizes back. It's about all he has left. Anyway, I appreciate your letter very much. It is the first real information I've ever received on this subject. Sincerely, Grant Rice."

IT WAS IN 1915 that Jack Cusack lured Thorpe to Ohio to play his first professional football game for the Canton Bulldogs against the rival Massillon Tigers. Jim was in the prime of his career then, a twenty-eight-year-old multisport star drawing $250 a game as the best-paid player in the Ohio League. Now, on the evening of January 30, 1952, Canton was luring Thorpe once again, this time for a testimonial dinner that attracted "the rich and mighty in industry, sports and politics" to the Onesta Hotel ballroom to honor a "sick and poor" man nearing his sixty-fifth birthday.

Every seat at every table was filled, the ballroom throbbing with 703 banquet guests. Old Cy Young was there, an Ohio legend whose first of a major league record 511 career wins was with the Cleveland Spiders. So was Woody Hayes, just finished with his first season as Ohio State's football coach. And Marion Motley, the brilliant black fullback for the Cleveland Browns, along with Jim's old college and pro teammate Pete Calac. Among the dignitaries at the head table were Frank J. Lausche, Ohio's governor; Benjamin Fairless, president of U.S. Steel; John Galbreath, owner of the Pittsburgh Pirates; and four congressmen.

Branch Rickey, the baseball executive who had recruited Jackie Robinson to desegregate major league baseball and was now general manager of the Pirates, was the evening's principal speaker. Rickey had played pro football briefly in the Ohio League more than a decade before Thorpe and was a front office man for the Browns and Cardinals in St. Louis during the years Jim played in the majors. He knew Thorpe, though not well, and spent days researching Jim's life in preparation for the speech. His notes included a chronology of Thorpe's entire athletic career as well as many of the myths that accompanied Jim's multitudinous accomplishments. But this was not a speech of yards gained and balls hit. Rickey was an ornate orator who spoke with the air of a man who knew more than anyone in the room, taking his listeners on a grand tour of history, religion, and philosophy on the way to making his points. He thought he knew more than he did, but in this case his verbosity was in service to a righteous cause—the return to athletic grace of Jim Thorpe.

He began by connecting the stripping of Thorpe's medals to the mistreatment of American Indians throughout history. "Many years ago, our distant forebears discovered a new race on this continent—a copper colored race," Rickey began. "That race originally gave us a gladsome and generous welcome. We have pushed them back and further back, here and there in comparative ultimate isolation to unwanted lands. . . . I regret that history may have the chance or even the right to point back to the prudery, if not the snobbery, of this present day when America cap-sheathed its injustice by stripping the race's foremost athletic representative of his Olympic medals which were fairly earned."

Then Rickey tapped into his audience's patriotism to make his case, placing Thorpe's mistreatment in the context of crime and the anticommunist fervor gripping the nation as American troops fought against the reds in Korea. Thorpe, he said, had been denied what he was due for nearly forty years. "There are those who violate the privacy of property with great design and malice—thievery, fraud, deceit, arson, and burglary—and they don't get a life sentence or even forty years. Then too, in the depths of moral turpitude, there are those who violate . . . the right of public assemblage, and the freedom of speech and the right to worship as one wishes; only traitors and communists do that, and with difficulty the traitor gets five years and the communist continues to test the national existence with a policy of no peace and now war." All treated better than the great Indian athlete.

He then turned to Thorpe's magnificent performance in Stockholm and the summer baseball seasons that cost him his medals. Like Pop Warner and Patsy Thorpe and so many others, Rickey misstated the facts of what happened in the Eastern Carolina League while making the argument that Jim was both innocent and ignorant. "He did not seek honors at the expense of honor, and when he took two dollars a day to play what was little more than semi-professional summer baseball down in North Carolina in 1910 it never occurred to him that he was violating any amateur rule or jeopardizing his standing in further competition. The innocent sin but are forgiven. The ignorant know not the wrong and therefore never seek nor need forgiveness, and it is a sound thesis advanced by a great many philosophers that in this sense the ignorant have more power and virtue than the innocent."

Rickey was deep into his element now, preaching his way to a florid climax. "It is indeed a cruel world that sets up a worthy idol just to knock him down, to be more sinned against than sinning. . . . What is condonation? What is retribution? What is the limit of penalty? Where is the face of justice without mercy? What is the price of excellence—par excellence, aye, supra excellence? The restoration of the medals to Jim Thorpe will meet not only the expected hopes of the youth of America but will have the quick approval of the measured judgment of mature sportsmen through the world."

As Thorpe sat nearby at the head table, Rickey concluded: "He stands before you . . . unassuming, unmasking, but uncrowned." A rousing standing ovation ensued.

The evening concluded with Thorpe, in a characteristically concise fifty-word speech, thanking the enraptured audience—"I can see I am not a forgotten man," he said—and receiving a $1,000 check, with the promise for more once the event's $10-a-ticket receipts were counted. He also was given a fancy watch inscribed "Jim Thorpe—Canton Bulldogs—From your many friends in Canton, the cradle of professional football." And he left with a promise from the four congressmen that they would take up the matter of Jim's medals with the House subcommittee on Indian affairs. This gave him hope, however fleeting. Shortly after the banquet, Jim wrote optimistically to a friend: "The trophy deal is pending in Congress at the present writing, and I hope that an act will be passed to regain them—I do know that if Congress goes after them I'll get them back."

If he thought pressure was building, Thorpe did not understand the relationship between American officials and Avery Brundage, who despite his protestations to the contrary was the one with all the power. Brundage would not budge.

One week after the night in Canton, Thorpe was in another city where he had good memories. Boston was the first place he had visited after returning from Stockholm with his gold medals. Nearby Cambridge was where he single-handedly ran and kicked his Carlisle squad past mighty Harvard in 1911, a game that lifted Jim into the ranks of college football immortals. And in 1919, it was with the Boston Braves that he had his finest season in the majors. Now he was back to sign autographs at a sports show at Mechanics Hall.

His seatmate was Ted Williams, the Red Sox star who had just heard that he would be called from a list of inactive Marine Corps reserves for duty as a pilot in the Korean War. Thorpe and Williams were almost a tag team now; they had traveled up to Boston after appearing together at another event in New York. There is a photograph of the two arm-wrestling in a hotel room there, both smiling broadly, Jim dressed in a buckskin fringed jacket, Ted in a polo shirt, though no documentation as to who won. Williams was the biggest draw in Boston, the marquee name loved and booed with equal passion by Beantown baseball fans. He had finished the 1951 season with batting statistics that were average for him but career marks for any other hitter—a .318 average, 30 home runs, 126 runs batted in. Within three months, Williams would be flying combat missions over Korea, wingman in a fighter jet piloted by future astronaut John Glenn. Promoter Sheldon Fairbanks paid Williams $12,000 for the two gigs and made his money back in drawing a record crowd to the Boston show. He would not reveal what he paid Thorpe, but reporters guessed that it was "about one-tenth that paid the slugger."

It was a buoyant time for Jim nonetheless. He was nearly twice Williams's age, but they bonded as the best of their generations, stubborn individualists who would rather be out fishing and hunting than performing any of the miraculous feats they undertook on the fields of play. Williams, whose mother was Mexican American, was a conservative in most respects but liberal on matters of race, an early supporter of Jackie Robinson and blacks in baseball. He considered himself an underdog against the elites and identified with what Thorpe endured as a Native American. "I was so impressed with how quiet and attentive he was, how he would listen to people. Here's Jim Thorpe, all-time, and he'd listen to anybody." Williams called Jim "Chief"—as in "The Chief is really something. What a wonder he must have been in his prime."

"The shrieks are for Williams but the deep-throated shouts of the middle-aged are for Thorpe," noted one reporter on the scene at Mechanics Hall. "Two years ago, when Williams made his fly-casting debut here he dominated the press room where top performers rest between shows. This time, it's all about Thorpe. What he did at Harvard stadium when he was attending Carlisle. What he did during the 1912 Olympics. What he did in baseball with the New York Giants, Boston Braves, and . . . with the Independents in nearby Lawrence, Mass."

Thorpe encountered myth and reality at the Boston show. The myth came when he was greeted by an old-school fan club of four creaking Irishmen, football players from New England who had played with him in Canton: Mark Devlin, Dan O'Connor, Bunny Corcoran, and Tom Whelan. With a gift for the blarney, O'Connor happily hyped the image of Thorpe as superman. "I've seen Thorpe do things on football fields that never happened before or since," he said. "I'll never forget the day I saw him run one-hundred yards in nine-point-four seconds wearing football cleats and as he slowed down at the high jump pit cleared the bar at six feet one inch." The reality came when Thorpe shook hands with a *Boston Globe* reporter named Roy Ruggles Johnson, who as a young county editor at the *Worcester Telegram* in January 1913 had broken the story that Thorpe played pro baseball in Rocky Mount. Johnson said he regretted that Jim had lost his medals because of the story. With equanimity, Thorpe told Johnson that he was only doing his job.

OF ALL THE movies that came out in 1951—including the classics *Strangers on a Train, A Place in the Sun, A Streetcar Named Desire, Show Boat, An American in Paris, The Day the Earth Stood Still,* and *The African Queen*—none had a wider showing when the drive-in movie season opened in the spring of 1952 than *Jim Thorpe—All-American.* From the Friendly Drive-in on Whiskey Road in Aiken, South Carolina, to the Eastern Drive-in Theater in Union, New Jersey; from the massive 2,200-car Bel Air Drive-in on 8 Mile Road in Detroit to the Pine Motor Theater on Alameda Avenue in Roseburg, Oregon, the Thorpe story was on the bill at hundreds of outdoor theaters from March through October. It was riding the wave of postwar America, when the number of drive-ins increased exponentially, from 820 in 1948 to more than 3,000 by June 1952, accompanying the baby boom population eruption. Drive-ins became another representation of 1950s freedom—freedom of the automobile and freedom of entertainment for parents without need for a babysitter.

Wherever Thorpe traveled that year, he was bound to see an advertisement in the local newspaper promoting the celluloid version of his story. "Glorious as the Grand Guy it Glorifies—JIM THORPE, ALL AMERICAN—Starring Burt Lancaster—Charles Bickford—Steve Cochran—Phyllis Thaxter—Added Cartoon (Woody Woodpecker) and Football Thrills."

The grand guy kept moving. "I am feeling very good at the moment and hope to live to a ripe old age," Jim wrote to a friend later that February. The cancer was "really hard to have," but he felt he had beaten it. In his nomadic life so far, Thorpe had lived in nineteen states, in every region of the country. New York, New Jersey, Pennsylvania, Connecticut, and Massachusetts in the East; Ohio, Indiana, Illinois, and Wisconsin in the Midwest; North Carolina, Florida, South Carolina, and Tennessee in the South; Texas, Oklahoma, and Kansas in the southern plains; and California, Oregon, and Montana in the West. Now Nevada made it twenty.

Here was another answer to what happened to the money people raised after learning Jim was broke. Patsy found another nightclub for them to run, this time in the small town of Pittman, south of Las Vegas. The establishment on South Boulder Highway was in a semicylindrical corrugated steel Quonset hut built during World War II. It had been operating for years as the Hut Club, but Jim and Patsy renamed it Jim Thorpe's All American Club, stocked it with photographs and other memorabilia of his athletic career, then went off to Reno to apply for a gambling license to supplement the food, liquor, and occasional weekend entertainment.

The grand opening, advertised on coasters Patsy ordered, was May 28,

1952. Jim said the opening marked his sixty-fourth birthday. Throughout his life, he got his birth date wrong by one year and six days. He had already turned sixty-five on May 22. His job was the usual one, to sit there and be the famous Jim Thorpe, or the shadow of his former self. Patrons were few, but Phillip I. Earl of the Nevada Historical Society found some local residents decades later who recalled that Thorpe sat at the end of the bar drinking a beer, while Patsy and Chuck Montag, the bartender and club manager, served customers. They said Jim seemed quiet, modest, and somewhat embittered.

On the afternoon of June 18, the Nevada Tax Commission in Carson City granted a batch of gambling licenses around the state to big shots and small fries. One went to Clifford "Big Juice" Jones, the state's lieutenant governor, a corporation lawyer who had a stake in Las Vegas's Thunderbird Hotel and other mob-run casinos and was later forced to resign after a sting operation recorded him describing how to fix gambling licenses. And another went to James F. Thorpe, proprietor of the steel hut in the boondocks twenty miles south of the bustling Strip. South Boulder Highway was not a path lit by lightning.

The following weekend, Thorpe traveled to Los Angeles at the invitation of Bob Hope, his old benefactor, who along with Bing Crosby was holding an overnight telethon to raise money for the U.S. Olympic team that would be traveling to Helsinki in mid-July to participate in the 1952 summer games. The Hope-Crosby telethon aired nonstop on CBS and NBC for twelve and a half hours from Saturday night through Sunday morning and raised a million dollars. With hundreds of prominent guests participating, dueling egos were unavoidable, but no encounter seemed more awkward than when Thorpe and Avery Brundage showed up at the El Capitan Theatre at the same time. Photographers immediately staged a handshake between Jim and his longtime nemesis in front of the U.S. Olympic shield for a wirephoto that appeared in newspapers around the country; Brundage appears apprehensive, and Jim declines to look the "stuffed shirt" in the eye. The meeting was nonetheless described as "historical"—their first handshake since Thorpe and Brundage had been Olympic teammates forty years earlier.

As Jim was heading back to Pittman, the *Los Angeles Times* ran a promotion for an article that was to appear in the following Sunday's supplement, *This Week* magazine. "For many years the Olympic Games have bred scandals and bitterness involving some of the world's best athletes," the ad began. "In the center of many such controversies has stood Avery Brundage. . . . Next week Mr. Brundage, in an exclusive article, for the first time tells the inside story of the Games. . . . Don't miss 'THE TRUTH ABOUT THE OLYMPICS.' "

Brundage's piece was published on June 29. One of his "truths" was a blatant lie that his own archive at the University of Illinois refutes. In the article, he claimed that he and other Olympic officials prevented Hitler from using the 1936 games for Nazi propaganda purposes and expressed shock that he and his Olympic compatriots "were even accused of being pro-Nazi." Files in his archive bulge with letters he exchanged with Nazi officials as they conspired to discredit the Jewish-led boycott against the games, which served as a stage for Hitler and his propagandists. In one letter to Carl Diem, a German Olympic official, he blamed American Jews for spreading false propaganda about Germany and asked Diem if he could provide data "showing Jews going about their business in Germany as far as sports are concerned."

The section of the article devoted to Thorpe was manipulative and misleading. Again, as he did with American Jewish opposition to the Nazi games, Brundage attempted to belittle and discredit his opponents. "Some of the 'reports' [in support of Thorpe] are the result of gross ignorance. Others come from those who would stir up bad feeling," Brundage wrote. "To this day Thorpe is said to have been the victim of the worst swindle in sport history." Brundage then unleashed what he considered to be an irrefutable witness for the prosecution. He turned to Pop Warner to make his case. "Yet what does Pop Warner, who coached Jim Thorpe in 1912 have to say? 'He made an innocent mistake, but innocence never has been part of the definition of an amateur. What's fair for one is fair for all.' "

Back in Nevada, Jim was not much of a presence in Pittman or nearby Henderson, keeping close to his nightclub, avoiding most requests for public appearances. He did show up for an American Legion baseball game on the Fourth of July; one witness recalled him stumbling to the mound to throw out the first pitch. He also came out to greet Dwight D. Eisenhower when Ike landed at McCarran Field in Las Vegas on a campaign swing shortly before receiving the nomination for president at the Republican National Convention in Chicago that summer. Thorpe and Eisenhower were seeing each other for the first time since 1912, when Jim rumbled over and around Ike on the football field at West Point. Unlike the reacquaintance with Brundage, this encounter prompted no ill will, just the memories of two old warriors. Ike, who loved sports, talked often of Jim on his way to the presidency. "I played against the greatest football player of them all back in 1912," he would say. Or self-deprecatingly: "It was a pleasure to see a guy like Thorpe running by." Or: "I once tackled Thorpe." By "once," he made clear, he meant literally only once in that game.

Las Vegas was booming in the summer of 1952. Frank Sinatra had made his first appearance at the Desert Inn months earlier; the riverboat-style Binion's Horseshoe Casino had just opened; Vegas Vic, the forty-foot-high cowboy, as symbolic of the city as the HOLLYWOOD sign was of LA, beckoned tourists from above the Pioneer Club; the Sands and the Sahara were being constructed and would open before the year was out. But whatever slim chance the Thorpes had of cashing in on the boom with the new gambling license at their joint twenty miles south of the Strip disappeared early on Friday morning, August 8, when Jim told Patsy he was "not feeling well" and lay down to rest.

It had been less than a year since his cancer surgery. And a few weeks earlier, he had been taken to the hospital briefly with a broken nose and several cuts on his face, arms, and legs, the result of a traffic accident in which he was a front-seat passenger in a pickup truck. Was he still worn out from the effects of all that trauma?

Worse. His collapse this time was from a heart attack, the second of his life, nine years after he was felled in Detroit. He was unconscious when he reached Rose De Lima Hospital in Henderson and was rushed to an oxygen tent for breathing support. "Doctors don't know if they can pull him through," Patsy said. But Thorpe was a tough old bird. Dr. J. F. Coogan soon described his condition as serious but not critical. It would be a slow recovery. Coogan said, requiring at least a week of treatment and rest at the hospital. Just as in Philadelphia, press photographers were allowed into his hospital room to snap pictures of him resting in his hospital bed. "JIM THORPE DOWN—BUT NOT OUT," read the cutline.

Perhaps, but Jim Thorpe's All American Club was soon out. Two weeks after Jim suffered his heart attack, Chuck Montag was killed when he was thrown from a speeding car that skidded out of control on the Vegas Wash highway outside of Henderson. The owner with a weak heart, the manager killed—bad luck upon bad luck. In September Jim and Patsy sold the club and moved back to California.

ANOTHER TOWN, ANOTHER bar. Jim and Patsy relocated in the Harbor region south of Los Angeles. They found an establishment on East Anaheim Street in the town of Wilmington and renamed it the Sports Café. Beer and wine. Steaks and chops. Booths commodious enough for families. The walls decorated in familiar fashion, as a photo museum of Jim's life and times, with 157 framed pictures of famous people in sports, movies, and politics, all autographed to Jim. Bing Crosby. Bob Hope. Ted Williams. Gary Cooper. California Governor Earl Warren. Golfer Cary Middlecoff. A flowing Indian headdress on a hook where Jim could reach it for special occasions. Jim sitting on a stool, the sphinxlike curiosity.

Patsy said they chose Wilmington because they liked a small town for business. She announced that they would be there to stay. Jim's traveling days were over, she said. None of it true.

Whatever money they'd been paid for the Quonset hut in Nevada went into the new place or vanished. Patsy and Jim had a knack for making money disappear, a combination of her profligate spending and his naïve generosity. Their symbiotic relationship was fraying after seven exhausting years. Patsy had wrung about as much financial gain as she could out of his fading fame. Jim had once welcomed her aggressive nature, thinking he needed it to get what he deserved; but after two heart attacks and cancer, his ambition was fading, and now he saw it more as a form of hectoring.

His daughter Gail thought he had never seemed more disconsolate. "He was just like a puppet," she recalled of a visit during that period. "He just sat there, holding my hand. He wouldn't even talk. He was like a dead man alive. He just held my hand. She [Patsy] did all the talking and she did nothing but just sit there and bitch about him. He just sat there. It was sad to see the deterioration."

Jim and Patsy fought and drank and separated and reconciled in a final act of codependence, a scene played out in a trailer park home in Lomita, just off the Pacific Coast Highway five miles to the west of Wilmington. According to friends, the money to buy the trailer came from Ted Williams.

With the new year of 1953 came a back-to-the-future revision in college football, a move Jim heartily endorsed. A new NCAA rule put an end to the two-platoon game with separate players for offense and defense, and a return to one-platoon or iron man football. The platoon system had been around for only a decade, employed to great effect by Fritz Crisler at Michigan and Red Blaik at Army. Some old-school coaches including Robert Neyland at Tennessee called it "chickenshit football" and longed for the days of sixty-minute men. They got their wish now from the game's governing body, mostly due to financial concerns at the universities. One platoon required fewer players and hence fewer scholarships.

Although Patsy had said Jim's traveling days were over, he was in New York when the changes were announced, making appearances and staying with his faux son Buddy for a few weeks. The rule change rekindled memories of Carlisle, when Jim and his teammates played both ways and never came out of a game. "We'll once again have real all-Americas, not half-Americas," he said. "We'll know that a man who gains such an honor can not only move that old pigskin forward but can also stop the other team. I just wish I was a few years younger so I could play again. It is going to be my kind of football and I sure would like to be able to run that ball and smack them over as I did years ago."

One night while in New York in early February, Jim had the opportunity to reminisce more about the Carlisle days. He was invited to speak at the Lambs Club, the hangout of actors, writers, and other notables, at their lair on West Forty-Fourth Street. "What was your greatest football game, greatest in your estimation?" someone asked.

"Army in 1912," Thorpe answered. Here was a rare time when he infused sports with a larger political meaning, at least in his public comments. The older he got, the more uncertain his life became, the more he connected with his Indian roots. The Army game was different from all the others, he said. "This was the game we wanted to win. There wasn't a boy on that Indian team who didn't carry the scars of family feud with the Long Knives—that's what the Indians called the cavalry—and when we got to West Point we vowed to wipe out some of those debts with touchdowns against the Cadets. I don't believe I ever ran as hard as I did in that game. . . . We beat them hands down, and that night we felt we had done something for our fathers."

Two days later, on February 10, Jim cut short his New York stay, saying he had received a call from Patsy who said she was seriously ill with a heart ailment and needed to enter a hospital. When Jim arrived back in California, he found her "up and around," and headed not for the hospital but for a less beneficent institution, and taking Jim with her. Police visited the Sports Café and arrested and detained them on an old warrant charging that they had violated the state labor code for failing to pay $320 owed to Thomas F. Murray, who had worked at a restaurant Patsy operated in Hollywood in 1951 under Jim's name. After a judge set bail at $200 each, they were led to the lockup, but quickly bailed out by one of Patsy's former restaurant pals, Slim Harrison. The case was dropped when Murray refused to press charges, saying Jim had promised to pay and anyway it was Brotherhood Week. His initial complaint was wholly understandable—but why did the cops decide to enforce it months after it was filed, and why did they find it necessary to throw Jim and Patsy into the hoosegow? Was it a matter of overzealous and perhaps racist police out to get Jim? Or were they after Patsy, who often seemed one step ahead of trouble? Those questions remained unresolved.

Slim Harrison had a particular reason for posting bail for Jim and Patsy. He had known Patsy for twenty years, and through her became friends with Jim, often stopping to talk with him on his way home from work. When the Catholic church in San Pedro, Mary Star of the Sea, was planning its fourth annual sports banquet, Monsignor George Scott asked Slim if he could persuade Jim to be one of the athletic celebrity guests. Harrison arranged it, only to find that Thorpe needed to be bailed from jail the day before the event. Jim attended the banquet as though nothing out of the ordinary had just happened, smiling and glad-handing through the evening with Beans Reardon, an old major league umpire; Hamp Pool, coach of the Los Angeles Rams; and Christy Walsh, the sports agent who had represented Babe Ruth and Ty Cobb. According to Bill Hollohan of the *San Pedro News-Pilot*, when Thorpe was announced to the throng of sports fans, he drew "one of the finest standing ovations these old ears have ever heard."

IT WAS THE next to last ovation of Jim's life. The last was on March 2, when he waved from the back seat of Del Dryer's sports roadster during a benefit parade for the local Booster Association. It turned out he was waving good-bye.

The end came later that month. A Saturday. March 28, 1953. A mid-afternoon meal, late lunch or early dinner. Jim and Patsy were in the mobile home near the back of the trailer park. Jim had another trip to New York coming up, but he planned to spend a relaxing summer closer to home, fishing at the Redondo pier. As he was eating, he slumped and collapsed. It was another heart attack, his third. Patsy screamed so loud a neighbor, Colby Bradshaw, heard her and came running. Patsy called for help, reaching the Rolling Hills unit of the fire rescue squad.

Bradshaw administered artificial respiration—twelve breaths a minute from his mouth into Thorpe's—until Captain Ben Reynolds and fireman Gerald Hibbard arrived and took up the effort. Patsy was still screaming. Now her screeches were directed at the rescuers—to save Jim. Sometime between 3:15 and 3:25 he briefly revived. He opened his eyes, looked around, said a few words, then collapsed again. Dr. Rachel E. Jenkins of the Hillside Emergency Clinic shot adrenaline into his heart to try to revive him again, but it was no use. This time it was fatal. James Francis Thorpe was pronounced dead at 3:52 p.m., although the death certificate a few days later would place the time of death at 3:25. It also listed his age wrong, using the May 28, 1888, date instead of the correct May 22, 1887. He died not quite two months short of his sixty-sixth birthday.

What to do with the body? Thorpe's corpse remained in the trailer deep into the night until Slim Harrison and a friend arrived and arranged for it to be taken to the Gamby Mortuary in Lomita. But Patsy said she had no money to pay the undertaker, so nothing more was done until late Monday when friends intervened again and found another funeral parlor, Malloy and Malloy on Flower Street in downtown LA, whose proprietor admired Jim and promised to handle the arrangements gratis.

By then the world knew Thorpe was gone. One after another came the exaltations.

From the Olympic potentate who refused to give Jim his medals: "I'm sorry to hear of his passing," said Avery Brundage. "Jim was one of the greatest athletes of all time."

From the coach who feigned ignorance of Jim's seasons in the Eastern Carolina League to save his own reputation: "I certainly regret to hear it," said Pop Warner. "What can you say at a time like this? I've never had or seen an athlete to compare with Jim Thorpe. It was a wonderful privilege for me to have been his coach in football and track. . . . Although we had not seen much of each other in recent years, I always thought of him as one of my closest friends."

From the top politician in his home state: "As well as being one of Oklahoma's most famous sons, Jim Thorpe was also a favorite person with all who knew him," said Governor Johnston Murray. "Those of us with native American blood in our veins take special pride in his great triumphs."

From an old linebacker who tried and failed to knock the Carlisle star out of that momentous Army versus Indians game on the Plain in 1912: "I learned with sorrow of the death of my old friend, Jim Thorpe," said Dwight D. Eisenhower, president of the United States. "Jim has long been recognized as one of the outstanding athletes of our time and has occupied a unique place in the hearts of Americans everywhere. As one who played against him in football more than forty years ago, I personally feel that no other athlete has possessed his all-around abilities in games and sports."

From the Swedish decathlete who finished second to Thorpe at Stockholm but later was awarded the gold medal after Jim's disqualification: "Thorpe was a live wire and a nice guy," said Hugo Wieslander, now a cartographer at the Swedish Geodetic Society. "He celebrated his victory rather thoroughly, I remember, and scared the Stockholmers with some of his war-whoops. I thought a lot of him."

From the sports editor of the *Chicago Tribune*: "No author of fiction would have dared create a character as fabulous as Jim Thorpe," wrote Arch Ward, a spinner of sporting myths who got his start doing publicity for Knute Rockne at Notre Dame and conceived of the major league All-Star Game. "Yet our grandchildren, when we tell them tales of Big Jim in years to come, will be skeptical that we only are inventing this super Frank Merriwell."

From a *Los Angeles Times* sportswriter who watched Jim closely during his final troubled years: "An unfortunate fact that might be construed to be a sad commentary on the human race is that its greatest athlete of all time, Jim Thorpe, spent most of his life surrounded by heartbreak and disappointment," wrote Paul Zimmerman. "P.S. Jim Thorpe's frustration and heartbreak is at an end."

His three eldest boys, all in their twenties, were in the military service when they got the news. Phil and Bill came from overseas. Dick was close by with the Navy Air Corps in San Pedro. Jack was still at the Chemawa Indian School in Oregon; he heard it on the radio. Daughters Gail, Charlotte, and Grace were in their thirties with growing families of their own. The Thorpe women had endured separation and dysfunction from an early age. They were often apart from their father, but they had a deep understanding of him—the gentleness, the weaknesses, the joy and sadness, the competing instincts of calm and restlessness.

Grace would not forget the last time she saw him alive. It was in Pearl River. Jim was returning to New York City after a brief visit with the family. He was getting around by bus, so she dropped him at a stop on Central Avenue to catch the coach to Manhattan thirty miles down the Palisades.

She idled across the street until she saw the big gray-and-red bus approach, then took a last look at her father before driving away. Brown suit, broad-brimmed hat, threadbare tweed overcoat in the crook of his left elbow, an old cowhide suitcase—as weary and well-traveled as he was—in his massive right hand. Jim caught her eye from across the street and smiled self-consciously, seemingly unaware of what loomed above. It was the marquee of the Pearl River Theater, where his name beckoned in large block letters: **JIM THORPE—ALL AMERICAN.** The story of his life, playing in a return engagement. Grace waved good-bye to her Sac and Fox father, the greatest athlete in the world, as he stood there quiet and alone, until the door sighed open and he got on board.

Epilogue

The Great Spirit

A COLD WIND RUSTLED THE BLACKJACK OAKS ON A HILLside above Ed Mack's farmhouse when the big black coffin holding Jim Thorpe's body arrived. Two weeks had passed since Jim had died of a heart attack in his house trailer in southern California. After a forty-five-hour passage east from Los Angeles to Oklahoma by train, his casket had been unloaded from the baggage car into a hearse, an effort that required the strength of nine men; and now, a day later, another cortege of mourners hauled him up the hill and home. The Mack farm was ten miles northeast of Shawnee and an equal distance another direction from the cabin above the North Canadian River where Jim was born. He was being taken back to his roots, to land that was Indian Territory at the time of his birth, into the embrace of the people of the Sac and Fox and Potawatomi nations from which he rose to world fame.

The Mack farm was now sacred ground, a closing of the circle for *Wa-tho-huk*. As a boy, he had been told by his mother that he was the reincarnation of Black Hawk, the Sac and Fox warrior. He had been reared Catholic, and a requiem mass was being planned at a church in Shawnee, but this outdoor rite on the hillside held a deeper spiritual meaning. In keeping with tradition, the casket was placed in a ceremonial wickiup, a makeshift shelter of canvas stretched over a dome of oak branches. Moccasins and herbal medicines were placed inside the coffin as totems to accompany Jim on his journey to the Spirit World. Cars and pickup trucks spotted the grounds near the farmhouse as friends and family paid tribute with bags of corn and pots of beef and chicken. Campfires flickered. Jim's children were there, along with other relatives and Carlisle teammates

Albert Exendine, William Newashe, and Joe Guyon. An elder led the gathering in hours of Sac and Fox song and prayer, a grieving process meant to go on through the night until dawn, when Jim's soul would be set free on a journey toward the western horizon.

The ritual never got that far. They were in the middle of the feast when Patsy Thorpe arrived from the Aldridge Hotel in downtown Shawnee, accompanied by a hearse and a cadre of officers. This cold hillside was no place for her husband, even if only for a night, she declared. As the widow, she had the power over his body, and she ordered her squad of men to haul away the coffin. "My brothers and I, along with many tribal members who were in attendance, were all very upset that Patsy had the body removed from the ceremony," recalled Bill Thorpe, who'd come home on leave from army service in Korea after his father's death. His younger brother Jack called Patsy's intervention "a slap in the face to all Indian people." They looked on in astonishment, helpless to prevent what they viewed as a sacrilegious act of psychic terror that would strand the dead man's soul in limbo if the ceremony was not completed.

Lo, the poor Indian, one more time.

It was an unsettling moment, but one that fit the pattern of Jim Thorpe's epic life. Once again, a white person was deciding what was best for an Indian. Jim was born and died in years of seminal significance in white society's mistreatment of indigenous people. He came into the world the same year as the 1887 Dawes Act that stripped Native American nations of millions of acres of communal reservation property and pushed most Indians onto smaller individual allotments. And he left in the year of the Indian Termination Policy of 1953, an act seen as a final dissolution that attempted to disband American Indian tribes altogether, or at least the federal government's recognition of them. The goal in both cases was forced assimilation. The result in both cases was the loss of Indian lands and an assault on ancient cultures.

Patsy's hijacking of the coffin during the ceremony was the first in a series of peculiar events after Thorpe's death. Just as she had during eight years of marriage, Jim's third wife played the angles as his self-assigned agent and promoter, looking for the best deal. She maintained that she was defending his interests, but her involvement was greeted with skepticism and often scorn by others who thought she was self-serving if not greedy, and that she knew little and cared less about indigenous traditions.

Jim had stressed to his sons over the years that he wished to end up in Sac and Fox country. Bill Thorpe later cited three instances where his father asked to be buried near where he was born. The first mention came after Jim had a heart attack while working at the Ford Motor Company when he and the boys were living near Detroit. The second was when Bill was a boarding student at the Sherman Indian Institute in Riverside, California, and Jim visited to watch Bill play in a baseball game, after which father and son discussed the old man's vulnerable health. And the final instance came when Bill was working as a salesman in Buffalo after the war and Jim was barnstorming through New York state as the manager of wrestler Suni War Cloud. "I contacted my father while we were both in Buffalo and we had dinner," Bill later reported. "As part of this discussion my father again mentioned his desire to be returned to Sac and Fox country for his last rites and burial."

If Jim made those wishes known to Patsy—and he almost certainly did—they were only one factor, and not the decisive one, in her deliberations. Would he end up in his native Oklahoma, in a cemetery in Shawnee or Anadarko, both of which expressed interest? Or at the old cemetery at the Carlisle Indian Industrial School in Pennsylvania where he rose to fame and where civic and military leaders now said he belonged? Or would he be put to rest in California, where he'd spent most of his final two decades? For the first week after Jim's fatal heart attack, Patsy remained noncommittal, playing various suitors against one another.

As it turned out, Thorpe had a viewing, a partial ceremony, and a full funeral service—but no burial anywhere in the days and weeks after his death in the spring of 1953.

The viewing was in Los Angeles days before Patsy cut short the ceremony at the Mack farm. Jim's embalmed body, outfitted in a beaded buckskin jacket and moccasins, a rosary and prayer book at his side, lay under glass at the Malloy and Malloy mortuary on South Flower Street as a few thousand visitors, ranging from sports and film celebrities to Indians from nearby Riverside, trooped past his coffin. That very day a headline in a Muskogee newspaper declared, "Widow of Thorpe Refuses Sending Body Back Home." Two days later, Patsy relented when Jim's children prevailed on her to put the body on the train to Oklahoma, where it seemed the state would finance a memorial to meet her grand expectations. Then came the truncated Sac and Fox ceremony interrupted by Patsy, followed the next day by a requiem mass at St. Benedict's Roman Catholic Church in Shawnee, where Patsy was the grieving widow, at one point wailing, "Good-bye dear, I've brought you back home!"

Not quite. The expectation was that Jim would then be buried in Row 2 of the cemetery at nearby Garden Grove, in the family plot near his father, Hiram, and long-departed twin brother, Charlie. It never happened. Patsy kept the coffin above ground, waiting for the state to follow through on its promise of a suitable memorial. She could be stubborn and self-centered, but her distrust of others was not always without reason. When a bill to fund the memorial reached the desk of Governor Johnston Murray, everyone expected him to sign it. Murray had played football and baseball like Jim, was born on Chickasaw Nation land in Indian Territory, and kept a portrait of Thorpe in the Blue Room next to his office at the state capitol. Ross Porter, the wealthy general manager of the *Shawnee News Star*, who had been recruited by Murray to serve on a Thorpe memorial commission, said the governor promised the project would succeed. "I'm part Indian myself," Murray told Porter. "Oh, no, this thing goes through. Don't worry about it."

Despite that reassurance, Murray vetoed the Thorpe memorial funding bill two months later, claiming he had to because of a revenue deficit. "He double-crossed us," Porter said of Murray, who during his single four-year term set a state record with forty vetoes. Patsy felt vindicated and continued her effort to find the best deal. Before summer's end, she had moved Jim's body from the mausoleum at Fairview Cemetery in Shawnee to the Rose Hill Mausoleum in Tulsa, hoping that Oklahoma's second-largest city might host him. That idea also went nowhere. The Thorpe sons and others maintained that Patsy was looking not only for the grandest memorial but also for cash for her efforts. "What she was looking for was money," said Bill Thorpe. Her history lent some credence to that assertion, but it fell into the category of supposition and in the decades since then no documentation has surfaced to support the allegation.

In any case, she was through with Oklahoma, again, and turned her attention to Pennsylvania, the other region with strong ties to her late husband. She commuted between Tulsa and Philadelphia, where with the help of lawyers she formed a Thorpe foundation to promote her cause. Philadelphia might be the right place for an ambitious scheme, she thought. Or Pittsburgh, or Harrisburg, or Carlisle. But there were problems with each, either no interest or confoundment over Patsy's demands. Finally, during the height of the fall foliage season, and quite by accident, she found her match in the most unlikely place, on ground where Jim had never set foot.

ONE OF PATSY'S key contacts in Philadelphia was Bert Bell, who had served as commissioner of the NFL since 1946. Bell grew up in a football family and as a teenager watched in awe as Thorpe led the Carlisle Indians in their annual rivalry games against the University of Pennsylvania Quakers in 1908, 1911, and 1912—an era when Bell's father, a former Penn football player, was a school trustee. Bert played football himself at Penn years later and after leaving school went into assistant coaching at Penn and Temple, where he eventually was let go by none other than Pop Warner in 1933 when Pop, after leaving Stanford, was named head coach. It was then that Bell became involved with the NFL, first as founding owner of Philadelphia's pro franchise, the Eagles, and later as commissioner, a more powerful iteration of the job Thorpe held at the dawn of the league. To Bell, Thorpe was a sporting god. When Thorpe's widow approached him for support, he was immediately receptive.

As Patsy later told the story, she was in Philadelphia for a meeting with Bell and foundation lawyers that October when "a stroke of fate" redirected her mission. One evening, after she had returned to her room at the Bellevue-Stratford Hotel, she switched on the television to watch her preferred news program. In the early 1950s, TV sets were erratic and reception iffy. Philadelphia had three main channels—3, 6, and 10. Patsy kept twisting the dial trying to get 6 or 10, but could only pick up 3, WPTZ, one of the oldest stations in the nation. Dick McCutchen's *Esso Hour* was on the air with a feature on two small towns struggling with economic decline in the anthracite coal country of the Pocono Mountains between Scranton and Allentown.

The twin boroughs were Mauch Chunk and East Mauch Chunk. (Mauch as in *mock*.) The name derived from the indigenous Munsee-Lenape language and was translated as "sleeping bear" or "bear mountain." The towns were separated by the deep gorge of the Lehigh River, nestled between mountains with vistas so majestic local boosters called the region the Switzerland of America. Coal and tourism had put the towns on the map, but as McCutchen's show revealed, tourists had stopped coming decades ago, and the coal business was dying, and the towns along with it. To revive the economy, a local newspaper editor had started a "Nickel a Week" fund-raising drive with the goal of raising enough money in modest increments to build an industrial park, a movement that brought McCutchen there to chronicle the story. As Patsy watched his program, she became enthralled by the beauty of the area and struck by its need for a fresh start. Combining those two elements, beauty and desperation, she conceived her latest great notion and made a trip up to "the Chunks" to see if her idea might work.

The widow Thorpe's visit to the mountain towns had some of the flavor of Harold Hill's arrival in River City in *The Music Man*. She was not a professional con artist like Hill, but like him arrived with a bounteous supply of boasts and sweet-talking promises to bestow upon unsuspecting townsfolk. Saying she was thrilled by the scenery and taken by the friendliness of the people, she broached the subject of making this the final resting place for her late husband—and so much more. How about a five-hundred-bed Jim Thorpe heart and cancer hospital? And a Jim Thorpe recreation center? And maybe even a Jim Thorpe College. And why not locate a pro football hall of fame there someday? Patsy oozed charm and grace. She found a willing local believer in Joseph L. Boyle, editor of the *Mauch Chunk Times-News*, and a courtship ensued.

In early November, Boyle formed a citizens' committee that proposed merging the boroughs and renaming them Jim Thorpe, Pennsylvania, and turning them into a shrine to the great athlete featuring his tomb, the hospital, and all the rest. In a letter sent to David Shinberg, the lawyer for the Thorpe foundation, Boyle said his committee members were "ardent admirers of the late Jim Thorpe," and that there was a "prevailing sentiment" in the towns to go forward with the scheme "if Mrs. Thorpe consents to have his body brought here for permanent interment." When word of the letter reached Patsy in Tulsa, she sent back a telegram stating that the news "delights and brings great happiness." She would return to the area soon to discuss details, she said. "Advise Dave [Shinberg] of my approval and acceptance. Most Cordially, Patricia G. Thorpe."

Patsy swept into town after what she called a fatiguing train ride from Oklahoma late on Thursday, November 20, in the company of Jim's favorite old dog, sixteen-year-old Butch, a suitcase full of Thorpe memorabilia, and one of his daughters, Charlotte Koehler, who joined her from Chicago. Charlotte's presence revealed a split within Jim's family. The four sons wanted nothing to do with Patsy and were enraged when she declined to bury Jim in Oklahoma. But she had a smoother relationship with Charlotte, Grace, and Gail. They viewed her not as a slick manipulator looking out only for her own interests but as a strong if melodramatic woman devoted to trying to give their father his due. As diametric as the two viewpoints seemed, they both accommodated some measure of truth.

While Patsy signed the register at the American Hotel in Mauch Chunk, Charlotte turned to a local reporter and declared that "the family is thrilled with the plan." Patsy then praised the local citizenry, saying the people were the salt-of-the-earth sort Jim loved. Broaching the concept of the hospital and other future developments, she said the possibilities of her relationship with the town were "unlimited."

In a weeklong lobbying campaign, Patsy took part in a noon radio program at Bright's Store; revealed that she had written six chapters of a book about her late husband that would be titled "Jim Thorpe, the Man," with all profits from the proposed book going toward the Thorpe enterprise; sat for an interview with sportscaster Chick Whittier that would be featured on Bill Stern's coast-to-coast radio broadcast (now on ABC); and gave another interview to Dick McCutchen, who drove up from Philadelphia with his crew to do a show about her. She was also escorted to nearby Lehighton with Charlotte where they were honored guests at the annual Carbon County parade, riding in a sedan with leaders of the Mauch Chunk industrial association; was saluted at the head table of a Bear Mountain Lions Club dinner; and addressed three hundred citizens at a public hearing at Mauch Chunk High School. For the plan to go forward, it required first a successful petition drive and then a referendum vote the following spring.

The success of Patsy's goodwill tour was reflected in both positive sentiments expressed at the public hearing and in glowing press she received. After meeting her, Betty Cossman, a feature writer at the *Morning Call* in Allentown, came away entranced. She called Patsy "a woman driven by her unselfish burning desire to have her husband's name enshrined in a place for all the world to see and remember" and described her "mature beauty that is lighted from within when she speaks of 'My Jim.'" Patsy, she wrote, was "an interesting conversationalist" who shrugged off discussing her own life but could not stop talking about Jim. In a "low, rather husky voice, she begins to weave word pictures of the early, golden days when the young Indian athlete was the idol of the world. The huskiness deepens as she describes his later life, when the early golden days were gone and the world had turned to new idols. As she continues, her face softens, changes, and becomes young again, making you wish you had been born earlier so that you, too, could have known Jim Thorpe." Her business affairs kept her on the move around the nation, Patsy said, but the connection she felt to this little pocket of Pennsylvania was so strong she vowed to establish residence in "Jim Thorpe, Pa.," and complete her book there. Maybe even run a tepee-themed hotel.

It was six months until the local election on May 18, 1954. In the middle of that time, in February, Patsy became confident enough of the outcome to have Jim moved from Tulsa. This time, there was nothing surreptitious about the leave-taking. It was treated as a solemn celebration. After a two-day journey by rail, the body arrived in Allentown early on the morning of February 7. Patsy collapsed at the sight of the casket and wept as she was assisted into a sedan for the thirty-car caravan from Allentown to East Mauch Chunk's Evergreen Cemetery mausoleum. The skies were a dreary gray. Snowbanks encrusted with dirt lined the roads along the route. As the cortege neared the Chunks, fire sirens alerted townspeople so they could view the passing scene, joining schoolchildren who had been excused from their morning sessions. Church bells pealed on both sides of the Lehigh gorge. At the cemetery, veterans formed an honor guard and a cordon of local athletic coaches lined up as pallbearers, slowly toting Thorpe's casket from the hearse to Crypt No. 10.

When the votes were counted on election night three months later, the referendum passed by an overwhelming ten-to-one margin in both boroughs—1,025 to 90 on the west side of the river and 1,178 to 109 on the east. Mauch Chunk and East Mauch Chunk were no more. From now on, they were one municipality—Jim Thorpe. The great man's widow declared herself eternally grateful. The Fraternal Order of Eagles vowed to get started on building a shrine on land set aside on the east side of the river. Bert Bell, newly named chairman of the foundation for the shrine and hospital, said he was delighted by the vote and called the people of the coalfields "as honest as the day is long." In the spirit of the "Nickel a Week" campaign, he said it would be better to fund the hospital with a million small donations than a few donations of millions. It was left to an editorial in the *Scranton Times-Tribune* to lend a sanguine perspective to what had happened: "Whether the people of Mauch Chunk and East Mauch Chunk acted wisely in voting to change the name of their communities—conceding all the time that Jim Thorpe's name is worthy of preservation—remains to be seen. Fame is fleeting, and it could be that a few years hence, if the hopes of those who urged the change of name are not fulfilled, that the town will again be called Mauch Chunk."

The day after the vote, town officials and Patsy Thorpe finalized the deal. The first "therefore" in their official agreement proved to be the most important. "The first party agrees for herself, her heirs, administrators and executors that neither she nor any of them will remove or cause to be removed the body of her said husband, Jim Thorpe, from the confines of the boroughs."

Jim was 1,340 miles from where he was born, in a place he had never been and where no one had ever known him. The fight over his bones seemed done. In fact, it had only just begun.

GRANTLAND RICE, THE bard of athletic heroism, came in with Thorpe and left with Thorpe, and during the decades of his prolific career tapped out as many odes to Jim as to Babe Ruth, Bobby Jones, Jack Dempsey, or any of the other sporting idols of the first half of the twentieth century. Rice wrote his first newspaper column in New York in 1911, just as Jim was reaching national fame as an All-American halfback at Carlisle, and died of a stroke at his typewriter on July 13, 1954, only a few months after Jim had reached his final resting place in a town renamed in his honor. In dozens of columns during those forty-plus years, Rice extolled Thorpe as the greatest of all athletes and campaigned persistently for the restoration of the gold medals and records that were stripped from him after the 1912 Stockholm Olympics.

Along with his immortal opening paragraph describing the Four Horsemen of Notre Dame outlined against a blue-gray October sky, Rice was known for hundreds of purple prose odes he wrote about athletic pursuits, none more famous than a rhyming stanza he conceived near the dawn of his career in a poem titled "Alumnus Football" that would be recited by generations of sports fans.

For when the one Great Scorer comes to mark against your name
He writes—not that you won or lost—but how you played the game.

Rice was awestruck by the way Thorpe played the game and believed the Great Scorer had done him wrong, or in this case the great scorers—of the amateur and Olympic movements, and above all Avery Brundage. Only months before he died, Rice made his last plea for justice for Thorpe while finishing his posthumously published memoir, *The Tumult and the Shouting*. "I seldom go out on limbs to crusade for individuals, much less a sport, my attitude toward public projects of this sort being with the 'sink' or 'swim' school," Rice wrote. "However, if ever an individual was pilloried by the shabby treatment he received . . . Jim Thorpe is that man." Rice argued that Jim was as misused and abused in life as in sports, but saved his most damning words for Brundage. "I wrote several letters in later years to Avery Brundage . . . stating the case for Thorpe. Brundage's replies were weak and implied a 'who, what . . . it's dead and forgotten' attitude. The treatment accorded Thorpe, in my opinion, is one of the cruel turns of all American sport."

With Rice gone, Brundage remained the target for those fighting to restore Jim's medals for the next two decades, until he relinquished his iron-fisted presidency of the IOC. His retirement came after the deadly Munich Olympics of 1972, when eleven members of the Israeli delegation were kidnapped and murdered by the Black September terrorist group. "The games must go on," Brundage declared shortly after the Israelis were killed. It was the defining statement of his life, a commitment to his notion of the Olympic ideal that overwhelmed any contrary notions of common sense and political reality. It was part of a Brundage pattern that included his support of the Nazi Olympics in 1936 and his stubborn refusal to consider the inequities in the treatment of athletes he deemed somehow impure, first and foremost Jim Thorpe. In that realm, Brundage was resistant to the end, making it sound as though he were the aggrieved party. "Any time they wanted publicity . . . they'd write that old Brundage should be made to give back Jim Thorpe's trophies," he complained in an interview with *Sport* magazine. "I had nothing to do with taking them away. I was an athlete just like he was at the time but I've been the whipping boy for it ever since."

The eventual elimination of strict amateur rules seemed inevitable in the post-Brundage period. Part of it had to do with so many blatant examples of athletes being punished for trivialities, such as when the great hurdler Lee Calhoun was suspended in 1958 for appearing with his wife as newlyweds on the television show *Bride and Groom,* an act said to violate General Rule VII, Section 1D forbidding athletes from "capitalizing on their athletic fame." Part of it had to do with the uneven international playing field Brundage had tried to ignore—the reality that athletes in the Soviet Union and its satellite nations had been professionals all along, funded by the state in service of Cold War bragging rights. And part of it had to do with a larger cultural shift in the 1960s and 1970s away from the archaic sensibility of elitist old boys competing for the pure love of sport, blissfully unconcerned with the economic necessities of most athletes. But if change was coming, it was at a glacial pace. It was not until 1973 that Olympic athletes were finally allowed to accept aid for training. Soon thereafter the amateur requirement was stricken from the Olympic charter, but the deletion was Pyrrhic; nothing was modified in the Olympic rule book.

The movement to restore Thorpe's medals waned and waxed year by year. As Patsy's health declined, her role as Jim's promoter diminished, but there was no shortage of others to take up the mission. Jim's children, sportswriters, biographers, fraternal organizations, politicians—every few years someone would resuscitate the cause. The first step toward restoration came when the AAU changed course and retroactively recognized Thorpe's amateur status. The move led President Richard Nixon to declare Jim Thorpe Day on April 16, 1973, saying that "millions of young people who aspire to great achievements transcending a disadvantaged background continue to take heart from Jim Thorpe's example." Two years later, after Patsy died in Hesperia, California, at age seventy-seven, the movement regained momentum in Washington. Grace Thorpe was working on Capitol Hill in 1975 as an intern in the office of James G. Abourezk, a Democratic senator from South Dakota and chairman of the Senate Committee on Indian Affairs. At the urging of Grace and her siblings, Abourezk cosponsored a Senate resolution calling on the IOC to follow the AAU's lead and restore Thorpe's amateur status. Grace saw it as the first move in a two-step process that eventually would lead to the return of his medals. First clear his name, then restore his Olympic achievements.

In tandem with the Senate resolution came another endorsement from the White House, this time a letter from President Gerald R. Ford to Brundage's successor at the IOC, Michael Morris of the United Kingdom, known by the title Lord Killanin. "To Americans of Indian heritage, Mr. Thorpe . . . is a hero, and in the American Indian's struggle for human dignity and freedom, Jim Thorpe represents a man who was able to contribute significantly to American society while retaining the values of his cultural ties with the past," Ford wrote. "For this reason, I urge your committee to consider the AAU's request." Ford, who excelled as a football center at the University of Michigan, said he was writing as a private citizen "with a lifetime interest in sports." He hoped the IOC would "act with a sense of equity in the light of history and the contribution that Jim Thorpe has made to the world of sports."

Still, the old guard resisted. When Jack Thorpe took the cause to Montreal during the 1976 Olympics, the IOC executive committee placed the question on its agenda but swiftly tabled the matter. The Thorpe children felt demoralized, but the campaign continued. More petition drives, more newspaper columns, more statements of support from fraternal and business organizations in Oklahoma, Ohio, and Pennsylvania, more support from the White House (now from the administration of Jimmy Carter), more letters by the bagful from schoolchildren around the country. Still nothing but dismissiveness from the Olympic powers that be. When sixth-grade students at Little Axe Elementary School in Norman, Oklahoma, conducted a letter-writing campaign, Robert Paul, longtime director of communications for the United States Olympic Committee, wrote back with responses that seemed jarringly disproportionate in their biting sarcasm to the young audience he was addressing.

To Autumn Colwell he wrote: "Really, Autumn, the medals are not part of the rich heritage of your state or the Sac and Fox tribe. Mr. Thorpe had left Oklahoma by then and the medals were ill-gotten."

To Belinda Thornhill he replied: "May I ask you, Belinda, if you win a prize and disobey the rules of the contest would you consider that you had won the prize fair and square? That is what you are faced with in judging Mr. Thorpe."

And to James Ray: "I have promised other members of your class that I shall never enter the state of Oklahoma because of statements which I made based on facts that were not acceptable to the members of your school."

Finally, in the early 1980s, the resistance broke. A combination of the relentless efforts of Jim's supporters, a change in leadership in the Olympic movement, and the imminent return of the games to Los Angeles made the difference. When the long-sought victory arrived, even though it turned out to be partial, there was considerable jockeying for credit. All seven Thorpe children played roles, even as disagreements arose among them and Charlotte in particular felt she was unfairly overshadowed. Robert Wheeler, Thorpe's first biographer, and his wife, sociologist Florence Ridlon, were tireless once they turned from chroniclers of the Thorpe saga to promoters of the cause, forming another Thorpe foundation and bringing aboard a roster of luminaries, including House Speaker Tip O'Neill; decathlete Rafer Johnson, who assumed Thorpe's title as the greatest athlete in the world at the Rome 1960 Olympics; and Billy Mills, the long-distance runner from the Oglala Sioux Nation who stunned the world by winning the 10,000-meter race at the 1964 Olympics in Tokyo.

The role that Wheeler and Ridlon played was vital and should not be undervalued. But it can also be noted that the one decisive legal argument they were said to have unearthed serendipitously while researching at the Library of Congress—an Olympic bylaw that said any protest regarding a contestant on the grounds of professionalism had to be filed within thirty days of the prizes—was nothing new. It was something that Swedish authorities and the *New York Times* correspondent in Stockholm had made abundantly clear as soon as the controversy broke in 1913. As the *Times* reported then, the Swedes' first response was to say that it was too late to strip Thorpe of his medals because 180 days had passed by the time his pro baseball history was exposed.

The revelation of that long-ignored rule nonetheless added legal weight to the moral and common-sensical arguments in Thorpe's favor. In quick succession, Congress passed a concurrent resolution calling on the IOC to recognize Thorpe's records and return his medals, and William E. Simon, the former treasury secretary under Nixon who had become chairman of the United States Olympic Committee, felt he had enough ammunition to persuade the IOC executive board, now led by president Juan Antonio Samaranch of Spain, to change its position. On October 12, 1982, Olympic authorities restored Jim's amateur status and scheduled a ceremony at which his children would be presented with the medals.

That moment arrived on January 18, 1983, at the Crystal Ballroom of the Biltmore Hotel in Los Angeles, seventy years to the month after Jim had been stripped of his medals. Samaranch was there with a cavalcade of Olympic officials. Six of the seven Thorpe children came along with more than thirty grandchildren and great-grandchildren, whose high-pitched whoops of appreciation during the event seemed to startle the executive suits in the room. For all of Jim's troubles—his struggles with alcohol, his nomadic lifestyle, his Sisyphean cycle of finding and losing jobs, his bad luck and mistreatment, his dysfunctional marriages, his time away from his sons and daughters when they were young—the Thorpe family did not wither but thrived from one generation to the next, producing military officers, government workers, college graduates, and Native American activists.

Carl Phillip retired as a lieutenant colonel who had served in the South Pacific during World War II, then Korea and Vietnam before earning a business degree from Maryland. Bill, another veteran, worked in the aircraft industry. Gail worked for the Girl Scouts of America, obtained a master's degree in tribal management, and helped shape Indian policy in Washington. Charlotte devoted herself to her father's cause, considering it emblematic of the larger mistreatment of Native people. Grace led the life of an activist, getting her start during the occupation of Alcatraz Island in late 1969, when she served as a publicist and negotiator for the American Indian protestors, a sensibility she passed along to her children and grandchildren. And Jack returned fully to his roots. As chief of the Sac and Fox Nation, he entered the Biltmore Hotel in a flowing headdress and the ceremonial regalia of his father's Thunder Clan. In the arc of the Thorpe story, as great as Jim's athletic achievements were, the productive if occasionally quarrelsome family he and his first two wives, Iva and Freeda, left behind was also an impressive legacy.

As it unfolded, the Los Angeles ceremony provoked a range of emotions. First came a sense of relief. Jack Thorpe said their hearts were overflowing with joy, that the spirit of his father was looking down on them, and that this marked "one of the first times in the history of the United States that an Indian has his honors restored to him." But there was also an unshakable sense of disappointment, as Bill Thorpe put it, that "this couldn't have been done thirty years ago." Burt Lancaster shared that sentiment, saying he "felt a certain cynicism that he didn't get it before. What does it mean now? There is a feeling of bitterness that it didn't get done in its own time."

The disappointment intensified as the hollowness of the gesture set in. The family did not receive Jim's old medals. After seven decades, they were missing. In their place, gold vermeil duplicates were cast from the original mold at the Swedish foundry. And the two trophies Jim had won and returned—the grand bronze pentathlon bust and silver decathlon Viking ship—were not part of the restoration. They remained at the Olympic headquarters in Switzerland. But the medals and trophies were only symbols of what Jim had achieved. Of more lasting importance would have been the acknowledgment of him as the clear winner in Stockholm and a rewriting of the official record to establish that fact. Instead, the IOC declared him cochampion with the athletes who finished second, Ferdinand Bie of Norway and Hugo Wieslander of Sweden, the runners-up who had been named gold medalists when Jim was disqualified. And even his status as cochampion was devalued when the IOC refused to modify the official report of the games, meaning that his record-smashing performances in the ten decathlon and five pentathlon events are missing from the documentation. As sportswriter and author Sally Jenkins, an astute and fierce critic of Olympic hypocrisy, later noted: "It made him an asterisk, not a champion. It was lip service, not restitution."

The campaign to restore the records would resume in the first decades of the twenty-first century, still without resolution, another dream deferred.

MOST OF WHAT Patsy promised would happen in Jim Thorpe, Pennsylvania, never materialized. The Jim Thorpe Heart and Cancer Hospital never came close to being built. It was proposed as a $10 million facility, but by the time Bert Bell, the foundation chairman, died of a heart attack while watching the Eagles play the Steelers at Franklin Field in 1959, they had raised about a thousand dollars. So much for that. No stadium named for Jim Thorpe either, and no recreation center or industrial park or college. Patsy had told the townsfolk that she loved the place so much she might move there and run a tepee-themed hotel, but she never did, nor did she finish her book about Jim. The Pro Football Hall of Fame opened in 1963, but it was located in Canton, not the town renamed for the hall's first iconic figure, though the fact that Jim played for the Canton Bulldogs and was there at the creation of the NFL was a key reason the Ohio site was chosen. (At the ceremonies in Canton that year, Thorpe was inducted into the inaugural Hall of Fame class, the brightest star of the first seventeen.)

What, if anything, did the river-split town in the hills of Pennsylvania end up with—besides the merger of the Chunks and the name change? A small park with a shrine to Jim Thorpe, including a twenty-ton gravestone made of Minnesota red granite, perched on a grassy slope on the east side of the Lehigh River just off State Road 903, a truck route wending through a neighborhood of ranch houses, pickup trucks, and a vocational school on the way out of town. The vault holding Jim's bones was dedicated on May 30, 1957, surrounded by a finely crafted sculpture garden of Jim toting a football and throwing a discus with markers that outlined the story of his fabled career. Here one could read about the famous line from the king of Sweden calling Jim the greatest athlete in the world, as well as an account of his records in the pentathlon and decathlon and his All-American football days at the Carlisle Indian Industrial School and his career in major league baseball. All waiting for a stream of visitors that never came in the numbers he deserved.

Jim was no Ozymandias. He never demanded attention as an arrogant king of kings. At the moment of his greatest acclaim, after his triumph in Stockholm, when he was placed at the head of a jubilant parade down Fifth Avenue in New York and was hailed by the multitudes and showered with confetti, he pulled his hat down low over his face and pinched his knees together as though he wanted nothing to do with fame. And now it came to this, a roadside shrine in the distant hills, not neglected but mostly forgotten as soon as it was built. It was not Shelley's "colossal wreck, boundless and bare," where "lone and level sands stretch far away," but it stood as a misplaced if not melancholy reminder that all of life's wonders diminish and decay.

The Scranton newspaper's warning that the citizens of Jim Thorpe might come to regret the town's name change proved prescient. By 1963, after it became obvious that none of Patsy's grand plans were to be realized, a noisy faction of locals known as Chunkers started petitioning for reversion to the old name. Chunkers versus Thorpians. The question was put to a public vote two consecutive years, 1964 and 1965, and both times the Thorpians narrowly prevailed, though the Chunker sentiment persisted in a low grumble for years. In 1970, *Detroit News* columnist Pete Waldmeir came to town and interviewed a disgruntled retired police sergeant named Fred Kemmerle. "It was a confidence job that's all it was," said the old cop. "Thorpe's wife came in here with a song and dance and we fell for it."

Gene Kilroy, who was Muhammad Ali's business manager, recalled the April day in 1974 when he and Ali hopped into Kilroy's blue and white Cadillac after the champ's morning road work and drove over to see the Thorpe memorial from nearby Deer Lake, where Ali was training for his heavyweight bout in Zaire with George Foreman, the "Rumble in the Jungle." "We drive up and see the big pink monument on the side of the road and Ali gets out and looks at it against the mountains in the background and says, 'Jim Thorpe can finally rest now.' And as we're standing there this couple pulls up and gets out of their car because they recognize Ali, the most recognizable person in the world, and they say, 'Oh my God, it's Muhammad Ali, thank you for coming,' and he says, 'Yeah, I just came to visit Jim Thorpe,' and they say, 'We paid thousands of dollars for this and no one comes here and all we got is a dead Indian.' We get in the car and there is dead silence. Finally, Ali says, 'Man, Poor Jim Thorpe. Even in death he can't rest in peace. That's how life is: yesterday's history, tomorrow's a mystery.' "

By the early 1980s, Jim Thorpe, Pennsylvania, had undergone a revival as a quaint Poconos resort for mountain bikers, hikers, whitewater rafters, and weekend antiques browsers—and the script flipped. The debate was no longer so much about the name, but about the bones. Jim's sons wanted to return him to Sac and Fox country and raised the issue more frequently. "Now if we can only bring my father's body back to Oklahoma, his spirit will finally have peace," Jack Thorpe said as he left the Biltmore Hotel on that January day in 1983 when he and his siblings received the replica Olympic medals. Jack visited Jim Thorpe, Pennsylvania, several times to make the case for repatriation, not as a demand but as a polite request. Nothing against the town, he said. He was just trying to respect his father's wishes. No dice, responded civic leaders. When Olinka Hrdy, a well-known artist from Prague, Oklahoma, within a few miles of where Jim was born, sent the community a thousand dollars hoping to prompt the repatriation of Jim's bones, the city council voted not to keep her check.

The Thorpe sisters, who never shared their brothers' negative feelings about stepmother Patsy, came to accept the location of the gravestone, as did their descendants. Charlotte had been there from the beginning, accompanying Patsy to the Chunks when she first made the deal in the late winter of 1954. Gail and Grace, with their histories as American Indian activists, eventually accommodated conflicting impulses by conducting spiritual ceremonies at the site complete with dirt from the Sac and Fox reservation. Jim's soul was rested, they said. The debate ebbed and flowed. At times the brothers seemed resigned to their father's unlikely resting place, just as they had once felt resigned to the idea that the Olympic wrongs would never be righted. Then, in 2010, feeling the mortality of his generation of Thorpes, Jack decided that if action was not taken then it would never happen. He went to federal court and sued to bring his father home.

BONES. THE MYSTERY and meaning of what remains. Jim Thorpe was told by his mother that he was the reincarnation of Black Hawk, his tribal ancestor in the Thunder Clan of the Sac and Fox nation. Black Hawk the warrior, Thorpe the athlete, the best-known American Indians of their times, both paraded through white America as noble oddities, one a prisoner of war, the other a prisoner of fame. The myth in each instance outlived the man.

When Thorpe died of a heart attack at his trailer home in California in 1953, he was destitute, desperate, and drinking cheap wine, far removed in time and distance from his fields of glory. When Black Hawk died of a sudden illness at a remote lodge along the Des Moines River in south-central Iowa on October 3, 1838, he was feeble and shriveled "like an old leaf" by age and whiskey, a shadow of his former rebellious self. Jim went into his coffin honoring his indigenous roots, dressed in a beaded buckskin jacket with moccasins and herbal medicines at his side. Black Hawk was buried in a Sac and Fox wickiup, in the traditional sitting-up position, but dressed in the fashion of his final years, a once-proud warrior who had succumbed to white societal norms. His death suit was the uniform of his former enemies: a bemedaled U.S. Army tunic presented to him by President Jackson, the Indian killer. At his side was a silver-handled walking stick, a gift from Senator Henry Clay of Kentucky, the Great Compromiser who supported indigenous land rights but believed Indians were a lower form of human life.

Black Hawk's bones had their own strange story. It was not precisely the same as Thorpe's but similarly unsettling. In July several months after he was put to rest in the wickiup at the Iowaville Cemetery near the town of Selma, his relatives came to check on him and discovered that his skull was missing. At their next visit, his remains were entirely gone. The grave robber turned out to be Dr. James Turner, a physician and Black Hawk aficionado who lived in the village of Quincy 150 miles to the west. When it became known that Turner had assembled Black Hawk's bones into a skeleton which he displayed in his office, the public clamor reached Robert Lucas, governor of the Iowa Territory. Lucas had his men seize the bones, but rather than return them to Iowaville he sent them to the Geographical and Historical Society in Burlington, where his territorial government was quartered. What remained of Black Hawk was on display there for seventeen years, until the skeleton was destroyed by a fire that ravaged the building in 1855.

Thorpe's bones were not lost to fire, but during the time of intense opposition to the name change in the mid-1960s an irate Chunker took a hammer to the granite base of his crypt, inflicting chips and scratches. Earlier, before the shrine was completed, some local skeptics were worried that Patsy had deceived them and failed to put his bones in the casket they were about to entomb. A surreptitious peek inside erased their doubts.

White men had been looting Native American gravesites for generations before Dr. Turner absconded with Black Hawk's bones. Thomas Jefferson was not the first to do it, but perhaps the most famous. The reason he opened a burial site near his home in Virginia in 1788 fit a pattern. The site near Monticello, which held as many as a thousand remains, was unearthed out of scientific curiosity, with no thought given to the deep significance burial mounds evoked in indigenous cultures. Sometimes the motivations were benign, but more often they were malignant. Polygenists seeking to demonstrate the superiority of the Caucasian race dug up the skulls of countless Native Americans for use in phrenology, a racist pseudoscience popular in the nineteenth and early twentieth centuries that claimed to determine personality and intelligence traits through the shape of the skull. It was phrenology that was used in the bogus analysis of Black Hawk based on a plaster cast made of his face during his East Coast tour as a prisoner of war in 1833.

Some grave robbers were unscrupulous private collectors, but more often they were public museums or federal agencies who thought they were advancing the disciplines of anthropology and archaeology. The most prominent included the American Museum of Natural History in New York, the Field Museum in Chicago, the Smithsonian Institution in Washington, and the Army Medical Museum, which started collecting during the wars against Indians after the Civil War and was interested only in skulls. Over the decades, hundreds of thousands of skeletons were dug up from indigenous gravesites and stored at museums—nineteen thousand at the Smithsonian alone. A movement to repatriate them to home soil finally gained legal momentum in 1990, when Congress passed the Native American Graves Protection and Repatriation Act.

It was through that act twenty years later that Jack Thorpe sued the city of Jim Thorpe, Pennsylvania, seeking the return of Jim's bones to Oklahoma. His sensibility in going to court was later captured in a play titled *My Father's Bones* written by Mary Kathryn Nagle, a playwright and lawyer specializing in tribal sovereignty cases, and Suzan Shown Harjo, a key activist in the fight for grave repatriation. "I spent years tryin' to bring Dad back," the Jack character says in the first scene as he stands in a corner of the family graveyard in Sac and Fox country. "I begged. I pleaded. I prayed. And when that didn't work, I did what you non-Native folks do all the time. I filed a lawsuit."

The case was heard by Judge Richard A. Caputo of the U.S. District Court for the Middle District of Pennsylvania. Jack said on the day he filed suit that he understood the conflicting sentiments. On the one hand, he noted, his father was "the greatest all-around athlete this country has ever produced," but he was also "Native American, and he had his tribe and his family, so you've always had two different cultures butting heads." But the earth in Oklahoma was sacred in Jim Thorpe's life, while the town in Pennsylvania had no meaning to him. "The bones of my father do not make or break your town," he said to the defendants. "I resent using my father as a tourist attraction."

A year later, while the case was still in court, Jack Thorpe died of cancer at age seventy-three, but the lawsuit did not die with him. It was picked up by his brothers Bill and Dick along with the Sac and Fox nation. First came a victory. On April 19, 2013, Judge Caputo ruled in favor of the sons and the tribe, deciding that the congressional act on repatriation, known as NAGPRA, took precedence over the contract Patsy Thorpe signed with the Mauch Chunks back in 1954. But that was followed by two defeats in succession. First a three-judge appeals panel overturned the decision, ruling that the town did not meet the act's definition of a museum, that the original contract was lawful, and that Caputo's ruling was an "absurd" interpretation of congressional intent. Then the U.S. Supreme Court declined to hear the case, and it was over.

• • •

MOST OF THE buildings that once housed the Carlisle Indian Industrial School still stand. They can be found on the edge of Carlisle on the grounds of the U.S. Army War College, 106 miles to the south and west of Thorpe's red granite tomb. Jim was but one of eight thousand or more young Native Americans sent to this national boarding school in the name of forced assimilation from 1879 to 1918, but he was the one who made it famous. The entrance road into the military installation is Jim Thorpe Drive. What once was the athletic dormitory has been turned into guest quarters known as Jim Thorpe Hall. There is a marker honoring Jim Thorpe at the gymnasium, and the soldiers stationed there celebrate Jim Thorpe Day with a round of sporting events at Indian Field every April.

On the far west end of the grounds, the white clapboard house where Pop Warner lived is still there on Garrison Lane, perched above a stretch of Letort Creek that in winter was flooded to create a skating rink. Across the lane is the Leupp Art Studio where Angel De Cora and Lone Star Dietz painted and taught in the company of their wolfhounds. The pillared mansion that once housed founder Richard Henry Pratt and his successors William Mercer and Moses Friedman sits at the top of a verdant expanse rising gently eastward with its replica of the bandstand where misbehaving students were forced to march in circles with DRUNK signs on their backs. To the south stands the old Guard House where Jim once spent the night after he was caught trying to run away from school, an indestructible structure built by Hessian prisoners during the Revolutionary War.

And finally, the cemetery and the matter, again, of funerary rites and the repatriation of Native American bones. At least 186 children were buried there after dying at school. Many more were sent home to die. The reason for that was appalling—so that the fatality numbers would draw less scrutiny—but the outcome was better for those young people. At least they were not put into the ground hundreds or thousands of miles from their families. The original Carlisle Indian Cemetery was near Poor House Road, not far from the athletic fields, but it was moved in 1927 to make way for new construction and a parking lot. All the skeletons, starting with

Abe Lincoln and Amos LaFramboise, the first two students to die during the school's inaugural season, were dug up and reburied at the new site on the edge of the military campus between what is now a commissary with a Subway sandwich franchise and the traffic on Claremont Road. There are six rows of headstones, each row about seventy yards long, with a stone historical marker at the entrance, a weeping cherry tree in the middle, and a black iron fence around the perimeter. The headstones, replaced twice over the years, reflected military ignorance or a lack of respect for the dead, or both. The names of many students and their tribal affiliations were misspelled. La*Fram*boise was turned into La*Farm*boise. The headstone for Cooki Glook, the Inuit girl from Port Clarence, Alaska, who died just before Thorpe arrived in 1904, called her Cookinglook. On the markers for James Wolfe and Fred Senachi, Sac and Fox was rendered *Sax* and Fox. And each of the oblong headstones was marked by a small Christian cross, with no apparent consideration given to the spirituality of indigenous cultures.

The bones of these Carlisle students, like Thorpe's, rest under Pennsylvania soil far from home. But at least for them the process of repatriation finally got underway. After decades of rebuffing family requests, the army reversed course in 2016. Tribes from Alaska to South Dakota to Wisconsin sent delegations to Carlisle for ceremonies at which bodies were exhumed for return to their native lands. To the home soil of the Rosebud Sioux went the remains of One That Kills Horse and Rose Long Face and Dennis Strikes First and Maud and Ernest Knocks Off and Bear Paints Dirt and Friend Hollow Bear and Little Girl. Home to the Oneida reservation in northern Wisconsin went Jemima Metoxen (whose gravestone at Carlisle was misspelled Meloxen), along with Sophia Coulon and Ophelia Powless; the first died of meningitis, the second from tuberculosis, and the third of pneumonia. As their bodies were exhumed, a great-niece of Jemima's sang out a version of "Amazing Grace." She recited it in the Oneida language.

What happened at the Carlisle Indian Industrial School was in many ways illustrative of the larger treatment of American Indians by white society. Under the guise of knowing what was best, with intentions considered pure and enlightened, the federal government forced thousands of Indian children to assimilate and acculturate to white norms and expectations. *Kill the Indian, save the man.* Some resisted, many suffered, some thrived, most learned the nuances of how to survive while maintaining their identity as Native Americans. Jim Thorpe became a symbol for almost all of that. At times he resisted. At times he suffered. At times he thrived. And he survived.

One evening in May 1968, Grace Thorpe was invited to speak at a banquet sponsored by the Carlisle Junior Chamber of Commerce for the first celebration of Jim Thorpe Day. She labored over the speech, wanting to get it right, practicing it over and again in front of a mirror in her hotel room, timing it at twenty-one minutes, telling herself to speak with more animation, stop sniffling, smile while talking, don't make it too singsongy, get close to the microphone. Some of her notes were in longhand, some typewritten, words crossed out and replaced for rhythm and meaning. She arrived in Carlisle a day early so she could roam the campus and think about where her father had spent seven years of his life, where he reached athletic stardom on the track and football field, and where he met Iva Miller, her mother. She talked to whoever she could find who still had stories to tell about her dad, from Pop Warner's old secretary to a haberdasher at Blumenthal's Men's Store downtown.

It is human nature to try to repress some memories and revive and reshape others. None of Jim's seven children were able to spend much time with him when he was alive, yet all of them in different ways revered him and strove to honor and redeem him once he was gone. Grace was no exception. Once, when she was eight and a boarding student at Haskell, she barely recognized Jim when he came to perform at halftime, so seldom had she seen him. Her life was marked more by his absence than his presence. Yet now that he had slipped into history, into American mythology, she could reclaim his ghost. He was a public monument, but also again a father.

The question she was asked most often, Grace said, was what it was like to be Jim Thorpe's daughter. "The answer to that is I don't feel any different than anyone else. My dad was famous when I was born. I'm used to it. It's like how do I feel about being female? Since I've always been one, how can I judge? To me, my father was not an amazing athlete, or a world-renowned figure, or a walking legend. To me, he was just plain . . . my dad." She recalled staying with him at the Oklahoma ranch of her aunt, Big Mary, when she was a teenager, and how he got up before sunrise one morning, shot squirrels out of the pecan trees down by the creek, and made a delicious breakfast of baking powder biscuits, pork chops, oatmeal, eggs, fried potatoes, and fried squirrel with gravy. He loved to hunt and fish more than anything, she said. He liked family picnics with old friends, and reading both the morning and evening paper, and having a smoke just before he retired for the night. He was a bear of a man who was light on his feet, a great dancer, and could sketch anything, but didn't talk much and almost never about himself.

After Grace finished speaking that night, the Jaycees were planning to end the evening in the auditorium at Carlisle High School by showing *Jim Thorpe—All-American*, the movie starring Burt Lancaster that happened to be on the marquee at the Pearl River Theater on the day in 1953 when she last saw her father alive, not long before he died in the trailer park across the continent. "Before the movie starts, and in conclusion, I would like to say this," Grace said. "What does the word *great* mean? Webster's dictionary defines it like this, and I quote: 'Remarkable in magnitude, degree, or effectiveness.' My father had his faults. Who doesn't? He was not a businessman and he left only a small estate when he died. He dug ditches to support his family during the Depression when he was too old for athletics. But in his chosen field he had no peers. He stood alone. He was remarkable in magnitude, degree, and effectiveness. He was great."

Gratitude

Nearly two decades ago, in the fall of 2003, my travels around America to talk about *They Marched into Sunlight*, a book on the Vietnam War, took me to the Denver Press Club. After a session with journalists there, I was approached by Norbert Hill Jr., a writer from the Oneida nation in Wisconsin, my home state. He had an idea for my next book. "Write a biography of Jim Thorpe," he said. I thanked him, explained that I was already working on a biography of Roberto Clemente, that I had other projects beyond that lined up, and that the subjects of my books had to be things about which I was obsessed. I did not realize that a seed had been planted that day. It took a long time to grow, but grow it did, and four years ago my interest in Jim Thorpe sprouted into obsession. I owe this book to Norbert Hill, with belated gratitude.

Before launching into the project, I wrote to Patty Loew, director of the Center for Native American and Indigenous Research at Northwestern University and a professor at the Medill School of Journalism. Loew, a member of the Bad River Band of Lake Superior Ojibwe, had come to Northwestern from the University of Wisconsin, where I knew her as a prodigious documentarian and public television host who loved sports and was an expert on indigenous athletics. I asked her whether she thought Jim Thorpe was worth another look and whether I could be the one to do it. "Yes . . . and emphatically YES!" she responded, and that made all the difference. Of course, she is not responsible for any mistakes I've made, but I would not have started had her response been otherwise, and I've benefited from her wisdom all along the way.

One of the first research calls I made was to Suzan Shown Harjo, a longtime American Indian activist who was involved in virtually every important campaign for indigenous rights over the last half century. Harjo,

Cheyenne and Hodulgee Muscogee from Oklahoma, was instrumental in the development of the Smithsonian's National Museum of the American Indian and honored with a Presidential Medal of Freedom in 2014. Her mother's grandfather was in Richard Henry Pratt's first class at the Carlisle Indian Industrial School in 1879, and her mother's mother was born in Carlisle. It was in my discussions with Harjo that I began to understand how the "civilizationist" philosophy at Carlisle and other Indian boarding schools affected generations of Native Americans. But it was something more personal that struck the most powerful chord—her description of what happened to her father, Freeland Edward Douglas, as a boy. "My dad used to say that when he was in federal boarding school in Oklahoma at age nine, he didn't know why he was getting beat up," she told me. "That he was getting beat up in the lunchroom where they served the food and he thought they didn't want talking around food. Then he thought, no they don't want talking in line, no they don't want talking in Indian, in Muscogee, his language. He said he was beaten with boards. When you think about it, a nine-year-old! To his last days, he was always uncomfortable speaking at dinner or at the table."

Harjo also recalled her father telling her about the time as a boy in Okmulgee, Oklahoma, when he was standing near the Newtown United Methodist Church and saw a big black car pull to the curb. When he asked who it was, he was told it was "the great man"—Jim Thorpe, there to visit one of his sisters, Fannie. "He shook my hand and talked to me," Douglas told his daughter "I remember he talked to me real good, real good, and I was happy to meet him."

Researching a book can be a methodical process, but there is always a certain serendipity to it. Harjo told me that an associate of hers had once interviewed her father about meeting Thorpe. Who was that? I asked. She said it was David Hurst Thomas, curator of North American Archaeology at the American Museum of Natural History in New York, who had also served with her as a founding trustee at the National Museum of the American Indian on the National Mall. When I contacted Thomas, he invited me to meet with him at his office on the fifth floor of the grand neo-Romanesque building on the Upper West Side. Thomas sat casually in a room stuffed with old books, maps, and artifacts, his western boots occasionally propped on his desk—an artifact in and of itself, having once belonged to his late colleague at the museum, the legendary anthropologist Margaret Mead. He talked about Thorpe and the museum and his support of the repatriation of bones and cultural artifacts taken from indigenous sites over the centuries, and near the end of our conversation, he told me that he had been obsessed with the Thorpe story and spent years conducting research for a biography that for various reasons he never wrote. As a football fan who had once worked for Al Davis of the Oakland Raiders, he had read my book on Vince Lombardi, he said, and was thrilled that I was now as obsessed with Thorpe as he was. And that is how I inherited what I now call the David Hurst Thomas Archive, eight boxes of invaluable material that my friend Chip Brown later helped me pile into a station wagon for the drive back to my home office in Washington. I remain everlastingly grateful to David for his generosity.

Biographers are miners panning for gold in old rivers, and when dealing with a well-known subject there are always people who had worked the waters earlier. Thomas was one among many who in various ways contributed to my understanding of Jim Thorpe. Soon after I started, I wrote to Kate Buford, a fellow biographer who had written a finely documented book about Thorpe a decade earlier. When I told her what I was doing, she responded with characteristic grace, welcoming me to the story and inviting me to explore the personal archive she had accumulated, which led to a rewarding day rummaging through several well-kept boxes in her Charlottesville, Virginia, basement. My *Washington Post* colleague Sally Jenkins, who had written a book about the Carlisle football team, was also generous and helpful, as was Texas writer Bill Crawford. Scott and Tod Newcombe, the sons of the late *Life* magazine writer Jack Newcombe, sent me a box of typed and handwritten notes their father had taken in the 1970s to write his book about the Carlisle athletic boys. Robert W. Wheeler was the first Thorpe biographer, providing valuable research at a time when many of Thorpe's contemporaries were still alive. James E. Elfers was generous with documents and information about baseball and the 1913 world tour.

Archivists and librarians around the country helped me find my way through documents. They included Linda Stahnke and William J. Maher at the University of Illinois Library's Avery Brundage Collection; David S. Sager at the Recorded Sound Research Center at the Library of Congress; Sara Powell at the Beinecke Rare Book and Manuscript Library at Yale; Nathan Sowry at the National Museum of the American Indian Cultural Resource Center; Mallory Covington at the Oklahoma Historical Society; Bill Francis at the National Baseball Hall of Fame and Museum; Tom Haas at the McKinley Presidential Library and Museum in Canton, Ohio; Elizabeth E. Fuller at the Rosenbach in Philadelphia; researcher Tanya Parlet at the University of Oregon; and Richard Tritt at the Cumberland County Historical Society. Also thanks to Jim Kossakowski, Leigh Montville, Gene Kilroy, Jeff Benjamin, Bill Mallon, Alec Albee, Vicky Armstrong, Brian Wright O'Connor, Tom Salva, Tonya Hamilton, Ned Blackhawk, Louis Clark, Trace L. Hentz, and Aaron Bird Bear for bits of information and inspiration. The internet is a neutral force that can be used for bad or good, but writers of history appreciate the ways the digitization of primary documents has made their lives easier. I still love to comb through musty folders, but finding newspapers online through Newspapers.com and digitized documents through the Carlisle Indian School Digital Resource Center saved me from months of labor at microfilm machines.

The pandemic made this book unavoidably different from my previous twelve. My motto had always been *Go there, wherever there is,* but partway through my research I had to stop traveling to protect myself and my family from Covid-19. This meant I never got to Stockholm, the site of Thorpe's great triumph at the 1912 Olympics, among other places, but through the miracle of hours of old film compiled and modernized by documentarian Adrian Wood I felt I was there. One adventure I did take, which informed the book though it did not find its way directly into the manuscript, was a boat tour of Lake Mendota in Madison with Steve Holtzman and Don Sanford, who wrote a social history of the wondrous glacial lake and expertly showed me the many Indian mounds that rise on its banks and the cave on the south shore where Black Hawk hid when he and his party were being chased by troops in 1833 during what became known as the Black Hawk War.

For much of the project I was lucky to have the assistance of Erin Paulson, a brilliant young graduate of James Madison University who showed remarkable ingenuity and diligence handling the tasks I assigned her. She's a Purdue Boilermaker now, a graduate student in creative writing, and I can't wait to see what she creates. Teddy Brokaw first filled that role briefly and effectively before heading off for law school. Margot Williams, my longtime friend and former colleague at the *Washington Post*, was miraculous as usual in helping me locate people and documents. Barbara Landis, the former archivist at the Cumberland County Historical Society, is a walking encyclopedia of knowledge about the Carlisle Indian Industrial School. I'll never forget the time my wife and I spent walking the grounds of Carlisle with her and I'm grateful for all of her wisdom on the history of the school.

This book is dedicated to Alice Mayhew, the inimitable force of nature who edited all of my earlier books with Simon & Schuster and along the way became a wonderful friend. Like most of her writers, I never knew how old Alice was until she died on February 4, 2020. It turned out she was eighty-seven. I started this project with her around, and in our many conversations about it she was vibrant and supportive to the end. If Alice was irreplaceable, it was my great good fortune to find Bob Bender, another excellent editor who seamlessly picked up where Alice left off, adding his own seasoned perspective and keen eyes to the manuscript, along with the efficient help of Johanna Li. I am also grateful for support from Jonathan Karp, the S&S chairman; Dana Canedy, the publisher; and especially my A-team of Julia Prosser, Cat Boyd, Stephen Bedford, and Jackie Seow. I bow in thanks to the book's copy editor, the poet Joal Hetherington, and to production editor Kayley Hoffman.

I'm old-school when it comes to loyalty. One football team (Packers), one baseball team (Brewers), and one agent and one newspaper. None of this would be possible without my agent and friend, Rafe Sagalyn, and all of my amazing colleagues during a forty-plus-year career at the *Washington Post*.

Many thanks to the writers who commented on parts of the manuscript, including Patty Loew, Blaine Harden, Glenn Frankel, Chip Brown,

Pat Toomay, Jane Leavy, Anne Hull, Bruce Oppenheimer, Jim Warren, and my brother Jim Maraniss, and to great friends Neil Henry, John Feinstein, Robert Samuels, Ines Pohl, Mike Tackett, Michael and Rebekah Weisskopf, Kim Vergeront and Andy Cohn, Michael and Beth Norman, Rick and Jane Atkinson, Bob Woodward and Elsa Walsh, Jenny Chandler-Hauge and Steve Berk, and also to Tom Schwartz, Alan Wiseman, Bob Barsky, and my other colleagues at Vanderbilt University. I'm eternally thankful to have such a wonderful extended family, including sister Jean and her husband, Michael Alexander, brother Jim and his, wife Gigi Kaeser, Carol and Ty Garner, Dick and Mary Ann Porter, Doug and Cathy Williams, and a voting bloc of equality-pushing, democracy-loving cousins, nieces, and nephews.

Despite the heartbreak, meanness, and idiocy of this messed-up world, there is also enough beauty and soul around to keep me going, and much of it comes from the home team: son, Andrew and his wife, Alison; daughter, Sarah and her husband, Tom; and four inspired and inspiring grandchildren—Heidi, Ava, Eliza, and Charlie. They make me feel better about the future. Linda is my past, present, and future, the quirky saint who has been my partner for more than a half century. She read the manuscript from beginning to end and kept me safe and sane during the long slog of Covid times, especially the brutally hot summer months in Washington when I would quit writing precisely at three for our daily ritual of playing in the hose in our front driveway and cooling off with a tree bath. As I was finishing *Path Lit by Lightning*, Linda, whose religion is the wonder of the natural world, was reading *Braiding Sweetgrass* by Robin Wall Kimmerer, a professor and naturalist and member of the Citizen Potawatomi Nation. Linda said she loved how Kimmerer described the way the Potawatomi would recognize the world of water and grass and trees and animals with the words "Greetings and thanks. Now our minds are one."

All greetings and thanks to Linda. Our minds, now and always, are one. Even in her crazy dreams.

Notes

The narrative of this book was shaped primarily from documents, letters, oral histories, and contemporaneous accounts from the following archival sources:

Beinecke Rare Book and Manuscript Library, Yale University
Carlisle Indian School Digital Resource Center, Dickinson University (CISDRC)
Carlisle Industrial School Site, Barbara Landis/Genevieve Bell
Cumberland County Historical Society, Carlisle, Pennsylvania (CCHS)
David Hurst Thomas Collection (DHTC)
Glenbow Western Research Centre, University of Calgary
Grace F. Thorpe Collection, National Museum of the American Indian Cultural Resources
Center, Suitland, Maryland (NMAI)
International Olympic Committee Archives, Lausanne, Switzerland
Jack Newcombe personal papers
James Elfers personal papers
Jim Thorpe House, Yale, Oklahoma
Kate Buford personal papers
Mike Koehler unpublished manuscript
Library of Congress Manuscript Division (LOC)
Library of Congress Sound Research Center
National Archives and Record Administration, Record Group 75 (NARA)
National Baseball Hall of Fame, Cooperstown, New York
National Museum of the American Indian, Washington, D.C.
Newberry Library (Chicago) Carlos Montezuma Collection
Newspapers.com
Oklahoma Historical Society (OHS)
Pro Football Hall of Fame, Canton, Ohio

Rosenbach Museum and Library, Philadelphia
University of Illinois Archive, Avery Brundage Collection (UIABC)

CHAPTER 1: "THE STUFF HIS PEOPLE ARE MADE OF"

5 *The first public stop*: Depiction of scene in Boston from local newspapers, *Boston Herald, Boston Globe, Boston Traveler, Los Angeles Herald,* Aug. 10–11, 1912. "Thorpe would not make a speech," wrote the *Globe.* "But he had to stand up while those around cheered him": also "Red Son of Carlisle" unpublished manuscript, 48. Honey Fitz was a devoted fan of the Boston Red Sox and had thrown out the first pitch that April 20 to open the inaugural season of the team's new home, Fenway Park.

5 *Speechwriters for William Howard Taft*: Text of Taft's letter in Thorpe Student File, Carlisle Indian School Digital Resource Center. The federal government would not acknowledge Thorpe as a U.S. citizen until 1916.

7 *Thorpe stayed behind*: *Boston Herald,* July 29, 1912. John H. Hallahan of the *Herald* was among the journalists accompanying Thorpe's crew to Paris, and for years thereafter he told variations of this story of Thorpe and his teammates in the City of Light: Thorpe and Ted Meredith, one of the speediest runners of his day, went on a tour of Paris with Hallahan and eventually found themselves in the rough Apache district. Suddenly a tough darted from a doorway and grabbed Hallahan's watch and chain and sped down an alley. "The poor guy didn't realize what a terrible mistake he was making. I had Meredith to catch him and Thorpe to beat his brains. What a combination!"

7 Get to New York soonest: "Red Son of Carlisle," unpublished manuscript, 48. Before reaching Carlisle, the trio stopped in Hershey, Pennsylvania, where Thorpe said he "let down on training sufficiently to do justice to the sweets."

7 *The festivities in Carlisle*: Account of Carlisle celebration drawn from *Carlisle Arrow* (CIS student newspaper), Sept. 13, 1912; also Aug. 17, 1912 editions of *Pittsburgh Post-Gazette, Carlisle Evening Herald, Boston Globe,* and *Philadelphia Inquirer,* and "Red Son of Carlisle," 52. "It was a nice reception and the memory of it has remained with me throughout these years," Thorpe wrote.

10 *Eight days later*: Account of parade in New York drawn from Aug. 25, 1912 editions of the *New York Times, New-York Tribune, New York Sun, Brooklyn Daily Eagle,* and *Buffalo Courier.*

11 *From New York it was on*: Account of celebration in Philadelphia drawn from Aug. 25–27, 1912 editions of *Philadelphia Inquirer.*

11 *the artist George Catlin arrived at Jefferson Barracks*: Reich, *Painting the Wild Frontier,* 45–48: "The sight of Black Hawk in chains strengthened George's resolve to help white people understand and respect the Indian peoples"; also Eisler, *The Red Man's Bones,* 155–157.

11 *For a few months*: Depiction of Black Hawk War drawn from Trask, *Black Hawk,* chapters 9–12; *Life of Black Hawk, Dictated by Himself,* 66–85; "Event of the Black Hawk War," Wisconsin Historical Society; Anthony F. C. Wallace, *Prelude to Disaster: The*

Course of Indian-White Relations Which Led to the Black Hawk War of 1832; Holman Hamilton, "Zachary Taylor and the Black Hawk War," *Wisconsin Magazine of History*, March 1941.

13 *Black Hawk's trip east*: Account of Black Hawk tour as prisoner of war drawn from *Life of Black Hawk, Dictated by Himself*, 88–98; Trask, *Black Hawk*, 297–302; also *York (PA) Gazette*, May 21, 1833; *New York Evening Post*, June 15, 1833; *Long Island Star*, June 19, 1833; *Wilmington People's Press & Advertiser*, June 26, 1833; *Boston Atlas*, June 27, 1833; *National Gazette* (Philadelphia), July 1, 1833; *London Morning Chronicle*, July 17, 1833; *Pittsburgh Weekly Gazette*, Nov. 28, 1833.

16 *Phrenology was a trendy pseudo-science*: Account of study of Black Hawk's head from *American Phrenological Journal*, November 1838. The study began: "Having given the measurements of the head of Black Hawk, and the relative size of his organs, we will now deduce the phrenological analysis of his character and then present the coincidence between what phrenology describes his character to be, and what his life thus far shows that it really is." Also R. L. Jantz, "Franz Boas and Native American Biological Variability," *Human Biology*, Vol. 67, No. 3, June 1995.

17 *Thorpe was put to his own*: Anthropometric study of Thorpe drawn from *Boston Herald*, Dec. 19, 1912; *Carlisle Evening Herald*, "Experts Measure and Find James Thorpe 'The Perfect Man,'" Dec. 30, 1912; Robert J. Park, "Taking Their Measure," *Journal of Sports History*, Summer 2006.

19 *Wilson was the George Catlin*: Depiction of how Wilson drew Thorpe portrait drawn from article he wrote in *Oklahoma's Orbit*, September 1967.

CHAPTER 2: PATH LIT BY LIGHTNING

20 *Hiram Thorp had five wives*: Hiram Thorpe probate document filed after testimony and investigation to determine his heirs, Hiram Thorpe individual file, Oklahoma Historical Society (most documents spelled his name without an *e* on the end); also 1900 Census, Dent Township, village of Keokuk Falls, Oklahoma; "Memories of Dad Notes," Grace Thorpe Collection, Series 1, NMAI.

20 *Jim was called* Wa-tho-Huk: It has also been spelled *Wa-tha-Huk*, and a more concise if less poetic translation of the name was Bright Path.

21 *He was part of both*: Dagmar Thorpe, "Ancestors of Jim Thorpe," September 2002; Grace Thorpe, "The Jim Thorpe Family," Parts I and II," *Chronicles of Oklahoma*, Spring and Summer 1981; Newcombe, *The Best of the Athletic Boys*, 28–31; "Red Son of Carlisle," 4–5; "Memories of Dad Notes," Grace Thorpe Collection, Series 1, NMAI.

21 *The specifics of the Dawes Act*: Bloom, *To Show What an Indian Can Do*, xiv–xv; Hoxie, *A Final Promise*, 77–81; Thomas, *Skull Wars*, 67–69; Adams, *Education for Extinction*, 17; Stephen Pevar, "The Dawes Act: How Congress Tried to Destroy Indian Reservations," Oxford University Press blog, Feb. 8, 2012.

22 *The Sac and Fox were . . . wary*: *Wichita Eagle*, June 10, 1887; *Pawnee Rock Leader*, June 17, 1887.

23 *A government agent reported*: Leo Bowers, "A History of the Sac and Fox Until After

the Opening of Their Reservations in Oklahoma," Oklahoma A&M University, 1940; 1890 Census Data on Sac and Fox Indians and report of U.S. Indian Agent Samuel L. Patrick.

23 *it was Charlie who more resembled*: Jim Thorpe, "This Is My Story," *Sports World*, September 1949; Michael Koehler unpublished manuscript of his grandfather.

24 *Hiram was a big man*: Portrait of Hiram Thorpe drawn from Grace Thorpe, "The Jim Thorpe Family Part II"; Newcombe, 47–51; Hiram Thorpe file, DHTC; "Red Son of Carlisle," 4–5.

25 *The history of alcohol*: John W. Frank, Roland S. Moore, and Genevieve M. Ames, "Historical and Cultural Roots of Drinking Problems among American Indians," *American Journal of Public Health*, March 2000; J. K. Cunningham, T. A. Solomon, and M. L. Muramoto, "Alcohol Use among Native Americans Compared to Whites," *Journal of Drug and Alcohol Dependence*, February 2016.

26 *Charlotte came from Kansas*: Grace Thorpe, "The Jim Thorpe Family, Part I," 97–102; Buford, *Native American Son*, 7–8; Dagmar Thorpe, "Ancestors of James Thorpe"; Lisa A. Kraft, "Citizen Potawatomi," Encyclopedia of Oklahoma History and Culture (online), OHS.

27 *The trail of forced migrations*: Timothy James McCollum, "Sac and Fox," Encyclopedia of Oklahoma History and Culture; Grace Thorpe, "The Jim Thorpe Family, Part I"; The Indians of Oklahoma, Extract from the Governor's Report, July 1, 1901. OHS; Sac and Fox Nation Official Website: Hagan, *The Sac and Fox Indians.*

27 *The descendants of Jim Thorpe*: Grace Thorpe, "The Jim Thorpe Family, Part II"; Hiram Thorpe probate document, Hiram Thorpe file, OHS.

29 *Paul Gokey was with his parents*: From oral histories of Sac and Fox members for the Indian Pioneer Histories project in April 1937. Gokey told interviewer Lenna M. Rushing that he was born in Kansas in 1871 and migrated to Oklahoma with his parents when the Sac and Fox were forced into Indian Territory.

29 *Jim remembered his father*: "Red Son of Carlisle," 9. Hiram was there with one of his mongrel dogs, and one of the surveyors had a bulldog. As Jim told the story, the surveyor told Hiram to keep his dog away or the bulldog might kill him. " 'I think my dog can take of himself,' my father said. In a few minutes the dogs were fighting and the surveyor was pleading with my father to tear the mongrel's hold from his bulldog's throat."

29 *Men like Dewitt Dever*: Dever was a great-grandfather on my mother's side. He kept a journal of his experiences during the Oklahoma land run.

30 *Charlotte filed for divorce*: Details from Hiram Thorpe probate document, OHS. When Charlotte and Hiram reunited, according to the probate investigation, there was no official marriage license but it was "under the Indian custom."

30 *He told of boys roaming free*: Jim Thorpe, "This Is My Story."

30 *the Sac and Fox also clung*: Indian-Pioneer Histories, OHS, 1937 field worker interviews concerning "Games, Sac and Fox Indians" with Mrs. Frank Smith (*Bo-no-we*), Sarah Jefferson, and Ben Smith; also "Red Son of Carlisle," 8.

31 *"From the time I was six"*: Jim Thorpe, "This Is My Story"; "Red Son of Carlisle," 5–6.

31 *Stella Reuben recalled being deprived of food*: Interview with Stella Reuben for Indian-Pioneer Histories project, 1937, OHS.

31 *Jim and Charlie were sent*: Details of Jim's experiences at the school drawn from *Red Son of Carlisle*, 10–11; Newcombe, 39–45; Buford, 24–26; Sac and Fox school file, DHTC; Stella Reuben oral history, OHS.

33 *On the first weekend*: *Lawrence Daily Journal*, Sept. 5, 1898. Arthur St. L. Mosse, captain of the KU team, told reporters meeting the train that he was "feeling good though he is not as fleshy as he was when he left school last spring."

34 *In the middle of one of Jim's first nights*: *Lawrence Daily Journal*, Sept. 5, 1898.

34 *When the school opened*: "Two Visions of Haskell's Purpose," Document A, Kansas Historical Society.

34 *Some students did not want to be saved*: *Topeka State Journal*, March 28, 1898. Another story in the *Nortonville Herald* said a truant officer who was looking for three girls who had run away from Haskell "complained bitterly" that local authorities "instead of assisting him in the search tried to throw him off track."

35 *The season when Haskell started to emphasize football*: " 'Sal Walker' Is a Coach," *Kansas City Journal*, Aug. 24, 1898: "His charges are the redskinned students at the Haskell Indian School . . ."; Keith A. Sculle, "The New Carlisle of the West," *Kansas History*, Autumn 1994.

36 *Jim was only eleven*: NARA Central Plains Region digital archive: "James Thorpe entered Haskell Institute September 4, 1898, at the age of eleven. . . . His record does not indicate the exact subjects he studied, however the subjects covered would probably be . . . reading, writing, arithmetic, and spelling."

36 *"It was at Haskell I saw"*: "Red Son of Carlisle," 19.

36 *Chauncey Archiquette was an Oneida*: Benjey, *Wisconsin's Carlisle School Immortals*, 89; Sculle, "The New Carlisle of the West."

37 *It started when a classmate*: "Red Son of Carlisle," 12–13; Buford, 29; Newcombe, 57.

CHAPTER 3: "THIS IS THE INDIAN'S HOME"

38 *It was the flagship school*: Description of the Carlisle school drawn from Richard Henry Pratt papers, box 22, folder 716; box 30, folders 813–833; and box 30, folder 769, Transcript of interview of Pratt by Mr. Spears of the *New York Sun*, Oct. 4, 1896, Beinecke; Carlisle folder, box 8, M. Scott Momaday files, Beinecke; also a depiction by student Charles Mitchell of the Crow tribe in Montana, *Carlisle Arrow*, May 15, 1908, and Wheeler, *Jim Thorpe: World's Greatest Athlete*, 30.

40 *It was on the warm but drizzly evening*: *Carlisle Evening Herald*, Feb. 4–7, 1904; Carlisle *Sentinel*, Feb. 4–7, 1904; *Red Man and Helper*, Friday, Feb. 5, 1904; Jim Thorpe student file, CISDRC; also Carlisle file, DHTC.

40 *In Carlisle's leather-bound ledger*: Photocopy of Descriptive Record of Students As Admitted, 1899–1905, CISDRC, volumes located at NARA, Record Group 75, Series 1324.

41 *The events that took Jim*: Depiction of Thorpe in Oklahoma before arriving at Carlisle drawn from Grace Thorpe, "The Thorpe Family Story, Part II," *Chronicles of Okla-*

homa, Summer 1981; *Red Son of Carlisle*, 14–15; Carlisle file, DHTC; Buford, *Native American Son*, 29–31; Mike Koehler unpublished manuscript, chapter 4, 16–18; Telegram from Hiram Thorp to U.S. Indian Agent, Sac & Fox Agency, issued Dec. 13, 1903, OHS.

43 *On the day before Jim arrived*: *Red Man*, Feb. 5, 1904. Also in that edition: "The groundhog saw his shadow on Tuesday and there are those at Carlisle who are sorry for it for we have had enough winter."

44 *That was the theme*: Depiction of scene at commencement and of appearance of O. O. Howard and Chief Joseph drawn from Pratt papers, box 22, folder 716, Beinecke; *Red Man*, Feb. 19, 1904. Also John H. Carpenter, "General Howard and the Nez Perce War of 1877," *PNQ*, October 1958; and interview with historian Barbara Landis, CCHS.

47 *Pratt was a long-limbed crane*: Depiction of Richard Henry Pratt drawn from Pratt papers, boxes 813–833, Beinecke; Elaine Goodale Eastman, *The Red Man's Moses*, Literary Licensing LLC, 2011. When Pratt's daughter wrote a letter questioning Eastman's portrayal of Pratt, even though it was largely flattering, Eastman responded: "The public nowadays doesn't care to read about noble self-sacrificing and practically perfect characters: what appeals far more is the entirely human individual, with plenty of rough edges, making occasional mistakes and getting himself disliked as well as loved." Also Jenkins, *The Real All Americans*, chapter 2; Adams, *Education for Extinction*, 36–51; Pratt file, DHTS.

49 *"Arrived safely at midnight"*: Richard Henry Pratt digital file, CISDRC.

49 *It was not an easy sell*: Description of Pratt recruiting first Sioux students drawn from Pratt papers, box 30, folder 769, Beinecke; Adams, *Education for Extinction*, 97–103.

51 *Among the boys Pratt took east*: Luther Standing Bear described his first experiences at Carlisle in *My People, the Sioux*, 60–69; also Adams, *Education for Extinction*, 101.

52 *When the one-year anniversary*: Pratt papers, box 22, folder 716, Beinecke.

53 *Two of the original group were not alive*: Depiction of the first two student deaths and the alarming rate of death in early years drawn from cemetery information and mortuary documents related to Abraham Lincoln, member of the Cheyenne nation, and Amos LaFramboise, member of the Sioux nation, CISDRC; Natalia Flores, "Life and Death in the Carlisle Indian Industrial School," St. Mary's University Research Scholars, March 8, 2018. Jacqueline Fear-Segal, "Institutional Death and Ceremonial Healing Far From Home," *Museum Anthropology* Volume 33, Issue 2, Fall 2010; also interview with Barbara Landis, CCHS.

54 *Luther Standing Bear . . . would become*: Standing Bear, *My People, the Sioux*; box 8, Momaday files, Beinecke.

55 *He was a believer in using the media*: Pratt papers, box 30, files 813–833, Beinecke.

55 *That some would go back*: "Breaking Away from the Reservation," April 21 1894, address to students, Pratt papers, folder 650, Beinecke.

56 *The early months of 1904*: Cemetery information and mortuary documents related to Cooki Glook from Point Barrow, Alaska, and Wade Ayers from the Catawba nation in South Carolina; *Carlisle Arrow*, January 1904.

56 *Pop Warner took his leave*: *Red Man*, Feb. 5, 1904. "Announcement that Mr. G.S. War-

ner, our able football coach for five years, has been recalled to his Alma Mater, Cornell, to resume his former place as coach with ample powers. . . . Our loss is Cornell's gain."

56 *Pratt . . . was also on his way out*: "Report of School at Carlisle, Pa.," Department of the Interior, Fiscal Year Ended June 30, 1904; Pratt papers, folder 654, Beinecke, CISDRC. Pratt said of Leupp: "I doubt if there is one Indian in the United States who will say that Mr. Leupp took him by the hand and encouraged and materially aided him to enter the avenues of higher education and usefulness looking to citizenship."

58 *On the first two days of April*: *Red Man*, April 1, 1904.

58 *The Outing system had been run*: History of Outing system in *Carlisle Arrow* and *Red Man*, June 7, 1918.

59 *"I was anxious to go"*: "Red Son of Carlisle," 17–19; James Thorpe Student File, James Thorpe Progress Card, CISDRC.

CHAPTER 4: HIGH JUMP

61 *the truck farm of Harley Bozarth*: *Red Son of Carlisle*, 18–19; 1905 New Jersey State Census for Hamilton Township; James Thorpe Progress Card, CISDRC; *A Narrative History of Hamilton Township, Mercer County, NJ (Written by People Who Live Here)* Historical Society of Hamilton, N.J., January 1990; interviews with Barbara Landis, CCHS, and Tom Salva, local researcher Robbinsville, N.J.; Outing Reports of Cleveland Schuyler, Leonard Lester, and James Pino at Bozarth Farm, CISDRC.

61 *"James Thorpe is in the guardhouse"*: Newcombe, *The Best of the Athletic Boys*, 65.

62 *"rankled in my heart for many years"*: "Red Son of Carlisle," 19.

62 *The tale was refashioned*: Account of Thorpe at the high jump pit drawn from Warner, *Pop Warner: Football's Greatest Teacher*, 30–31; "Red Son of Carlisle," 20; Miller, *Pop Warner*, 78–79: Pop Warner, "Red Menace," *Collier's*, October 1931.

63 *Warner saw enough promise in Jim*: Wheeler, *Jim Thorpe: World's Greatest Athlete*, 52; Buford, *Native American Son*, 42.

64 *The spring was unusually wet*: *Carlisle Arrow*, April 19 and April 26, 1907, account of Field Day competition. "Saturday afternoon will long linger in the memory of the student body as one of the most successful Class-contest days in the history of the school."

64 *President Roosevelt had established Arbor Day*: *Carlisle Arrow*, Feb. 11, 1907; April 27, 1907; and April 19, 1912.

65 *Jim had success that track season*: *Carlisle Arrow*, May 3, May 10, May 17, May 24, May 31, 1907.

65 *The three were well-known*: Account of three Carlisle players in Sunset League from *Carlisle Arrow*, Aug. 23 and Sept. 20, 1907; Student Files Michael Balenti, William Newashe, and William Garlow, CISDRC; *Baltimore Sun*, July 21, 1907; *Washington Post*, Aug. 8, 1907; *Frederick Magazine* (Md.), April 29, 2013; Class D Blue Ridge League History: "The Sunset League, which got its name because the games were played in the late afternoon and lasted until the sun had set into darkness, lasted until 1911."

66 *Jim remained at Carlisle*: *Carlisle Arrow*, July 12, July 19, and Aug. 23, 1907; Newcombe, 98–99.

67 *Pratt's successor*: Personnel File of William A. Mercer, Superintendent, July 1, 1904–Feb. 1, 1908; *Carlisle Arrow*, April 20, 1904; *Army and Navy Journal*, July 9, 1904; Joseph Cress, "Tour Through Time," Carlisle *Sentinel*, July 9, 2021.

67 *The arts program was run*: Depiction of De Cora and Lone Star Dietz drawn from Linda Waggoner, "On Trial," *Montana* Spring 2013; Angel De Cora Personnel File, De Cora Reports on the Condition of the Art Department at Carlisle, CISDRC; *Indian Craftsman*, February 1909.

69 *All money from ticket sales*: Carlisle Indian School Hearings before the Joint Commission of the Congress of the United States to Investigate Indian Affairs, Part II, Feb. 6, 7, 8, and March 25, 1914.

70 *That freedom was the main reason*: Miller, *Pop Warner*, 73–75; Warner, *Pop Warner*, 115–16.

70 *The game seemed a case*: Depiction of injury reports and early football drawn from *Spokane Press*, Nov. 30, 1905; Oriard, *Reading Football*, 164–165, 170–171; "How Teddy Roosevelt Saved Football," *Washington Post*, May 29, 2014; Peterson, *Pigskin*, 17–20, 45–47.

71 *Warner encountered the Indians*: Depiction of Warner drawn from Warner, *Pop Warner: Football's Greatest Teacher*, 37–57; Jenkins, *The Real All Americans*, 165–166, 247–251; *Indian Craftsman*, vol. 1, no. 2; Newcombe, 83–86; Buford, 62; Warner documents in CISDRC.

72 *In that fall of 1907*: *Carlisle Arrow*, Sept. 6 and 13, 1907.

73 *The first football practice*: (Special to) *Minneapolis Tribune*, Sept. 1, 1907; *Harrisburg Telegraph*, Sept. 3, 1907; *Carlisle Arrow*, Sept. 6, 1907. Of the move to new quarters, the student paper reported: "They like the move very much, especially the training tables."

73 *As Thorpe later told the story*: Depiction of Thorpe joining football team and being mentored by Exendine drawn from "Red Son of Carlisle," 21; Newcombe, 107–109; *Carlisle Arrow*, Sept. 6, 1907; Wheeler, 52–54; Anderson, *Carlisle vs. Army*, 139–40.

75 *The Lebanon Valley opener*: Account of first five games of 1907 drawn from *Philadelphia Inquirer, Boston Globe, Pittsburgh Press*, Sept. 22, 1907; *York (PA) Gazette, Philadelphia Inquirer*, Sept. 29, 1907; *Pittsburgh Daily Post*, Oct. 3, 1907; *Pittsburgh Press, Philadelphia Inquirer*, Oct. 6, 1907; *Buffalo Times, Rochester Democrat and Chronicle*, Oct. 13, 1907; *Carlisle Arrow*, Sept. 27, Oct. 4, and Oct. 11, 1907.

75 *Now came Bucknell*: *Philadelphia Ledger, Philadelphia Press, Philadelphia Inquirer*, Oct. 20, 1907; *Carlisle Arrow*, Oct. 25, 1907.

76 *The game illuminated*: Account of Carlisle game against Penn drawn from *Philadelphia Inquirer, New York Times, Chicago Inter Ocean, Harrisburg Courier*, Oct. 27, 1907.

76 *Thorpe's memories of the Penn game*: "Red Son of Carlisle," 22.

77 *The teams played in a steady downpour*: Account of Princeton game drawn from *New York Times, Philadelphia Inquirer, Brooklyn Daily Eagle*, Nov. 3, 1907; *Carlisle Arrow*, Nov. 8, 1907; "Red Son of Carlisle," 23.

78 *Jim was promoted*: *Carlisle Arrow*, Oct. 18, 1907.

78 *"We had a private car"*: "Red Son of Carlisle," 24; Minneapolis Tribune, Nov. 14, 1907: "The Carlisle football team, composed of 20 redskin players . . . left here at noon yesterday in the private car 'Youngstown' on their Western football trip."

79 *That game . . . was an all-star*: Account of game against Chicago and football injuries drawn from *Chicago Tribune*, Nov. 24, 1907.

CHAPTER 5: ATHLETIC DUTIES ABOVE EVERYTHING

81 *It came in the form of a guest article*: *Chicago Tribune*, Nov. 24, 1907.

82 Wassaja *was Montezuma's birth name*: Description of Montezuma's early life from Maurice Crandall, "Wassaja Comes Home," *Journal of Arizona History*, Spring 2014; Peter Iverson, *Carlos Montezuma and the Changing World of American Indians* (University of New Mexico Press, 1984), 1–15.

83 *He arrived at Carlisle*: Iverson, *Carlos Montezuma*, 24; Carlos Montezuma Collection, letters to Richard Henry Pratt, Newberry Library. Pratt and Montezuma corresponded over many decades and most of the letters have been digitized by Newberry.

83 *There was "no such thing as Indian art"*: Draft of article on Carlisle and the art studio, undated, Montezuma Collection, Newberry Library.

84 *Thompson wrote Montezuma*: CCHS copy of letter; also Jenkins, *The Real All Americans*, 242.

84 *Montezuma took up the cause with fervor*: *Chicago Tribune*, Nov. 24, 1907.

85 *Montezuma's complaint was soon amplified*: *Minneapolis Tribune*, Dec. 5, 1907, from "Accusations of Professionalism on the Carlisle Football Team" file, CISDRC.

85 *the first return volley*: *Tomahawk*, Nov. 28, 1907, republished by *Star Tribune* and *Carlisle Arrow* later, archived by CISDRC, along with Little Boy personal file.

86 *His mission was to save*: *New York Times*, Dec. 7, 1907. The *Times* simply republished Warner's response under the headline "Indians' Famous Coach Answers Critics of Successful Football Team."

87 *Superintendent Mercer . . . called the controversy*: "Accusations of Professionalism on the Carlisle Football Team," CISDRC. Mercer claimed, without substantiating evidence, that Montezuma's story in the *Tribune* "was prepared and held with the intention of not publishing it in case Carlisle lost the game."

87 *Left unsaid was the fact*: Account of Carlisle football financial situation drawn from "Accusations of Professionalism on the Carlisle Football Team" file, CISDRC; also Carlisle Indian School Hearings before the Joint Commission of the Congress of the United States to Investigate Indian Affairs, Part II, Feb. 6, 7, 8, and March 25, 1914.

88 *"You and I know that no one"*: Montezuma letter to Thompson, Montezuma files, Jan. 12, 1907, CISDRC.

89 *On the Monday of Christmas week*: *Carlisle Arrow*, Dec. 27, 1907.

89 *Among those celebrating*: Richard Kesetta Progress Card, CISDRC.

89 *Her Lipan name*: Account of Kisetta Roosevelt drawn from Kisetta Roosevelt Student Information Cards, Cover Letter Concerning Receipt of Two Lipan Children, Correspondence Concerning Richard Kesetta, CISDRC; also interview with Barbara Landis, CCHS.

90 *Superintendent Mercer's gift*: Letter from Secretary of the Interior to the Secretary of War, Dec. 26, 1907, Mercer Personnel File, CISDRC. In his resignation letter, Mercer also wrote: "Though in good physical health, I have, for the past several months, experienced at frequent intervals severe pains in my head with consequent temporary loss of brain power."

CHAPTER 6: THE NEWEST STAR

91 *One mid-February night in 1908*: *Carlisle Arrow*, Feb. 21, 1908.

92 *Two weeks later, on February 27*: *Carlisle Arrow*, Feb. 28, 1908; *New York Evening World*, Feb. 24, 1908.

93 *He was the star of the spring*: Account of Thorpe's 1908 track season drawn from *Carlisle Arrow*, May 1, 8, 15, and 22, 1908; "Red Son of Carlisle," 25; *Elmira Star-Gazette*, May 14–15, 1908: "Two thousand people shivered in the grandstand or stood in the drizzling rain on the field and at the track side from 2 in the afternoon until after 6 and never for a minute lost their interest or enthusiasm."

93 *"he makes a fine teacher"*: *Carlisle Arrow*, May 22, 1908.

93 *"James Thorpe . . . went to his house"*: Account of Thorpe in Oklahoma drawn from *Carlisle Arrow*, June 19, 1908; "Red Son of Carlisle," 26–27; Newcombe, *The Best of the Athletic Boys*, 129–132; Mike Koehler unpublished manuscript.

95 *The first attempt . . . came in November 1876*: Account of early football organization and rules drawn from Peterson, *Pigskin*, 15; Oriard, *Reading Football*, 164; Danzig, *The History of American Football*, 70–71; *Minneapolis Tribune*, Nov. 22, 1908.

95 *The team Pop Warner fielded*: Lineup from *Philadelphia Inquirer*, Oct. 24, 1908; "Red Son of Carlisle," 29; player information from student information files, CISDRC.

96 *what was the national landscape*: "1908 College Football National Championship," Tiptop25.com; *Spalding's Football Guide, 1909*; "1908 College Football Schedule and Results," Sports Reference website.

97 *When Chicago played Wisconsin*: *Chicago Inter Ocean, Chicago Tribune*, Nov. 22, 1908.

98 *Thorpe seized national attention*: *Wilmington News Journal*, Sept. 24, 1908; *Philadelphia Inquirer*, Sept. 27, Oct. 4, 1908; *Wilkes-Barre News*, Oct. 5, 1908; *Buffalo Times*, Oct. 11, 1908; *Brooklyn Daily Eagle*, Oct. 11, 1908; *Carlisle Arrow*, Sept. 25, Oct. 2, Oct. 9, Oct. 16, 1908.

98 *At the Wednesday practice*: Account of week of rivalry Penn game drawn from *Carlisle Arrow*, Oct. 30, 1908; *Philadelphia Inquirer*, Oct. 22–25, 1908; *Washington Star*, Oct. 25, 1908; *Buffalo Enquirer*, Nov. 3, 1908; "Red Son of Carlisle," 27–28.

100 *One of the losses was to Harvard*: *New York Sun*, Nov. 8, 1908; *St. Louis Post-Dispatch*, Nov. 9, 1908; *Boston Globe*, Nov. 8, 1908; *Carlisle Arrow*, Nov. 13, 1908.

101 *Friedman was the third superintendent*: *Carlisle Arrow*, March 6, 1908; Rabbi Charles J. Freund, "Moses Friedman an Apostate—An Interesting Communication," *American Israelite*, July 1915; Buford, *Native American Son*, 74; Crawford, *All American*, 89–90.

103 *The first stop*: *Pittsburgh Daily Post* and *St. Louis Globe-Democrat*, Nov. 15, 1908; *Carlisle Arrow*, Nov. 20, 1908.

103 *Minnesota threw the ball*: Account of game and postgame celebration in *Minneapolis Tribune*, Nov. 22, 1908; *Carlisle Arrow*, Nov. 27, 1908.

104 *For Carlisle, the long road trip continued*: *Official Guide of the Railways, 1908–1910*.

105 *On the day before Thanksgiving*: Account of unveiling of Sheridan statue drawn from *Washington Post, Philadelphia Inquirer*, et al., Nov. 2, 1908. The event was front-page news in papers from Bemidji, Minnesota, to Emporia, Kansas.

106 *The coming of the Indians thrilled*: *St. Louis Post-Dispatch*, Nov. 26–27, 1908.

107 *The Carlisle squad had five days*: Account of Carlisle team in Nebraska drawn from *Lincoln Star Journal*, Nov. 28–Dec. 4, 1908; *Nebraska State Journal*, Nov. 29–Dec. 3, 1908.

108 *It was George Flippen*: *Lincoln Star Journal*, Dec. 4, 1908; Jon Johnston, "Nebraska's George Flippin and a History of Black Football Players in the Big Ten," June 23, 2011, Corn Nation (website).

109 *Denver was Carlisle's last stop*: Account of Denver game and controversy of whether the game would be played drawn from *Butte Daily Post*, Dec. 1, 1908; *San Francisco Examiner, New-York Tribune, Chicago Inter Ocean, Denver Post*, Dec. 6, 1908; *Carlisle Arrow*, Dec. 11, 1908; CISDRC file on Denver controversy including letters and telegrams to and from the White House from Nov. 17 to Dec. 1, 1908.

110 *Joseph Twin was a Winnebago*: Depiction of the elopement drawn from Joseph W. Twin Student Information File, CISDRC; exchange of letters between Supt. Friedman and Dept. of Interior, CISDRC; "This Indian Couple Eloped from Carlisle," *Altoona Tribune*, Dec. 3, 1908.

110 *Thorpe returned to Carlisle in time*: *Hartford Courant*, Dec. 17, 1908; *Kansas City Times*, Dec. 23, 1908; *Carlisle Arrow*, Nov. 13, 1908. In account of Little Boy being denied captaincy, reporter added: "Fritz Hendricks will also be prevented from playing again on account of the four-year eligibility rule."

111 *Twice that winter*: Student Information Cards, Thorpe and Burd, CISDRC; *Carlisle Arrow*, Feb. 12 and 19, March 26, April 16, 23, and 30, May 7 and, 14, 1908; *Harrisburg Daily Independent* and, *Philadelphia Inquirer*, May 30, 1909.

113 *During much of April and May*: *Philadelphia Inquirer*, April 4, 1909; *Washington Post*, April 19, 1909; *Carlisle Arrow*, April 23 and 30, May 7, 14, 21, and 28, 1909; Crawford, 93–94.

CHAPTER 7: RAILROADED

114 *The publisher of the Rocky Mount Record*: *Rocky Mount Telegram*, July 12, 1959, reprinting recollections of Sam Mallison, cub reporter in 1910. Also recalled in Mallison's memoir, *Let's Set a Spell*, Education Foundation, Inc., January 1962.

114 *The most important lie*: Warner, *Pop Warner*: *Football's Greatest Coach*, 127.

115 *Wrong in every respect*: Thorpe Student Information Card and Progress Card, CISDRC; Crawford, *All American*, 119; Newcombe, *The Best of the Athletic Boys*, 139.

115 *By Thorpe's own account*: "Red Son of Carlisle," 30.

115 *Bender was an Ojibwe*: Albert Bender Student File, CISDRC. Like Thorpe's, Bender's

file at Carlisle includes biographical clippings from national newspapers and the *Carlisle Arrow.*

116 *One among the hundreds*: *Sporting News,* June 28, 1945; Associated Press, June 28, 1945; Kansas State League records; Finn quoted in article ghosted for Christy Mathewson, McClure Newspaper Syndicate, Feb. 3, 1912.

116 *"Few Rocky Mount citizens"*: Mallison story recounted in *Rocky Mount Telegram,* Oct. 10, 2010; also in Mallison, *Let's Set a Spell.*

117 *Just being a ballplayer*: Newcombe, *The Best of the Athletic Boys,* 141; more detail in interview with Tom McMillan Sr., Jack Newcombe personal papers; *Rocky Mount Telegram,* Dec. 12, 1951.

117 *Rocky Mount was mostly flat*: *Rocky Mount Record,* Jan. 30, 1909; Roger Biles, "Tobacco Towns," *North Carolina Historical Review,* April 2007; National Register of Historic Places, Dept. of the Interior, Rocky Mount Central Historic District report; Elijah Gaddis, "The June Germans," NCpedia (website), 2013; Charles Dunn, "Taking a Walk Down the Streets of Old Rocky Mount," oldrockymount.pbworks.com.

118 *The Railroaders were on the road*: *Raleigh News & Observer, Raleigh Times,* June 15–17, 1909.

118 *That promising start*: Leverett T. Smith, "Minor League Baseball in Rocky Mount," Society for American Baseball Research/SABR (website); "Jim Thorpe Register Batting and Pitching." Baseball Reference (website).

119 *The year Thorpe came*: Account of North Carolina prohibition and its connection to white supremacy drawn from Ben Steelman, "North Carolina Has Complex History with Liquor," *Wilmington Star News,* Mar. 6, 2010; *Charlotte Observer,* Aug. 10, 1909; *Raleigh News and Observer,* Sept. 7, 1910; Richard L. Watson Jr., "Furnifold Simmons and the Politics of White Supremacy," *Dictionary of North Carolina Biography.*

120 *"But when something was unfair"*: Libby interview in Mike Koehler unpublished manuscript.

120 *That was but one of many stories*: Interview with E. G. Johnston Sr., *Rocky Mount Telegram,* Oct. 31, 1960.

121 *"Big Chief Goes on Warpath"*: *Raleigh Times, Raleigh News & Observer,* Aug. 26, 1909.

122 *In response to accusations*: Account of executive controversy in the ECL drawn from *Raleigh News & Observer,* Aug. 23–27; *Raleigh Times,* Aug. 26; *Wilmington Morning Star,* Aug. 31, 1909.

124 *When the season ended*: "Red Son of Carlisle," 31; Newcombe, 142–43.

125 *But Jim did not cut all ties*: *St. Louis Globe Democrat,* Nov. 25–26, 1909; Buford, *Native American Son,* 90; Crawford, 126.

125 *One month after going on the hunt*: *Carlisle Arrow,* Dec. 31, 1909; Moses Friedman files, CISDRC; Newcombe, 143.

126 *1910, was a lost year for Thorpe*: Account of Thorpe in Rocky Mount and Fayetteville drawn from *Winston-Salem Journal,* July 21, 1910; *Raleigh Times,* July 28, Aug. 11, Aug. 13, 1910; *Wilmington Dispatch,* Aug. 1, 1910; *Raleigh News & Observer,* Aug. 10, Oct. 23, 1910; also Crawford, 130; Buford, 93.

CHAPTER 8: ALMOST THERE

128 *Ex was a man on the move*: Account of Thorpe in Anadarko and meeting Exendine drawn from *Oklahoma's Orbit*, Sept. 3, 1967; DHTC Exendine file; *Guthrie Daily Leader*, Dec. 2, 1912; Crawford, *All American*, 133.

129 *"The personnel of the Olympic team"*: *Pop Warner*, "Red Menaces," *Collier's*, Oct. 31, 1931.

129 *Thorpe was still in Anadarko*: Sac and Fox-Shawnee Agency Records/Carlisle Indian School, box 542, folder 6, OHS; also Newcombe, *The Best of the Athletic Boys*, 149; DHTC Thorpe Letters file.

130 *During the first week of September*: *Carlisle Arrow*, Sept. 15 and 22, 1911.

131 *Garlow had sent a postcard*: Postcard postmarked May 11, 1911, William Garlow Student File, CISDRC.

131 *Pop had set the schedule*: Carlisle beat Lebanon Valley 53–0, Muhlenberg 32–0, and Dickinson 17–0 before St. Mary's College scored the first points for the opposition, losing 46–5.

131 *"his happiest years were spent at Carlisle"*: Grace Thorpe telephone interview with author John Bloom. As a critic of the boarding schools, Bloom recalled, he "laughed nervously" at Grace's comment, but then understood it in context: "She understands [Carlisle] as a school that provided him the opportunity to . . . become one of the few Native Americans recognized and admired both nationally and internationally."

131 *"unusual sounds coming to our ears"*: *Carlisle Arrow*, Oct. 6, 1911; Carlisle *Sentinel*, Sept. 29, 1911; *Adams County News*, Sept. 23, 1911; "List of Air Show Accidents and Incidents, 1904–1911," exhaustive list on Wikipedia.

132 *another visage from the past*: Visit of Luther Standing Bear drawn from *Carlisle Arrow*, Oct. 13, 1911; biographical material from N. Scott Momaday collection, Beinecke, and Standing Bear, *My People, the Sioux*.

133 *A few days before the game*: Warner letter to John Newhall, Newhall family papers.

134 *At Pittsburgh that Saturday*: Account of Pitt game drawn from *Pittsburgh Leader, Pittsburgh Dispatch, Pittsburgh Post*, Oct. 22, 1911.

134 *One day that fall*: Typed and handwritten notes of Jack Newcombe interview with Iva Miller, Newcombe personal papers.

135 *Iva was six years younger*: Depiction of Iva Miller drawn from Iva Miller Student File, Application for Enrollment, Progress Card, Physical Record, Descriptive and Historical Record, Trade Record, Outing Record, and Character Book, also *Red Man*, January 1912 and, *American Indian*, November 1926, all from CISDRC. Also *St. Louis Republic*, May 10, 1904; *St. Louis Globe-Democrat*, Oct. 26, 1904, *St. Louis Post-Dispatch*, May 4, 1904.

137 *he picked the wrong game*: Account of Penn game drawn from *Carlisle Arrow*, Nov. 10, 1911; *Philadelphia Inquirer* and *Philadelphia Ledger*, Nov. 5, 1911; Carlisle *Sentinel*, Nov. 6, 1911.

139 *Next came a trip*: *Boston Globe*, Nov. 9, 1911; *Buffalo Commercial*, Nov. 8, 1911.

139 *Earlier that week, as Dr. Charles William Eliot*: Associated Press, Nov. 7, 1911.

139 *In the crowd were eighteen Carlisle girls*: *Boston American*, Nov. 12, 1911; *Carlisle Arrow*, Nov. 17, 1911. "The game came to an end at last and a new pleasure awaited us," Ella Johnson wrote. "We were invited to go to the Plymouth Theater where we had the privilege of seeing the quaint old-fashioned play, *Pomander Walk*, excellently acted."

140 *Jim stepped on the field gingerly*: Account of Harvard game drawn from *Carlisle Arrow*, Nov. 17, 1911; *Washington Times*, Nov. 10, 1912; *Boston Globe, Boston Post, Boston Herald*, and *New York Times*, Nov. 12, 1911; "Red Son of Carlisle," 34; Pop Warner, "Heap Big Run Most Fast," *Collier's*, Oct. 24, 1931; *Daily Oklahoman*, Nov. 16, 1930; Newcombe, 163–65.

141 *Labor conquers all things*: *Carlisle Arrow*, Nov. 17, 1911.

141 *The only loss*: Account of remainder of 1911 season drawn from *Carlisle Arrow*, Nov. 24, Dec. 1, Dec. 8, Dec. 16, 1911; *New York Times* and *Buffalo Courier*, Nov. 19, 1911; *Baltimore Sun* and *Brooklyn Daily Eagle*, Nov. 26, 1911; "Red Son of Carlisle," 37–38; Miller, *Pop Warner*, 98; Newcombe, 169–70.

141 *Thorpe's national reputation*: *Pittsburgh Spectator*, Dec. 1, 1911; *Louisville Courier-Journal*, Dec. 10, 1911.

142 *Trachoma swept through Carlisle*: Account of trachoma at Carlisle and treatment of Thorpe drawn from Synopsis Eye Examination Carlisle School, Dr. Daniel W. White, March 12, 1912 (for work done in 1911); letter from Charles E. Pierce, Supervisor of Indian Schools (Fifth District) to Moses Friedman after general inspection, Jan. 23, 1912, CISDRC; Diane T. Putney, "Fighting the Scourge: American Indian Morbidity and Federal Policy, 1897–1928," (dissertation, Marquette University, April 1980); *Red Man*, Oct. 11, 1911; "Trachoma," Museum of Family History, Statue of Liberty National Monument website; also Buford, *Native American Son*, 111.

144 *The roster of employees*: Document listing employees at school in 1911, CISDRC.

144 *Miss Moore, as she was known at Carlisle*: Account of Marianne Moore at Carlisle drawn from material in Marianne Moore papers at Rosenbach Museum and Library, including: "Coming About," her unfinished and unpublished memoir; *Selected Letters of Marianne Moore*, 73–75; Linda Leavell, *Holding on Upside Down: The Life and Work of Marianne Moore*, 118; George Plimpton *Harper's* interview with Moore, Leavell appendix, 682; Moore letter from brother John W. Moore, Oct. 21, 1911; letters exchanged between John W. Moore and Moses Friedman, Jan 7 and Jan. 10, 1912; Charles Molesworth, *Marianne Moore, A Literary Life*, 90–91; and Robert Cantwell, "The Poet, the Bums, and the Legendary Red Men," *Sports Illustrated*, Feb. 15, 1960.

147 *When springtime bloomed*: "Red Son of Carlisle," 40–41; Jack Newcombe interview with Iva Miller, Newcombe personal papers.

147 *Pop Warner noticed a similar practicality*: Pop Warner, "Red Menaces," *Collier's*, Oct. 31, 1931: *Physical Culture*, February 1912; *Pittsburgh Post-Gazette*, March 10, 1912.

148 *If Jim was wondering*: Newcombe, *The Best of the Athletic Boys*, 182.

149 *his training partner was Sylvester Long*: *Carlisle Arrow*, April 19, 1912; "Red Son of Carlisle," 40.

149 *The class of 1912 was among the largest in school history*: *Carlisle Arrow*, April 19, 1912.

149 *Iva, chosen by her peers*: *Carlisle Arrow*, April 19, 1912.

150 *On Memorial Day, Marianne Moore*: Plimpton interview, Leavell appendix, Rosenbach; Siobhan Phillips, "The Students of Marianne Moore," Poetry Foundation website, March 14, 2017.

150 *In the days before graduation*: Iva Miller and Jim Thorpe Character Books, CISDRC; also Long Lance miscellaneous papers, Glenbow.

CHAPTER 9: STOCKHOLM

152 *The young men mustered*: Account of Olympians preparing to sail from New York drawn from *New York Evening World, New-York Tribune, New York Times*, June 14, 1912; *Fall River Daily Globe* (photograph), June 27, 1912; James E. Sullivan, "The Steamship *Finland* Trip," *The Olympic Games, Stockholm 1912*, 37–49; Avery Brundage unpublished manuscript, chapter 1, "1912," UIABC; Blumenson, *The Patton Papers*, 229; *Los Angeles Times*, July 12, 1912.

154 *In the holds below*: *New-York Tribune*, June 14, 1912; Sullivan, "The Steamship *Finland* Trip."

155 *Workmen had installed*: *San Francisco Call*, June 13, 1912; Associated Press dispatch, "Athletes Train Aboard Ship," June 16, 1912; Wheeler, *Jim Thorpe*, 100; *Washington Evening Star*, July 7, 1912; *Pittsburgh Daily Post*, June 17, 1912; *Harrisburg Telegraph*, June 18, 1912.

155 *The excitement of the occasion*: *Washington Evening Star*, June 5, 1912; *Tampa Times*, April 16, 1912: "With the horrors of the great *Titanic* disaster still before them . . ."

156 *The waters of the Atlantic were smooth*: *New-York Tribune*, June 15–16; *New York Evening World*, June 17, 1912.

156 *He wrote to her nearly every day*: Jack Newcombe interview with Iva Miller, Newcombe personal papers; Mike Koehler unpublished manuscript, chapter 8, pp. 5–6.

156 *There were two versions*: Sullivan, "The Steamship *Finland* Trip"; *Brooklyn Daily Eagle*, July 5, 1912; *New-York Tribune*, June 19, 1912; Crawford, *All American*, 169; also several articles by Jeff Benjamin, a Staten Island track enthusiast who studied Kiviat's career.

157 *Jim was not naturally talkative*: Kiviat interview in Lewis H. Carlson and John J. Fogarty, *Tales of Gold* (Contemporary Books, 1987), 8; Koehler manuscript, chapter 8, p. 6; Jim Costin column, *South Bend Tribune*, Feb. 13, 1943.

157 *Silent Mike—as Murphy was known*: Associated Press, June 16, 192; Wheeler, 100; *Washington Evening Star*, July 7, 1912; *Brooklyn Daily Eagle*, July 5, 1912; University of Pennsylvania archives biography. Murphy died of tuberculosis one year after the 1912 Olympics. He showed signs of illness in Stockholm, where he missed a few days of practice and friends were "endeavoring to ward off a serious collapse."

158 *Whether Thorpe followed Murphy's*: Rice, *The Tumult and the Shouting*, 229; Wheeler, 102.

159 *"My program on the* Finland": Patton Report to the Adjutant General, U.S. Army, Sept. 19, 1912; George S. Patton papers, box 75, folder 7, LOC.

159 *After steaming through the English Channel*: Sullivan, "The Steamship *Finland* Trip," 43;

New York Sun, June 27, 1912; *New York Times*, June 26, 1912; *The Patton Papers*, 230; DHTC unpublished material, 34; Brundage manuscript, chapter 1, "1912," UIABC.

160 *Brundage . . . was overcome*: Brundage manuscript, chapter 1, "1912," UIABC.

160 *The big ship docked in Stockholm*: "Red Son of Carlisle," 44; Sullivan, "The Steamship *Finland* Trip," 43; Brundage manuscript, chapter 1, "1912," UIABC: "A ship for living quarters, even though it was the largest ever to visit Stockholm, was not a success."

160 *On the morning of July 2*: *Washington Times*, Special Cable Dispatch, July 3, 1912: "Thorpe's back was in bad shape and he was ordered to the hotel for treatment." The leading American correspondents in Stockholm included Edward T. Brennan of the AP, James S. Mitchel of the *New York Herald*, John Hallahan of the *Boston Globe*, Howard Valentine of the *New York Globe*, F. P. Albertini of the *New York Evening Mail*, and W. G. Shepherd of the United Press. All reported on Thorpe's injury.

161 *Curious Swedes inevitably*: "Red Son of Carlisle," 44–45.

162 *It was at Stockund that Johnny Hayes*: Rice, *The Tumult and the Shouting*, 228–29; Crawford, 169.

162 *The games opened in glorious weather*: Associated Press, July 6, 1912: "The day was perfect; there was a clear blue sky overhead"; *New York Herald, New York Times*, July 7, 1912; Mallon and Widlund, *The 1912 Olympic Games*, 21; depiction of scenes inside and outside the stadium drawn from the IOC official film *The Games of the V Olympiad, Stockholm, 1912*, Adrian Wood, director (2017).

164 *For the heats in the dash*: *St. Louis Post-Dispatch*, July 8, 1912; "Springfield High School Star Howard Drew was original 'World's Fastest Human,'" Mass Live website, March 20, 2011; "Red Son of Carlisle," 48. That Murphy would call Drew a "colored boy" reflected the casual racism of the times. Two months earlier, when the Olympic athletes from southern California were raising money for the trip to Stockholm, they held a minstrel show that was covered by the *Los Angeles Times*: "The first part of the show will consist of a black-face bill . . . in the cast will be a big bunch of active and retired athletes from the colleges. . . ."

164 *Thorpe faced his own measure*: *Los Angeles Times*, June 12, 1912; *Chicago Inter Ocean*, July 6–7, 1912.

164 *So much for that idea*: Account of Thorpe winning the pentathlon drawn from *The Olympic Games of Stockholm 1912 Official Report*, 412–14 (although Thorpe's scores were stricken from the records, the official report in its description of each event inadvertently described his performances, perhaps because the writers forgot to exercise those comments); *Chicago Inter Ocean, New York Times, New York Herald, Austin American-Statesman, St. Louis Post-Dispatch, Buffalo Express, Daily Oklahoman, Davenport (IA) Times, Washington Times, Washington Post*, July 8, 1912; Warner, *Pop Warner: Football's Greatest Teacher*, 134–35; Wheeler, 104–106; Mallon and Widlund, 121.

166 *The next day was Lewis Tewanima's*: Account of Tewanima's race in the 10,000 meters and his backstory drawn from *New-York Tribune, New York World, St. Louis Post-Dispatch*, Associated Press, July 9, 1912; Tewanima Student File, CISDRC; *Wall Street Journal*, Aug. 11, 1972; *New York Daily News*, Jan. 21, 1969; Associated Press,

Jan. 20, 1969; *Carlisle Arrow*, Feb. 1, 1907; *Indian Craftsman*, April 1909; Bill Crawford, "Tewanima," July 28, 2021, draft of paper provided to author.

168 *The modern pentathlon had started*: Account of Patton's performance and use of opium in race drawn from D'Este, *Patton: A Genius for War*, 162; Patton Report to the Adjutant General, U.S. Army, Sept. 19, 1912, box 75, folder 7, LOC; Rusty Wilson, " 'The Truth and Anything But the Truth': The Consequences of Gen. George S. Patton's 1912 Olympic Report," Seventh International Symposium for Olympic Research; Harold E. Wilson. "A Legend in His Own Mind," *Olympika*, vol. VI, 1997; *Los Angeles Times*, July 7–12, 1912; *Los Angeles Examiner*, July 7–12, 1912; *St. Louis Globe-Democrat*, July 13, 1912; Blumenson, *The Patton Papers*, 227.

170 *The Swedish Organizing Committee assigned*: Account of filming of games drawn from author interview with Adrian Wood, Oct. 13, 2020; official film *The Games of the V Olympiad, Stockholm, 1912*; Yttergren, *The 1912 Olympics*, 49.

171 *The decathlon was held*: Account of first two days of decathlon competition drawn from *The Olympic Games of Stockholm 1912 Official Report*, 414–19; Mallon and Widlund, 118–19; Wheeler, 107; Buford, *Native American Son*, 129; "Red Son of Carlisle," 46; Yttergren, 244; also *Los Angeles Times, New York Herald, New York Times, Chicago Tribune, St. Louis Post-Dispatch, Brooklyn Citizen, San Francisco Call*, July 15–17, 1912.

174 *Much of the Olympic attention*: Account of marathon competition, death of Lázaro, and disappearance of Kanakuri drawn from Yttgergren, 50; Mallon and Widlund, 83–84; *San Francisco Chronicle, Washington Post, St. Louis Globe-Democrat, Chicago Tribune, New York Herald*, July 16, 1912; *Japan Times*, July 15, 2012; *Washington Post*, Aug. 6, 2021; Roger Robinson, *Outside*, August 4, 2020; IOC official film *The Games of the V Olympiad, Stockholm, 1912.*

176 *Avery Brundage did not even try*: Account of Brundage dropping out of competition drawn from Brundage manuscript, chapter 1, "1912"; David Hurst Thomas interview with decathlon expert C. Frank Zarnowski, DHTC.

177 *With the field down to twelve*: Account of final day of decathlon competition and Thorpe competing with mismatched shoes drawn from "Red Son of Carlisle," 45; *The Olympic Games of Stockholm 1912 Official Report*; Mallon and Widlund, 118–19; Pop Warner, "Red Menaces," *Collier's*, Oct. 31, 1931; Dan Evon, "Did Jim Thorpe Wear Mismatched Shoes at the 1912 Olympics?" Snopes.com, Jan. 25, 2019; *Washington Times, Washington Herald, Buffalo Times, Los Angeles Times, Chicago Tribune, New York Times*, July 16, 1912; Buford, 129–30.

177 *At five that afternoon*: Account of Thorpe receiving trophies from King Gustav V drawn from IOC official film *The Games of the V Olympiad, Stockholm, 1912; New York Times, New York Herald, Boston Globe, Chicago Tribune, St. Louis Post-Dispatch, Washington Post, Brooklyn Times*, July 16–17, 1912; "Red Son of Carlisle," 46; Crawford, 175–76; Buford, 131.

180 *The next day, for the enjoyment of Swedish fans*: *New York Sun*, July 7 and 16, 1912.

180 *The scene aboard ship*: Ship comportment and exhibition baseball both in dispatch from Associated Press, July 17, 1912.

181 *something happened that added*: Account of inaccurate stories about Thorpe spurn-

ing King Gustav V drawn from International News Service dispatch, July 17, 1912; special cable to *Buffalo Courier*, July 18, 1912; Associated Press, July 22, 1912; The Summary, newsletter, Stockholm, July 17, 1912; Rice, *The Tumult and the Shouting*, 230; Wheeler, 113; "Red Son of Carlisle," 46–47.

CHAPTER 10: NEAR CUSTER'S TOMB

183 *There was . . . "something in the air"*: N. Scott Momaday papers, box 8, Beinecke.

183 *Within walking distance*: *New York Herald*, Oct. 11, 1877; *Harper's Weekly*, Oct. 27, 1877; George Pappas, *To the Point: The United States Military Academy, 1802–1902* (Praeger, 1993). P. Willey and Douglas D. Scott, "Who's Buried in Custer's Grave?" *Journal of Forensic Science*, 1999.

183 *"Unlike their fathers and grandfathers"*: Momaday, box 8, Beinecke. Of the motivations for the Carlisle players, Momaday explained: "They weren't like the Harvard or Princeton or Cornell kids, caught up in Ivy League loyalty to alma mater. They were having fun. But I'll tell you what they did have, and when they most needed it. Unlike their fathers and grandfathers, they were given an honest chance, and that was worth more to them than you and I will ever know."

184 *As Pop made his case*: Newcombe, *The Best of the Athletic Boys*, 193; Pop Warner, "Red Menaces," *Collier's*, Oct. 31, 1931.

185 *This caught the attention*: Account of Jim's courtship by major league teams and controversy between the Brotherhood, Moses Friedman of Carlisle, and officials at the Interior Department drawn from *Pittsburgh Press*, Aug. 11, 1912; *Washington Post*, Feb. 11, 1913; also Thorpe Carlisle Indian School Files, 89680 (1912), NARA; and Thorpe Student Files, CISDRC.

186 *When Jim decided to return*: Jim Thorpe and Edward Thorpe Student Files, NARA; Carlisle Indian School, File 88975.

187 *This was their first year*: Joseph Guyon Student File, Pete Calac Student File, CISDRC; Recorded interview with Pete Calac conducted by Robert W. Wheeler, Jim Thorpe, two record set, 1983.

188 *For the fifth game, on October 5*: Account of game against Washington and Jefferson and dustup between Thorpe and Pop Warner afterward drawn from *Pittsburgh Daily Post, Pittsburgh Press, New York Sun, La Crosse (WI) Tribune*, Oct. 6, 1912; Arthur Daley, "Pop Warner Discusses Jim Thorpe," Sports of the Times column, *New York Times*, Nov. 20, 1947; *Esquire*, Sept. 1, 1952; "Interview with Eddie Brannick," Associated Press, Feb. 20, 1943; Howitzer 1913; USMA yearbook (United States Military Academy); *Carlisle Arrow*, Nov. 22, 1912.

190 *By the next weekend*: Carlisle *Sentinel*, Oct. 14, 1912; *Buffalo Courier*, Oct. 13, 1912; Daley, "Pop Warner Discusses Jim Thorpe"; "Red Son of Carlisle," 57.

191 *Always looking for an edge*: Wheeler, *Jim Thorpe: World's Greatest Athlete*, 128–29; Anderson, *Carlisle vs. Army*, 3.

191 *What was happening in practice*: Miller, *Pop Warner*, 103–4; Jenkins, *The Real All Americans*, 283; Warner, *Pop Warner: Football's Greatest Teacher*, 141; Anderson, 261.

192 *At game time*: Scene at start of game drawn from *New York Sun, New-York Tribune, New York Times*, Nov. 10, 1912.

192 *Eisenhower arrived at West Point*: Depiction of how both teams schemed to take out the best player on the other team drawn from Kenneth Davis, *Dwight D. Eisenhower*, 141; *Esquire*, Sept. 1, 1952; Wheeler, 128; also recorded interview with Dwight D. Eisenhower, Wheeler, two-record set.

193 *The first period was scoreless*: Account of game drawn from *New York Sun, New York Herald, New York Times, Washington Evening Star, Philadelphia Inquirer*, Nov. 10, 1912: Jenkins, 283–85; Warner, *Pop Warner*, 141; *Esquire*, Sept. 1, 1952; Anderson, 278–80; K. Davis, 137.

195 *Thorpe made the most memorable*: Account of the play and the mythology that arose from it drawn from *New York Sun, New York Times*, Nov. 10, 1912; *Esquire*, Sept. 1, 1952; Bob Wolff WOL radio interview with Thorpe, 1951, Library of Congress Sound Research Center.

195 *As the game neared an end*: *Brooklyn Daily Eagle, New York Herald*, Nov. 10, 1912; Jenkins, 28; Anderson, 291; K. Davis, 141.

196 *In the dejected Army locker room*: Postgame scene drawn from Memories of Col. W. H. Britton to the Map and Manuscript Librarian Marie T. Capps, June 2, 1978, USMA archive; Anderson, 292.

196 *The press corps agreed*: *New York Herald, New York Times*, Nov. 10, 1912.

196 *As the southbound train*: Wheeler, 132; Jenkins, 286; Anderson, 295.

197 *Hopes for an undefeated season*: *Carlisle Arrow*, Nov. 22, 1912; Daley, "Pop Warner Discusses Jim Thorpe"; *Philadelphia Inquirer*, Nov. 17, 1912.

197 *Some openly despised him*: The player animus toward Warner became public more than a year later, when a special congressional committee investigating Carlisle focused much of its attention on Warner and the athletic program. Welch and other players testified against Warner; transcript of the Joint Commission of the Congress of the United States to Investigate Indian Affairs, Feb. 6, 7, 8, and March 25, 1914.

197 *Late in November, Warner took the squad*: *Hartford Daily Courant, Fall River Evening Herald, Philadelphia Inquirer*, Nov. 25, 1912.

198 *Those sentiments overwhelmed him*: "Red Son of Carlisle," 62–63.

198 *"Imagine what Jim would do"*: Column syndicated by Robert Edgren, Nov. 20, 1912.

199 *In the final month*: "Jim Thorpe, Carlisle Indian, Is Ranked First Place by James Sullivan, Head of Amateur Union," *East Liverpool (Ohio) Evening Review*, Dec. 5, 1912.

CHAPTER 11: LO, THE POOR INDIAN!

200 *Roy Ruggles Johnson was at work*: *Boston Globe*, Feb. 12, 1950. Decades after he broke the story, Johnson, then working at the *Boston Globe*, recalled the story in detail to his colleague Roger Birtwell. The italic precede read: *"Many newspapermen have claimed that the story behind Jim Thorpe's amateur disbarment is a mystery. But the inside story of the Thorpe incident has been resting, unmentioned for decades, in the memory of the man who was there—Roy R. Johnson of Upton, night news editor of the* Globe."

202 *The first two paragraphs*: *Worcester Telegram*, Jan. 22, 1913.

203 *In considering what happened*: Conclusions about who knew what and when drawn from material documented in chapters 7 ("Railroaded") and 8 ("Almost There").

205 *The* Telegram *article reached Sullivan's desk*: Daniel Ferris letter to Robert Paul, 1972, UIABC. Ferris was then Sullivan's secretary.

205 *"As a matter of fact and record"*: Account of immediate reactions by Sullivan and Warner drawn from *New York Times, Paterson (NJ) Morning Call*, Jan. 25, 1913; *New-York Tribune, Philadelphia Inquirer, Washington Herald, Washington Times*, Jan. 26, 1913; James Ring Adams, "The Jim Thorpe Backlash," *American Indian*, Summer 2012; Crawford, *All American*, 200–201.

206 *Jim had returned to Carlisle*: Account of Thorpe in oil boom Oklahoma drawn from *Guthrie (OK) Leader*, Jan. 23, 1913; *Yale (OK) Record*, Oct. 13, 1913; *Honesdale (PA) Citizen*, Jan. 24, 1913; *Carlisle Arrow*, Dec. 27, 1912; Kenny A. Franks, "Petroleum Industry," Encyclopedia of Oklahoma History and Culture (online).

207 *In Warner's own autobiography*: *Pop Warner: Football's Greatest Teacher*, 143.

208 *By Thorpe's later account*: "Red Son of Carlisle," 64.

208 *By then, Clancy's second-day denial*: Account of Sam T. Mallison from *Rocky Mount Telegram*, Oct. 10, 2010; also Mallison, *Let's Set a Spell*, Education Foundation, Inc., January 1962.

208 *He wrote a letter of confession*: Letter from Thorpe addressed to James E. Sullivan, January 26, 1913; letter published in Carlisle *Sentinel*, Jan. 28, 1913; also *New York Times*, Jan. 28, 1913; Crawford, 205. William Cook, in a biography of Thorpe, quoted an eyewitness (Welch) claiming that Warner wrote the letter. Welch's loss of faith in Warner culminated in his testimony before the congressional commission in 1914.

212 *One of the most common*: From Epistle 1 of the Pope poem *An Essay on Man*.

212 *What did L. C. Davis*: "Sport Salad" by L. C. Davis, *St. Louis Post-Dispatch*, Jan. 28, 1913. Sportswriters and columnists across the country almost uniformly sympathized with Thorpe and scorned Sullivan and the amateur officials who rescinded Jim's gold medals.

212 *From the opening* My Dear Sir: Friedman letter printed verbatim in *New York Times*, Jan. 28, 1913.

213 *The point of the letter*: Sullivan letter published in Carlisle *Sentinel*, Jan. 28, 1913.

214 *The first response from Swedish authorities*: *New York Times*, Jan. 29, 1913; *Dagens* Nyheter (largest newspaper in Sweden, translated as News of the Day), Jan. 29, 1913.

215 *But the trophies*: *Philadelphia Inquirer*, Feb. 1, 1913.

215 *Here was columnist Herbert Slater*: *Oakland (CA) Tribune*, Feb. 2, 1913.

215 *Here was a columnist writing*: London *Daily Mail*, Feb. 1, 1913.

216 *Here was Vilhelm Salchow*: *Dagens Nyheter*, Jan. 31, 1913.

216 *As Leif Yttergren . . . later pointed out*: Yttergren, *The 1912 Olympics*, 87.

216 *Here was Colonel William T. Chatland*: *Pittsburgh Press*, Feb. 1, 1913.

217 *"It is no trouble to find Mr. Thorpe"*: *Sporting News*, Feb. 6, 1913.

218 *"While my castle fell"*: "Red Son of Carlisle," 65.

CHAPTER 12: AMONG THE GIANTS

219 *Pop Warner . . . wasted no time*: *Washington Evening Star, Washington Post, Baltimore Evening Sun*, Feb. 1, 1913; *Pittsburgh Daily Post*, Feb. 2, 1913.

220 *The business office*: Scene of Thorpe, Warner, and McGraw at press conference drawn from *New York Sun, New York Times, New-York Tribune, Chicago Tribune, Boston Globe*, Feb. 2, 1913; *Washington Post*, Feb. 3, 1913; "Red Son of Carlisle," 66.

221 *Another reason for McGraw's gambit*: *New York Times, Brooklyn Daily Eagle, Chicago Inter Ocean*, Feb. 2, 1913. "The two teams will start their trip immediately after the world's series in October. . . ."

222 *There was no Grapefruit League*: "Spring Training Sites for all National League and American League Baseball Teams," Baseball Almanac (website); "MLB Spring Training Locations by Franchise Since 1900," Baseballguru.com; "Baseball's Golden Days in Hot Springs," Hot Springs Arkansas Historic Baseball Trail (website); Frank Vargo, "The Origins of Spring Training," Whiting-Robertsdale Historical Society, March 2019.

223 *McGraw and crew traveled*: *Sporting News*, Feb. 17, 1913; *Detroit Free Press*, Feb. 19, 1913.

223 *Baseball fans and sportswriters*: *Sporting News*, Feb. 22, 1913. Correspondent E. F. Fife was on the train. "John McGraw accompanied by 28 players and a staff of sports writers from New York reached Marlin Feb. 19."

224 *Thorpe was assigned a room*: Associated Press, Feb. 13, 1913. A headline in the *New Castle (PA) Herald* read: "Lo the Poor Indian to Be Real Factor in Baseball in 1913." The racist depiction of the grounds crew ended with the comment: "They may be sloughed there for all one knows."

224 *Oscar Colquitt, the Texas governor*: *Sporting News*, Feb. 22, 1913.

225 *Mathewson . . . was the team's immortal*: Mathewson statistics, Baseball Reference (website); "James Thorpe Does Well in Work-Outs at Marlin," by Christy Mathewson, *New-York Tribune*, Feb. 23, 1913. John Neville Wheeler, his ghostwriter, went on to become general manager of the North American Newspaper Alliance and sent Ernest Hemingway to Madrid to cover the Spanish Civil War.

226 *"THORPE IN GIANT WAR PAINT"*: *Sporting News*, March 2, 1913.

226 *The baseball writers came to Marlin Springs*: "Thorpe Doing Great Work," *Sporting News*, March 6, 1913; "Why Thorpe Will Make Good," *Sporting Life*, March 1, 1913; *New York Times*, March 12, 1913.

226 *As spring training neared an end*: *Sporting News, New York Evening Journal*, March 22, 1913.

227 *"I see they are panning me"*: John J. McGraw, "Jim Thorpe Is Fine Prospect; He Will Stick the Season," *Atlanta Constitution*, April 6, 1913.

227 *The 1913 season was a frustrating one*: Thorpe statistics for 1913, Baseball Reference (website); Don Jensen, "Jim Thorpe," SABR (website), 2004.

228 *Thorpe later praised McGraw*: "Red Son of Carlisle," 66.

228 *Jim's roommate . . . called him*: W. J. O'Connor, *St. Louis Post-Dispatch*, June 3, 1913.

228 *One oft-repeated story*: Buford, *Native American Son*, 181.

229 *With Thorpe that season*: International News Service, May 19, 1913; *Chicago Inter Ocean*, June 10, 1913.

229 *It was not until late September*: *New York Times, New York Sun*, Oct. 1–3, 1913; *Boston Globe*, Oct. 1, 1913; *Lansing (MI) State Journal*, "Hans Lobert Beats Jim Thorpe in 100 Yard Dash," Oct. 7, 1913.

229 *Then it was back to the bench*: Wire service stories in *Chicago Inter Ocean, Baltimore Sun, Pittsburgh Daily Post, Philadelphia Inquirer, New-York Tribune*, Oct. 9, 1913. "Gotham Greets Giants."

230 *After a fifteen-month long-distance courtship*: Account of imminent wedding of Jim and Iva drawn from notes of Jack Newcombe interview with Iva, Newcombe personal papers; also *New York Herald, Philadelphia American, Allentown Democrat, Meriden (CT) Daily Journal*, Oct. 2, 1913; also *Port Huron (MI) Times Herald*, Oct. 1, 1913: "Apparently Jim Thorpe is not anxious to emulate Lo, the poor Indian."

CHAPTER 13: AROUND THE WORLD

231 *Now on a bright Tuesday*: Account of Jim and Iva wedding drawn from *Carlisle Arrow*, Oct. 17, 1913; Carlisle *Sentinel, Harrisburg Telegraph, New York Times*, Oct. 14, 1913.

232 *The train departing*: Scene at train station drawn from *New York Evening World, New-York Tribune, New York Times, Harrisburg Telegraph, Meriden (CT) Daily Journal, Long Branch (NJ) Daily Record*, Oct. 18, 1913. "The feature of jollification was in a measure a compensated loss for the Thorpes for the loss of their luggage which is kicking around Manhattan somewhere," wrote the *Times* reporter.

233 *Ty Cobb and Nap Lajoie*: Elfers, *The Tour to End All Tours*, 21–22.

233 *starting on a blustery afternoon*: *Cincinnati Enquirer, Chicago Tribune*, Oct. 18, 1913; *New York Tribune*, Oct. 19, 1913; Ted Sullivan, *History of World's Tour: Chicago White Sox, New York Giants*, 9–10 (1914). Sullivan, the managing director of the tour, was most interested in the social aspects of the trip. At the first stop in Cincinnati, he raved about the German Luncheon hosted by Reds owner August Hermann, who was also the equivalent of the baseball commissioner during that era. In an interview, historian James Elfers said of Sullivan: "He was a pompous, racist, xenophobic windbag, every negative stereotype foreigners had about Americans."

233 *five steel rail cars*: *Chicago Tribune*, Oct. 16, 1913.

234 *"Polo Grounds fans who have delighted"*: Article by John J. McGraw, Special Correspondent of the *New York Times*, "Indian War Whoops for Giants' Red Men," *New York Times*, Oct. 24, 1913.

234 *The road show moved south from there*: Elfers, 45.

234 *The weather turned nasty*: *Kansas City Times*, Oct. 27, 1913. "And 5,000 Shivered While the Giants Were Beating the Red Sox."

234 *The marquee game*: Account of tragic game in Tulsa drawn from *Tulsa Daily World, Daily Oklahoman*, Oct. 28–29, 1913. Some newspaper accounts, like the one in the

Muskogee Daily Phoenix, focused on the Mathewson-Johnson matchup and treated the bleachers collapse as a secondary matter.

236 *"Oh, you dear boy"*: *Boston Globe*, Nov. 12, 1913. The headline and subheads on Axelson's story read: "Wives Having Time of Lives, Players' Tour Has Its Comedy Side, Not a Little Contributed by Honeymoon Squad."

236 *"It was water that scared"*: Account of Mathewson's fears and the financial success of continental trip from McGraw report written from Seattle, Nov. 19, and published in the *New York Times*, Nov. 23, 1913.

237 *Iva brought a travel journal*: Copy of travel journal obtained from James Elfers, who had received a photocopy from Grace Thorpe. At the top of each page Iva filled in Date and Place.

237 *Day by day the storm intensified*: Frank McGlynn, "Striking Scenes from the Tour Around the World, Part I," *Baseball*, February 1914; Iva Thorpe journal, Nov. 20, 1913 entry.

237 *In an imperial suite*: Comiskey testimonial for Indestructo trunks appeared in Sullivan's published account: "They have stood the strain and stress and today I am an enthusiastic Indestructo rooter." Spink's satirical poem appeared in *The Homecoming* by Ring Lardner and Edward Heeman.

238 *Every sportswriter a poet*: Characterization of Jack Keefe based on the short story "The Busher Beats It Hence" in Lardner's *You Know Me, Al.*

239 *"Sixth day awoke feeling excellent"*: Iva Thorpe journal, Nov. 25 and Nov. 27, 1913 entries.

239 *"He has shown the boys"*: Special Correspondent McGraw, datelined "On Board the Steamship *Empress of Japan*," *New York Times*, Dec. 4, 1913.

239 *When the* Empress *reached port*: McGlynn, Part I, 67; Iva Thorpe journal, Dec. 6, 1913 entry; Elfers, 107–108.

240 *The sentence in that entry*: Account of whether Iva was an American Indian drawn from Iva Miller Student File, CISDRC; Grace Thorpe, "Mother Thought She Was Indian," Grace F. Thorpe Collection, Series 1, NMAI.

241 *From Tokyo the players*: McGlynn, "Striking Scenes, Part II," *Baseball*, 70; Iva Thorpe journal, Dec. 7–9, 1913 entries.

242 *From Nagasaki the* Empress *sailed*: Account of sail to Shanghai and rained-out game drawn from McGlynn, Part II, 72; Elfers, 122–23; Sullivan, 14; Iva Thorpe journal, Dec. 12, 1913 entry.

242 *Aboard ship the following night*: Iva Thorpe journal, Dec. 14, 1913 entry; McGlynn, Part II, 72–73.

243 *The Hong Kong stop*: McGlynn Part II, 73–74; Iva Thorpe journal, Dec. 14, 1913 entry; Sullivan, 16–17; Elfers, 128–31.

243 *the* Empress *was gone*: McGlynn, Part II, 74–75; Elfers, 134–35; Sullivan, 17–18.

243 *Under the midnight stars*: McGlynn, Part II, 75; Elfers, 137; Iva Thorpe journal, Dec. 17–18, 1913 entries.

244 *Seven straight days at sea*: Iva Thorpe journal, Dec. 21–27, 1913 entries; McGlynn,

Part II, 76–78. He described the *St. Albans* as "a tidy little steamer, most comfortable in every way."

244 *The first stop in Australia*: Elfers, 150–51; Iva Thorpe journal, Dec. 28, 1913 entry; McGlynn, Part II, 79.

244 *The traveling party celebrated*: Iva Thorpe journal entries, Jan. 1–5, 1914.

245 *Melbourne . . . delighted her*: Iva Thorpe journal entries, Jan. 6–8, 1914.

245 *The overland train*: McGlynn, "Striking Scenes, Part III," 66; Iva Thorpe journal, Jan. 9–12, 1914 entries.

246 *"Of course, we were crazy to learn"*: Iva told the story of learning the "onion glide" at sea out of Adelaide after arriving back in New York, *Washington Post*, March 6, 1914; also Elfers, 172–73.

246 *It was a Sunday when they reached Colombo*: McGlynn, Part II, 67–68; Sullivan, 30; Elfers, 176–78.

246 *After a "sumptuous breakfast"*: McGlynn, Part III, 70; Iva Thorpe journal, Feb. 1–4, 1914 entries.

247 *the fertile imagination of E. L. Doctorow*: Doctorow mentioned the Giants twice in *Ragtime.* In a section before the Sphinx scene, he wrote of McGraw: "The manager . . . unleashed the most constant and creative string of vile epithets of anyone."

247 *"My Snooks played some ball"*: Iva Thorpe journal, Feb. 4, 1914 entry.

247 *The men wore evening suits*: Account of the group meeting Pope Pius X drawn from McGlynn, "Striking Scenes, Part IV," 76–78; Iva Thorpe journal, Feb. 9–13, 1914 entries; Elfers, 206–209.

248 *A year had now elapsed*: Damon Runyon, International News Service, Feb. 18, 1914. "McGraw says Thorpe has developed into a corking player."

248 *Chicago writer Gus Axelson*: *Chicago Record-Herald*, Feb. 25, 1914.

249 *Damon Runyon . . . was waiting for them*: Runyon's account of the group in Paris from Special to the *Washington Herald*, Feb. 17, 1914.

249 *During five rainy days*: Iva Thorpe journal, Feb. 18–23, 1914 entries.

250 *The scene was delicious material*: *San Francisco Examiner*, Feb. 20, 1914.

250 *An upstart organization*: "Federals to Meet Tourists," *Chicago Tribune*, Feb. 24, 1914; Runyon, INS, Feb. 19, 1914; " 'Feds' Go After Mathewson," *Chicago Tribune*, Feb. 25, 1914; Elfers, 204.

251 *Last stop, London*: McGlynn, "Striking Scenes, Part V," 86–87; Iva Thorpe journal, Feb. 23–28, 1914; McGraw, *The Real McGraw*, 243; *New York Times* and *Chicago Tribune*, Feb. 27, 1914.

252 *A future unknown to Iva and Jim*: Depiction of arrival in New York drawn from *New York Times*, *Washington Post*, March 7, 1914; McGlynn, Part V, 87–88; Elfers, 238–40.

CHAPTER 14: THE RECKONING

254 *Marianne Moore was still teaching*: Account of Moore at Carlisle drawn from "Coming About," unpublished Moore autobiography manuscript, and Moore letters to brother, Rosenbach; Linda Leavell, *Holding on Upside Down*, 117–18; Charles Molesworth, *Marianne Moore: A Literary Life*, 90–91.

254 *Hardin arrived at Carlisle*: Account of Julia Hardin case drawn from Julia Hardin Student File, CISDRC; also testimony of Julia Hardin, Carlisle Indian School Hearings before the Joint Commission of the Congress of the U.S., Part II, 1100–106; Claude Stauffer testimony, 1243–46; Moses Friedman testimony, 1251–53; Anna H. Ridenour (matron) testimony, 1196; principal teacher John Whitwell, 1082.

256 *The relationship between students*: Account of findings of Inspector E. B. Linnen drawn from Linnen's "Report on the Carlisle Indian School," Feb. 24, 1914; Joint Commission transcript, Part II.

259 *Soon after Welch filed*: Exhibit I, affidavit of Gus Welch, "Report on the Carlisle Indian School," 1341.

259 *"I know he is kind of good"*: Exhibit J, affidavit of Elmer Bush, "Report on the Carlisle Indian School," 1340.

259 *Gus Welch was harsher*: Exhibit I, affidavit of Gus Welch, "Report on the Carlisle Indian School," 1341.

260 *John Wallette, a Chippewa*: Affidavits from John Wallette, Exhibit N; Joe Guyon, Exhibit M; Pete Calac, Exhibit O; and William Newashe, Exhibit P, all from "Report on the Carlisle Indian School," 1341–42.

260 *It also came out*: Testimony of Glenn S. Warner, Joint Commission transcript, 1226.

261 *Much of the anger*: "Report on the Carlisle Indian School," 1370. Linnen wrote: "John M. Rudey (former assistant disciplinarian) states that the students hate Superintendent Friedman, have no respect for him, and that both the boys and girls call him 'Old Mose,' 'Old Sheeny,' etc."

261 *Warner rewrote history*: Warner: *Pop Warner: Football's Greatest Teacher*, 150.

262 *Carlisle expelled Julia Hardin*: Letters from Supt. Carlisle School to John A. Buntin, The Shawnee Agency, Shawnee, Oklahoma, May 29, 1914; letters from Dept. of Interior to Supt. Carlisle School, May 29 and June 1, 1914; letter from Office of Commissioner of Indian Affairs to Miss Julia Hardin, Shawnee, Oklahoma, June 16 1914, all in Julia Hardin Student File, CISDRC.

CHAPTER 15: THE MYTH OF A VANISHING RACE

263 *The Bulger story appeared*: Bulger's stories for the *New York World* were published in papers across North America. For instance, his Thorpe column ran in Manitoba's *Winnipeg Tribune* on May 8, 1915.

264 *The end of the trail*: Account of San Francisco's 1915 Panama-Pacific International Exposition and *The End of the Trail* statue drawn from Abigail Markwyn, "Beyond the End of the Trail," *Ethnohistory*, April 2016; Hoxie, *A Final Promise*, 93–94; Chandra Boyd, "End of the Trail," Encyclopedia of Oklahoma History and Culture, OHS; *San Francisco Examiner*, Dec. 4, 1915; *Los Angeles Times*, July 23, 1915; *End of the Trail*, National Cowboy & Western Culture Museum pamphlet on artist James Earle Fraser; "100 Years, Panama-Pacific International Exposition, 1915–2015," California Historical Society.

264 *The precise number*: Russell Thornton, "Who Counts? Indians and the U.S. Census," in Ratteree, *The Great Vanishing Act*, 142–53.

266 *McGraw's decision to send him*: *New York Herald*, May 1, 1915; *Buffalo Courier*, May 4, 1915; *Ottawa Citizen*, May 5, 1915; *Pottsville (PA) Evening Herald*, May 11, 1915; *Sport*, February 1949.

266 *His life took another turn*: "Red Son of Carlisle," 67; *Arkansas City (Kansas) Traveler*, May 19, 1915; Buford, *Native American Son*, 195.

266 *Jim was off on a road trip*: *Rochester Democrat and Chronicle*, May 18, 1915.

267 *Although the Skeeters were dwelling*: Associated Press, May 24, 1915; *Brooklyn Daily Times*, May 25, 1915: "Jim Thorpe . . . has shown flashes of brilliant playing ability."

267 *Then his luck turned*: International News Service, July 21, 1915: "The robbery occurred at the end of the game between the Jersey team and the team from Buffalo when the rooms were left unguarded."

267 *His tenure on the Skeeters*: *Carlisle Evening Herald, York (PA) Dispatch, Wilmington Daily News (DE)*, July 24, 1915.

267 *Jim was received as a hometown hero*: *Carlisle Evening Herald, Harrisburg Telegraph*, July 24–26, 1915.

268 *His best friend on the team*: Wheeler, *Jim Thorpe: World's Greatest Athlete*, on Schacht, 158–60. Wheeler's valuable book is enriched by many verbatim interviews with subjects who died long ago, including one with Schacht. Also Larry Amman, "The Clown Prince of Baseball," *Baseball Research Journal*, 1982; Ralph Berger, "Al Schacht," Society for American Baseball Research (online).

269 *Schact's memory was imprecise*: International News Service, June 15, 1915; *Passaic (NJ) Herald News*, June 3, 1916.

269 *Harrisburg took advantage*: *York (PA) Gazette*, Aug. 10, 1915; *Harrisburg Telegraph*, Aug. 17–18, 1915; *Carlisle Evening Herald*, Aug. 14 and 18, 1915. The *Evening Herald* article described him as "Big Chief James Thorpe."

269 *What was daily existence*: Account of life in the International League drawn from *Harrisburg Courier*, Aug. 15, 1915; *Harrisburg Telegraph*, Aug. 19–20, 1915. "Arrests Will Be Made," was the subhead in the story about rowdyism. In his article about the trip to Chambersburg, Wellington G. Jones called the outing "unique and enjoyable."

270 *A few days later, Iva*: *Harrisburg Telegraph*, Aug. 17 and 26, 1915.

270 *Iva and Junior had no sooner*: *Harrisburg Courier, Carlisle Evening Herald, New York Tribune, Chicago Tribune*, Aug. 29, 1915. All ran variations of the *Tribune* headline: "Harrisburg Cans Thorpe."

272 *Earlier that year, a rumor flitted*: *Brooklyn Times Union*, May 15, 1915: "About the only thing that will bar Columbia from gaining Thorpe's services is the coin of the realm." Also *Tucson Citizen*, May 7, 1915; *Salt Lake Telegram*, May 10, 1915.

272 *But Jim did not stop looking*: *Bloomington Evening World*, Sept. 2, 1915.

CHAPTER 16: NEVER LOOK UP

273 *When Clarence Childs coached*: "Midwestern Pioneer," Indiana University website; Ken Bikoff, "A God in Bloomington," *Hoosier Beginnings* (Well House Books, 2020), chapter 7, 134–41.

273 *His arrival was awaited*: *Bloomington Evening World*, Oct. 7, 1915; *Bloomington Daily Telephone*, Oct. 8, 1915.

273 *No time to waste*: *Indianapolis Star*, Oct. 9, 1915.

274 *The next day offered*: *Indianapolis Star*, Oct. 10, 1915.

274 *But as a tutor of kickers*: *Indianapolis News*, Nov. 11, 1915: "Good Punter Has Use for English Same as Pitcher, Says Jim Thorpe." Thorpe expanded on his punting theories later in a speech quoted in Wheeler, *Jim Thorpe*, 203–204.

275 *"We lingered in the grass"*: *Bloomington Herald Tribune*, Nov. 24, 1979.

277 *But fans expected more*: *Indianapolis Star*, *Bloomington Evening World*, Nov. 12, 1915.

277 *Cusack sent Gardner*: Jack Cusack, "Pioneer in Pro Football," *Professional Football Researchers Association Annual*, 1987.

278 *Bob Carroll, the noted*: Bob Carroll and Bob Braunwart, *Coffin Corner* 3, no. 7.

278 *In some ways it was an inauspicious start*: Carroll and Braunwart; also *Akron Beacon Journal*, Nov. 15–16, 1915; *Mansfield (OH) News Journal*, Nov. 15, 1915.

279 *Town and team rivalries*: Account of Purdue game drawn from *Bloomington Daily Telephone*, *Lafayette Journal*, *Bloomington Evening World*, *Indianapolis Star*, *Martinsville (IN) Reporter*, Nov. 22, 1915.

280 *Jim found a pro match*: *Bloomington Evening World*, Nov. 23, 1915; *Indianapolis Star*, Nov. 25, 1915.

281 *The next day Thorpe traveled*: Account of second Canton vs. Massillon game drawn from "Thorpe Arrives, 1915," PFRA Research website; *Pittsburgh Post-Gazette*, *Akron Beacon Journal*, Nov. 29, 1915; *Carlisle Evening Herald*, Dec. 1, 1915; Cusack, "Pioneer in Pro Football."

283 *The triptych of his life*: *Bloomington Daily Telephone*, Dec. 1, 1915; *Yale (OK) Record*, Dec. 7, 1915.

283 *During a warm February*: *Tulsa World*, Feb. 19, 1916.

CHAPTER 17: GAINS

284 *At the end of 1916*: Grace Thorpe, "The Jim Thorpe Family, Part II," *Chronicles of Oklahoma*, Summer 1981, 185; Jim Thorpe file 322, OHS; Buford, *Native American Son*, 208–209.

285 *Here was another action*: Communication from Patty Loew, Sept. 22, 2021.

285 *The past year had been uneven*: Associated Press, April 5, 1915; also *Tulsa Daily World*, March 18, 1916: report from Giants' training camp headlined "This Is Thorpe's Last Chance."

286 *Rather than give up*: Thorpe remained a drawing card throughout the league and attracted headlines in every town: *Pine Bluff (AR) Daily Graphic*, April 4, 1916; *Indianapolis News*, April 27, 1916; *Louisville Courier-Journal*, April 30, 1916; *Indianapolis Star*, July 22, 1916; *Minneapolis Tribune*, July 27, 1916. Also "Now Batting for the Brewers . . . Jim Thorpe?" Borchertfield.com, April 29, 2009; Jim Thorpe minor league statistics, Baseball Reference website.

286 *Had the Little Napoleon*: *New York Herald*, March 20, 1916; Warner quoted in *New York Times*, Nov. 20, 1947.

286 *In football, Thorpe's talents*: Account of Thorpe's 1916 season with Canton drawn from "The Super Bulldogs, 1916 Season," PFRA website; Canton Bulldogs 1916 statistics, Pro Football Archives website; also *Akron Beacon Journal*, Oct. 14 and 21, Dec. 4, 1916; *Lancaster (PA) News-Journal*, Nov. 18, 1916; *Canton (OH) Evening Repository*, Dec. 4, 1916; *Carlisle Evening Herald*, Dec. 7, 1916.

287 *"Introverted is not the way"*: *Fort Worth Star-Telegram*, April 6, 1972.

287 *Jim wrote letters and little poems*: "The Personal Life of Jim Thorpe," handwritten notes of Grace Thorpe for speech May 10, 1968; Grace F. Thorpe Collection, NMAI, Series 5.

287 *Jack Cusack, the Canton owner*: *Sport*, December 1966; *Fort Worth Star-Telegram*, April 6, 1972.

288 *"I'd never seen him drunk"*: Jack Newcombe notes from interview with Iva Thorpe, Newcombe personal papers.

289 *At spring training with the Giants*: *New York World*, April 16, 1917.

289 *He was sold outright*: *Dayton Daily News*, April 23, 1917.

289 *In a letter, Iva described*: Iva Thorpe letter to Carlisle superintendent, Aug. 1, 1917, Iva Miller Student File, CISDRC.

289 *"I was up against it"*: *New York Evening World*, April 30, 1917.

290 *The change seemed promising*: *New York Herald*, June 12, 1917; *Dayton Daily News*, July 18, 1917.

291 *What did Jim do?*: *Carlisle Evening Herald*, July 19, 1917; *Philadelphia Public Ledger*, July 18, 1917.

292 *Before any move*: *Pittsburgh Press*, Aug. 9, 1917; *Fall River(MA) Daily News*, Aug. 9, 1917; *Brooklyn Daily Eagle*, *New York Sun*, Aug. 19, 1917.

292 *Iva had not seen Clyde*: Iva Thorpe letter to Carlisle, Aug. 1, 1917, and Clyde Miller letter to Iva, July 1917, Iva Miller Student File, CISDRC.

293 *With the Yanks now*: "Carlisle Indians Joining U.S. Army, Jim Thorpe's Brother, Edward, Among Recruits," Associated Press, July 12, 1917; Gus Welch Student File (undated clippings from Luce's Press Bureau), CISDRC.

293 *Another Carlisle friend*: Account of Sylvester Long's amazing life, real and imagined, drawn from *Washington Post*, July 29, 1917; description of Sylvester Chahuska Long-Lance on Enlistment, Personnel Records of the First World War, Library and Archives Canada, RG 150, box 5729-66.

294 *Jim finished the Giants season*: "Who's Who in World Series," by Jack Veiock, INS, Sept. 10, 1917; Kevin Larkin, "October 13, 1917: White Sox's Big Push Brings Bedlam in Game 5 Comeback," SABR website.

294 *By the time he reached Canton*: Account of Thorpe's 1917 season with Canton Bulldogs drawn from *Sport* December 1966 interviews with Pete Calac, Joe Guyon, and Jack Cusack; *Akron Beacon Journal*, Nov. 12, 1917; *New Philadelphia Times*, Nov. 24, 1917; "Canton Wins Again, 1917," PFRA website; Peterson, *Pigskin*, 174.

297 *That winter . . . back in his Oklahoma homeland*: Grace Thorpe, "The Jim Thorpe Family, Part II," *Chronicles of Oklahoma*, Summer 1981, 188; Mike Koehler unpublished manuscript; Buford, 212–13.

CHAPTER 18: LOSSES

298 *The decline and fall*: Account of last days of the Carlisle Indian Industrial School drawn from Closure of the Carlisle Indian School File, CISDRC; Part 1.2 Transfer of Land, Transfer of Property, Transfer of Students, Notice of Closure for School Agents, Proposal of Closure of School, 173 pages (from National Archive records of the Department of Interior and Department of War). Also *Kansas City Star*, Aug. 1, 1918; *Hazleton (PA) Plain Speaker*, Aug. 7, 1918; *Los Angeles Times*, Aug. 10, 1918; *Philadelphia Inquirer*, Aug. 26, 1918; Carlisle *Sentinel* and *Carlisle Evening Herald*, Aug. 27, 1918; Carlisle *Sentinel*, May 26, 2017.

301 *"Taking Jim Thorpe to Texas"*: International News Service, March 29, 1918.

302 *True to form, Jim played*: *New York Times*, March 21, 1918; *New York Evening World*, March 25, 1918; Jim Thorpe statistics for 1918, Baseball Reference website.

302 *When the military began drafting*: Barry, *The Great Influenza*, 301; Naomi Coquillon, "Baseball and World War I," Library of Congress blog, Sept. 27, 2018; Matt Kelly, "On Account of War," Baseball Hall of Fame website; "1918: All Work and Fight or No Play," This Great Game: The Online Book of Baseball.

303 *The Red Sox batting order*: Randy Roberts and Johnny Smith, "Babe Caught the 1918 Flu—Twice," Slate, March 26, 2020 (material from their book *War Fever*).

303 *Branch Rickey, in a break*: John Rosengren, "Hall of Famers Served in World War I Gas and Flame Division," Baseball History Series, National Baseball Hall of Fame website.

304 *Some historians trace the influenza*: The role of Haskell County, Kansas, and Camp Funston in the 1918 flu drawn from John M. Barry, "How the Horrific 1918 Flu Spread across America," *Smithsonian*, November 2017 (from material first presented in Barry's seminal book, *The Great Influenza*). Barry states that it cannot be determined for certain that Haskell was the epicenter, but a report from there "stands as the first recorded anywhere in the world of unusual influenza activity that year." Also "Flue Epidemic of 1918," Kansas Historical Society; "The Great Influenza at Camp Funston," Johnson County History blog, Oct. 29, 2018; Clark Bluster letters to family, Kansas Memory, Kansas Historical Society; *Wichita Eagle*, Feb. 19, 2018.

305 *One of the dead*: *Harrisburg Evening News, San Francisco Examiner, Los Angeles Herald*, Oct. 31, 1918; David Larvie Student File, CISDRC.

305 *From the Philadelphia Naval Shipyard*: Account of influenza sweeping across Pennsylvania to Carlisle, and how it entered New York, drawn from reports by Joseph Cress in Carlisle *Sentinel*, May 26, 2017, and Oct. 5, 2018; Mira Shetty, "Penn and the 1918 Influenza Epidemic," Penn University Archives and Records Center, "Philadelphia Parade Exposes Thousands to Spanish Flu," History.com; "New York and the 1918–1919 Influenza Epidemic," Influenzaarchive.org.

306 *The baseball world was not immune*: Bill Francis, "1918 Flu Pandemic Did Not Spare Baseball," Baseball History Series, National Baseball Hall of Fame website; Roberts and Smith, "Babe Ruth Caught the 1918 Flu—Twice"; Melissa August, Spotlight Story, *Time*, Oct. 23, 2020.

306 *The second flu wave*: Brad Agnew, *Tahlequah (OK) Daily Press*, March 21, 2020.

307 *On the journey . . . from New York*: "Red Son of Carlisle," 69; Buford, *Native American Son*, 214.

307 *Dr. Newell listed the cause of death*: Death Certificate, Oklahoma State Board of Health, Bureau of Vital Statistics, Registered No. 43, Sept. 28, 1918.

307 *But according to a leading expert*: Interview with Dr. Stuart Berger, chief of cardiology, Lurie Children's Hospital, Chicago, Jan. 27, 2021.

308 *"We went home then"*: "Red Son of Carlisle," 69; Mike Koehler unpublished manuscript; *Washington Herald, Baltimore Sun, Buffalo Courier*, Sept. 29, 1918.

CHAPTER 19: GAMBLERS

309 *John McGraw was a win-at-all-costs*: Jack Veiock, INS feature story in *Buffalo Enquirer, Appleton (WI) Post-Crescent*, Sept. 18, 1919.

309 *McGraw traded Jim Thorpe*: *Boston Globe, New York Herald*, May 22, 1919.

309 *than the sight in Boston Harbor*: *Boston Globe*, May 23, 1919. "A spectacular and striking Naval parade such has not been seen in Boston Harbor since the present war began."

310 *Gowdy, the gifted catcher*: *Boston Globe*, May 24, 1919; *Brooklyn Times Union*, May 25, 1919; John DiGonzo, "Hank Gowdy Day at Braves Field," SABR website, 2015.

310 *When Stallings inserted Thorpe*: Boston Nationals batting statistics, *Boston Globe*, June 2, 1919; "Jim Thorpe in Batting Lead," Associated Press, July 5, 1919: "Jim Thorpe . . . has stepped out in front among batters of the National League with an average of .411." Also "Where Did They Steal Those Bats?" Fred Turbyville, NEA Sports Writer, Aug. 1, 1919; "Cravath Forces Jim Thorpe into Second Place . . .", Associated Press, Aug. 16, 1919.

311 *A few weeks later*: "Red Son of Carlisle," 70; Burford, *Native American Son*, 217; *New York Times*, Sept. 17, 1919.

311 *Damon Runyon, vernacular poet*: *New York American*, Oct. 2, 1919.

311 *As it turned out, Runyon was right*: Diana Goetsch, "Baseball's Loss of Innocence," *American Scholar*, March 2, 2011; Mike Vaccaro, "Inside the Black Sox Scandal 100 Years after It Scarred MLB," *New York Post*, Oct. 22, 2019; "Hugh S. Fullerton Vividly Describes the Full Details of Great Baseball Scandal," *New York World*, Oct. 3, 1920.

312 *Consider McGraw*: Account of John McGraw's dealings with corrupt ballplayers and being expelled from Lamb's Club drawn from *Washington Post*, Oct. 18, 1908; "John McGraw's Troubles at the Lambs," The Baseball Historian blog, Dec. 11, 2011; Dan Jensen, "John McGraw," SABR website; *New York Times*, Aug. 10, 1920; Associated Press, Aug. 16, 1920; Jacob Pomrenke, "The Whitewashing of Hal Chase," TheNational PastimeMuseum.com, *Nashville Banner*, July 24, 1936; Robert C. Hole, "The Hal Chase Case," SABR Research Journals (online).

313 *"Pure fiction!" said Jack Cusack*: Jack Cusack, "Pioneer in Pro Football," *PFRA Annual* 1987.

314 *"This bribery of athletes is a terrible thing"*: Associated Press interview with Thorpe in Memphis, Sept. 3, 1951.

314 *The new owner was Ralph Hay*: Bob Carroll, *Bulldogs on Sunday, 1919*, PFRA publication.

316 *In moving through the schedule*: *Chicago Tribune*, Aug. 29, 1919; Peterson, *Pigskin*, 62–63; Carroll et al., *Total Football*, 12–13.

317 *Among other Ohio League players*: Depiction of Frederick (Fritz) Pollard from Carroll et al., *Total Football*, 270–71; Peterson, 62–63.

317 *"The game was another demonstration"*: *Canton (OH) Repository*, Nov. 17, 1919.

318 *When the season ended*: Account of Thorpe returning to Oklahoma, the emergence of an incipient Klan, and Jim dealing with sister-in-law in Yale drawn from Grace Thorpe, "The Jim Thorpe Family, Part II," *Chronicles of Oklahoma*, Summer 1981, 188; *Yale (OK) Record*, April 1, 1920; Larry O'Dell, "Ku Klux Klan," OHS; Carter Blue Clark, *A History of the Ku Klux Klan in Oklahoma*, University of Oklahoma, 1976; Mike Koehler unpublished manuscript; Buford, *Native American Son*, 213; Kate Buford personal papers, interview with Grace Thorpe.

CHAPTER 20: START TO FINISH

319 *The sporting worlds of Jim Thorpe*: *Akron Evening Times*, Sept. 18, 1920; Jim Thorpe minor league statistics, Baseball Reference website; *Akron Beacon Journal*, Aug. 20, 1920; *Brooklyn Daily Eagle*, Dec. 17, 1920: "Thorpe was fifth among the IL sluggers last summer, hammering the really good hurlers of that circuit for the following averages—128 games, 522 at bats, 102 runs, 188 hits, 290 total bases, 16 home runs, 32 stolen bases, .360 average. He has a very pleasant personality. He has broadened about the neck and shoulders."

319 *A few hours after the game*: Account of APFA organizational meeting in Ralph Hay's Hupmobile showroom drawn from Beau Riffenburgh and Bob Carroll, "The Birth of Pro Football," *PFRA Annual*, 1989; "Happy Birthday NFL?", *Coffin Corner* 2, no. 8, 1980; Peterson, *Pigskin*, 67–68; *Akron Evening Times, New York Times, Harrisburg Telegraph, Detroit Free Press, Davenport (IA) Daily Times, Muncie Star Press, Fort Wayne Sentinel*, Sept. 19, 1920; "One Car Showroom, 15 Men," *Newsday*, Sept. 15, 2020; "Remembering Pro Football's Ralph Hay," CantonRep.com, Sept. 8, 2019; "Liquor Dried Up 100 Years Ago," *Akron Beacon Journal*, Jan. 13, 2020; *Halas by Halas*, 60–61; J. Davis, *Papa Bear*, 63.

323 *Next came the Akron Pros*: *Akron Beacon Journal*, Oct. 26–Nov. 1, 1920.

323 *Pollard played for Akron*: *Coffin Corner* 27, no. 3, 2005; Peterson, *Pigskin*, 171–72; Gary Waleik, "Fritz Pollard: The Small Running Back Who Broke Big Barriers," WBUR, Jan. 13, 2018; Stephen Eschenbach and Brett Hoover, "Fritz's Fame," *Brown Alumni Magazine*, Aug. 10, 2007; Aaron Dodson, "Fritz Pollard Was a True Football Pioneer," Undefeated website, Sept. 21, 2017.

325 *"There is a tendency"*: *New York Herald*, Nov. 19, 1920.

325 *"He was the evangelist of fun"*: Bruce Barton eulogy to Grantland Rice, July 16, 1954, Brick Presbyterian Church, New York.

326 *Near the end of the 1920 season*: *Leslie's Weekly*, Dec. 10, 1920.

326 *Even home with his family*: *Yale (OK) Record*, Jan. 27, 1921.

327 *Next stop, Toledo*: *Akron Beacon Journal*, Jan. 14, 1921; *Nashville Tennessean*, Jan. 15, 1921; *Lincoln Journal Star*, March 26, 1921.

327 *The American Association of 1921*: *Washington Evening Star*, April 29, 1921; John E. Kleber, Encyclopedia of Louisville, 72; John McMurray, "Joe McCarthy," SABR website, last revised Feb. 17, 2021; McCarthy managerial statistics, Baseball Reference website.

327 *But Jim did not struggle*: Jim Thorpe minor league statistics, Baseball Reference website; *Washington Evening Star, Baltimore Sun, Tampa Times*, July 14, 1921; Associated Press, Oct. 2, 1921, final American Association statistics.

327 *While Thorpe played for the Mud Hens*: *Akron Beacon Journal*, "Joe Carr Is Elected President National Pro Football Body, Succeeds Jim Thorpe," May 2, 1921; Carroll et. al, *Total Football*, 15; Peterson, 76.

328 *When the 1921 season began*: John Cusack, "Pioneer in Pro Football," *PFRA Annual*, 1987; Peterson, 79–80; "1921 Cleveland Indians Statistics and Players," Pro Football Reference website.

329 *The last scheduled game*: *New York Daily News*, Dec. 3, 1921; Keith Yowell, "Today in Pro Football History," blog, Dec. 3, 2011; *Boston Globe*, Dec. 6, 1921; Sid Mercer, *Buffalo Enquirer*, Dec. 10, 1921.

330 *Other than Thorpe's run*: Cusack, "Pioneer in Pro Football."

330 *In what had become an annual tradition*: The column by Norman E. Brown ran in scores of newspapers, including the *Oklahoma City Times*, Dec. 28, 1921, and *Muskogee Daily Phoenix*, Dec. 30, 1921. Usual headline: "Sun Sets on Thorpe's Athletic Career."

331 *It was happening again*: "Famous Indian to Play with Beaver Club," *Oregon Daily Journal*, Feb. 9–10, 1922.

332 *The* Journal *did Klepper's bidding*: *Oregon Daily Journal*, Feb. 22, 1922.

333 *"Jim Thorpe is a great big good-natured fellow"*: Bertz column in *Oregon Daily Journal* from training camp in Pasadena, March 16, 1922.

333 *His value to the team*: *Oregon Daily Journal*, April 23–24, 1922.

333 *Life in the Northwest*: "Beaver Outfielder Lands First Salmon," *Oregon Daily Journal*, April 27, 1922. McFarland, a dentist and Republican state legislator, was from one of the first families of eastern Oregon.

333 *Then his luck turned again*: *Oregon Daily Journal*, June 1, 1922. "Another reason was that a 20-man limit was going into effect in the league and Thorpe was one of three players Portland cut to get to the limit."

334 *"I think Jim will take it"*: *Hartford Courant*, June 6, 1922.

334 *Jim and Iva and the three girls*: *Hartford Daily Times*, June 12–13, 1922; *Hartford Courant*, June 14, 1922.

334 The Hartford Courant *greeted Jim's arrival*: *Hartford Courant*, June 13, 1922.

335 *During his first month*: *Hartford Courant*, June 15 and 23, July 2 and 6, 1922.

335 *Jim seemed on his way*: Black and White Taxi Service ad appeared in the *Courant* on June 17, 1922; the ad and feature story on the Buick Roadster ran June 18.

336 *Then it fell apart, again*: Account of Jim's behavior in games against Waterbury, New Haven, and Springfield drawn from *Hartford Courant*, July 11–12, Aug. 9–19, 1922; *Boston Globe*, Aug. 11, 1022; *Berkshire (MA) Evening Eagle*, July 11, 1922; *Oregon Daily Journal*, July 12, 1922; Buford, *Native American Son*, 231.

337 *The next night a reporter*: *Hartford Courant*, Aug. 12 and Aug. 15, 1922.

338 *The first games Jim played*: *Hartford Courant*, Aug. 18, 1922.

339 *"We had friends who were priests"*: Transcript of Iva Thorpe interview, Jack Newcombe personal papers.

CHAPTER 21: OORANG INDIANS

340 *The Oorang part*: "Mankind's Best Friend," *Oorang Catalog No. 26*; "The Oorang Indians," *Coffin Corner* 3, no. 1, 1981; "The Team that Went to the Dogs," *Ohio*, July 1986; *Dayton Daily News*, Feb. 19, 1922.

340 *brought outdoorsmen of all sorts*: *Marion(OH) Star*, Nov. 20, 1988.

341 *It was perhaps inevitable*: *Coffin Corner* 3, no. 1, 1981; *Hartford Courant*, June 28, 1922; *Akron Beacon Journal*, Jan. 24, 1995.

341 *The plan was that players and dogs*: *Oorang Catalog No. 26*, interview with Lingo by Albert Sidney Gregg.

341 *In a two-tone Pierce-Arrow sedan*: *Marion Star*, Sept. 28, 1922.

342 *The first to arrive was Nick Lassa*: *Marion Star*, Sept. 5, 1922. The headline inverted his name: "Chief Sleep Long Time first to reach LaRue."

342 *The oldest among them*: Interview with historian Patty Loew, who conducted research on Native American athletes from Wisconsin; also *Marion Star*, Sept. 27, 1922.

342 *William Guthery, one of the high school players*: Chris Wills, "Remembering the Oorang Indians," *Coffin Corner* 24, No. 3, 2002.

343 *Hardly a great battle*: *Dayton Herald, Dayton Daily News, Marion Star*, Oct. 2, 1922.

343 *No story was more egregious*: *Akron Beacon Journal*, Oct. 28, 1922.

344 *The halftime shows played into this*: Bloom, *To Show What an Indian Can Do*, 120.

344 *"White people had this misconception"*: *Ohio*, July 1986.

344 *They became actors*: Account of the hunt for the fabricated lion drawn from United Press, "Indians and an Airplane Hunt Lions at Kenton," Oct. 3, 1922; Cosmopolitan News Service, "Angry Farmers Surround Ohio Lions in Wood," Oct. 4, 1922; Associated Press, Oct. 4, 1922; *Marion Star*, Oct. 5–7, 1922.

346 *Late on Halloween afternoon*: *Marion Star*, Nov. 1, 1922.

346 *The night before the Chicago game*: Account of Bears game drawn from *Chicago Tribune*, Nov. 10–13, 1922; *Racine Journal Times*, Nov. 10, 1922; Associated Press, Nov. 12, 1922; *Coffin Corner* 3, no. 1, 1981; *Rock Island (IL) Argus*, Nov. 7, 1922; *White Earth (MN) Tomahawk*, Nov. 23, 1922; Moline Dispatch, Nov. 14, 1922; *Collyer's Eye*, November 1922.

347 *Something more epic occurred*: Account of match between Jim Thorpe and Paul Robeson drawn from *Racine Journal Times, Louisville Courier Journal*, Nov. 18, 1922; *Milwaukee Journal, Milwaukee Sentinel, Green Bay Press Gazette, Marion Star, Chicago Tribune, Kenosha News, Fort Wayne Journal Gazette*, Nov. 20, 1922; J. Gordon Hylton,

"Paul Robeson and the Marquette Law School," Marquette U. Law School Faculty blog, June 4, 2010.

349 *The Indians traveled the country*: *Buffalo Express*, Nov. 23, 1922; *Buffalo Times*, Nov. 25, 1922; *Buffalo Enquirer*, Nov. 27, 1922; *Baltimore Sun*, Dec. 7 ("Old Master to Play Saturday"), Dec. 9–10, 1922.

349 *Lingo suggested they also visit the White House*: *Yale (OK) Record*, July 26, 1923; Chris Willis, *Walter Lingo, Jim Thorpe, and the Oorang Indians* (Rowan & Littlefield Publishers, 2017), 146.

350 *Barnstorming was a regular part of life*: Account of Thorpe and the Toledo Maroons drawn from *Tulsa World*, Dec. 28–30, 1922; *Oklahoma City Times*, *Aline (OK) Chronoscope*, Jan. 5, 1923; *Daily Oklahoman*, Jan. 6, 1923; *Oklahoma Leader*, Jan. 8, 1923; Steve Owen, *My Kind of Football*, 28–30.

351 *When the barnstorming ended*: *Marion Star*, March 7 and 17, 1923; Buford, *Native American Son*, 236.

351 *Jim could not get baseball*: *Bucyrus (OH) Telegraph-Forum*, July 20, 1923.

351 *When Lingo decided to keep*: *Green Bay Press-Gazette*, Sept. 26, 1923; *Minneapolis Star*, Oct. 10–14, 1923; Wheeler, *Jim Thorpe*, 246; *Buffalo Courier*, *Buffalo Times*, Oct. 22, 1923. The Custer analogy came after the Indians lost 57–0 to the Buffalo All-Americans.

352 *It had been ten years*: Account of dissolution of marriage drawn from "Red Son of Carlisle," 72; Buford, 238–39; Mike Koehler unpublished manuscript; *Marion Star*, March 9, 2007.

CHAPTERS 22 & 23: LETTERS I AND LETTERS II

354 *A batch of letters written*: Provenance of letters from Thorpe to Freeda 1924 through 1926: now archived at Cumberland County Historical Society, purchased at a Sotheby's auction in 2007, before that kept in Thorpe family by Bill Thorpe, Jim and Freeda's son.

354 *He was in Massachusetts*: Account of Twilight League and Thorpe's play with Lawrence Independents drawn from *Lawrence (MA) Telegram*, May–July, 1924. The entire league schedule was compiled by *Telegram* reporter Peter L. J. Pomerleau, who covered most of the Independent games. Albert J. Woodlock of the *Boston Globe* also wrote about the league that year.

359 *Charles F. Michael was the richest man*: "Locomotive Crane History," American and Ohio Crane Company website, 2007.

359 *On the last Sunday in July*: *Boston Globe*, July 28, 1924. "Jim Thorpe and Others Hear Rev. Harold C. Cutbill, 'The Flying Parson,' Declare Athletes Must Live Clean and Have Regular Habits to Succeed."

362 *Jim's arrival in Rock Island*: Rock Island Independents file, DHTC; *Rock Island (IL) Argus*, Oct. 20, 1924; *Davenport (IA) Daily Times*, Oct. 11, 1924.

363 *Jim remained an itinerant athlete*: Account of Thorpe marrying Freeda, playing one game with the New York Football Giants, then being released by the team drawn from *Philadelphia Inquirer*, Oct. 17, 1925; Associated Press, *Boston Globe*, *Hartford Courant*,

Philadelphia Inquirer, Oct. 29, 1925; *Harrisburg Telegraph*, Oct. 31, 1925. Thorpe's marriage and football release were part of the same story.

364 *Thorpe had been divorced from Iva*: *Chicago Tribune*, March 24, 1925; *Harrisburg Telegraph*, April 25, 1925; Buford, *Native American Son*, 243.

365 *He wired Archie Bowlby*: A. H. Bowlby, business manager of the Rock Island Independents. He was a society figure in Rock Island and president of the local chamber of commerce. Bowlby brought Thorpe to Rock Island starting in the second game of the 1924 season, after which Jim took many of his players on a barnstorming tour through Texas, where they won games by a combined score of 76–7.

366 South Bend Tribune *reported from Bears camp*: "Bears Prepare for Tilt," *South Bend (IN) Tribune*, Dec. 30, 1925.

367 *The game did not turn out the way Jim hoped*: *Tampa Tribune*, Jan. 2, 1926.

369 *Thorpe and tackle Chet Widerquist*: Associated Press, *Minneapolis Star*, Jan. 4, 1926: "Jim Thorpe and Former Gopher Are Arrested in Tampa."

371 *The* Great Falls Tribune *announced*: *Great Falls (MT) Tribune*, March 21, 1926. "No athlete in America ever added more color to a football game, a baseball game, or a cinder struggle, than Jim Thorpe."

CHAPTER 24: WORLD FAMOUS INDIANS

372 *Baseball season in Montana*: Curt Syness, "Jim Thorpe Played Ball in Montana," *Helena Independent Record*, Aug. 9, 2006; "History of Montana Hi-Line," Big Sky Fishing.com; Daniel Vichorek, *The Hi-Line: Profiles of a Montana Land* (Farcountry, 1994), 7–9.

372 *In the decade and a half*: Sampson Burd Student File, CISDRC; Margaret Burgess Student File, CISDRC; Tom Benjey, "Sampson Burd Fights the Pandemic" (blog), March 28, 2020; American Indian Athletic Hall of Fame, AIAHOF.com.

373 *Freeda, he later wrote*: "Red Son of Carlisle," 74.

373 *Flush with Roaring Twenties cash*: Account of semipro baseball in Montana drawn from Richard D. Gibbons, "Joy in Minersville: A Study of the Butte Mines and Independent Leagues," (graduate thesis, 2004); Gary Lucht, "Scobey's Touring Pros," *Montana*, Summer 1970; *Havre Daily News*, May 26, 1926; *Helena Independent Record*, Aug. 9, 2006, and June 25, 2018; Jim Nitz, "Happy Felsch," SABR website, 2015.

374 *It was trying too hard*: Account of Thorpe's play for Shelby and Havre drawn from *Anaconda (MT) Standard*, March 26, 1926; *Great Falls (MT) Tribune*, May 6, June 11, 27, 28, Sept. 12, 1926; *Hartford Courant*, April 18, 1926; *Havre Daily News*, June 14, 20, 21, 1926.

375 *They were back in Ohio*: 1926 Canton Bulldogs statistics, Pro Football Reference website: *Minneapolis Tribune*, Oct. 3, 1926. "All you need in the line is strength, knowledge of the game, a few tricks and the old instinct," Thorpe said.

375 *He organized a barnstorming*: *Marion (OH) Star*, Dec. 17, 1926.

376 *The inaugural barnstorming tour*: *Indianapolis News*, Dec. 20; *Rushville (IN) Republican*, Dec. 15–20; *Muncie (IN) Star Press*, Dec. 22–24, 1926.

376 *At New Castle, it was the World Famous Indians*: "Palefaces Join Indian Five," *Richmond (IN) Item*, Dec. 30, 1926.

376 *The use of faux Indians*: *Uniontown (PA) Morning Herald*, Jan. 10, 1927; *Indiana (PA) Gazette*, March 3, 1927.

377 *When the team reached the Penn-Harris Hotel*: *Harrisburg Telegraph*, March 15, 1927.

378 *It had been fifteen years*: "Thorpe Is Greeted by Large Crowd," Carlisle *Sentinel*, March 19, 1927.

378 *He played baseball that summer*: *Akron Beacon Journal*, July 2, 1927. Thorpe's Collegians included football and baseball alumni from Ohio State, Miami of Ohio, Ohio Wesleyan, and Ohio Northern. Also "Red Son of Carlisle," 74.

378 *Jim had signed a contract*: "Full of Vim and Pep Jim Thorpe Takes Charge of Local Gridders," *Portsmouth (OH) Daily Times*, Sept. 14, 1927; Bob Gill, "Thorpe's Farewell Season," *Coffin Corner* 15, no. 23, 1993; *Portsmouth (OH) Daily Times*, Oct. 31, 1927; *Cincinnati Enquirer*, Nov. 21, 1927.

379 *Once again came a tale*: *Hartford Courant*, Dec. 21, 1928; Lawrence Perry, Consolidated Press syndicated column, *Harrisburg Telegraph*, Nov. 10, 1928.

380 *Weeks before those stories appeared*: *Chicago Tribune*, Associated Press, Nov. 30, 1928; "Red Son of Carlisle," 77.

381 *He went by C. C.*: International News Service obituary, Feb. 4, 1939; *Chicago Tribune*, "Red Grange's Own Story," Dec. 29, 1929.

381 *Pyle's idea was to recruit*: Susan Croce Kelly, *Route 66* (University of Oklahoma Press, 1990), 32–35; *Oklahoma Today*, May–June, 1998.

382 *The derby had not quite reached*: Associated Press, April 22, 1929. "It was announced today that Jim Thorpe . . . would join the caravan."

382 *In conversations with the Bunion Derby publicist*: Letter from Lon Scott to Thorpe, May 16, 1943, Kate Buford personal papers; Associated Press, May 1, 1929.

383 *The response . . . came from Daniel J. Ferris*: Associated Press, May 1, 1929.

383 *In Holdenville*: *Holdenville (OK) Daily News*, May 7, 1929.

383 *The trip west offered Jim a chance*: *Fort Worth Star-Telegram*, April 6, 1972, interviews with Exendine and Cusack.

384 *The caravan left Mesa*: *Arizona Republic*, June 7, 1929.

384 *At the end of the road*: Account of consolation race and Thorpe and runners being shorted by Pyle drawn from *Los Angeles Express*, July 12, 1929; Associated Press, July 30, 1929; *San Bernardino County Sun*, Aug. 4, 1929; Walter Trumbull, *Washington Evening Star*, Aug. 27, 1929: "A native American, the best all around athlete of his time, cheerful and swift, game and strong, Jim was quite a fellow. Knowing nothing of the merits of the controversy, if Mr. Pyle owes Jim Thorpe any legitimate expense money, I certainly hope Jim gets it."

385 *"We took a little house"*: "Red Son of Carlisle," 77–78.

385 *He had all he needed*: *Los Angeles Times*, Sept. 13, 1929; *Sacramento Bee*, Oct. 5, 1929; *San Pedro News-Pilot*, Nov. 14, 1929.

386 *Drawn to the struggles*: United Press, Sept. 25, 1929.

386 *One of his most successful friends*: Account of Sylvester Long's invented life drawn from Donald B. Smith, *Chief Buffalo Child Long Lance, The Glorious Imposter* (Red Deer Press, 2002); Melinda Micco, "Tribal Recreations: Buffalo Child Long Lance and

Black Seminole Narratives"; Sylvester Long, *The Autobiography of a Blackfoot Indian Chief Re-Placing America* (University of Hawaii Press, 2000); letters between Thorpe and Chief Long Lance, Dec. 30, 1929, and Jan. 3, 1930, DHTC.

389 *"I could understand why"*: Mike Koehler unpublished manuscript.

389 *Grace was at Haskell*: Account of Jim and daughter Grace meeting at Haskell and events of 1930 Haskell powwow drawn from "Memories of Dad" by Grace Thorpe and handwritten notes for that story, Grace F. Thorpe Collection, Series 5, NMAI; "Red Son of Carlisle," 13, 78–79; *Pittsburgh Press*, Sept. 21, 1930; *Miami (OK) Daily News-Record*, Oct. 8, 1930; *Kansas City Times*, Oct. 7–10, 1930; *St. Joseph News-Press*, Oct. 9, 1930, Associated Press, Oct. 9–10, 1930; United Press, Oct. 9, 1930; Grann, *Killers of the Flower Moon*, 291; United Press, Nov. 27, 1930; *Daily Oklahoman*, Nov. 23, 1930; "Magpie," Oklahoma Historical Society; T. J. Stiles, *Custer's Trials* (Vintage, 2016), 317; Warren, *The Quest for Leadership*, 158.

CHAPTER 25: PICK AND SHOVEL

394 *When the American Football Coaches Association*: L. S. Cameron, United Press Sports Editor, Dec. 28, 1930.

394 *This was their first meeting*: Associated Press, Dec. 27–30, 1930; *York (PA) Daily Record*, Dec. 30, 1930.

394 *There was even a prize*: Foster Hailey, Associated Press Sports Writer, "Welch's Story of Lazy Guard Wins 'Iron Hat,'" Dec. 30, 1930; *Rochester Democrat and Chronicle*, Dec. 30, 1930.

396 *Consider the case*: American Football Database website. Cavanaugh gave this advice to fellow coach Joe McKenney.

396 *When Jim left Kansas*: Associated Press, Ponca City, OK, Oct. 13, 1930; Mike Koehler unpublished manuscript. "Thorpe visited his two children who are attending Chilocco Institute."

396 *His athletic career seemed distant*: "Rockne Picks His All-Time Backfield," Associated Press, Dec. 6, 1930; advertisement in *Cincinnati Enquirer*, Nov. 3, 1930; "Then and Now," *Vineland (NJ) Daily Journal*, Dec. 16, 1930.

397 *Scrapping around for another way*: "Pro Grid Circuit Planned," *Los Angeles Times*, Jan. 25, 1931.

397 *Jim's next job*: "Red Son of Carlisle," 79; Buford, *Native American Son*, 264.

398 *With that in mind*: Account of Thorpe working as laborer drawn from *Red Son of Carlisle*, 79; Jean Bosquiet, Associated Press, March 2, 1931 ("The once mighty Indian of Carlisle . . . is not ashamed of his job."); AP wirephoto, *Austin American Statesman*, March 12, 1931; Lawrence Perry column, *Oakland Tribune*, March 6, 1931; Newspaper Enterprise Association article, March 14, 1931.

399 *Pop Warner was also on the West Coast*: Stanford coaching record, College Football, Sports Reference website.

399 *As for the real Indians*: *Collier's*, Oct. 24 and 31, 1931.

400 *In the days leading up*: Account of Thorpe's treatment leading up to the 1932 Olympics drawn from *Stockholms-Tinningen*, April 21, 1964; *Los Angeles Times*, May 11,

1932; *Los Angeles Times* advertisement, July 17, 1932 ("Great American Athlete Now an Author"); United Press correspondent George H. Beale, July 21, 1932; *Los Angeles Times*, Associated Press, Aug. 1, 1932; 1932 Olympics file, DHTC; Buford, 275–76.

CHAPTER 26: "A MAN HAS TO KEEP HUSTLING"

403 *His closest neighbors*: Interview with Vicky Armstrong, Frank and Kate Miller's granddaughter, Dec. 18, 1920.

404 *At one point her field*: Michael E. Welsh, "The Road to Assimilation: The Seminoles in Oklahoma, 1839–1936," University of New Mexico dissertation, 1983; letter from Acting Field Clerk C. L. Ellis to Department of Interior, June 21, 1927, drawn from DHTC Harjo's Indians files and RG75, Central Classified Files, Seminole, 34605, NARA.

404 *This was an ambitious enterprise*: "Hardball and Headdresses: Jim Thorpe, Harjo's Indians, and Playing Social Stereotypes in Oklahoma Native American Baseball," Horsehide Historian blog, Feb. 3, 2017; Associated Press, April 28, 1933; *Sioux City Journal*, May 22, 1933; *Camden (NJ) Morning Post*, July 20, 1933; *Drumright (OK) Daily Derrick*, May 17, 1933.

406 *The first game was on May 21*: "Big Crowd Sees Game," *Emporia Gazette*, May 22, 1933.

406 *After a game in Topeka*: Postcard provided by Miller granddaughter Vicky Armstrong.

407 *The Monarchs were now managed*: *Tulsa Daily World*, May 28, 30–31, 1933; *St. Joseph (MO) News-Press*, June 3, 1933; Charles Wilber (Bullet) Rogan entry, National Baseball Hall of Fame website. Rogan began his career playing baseball in the army for the all-black Twenty-Fifth Infantry before spending nineteen seasons with the Kansas City Monarchs. Along with his excellent pitching, he also batted cleanup.

407 *the Indians again faced an all-black club*: "The Pittsburgh Crawfords," Negro Leagues History website; "1933 Pittsburgh Crawfords," Negro Leagues Database, Seamheads .com; *Akron Beacon Journal*, June 19–22, 1933. In the 16–1 drubbing, the Crawfords "scored four times in the first, twice in the second, three times in the third, seven times in the fifth and could have been scoring yet if they had been so minded."

407 *When Jim reached Pittsburgh*: *Pittsburgh Press*, June 23, 1933.

408 *The Harjo's bus rolled across*: *Altoona Tribune*, June 24–26, 1933; *Shamokin (PA) News-Dispatch*, June 26, 1933; *Philadelphia Inquirer*, June 27, 1933.

409 *Iva had remarried*: Account of Iva's new life as Iva Davies and her relationship with her daughters drawn from *Fort Worth Star-Telegram* article on the wedding, Dec. 27, 1929; Mike Koehler unpublished manuscript; Grace F. Thorpe Collection, Series 5, *NMAI*; Buford, *Native American Son*, 244–45.

410 *Nat C. Strong, a promoter and owner*: Layton Revel, "Early Pioneers of the Negro Leagues: Nat Strong," Center for Negro League Baseball Research website; *New York Age*, Feb. 6, 1926.

410 *"The Indians are coming"*: Account of Harjo's Indians playing in New York and New Jersey drawn from *Brooklyn Times Union*, June 15, 28, 30, July 3, 1933; *Brooklyn Daily*

Eagle, June 29, 1933; *Hackensack Record*, June 29, July 1, 1933; *Middletown (NY) Times Herald*, July 5, 1933; *Camden (NJ) Morning Post*, July 20, 1933.

410 *During a break in the schedule*: Frank (Buck) O'Neill, International News Service sportswriter, "Jim Thorpe Tells Bambino How He Chased Curve Ball," July 22, 1933.

411 *"My dear Frank"*: Letter provided by Vicky Armstrong.

412 *In truth, Jim's time on the road*: *Poughkeepsie Eagle-News*, Aug. 2, 1933; *Fitchburg (MA) Sentinel*, Aug. 18, 1933; *Boston Globe*, Aug. 14, 1933.

413 *In the first game*: *Hartford Courant*, Aug. 7 and 21, 1933.

413 *On a return trip*: "Calling 'Em Right with Albert W. Keane, Sports Editor," *Hartford Courant*, Aug. 24, 1933.

414 *Ben Harjo . . . had no money*: Account of Thorpe's struggles to get paid drawn from *Daily Oklahoman*, Nov. 17, 1933; telegram from Thorpe to Commissioner of Indian Affairs, Oct. 4, 1933; letter from Commissioner Collier to Susey Walker Harjo, Oct. 7, 1933; letter from Thorpe to Senator William McAdoo, Oct. 7, 1933; letter from Harjo to Collier, Oct. 10, 1933; letter from Thorpe to Collier, January, 1935; letter from Thorpe lawyer E. A. Kline to Oklahoma governor E. W. Marland, Nov. 12, 1935; Marland letter to Kline, Nov. 22, 1935; Thorpe letter to Collier, May 22, 1935; Thorpe letters to President Roosevelt, Feb. 1, 1935 and May 31, 1937, all in DHTC Harjo's Indians file and RG75, Central Classified Files, Seminole, 34605, NARA.

CHAPTER 27: *AKAPAMATA* IN HOLLYWOOD

416 *For the rights*: *Brooklyn Standard Union*, Dec. 26, 1931; Buford, *Native American Son*, 272; *Life*, Nov. 28, 1960; *Time*, Aug. 31, 1936.

416 *He landed his first credited role*: *Films in Review*, July 1966; "Jim Thorpe," IMDb.

417 *Thorpe's career in movies*: United Press, Aug. 10, 1932; Dan Thomas, "Hollywood Gossip," *Waterbury Democrat*, Aug. 13, 1932; United Press, March 30, 1935; *Hollywood Citizen*, April 11, 1935 and May 30, 1938; *Chicago Tribune*, Sept. 17, 1937.

418 *But those Hollywood years were affirming*: Bob Wheeler, Florence Ridlon, and Rob Wheeler, "Akapamata: The Forgotten Hollywood Legacy of Jim Thorpe," *American Indian*, Spring 2015.

418 *Concerns about how Hollywood treated Indians*: *Moving Picture World*, March 18, 1911.

418 *After a few years in Hollywood*: "Luther Standing Bear," IMBd; Aleiss, *Making the White Man's Indian*, 54, 184; *New York Times*, April 14, 1916. In 1935, Luther Standing Bear was arrested and jailed for eight months for making inappropriate advances toward an eight-year-old Paiute girl, *Los Angeles Times*, March 19, 1935.

419 *The stereotypes . . . were encrusted*: Associated Press, March 15, 1934; *Los Angeles Times*, Jan. 28, 1934; "Indians Object to Being Imitated in Movies," *Chicago Tribune*, June 8, 1932; Aleiss, 54–55.

420 *One film in which he was an extra*: Details of filming *Under Pressure* drawn from *Detroit Free Press*, Sept. 25, 1934; *New York Daily News*, Sept. 27, 1934; "*Under Pressure*," Letterbox.com; author viewing of movie.

421 *It was not a classic western*: "*Behold My Wife!* Synopsis," TCM.com; "*Behold My Wife!*"

IMDb.com; "Sylvia Sidney Excels in Role of Indian Girl," *Paducah Sun-Democrat*, Dec. 23, 1934.

421 *As Jim became more of a presence*: George Kirksey, United Press Staff Correspondent, March 30, 1935.

422 *An investigation requested by the Swedes*: International News Service, April 22, 1935; Associated Press, April 22, 1935; *Los Angeles Times*, June 8, 1936.

423 *The accolades made Jim take notice*: Associated Press, June 29, 1935. "Seldom given to vain regrets of any sort, Jim Thorpe, the super-athlete of an era long gone, is harboring one now. It comes from envying Jesse Owens."

423 *A wirephoto in newspapers*: Associated Press, April 10 and 24, 1935.

424 *Hitler found a strong ally*: Andrew Maraniss, *Games of Deception*, (Viking, 2021), 36–42; David Maraniss, *Rome 1960*, (Simon & Schuster, 2008), 67.

424 *Thorpe's position . . . evolved*: Hollywood column by Sidney Skolsky, *New York Daily News*, July 6, 1935 and Dec. 7, 1935; *Wisconsin Jewish Chronicle*, July 10, 1936. (WNS newsletter) "Opposition to American participation the Berlin Olympics was expressed by Jim Thorpe. . . ."

425 *Wilcox was the newly minted*: *Hollywood Reporter*, July 21, 1935.

426 *Phil later told the writer Paul Zimmerman*: Paul Zimmerman, "Calling Signals," *Cincinnati Enquirer*, Oct. 26, 1974.

427 *After a trip to the Midwest*: *People*, Jan. 8, 1996; Bob Greene column, *Chicago Tribune*, Aug. 10, 1992.

428 *Now came a third variation*: *Santa Rosa Republican*, May 28, 1935; *Los Angeles Times*, May 30, Sept. 9, Sept. 20, 1935.

429 *"Lo, the poor Indian"*: United Press, Hollywood, Sept. 24, 1936; *Los Angeles Times*, Sept. 24, 1936. "Jim Thorpe Takes Warpath."

430 *In this case, it was not just the hiring*: Aleiss, 56.

430 *Enraged by it all*: Louella Parsons, Universal Service, Oct. 19, 1936. DeMille wrote a letter to Parsons the next day arguing that he cast two white actors to play Indian chiefs because "after we had conscientiously auditioned all the real Indians available, we found them inadequate for the roles."

430 *"Hollywood's 250 Po Lo's"*: *Variety*, Sept. 30, 1936.

431 *Every few years, Grantland Rice*: Column by Grantland Rice, North American Newspaper Alliance, Dec. 17, 1936.

432 *The question of whether Owens*: *New York Daily News*, Aug. 6, 1936.

432 *It was left to Damon Runyon*: "Runyon Says," Universal Service, July 27, 1936. "Aha," Runyon's column began. "So there were goings-on aboard the good ship Manhattan, eh?"

433 *He drove across America*: Account of Ernie Pyle's columns from the road and interview with Thorpe drawn from "The Hoosier Vagabond: On the Road with Ernie Pyle," Ray E. Boomhower's Books (blog), Aug. 1, 2019; Ernie Pyle, "Once Famous Athlete Is Just a Nobody Now," Hawthorne, CA, Jan. 6, 1937, Scripps-Howard syndicate.

437 *Jim Thorpe opposed part*: Account of Thorpe lobbying against new Sac and Fox con-

stitution drawn from Arthur Edson, North American Newspaper Alliance, Dec. 26, 1937; *Oklahoma News*, Dec. 5–6, 1937; *Cushing (OK) Daily Citizen*, Dec. 6, 1937; Associated Press, Dec. 6–9, 1937; ("Thorpe into Politics" read a headline on the AP story in the *Manhattan (Kan) Mercury*); "Sic Transit Jim Thorpe," *Kansas City Times*, Dec. 10, 1937; Constitution and By-Laws of the Sac and Fox Tribe of Indians of Oklahoma, Ratified Dec. 7, 1937, U.S. Government Printing Office; Buford, 302–303: Brian F. Rader, "Oklahoma Indian Welfare Act," OHS.

439 *His Indian compatriots*: Wheeler, Ridlon, and Wheeler, "Akapamata"; Buford, 264.

CHAPTER 28: NEVER FORGOTTEN

440 *Rockne, born in Norway*: *Time*, April 6, 1931; Chelland, *One for the Gipper*, 78; Knute Rockne coaching record, College Football, Sports Reference website.

441 *Nothing gilds a legend*: AP Bulletin, Cottonwood Falls, KS, March 31, 1931: "A loud explosion and spurting flames in a murky sky heralded the disaster," Also *Time*, April 6, 1941; Jim Lefebre, "Explaining the Rockne Crash," Forever Irish on ND Football History website.

441 *In 1940, Warner Bros.*: Associated Press, April 13, 1940; "*Knute Rockne, All American*, Full Cast and Crew," IMDb; Frederick C. Othman, United Press Hollywood Correspondent, April 12, 1940. Othman quoted Rockne's widow as saying O'Brien in makeup looked so much like her husband "I almost expect him to make love to me."

441 *There were also two Thorpe sightings*: Associated Press, April 6, 1940; "*Knute Rockne, All American*, Full Cast and Crew," IMDb; author observations after viewing movie. According to a report that made its way to a sports columnist in Massachusetts, Thorpe during the movie at age fifty-two "got away a punt which went 52 yards on the fly and then contributed another which, including the bound, covered 72 yards."

442 *Rockne's was a journey*: Account of the Rockne movie and comparisons with Thorpe drawn from author viewing of *Knute Rockne, All American.*

444 *Then there is the matter*: Coles Phinizy, "Win One for the Gipper," *Sports Illustrated*, Sept. 17, 1979; Chelland, chapter 11, "Problems of a Superstar," 128–39; full text of Rockne's "Win One for the Gipper" speech in movie, University of Notre Dame Archives.

445 *He had given speeches*: "Indian Jim Thorpe's Life Just Beginning at 50," *Los Angeles Times*, Feb. 2, 1940; Wheeler, *Jim Thorpe*, 199; Stanley Woodward, "Views of Sport: A Visit with Jim Thorpe," *New York Herald Tribune*, Dec. 23, 1941; *Chicago Tribune*, Sept. 24, 1940; promotional brochure from W. Colston Leigh, Inc., DHTC Colston Leigh file.

446 *"I came from the Sac and Fox tribe"*: Wheeler, 203–204.

446 *When the tour took Jim to New York*: Stanley Woodward, "Views of Sport."

447 *A collegiate All-Star football game*: "British Relief Grid Tilt Is Cancelled; Tom Harmon, Mates are Called 'Pros,'" Associated Press, Jan. 4, 1941; Louella Parsons, International News Service, Jan. 4, 1941.

448 *One summer night*: DHTC Thorpe Letters file.

448 *Less than a week later*: *Marion (OH) Star*, Aug. 13, 1941.

449 *"We spent the evening chatting"*: Luella Hoffmire remembrance in DHTC Carl Hoffmire file.

450 *Freeda had definitively reached that conclusion*: *Los Angeles Times*, Oct. 30, 1941; Final Judgment of Divorce, Freeda Thorpe Plaintiff vs. James F. Thorpe, Defendant, Docket no. 204206, Superior Court of the State of California; International News Service, Oct. 30, 1931. ("Although he once was the sports idol of America, Jim Thorpe . . . proved a neglectful husband . . ."); "Champ's Image Tarnished, Freeda Thorpe Has Bad Memories of Marriage," Associated Press, Aug. 31, 1996.

451 *"Dear Friend Gus"*: DHTC Thorpe Letters file.

452 *With America at war again*: Jimmy Corcoran, "Ol' Jim Thorpe Would Do Bit," *Chicago Record-Herald*, Jan. 31, 1942; Hugh Fullerton Jr., Wide World Sports Writer, Associated Press. April 27, 1942; *Medford (OH) Mail Tribune*, April 22, 1942; *Nashville Banner*, May 8, 1942.

453 *the connection to Ford went back*: Pete Calac Student File, CISDRC; "Carlisle Boys Making Good in a University of Citizenship," *Carlisle Arrow*, May 7, 1915; "Ford Motor Company's School," *Carlisle Arrow*, March 31, 1916.

453 *Bennett and his top lieutenant, Stanley Fay*: Account of Thorpe's work at Ford Motor Company drawn from Watson Spoelstra, "Through the Gates of Ford Empire Pass World's Greatest Athletes," Associated Press, May 1942; Frank Scully and Norman Sper, "The Little Man in Henry Ford's Basement," *American Mercury*, May 1942; letter from Sharon James, Request Coordinator, Ford Motor Co., to Grace Thorpe, Aug. 13, 2002, and Robert Wheeler interviews with Luther Bass and Chief Nevitt, plant security, Kate Buford personal papers.

454 *On May 4*: DHTC Thorpe Letters file.

454 *On one shift that summer*: Letter from FBI, Detroit, to Washington, D.C., July 17, 1942, Kate Buford personal papers.

455 *It was also that summer*: Jack Thorpe remembrance, Kate Buford personal papers; DHTC Ford Motor Co. file; Wheeler, *Jim Thorpe*, 207, citing undated column by Jim McCulley of the *New York Daily News* in Jim Thorpe's personal scrapbook; Grace F. Thorpe Collection, Series 5, NMAI.

455 *Doctors determined*: Associated Press, Feb. 11, 1943; *Sport*, February 1949; Whitney Martin, Associated Press, Feb. 19, 1943; "Scully's Notebook," *Variety*, Aug. 29, 1951; Buford, *Native American Son*, 320; "Jim Costin Says," *South Bend (IN) Tribune*, Feb. 13, 1943. "So the old ticker is running out on Jim Thorpe . . ."

455 *What happened next is unclear*: Associated Press, Feb. 19, 1943; Thorpe letter to Lon Scott, March 28, 1943, Lon Scott file, Jim Thorpe House, Yale, Oklahoma.

455 *When news of Jim's heart attack*: *Sport*, February 1949; DHTC Ford Motor Co. file.

456 *The piece drew the attention*: Associated Press dispatch in *Tulsa Daily World*, Feb. 12, 1943; letter from Lon Scott to Personnel Director, Ford Motor Co., Lon Scott File, Jim Thorpe House.

456 *He reached out while Jim*: Account of Scott trying to help Thorpe with a job and placing his sons in schools in Oklahoma drawn from letters from Scott to Thorpe, April 10,

May 16, June 12, June 16, July 15, 1943; Thorpe to Scott, March 28, June 4, Aug. 22, 1943; Scott to Col. L. E. Angle, June 12, 1943; Gov. Kerr to Scott, June 29, 1943; Burton Logan to Thorpe, July 8, 1943; Emmet Brown memos, June 11, Aug. 10, 1943, all found in Lon Scott file, Jim Thorpe House, Yale, OK; DHTC Lon Scott file; Kate Buford personal papers, Lon Scott file.

458 *Most of the problems*: *Tulsa Daily World*, Sept. 18, 1943.

CHAPTER 29: ROAD TO UTOPIA

459 *The Pawnee Indian School*: Pawnee Agency and Boarding School Historic District, National Register of Historic Places Registration Form, National Park Service; Jack Thorpe file, Kate Buford personal papers; "The Gravy Had No Lumps," Theda Good-Fox Kresge, *Native Times*, June 15, 2009.

460 *Jim was long gone from Oklahoma*: Associated Press, March 9, Oct. 26, 1943; United Press, July 29, 1943; AP, Nov. 9, 1943; "Jim Thorpe Dream Fades; Goes West." Also Lon Scott letter to George Reif, traffic section, Tulsa police, Sept. 21, 1943, Lon Scott file, Jim Thorpe House, Yale, OK; DHTC Scott file.

460 *"Well, Xmas is over thank God"*: Lon Scott papers, Jim Thorpe House, Yale, OK; Scott file, Kate Buford personal papers.

461 *The banquet was the first annual*: *Los Angeles Times*, Dec. 28, 1943.

461 *The opportunity to rub shoulders again*: *"Road to Utopia,"* TCM.com; *"Road to Utopia,"* IMDb; author observations of movie.

462 *he obtained a seaman's certificate*: Seaman's Certificate Application. United States Coast Guard, Port of Los Angeles, May 19, 1945. Certificate of identification No. Z-612083, National Personnel Records Center, St. Louis.

462 *His third wife was different*: DHTC, Thorpe outline, 68; Al Zagofsky, *Jim Thorpe (PA) Times News*, July 13, 2013; Mike Koehler unpublished manuscript; Wheeler, *Jim Thorpe*, 209; Buford, *Native American Son*, 329; UPI, *San Bernardino County Sun*, April 8, 1975.

463 *At four on the afternoon*: Details of the preparations and voyage of SS *Southwestern Victory* drawn from: SS *Southwestern Victory* No. 29683, NARA, Northeast Region, NY; General Records of the Bureau of Naval Personnel, RG 24.2.2. Operational and Signal Logs of U.S. Navy Armed Guard units. Class: Liberty ship. Type, VC-2-AP2. Keel laid: March 6, 1945. Delivered: May 23, 1945.

464 *"He had lots of tales"*: Letter from Wesley A. Nimitz to Buford, Kate Buford personal papers.

464 *That commander was . . . Robert R. Neyland*: Connie L. Lester, "Robert Reese Neyland," Tennessee Encyclopedia (online); U.S. Army Corps of Engineers website, November 2001; DHTC outline, 68; Tennessee Historical Society Neyland profile; Wheeler, 209; *Tiger Rag*, Bengal Air Depot, July 28, Aug. 11, 1945.

465 *"The captain of our ship"*: DHTC Merchant Marine file.

465 *"As you know, Jim"*: Letter from Patricia G. Thorpe to Lon Scott from 26208 Belle Porte Ave., Lomita Cal, in Lon Scott file, Jim Thorpe House, Yale, OK; Kate Buford personal papers.

467 *a young man named William Thourlby*: Account of the bond between Thorpe and William Thourlby, who came to be called Buddy Thorpe, drawn from Furman Bisher, "Jim Thorpe's Adopted Son," *Atlanta Journal and Constitution* magazine, March 19, 1972; *Atlanta Constitution*, March 22, 1988; *Port Huron (MI) Times Herald*, July 1, 1953, July 25, 1992 ("'Marlboro Man' returns to St. Clair today"); *Los Angeles Times*, May 26, 2002; Harvey MacKay, "Outswimming the Sharks," *Minneapolis Star Tribune*, Sept. 4, 2017; Buford, 350–52.

469 *Thourlby recounted that story*: Correspondence to author from Kate Buford, April 25, 2021.

470 *"knots all over my head"*: Associated Press, Jan. 25, 1946.

470 *Freeda put Dick on a bus*: Buford, *Native American Son*, 333.

471 *The* Miami News *ran a multipart series*: Bylined "By Jim Thorpe (As Told to Guy Butler, Sports Editor, The Miami Daily News)," it ran. March 3–28, 1946. "Thorpe is now visiting in the area and he was induced to tell the story of his life from the time of his birth . . . up to the present day."

471 *Jim tried to get a job as wrestling*: Associated Press, March 5, 1947.

471 *When Eddie Allen of North Carolina's* Charlotte Observer: Eddie Allen's Sports Asides, "Pity the Poor Indian?—Not Jim Thorpe," *Charlotte Observer*, July 23, 1947.

472 *While in Charleston*: Dan Parker, *Broadway Bugle*, June 28, Aug. 13, 1947.

473 *The resulting headline*: Associated Press, Atlanta, Oct. 13, 1947.

473 *He also took a job as a greeter*: United Press, Chicago, "Thorpe Acts as Greeter in Saloon," Nov. 18, 1947.

474 *Three weeks before Christmas*: Associated Press, "Jim Thorpe Robbed," Dec. 3, 1947.

CHAPTER 30: THUNDERBIRDS

475 *They stayed at the Pennsylvania*: *New York Times*, March 22, 1948.

476 *When a reporter in Dallas*: Harold V. Ratliff, Associated Press, April 6, 1948. Brundage had arrived in Dallas from Austin where he had refereed the Texas Relays.

476 *As part of his job in Chicago*: *Chicago Tribune*, May 5, 1948.

476 *His city personnel records*: Transcript of Supplementary Personnel Card. Thorpe, James. Chicago Parks Department, 1948.

477 *In May, a photograph went out*: AP wirephoto and caption, May 8, 1948; Associated Press article, June 8, 1948. "Here Thorpe gives an autograph to his young pupils and coaches them on passing a relay baton."

477 *And there he was in July*: *Chicago Tribune*, July 5–9, 1948; National Archives Exhibit, Freedom Train, Sept. 17, 1949. The seven-car train traveled America from September 1947 to January 1949 and was visited by more than 3.5 million people.

478 *Sullivan had spotted Jim*: Little Old New York column by Ed Sullivan, "I Have News for You," Aug. 19, 1948; "50,000 Pass Ruth's Bier," *New York Daily News*, Aug. 18, 1948.

478 *After reading about Ruth's death*: "How About a Job for Jim Thorpe?" *Pittsburgh Sunday Sun-Telegraph*, Aug. 22, 1948.

479 *A month after his Thorpe column*: *Pittsburgh Sun-Telegraph*, Sept. 28, 1948; *"The Stratton Story* (1949)," IMDb; author viewing of movie.

480 *The Israeli team*: *New York Daily News*, Sept. 22, 1948; Associated Press, Sept. 20–21, 1948; AP wirephoto, "Mighty Redman," Sept. 28, 1948.

480 *That same week, Jim and Patsy*: Account of revival of Thorpe movie and Patsy's behavior drawn from Louella O. Parsons, "In Hollywood," International News Service, Sept. 27, 1948; "On the Line with Bob Considine," syndicated column, Feb. 11, 1948; Erskine Johnson, "Hollywood Notes," Newspaper Enterprise Association column, Nov. 23, 1948: Vincent X. Flaherty, IMDb biography; Buford, *Native American Son*, 340–41; *Los Angeles Times*, Freeman obituary, Jan. 26, 1991.

483 *Softball was the rage*: Account of Jim and Patsy's time running the Thunderbirds softball club drawn from Ray Silvius, "Jim Thorpe, Famed World Athlete, Turns Attention to Girls Softball," *Arizona Republic*, April 10, 1949; also *Arizona Republic*, April 17, 26–29, 1949; *Los Angeles Daily News*, April 16, 1949; Paul Zimmerman, "Sportscripts," *Los Angeles Times*, April 24, 1949; Al Zagofsky, "Jim Thorpe Once Owned a Woman's Baseball Team," Times News Online (Lehigh Valley, PA), July 13, 2013; Associated Press, April 23 and 24, 1949; *Wilmington (CA) Daily Press Journal*, April 23, 1949.

485 *The friend and proprietor*: Associated Press, Los Angeles, "Jim Thorpe Lonely in New Role," June 4, 1949.

486 *Grantland Rice did not need much*: Letter exchange between Rice and Brundage from Brundage Collection, box 42, Individuals, Jim Thorpe, UIABC.

487 *It had been thirty-six years*: Letter likely ghostwritten from Patsy Thorpe to Mahoney, dated September 1949, "Poignant Appeal: Jim Thorpe Letter Begs for Return of Olympic Medals," posted in sportscollectorsdaily.com.

488 *Jim lamented*: Aline Mosby, United Press, Hollywood, Aug. 2, 1949.

488 *The movie was going forward*: "Albums to be Flown to Hollywood for Jim Thorpe Movie," Carlisle *Sentinel*, Aug. 3, 1949; Freeman letter to Warner, *Jim Thorpe—All American* production file, University of Southern California.

489 *Thorpe had a soft voice*: Recordings of Thorpe interviews with radio broadcaster Bob Wolff, June 1951, Library of Congress Sound Research Center.

489 *Asking the public to identify*: Walter Winchell, "Broadway Ticker," *New York Daily Mirror*, Nov. 2, 1949; *Berkshire Eagle*, Sept. 12, 1949; *Lincoln Star*, Aug. 7, 1949; *San Francisco Examiner*, June 25, 1949; *St. Louis Globe-Democrat*, March 6, 1949; *Odessa American*, Aug. 14, 1949; "Chip Off Old Block: Jim Thorpe's Son Starring on Gridiron," Associated Press, Fort Monmouth, NJ. Nov. 10, 1949.

490 *The past circled back*: *Washington Post*, Dec. 30, 1949; Associated Press, Jan. 25, Feb. 12, 1950; "Jim Thorpe Named Male Athlete of Era—1900–1950, Star in Track, Football, Baseball; Ruth, Dempsey, Cobb Far Back," *Boston Globe*, Feb. 12, 1950.

492 *"He's the ugliest man"*: Associated Press, March 23, 1950.

493 *In the first step*: Account of Thorpe as manager of wrestler Suni War Cloud drawn from "Jim Thorpe Returns to Pro Sports to Manage Second Young Indian Wrestler," Associated Press, Buffalo, NY, March 24, 1950; *Troy Record*, March 24, 1950; *Binghamton Press and Sun-Bulletin*, March 30, April 9, 12, 21, 1950; *Syracuse Post-Standard*, April 5, 9, 1950; *Ottawa Journal*, May 2–3, 1950.

494 *"Why, Mike Regan, you old so and so"*: "Pair of 'Bushers' Have Brief Reunion," Associated Press, Albany, March 28, 1950.

494 *The envelope said*: March 28, 1950 letter from Patricia Thorpe to Mrs. FW Seely [Jim's daughter Grace], on Statler Hotel stationery, Grace F. Thorpe Collection, Series 5, NMAI.

CHAPTER 31: HAVE YOU SEEN THE MOVIE?

497 *But along with its conflations*: Descriptions and opinions of *Jim Thorpe—All-American* based on author's multiple viewings of the 1951 Warner Bros. film.

498 *In an internal memo*: Memo from Morrow to Trilling, Sept. 1, 1950, *Jim Thorpe—All-American* production file, Warner Bros. Collection, USC.

499 *Jim was played by Billy Gray*: Billy Gray interview, May 17, 2021.

499 *"a faithful interpretation"*: Sidney Skolsky, *Hollywood Citizen-News*, Sept. 8, 1950.

500 *The third Carlisle student*: *Los Angeles Times*, Sept. 15, 1950; Associated Press, Sept. 11, 1950. "Director Michael Curtiz . . . tested 35 actors before discovering Bighead. The role will mark his debut as an actor."

501 *Even before the news*: "Muskogee Getting Ready for Movie of Thorpe's Life," *Daily Oklahoman*, Aug. 8, 1950.

501 *In preparation for the location shoot*: "Warner Couldn't Have Picked Better Site," *Muskogee Daily Phoenix*, Aug. 19, 1951.

501 *"I'm used to high heels"*: Erskine Johnson, NEA, *Shamokin (PA) News-Dispatch*, Oct. 1, 1950.

502 *Curtiz was a veteran director*: Rode, *Michael Curtiz: A Life in Film*, 452–54.

502 *"Do what I meant"*: Billy Gray interview, May 17, 2021.

502 *The cast and crew descended*: *Muskogee Times-Democrat*, Aug. 16, 1950.

502 *To absorb the role of Thorpe*: Wheeler, *Jim Thorpe*, 251; *New York Daily News*, Aug. 20, 1950; Harrison Carroll, "Behind the Scenes in Hollywood," Hearst syndicate, Sept. 5, 1950; *Rock Island (IL) Argus*, Aug. 15, 1950.

503 *Thorpe was also on hand*: *Muskogee Daily Phoenix*, Sept. 1, 1950; DHTC, Muskogee file.

503 *At Patsy's urging*: Erskine Johnson, NEA, "Big Jim Thorpe Wins Round with Face Lifting Surgery," Aug. 24, 1950; "Confessions of a Plastic Surgeon," *Esquire*, June 1951.

503 *Lancaster had been training*: Wheeler, 251; Rode, 452–54; *Muskogee Daily Phoenix*, Aug. 19, 1951; Kate Buford, *Burt Lancaster: An American life* (Da Capo Press, 2001), 110.

504 *Mrs. Dwight D. Sanders*: Undated letter from Mrs. Dwight D. Sanders, "Images of Oklahoma through the Eyes of Bacone College," Bacone College archive.

504 *Among those watching*: Photo caption "Thorpe Scene at Bacone College," *Muskogee Daily Phoenix*, Aug. 19, 1951: "James Lancaster, father of Burt . . . may be detected applauding in front of the receiving platform." Also "Local Men Have Part in the Film," *Stillwell Democrat-Journal*, Aug. 31, 1950.

504 *As the Thorpe movie*: Account of convention drawn from Records of the National Congress of American Indians, NMAI.AC.010, Series 1, Conventions and Mid-Year

Conferences; Mission and History, NCAI.org; Norman Transcript, Sept. 3, 1950. Also *Boston Globe*, Aug. 31, 1950; *Salem (OR) Capital Journal*, Sept. 1, 1950.

505 *As the location shooting*: "Hollywood Remembers Bacone with Gifts of Scholarships," *Bacone Indian*, Oct. 27, 1950.

505 *Jim, back in Los Angeles*: *Los Angeles Daily News*, Sept. 12, 1950.

505 *opens newsreel style*: "*Jim Thorpe—All-American* Synopsis," IMDb, and analysis by author after multiple viewings of film.

510 *Before the movie came out*: "Face Lift Job? Say it Ain't So, Jim," Associated Press, March 27, 1951.

510 *When he was in New York*: *Atlanta Journal and Constitution* magazine, March 19, 1972; Thourlby file, Kate Buford personal papers.

511 *"I look about twenty years younger"*: Thorpe letter to Grace on Jim Thorpe Sports Enterprises stationery, April 29, 1951, Grace F. Thorpe Collection, NMAI.

511 *Using her many contacts*: Patricia Thorpe letter to Grace, May 5, 1951, NMAI.

511 *"We are getting no place fast"*: Patricia Thorpe letter to Grace from Hotel Belvedere, Manhattan, NMAI.

512 *Among Patsy's skills*: "Voice of Broadway," Dorothy Kilgallen syndicated column, June 4, 1951.

512 *Wolff began by noting*: Bob Wolff interview with Thorpe, recording Part 1, Library of Congress Sound Research Center.

513 *It was ninety-five degrees the next day*: "On the Line with Bob Considine," syndicated column, June 3, 1951; *Washington Post*, Associated Press, United Press, June 3–4, 1951.

514 *"The church bells are ringing"*: Patricia Thorpe letter to Grace from Milwaukee, June 25, 1951, Grace F. Thorpe Collection, NMAI.

514 *Thorpe's biggest event*: United Press, July 12, 1951: "At the start of the mile, Jim Thorpe, now a Milwaukee resident . . ."

514 *That was when the movie*: Account of movie premieres in Muskogee and Oklahoma City drawn from *Muskogee Daily Phoenix* June 18, Aug. 9, Aug. 20–21, 1951; full-page advertisements in Muskogee and regional newspapers, "Muskogee extends to All the World a cordial invitation to be our guest for our day-long celebration and the colorful World Premiere of Warner Bros. Greatest Indian Production of All Time," August 1951; "Thorpe's Absence Fails to Dim Movie Premiere," *Tulsa World*, Aug. 20, 1951; "Jim Thorpe Calls Moviemakers Stinkers," *Daily Oklahoma*, Aug. 22, 1951.

515 *Jim returned to the scene*: "World Premiere of Thorpe Movie a Great Success," Carlisle *Sentinel*, Aug. 24, 1951; "Thorpe Back at Carlisle," International News Service, Aug. 23, 1951.

516 *"We have rented a beautiful old place"*: Patricia Thorpe letter to Grace from Memphis, Sept. 6, 1951, Grace F. Thorpe Collection, NMAI.

517 *When the film came to Pearl River*: "People Still Remember the Name Jim Thorpe," Grace Thorpe, Grace F. Thorpe Collection, NMAI.

CHAPTER 32: WAVING GOOD-BYE

519 *That venture was cut short*: Trace Lara Hentz, "Honor Restored," *Olympics at the Millennium*, (Rutgers Press, 2001), July 11, 2015; Associated Press, Nov. 9–10, 1951; *Philadelphia Inquirer*, Nov. 17, 1951.

520 *"Don't smile too much, honey"*: Arthur Daley, "A Visit with Jim Thorpe," Sports of the Times column, *New York Times*, Nov. 20, 1951; Whitney Martin, Associated Press, Nov. 21, 1951.

521 *Funds to raise money for Jim*: United Press, Jan. 30, 1952.

521 *Leigh Montville was a sports-loving*: Correspondence with Leigh Montville, July 4, 2020.

521 *After reading Arthur Daley's column*: Rode, *Michael Curtiz*, 453; DHTC movie file; Memos and Correspondence File, *Jim Thorpe—All-American*, Warner Bros. Collection, USC.

522 A man has to keep hustling: "Top Athlete Honored at Marlin Tilt," Associated Press, Dec. 8, 1951; "Jim Thorpe 'Convicted' of Theft in Mock Trial," United Press, Jan. 10, 1952.

523 *"I had the opportunity last evening"*: Letter from Miller to Brundage, Sept. 14, 1951, box 43, Individuals, Jim Thorpe, Avery Brundage Collection, UIABC.

523 *"Thanks for sending the information"*: Letter from Brundage to Miller, Sept. 17, 1951; UIABC.

523 *But the issue would not die*: Associated Press coverage of AAU convention in Daytona Beach, Dec. 1–4, 1951; Guy Butler, *Miami News*, Dec. 2, 1952.

524 *The Spokane Athletic Round Table*: *Spokane Chronicle*, Dec. 11, 1951; *Spokane Spokesman-Review*, Dec. 12, 1951; "Message from Spokane," *Dayton Daily News*, Dec. 26, 1951.

524 *Jim's two strongest proponents*: Grantland Rice column turned over to Patsy, North American Newspaper Alliance, Dec. 12, 1951.

525 *"You know Grantland Rice"*: Letter from Brundage to Kirby, Dec. 28, 1951, box 43, Individuals, Jim Thorpe, Avery Brundage Collection, UIABC.

525 *Kirby did as Brundage asked*: Letter from Kirby to Rice, Jan. 24, 1952, UIABC.

526 *From his winter perch*: Rice response letter to Kirby, Jan. 25, 1952, UIABC.

527 *Every seat at every table*: Account of Canton banquet and Branch Rickey speech drawn from box 73, Branch Rickey Papers, Library of Congress (speech typed on onionskin paper); Jim Schlemmer, "Legendary or Real, Jim Thorpe Has Night of Glory at Canton," *Akron Beacon Journal*, Jan. 30, 1952: also Associated Press, United Press, *Marion (OH) Star, Akron Beacon Journal*, Jan. 31, 1952; *Cleveland Plain Dealer*, Feb. 4, 1952.

530 *His seatmate was Ted Williams*: Bill King, "Thorpe Star at Boston Sports Show," Associated Press, Feb. 6, 1953.

532 *"I am feeling very good"*: Letter from Thorpe to "Dear Friend Walt," Feb. 28, 1952, DHTC letters file.

532 *Patsy found another nightclub*: *Reno Gazette-Journal*, May 21, 1952; Phillip I. Earl, "Mega-athlete Jim Thorpe Once Resided in Nevada," Nevada Historical Society column in *Elko Daily Free Press*, Aug. 22, 1995; Buford, *Native American Son*, 361.

533 *On the afternoon of June 18*: *Nevada State Journal*, June 19, 1952; "The Kefauver Hearing in Las Vegas," The Mob Museum (online); Cliff Jones obituary, *Las Vegas Sun*, Nov. 19, 2001.

533 *The Hope-Crosby telethon*: *Los Angeles Daily News*, June 25, 1952; Nadine Subotnik, "From Where We Sit," *Cedar Rapids Gazette*, June 19, 1952.

533 *Photographers immediately*: AP wirephoto published in papers from coast to coast starting June 22, 1952.

534 *As Jim was heading back*: "Mr. Olympics," *Los Angeles Times*, June 22, 1952.

534 *One of his "truths" was a blatant lie*: "My Biggest Olympic Battles" by Avery Brundage, President, United States Olympic Association, *Los Angeles Times*, June 29, 1952.

534 *Jim was not much of a presence*: "Mega-athlete Jim Thorpe," Aug. 22, 1995.

535 *He also came out to see Dwight D. Eisenhower*: Buford, 361; Leo H. Petersen, UP Sports Editor, "Ike Recalls His Tackle of Carlisle's Jim Thorpe," Oct. 29, 1952; Bill Corum, International News Service, Louisville, Nov. 7, 1952; Will Grimsley, Associated Press, Nov. 5, 1952.

535 *But whatever slim chance*: Account of Thorpe heart attack drawn from Associated Press and United Press dispatches from Henderson, NV, Aug. 8–10, 1952; Alex Kahn, UP report from Pittman, NV, Aug. 16, 1952; Gene Ward, *Chicago Tribune*, Sept. 3, 1952.

536 *Two weeks after Jim suffered*: *Reno Gazette-Journal*, Aug. 20, 1952. The driver, who survived, said the car skidded 250 feet and rolled over after she lost control on the highway's soft shoulder.

536 *Another town, another bar*: *Wilmington (CA) Press Journal*, March 2 and 21, 1953.

536 *Their symbiotic relationship*: Mike Koehler unpublished manuscript; Buford interview with Slim Harrison, Kate Buford personal papers.

537 *The rule change rekindled memories*: Orlo Robertson, "We'll Have Real All-Americas," Associated Press, Jan. 19, 1953; Loren McMullen, *Fort Worth Star-Telegram*, Jan. 20, 1953.

537 *One night while in New York*: Buck O'Neill, "Injun Jim Thorpe Recalls Past Glories on Gridiron," *New York Daily News*, Feb. 8, 1953.

538 *When Jim arrived back in California*: *Long Beach Press-Telegram*, *San Pedro News-Pilot*, Feb. 11, 1953; *Los Angeles Times*, Feb. 18, 1953.

538 *Slim Harrison had a particular reason*: Bill Hollohan, "Jim Thorpe, Rams' Coach Join Guests Honoring Athletes," *San Pedro News-Pilot*, Feb. 13, 1953.

539 *The last was on March 2*: *Wilmington (CA) Daily Press Journal*, March 2, 1953. "This will be a get acquainted night for Jim as well as the Boosters."

539 *The end came later that month*: Account of Thorpe's death at the trailer home drawn from Certificate of Death, State file 53-037265, County of Los Angeles, Registrar-Recorder/County Clerk; *Los Angeles Times*, March 28–29, 1953; *Long Beach Press-Telegram*, *Daily Oklahoman*, March 29, 1953; *Wilmington (CA) Daily Press Journal*, March 30, 1953; Buford, 363–66.

540 *One after another came the exaltations*: Associated Press, March 28, 1953; "Jim Thorpe Wins Praise from Nation," *Long Beach Independent*, March 29, 1953; *Daily*

Oklahoman, March 29, 1953; Western Union telegram from Dwight D. Eisenhower to Mrs. Patricia Thorpe, April 9, 1953, Grace F. Thorpe Collection, NMAI; *Dagens Nyheter*, March 30, 1953; Arch Ward, "In the Wake of the News," *Chicago Tribune*, March 30, 1953; Paul Zimmerman, "Sportscripts," *Los Angeles Times*, March 30, 1953.

541 *Grace would not forget*: *People*, Jan. 8, 1996; Grace Thorpe interview with Bob Greene, Oct. 14, 1992.

EPILOGUE: THE GREAT SPIRIT

543 *A cold wind*: Account of death rite drawn from Gilbert Hill, *Oklahoma City Times*, April 13, 1953; United Press, Associated Press, April 12–13, 1953; Erik Brady, *USA Today*, Aug. 10, 2015; Neely Tucker, *Washington Post*, March 16, 2012; Kurt Streeter, ESPN, July 28, 2016; Jack McCallum, *Sports Illustrated*, Oct. 25, 1982.

545 *Jim had stressed to his sons*: Affidavit of William K. Thorpe, U.S. District Court for the Middle District of Pennsylvania, John Thorpe, Richard Thorpe, William Thorpe and Sac and Fox Nation v. Borough of Jim Thorpe Pennsylvania, Dec. 28, 2012.

545 *The viewing was in Los Angeles*: Associated Press, April 2, 1953; *Muskogee Daily Phoenix*, April 2, 1953; *Los Angeles Times*, April 7, 1953.

546 *a requiem mass at St. Benedict's*: United Press, Associated Press, April 13–14, 1953.

546 *When a bill to fund*: *Daily Oklahoman*, June 21, 1953: "Gov. Murray swung a slashing veto ax Saturday" killing twenty bills that trimmed $890,000 from the state budget. Also Wheeler, *Jim Thorpe*, 192, 228.

547 *One of Patsy's key contacts*: *Pittsburgh Post-Gazette*, Jan. 15, 2001; *Sports Illustrated*, Oct. 25, 1982; Robert S. Lyons, *On Any Given Sunday: A Life of Bert Bell* (Temple University Press, 2009), 5–7; Bell obituary, Associated Press, Oct. 11, 1959.

547 *As Patsy later told the story*: *Mauch Chunk Times-News*, Nov. 17, 1953; *Allentown Morning Call*, April 4, 1954; *Sports Illustrated*, Oct. 25, 1982.

548 *In early November, Boyle formed*: "Telegram from Tulsa, Okla., Expresses 'Delight, Happiness,'" *Mauch Chunk Times-News*, Nov. 9–10, 1953.

549 *Patsy swept into town*: "Jim Thorpe's Widow and Daughter Happy with Local Proposal," *Mauch Chunk Times-News*, Nov. 21, 1953.

549 *In a weeklong campaign*: Patsy's whirlwind effort in town was front-page news in the *Mauch Chunk Times-News* each day Nov. 21–28, 1953.

550 *After meeting her, Betty Cossman*: "Patricia Thorpe Is a Woman with a Mission," *Allentown Morning Call*, Nov. 21, 29, 1953.

550 *It was treated as a solemn celebration*: *New York Sunday Mirror*, Feb. 7, 1953; *Mauch Chunk Times-News*, Feb. 8, 1953; *Allentown Morning Call*, Carlisle *Sentinel*, Feb. 9, 1983. *Sentinel* lede: "The much-traveled body of Jim Thorpe . . ."

551 *When the votes were counted*: *Allentown Morning Call; Hazleton (PA) Standard Sentinel*; United Press, Associated Press, May 19–20, 1954. An AP wirephoto showed a town leader standing next to a new Jim Thorpe, Pa., road sign.

551 *"Whether the people of Mauch Chunk"*: *Scranton Times-Tribune*, May 20, 1954.

551 *The first "therefore"*: Three-page document signed by Patricia G. Thorpe and the presidents of the Mauch Chunk and East Mauch Chunk Borough Councils, May 20, 1954.

552 *"I seldom go out on limbs"*: Rice, *The Tumult and the Shouting*, chapter 18, "Jim Thorpe the American Indian," 235–36; "Grantland Rice Completed Autobiography in Last Days," *Boston Globe*, July 24, 1954.

553 *"Any time they wanted publicity"*: *Sport*, December 1966.

554 *The move led President Richard Nixon*: "Notes on People," *New York Times*, Dec. 23, 1972; Proclamation 4209—Jim Thorpe Day, April 16, 1973, the American Presidency Project.

554 *At the urging of Grace*: Congressional Record, S10230, June 10, 1975.

554 *In tandem with the Senate*: Olympic Records, featuring materials related to Olympics from collections at Gerald R. Ford Presidential Library and Museum.

555 *Still sixth-grade students*: Letters to and from Robert Paul and the elementary school students in Norman, Oklahoma, October 1979, Thorpe Individual File, Avery Brundage Collection, UIABC.

555 *A combination of the relentless efforts*: McCallum, *Sports Illustrated*, Oct. 25, 1982; Trace Lara Hentz, "Honor Restored," July 11, 2015; *Olympics at the Millennium* (Rutgers Press, 2001), James Ring Adams, "The Jim Thorpe Backlash," *American Indian*, Summer 2012.

557 *That moment arrived*: "Thorpe's Victory," *Los Angeles Times*, Jan. 19, 1983; "Thorpe Medals Finally Returned," *New York Times*, Jan. 19, 1983; *Fort Worth Star-Telegram*, Jan. 21, 1983; Dave Anderson, "Jim Thorpe's Family Feud," *New York Times*, Feb. 7, 1983.

558 *Burt Lancaster shared*: New York Times News Service, Oct. 15, 1982.

558 *"It made him an asterisk"*: Sally Jenkins, "The All-American," *Smithsonian*, July 2012.

560 *The question was put to a public vote*: William Ecenbarger, "When Will Jim Thorpe's Soul Rest?" *Philadelphia Inquirer Magazine*, Aug. 8, 1982; Streeter, ESPN, July 28, 2016; Tucker, *Washington Post*, March 16, 2012.

560 *Gene Kilroy, who was Muhammad Ali's*: Interview with Kilroy, Sept. 14, 2021.

561 *"Now if we can only"*: *New York Times*, Jan. 19, 1983.

561 *When Olinka Hardy*: Associated Press, April 11, 1983.

561 *The Thorpe sisters*: Associated Press, June 24, 2010; John Branch, "Thorpe Family Split Over Sons' Lawsuit," *New York Times*, May 18, 2011; Streeter, ESPN, July 28, 2016.

562 *When Black Hawk died*: Account of Black Hawk's final days, death, and stealing of his bones drawn from Trask, *Black Hawk*, 303–304; *Keokuk (IA) Daily Gate City*, Dec. 13, 1961; *Ottumwa (IA) Courier*, Nov. 18, 1966; *Davenport (IA) Democrat and Leader*, Oct. 12, 1926; *Fairfield (IA) Daily Ledger*, Sept. 24, 1946; *Fort Madison (IA) Evening Democrat*, Feb. 25, 1939; *Burlington (IA) Hawk Eye*, April 25, 1979; DHTC, Black Hawk file.

563 *White men had been looting*: Robert E. Bieder, "A Brief Historical Survey of the Expropriation of American Indian Remains," Indiana University, April 1990; Report to Congress, "Native American Graves and Repatriation Act," U.S. Government Accountability Office, July 2010; Thomas, *Skull Wars*, 29–32.

564 *His sensibility in going to court*: Suzan Shown Harjo and Mary Kathryn Nagle, "My Father's Bones" (play), 2013.

564 *The case was heard*: Account of legal fight over Thorpe's bones drawn from *Daily Oklahoman*, April 20, 2013; *Philadelphia Inquirer*, June 3, 2015; *Allentown Morning Call*, Feb. 15, 2014; Joe McDonald, Reuters, May 6, 2013; Streeter, ESPN, July 20, 2016; Tucker, *Washington Post*, March 16, 2012.

565 *Most of the buildings*: Depiction of former grounds of Carlisle Indian School and student cemetery at what is now the Army War College drawn from walking tour with archivist and historian Barbara Landis.

566 *The bones of these Carlisle students*: Charles Fox, *Philadelphia Inquirer*, "Oneida Indian Reservation," Sept. 22, 2019; Amy Worden, "There Is One Less Child in This Cemetery," *Washington Post*, June 28, 2021; "Rosebud Sioux teens . . . return to claim relatives' remains from Carlisle Indian School Cemetery," *Philadelphia Inquirer*, July 18, 2021.

567 *One evening in May*: Final scene drawn from handwritten notes and typed copy of speech delivered by Grace Thorpe at Carlisle High auditorium, 1968, Grace F. Thorpe Collection, NMAI.

Selected Bibliography

Adams, David Wallace. *Education for Extinction: American Indians and the Boarding School Experience, 1875–1928.* Lawrence, KS: University of Kansas Press, 1995.

Aleiss, Angela. *Making the White Man's Indian: Native Americans and Hollywood Movies.* Praeger, 2005.

Anderson, Lars. *Carlisle vs. Army: Jim Thorpe, Dwight Eisenhower, Pop Warner, and the Forgotten Story of Football's Greatest Battle.* Random House, 2007.

Barry, John M. *The Great Influenza: The Story of the Deadliest Pandemic in History.* Penguin, 2005.

Benjey, Tom. *Carlisle Indian School Football Immortals.* Tuxedo Press, 2009.

Black Hawk. *Life of Black Hawk, Dictated by Himself.* Penguin Classics, 2008.

Bloom, John. *To Show What an Indian Can Do.* University of Minnesota Press, 2000.

Blumenson, Martin. *The Patton Papers.* Houghton Mifflin, 1972.

Buford, Kate. *Native American Son: The Life and Sporting Legend of Jim Thorpe.* Alfred A. Knopf, 2010.

Carroll, Bob. *The Ohio League: 1910–1919.* PFRA, 1997.

Carroll, Bob, Michael Gershman, David Neft, and John Thorn. *Total Football.* Harper Collins, 1997.

Chelland, Patrick. *One for the Gipper.* Regnery, 1973.

Child, Brenda J. *Boarding School Seasons.* University of Nebraska Press, 2000.

Crawford, Bill. *All American: The Rise and Fall of Jim Thorpe.* Wiley, 2004.

Danzig, Allison. *The History of American Football.* Prentice-Hall, 1956.

Davis, Jeff. *Papa Bear: The Life and Legacy of George Halas.* McGraw-Hill, 2005.

Davis, Kenneth S. *Dwight D. Eisenhower, Soldier of Democracy.* Doubleday, 1946.

D'Este, Carlo. *Patton: A Genius for War.* Harper Perennial, 1996.

Eisler, Benita. *The Red Man's Bones: George Catlin, Artist and Showman.* W. W. Norton, 2013.

Elfers, James E., *The Tour to End All Tours,* Bison Original, 2003.

Fear-Segal, Jacqueline. *Carlisle Indian Industrial School: Indigenous Histories, Memories, and Reclamations.* University of Nebraska Press, 2018.

Grann, David. *Killers of the Flower Moon: The Osage Murders and the Birth of the FBI.* Doubleday, 2017.

Hagan, William T. *The Sac and Fox Indians.* University of Oklahoma Press, 1998.

Halas, George, with Gwen Morgan and Arthur Veysey. *Halas by Halas: The Autobiography of George Halas.* McGraw-Hill, 1979.

Hoxie, Frederick E. *A Final Promise: The Campaign to Assimilate the Indians, 1880–1920.* University of Nebraska Press, 1984.

Lardner, Ring W. *You Know Me Al.* Scribner, 1960.

Jenkins, Sally. *The Real All Americans.* New York: Doubleday, 2007.

Lemann, Nicholas. *The Natural (ESPN Sports-Century).* ESPN Books, 1999.

Mallon, Bill, and Ture Widlund. *The 1912 Olympic Games: Results for All Competitors in All Events, with Commentary.* McFarland, 2002.

McGraw, Blanche S. *The Real McGraw.* Van Rees Press, 1953.

Miller, Jeffrey J. *Pop Warner: A Life on the Gridiron.* McFarland, 2015.

Newcombe, Jack. *The Best of the Athletic Boys: The World's Impact on Jim Thorpe.* Doubleday, 1975.

Oriard, Michael. *Reading Football: How the Popular Press Created an American Spectacle.* University of North Carolina Press, 1995.

Peterson, Robert W. *Pigskin: The Early Years of Pro Football.* Oxford University Press, 1997.

Pratt, Richard Henry. *Battlefield and Classroom: Four Decades with the American Indian. 1867–1904.* Yale University Press, 1964.

Ratteree, Kathleen, and Norbert Hill, eds. *The Great Vanishing Act: Blood Quantum and the Future of Native Nations.* Fulcrum, 2017.

Reich, Susanna. *Painting the Wild Frontier: The Art and Adventures of George Catlin.* Clarion Books, 2008.

Rice, Grantland. *The Tumult and the Shouting.* A. S. Barnes and Company, 1954.

Rode, Alan K. *Michael Curtiz: A Life in Film.* University Press of Kentucky, 2017.

Roessner, Amber. *Inventing Baseball Heroes: Ty Cobb, Christy Mathewson, and the Sporting Press in America.* Louisiana State University Press, 2014.

Rosenthal, Nicolas G. *Reimagining Indian Country: Native American Migration and Identity in Twentieth-Century Los Angeles.* University of North Carolina Press, 2012.

Sheinkin, Steve. *Undefeated: Jim Thorpe and the Carlisle Indian School Football Team.* Roaring Brook Press, 2017.

Standing Bear, Luther. *My People, the Sioux.* Houghton Mifflin, 1928.

Sullivan, Edward. *The Olympic Games, Stockholm 1912.* Spalding Red Cover Series, 1913.

Thomas, David Hurst. *Skull Wars: Kennewick Man, Archaeology, and the Battle for Native American Identity.* Basic Books, 2000.

Thorpe, Grace. "The Jim Thorpe Family, Parts 1 and 2." *Chronicles of Oklahoma* Volume 59, Numbers 1 & 2, Spring & Summer 1981.

Trask, Kerry A. *Black Hawk: The Battle for the Heart of America.* Henry Holt, 2005.

Treuer, David. *The Heartbeat of Wounded Knee: Native American from 1890 to the Present.* Riverhead Books, 2019.

Warner, Glenn S. *Pop Warner: Football's Greatest Teacher.* Gridiron Football, 1993.

Warren, Kim Cary. *The Quest for Citizenship: African American and Native American Education in Kansas, 1880–1935.* University of North Carolina Press, 2010.

Wheeler, Robert W. *Jim Thorpe: World's Greatest Athlete.* University of Oklahoma Press, 1981.

Wilson, Charles Banks. *Search for the Native American Purebloods.* University of Oklahoma Press, 1983.

Yttergren, Leif, ed. *The 1912 Olympics: Essays on the Competitions, the People, the City.* McFarland, 2012.Image Credits

IMAGE CREDITS

1 Getty Images
2 Oklahoma Historical Society
3 Cumberland County Historical Society
4 Cumberland County Historical Society
5 Library of Congress
6 Library of Congress
7 Cumberland County Historical Society
8 Cumberland County Historical Society
9 Library of Congress
10 Cumberland County Historical Society
11 Getty Images
12 Cumberland County Historical Society
13 Getty Images
14 University Archives; John R. Case Papers; Urbana, IL
15 Cumberland County Historical Society
16 Cumberland County Historical Society
17 Cumberland County Historical Society
18 Cumberland County Historical Society
19 Cumberland County Historical Society
20 Library of Congress
21 Library of Congress
22 Cumberland County Historical Society
23 Getty Images: Bettmann Archive
24 Library of Congress
25 Cumberland County Historical Society
26 Cumberland County Historical Society
27 Cumberland County Historical Society
28 Cumberland County Historical Society
29 AP Images
30 Getty Images
31 AP Images
32 Cumberland County Historical Society
33 Cumberland County Historical Society
34 Cumberland County Historical Society

35 Getty Images
36 Everett Collection
37 David Hurst Thomas
38 AP Images
39 Getty Images
40 AP Images
41 AP Images
42 AP Images
43 Getty Images
44 AP Images
45 Linda Maraniss
46 Linda Maraniss
47 Linda Maraniss
48 Linda Maraniss
49 AP Images
50 Cumberland County Historical Society

INDEX